Think
Pro/ENGINEER®
Wildfire 4.0

Steven J. Frey

Think Pro/ENGINEER® Wildfire 4.0
By Steven J. Frey

ISBN: 978-0-578-02945-0

First Printing: June 2009

Trademarks

Warning and Disclaimer

Quantity Sales

For information on academic or corporate bulk purchases, visit http://www.freyinnovations.com.

About the author

Steven J. Frey is an inventor, product design consultant, instructor and author. Steve began working in industry in 1985 with a pencil and a drafting machine, creating industrial piping layouts. In 1988, Steve made the switch to AutoCAD to design waste-to-energy incinerators and paving, drainage, water, and sewer layouts for residential developments and commercial properties. He started using Pro/ENGINEER (Release 9) in 1991 to design automotive components and systems. Steve became a PTC (Parametric Technology Corporation) Certified Engineering Provider (CEP) in 1998, before co-founding Universal Parametrics, Inc., an engineering consulting firm, specializing in the sales, implementation, training and use of PTC products for the automotive, heavy truck, aerospace, defense, medical and consumer products industries. From 1998 to 2001, Steve wrote the popular 'Pro/ENGINEER in the trenches' column for *Pro/E: The Magazine*, and served on the Editorial Advisory Board for several years, in addition to writing the magazine's 'Pro/ENGINEER Hardware Benchmark 2000' issue. In 2003, Steve became a PTC Certified Instruction Provider, and continues to deliver basic and advanced Pro/ENGINEER training courses to companies across the United States.

Acknowledgements

I would like to thank my wife Lori, and daughters Katie, Jackie and Rebecca for giving me the time and space needed for a project such as this, and for indulging me while I take on yet another project.

I'd also like to thank Lori for proof-reading the text, and Mike Hartmeyer for re-creating all of the Student Edition versions of the Pro/ENGINEER models included on the companion CD, and for his technical review of the techniques presented in this book.

Finally, I would like to thank C.L. for serving as my reminder that it is best to lead by optimism, enthusiasm and energy, not pessimism and cynicism, and for convincing me that it was time to write this book.

About the cover

The front cover image is a photograph taken by the author, January 12, 2008, of Auguste Rodin's *The Thinker* (*Le Penseur*), on the steps of the Detroit Institute of Arts (DIA). Made in 1904 by the Alexis Rudier Foundry for the German collector Dr. Max Linde in Lübeck, this is the first bronze casting made of the famous statue. After being sold by Linde, it was donated to the DIA in 1922 by Horace H. Rackham.

The back cover image is a 95th percentile male, human factors, Pro/ENGINEER assembly model.

Introduction

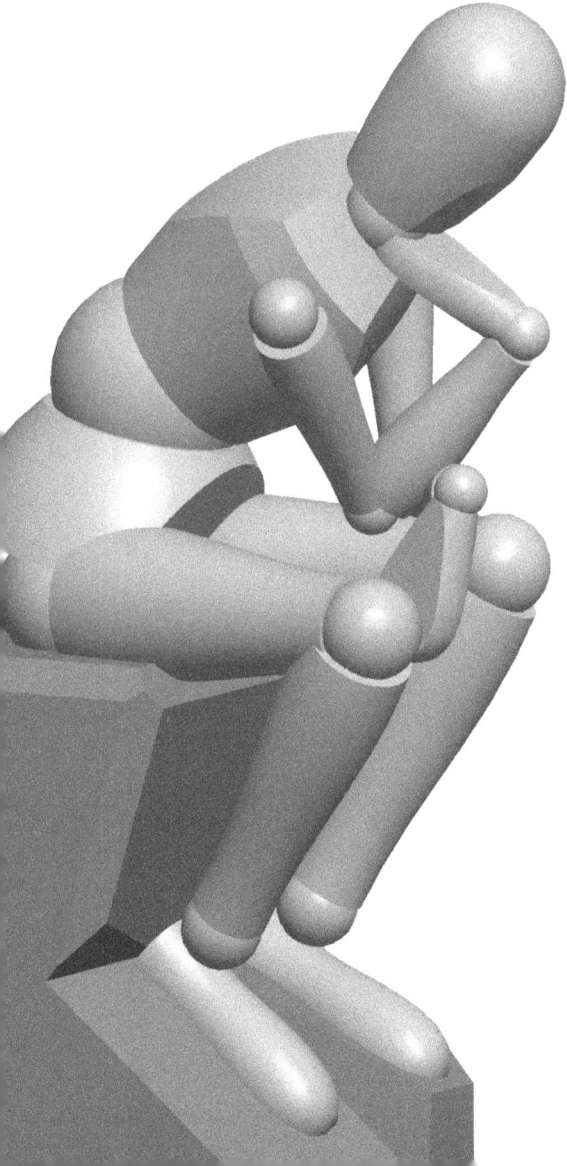

Pro/ENGINEER is quite simply, the best product development software currently on the market. It is the best, because it has the most complete and accurate suite of tools available to the product designer and manufacturer alike. Over the years, other CAD products and manufacturers have come and gone, and tried to paint the picture that Pro/ENGINEER is too hard to use, but one could argue that any CAD software is harder to use than drawing in the dirt with a stick. The more functionality the software has to offer, the more there is to learn, but that doesn't make it any harder. Incidentally, even experienced Pro/ENGINEER users only use a small percentage of the tools available, depending on their specific needs.

This book is written primarily for the beginning user. If you start with chapter one, and continue reading to the end, you will have a well rounded and functional understanding of Pro/ENGINEER, and you will have learned it in a logical and progressive manner. After you have completed the book, or if you are already an experienced user, you may use it as a convenient reference guide. More advanced techniques and practices will be covered in future works.

You will not find a single exercise in this book. A step by step, button click by button click set of instructions on how to create a coffee mug will teach you how to create that coffee mug, but nothing else. This book focuses on what features and commands are available, how to access them, how to use them, and most importantly, why to use them (or not). Also, all Pro/ENGINEER commands and techniques have basic or default settings, and this book discusses their use, but most commands also include advanced or optional settings. If this book included every single option and setting for every single command, it would need to be literally thousands of pages long. Who wants to read a book like that? Instead, I invite you to try the commands and settings I have illustrated, but also click all of the other buttons, tabs and settings as they present themselves. You will learn far more through personal discovery than by anything I, or any other author, could possibly write. There is no way you can break anything, so click on something, and see what happens!

Although I am not including any exercises in this book, the companion CD contains electronic copies of every Pro/ENGINEER file used to illustrate the text. You may also download the same files at **http://www.freyinnovations.com**. The files are organized by chapter, and their names correspond with the figure numbers in the text. For example, you may open the file named 9-8 and it will be the exact same file used to create Figure 9-8. This will allow you to work through the commands as I discuss them, and experiment with the options and settings, as you see fit. Once you have a file open, be creative and experiment!

If you do not have access to Pro/ENGINEER software either at your place of business or school, you may go to **http://www.freyinnovations.com** for information on downloading a **Free Trial** edition of the software, as well as purchasing both the Student and Professional versions.

Please also keep in mind that although I may have illustrated one or two different ways of using a command, there may be dozens of other ways to create the same geometry. Even as I continue to use Pro/ENGINEER to design and develop products for myself and my clients, I do not use the same techniques all the time. A truly advanced user does not believe that their way is the only way, and is always looking for a better, more efficient and accurate way to create their data.

Good luck, enjoy, and welcome to the world of Pro/ENGINEER!

Chapter 1

What is Pro/ENGINEER?

Philosophy of Pro/ENGINEER

3D Solid Models

Parametrics

Feature Based Modeling

Parents and Children

Design Intent

Pro/ENGINEER File Types

File Associativity

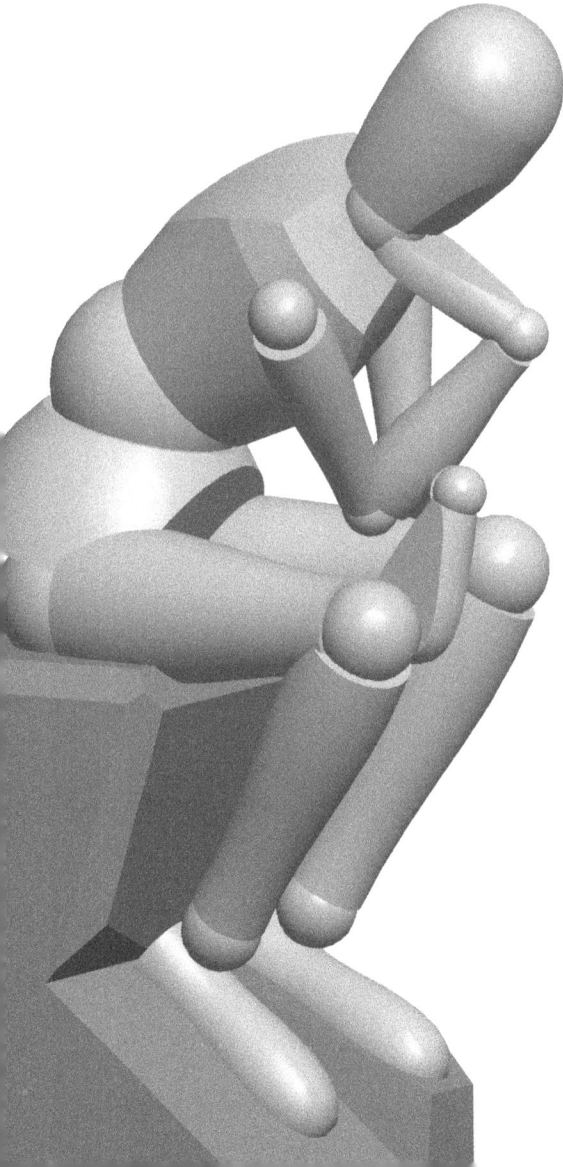

Philosophy of Pro/ENGINEER

From its beginning, Pro/ENGINEER was and continues to be the most versatile and advanced MCAD (Mechanical Computer-aided Design) software in the world.

Three-dimensional (3D) Solid Models

Before the introduction of Pro/ENGINEER in 1987, most computer drafting programs were just that, 'Drafting' programs. Even though a professional may have been called a 'CAD Operator' at the time, they were essentially doing the exact same work with a computer, as they were when they where called Draftsmen, using T-squares, triangles, and pencils. CAD Operators continued to produce two-dimensional drawings, albeit with greater neatness than with a pencil, but they were essentially electronic versions of the same drawings.

Autodesk introduced three-dimensional capability with their Release 10 of AutoCAD® at about the same time as Pro/ENGINEER was introduced, but three-dimensional 'drawings' created with AutoCAD® were limited to faceted, surface-only geometry.

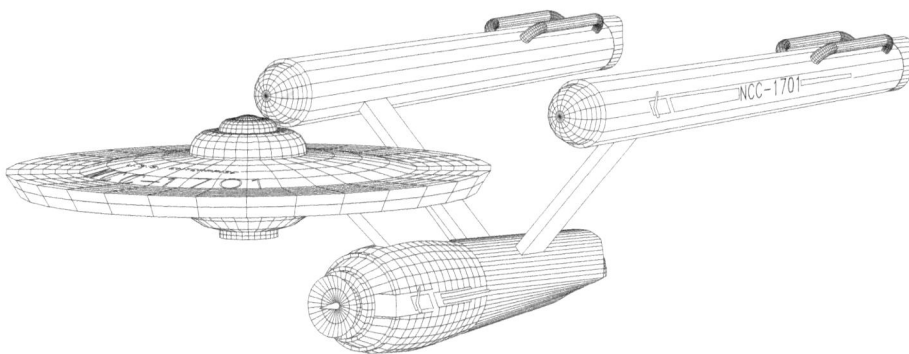

Fig. 1-1
Three-dimensional AutoCAD Rel. 10 drawing created by the author, circa 1987

What made Pro/ENGINEER different from its inception is that users did not think of creating a 'drawing', but rather a solid object first. Designers use various commands to add material to, or delete material from their current solid object, now referred to as a 'model'.

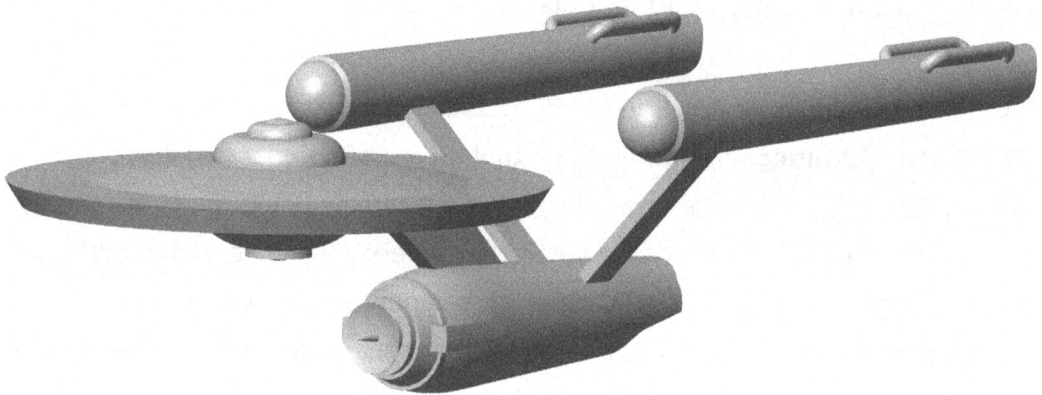

Fig. 1-2
Solid model using Pro/ENGINEER

Creating solid models has many advantages over two-dimensional drawings, or even three-dimensional surface and wireframe models. By assigning the appropriate material density to a model, the exact weight of the manufactured product may be determined in advance, as well as the object's center of gravity and moments of inertia. Sections may be cut into these models, as shown in Figure 1-3, and when creating designs comprising several individual parts, interferences between the parts may be checked to verify proper fit. Mechanisms may be designed with their full range of motion to prevent potential lock-up conditions.

Fig. 1-3
Cross sectional view of a Pro/ENGINEER solid model

Parametrics

Each Pro/ENGINEER design is driven by sets of values. These values can be in the form of dimensions to control the size and shape of the model, but they can also be in the form of parameters embedded into the model (See Chapter 20). By modifying these driving values, the design may be updated. To put it simply, a Pro/ENGINEER design is literally built from its list of values. Even if a designer is not at first concerned with defining an exact size or location of an object, Pro/ENGINEER still locates and defines the entities with a starting set of values, which may be modified by the user at any time.

Featured Based Modeling

As mentioned earlier, a Pro/ENGINEER model is created by literally adding or deleting material from the current design. This is accomplished by adding features to the model, one at a time. The model shown in Figure 1-4 contains a rectangular block and a cylinder which adds material to the model, window, and disk shaped cuts which remove material from the model, and several fillet type features (called rounds), some of which add material, and some of which delete material.

Fig. 1-4
Feature based model

The most important concept to remember with features is that they are added to the model sequentially, starting with feature number one, and adding as many features to the end of the list of features as necessary to complete the design. While the features may be reordered later (see Chapter 18), adding a feature to the end of the list, in no way modifies any of the features that occur before it. For example, the window shaped cut, as shown in Figure 1-4, removed material from the entire model in a Boolean operation. It did not change the definition of the cylinder in any way.

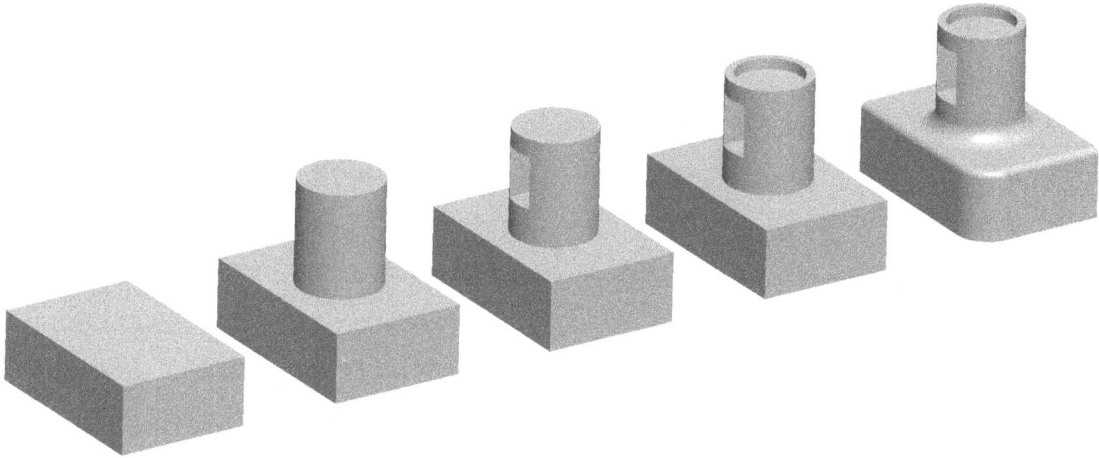

Figure 1-5
The progression of a design by adding features to the model

Parents and Children

With the exception of the default coordinate system and default datum planes (see Chapter 6), all features reference one or more other features or geometry, to determine their location in space. The feature being added becomes a 'child' of the features or geometry being referenced, which become the 'parents' of the feature. For example, the sharp edges of the rectangular block shown in Figure 1-4 are the parents of the round (or fillet) features added at the end of the list, by defining the location and extent of the rounds. In the same way, the disk shaped cut at the top of the part uses the cylindrical solid as its parent, to locate itself in space. Features may have several children, or none at all, but no feature (again with the exception of the default datums) may exist without one or more parents. A hierarchy of generations of parents and children may be created, but at no time will a feature be considered an 'orphan'.

Design Intent

Design intent is a general term to describe an overall philosophy of creating
Pro/ENGINEER designs which match and maintain the desired result. The type and
order of features used, and the features and geometry selected to be parents for
new features, insure design intent. When looking at the window shaped cut in the
part shown in Figure 1-4, it is not obvious if it is more important that the cut be
located relative to the top of the cylinder, or the bottom of the rectangular block. By
carefully choosing the appropriate parents while creating the cut, the design intent
may be captured and maintained. Figure 1-6 illustrates how the window cut is
located .375 inches down from the top of the cylinder.

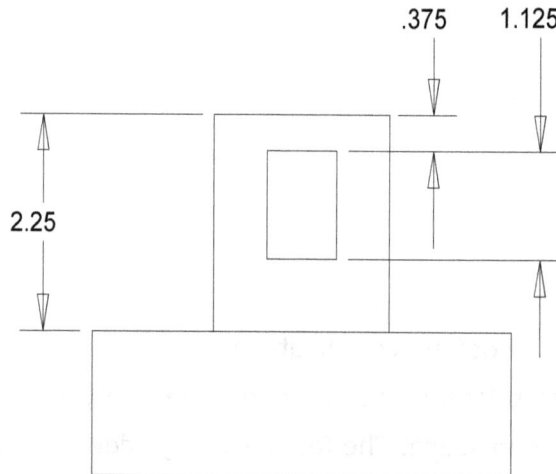

Fig. 1-6
Cut located from the top of the cylinder

The .375 dimension may be modified later, but no matter what value it is set to, the
cut will always be located a distance from the top of the cylinder. The top surface of
the cylinder is a parent of the cut. Figure 1-7 illustrates what happens to the cut
when the height of the cylinder is increased from 2.25 to 3.50. The cut physically
moves up in space because its parent (the top surface) moves up first.

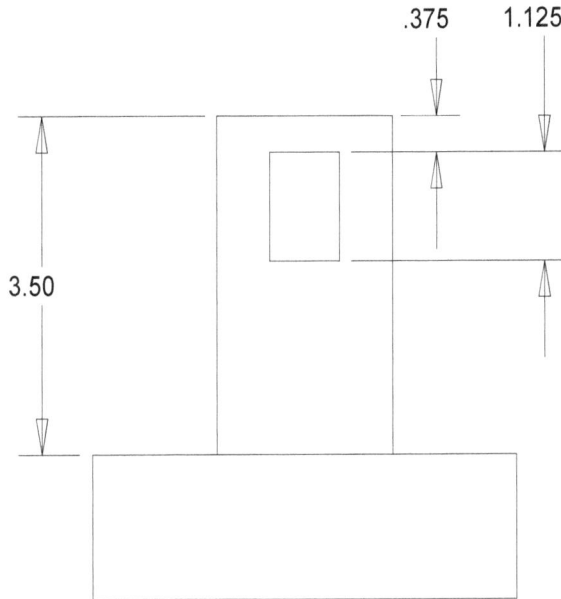

Fig. 1-7
Cut moves relative to the top of the cylinder

If the design intent is that the cut maintain its position in space, regardless of the height of the cylinder, then it should be defined as a distance from the bottom of the cylinder or the bottom of the rectangular block, as shown in Figure 1-8.

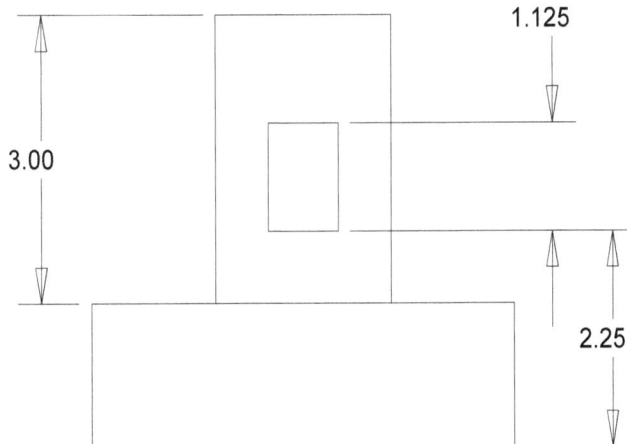

Fig. 1-8
Cut defined from the bottom of the part

A good designer will assume that during the lifetime of a design, many aspects of the model may be modified. By choosing the proper combination of features and parents for those features, the design intent of each feature will be maintained. The features may be redefined at any time, if it becomes necessary.

Pro/ENGINEER File Types

There are many types of files that are created by and used in conjunction with Pro/ENGINEER, but there are three basic types.

Parts

Part files are distinguished by the '.*prt*' file extension. When first creating the model, the file extension is automatically added to the file name based on the type of file being created. In simplest terms, a Pro/ENGINEER part represents the smallest, contiguous mass or boundary of a single material.

Figure 1-9
Single part file named *block.prt*

The Pro/ENGINEER model shown in Figure 1-9 is a representation of a product which is molded as a single item. Another example would be a single piece of lumber.

Assemblies

Assembly files are distinguished by the '.*asm*' file extension. As with the part file, the assembly extension is automatically added to the file name when it is created. Figure 1-10 is an example of a Pro/ENGINEER assembly.

Fig. 1-10
Assembly file named *stack.asm*

A Pro/ENGINEER assembly is a collection of one or more individual parts grouped together. The same individual part can be included as many times as appropriate. Typically these groups are put together to simulate actual conditions on the manufacturing or shop floor. Just as a Pro/ENGINEER part can represent a single piece of lumber, a Pro/ENGINEER assembly can represent an entire house.

Drawings

Drawing files are distinguished by the *'.drw'* file extension. Drawings are a two-dimensional representation of parts and assemblies. They may have unique names, or have the same base name as the part or assembly being illustrated. All of the information needed to manufacture or otherwise illustrate the design is included on the drawing, such as dimensions and notes. Figure 1-11 is a drawing of the block part, while Figure 1-12 is a drawing of the stack assembly.

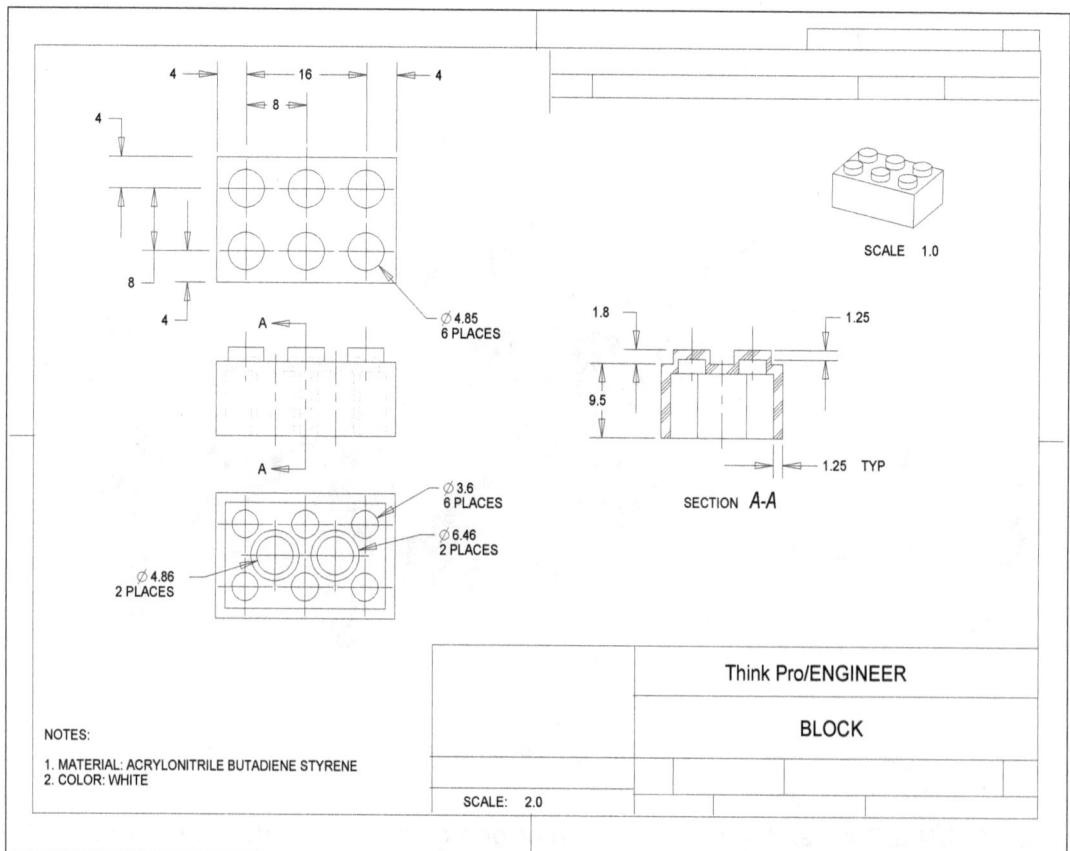

Fig. 1-11
Drawing file named *block.drw* showing the details of the block part

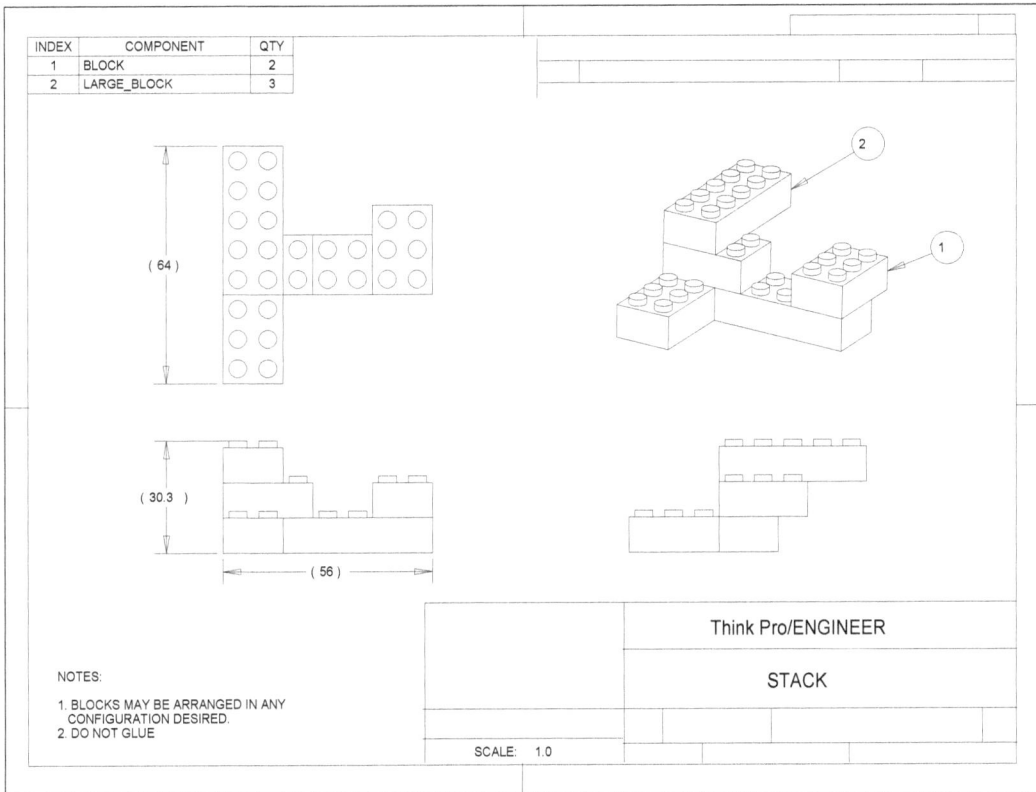

Fig. 1-12
Drawing file named *stack.drw* showing the details of the stack assembly

File Associativity

Pro/ENGINEER parts, assemblies, and drawings work with each other, and are dependant on each other. The stack assembly file shown in Figure 1-10 is a collection of individual part files, including the block part. It does not use copies of the block part, but the actual part file, several times. This associativity is always present, so that any changes to the individual parts are immediately reflected in any assemblies that may use those parts. This means that assembly files never need to be 'updated' since they are always up to date.

Drawings also have associativity with the parts and assemblies they represent. When looking at the block drawing shown in Figure 1-11, you are not seeing circles and lines, but rather the actual edges of the solid geometry. The individual drawing views are two-dimensional views of the three-dimensional part or assembly. As the geometry of the part or assembly changes, so will the two-dimensional views. This happens automatically, so there is never any need to 'update' a drawing, as it is always a perfect representation of the three-dimensional geometry.

This can be best illustrated in Figure 1-13 which is a Pro/ENGINEER part file inside a house. If you where to look through the front door, the part file would look a certain way. If you look through one of the windows on the side of the house, the part would look different, but it would be the same part. Even if you looked at the part from a bird's eye view, with the roof of the house removed, the part would look different, but it would still be the same part.

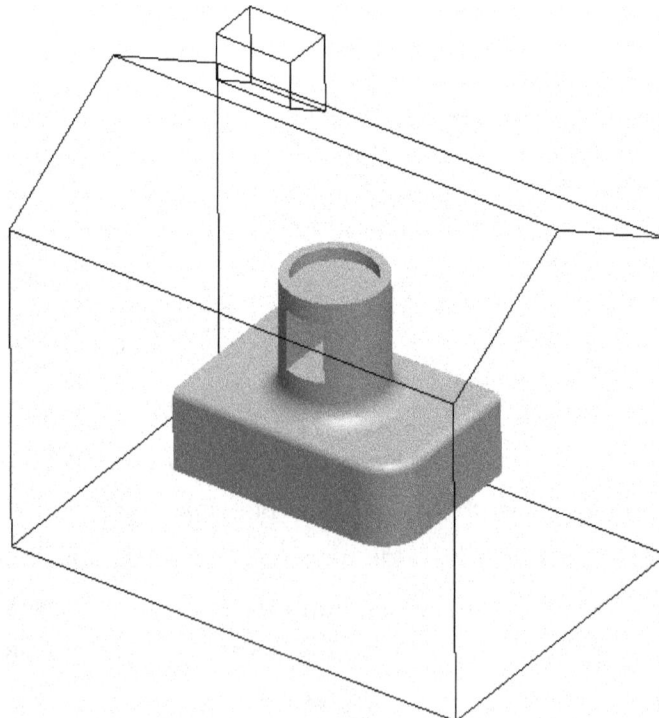

Fig. 1-13
Three-dimensional geometry inside a house

What would happen if someone were to change the height of the cylindrical shape of the part, or deleted the disk shaped cut on the top? The part would update, but you would not need to update the house, just to see the part through the windows. The same is true for Pro/ENGINEER drawings. They may be thought of as one or more windows (called views) to allow you to look at the actual three-dimensional geometry, as shown in Figure 1-14.

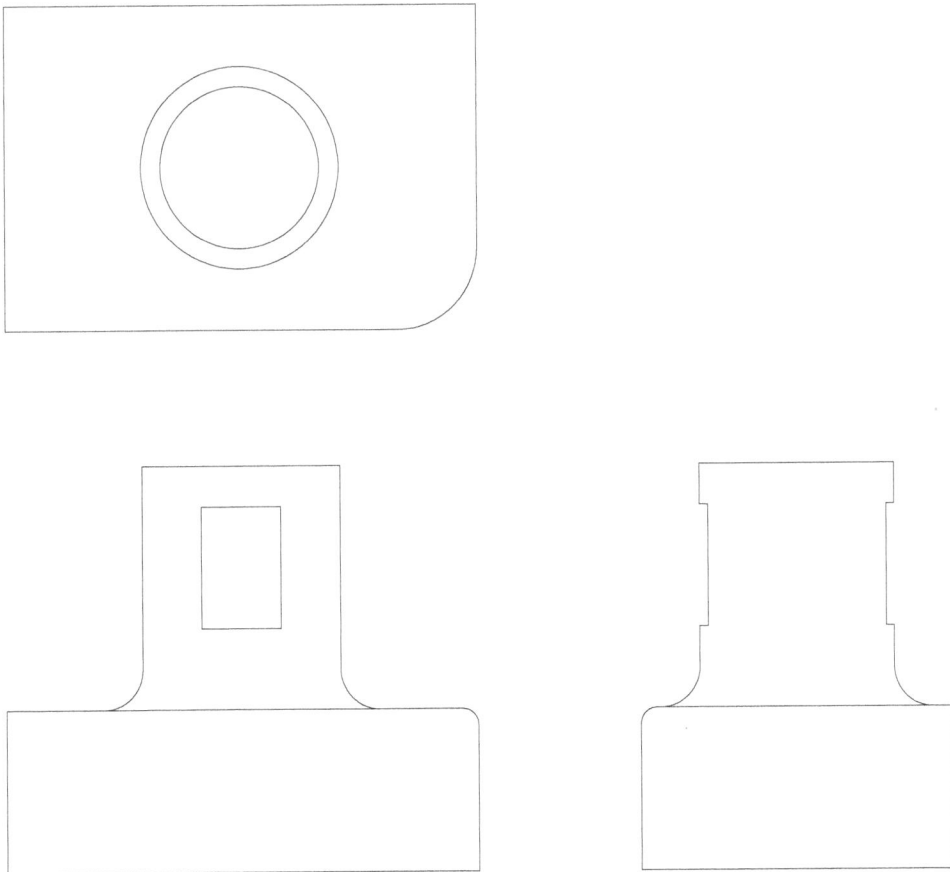

Fig. 1-14
Views of the three-dimensional object from the top, front and side

Just as assemblies use the actual part files, not copies, drawings use the actual three-dimensional geometry, not copies of it. This means that if you were to change the dimension of a feature while working on a part, the drawing will immediately reflect that change. The same is true if you modify a dimension on a drawing. The three-dimensional part geometry will automatically update. There is never a need to 'synchronize' the two files.

Many more aspects of Pro/ENGINEER's associativity and methods to maintain design intent will be discussed in later chapters.

Chapter 2

Pro/ENGINEER Environment

Screen Layout

Dialog Boxes

Pointing and Selection Devices

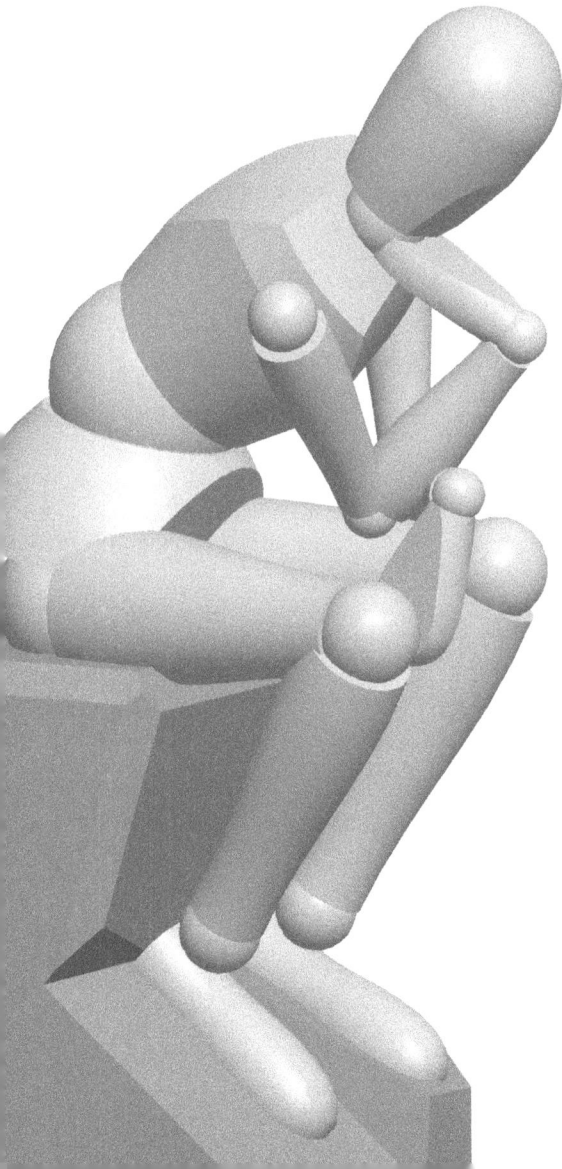

Screen Layout

The Pro/ENGINEER user interface is highly customizable, consisting of a few key areas.

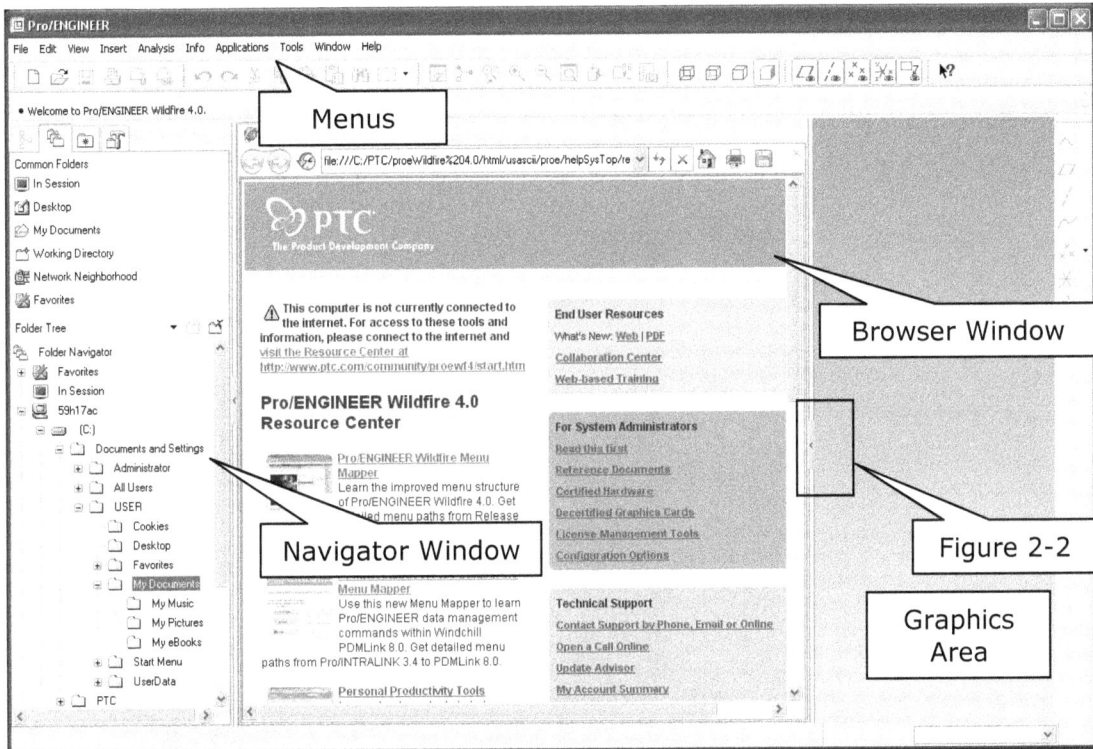

Fig. 2-1
The complete Pro/ENGINEER screen at startup

Browser Window

Located in the center of the screen, the Browser Window initially displays a default HTML (HyperText Markup Language) page. If your computer is connected to the internet, Pro/ENGINEER will connect to a 'landing page' located at the PTC web site. This page will contain tutorials and information related to the latest release of the software. If your computer is not connected to the internet, a local page will be displayed, as shown in Figure 2-1, containing technical support information.

In addition to displaying web pages, the Browser Window will display information about individual Pro/ENGINEER files and features. It will also display the contents of each folder, as they are selected in the Navigator Window.

At any time, the Browser Window may be resized by clicking on the edge of the window and dragging it, or it may be collapsed by clicking on the '**<**' (left arrow) as shown in Figure 2-2. A collapsed window may be re-expanded by simply clicking on the '**>**' (right arrow).

Figure 2-2
Click on the arrow to collapse

Navigator Window

When Pro/ENGINEER is first started, the Navigator Window will default to a Folder Browser, displaying a list of your computer's folders. The folders may be expanded and collapsed by clicking on the '**+**' (plus) and '**–**' (minus) signs to the immediate left of each folder name. Clicking on the name of each folder displays the contents of each folder in the Browser Window. The upper portion of the Navigator Window contains shortcuts to common or 'key' folders.

After a Pro/ENGINEER model is open, as shown in Figure 2-3, the Navigator Window automatically switches its display from a Folder Browser to the Model Tree. This is where all of the model's features are listed in chronological order and accessible for modifications.

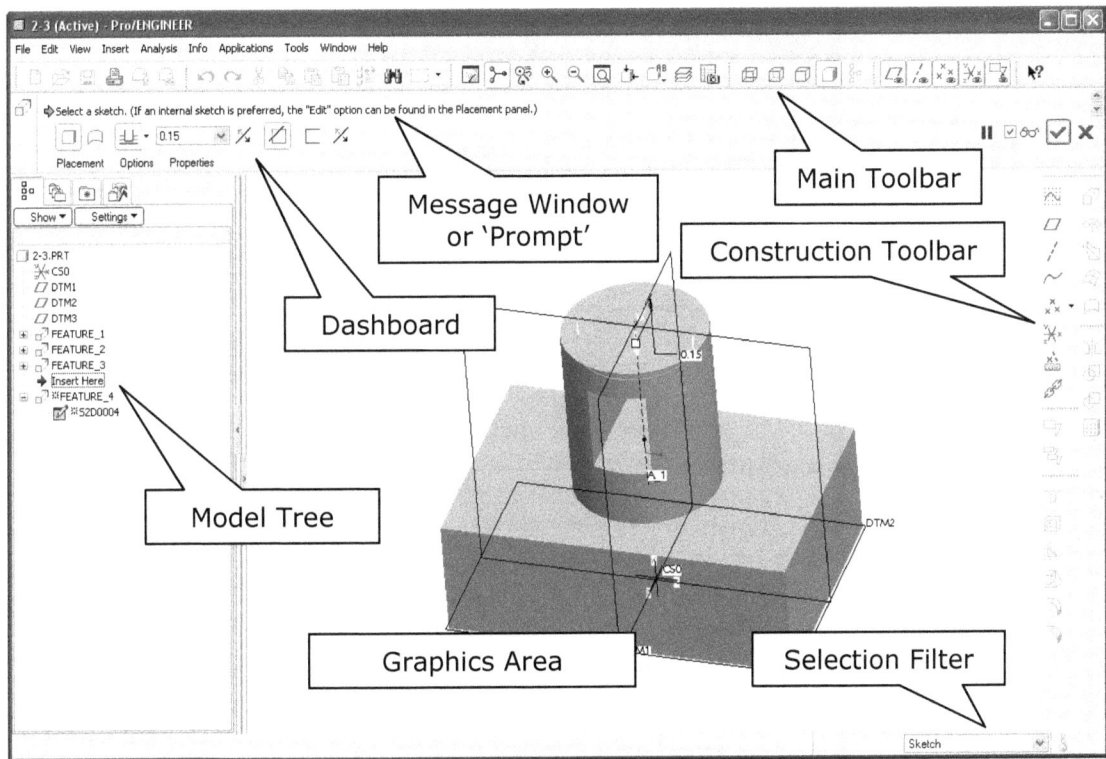

Fig. 2-3
Pro/ENGINEER model open

You can control the amount of information displayed in the window by clicking on the Settings tab at the top of the window, as shown in Figure 2-4.

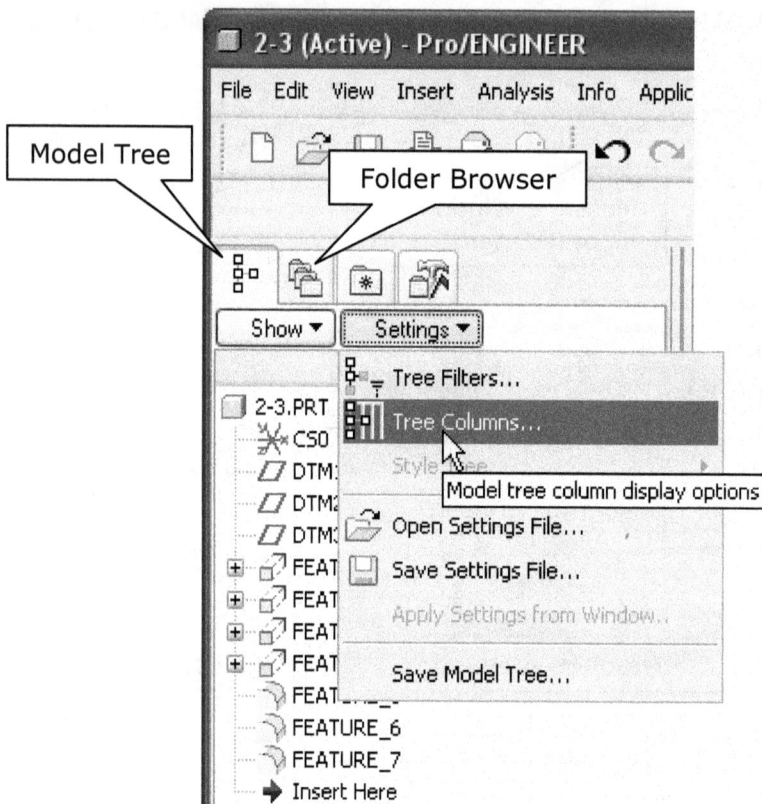

Fig. 2-4
Pro/ENGINEER Model Tree

To switch between the Folder Browser and Model Tree, simply click on the
appropriate icons as shown in Figure 2-4. Just as the Browser Window may be
collapsed, so too can the Navigator Window, by clicking on the '<' (left arrow) along
the edge.

Graphics Area

Behind the Browser Window is the Graphic Area. This is where your three-dimensional parts and assemblies, and two-dimensional drawings will be displayed. When a new file is created, or an existing file is opened, the Browser Window will automatically collapse to reveal the entire Graphics Area, as shown in Figure 2-3. If more graphics space is preferred, the Navigator Window may be collapsed, as discussed earlier.

Menus

The top of the Pro/ENGINEER screen contains pull-down menus, similar to most Windows®-based programs, as shown in Figure 2-5. These menus are used to access commands to create geometry, access system settings, and perform file operations such as opening, copying, and printing.

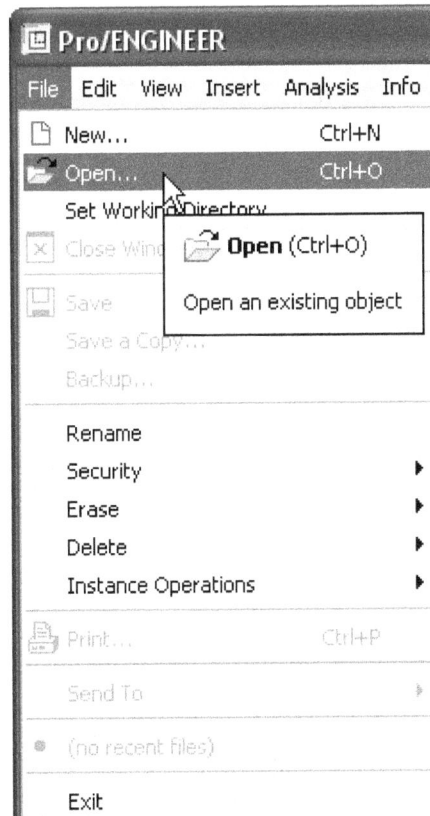

Fig. 2-5
Typical 'Pull-down' Menus

Main Toolbar

Just below the Menu is the Main Toolbar. This contains icons for commonly used system, environmental or 'global' type commands. Many of the commands listed in the pull-down menus are duplicated here. It is not necessary to memorize the function of each icon, as placing the cursor over each icon will cause a tag to appear, explaining the function of each icon, as shown in Figure 2-6.

Fig. 2-6
Icon tag

Construction Toolbar

Located to the right of the graphics area is the Construction Toolbar. Although this tool also contains commands duplicated from the pull-down menus, the Construction Toolbar only contains commands for creating (adding) new geometry features.

Dashboard

The Dashboard will appear automatically whenever a new feature is being created, or an existing feature is being redefined. The appearance of the Dashboard will vary depending on the type of feature being defined, but every aspect of the individual feature is accessible and controlled within the Dashboard.

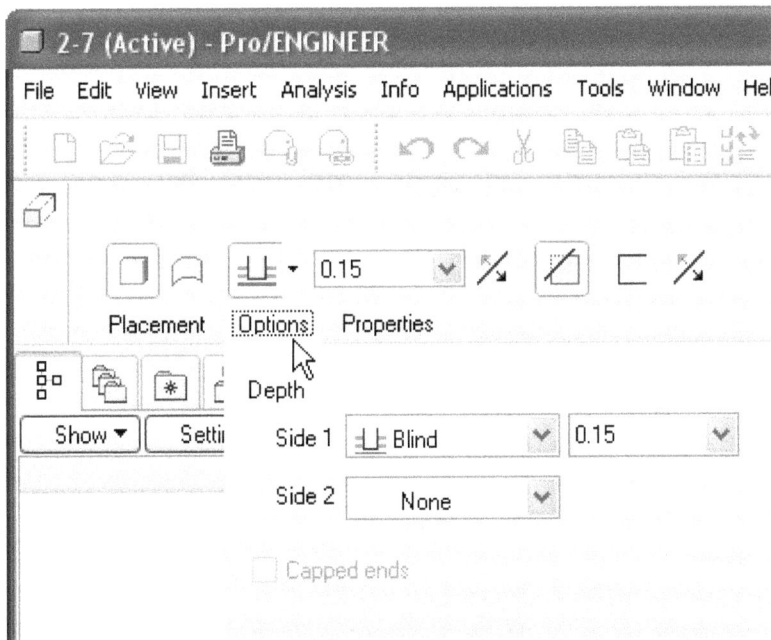

Fig. 2-7
Geometry controls for a cut, accessible within the Dashboard

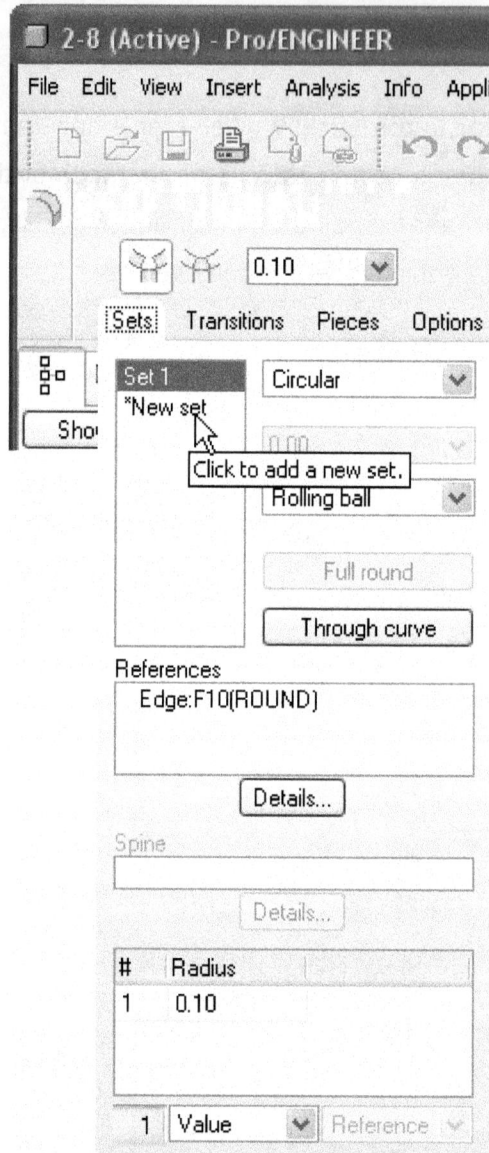

Figure 2-8
Geometry controls for a round, accessible within the Dashboard

The right side of the Dashboard contains icons to **‖** **Pause** the Dashboard, ☑ 👓

Preview the geometry being created or redefined (which automatically pauses the

dashboard), ▶ **Resume** the dashboard, ☑ **Apply** (accept) the current status of the geometry (as shown in Figure 2-9), or ✖ **Quit** the geometry definition and close the Dashboard.

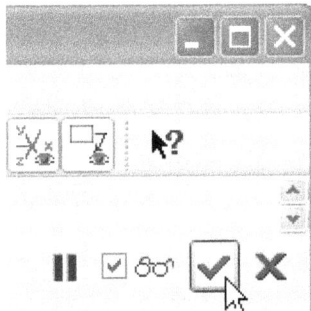

Applies and saves any changes you have made in the feature tool and then closes the tool dashboard.

Fig. 2-9
Dashboard control icons

Dialog Boxes

Depending on the feature being created, a Dialog Box may automatically pop-up. Simply fill in the appropriate information. Whenever typing text or values from the keyboard, be sure to hit the Return or Enter button to accept the entry. When all of the necessary information has been filled in, the Dialog Box will automatically close, or it may be manually closed if desired. Figure 2-10 shows one type of Dialog Box when creating datum features and Figure 2-11 shows another type of Dialog Box when creating some types of three-dimensional geometry.

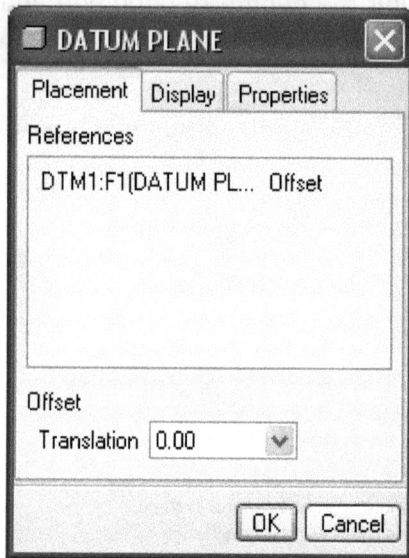

Fig. 2-10
Datum Feature Dialog Box

Fig. 2-11
Solid Geometry Dialog Box

Selection Filter

At times, you may wish to limit the possible
choices when selecting items for editing or
other manipulation. The Selection Filter
located at the lower right of the Pro/ENGINEER
screen will allow you to specify exactly which
type of geometry may be selected, as shown
in Figure 2-12.

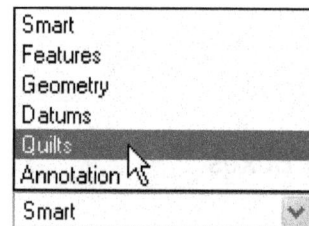

Fig. 2-12
Selection Filter

Message Window

Directly below the Main Toolbar is the Message Window. It is important to read the
messages that appear in this window, as they will indicate the current status of
features and commands, as well as prompt for required information.

Customization

The locations of the toolbars and windows may be modified at any time by selecting from the menu, **Tools** > **Customize Screen**, and make the appropriate choices in the dialog box as shown in Figure 2-13.

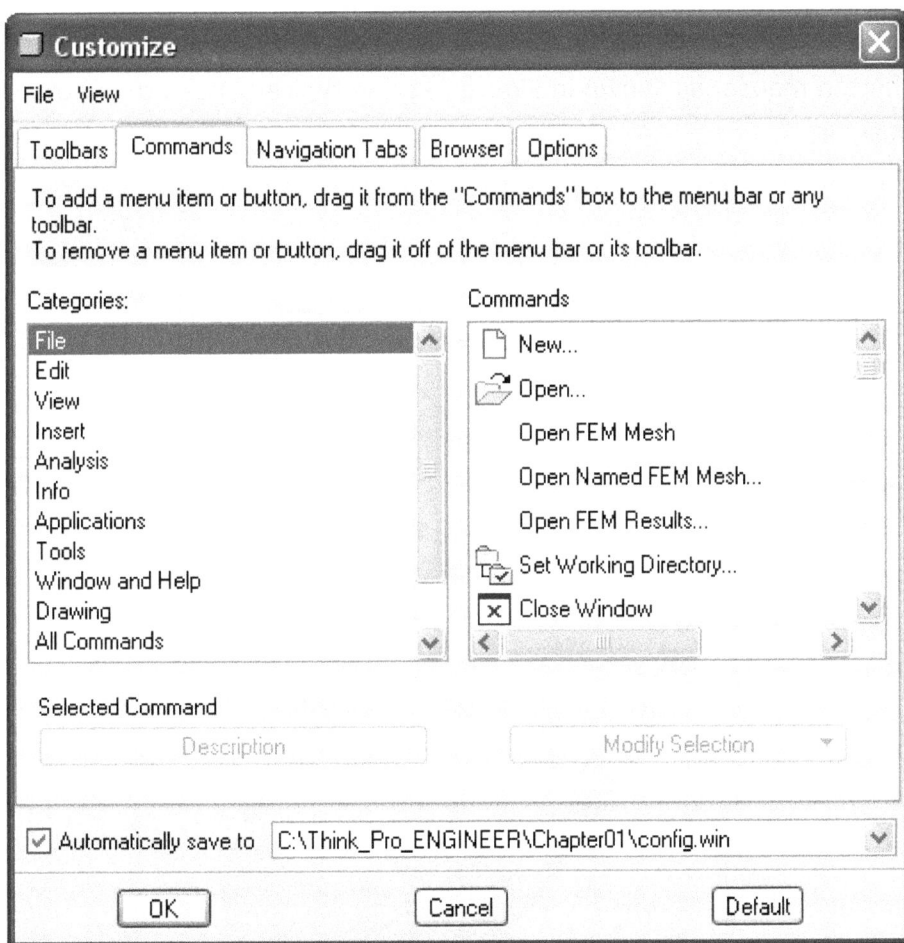

Fig. 2-13
Menu and screen customization

Pointing and Selection Devices

Many users of other MCAD systems enjoy using devices such as a 3D Mouse or Spaceball®. While Pro/ENGINEER supports the use of these devices, they are generally not necessary, due to Pro/ENGINEER's efficiency and ease of use.

Mouse

A three-button mouse, as shown in Figure 2-14, is typically used to control Pro/ENGINEER.

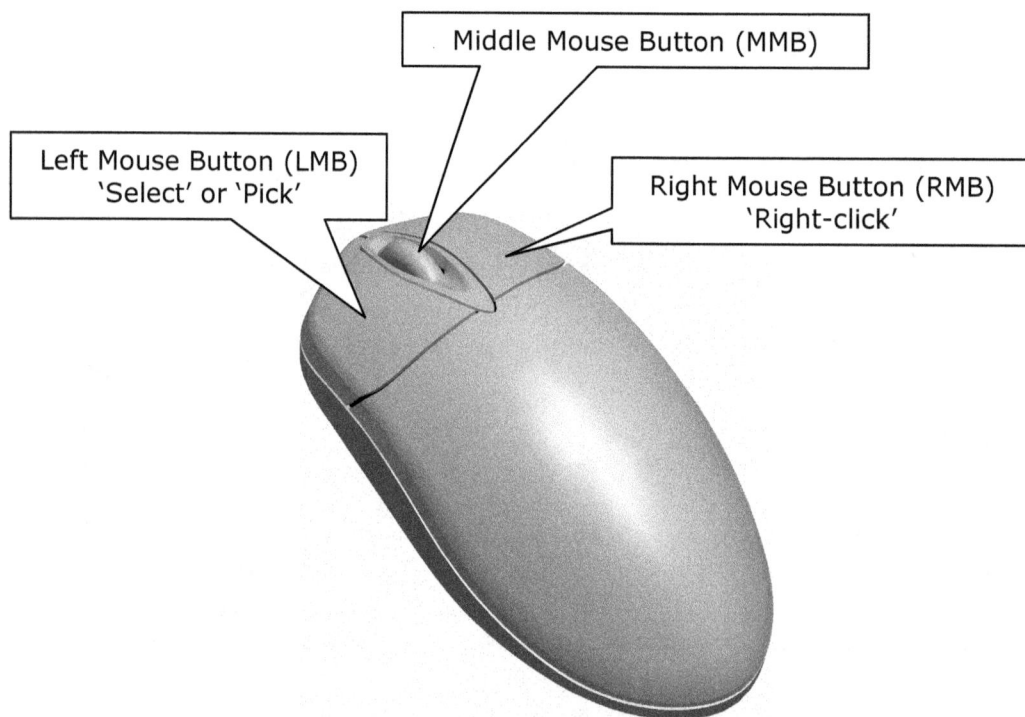

Middle Mouse Button (MMB)

Left Mouse Button (LMB)
'Select' or 'Pick'

Right Mouse Button (RMB)
'Right-click'

Fig. 2-14
Three-button scroll-wheel mouse

Holding the Mouse

To properly manipulate the buttons of the mouse, rest the index finger on the Left Mouse Button (LMB), and the middle finger on the Right Mouse Button (RMB), as shown in Figure 2-15.

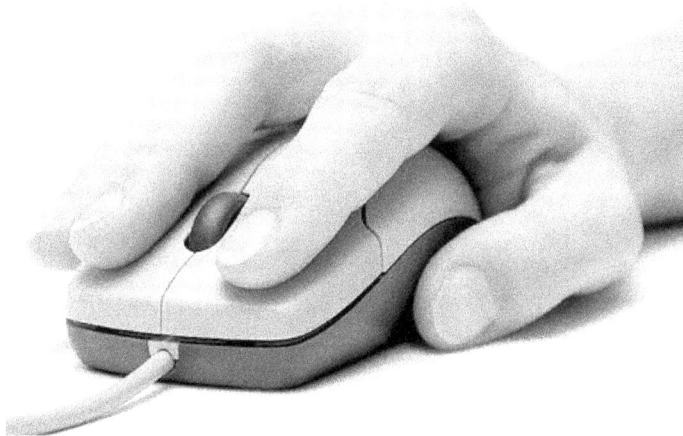

Fig. 2-15
Proper finger placement

The index finger is used to depress both the Left and Middle Mouse Buttons, and to manipulate the scroll wheel (if equipped).

Left Mouse Button (LMB)

This button is the 'select' or 'pick' button, used for selecting commands and geometry, sketching, and activating dialog boxes.

Middle Mouse Button (MMB)

This button is used primarily for spinning and orienting the Pro/ENGINEER geometry. It is also used to cancel commands and place dimensions on drawings and sketches.

Right Mouse Button (RMB)

The right mouse button has two main uses. It is used to query through various choices when selecting geometry (See Chapter 5), but its main function is to invoke a context sensitive menu, as shown in Figure 2-16.

To activate a 'mouse menu', first a feature or piece of geometry is selected with the left mouse button (LMB), then the right mouse button (RMB) is depressed, and held down. This technique is commonly referred to as 'right click' or 'right clicking'. To make a selection from the menu, simply move the mouse until the curser highlights the appropriate choice, as shown in Figure 2-16, and release.

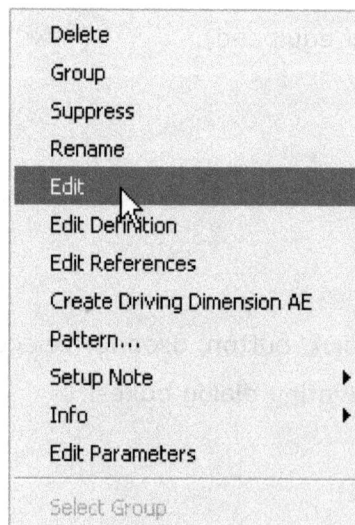

Delete
Group
Suppress
Rename
Edit
Edit Definition
Edit References
Create Driving Dimension AE
Pattern...
Setup Note ▶
Info ▶
Edit Parameters
Select Group

Fig. 2-16
Typical RMB 'Mouse Menu'

Keyboard

The keyboard is primarily used to enter alpha-numeric values and information, such as dimensions, notes, and names. The **Enter** or **Return** key (depending on the keyboard) is used to accept those values and choices. Figure 2-17 also shows the **Shift**, **Control** (**Ctrl**) and **Alt** Buttons which are frequently used in conjunction with the mouse for selecting geometry and orienting models.

Fig. 2-17
Special use buttons

Pro/ENGINEER also has the ability to use macros, also called 'keyboard shortcuts'. See Chapter 27 for information on how to program commonly used or complex commands into short keystrokes.

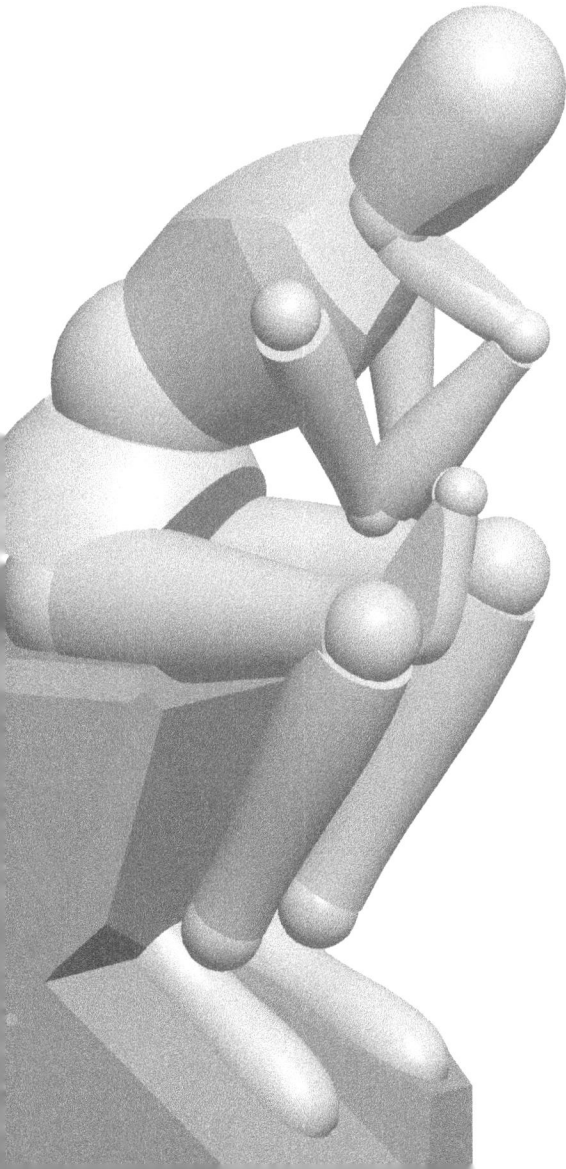

File Versions

As discussed in Chapter 1, Pro/ENGINEER creates several file types and extensions, most notably *filename.prt* for parts, *filename.asm* for assemblies, and *filename.drw* for drawings. In addition to a file name and extension, Pro/ENGINEER automatically adds a sequential version number suffix to the file name. When creating a new part named 'widget' the actual file Pro/ENGINEER creates is *widget.prt.1*. Each time a file is saved, Pro/ENGINEER creates a copy of the current file and increases its version number by one. So when the widget part is saved, *widget.prt.2* is created, while keeping the original *widget.prt.1*.

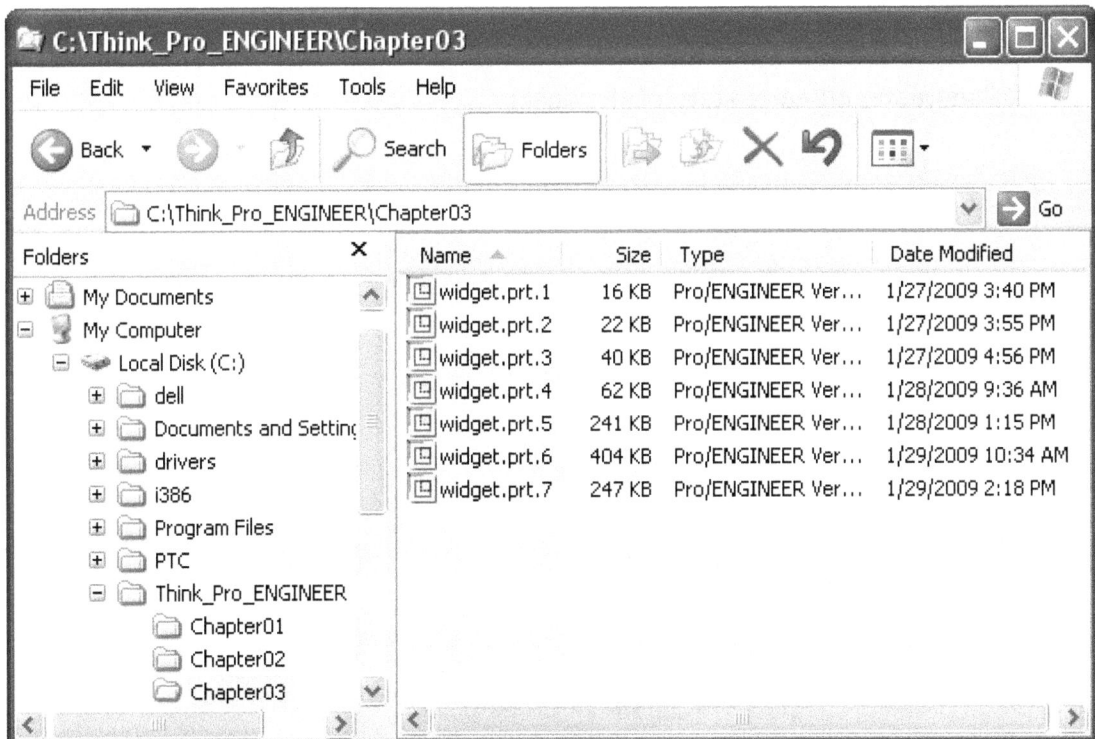

Fig. 3-1
Windows folder

To keep all the versions straight, Pro/ENGINEER always opens the highest version number of any given file, thus ensuring that only the latest design is opened. If a part is opened, worked on and saved various times over the course of one or more days, Pro/ENGINEER will create a new file each time it is saved. The computer folder may then look something like the folder shown in Figure 3-1.

Advantages

The multiple design versions created by Pro/ENGINEER represent 'snapshots in time'. Figure 3-2 shows the *widget.prt.3* version of the file (the third time it was saved), illustrating an early state of the design.

Fig. 3-2
widget.prt.3

After the part is revised and saved two additional times, *widget.prt.4* and *widget.prt.5* are created, and the part appears as it does in Figure 3-3.

Fig. 3-3
widget.prt.5

After the part is revised and saved twice more, *widget.prt.7* is created, shown in Figure 3-4.

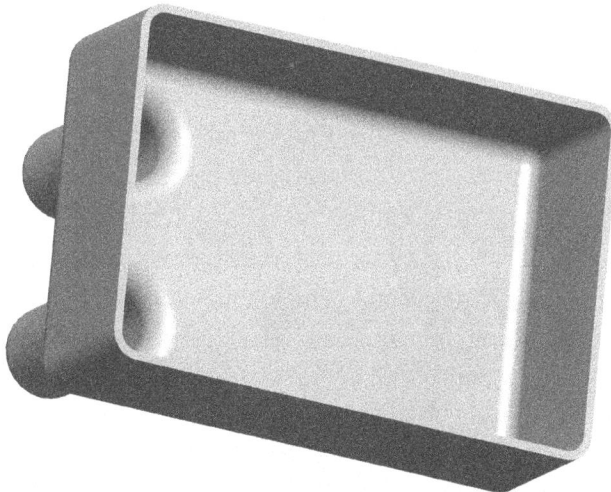

Fig. 3-4
widget.prt.7

At some point between saving version 5 and version 7, the notch on the top of the part was deleted, and the entire part was hollowed-out from the bottom. If it was decided that the part should no longer be hollow, it would be as easy as simply deleting the feature (called a Shell, see Chapter 14), but what if the notch needed to be put back into the part?

By simply deleting the *widget.prt.6* and *widget.prt.7* from the computer, or renaming them to different names, Pro/ENGINEER will open what is now the latest version of the Widget (*widget.prt.5*), effectively going back in time.

The multiple versions also allow you to experiment with parallel design paths. By simply renaming *widget.prt.4* to *new_widget.prt.1*, the new file may be opened, edited and saved without affecting the current Widget part, as shown in Figure 3-5.

Fig. 3-5
new_widget.prt.2

Disadvantages

When copying Pro/ENGINEER files to archive or send via FTP or email, it is important to be sure the highest version number is selected, to ensure the file represents the latest design.

Also, the larger the file size is, the more disk space will be required to maintain all of the Pro/ENGINEER file versions. If disk space is not an issue, then it should not be a concern. When looking at a list of files in the Pro/ENGINEER browser, as shown in Figure 3-6, the version numbers are hidden, and only the highest version is selectable.

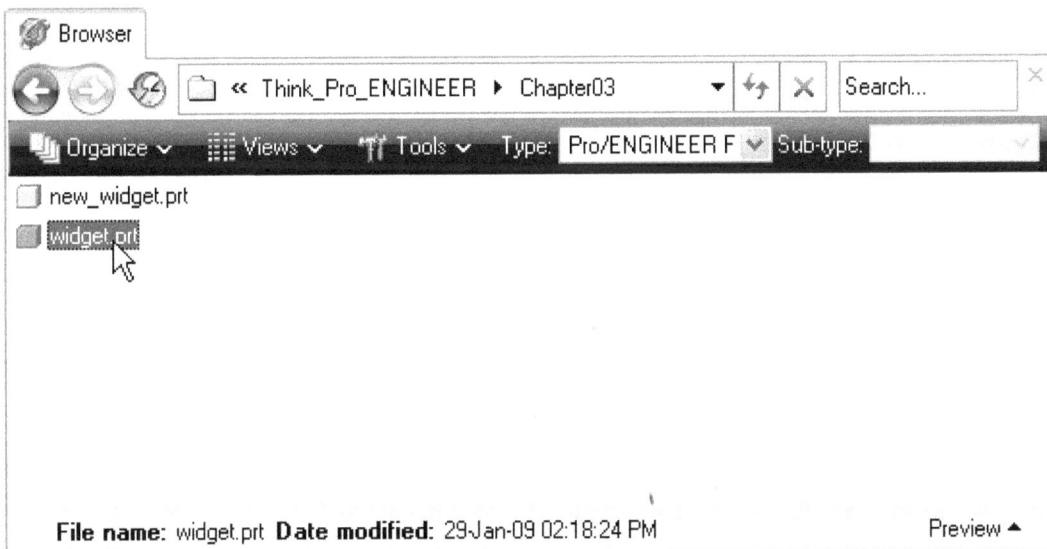

Fig. 3-6
Browser Window

If however file space is a concern, all of the old versions (every file except the highest version number) may be deleted from the computer by selecting from the menu, **File** > **Delete** > **Old Versions**. (Be sure not to select All Versions, unless that is your intent.)

File Locations

Pro/ENGINEER is able to access files from any drive and folder (directory) on a local or network computer. It can even access files from the Internet. If your installation of Pro/ENGINEER is using a PDM (Product Database Management) tool such as Windchill PDMLink, these tools will control how the data is accessed.

Regardless of what type of system you are using, your files will be stored in one or more locations. The standard convention is to organize your files into appropriate folders and sub-folders. For example, an engineering consultant with several clients would typically create a separate folder for each client, with sub-folders for each job. A company that manufactures widgets may create separate folders for each type of widget, while a company that is engaged in FEA (Finite Element Analysis) may divide the folders even further into individual iterations of a single design.

Working Directory

While files may be stored anywhere you like, the Working Directory is the single most important folder or directory. The Working Directory is not a permanent location, but rather a variable that the user sets as needed. The Working Directory is the first place Pro/ENGINEER will search when opening files with associativity to other files, such as when opening a drawing file. Pro/ENGINEER will search the current Working Directory for all of the parts and/or assembly files necessary to open the drawing. The best practice therefore is to store related files in the same folder.

If we wanted to continue working on our widget design and perhaps create a drawing of it, the first step would be to set the Working Directory by selecting **Set Working Directory** from the File Menu and selecting the appropriate folder.

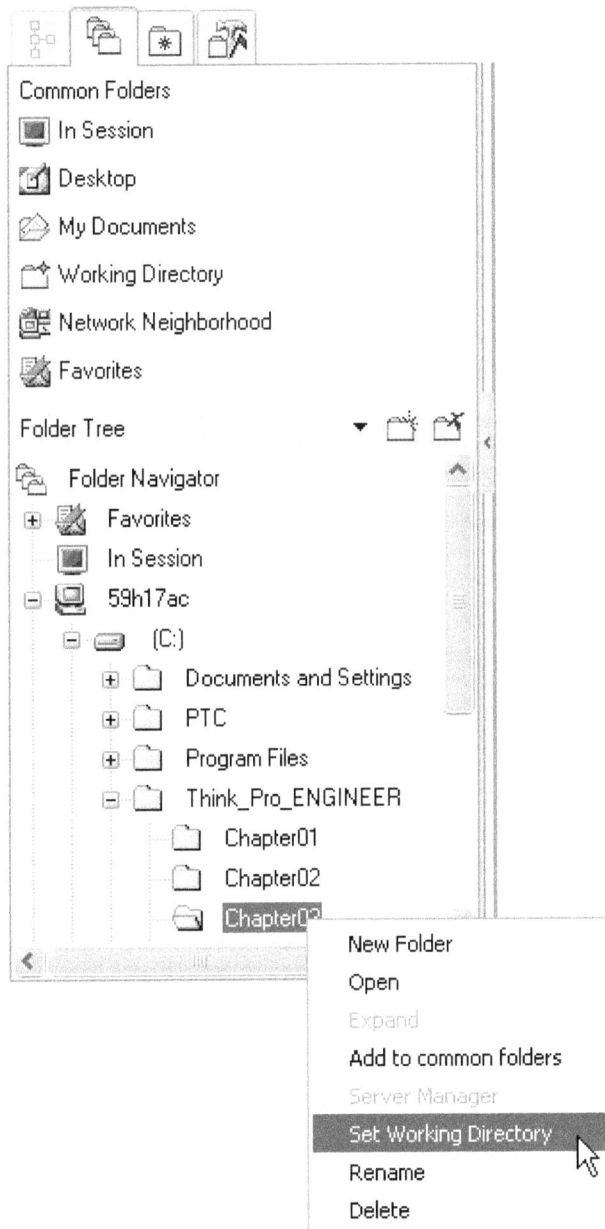

Fig. 3-7
Setting the Working Directory

It may be selected using the Folder Browser in the Navigator Window, as shown in Figure 3-7. Simply select the appropriate folder, hold down the **RMB**, and choose **Set Working Directory**. This will effectively create a 'short cut', so that when creating new files they can be easily stored in the Working Directory. Files that are not in the current Working Directory may still be accessed through the Folder Browser, but clicking on the Working Directory icon listed under the Common Folders at the top of the Navigator Window will quickly display the contents of the Working Directory in the Browser Window.

In Session

When a Pro/ENGINEER file is accessed, either by opening it directly or as a result of associativity to another file, it pulls all of the file's information from the hard-drive or server and places it in your computer's RAM (Random Access Memory). Even if you close the window displaying the model, the information is still in RAM. As long as you do not end your session of Pro/ENGINEER, these models may be accessed by simply selecting the **In Session** shortcut under the Common Folders in the Navigator Window. This allows you to open a model without needing to go back to the hard-drive or server. This also allows you to open new files that have been created and closed without remembering to save them first.

This functionality however, requires the Pro/ENGINEER user to be disciplined when naming files and organizing folders. For example, if we are working on our widget.prt in the Chapter03 folder and then closed the window, the information associated with that file name will be in RAM. If there was a completely different design in the Chapter02 (or any other) folder, but it had the same (widget.prt), the Widget that is in RAM will be opened, even if we select the file from the Chapter02 folder.

Erasing

Depending on your business, it may be necessary to have duplicate names for your files. Although it is not recommended, it is possible. In order to open the Chapter02 version of our widget, we first have to clear the Chapter03 version from RAM. To do this, simply select **Erase** from the File Menu, as shown in Figure 3-8.

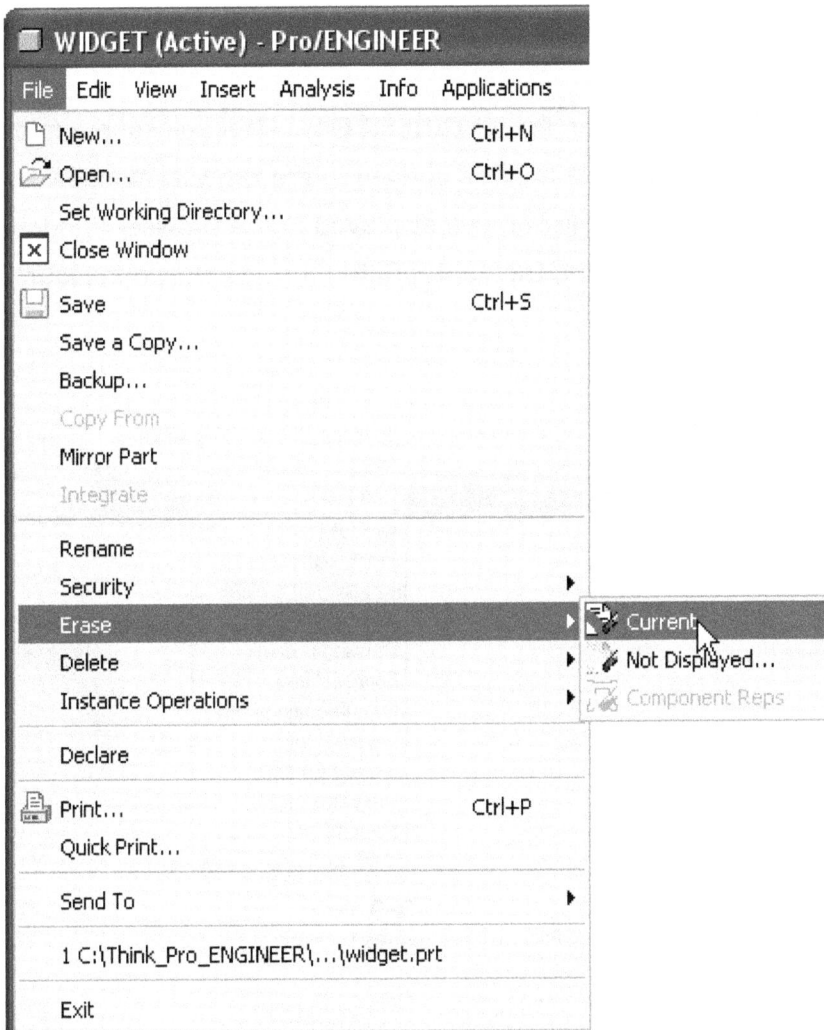

Fig. 3-8
Erasing a model from Session (RAM)

Select **Current** or **Not Displayed**, depending on whether you want to clear the data for the model that is currently open, or all other the models that have been opened but not currently displayed.

This will completely clear the RAM but in order to open the Chapter02 model, you need to first set Chapter02 as the Working Directory, since Pro/ENGINEER will always look in the Working Directory first, when opening a file.

Opening Files

There are several ways to open Pro/ENGINEER files. After selecting a folder in the Folder Browser, the desired file may be opened in the Browser Window by double-clicking on the file name. The list of files displayed in the Browser Window can be isolated by file type by selecting the appropriate filter, as shown in Figure 3-9.

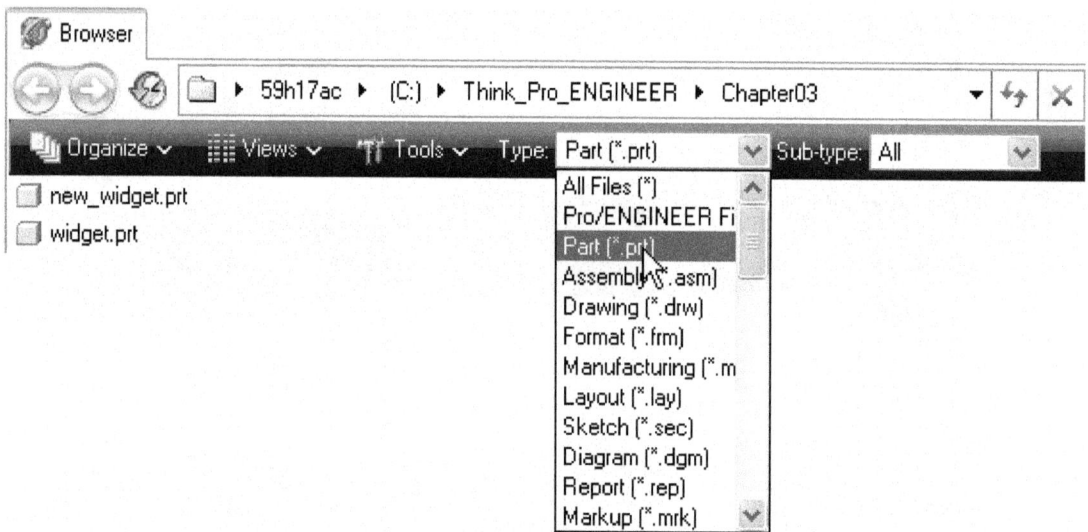

Fig. 3-9
Filtering file names by type

You may also select **Open** from the File Menu, and navigate to the appropriate drive, folder and file, or even drag a file using the **LMB** from the Browser Window or Windows Explorer into the Graphics Area.

Each time you open a file, it will open in a new window. You may have as many windows open as you wish, but only one window will be active at a time.

To switch between windows, select the file
name from the Window Menu. The current
active window will be indicated by a • (filled
dot), as shown in Figure 3-10.

Choose the model you wish to activate, or you
may choose **Close** to close the currently active
model. Remember that closed models are still
in RAM, and accessible **In Session**, until they
are erased or you exit Pro/ENGINEER.

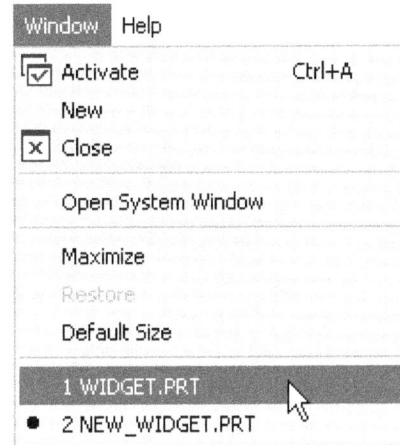

Fig. 3-10
Activating and closing windows

Saving Files

Since your current work is always being performed in RAM, you must save each

model if you wish to keep your changes. This is as simple as selecting 🖫 **Save**
from Main Toolbar or File Menu. You may also choose **Save a Copy** to create a new
file based on the current model. When doing so, you will be prompted for the new
file name, but you may also choose a new file type, such as IGES, STEP or STL for
export purposes, as shown in Figure 3-11.

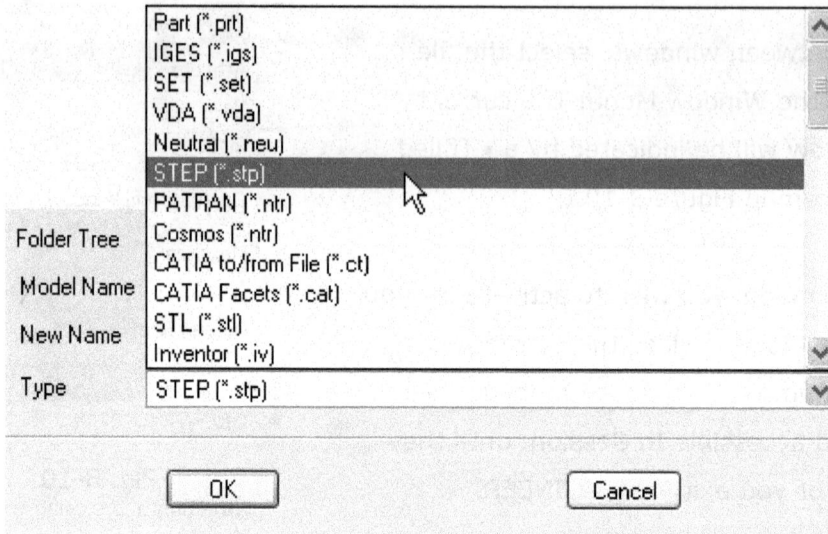

Fig. 3-11
Saving a Pro/ENGINEER model as a new type

Creating New Files

To create a new Pro/ENGINEER file, select ⬜ **New** from the File menu or Main Toolbar. Select the appropriate type of file from the list, as shown in Figure 3-12, and give the file a unique name. The file may be renamed later if desired, but the file name may not contain any spaces or special characters other than '-' (hyphen) or '_' (underscore). As discussed in Chapter 1, the proper file extension will automatically be created, so do not include it with the file name.

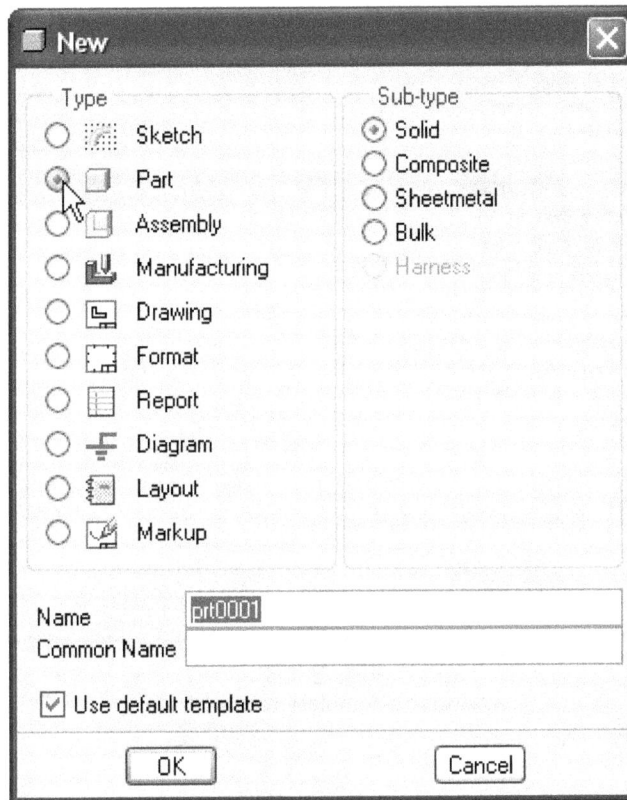

Fig. 3-12
Creating a new Pro/ENGINEER file

Leaving the **Use default template** box checked will create an exact duplicate of Pro/ENGINEER's default part, assembly or drawing as a starting point for the new model. Un-checking this box will allow you to choose any other existing file as a 'same as', by browsing to it, or if you choose, a completely empty (blank) file as shown in Figure 3-13.

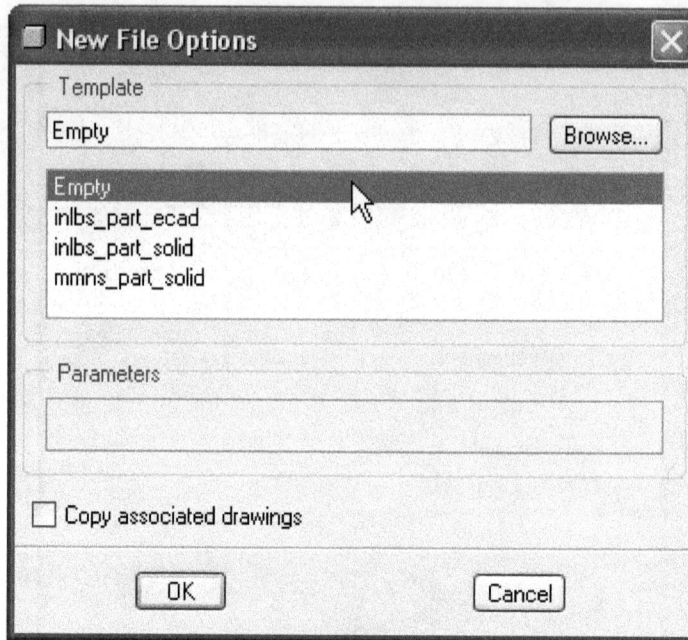

Fig. 3-13
Choosing a template to start from

File Setup

If a template is used, the new file's settings are the same
as the template, however, they may be modified by
selecting **Edit** > **Setup** from the menu. Pro/ENGINEER has
several common material specifications, such as 6061
Aluminum, Stainless Steel, Nylon, etc., that may be set by
selecting **Material** from the menu, as shown in Figure 3-14.
You may also select **Mass Props** to set a density value (by
default, a new part file has a density value of 1.0), or
manually enter a total mass value.

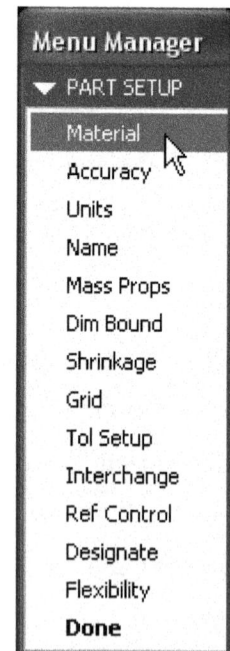

Fig. 3-14
Setup menu

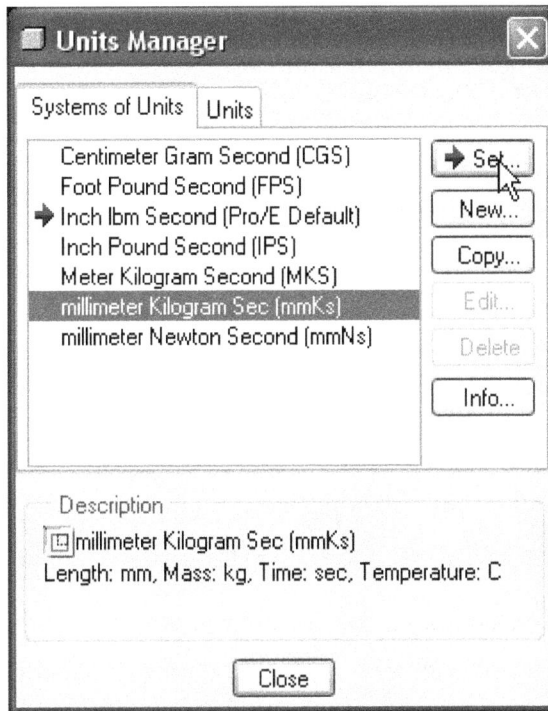

Fig. 3-15
Units Manager

Pro/ENGINEER's default units are Length: inches, Mass: pounds (LBS), Time:
seconds, Temperature: degrees F (Fahrenheit).

To change the units, select **Units** from the Menu to open the Units Manager, as
shown in Figure 3-15. Select the desired units, and select Set. When changing units,
you will need to choose whether or not to resize the model, as shown in Figure 3-
16.

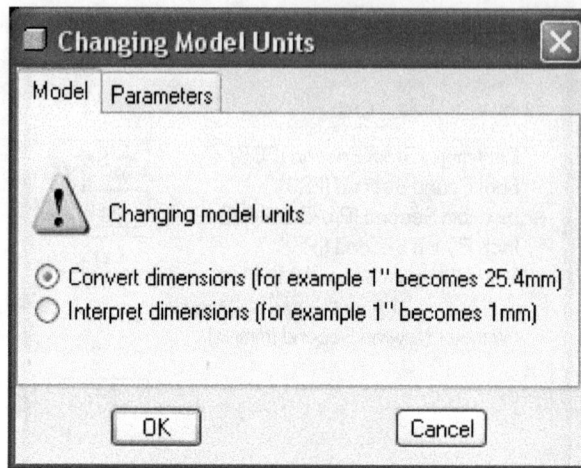

Fig. 3-16
Units Manager

If you choose **Convert dimensions**, the model will stay the same physical size, but the values will change. If you choose **Interpret dimensions**, the values of the dimensions will stay the same, but since you are changing the units, the physical size of the model will shrink or grow accordingly.

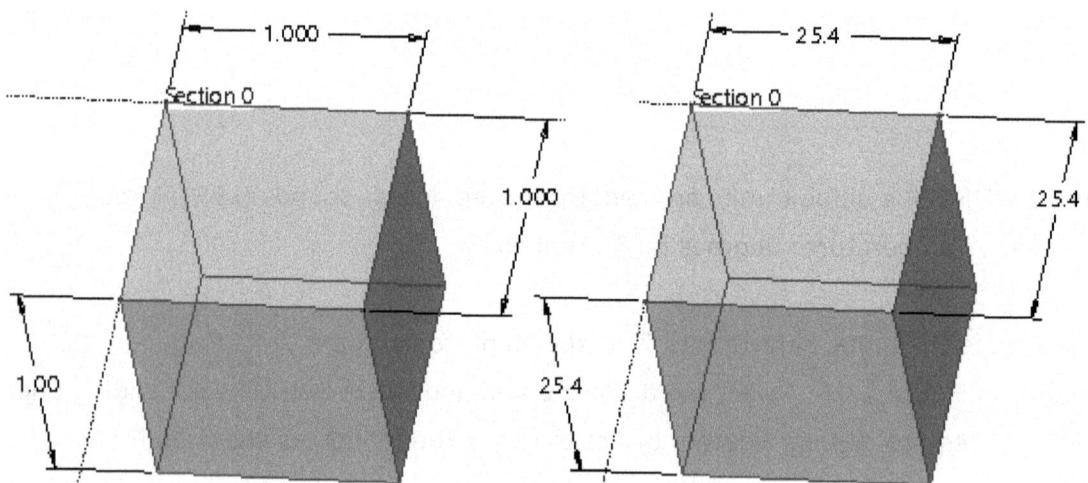

Fig. 3-17
Changed units

Figure 3-17 shows the exact same model, before and after changing the units from inches to millimeters, while using the **Convert dimensions** option.

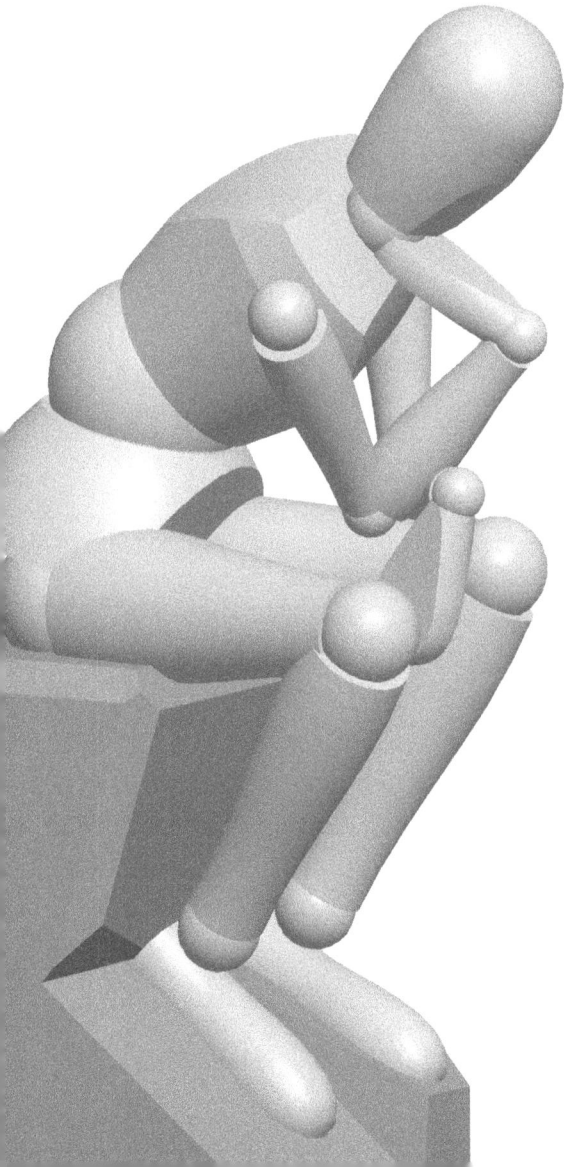

Chapter 4

Viewing Models

Display Styles
Zooming
Panning
Orientation
Spin

Display Styles

Three-dimensional models may be displayed with various styles.

Shading

The default style for Pro/ENGINEER is **Shading** (shaded mode turned on). This is a basic 'flat' shade, meaning that all surfaces oriented in the same direction are displayed with the exact same color and brightness, and that all surfaces will be illuminated equally according to a default light source.

Fig. 4-1
Three-dimensional model with Shading

Notice how the top of the cylindrical feature, shown in Figure 4-1, seems to blend with the top of the rectangular feature, which also blends with the top of the trapezoidal feature. This is usually sufficient for mechanical design purposes, but if a more sophisticated photo rendering or color variation is desired, those options may be set by selecting the **Color and Appearance**, **Model Setup** and **Display Settings** options found in the View menu.

By selecting the proper icon in the Main Toolbar, as shown in Figure 4-2, or by selecting **Tools** > **Environment** > **Display Style**, the display of the three-dimensional model may be changed from Shading to one of three additional types.

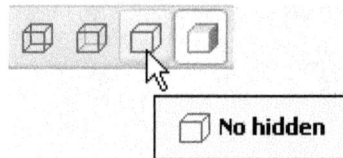

Fig. 4-2
Selecting the display style from the toolbar

No Hidden

The **No hidden** mode will display only the edges of the thee-dimensional model which are not obscured (hidden) by the rest of the model, as shown in Figure 4-3.

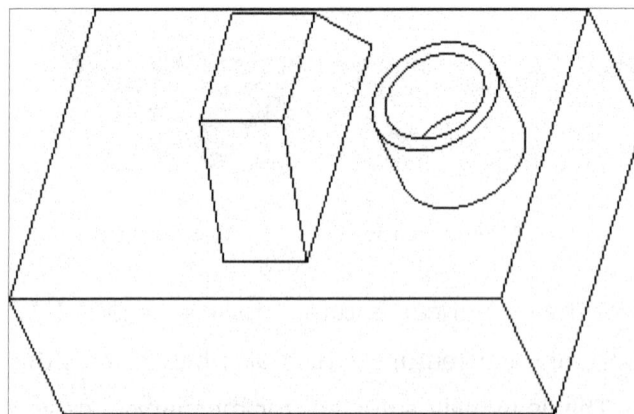

Fig. 4-3
Three-dimensional model with No hidden

All of the model's surfaces will appear the same as the background.

Hidden line

All of the model's edges are displayed in **Hidden line** mode, as shown in Figure 4-4, however, any obscured (hidden) edges will be displayed in grey.

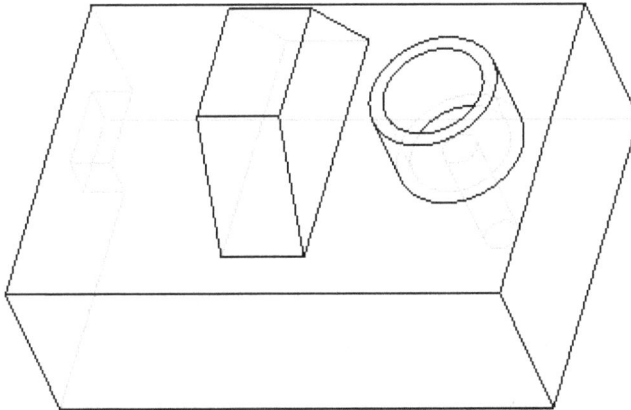

Fig. 4-4
Three-dimensional model with Hidden line

Notice that geometry which was not visible in **Shading** and **No hidden** modes is now visible in **Hidden line** mode.

Wireframe

By selecting **Wireframe**, all edges will be shown equally, regardless of their location on the model, as shown in Figure 4-5.

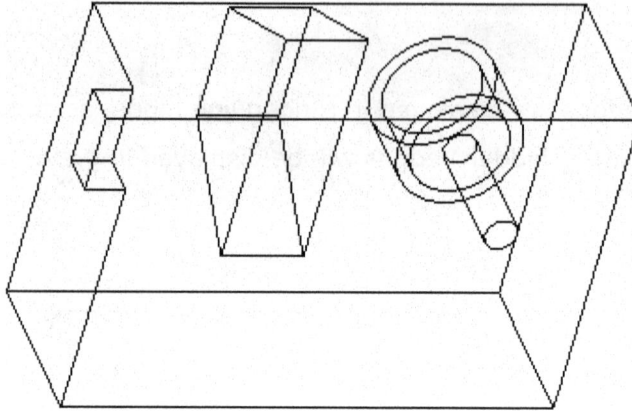

Fig. 4-5
Three-dimensional model in wireframe

Changing the display from **Shading** to **Wireframe** does not convert the model from a solid to a wireframe model. Regardless of which display mode is selected, the Pro/ENGINEER data remains the same, and the display mode only controls how the data is displayed on the screen.

Zooming

Zooming allows you to 'move in' close to see detail on a model, and 'move out' to see a larger portion, or entire model. The Pro/ENGINEER model remains a constant size and position in three-dimensional space, and only you the user are moving closer or further away from the model while zooming in and out.

Zooming with the Toolbar

You may zoom in to and out of a specified area by selecting the **Zoom In** and **Zoom Out** icons from the Main Toolbar. If at any time you have zoomed too far in or out, and would like to return the display back to its default setting, you may select the **Refit** icon.

Zooming with the Mouse

While holding down the **Ctrl** key with one finger, and the **MMB** simultaneously, drag the mouse up (away from you) to zoom out, and down (closer to you) to zoom in.

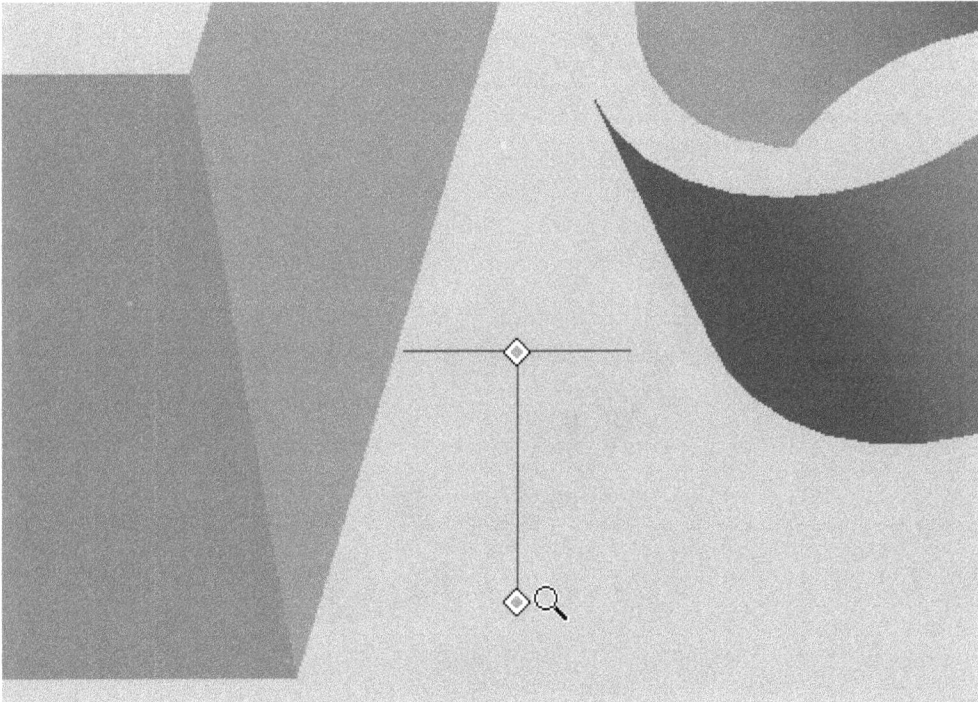

Fig 4-6
Zooming in with the mouse

A horizontal bar with a diamond will mark your starting position (zoom center), and as you drag the mouse, a vertical bar with a diamond will 'rubber-band', as shown in Figure 4-6, above or below the horizontal bar. You can control the zoom center simply by positioning the cursor before executing the command. When the desired amount of zoom is achieved, release both the mouse button and keyboard.

Zooming with the Scroll Wheel

The easiest way to zoom in and out is to place the cursor on the desired zoom center, and while leaving the mouse stationary, use the scroll wheel, as shown in Figure 4-7.

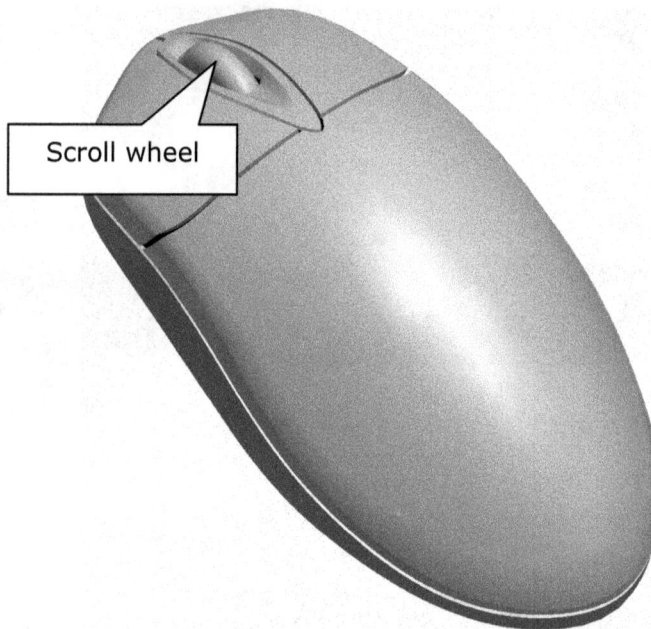

Scroll wheel

Fig. 4-7
Scroll wheel for zooming

Roll the wheel away from you to zoom out, and roll it toward you to zoom in.

Panning

Panning is a technique where the orientation and zoom factor of your model remains constant, but the view is shifted in any direction in a plane parallel to the screen. To pan, simply hold down the **Shift** key and **MMB** and drag the mouse. As with the zoom, you will see a starting diamond shape and a 'rubber-band', as shown in Figure 4-8. The view will move dynamically as you drag the mouse. Release both the keyboard and mouse to set the view.

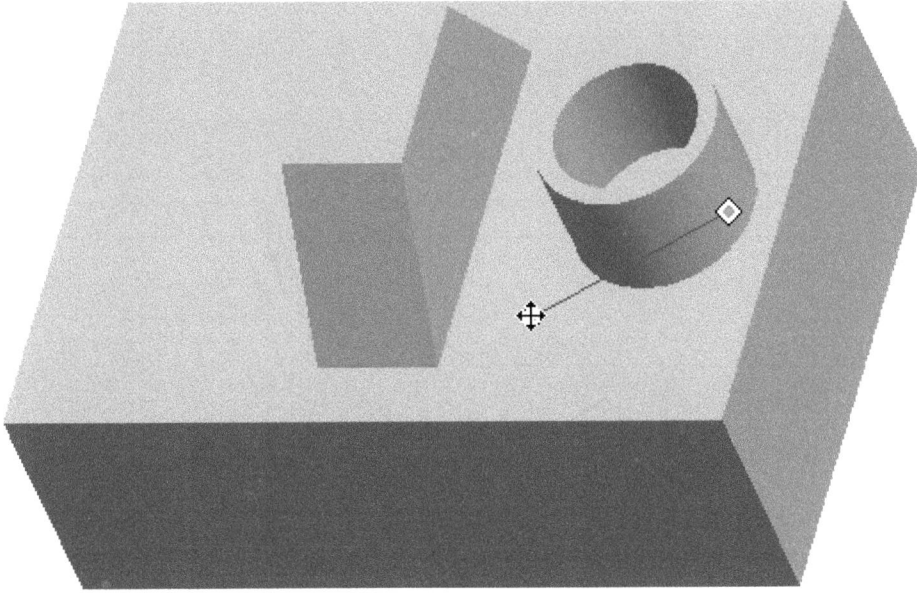

Fig. 4-8
Panning the view

Orientation

Trimetric Orientation

By default, Pro/ENGINEER displays three-dimensional models using trimetric orientation, where the direction of viewing is such that all of the three axes of space appear unequally foreshortened. The scale along each of the three axes and the angles among them are determined separately as dictated by the angle of viewing. The term trimetric comes from the Greek for 'three measure', reflecting that the scale along each axis of the projection is unique.

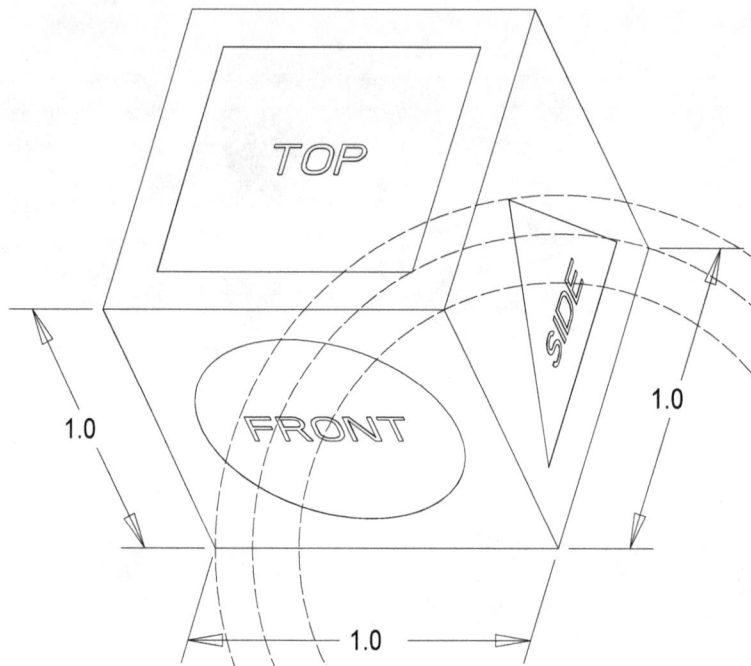

Fig. 4-9
Trimetric projection

Figure 4-9 shows a perfect cube in trimetric projection. It's length, width, and height are all equally set at one unit (1.0), yet appear to be of different values. It is important to note that this is only how the cube is displayed on the screen or a drawing, not how it was designed. The true size and shape of the solid model is not affected by the projection type.

Isometric Projection

Isometric projection is a form of axonometric projection, in which the three coordinate axes appear equally foreshortened and the angles between any two of them are 120°. The term isometric comes from the Greek for 'equal measure', reflecting that the scale along each axis of the projection is the same.

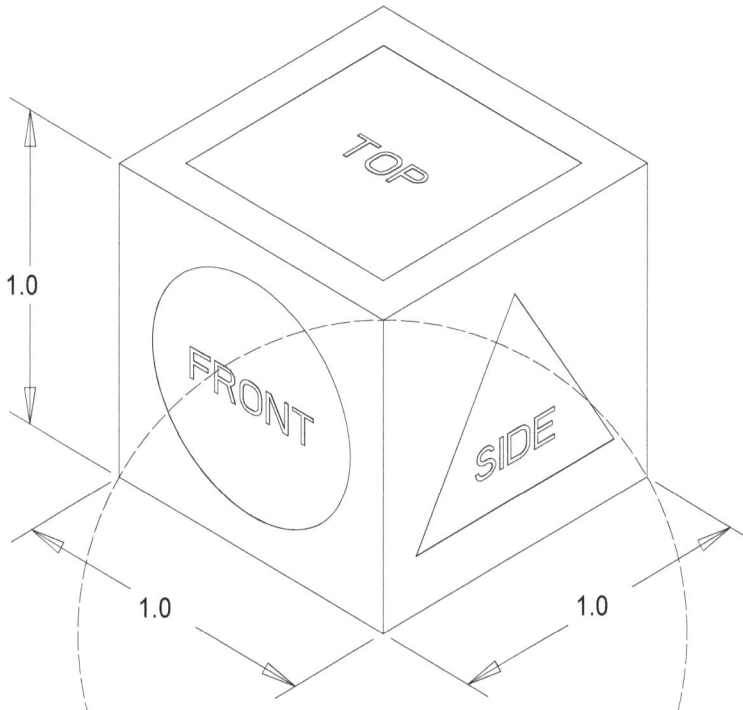

Fig. 4-10

Isometric Projection

Figure 4-10 shows the same perfect cube using isometric projection. Notice that the length, width, and height (which are equal in the solid model) are shown equally on the screen. To set the standard orientation to isometric, select from the menu, **Tools > Environment > Standard Orient > Isometric**.

Spin

Dynamic

To 'spin' your model (change its orientation), simply hold down the **MMB** and drag the mouse. The model will dynamically spin, meaning that any movement in the mouse is immediately reflected on the screen, about its default spin center. Figure

4-11 shows spinning the model dynamically, with the Spin Center turned on (default setting).

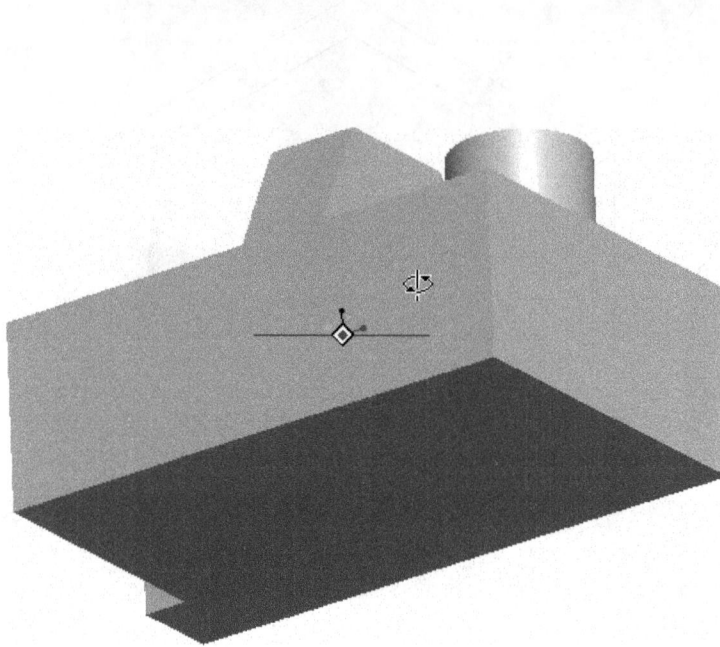

Fig. 4-11
Dynamic spin with Spin Center on

The Spin Center is automatically placed in the geometric center of the model, and is indicated by the three-lobed, green, red, and cyan icon, as shown in Figure 4-12.

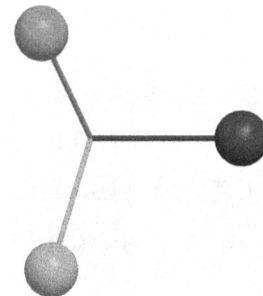

Fig. 4-12
Spin Center

When the Spin Center is turned off by selecting the **Spin Center** icon on the Main Toolbar, the model can be spun relative to where the cursor is placed on the screen with the **MMB**. Figure 4-13 shows the model being spun relative to an area near the corner of the model.

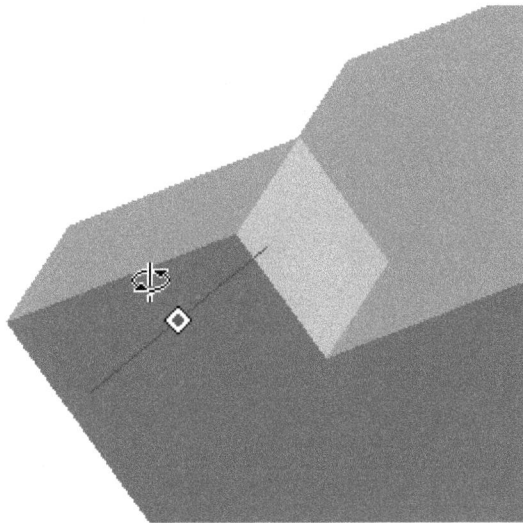

Fig. 4-13
Dynamic spin with Spin Center off

Orient Mode may be turned on by selecting the [icon] **Orient Mode** icon on the dashboard. This suspends the geometry creation abilities of Pro/ENGINEER, and allows for additional spin controls to be used to display the model.

These options are accessed by holding down the **RMB**, as shown in Figure 4-14, and selecting the desired spin type.

Anchored

The Anchored spin type is dynamic, but retains a 'rubber-band' from a triangle at the starting position to a triangle handle at the other end, as shown in Figure 4-15. Releasing the **MMB** in this position will set the orientation, but if the mouse is held down, the two triangles may be matched up so that the display may return to the original position.

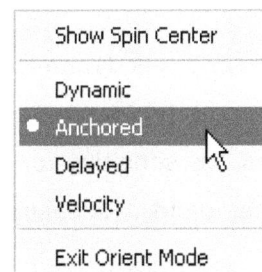

| Show Spin Center |
| Dynamic |
| ● Anchored |
| Delayed |
| Velocity |
| Exit Orient Mode |

Fig. 4-14
Selecting spin type

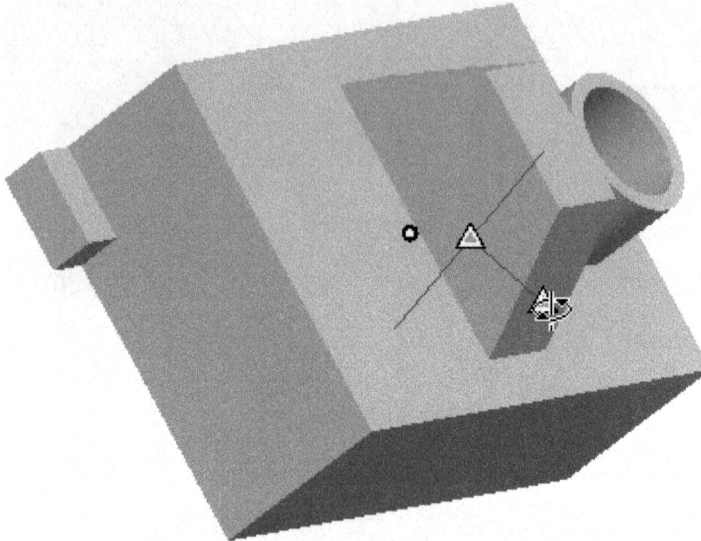

Fig. 4-15
Anchored spin

Delayed

Delayed spin operates the same as Anchored (uses squares instead of triangles), but it is not dynamic. The orientation of the model will not change until the **MMB** is released. This is useful for very large models which may take a long time to dynamically spin, or when the session of Pro/ENGINEER is being shared over the Internet.

Velocity

Velocity spin is dynamic, but the model will continue to spin in the same direction as the handle (circle, in this case) is being dragged. The speed of the automatic spinning is sensitive to the distance between the starting and ending handles (rubber-band). Releasing the **MMB** stops the spin.

To return to normal editing mode, select the **Orient Mode** icon to turn it off. See Chapter 22 for techniques to set and save exact view orientations.

Chapter 5

Selecting Items

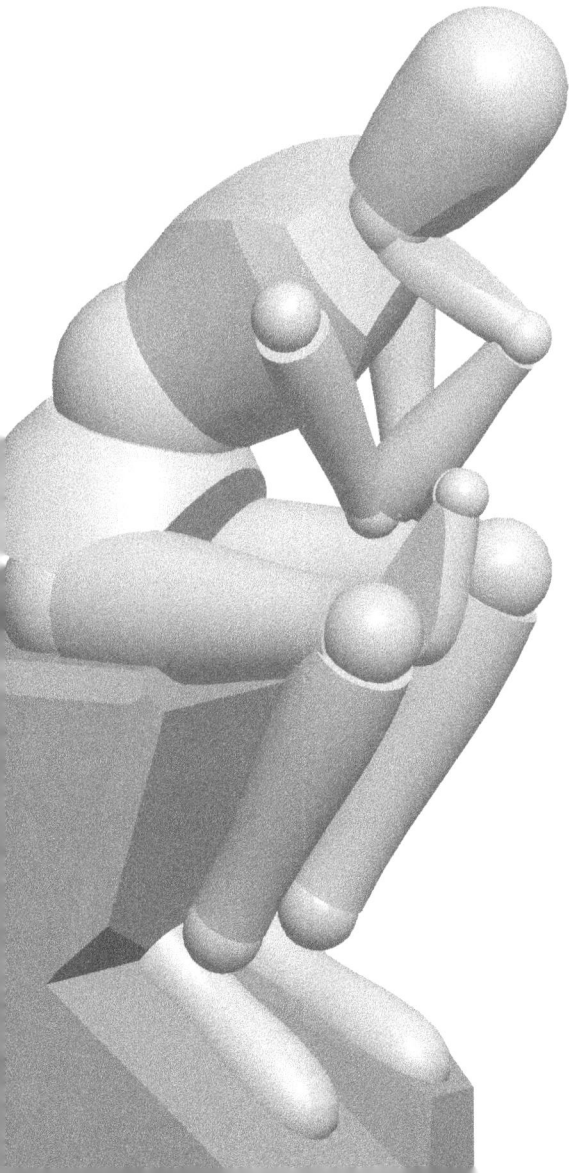

Selection Types

Chapter 2 discusses selecting commands from menus and icons with the **LMB**. When using these commands, you will also need to select models, features, and geometry from the three-dimensional design to complete the operation. Most operations in Pro/ENGINEER utilize a Flexible Work Flow, meaning you may select a command first, then apply that command to the design (Action – Object), or you may select some aspect of the design first, then affect that selection with a command (Object – Action). In either case, there are various ways to select items of the design.

Direct Selection

Figure 5-1 shows an assembly with several components. Perhaps we want to pick one of the parts from the assembly in order to delete it or revise its placement. The component may be directly selected one of two ways.

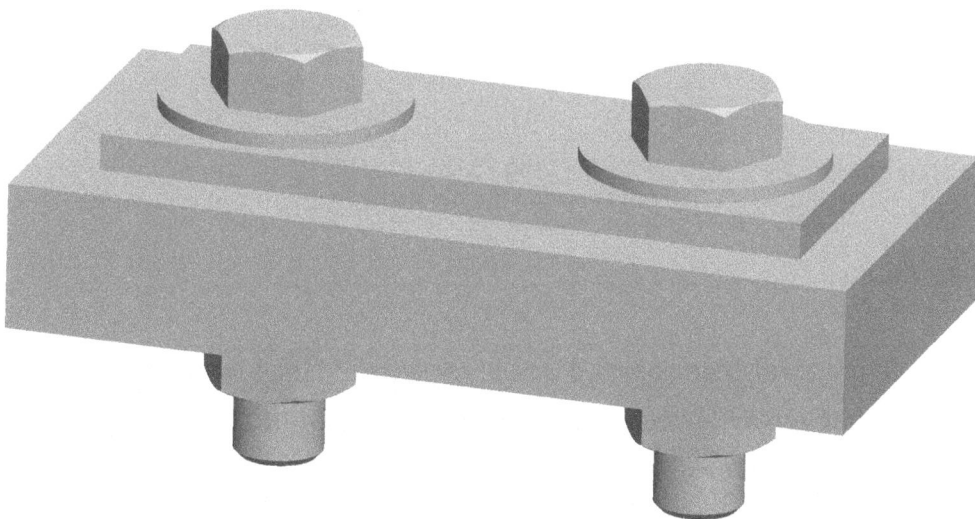

Fig. 5-1
Assembly of components

Model Tree

When an assembly is opened, the contents of the assembly are displayed in the Model Tree. To select and item, simply pick it from the list, with the **LMB**, as shown in Figure 5-2. The model tree will indicate the selected item with a blue field behind the text, and the selected item will be highlighted in the Graphics Area in red, wireframe.

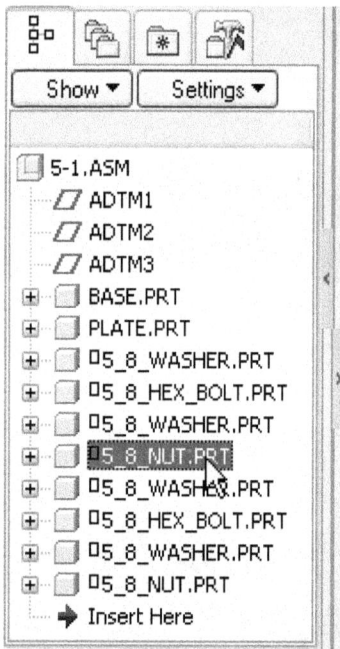

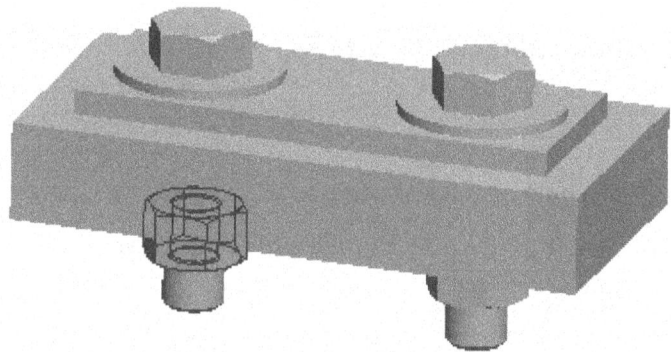

Fig. 5-2
Item selected from the Model Tree

Graphics Area

The same item may also be selected directly from the model in the Graphics Area, but to verify that you are selecting the desired item, Pro/ENGINEER uses Pre-select Highlighting. When you pass your cursor over the model various portions will highlight in cyan (light blue) wireframe, as shown in Figure 5-3. By holding the mouse still, a tag will also be displayed with the name or description of the item.

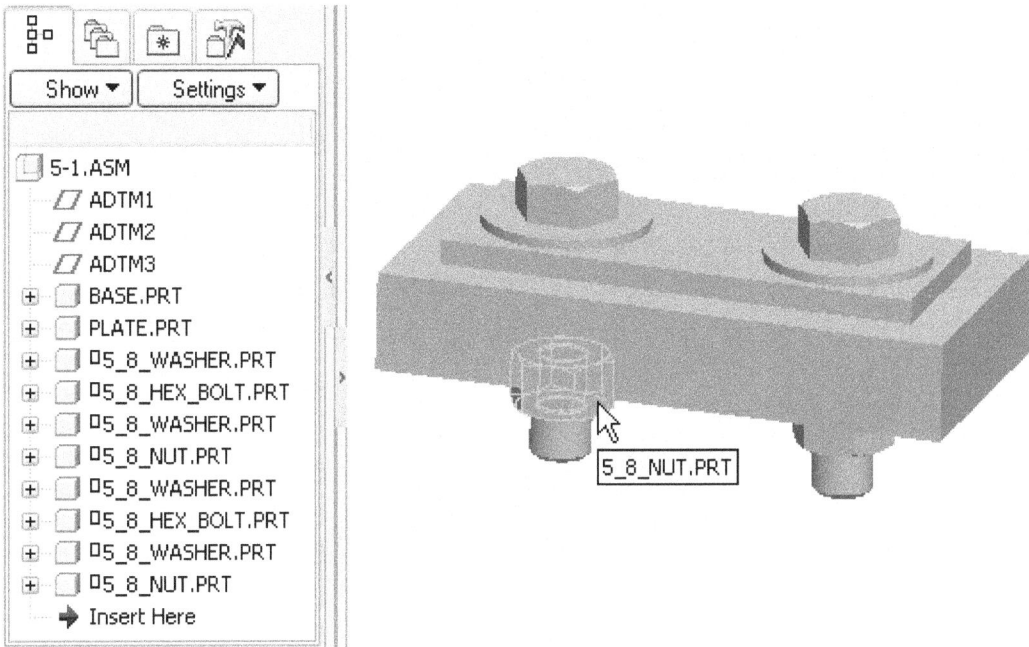

Fig. 5-3
Pre-select highlighting of an item

At this point, nothing has been selected, as this highlighting only serves as feedback to tell you that if you press the **LMB** now, this is the item that will be selected. Once you do so, the item will be selected, and the display will appear the same as it did in Figure 5-2.

Query Selection

The Direct Selection method from the Graphics Area only works for items that could be touched if your design was truly physical, rather than virtual. For example, you would not be able to physically touch the dishes inside a dishwasher if the door was closed, but you could if the door was open, and you could see the dishes inside. The same is true for your virtual designs.

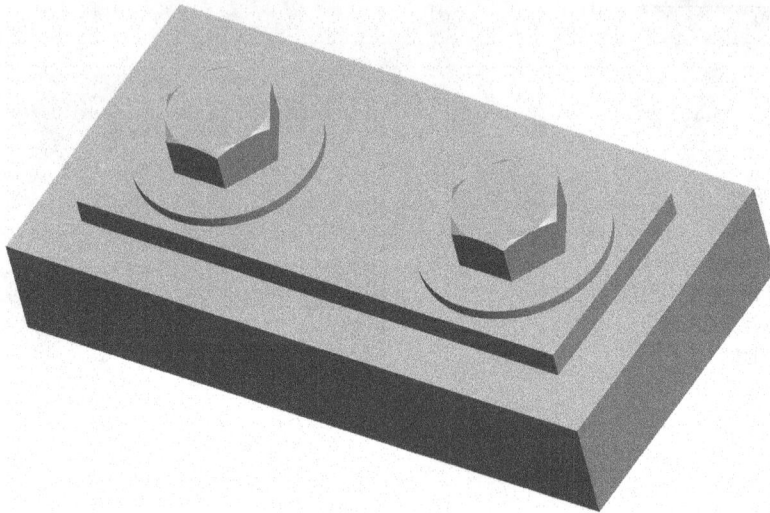

Fig. 5-4
Virtual design with obscured components

Figure 5-4 shows the same assembly, but it has been spun so that the nuts are no longer visible. When the mouse is passed over the model now, only the bolts, plate, base, and two of the washers will highlight. To be able to select the nuts, the easiest method would be to simply spin the model to an orientation that would allow direct selection, but sometimes this is not an option.

To query through possible selection choices, place the cursor on the model so that the desired item is directly behind the cursor. Imagine that your cursor is a laser cutter, and that you are trying to cut through the design to get to the item, as shown in Figure 5-5.

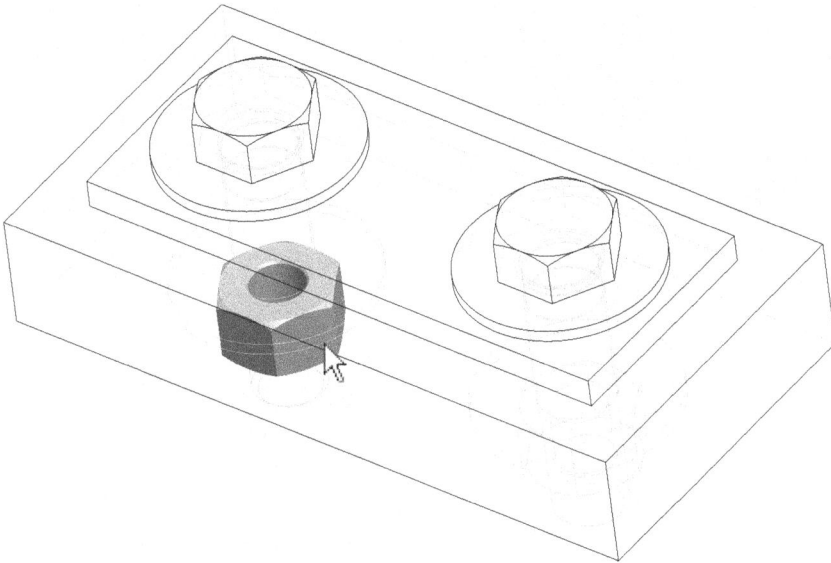

Fig. 5-5
Placing the cursor over the desired item

With the cursor in the proper position, click the **RMB** one time, and release. (Note that query selection is one of only two times that the **RMB** is used, but not held down.) This will cause one of the components to pre-highlight. Clicking the **RMB** again will pre-highlight the next possible choice. Continue clicking the **RMB** until the desired item is pre-highligted, as shown in Figure 5-6. The item can then be selected with the **LMB**.

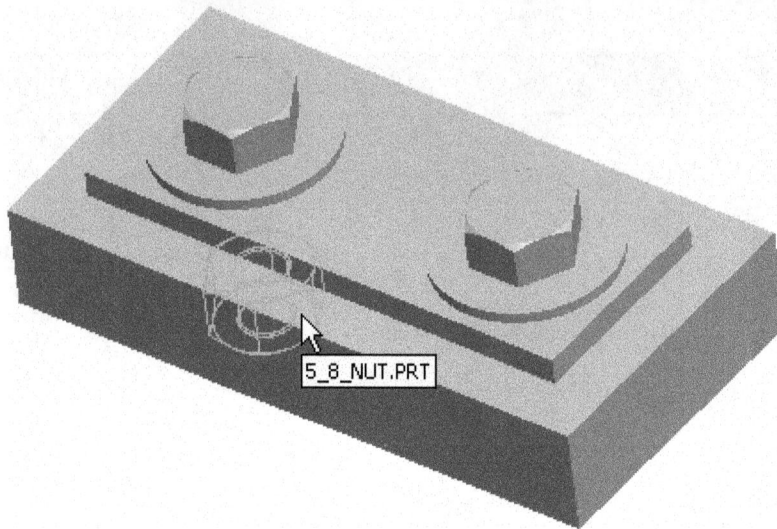

Fig. 5-6
Item pre-highlighted by query selection

Pick from List

With the cursor over the appropriate area, the **RMB** may be depressed, and held down. This will evoke a menu, as shown in Figure 5-7, from which you may choose **Pick From List**.

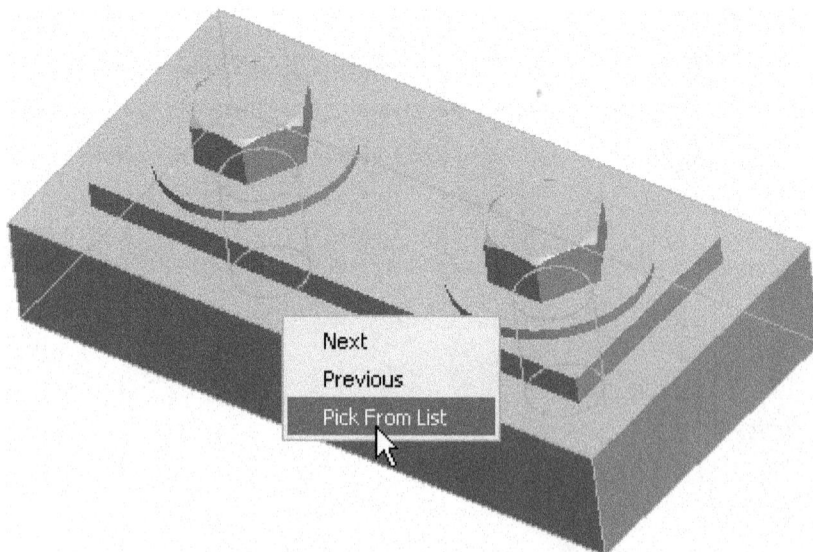

Fig. 5-7
Evoking a selection menu with the RMB

A separate menu will automatically pop
up, as shown in Figure 5-8, allowing you
to make the desired choice.

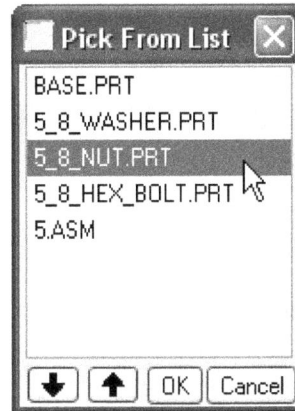

Fig. 5-8
Selecting items from a list

Searching

Items may be selected according to their name or type, whether they may be

visualized or not. Selecting the [icon] **Find** icon from the Main Toolbar will open the

Search Tool, as shown in Figure 5-9.

By using the drop-down menus and tabs within the tool, you can direct
Pro/ENGINEER to look for a particular type of item, and where to look, i.e. a hole in
a part. Using wildcards in the values, as shown in Figure 5-9, will result in one or
more possible choices being listed in the 'Found' window. Any desired item may

then be selected and added to the 'Selected' window with the [>>] **Add** button.

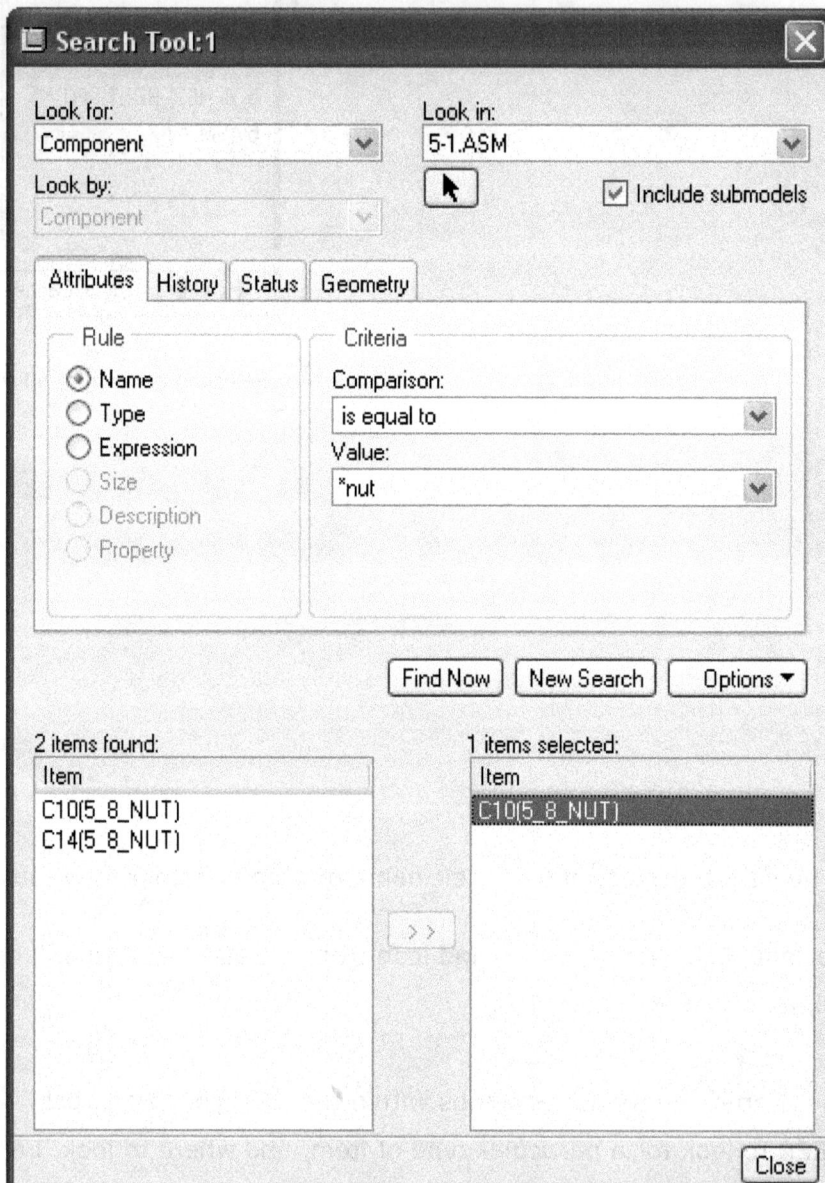

Fig. 5-9
Using the Search Tool

Deselecting

After an item has been selected, it is considered the 'current' item, and will remain the current item until a new selection is made to replace it, or it is removed from the selection set, much like how models may be erased from RAM (see Chapter 3). The selection set may be erased by selecting **Edit** > **Select** > **Deselect All**.

An item may be directly deselected by holding down **Ctrl** and selecting the same item again, however the easiest method is to replace the current selection with a null selection. By using the **LMB** to select an area of empty space within the Graphics Area, you can replace the current selection with an empty selection.

Selecting multiple items

Ctrl

When more that one item needs to be selected at the same time, such as when you want to pick several edges to round off together (see Chapter 11), hold down **Ctrl** while making the multiple selections. If after all the selections have been made and you decide to remove one or more from the set, hold down **Ctrl**, and select the item again, which will deselect only that one item.

Shift

When selecting items from the Model Tree, you may select one item, and while holding down **Shift**, select a second item, and all the items in between will be selected as well.

Selection Filter

Because Pro/ENGINEER offers a flexible workflow, the selection of items will vary depending on the operation you are performing. For example, if we want to create a chamfer (see Chapter 12) along the edge of our part, we could select the **Chamfer** tool (command) first. Pro/ENGINEER knows that you will be selecting an edge or surfaces, so it allows you to pick that geometry directly, as shown in Figure 5-10, and will indicate the possible choices with the pre-select highlight.

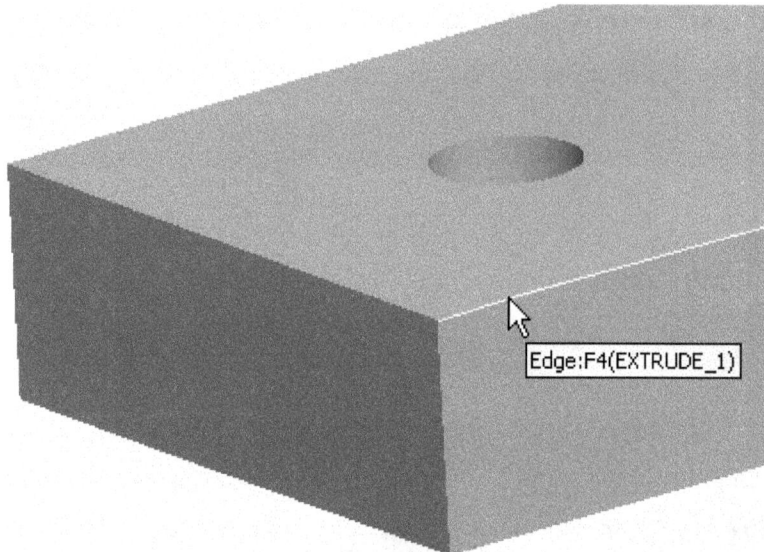

Edge:F4(EXTRUDE_1)

Fig. 5-10
Selecting an edge

This is an example of the Action – Object workflow, and is possible because the Selection Filter (located at the bottom right of the screen) defaults to **Smart**. It automatically allows for the proper selection type, depending on the operation at hand.

If however you want to select the same edge without selecting a command first (Object – Action), you can force Pro/ENGINEER to only pick geometry by setting the Selection Filter as shown in Figure 5-11.

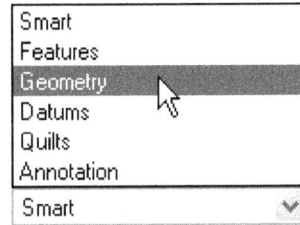

| Smart |
| Features |
| Geometry |
| Datums |
| Quilts |
| Annotation |
| Smart |

Fig. 5-11
Setting the Selection Filter

By leaving the filter set to **Smart**, you may use the hierarchy of the items to control selection. You can think of it in terms similar to the parent/child relationships. An edge does not exist without a solid piece of geometry first, so the first item that can be directly selected is the feature that forms the edge. After the feature is selected, passing the cursor over the feature will cause different pieces of geometry to be pre-selected (highlighted in cyan), such as edges, verticies, and surfaces, as shown in Figure 5-12, which then may be selected.

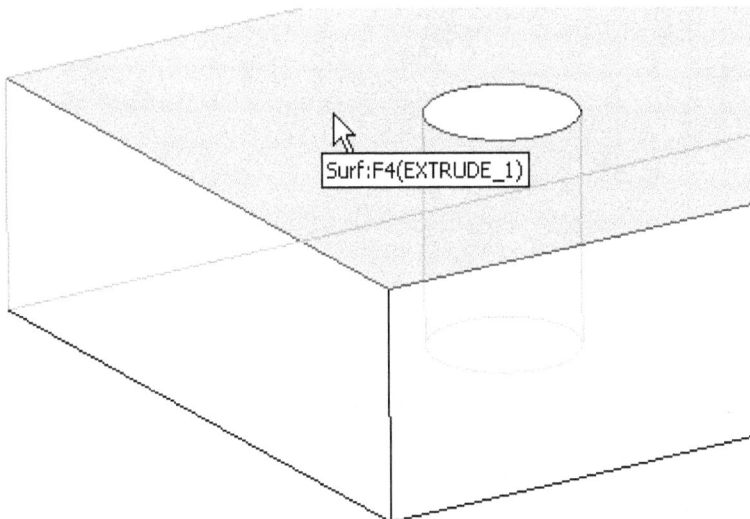

Surf:F4(EXTRUDE_1)

Fig. 5-12
Selecting a surface

Selecting a loop

You may also select a surface using the method described above, then while holding down **Shift**, select an edge of the surface. This will change the selection set from the 'seed' surface to all of the bounding surfaces, as shown in Figure 5-13.

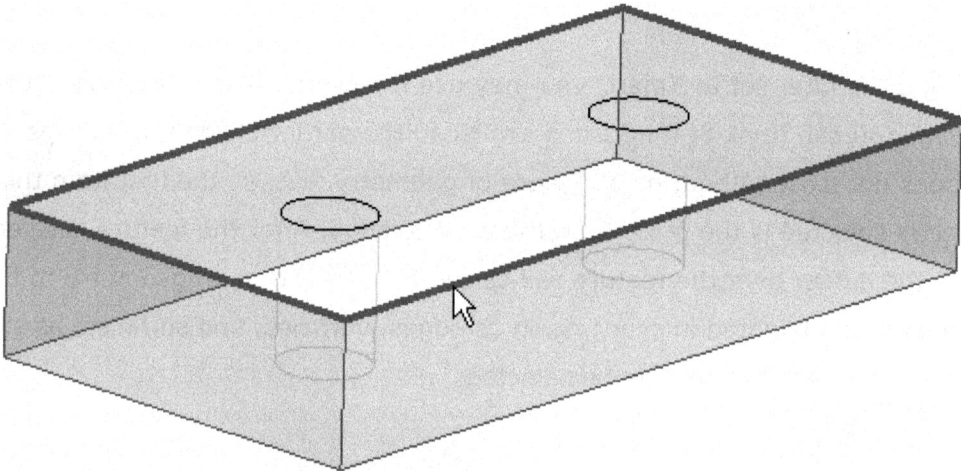

Fig. 5-13
Selecting a loop of surfaces

Reference Geometry

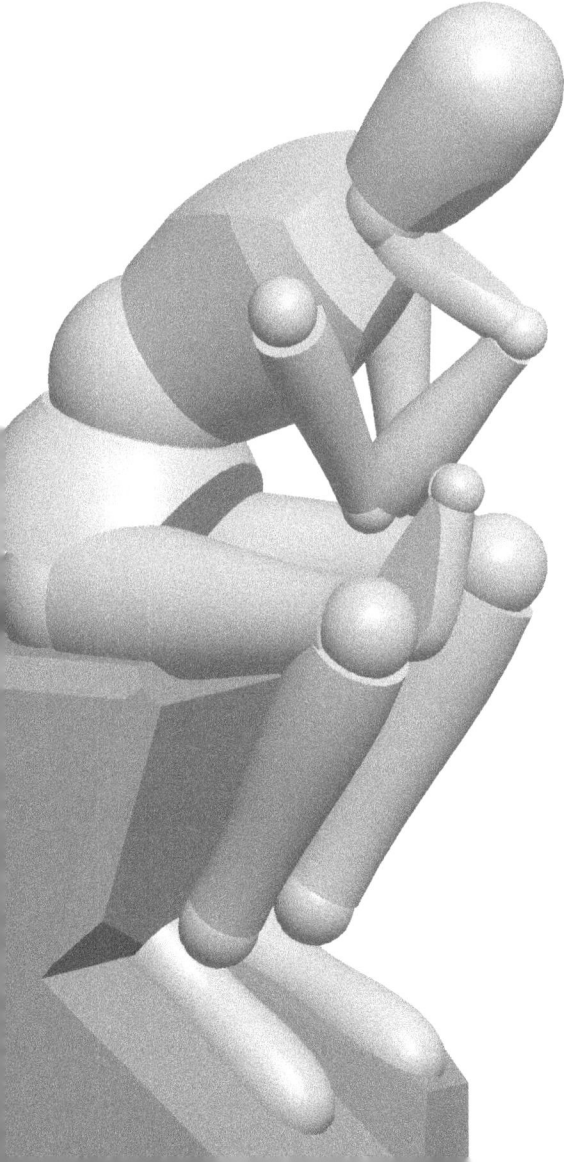

Chapter 5

Inference Geometry

As discussed in Chapter 1, it is necessary to reference existing geometry (parents) when creating new geometry (children). Due to the complexity of the new geometry, it may be necessary to have large amounts of data available to reference, but we may not want this reference geometry to appear as physical features in our manufactured product. We can create several reference features to control location, size, and shape of our physical features. To toggle the display (visibility) of datum features on or off, click on the appropriate icon in the Main Toolbar. (Notice the 'eye' in the icon.)

Coordinate Systems

In geometry, coordinate systems are used not only to describe the location of points, but also to describe the orientation of axes, planes, and rigid bodies.

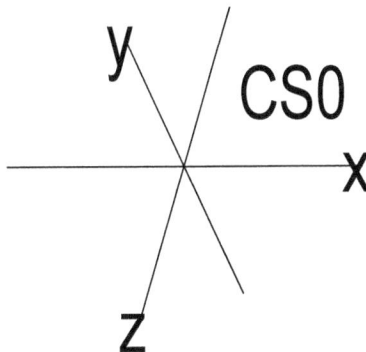

Fig. 6-1
Default Coordinate System

The default coordinate system in parts or assemblies, as shown in Figure 6-1, is the only feature in Pro/ENGINEER that does not require a parent feature. All other geometry is located and oriented relative to the default coordinate system, regardless if you have a coordinate system feature or not, as Pro/ENGINEER 'knows' where it would exist.

Additional coordinate systems may be added to parts and assemblies at any relative position or orientation, in order to locate parts within assemblies, and assemblies within other assemblies. They may also be used to locate geometry being imported from external sources, such as STEP (Standard for the Exchange of Product model) or IGES (Initial Graphics Exchange Specification) data.

Figure 6-2 shows a 1 inch solid cube that was created such that the lower, forward, left corner is located directly on the default coordinate system (CS0). Therefore, the coordinates of that corner is 0, 0, 0 in X, Y, Z format.

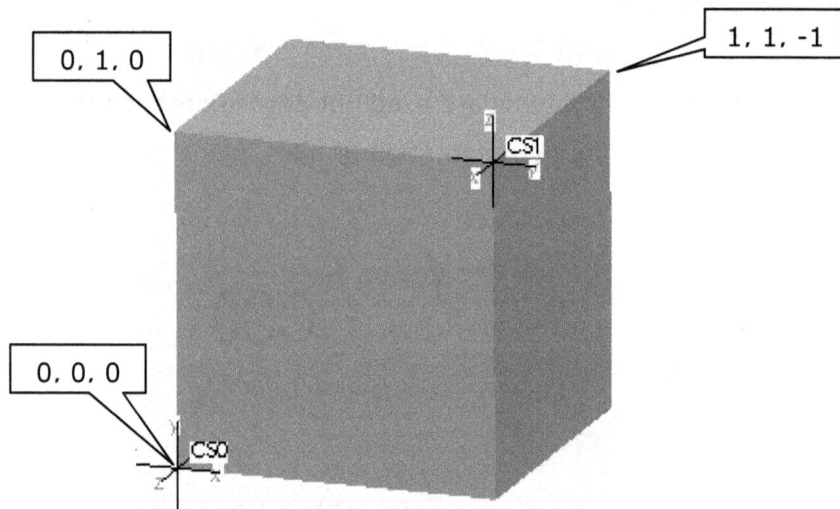

Fig. 6-2
Default coordinate system

The coordinates of the corner directly above is 0, 1, 0, and the coordinates of the opposite corner is 1, 1, -1.

Figure 6-2 also shows an additional coordinate system (CS1). Coordinate systems may be added to the model using any existing geometry to control its location and orientation by selecting the ⯐ **Coordinate System** icon from the Construction

Toolbar. To locate the origin (position) of the new coordinate system, the front, top and side surfaces of the cube are selected as references, as shown in Figure 6-3.

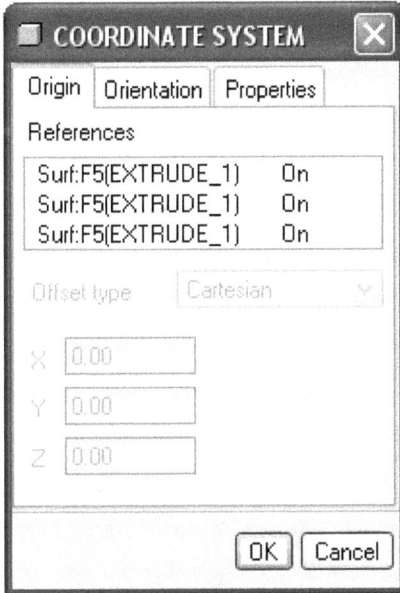

COORDINATE SYSTEM ⊠	COORDINATE SYSTEM ⊠
Origin Orientation Properties	Origin Orientation Properties
References	Orient by
Surf:F5(EXTRUDE_1) On Surf:F5(EXTRUDE_1) On Surf:F5(EXTRUDE_1) On	⊙ References selection ○ Selected CSYS axes
Offset type Cartesian	Use Surf:F5(EXTR...
X 0.00	to determine Z ∨ Flip
Y 0.00	Use Surf:F5(EXTR...
Z 0.00	to project Y ∨ Flip
OK Cancel	OK Cancel

Fig. 6-3
Setting origin

Fig. 6-4
Setting orientation

The CS1 coordinate shown in Figure 6-2 is also set at a different orientation than CS0. To do this, click on the Orientation tab, and select the desired references to set the preferred axes and directions, as shown in Figure 6-4.

Cartesian, cylindrical, and spherical coordinates may be created using any desired combination of references and controls from the dialog box.

Datum Planes

In geometry, a plane is a theoretical surface which has infinite width and length, zero thickness, and zero curvature (flat). In Pro/ENGINEER, datum planes are used as references for geometry to be created or define regions within a model. The first three datum planes created in a model are referred to as the default datum planes, as shown in Figure 6-5. Pro/ENGINEER uses the location and orientation of the default coordinate system (even if a coordinate system feature does not exist) for their references (parents).

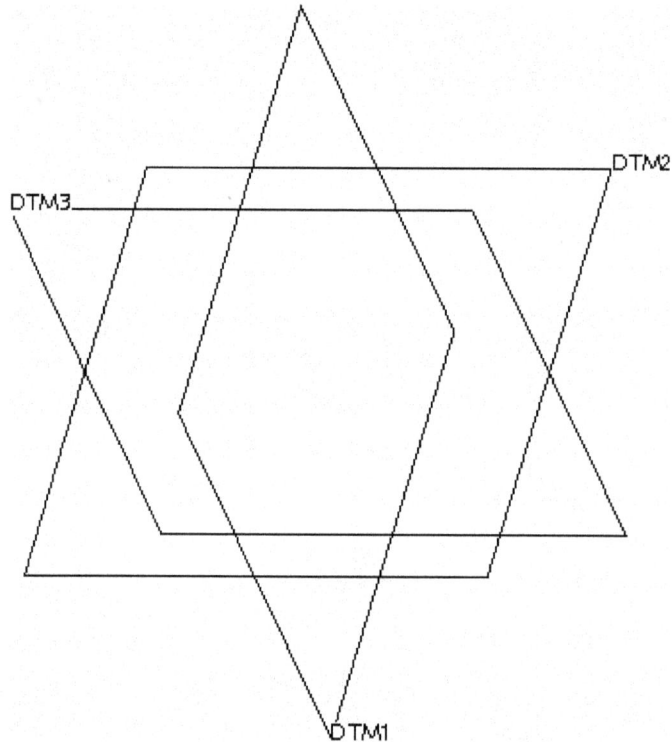

Fig. 6-5
Default datum planes

Since datum planes are perfectly flat, they can be used to sketch (see Chapter 7) directly on them, or they may be used as references to determine locations and

orientations for features. Datum planes are created by selecting the ▱ **Plane** icon from the Construction Toolbar. Similar to coordinate systems, creating datum planes are simply a matter of selecting the appropriate combinations of references and controls, as shown in Figure 6-6.

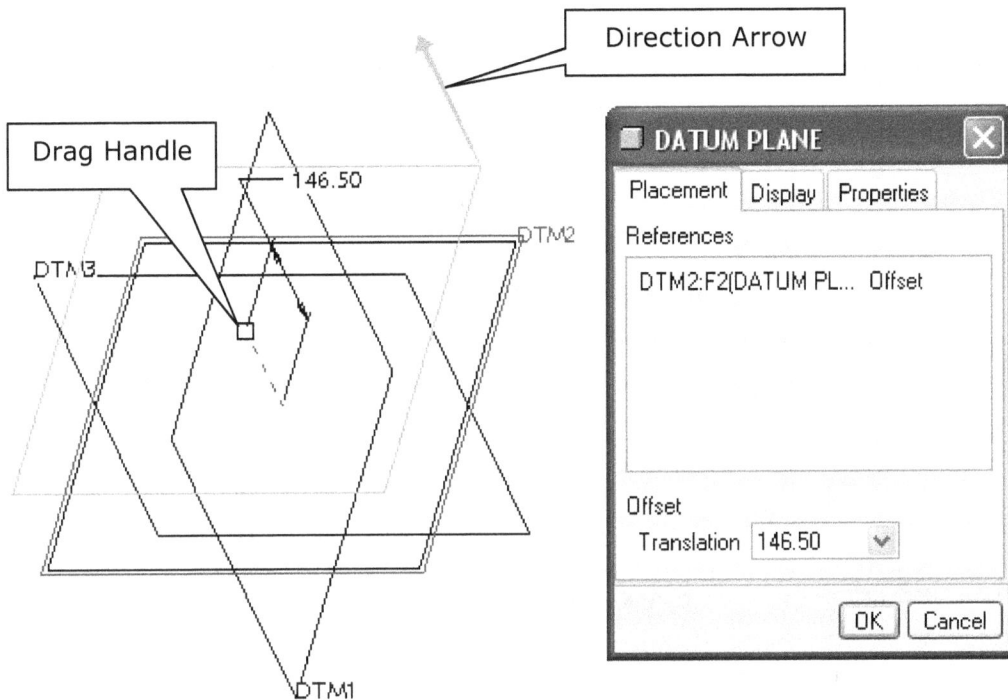

Fig. 6-6
Datum plane creation

In this case, DTM2 is being used as a reference, and the new plane is being located 146.50 units from the reference. The value of the offset may be set by moving the drag handle with the **LMB**, double-clicking the value in the graphics area, or entering the value in the dialog box. You will also notice a direction arrow. This is not the direction from the reference (which is controlled by positive or negative offset values), but rather which side of the new datum plane is the positive side. On a color monitor, you will notice that datum planes are brown on one side (indicating the positive side) and black on the other (indicating the negative side). This may be set by clicking on the arrow, or by selecting the Display tab in the dialog box and making the desired adjustments.

By selecting the appropriate combinations of references, a datum plane may be set in any position desired, as shown in Figure 6-7.

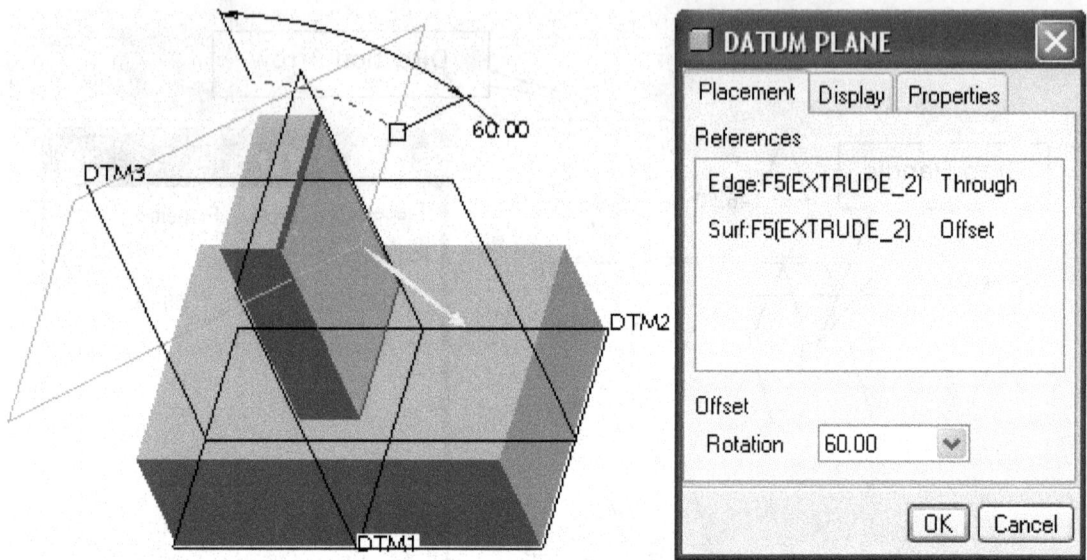

Fig. 6-7
Datum plane with rotational offset

This new datum plane (DTM4) can then be used as a reference for additional datum planes, as shown in Figure 6-8.

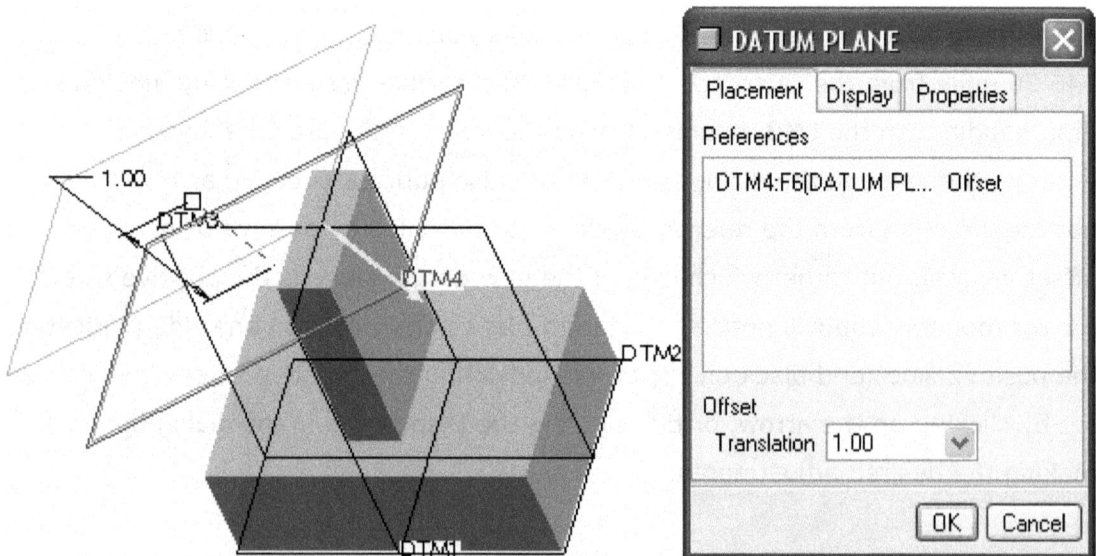

Fig. 6-8
Additional datum plane

Datum Axes

Just as a datum plane is infinitely long and wide, a datum axis is indefinitely long, but in a single direction. They are used to locate centers of geometry, such as holes, and also serve as centers of revolution, such as wheel hubs. To create a datum axis, select the ![axis icon] **Axis** icon from the Construction Toolbar. A dialog box will open, prompting for the features references. By selecting the appropriate geometry for both the References and Offset References, you can control exactly how the axis will be created.

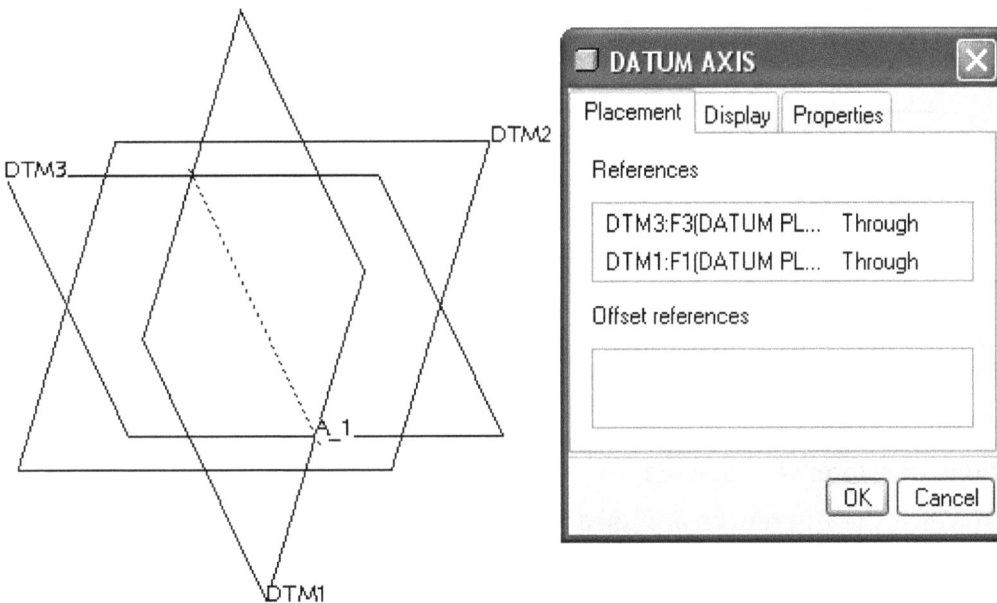

Fig. 6-9
Datum Axis through two references

Figure 6-9 shows the result when two intersecting datum planes are selected as references, and we are telling Pro/ENGINEER to create the axis 'through' each of them. The resulting axis is the only possible way a datum axis could be created, while satisfying all of the controls we are placing on it. Basically, Pro/ENGINEER will do exactly what we ask it to do, if it is geometrically possible.

Figure 6-10 shows an additional datum axis being added to the model, but this time we are asking Pro/ENGINEER to create the axis normal (perpendicular) to a reference datum plane, and located linearly from two others.

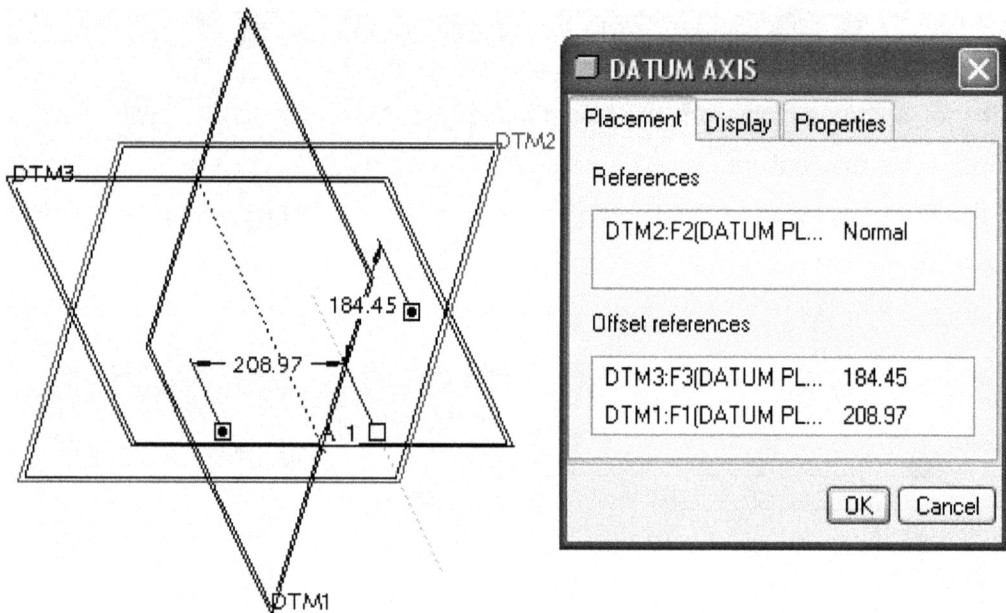

Fig. 6-10
Datum axis normal to a plane

Depending on the types and combinations of references selected, the manner in which the references are used may be adjusted, by selecting the controls in the dialog box, as shown in Figure 6-11.

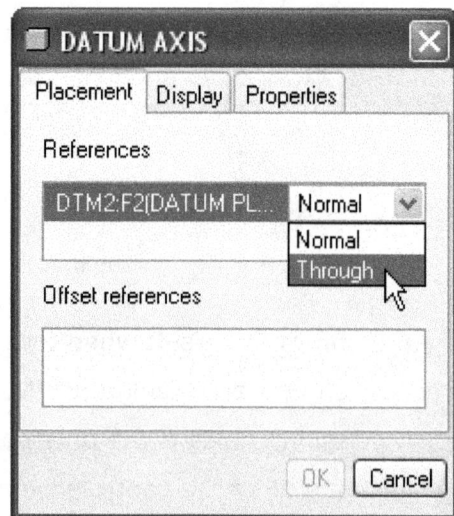

Fig. 6-11
Adjusting the reference

Fig. 6-12 shows the result of selecting a cylindrical surface as the only reference. Pro/ENGINEER will automatically create an axis through the center of the cylinder, because we have not given it any other control.

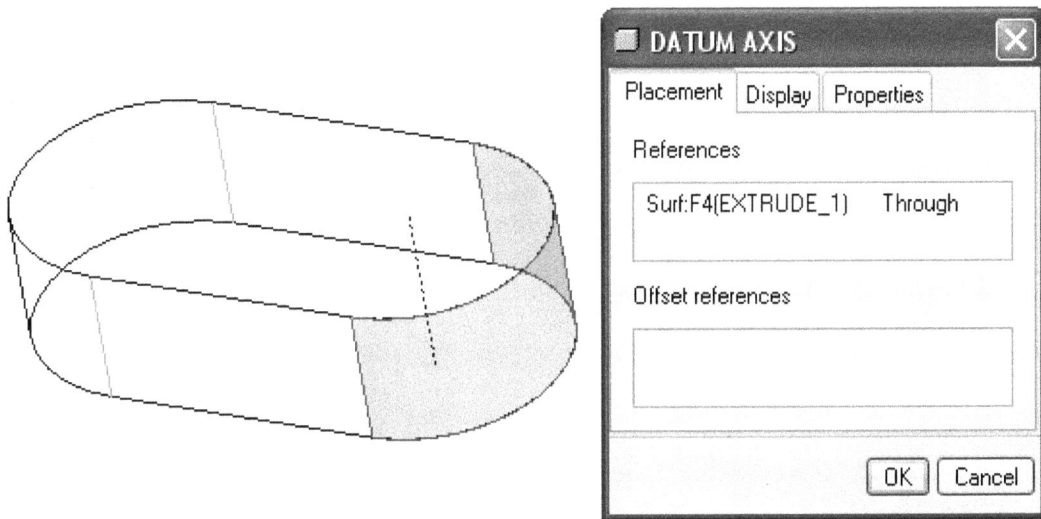

Fig. 6-12
Datum axis through a cylinder

Datum Points

A datum point indicates a single location in three-dimensional space, having a particular X, Y, and Z coordinate (value). They may be placed according to their coordinate, or by referencing existing geometry, much like datum planes and axes are placed. By clicking on the down arrow next to the Datum Point icon in the Construction Toolbar, as shown in Figure 6-13, you can access the various types of datum points.

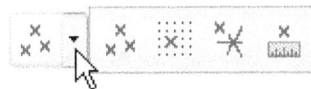

Fig. 6-13
Datum point construction options

A basic datum point may be created by selecting the ⁝ᵡᵡ Point icon. This will open a dialog box similar to creating datum planes and axes, as shown in Figure 6-14.

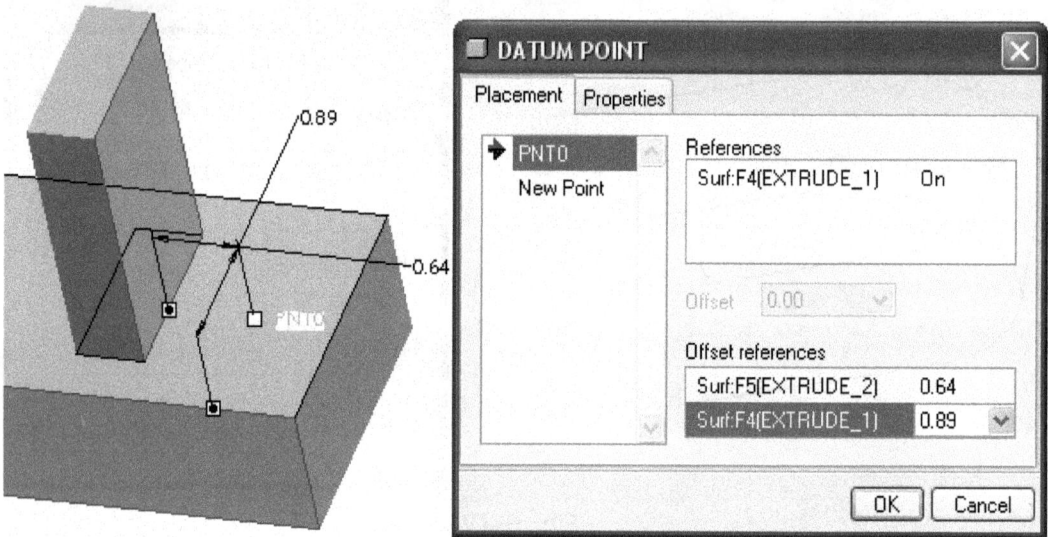

Fig. 6-14
Creating a datum point from references

This will create a single datum point feature. You may also click on **New Point** in the dialog box to add additional points to the same feature.

By selecting the ⁝ᵡ⁝ **Sketched** icon, you can create a sketched point (See Chapter 7 for information on how to set up and create sketches), as shown in Figure 6-15.

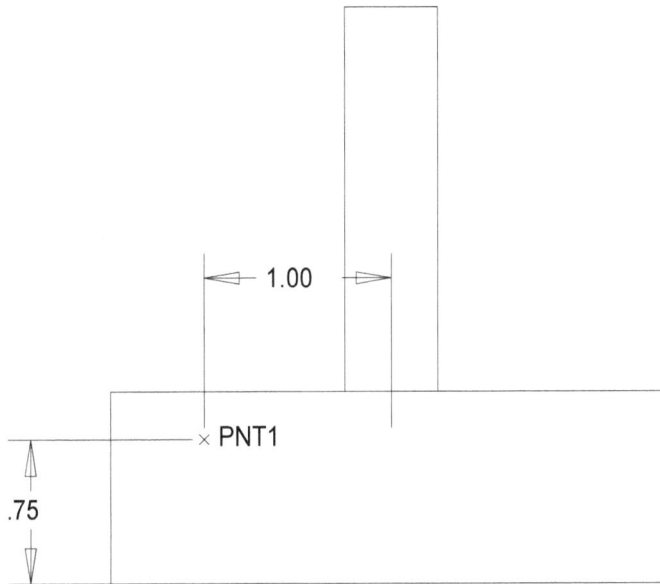

Fig. 6-15
Sketching a point

To create a single or array of datum points relative to a coordinate system, select

the ✳ **Offset Coordinate System** icon. This will open a dialog box, as shown in Figure 6-16. Select the coordinate system you wish to reference, and enter a list of points and their X, Y, and Z values.

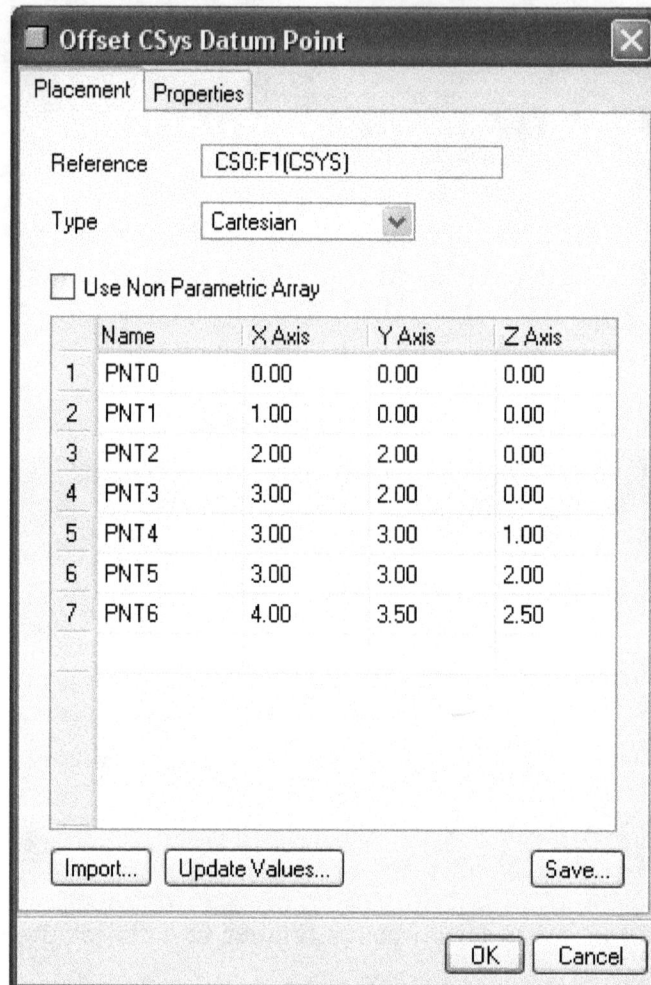

Offset CSys Datum Point

Placement | Properties

Reference   CS0:F1(CSYS)

Type   Cartesian

☐ Use Non Parametric Array

	Name	X Axis	Y Axis	Z Axis
1	PNT0	0.00	0.00	0.00
2	PNT1	1.00	0.00	0.00
3	PNT2	2.00	2.00	0.00
4	PNT3	3.00	2.00	0.00
5	PNT4	3.00	3.00	1.00
6	PNT5	3.00	3.00	2.00
7	PNT6	4.00	3.50	2.50

Import...   Update Values...   Save...

OK   Cancel

Fig. 6-16
Datum point 'cloud' offset from a coordinate system

The resulting point cloud created is shown in Figure 6-17. This information can then be used to drive additional geometry such as three-dimensional curves (see later in this chapter), as shown.

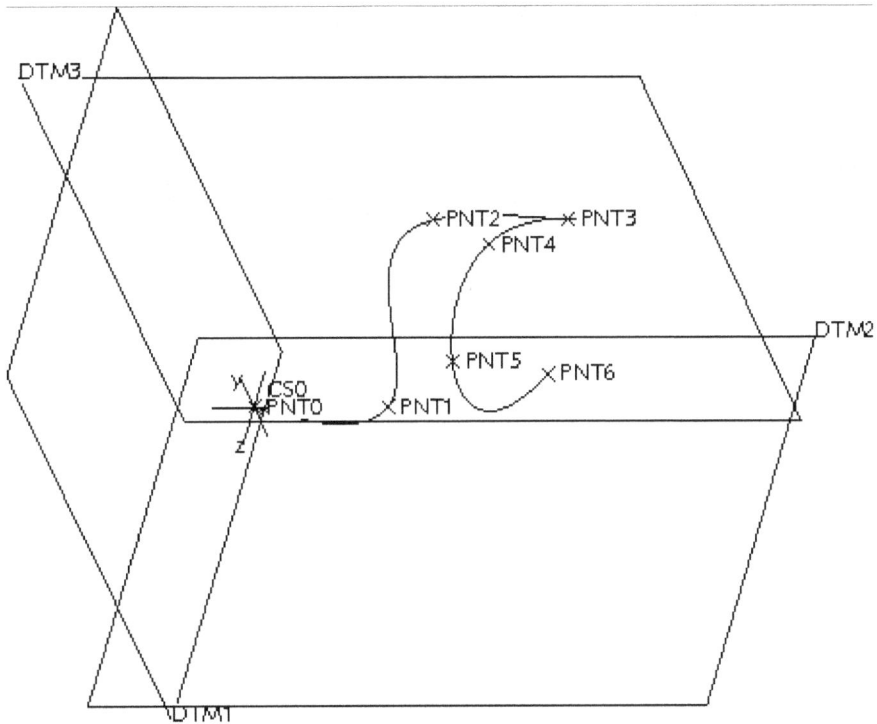

Fig. 6-17
Point array referenced by a three-dimensional curve

A ▦ Field point is a type of datum point intended for use in conjunction with user-defined analysis (UDA) and is not used for regular modeling.

Curves

Curve is a generic term used by Pro/ENGINEER to describe lines or a collection of lines in three-dimensional space. The term is misleading as the feature may be straight, or have curvature, as shown in Figure 6-17. There are two distinct types of curves.

Two-dimensional Curves

A two-dimensional curve that is sketched (drawn) on a planar surface is referred to as a Sketch, and created by selecting the ⟨⟩ **Sketch** icon in the Construction Toolbar. Figure 6-18 shows a curve that was sketched on datum plane DTM3. It may be used to define the shape of solid geometry. (See Chapter 7 for information on how to set up and create sketches.)

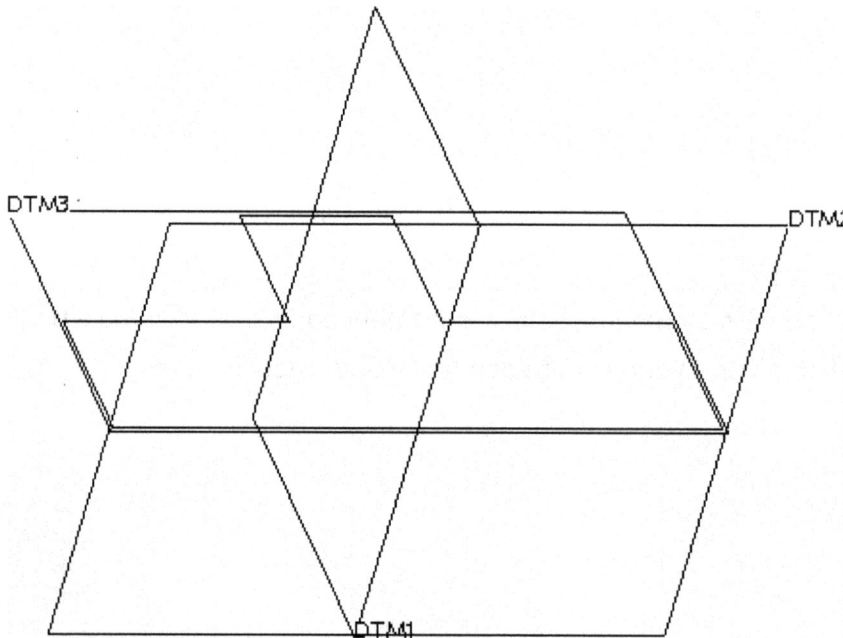

Fig. 6-18
Two-dimensional sketched curve

Three-dimensional Curves

Three-dimensional curves may be created

by selecting the ~ **Curve** icon on the
Construction Toolbar. This will open a
menu from which to choose the desired
curve type, as shown in Figure 6-19.

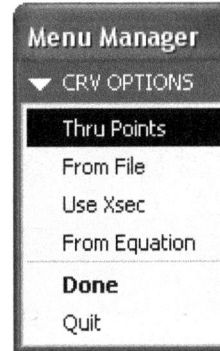

Fig. 6-19
Three-dimensional curve options

Curve data may be imported from external sources using the **From File** option, or
you may create an equation to control the curve using the **From Equation** option.
Figure 6-17 shows how the **Thru Points** option creates a curve through a set of
points, while Figure 6-20 shows the result of using the **Use Xsec** (cross section)
option.

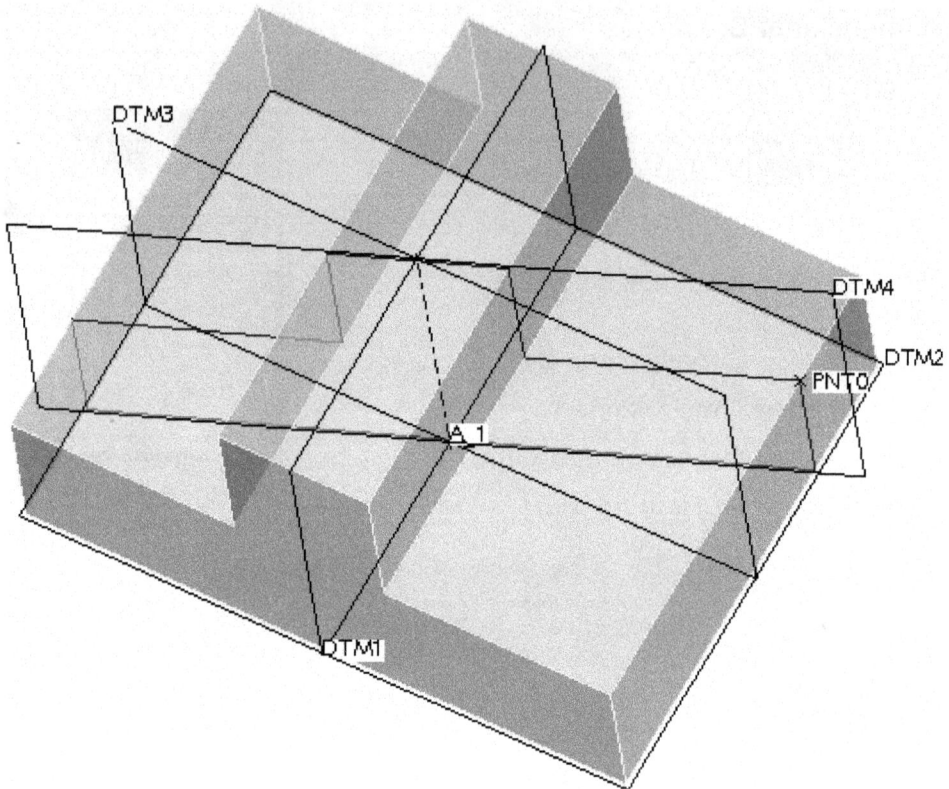

Fig. 6-20
Curve through a cross section

Figure 6-20 shows a curve created through a cross section (see Chapter 22 for information on creating cross sections). The cross section was created through a datum plane, which was created through a datum point (PNT0) which referenced two datum planes (DTM1 and DTM3) and a datum axis (A_1) which references the edge created by the solid object.

Since reference geometry does not create any physical surfaces or edges, you may create and reference as many as necessary to capture your design intent, and control your three-dimensional design.

Chapter 7

Sketching

Sketches
Sketcher
External Sketches
Internal Sketches
Embedded Reference Geometry

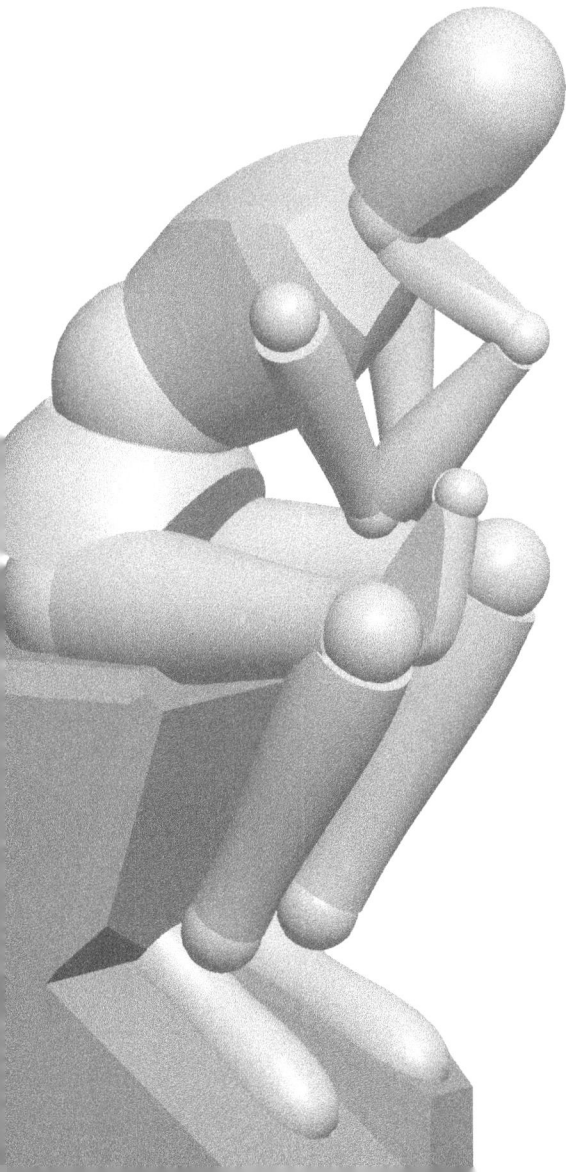

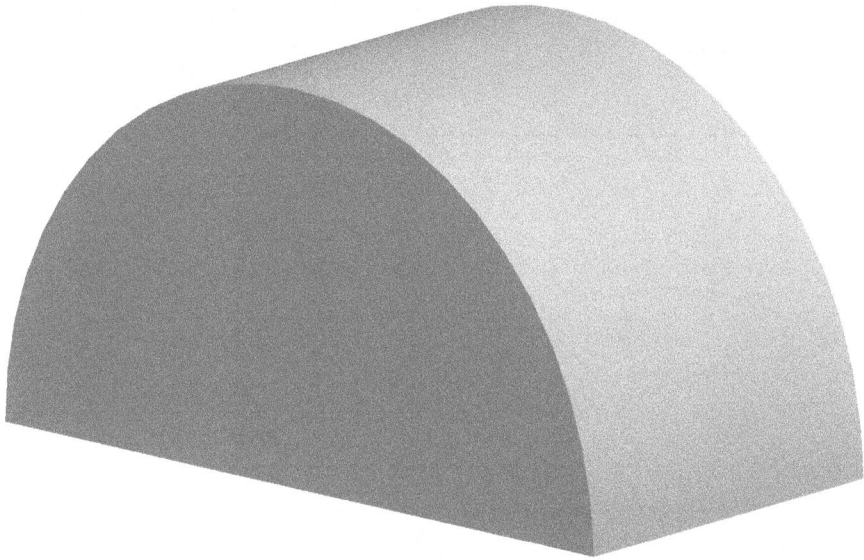

Fig. 7-1
Three-dimensional part

You will need to specify and control the shape of your parts and features. Quite often we do this by sketching a shape two-dimensionally, then give it a third dimension through a variety of techniques. These techniques may includes something as simple as extruding the shape to a given length or revolving the shape (see Chapter 9), but first we must define the objects basic shape two-dimensionally. Consider creating the part shown in Figure 7-1. What does it look like from the front? What does it look like from the side? What does it look like from the top or bottom? Figure 7-2 shows these two-dimensional views.

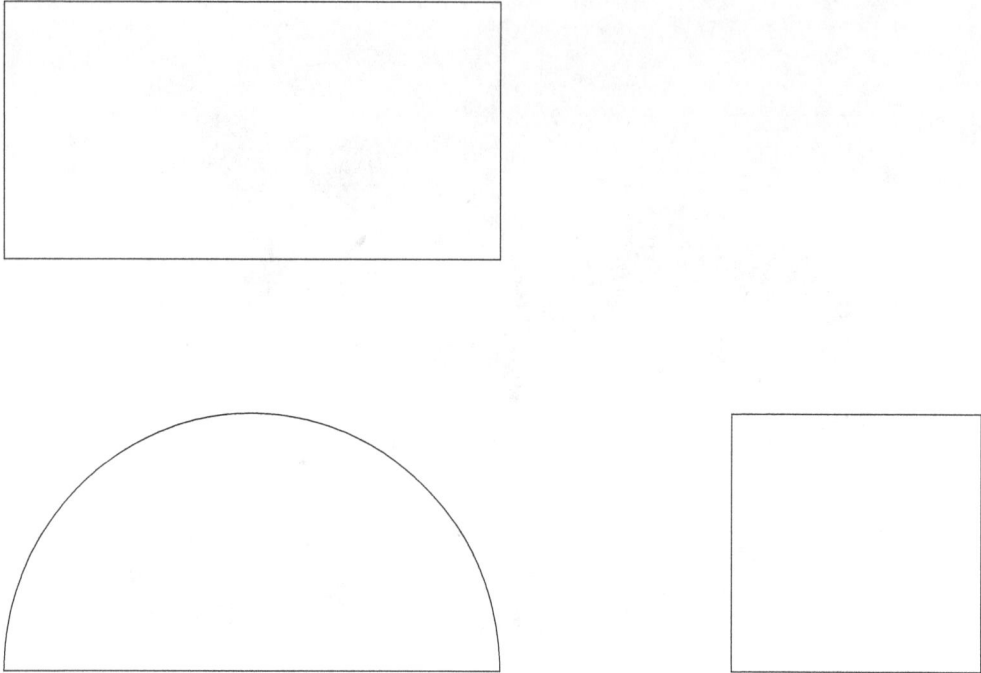

Fig. 7-2
Three views of the three-dimensional object

You will see that depending on which side you view the same object from, it can appear as a semi-circle, rectangle or square. When you define the shape of a feature, you will start with a two-dimensional sketch or 'drawing' of the feature. Therefore, it is advantageous to decide what shape best captures the design, and start there. For example, which of the three shapes above best captures the design intent of our three-dimensional part?

Sketches

As mentioned in Chapter 6, two-dimensional datum curves may be created as individual features called Sketches. These sketches can be used directly to control the shape of features, or you can use them to lay out a dimensioning scheme for additional sketches and features. Since sketches themselves are reference geometry features, you may use as many as you wish in a single design to capture your design intent. For example, we can use several sketches to lay out and create a solid model of the Great Pyramid of Giza, as shown in Figure 7-3.

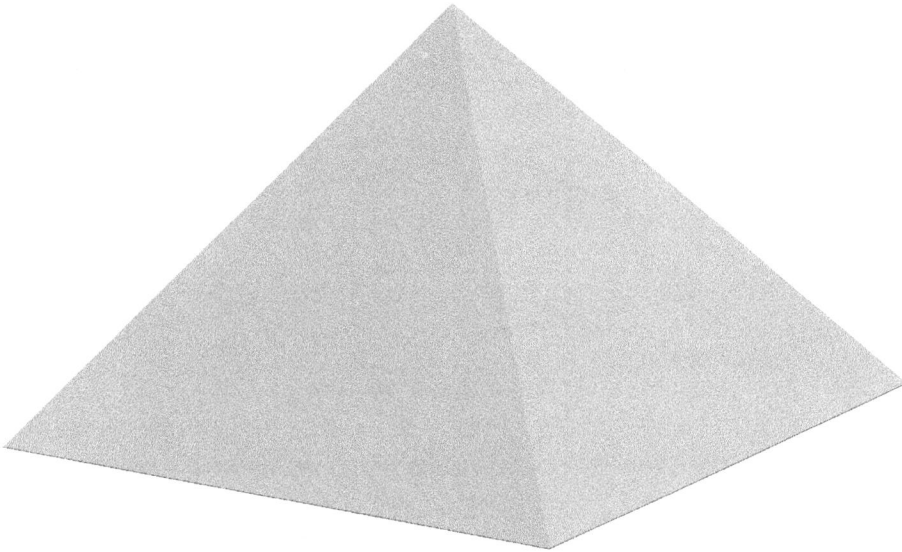

Fig. 7-3
Three-dimensional part

Perhaps the only dimensional information we have to work with is the pyramid's average size at the base (230,364 mm) and the angle of each side (51° 49' 38"). We can start by creating a sketch to represent the base, or bottom of our design, as shown in Figure 7-4.

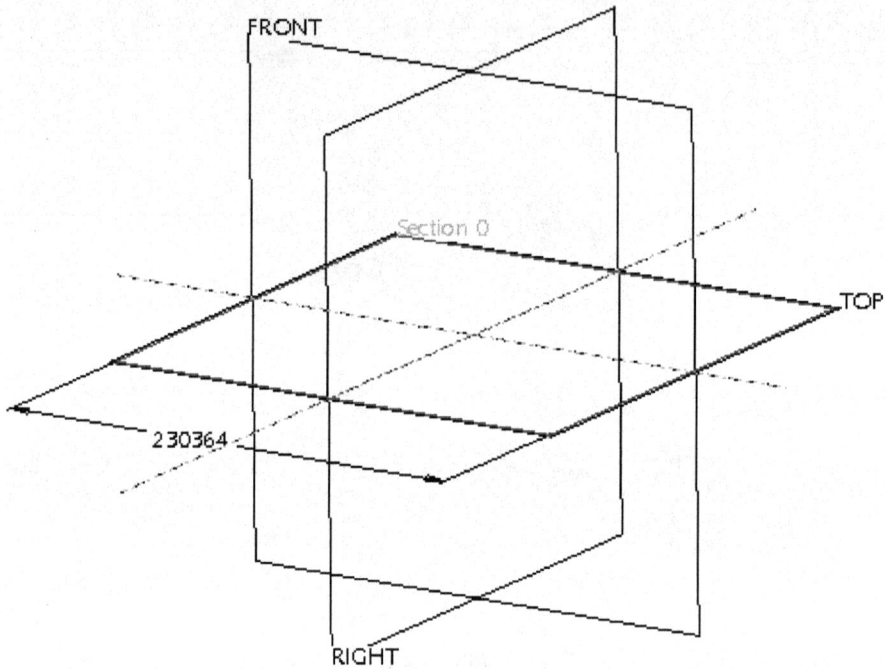

FRONT

Section 0

TOP

230364

RIGHT

Fig. 7-4
Sketch (square) for the pyramid base

If all we were trying to build is a cube, we could simple use this shape and extrude it to a vertical height, but for our pyramid, we need to continue creating additional sketches as needed. Figure 7-5 shows a sketch created on a vertical plane, to represent the definition of the sides of the pyramid.

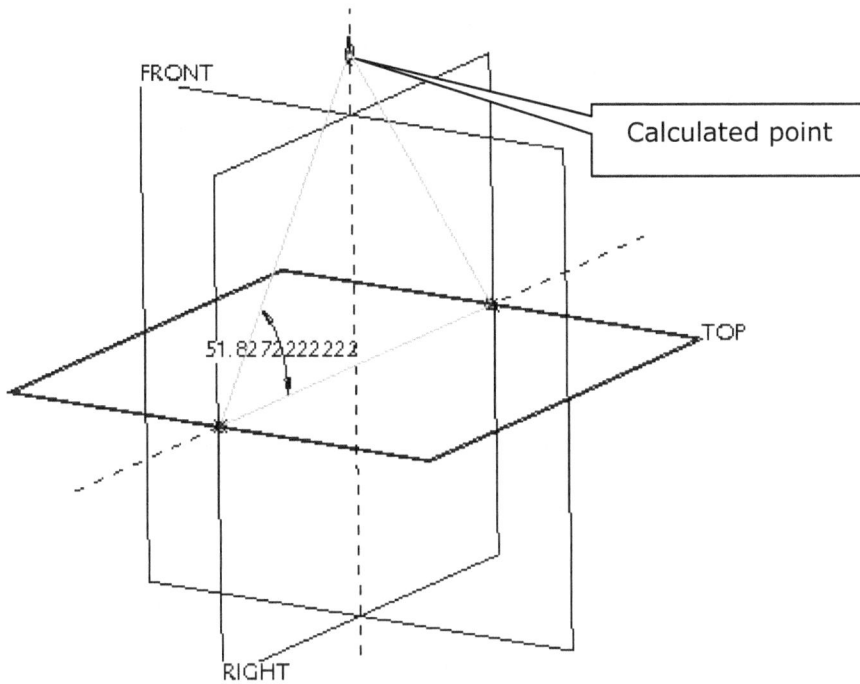

Fig. 7-5
Sketch (triangle) for the pyramid side

Now that we have used Pro/ENGINEER sketches to perform the trigonometry necessary to determine the apex (top) of the pyramid, the solid model can now be created using a variety of methods including a blend or a cube with angled cuts (see Chapter 9), or surface quilts merged together and solidified (see Chapter 10).

This is not to say that all of your three-dimensional features need to be built as wireframe models first, but it does demonstrate that complex geometry need not be created using a single complex feature, but can be built up from several simple features.

Sketcher

To create our sketches, there are several steps that must be performed, and it is best practice to complete these steps in the following order:

1. Sketching Plane

Sketches must be created on a datum plane or two-dimensional surface. If necessary, you may add datum planes to your models where needed, by following

the directions outlined in Chapter 6. To start a new sketch, select the ![sketch icon] **Sketch** icon from the Construction Toolbar. The Sketch Setup dialog box will appear, as shown in Figure 7-6.

Fig. 7-6
Sketch Setup dialog box

In this example, the datum plane DTM3 is selected as the sketching plane (the plane to sketch on).

2. Orientation

We also need to orient the sketch. Basically we need to tell Pro/ENGINEER which way is up, down, left or right. Pro/ENGINEER will typically automatically choose one of the default datum planes as an orientation reference, but we may choose any planar surface we wish. In this example, we have picked the datum plane DTM2 to face the top of our sketch. Remember that datum planes have positive and negative sides, and by selecting DTM2 to be the Top orientation, we are saying that we want the positive side of the datum plane to face the top of our sketch (facing the top of the screen).

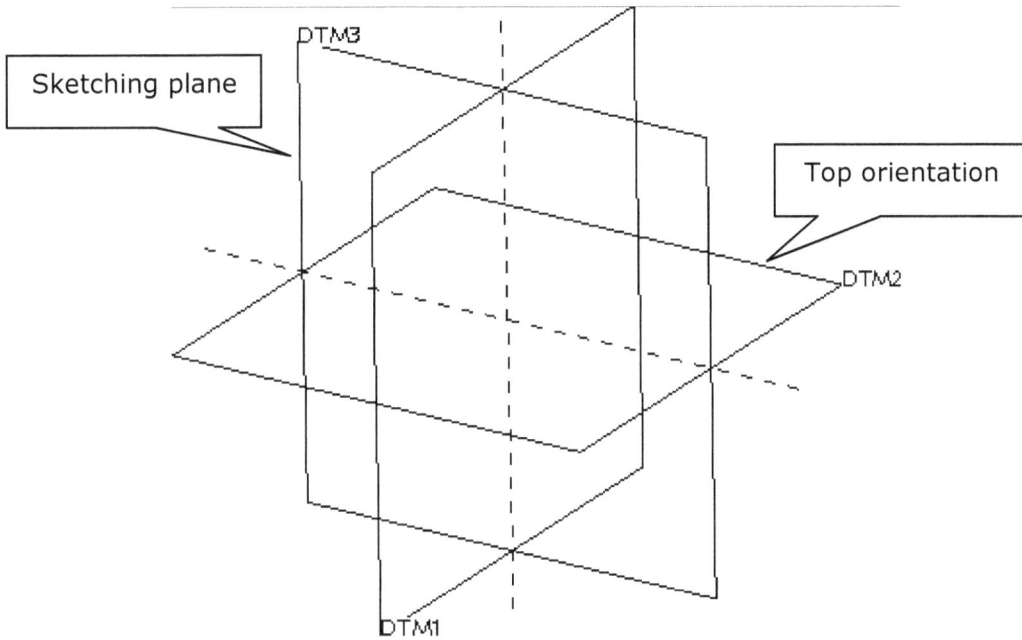

Fig. 7-7
Sketching plane and orientation reference

We may also use surfaces for our sketching plane and orientation reference, as shown in Figure 7-8.

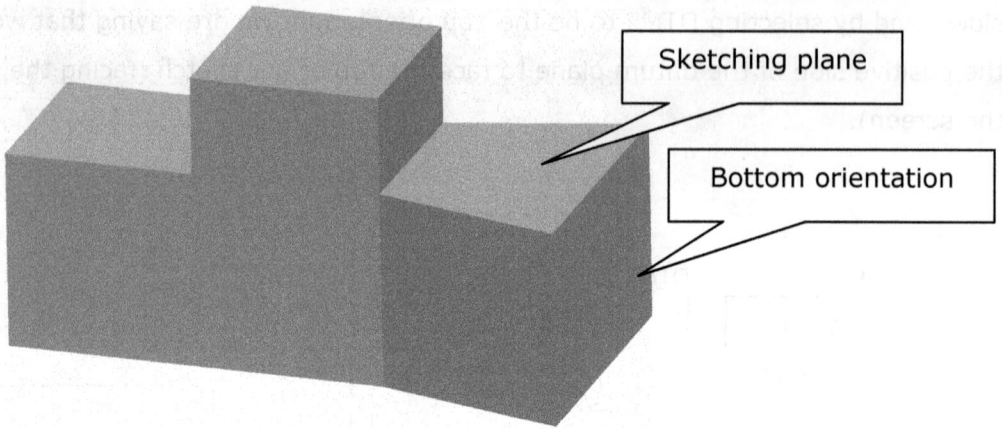

Fig. 7-8
Geometry surfaces

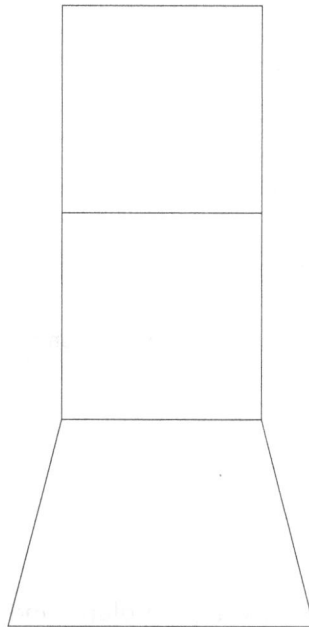

Fig. 7-9
Sketch view

After the sketching plane and orientation references are selected, you will be in sketcher mode, as shown in Figure 7-10.

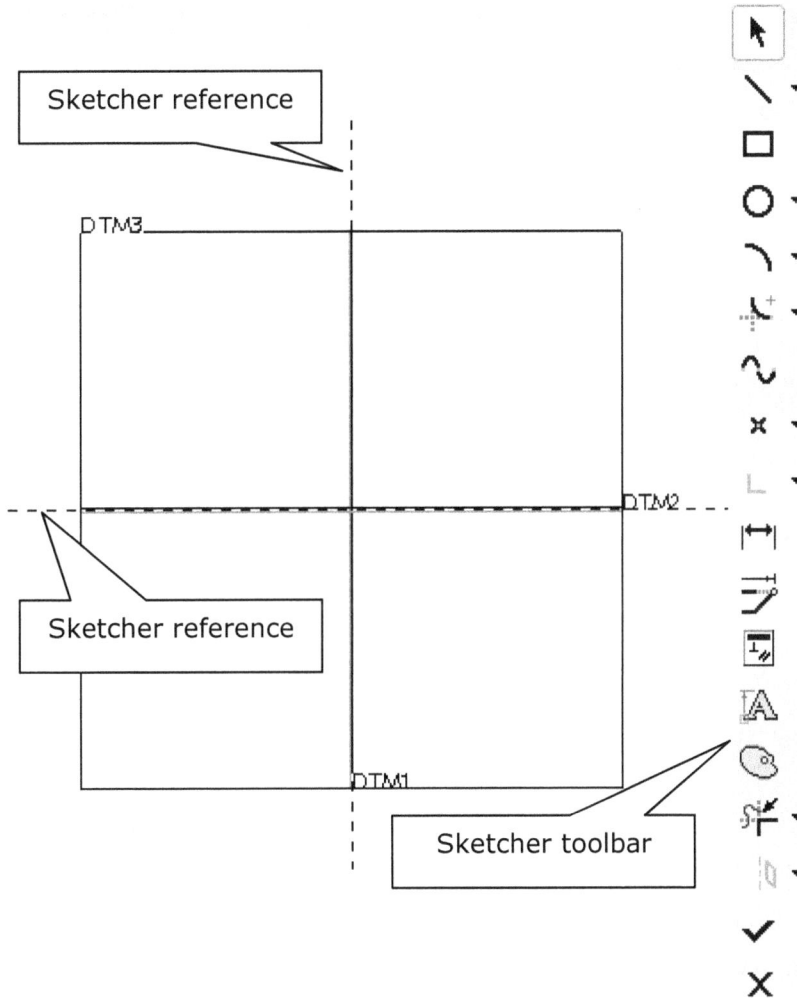

Fig. 7-10
Sketcher mode

3. References

You will notice dashed horizontal and vertical lines shown in a brown-orange color. These are sketcher references, and are necessary to locate your sketched entities relative to your part. If this is the first sketch in the part, Pro/ENGINEER will automatically choose your orientation reference as one of the references, along with the datum plane normal to it as another reference. These references become parents (see Chapter 1) of the sketch. If other geometry exists in your part that you wish to use as your references, or you simply want to add more references, you may select **Sketch** > **References**, from the menu, to open the References dialog box, as shown in Figure 7-11.

Fig. 7-11
References dialog box

You may delete unwanted references from the box, or select new references from the graphics area as desired, such as datum planes, axes, points, curves, and edges of solid geometry. The dialog box can be closed and reopened as needed.

4. Construction Geometry

When you start a new Pro/ENGINEER sketch, there are absolutely no features in it. If you have a datum axis feature in your model before the sketch, you will be able to see the axis while sketching, but remember, it is not part of the sketch. You may select the axis as a sketch reference, but in order to use it as a centerline in your sketch, you must create a centerline feature in the sketch, and align it to the existing axis. To create a centerline, expand the line command in the Sketcher toolbar by clicking the arrow next to the line icon, and select the centerline icon, as shown in Figure 7-12.

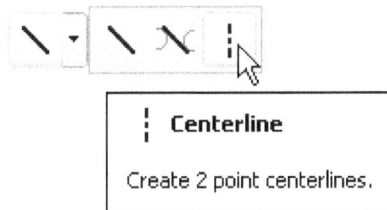

Fig. 7-12
Selecting the centerline tool

To place a centerline in your sketch, pick a location with the **LMB** and drag the cursor so that the centerline is at the orientation you wish (it will lock to horizontal or vertical) and pick again with the **LMB**. After you create an entity in sketcher, Pro/ENGINEER will keep the last command active, so if you want to create an additional centerline, just pick additional location points. To cancel the current command, click the **MMB**. You may also select the 🖈 **Select** icon from the Sketcher toolbar which allows you to select geometry. (Starting a new command automatically cancels the previous command.)

You may add additional centerlines to your sketch at any time, as well as other reference or construction entities such as points by selecting the ✗ **Point** icon. You may also create construction lines, circles and arcs by first creating them as solid (object) lines, then converting them to construction entities by selecting them and holding down the **RMB** and selecting **Construction** from the menu, as shown in Figure 7-13.

Delete	Del
Copy	
Cut	
Construction	
Properties...	
Line	
Rectangle	
Circle	
3-Point / Tangent End	
Centerline	
Fillet	
Dimension	

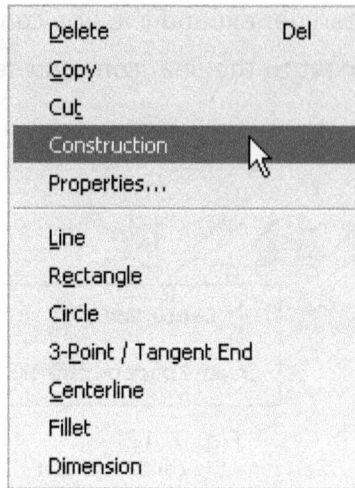

Fig. 7-13
Creating construction entities

It is a good idea to capture this information before proceeding, but you may always add additional construction entities as necessary to assist you in the layout of your sketch.

5. Sketched Entities

After your references are set, you may use a variety of common sketcher tools from the Sketcher Toolbar to create all of the necessary lines, circles, arcs, etc. to create your desired shape. (See Appendix A for a complete list of sketching tools available.) Remember it is not necessary to draw your entire part in one sketch, but rather capture what is the most important geometry for a single feature.

You will also see several dimensions automatically created, and shown dimmed, or grey in color, as shown in Figure 7-14. These dimensions are called 'weak' dimensions, and they are created automatically by Pro/ENGINEER based on the sketcher references that were used and the order you create your sketched entities. These are created because Pro/ENGINEER is parametrically driven, and needs to have all entities explicitly defined and located at all times, regardless if you have defined your desired position or not. While building your sketch, these weak dimensions should be completely ignored.

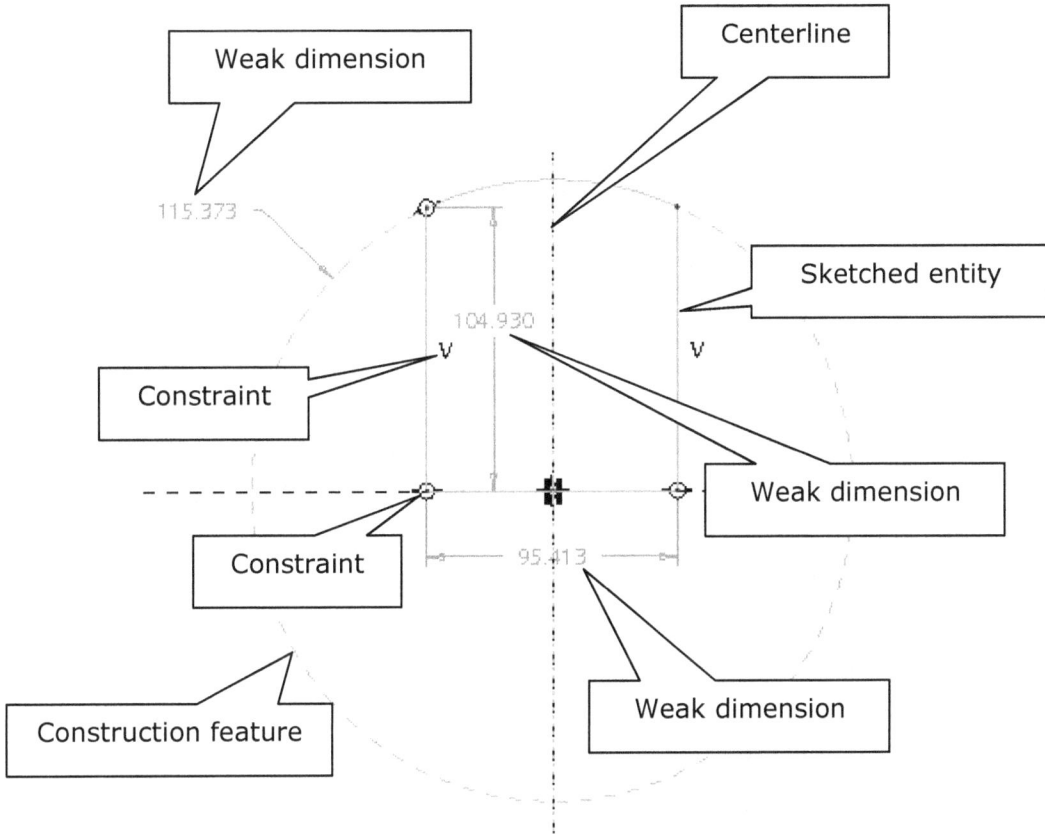

Fig. 7-14
Sketched entities, construction entities and weak dimensions

6. Constraints

When creating your sketched entities, Pro/ENGINEER will snap the ends of your lines, centers of circles, and corners of rectangles to your sketcher references and to other sketched entities. It will also make assumptions, such as vertical, horizontal, parallel, etc. When these assumptions are made, your sketched entities will snap into those positions, and will display that constraint on the screen. You will notice the two 'V' symbols in Figure 7-14 to indicate that both lines are vertical. If you do not want these automatic constraints, you may select and delete them. If you want to add any geometric constraint, select the [icon] **Constrain** icon from the Sketcher Toolbar. (See Appendix B for a complete list of constraints available.)

7. Dimension Scheme

After all of your sketched entities have been created, you will need to define your dimensioning scheme. This does not mean that you need to have the exact dimensional values, but rather specify the way you wish to control the sketch. For example, Figure 7-14 shows a 104.930 weak dimension that was automatically created from the horizontal reference to the endpoint of the vertical line. Is this how you would like to control this shape? Is this one of the dimensions you will want to display on a drawing later? If so, select the dimension, right-click and convert it to a strong dimension. If you would rather control the shape by specifying the height of the quadrant of the arc from the horizontal reference, as shown in Figure 7-15, then you may create that dimension by selecting the [icon] **Dimension** icon from the Sketcher Toolbar. Select one entity (the horizontal reference) then a second reference (the top of the arc), then place the dimension in the sketch with the **MMB**.

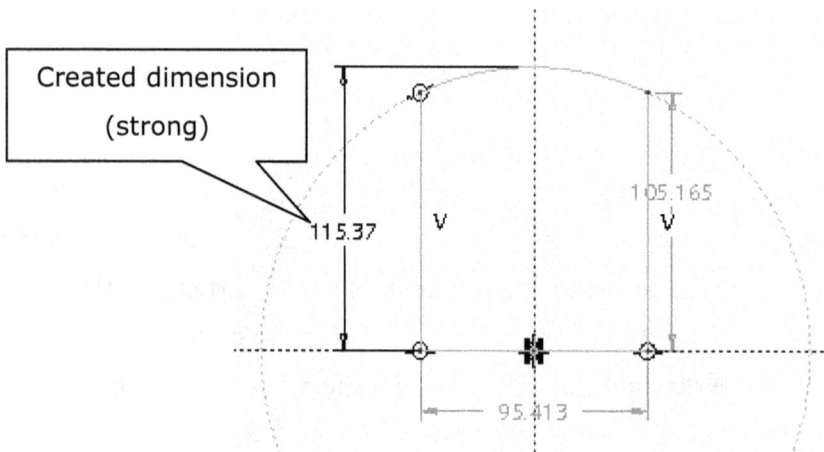

Fig. 7-15
Creating dimensions

Any dimension that you create is automatically a strong dimension (you cannot create a weak dimension). You will also notice that as you create strong dimensions, some weak dimensions will disappear, and some might appear. This is because Pro/ENGINEER always makes sure your sketches are fully defined, so it will create weak dimensions to compensate for under-dimensioned sketches. It is also impossible to over-dimension a sketch. This is the primary reason why the values of the weak dimensions should be ignored, as they are not intentional.

Figure 7-16 shows the same sketch, but we have added a horizontal dimension. Notice that the weak vertical dimension disappeared. This is because we are continuing to define the scheme we want to use.

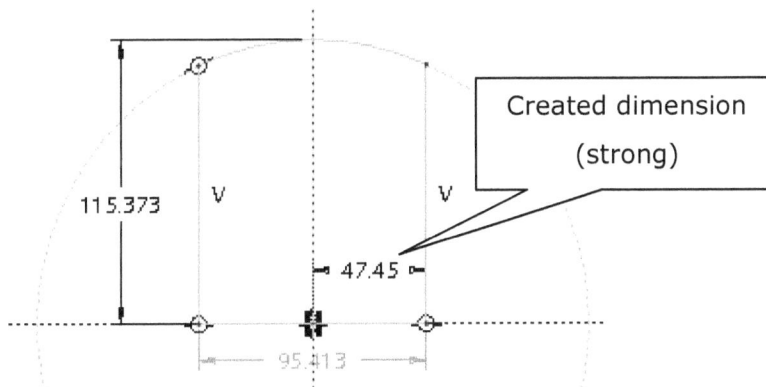

Fig. 7-16
Additional strong dimension

8. Values

Once the dimension scheme has been established, we can modify the dimensions to be the exact values we want. We can do this by double-clicking the dimension and entering the value, or we can select all the dimensions, right click, and select **Modify** to open the Modify Dimensions dialog box, as shown in Figure 7-17.

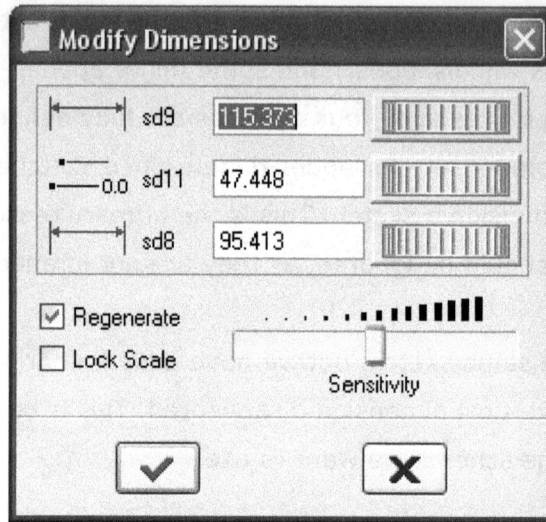

Fig. 7-17
Modifying dimensions

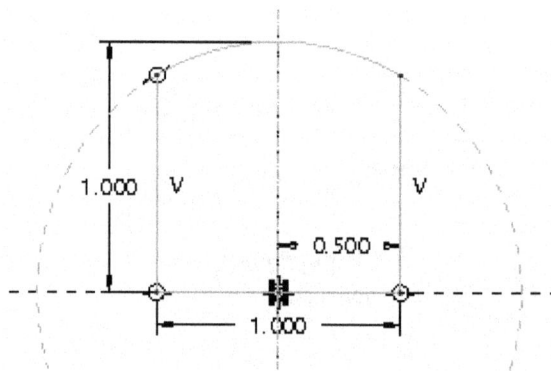

Fig. 7-18
Finished sketch

When you have finished defining your sketch, as shown in Fig. 7-18, you may

accept the definition by selecting the ✔ **Done** icon from the Sketcher Toolbar. If

you wish to cancel your sketch, you can exit by selecting the ✗ **Quit** icon.

Even though we need our sketches to be accurate, the value of the dimension is the

least important aspect of the sketch, as these values may be modified and any time.

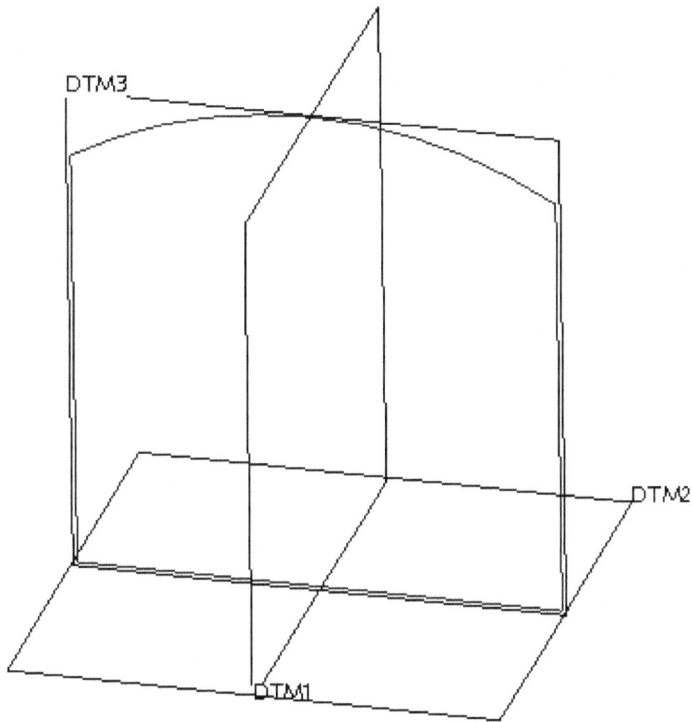

Fig. 7-19
Completed sketch feature

External Sketches

As mentioned earlier, sketch features may be used to define several three-dimensional shapes, provided the sketch is valid for the type of feature being created. For example, a sketch similar to Figure 7-20 cannot be used to extrude a shape, as it has intersecting entities.

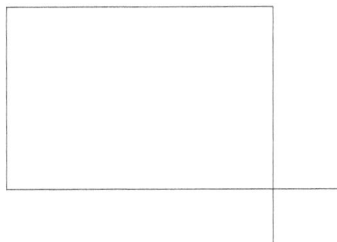

Fig. 7-20
Sketch unsuitable to extrude

If however the sketch is suitable, as shown in Figure 7-19 then it may be selected, and used as a reference for a variety of features, such as extrudes, revolves (see Chapter 9).

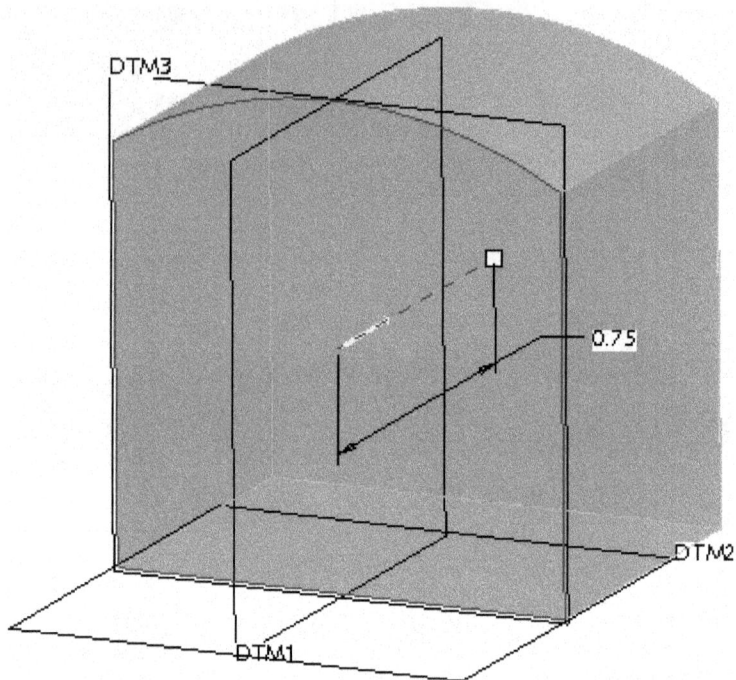

Fig. 7-21
Two-dimensional sketch controlling a three-dimensional feature

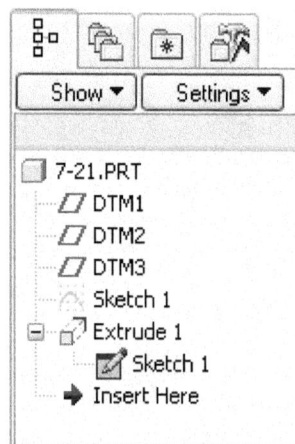

Fig. 7-22
Model Tree showing External Sketch

Figure 7-22 shows the Model Tree for the part shown in Figure 7-21. Notice how the fourth feature on the list is **Sketch 1**. This is the sketch created in Figure 7-19. When it is used directly to create an additional feature, the new feature uses it exactly as defined, and creates a link (which can later be broken) between the two. Notice how expanding the **Extrude 1** in the Model Tree reveals **Sketch 1** embedded into it.

In this case, we have used the sketch to define an extrusion. We could also use the same sketch again to define another feature, perhaps a revolved cut or other geometry. Each time, the new feature will be linked to the original sketch feature.

Internal Sketches

It is possible to create a sketch to define a feature that is unique to only that feature. If you start to create a feature that requires a sketch, such as extrude or revolve, and you do not have a sketch feature selected in advance, you may create a new sketch internal to the feature, by selecting the placement tab in the dashboard. You will notice that Pro/ENGINEER is prompting you to select an existing sketch (which you may), or you can define a new sketch, as shown in Figure 7-23.

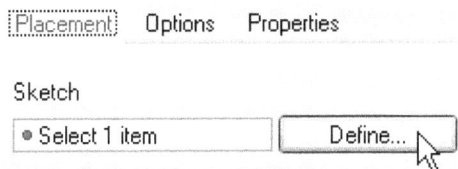

Fig. 7-23
Sketch selection

This will open the Sketch setup dialog box as shown in Figure 7-6, and you can define the sketch exactly the same as an external sketch. Figure 7-25 shows the internal sketch in the Model Tree. This internal sketch remains hidden, and cannot be used for any additional geometry.

Fig. 7-24
Additional feature created with an internal sketch

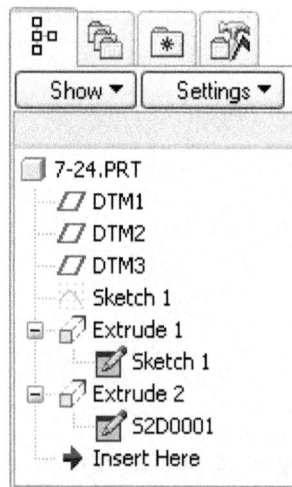

Fig. 7-25
Model tree showing internal sketch

Embedded Reference Geometry

Whether you are creating a Sketch feature or an internal sketch, there are times when you want to define a sketch, but do not have a datum plane or planar surface to select as the sketching plane. There are also times when you want to have datum features such as planes, points or axes to select for dimensional or placement reference for your features, but they may not exist either.

Pro/ENGINEER allows you to create these datum features while defining your intended geometry features. You will notice that when you begin a command, such as **Sketch** or **Extrude**, the Datum feature creation icons are available in the Construction Toolbar. While you are creating your feature, simply pick on the datum creation icon you would like. This will pause or 'suspend' the original feature creation and allow you to create as many datum features as you wish. These new datum feature are then available to be selected and used for sketching planes, and references. If needed the feature creation may be resumed by selecting the ▶ **Resume** icon.

Fig. 7-26
Datum construction tools

Figure 7-27 shows an extruded feature added to the model with two embedded datum planes that were created to properly define the feature. When embedding datum features, Pro/ENGINEER automatically hides them from the display (See Chapter 17). Expanding the Extrude 3 feature in the model tree, and un-hiding the datum planes reveals that a datum plane DTM4 was created tangent to the upper curved face, parallel to DTM2. An additional datum plane DTM5 was then offset from DTM4, and used as a sketching plane to create the internal sketch for the solid feature, as shown in Figure 7-28.

Fig. 7-27
Feature with embedded datum features

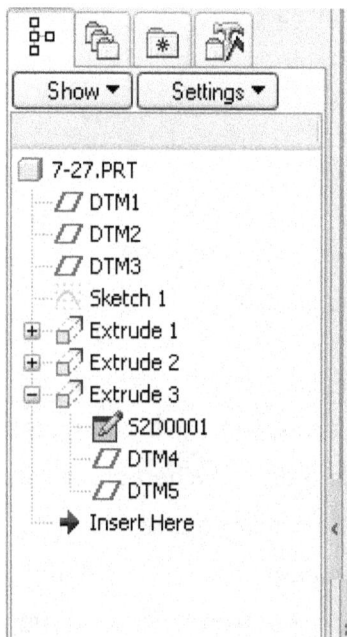

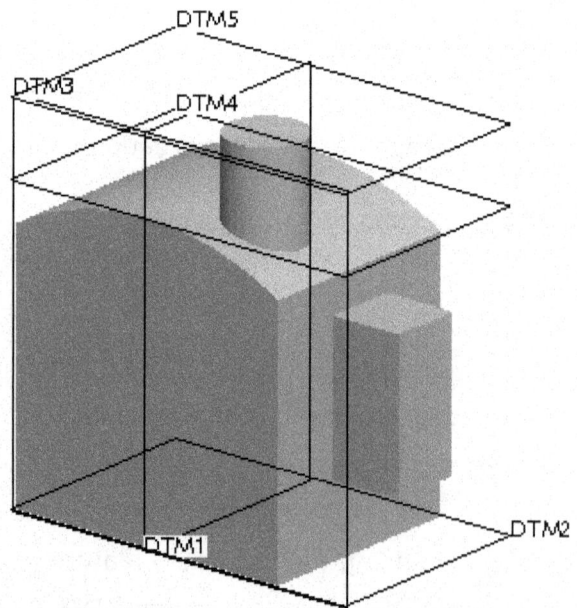

Fig. 7-28
Embedded datum features revealed

Chapter 8

Three-dimensional Feature Types

Solid Features

Quilts

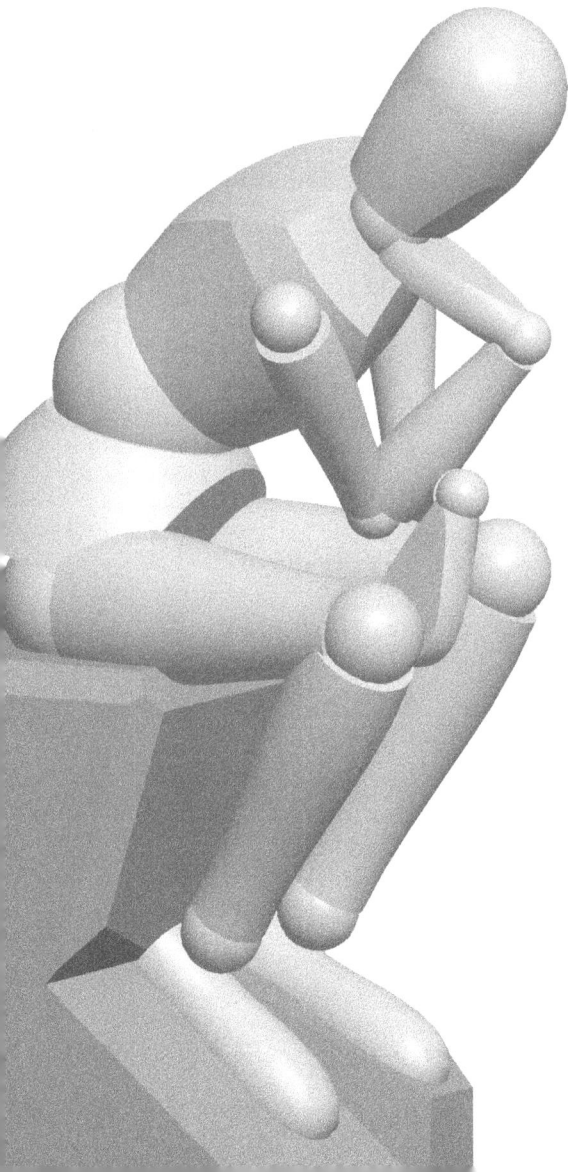

Chapter 6 discussed the creation and use of reference geometry. These are features that do not represent physical objects, but rather provide us with controls to lay out and define three-dimensional features in our design. When we create our three-dimensional features, as we will in the next few chapters, there are two basic feature types.

Solid Features

Solid features represent the actual geometry that is manufactured. These features not only have length, width, and height (making them three-dimensional), but they also have mass. Cutting a solid feature reveals its solid nature, as shown in Figure 8-1.

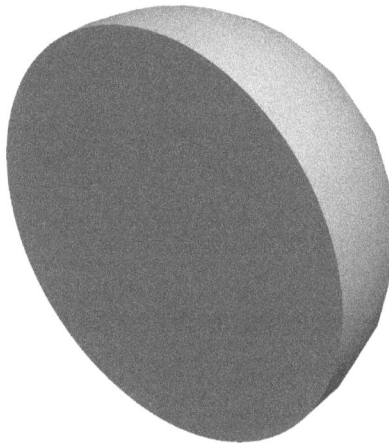

Fig. 8-1
Solid sphere cut in half

When creating solid features, there are two additional sub-types of features.

Default

Unless you tell Pro/ENGINEER otherwise, every face you create is treated as an exterior face, and Pro/ENGINEER will automatically fill in all of the material inside the shape. Figure 8-2 shows a 'T' shape that is being extruded (See Chapter 9).

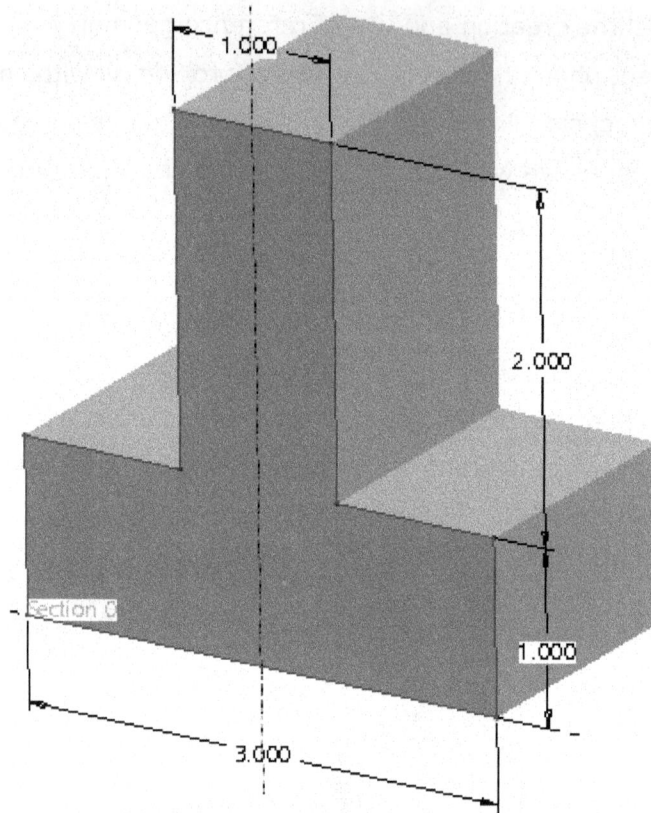

Fig. 8-2
Default solid feature

Also visible is the sketch that was used to define its shape. The lines in the sketch are used to create the faces of the solid, and Pro/ENGINEER automatically fills in the material. This works exactly the same as a cookie cutter would define the shape of a cookie.

Thicken Sketch (Thin)

Let's create the same feature as shown in Figure 8-2, but this time we can select

the ⬛ **Thicken Sketch** icon from the feature dashboard. When we do this, we are prompted to enter a thickness value. This takes the sketched entities and creates an offset of those entities the given value, and fills in all the material in between, as shown in Figure 8-3.

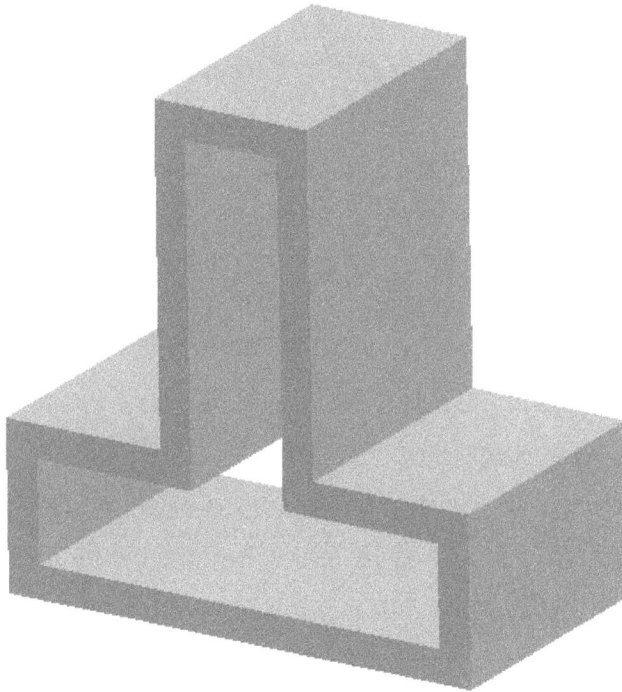

Fig. 8-3
Thickened sketch

Of course we could have created the exact same shape using the default setting, but we would have had to create twice as many lines in our sketch, and also create eight dimensions to control their placement. By using the **Thicken Sketch** option we can define the outside shape and give it a nominal thickness.

When defining a part that is normally specified by a thickness value, such as pipe or tubing, the **Thicken Sketch** option is the best method to maintain our design intent. Figure 8-4, shows a length of tubing that is specified as an outer diameter of 0.75" with a wall thickness of 0.035", yet only a single circle is needed to be created and dimensioned in the sketch.

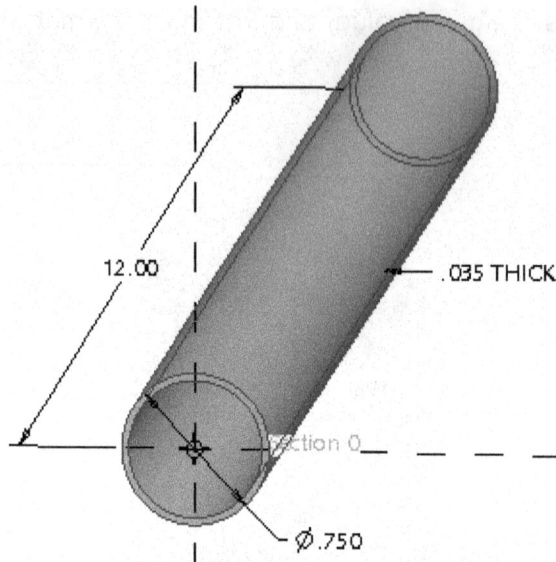

Fig. 8-4
0.75" O.D. x 0.035" wall

Of course if we wanted to control the inner diameter with a dimension we could have sketched it as such, and used the default setting. Some of the solid features you create in Pro/ENGINEER will have this thicken sketch option in the dashboard, while some other will have to be defined that way from the start, as a thin protrusion, or thin cut. You may also select a quilt feature (discussed later in this chapter) and select **Edit > Thicken**, from the menu, which will give you the options of whether you want to use that definition to add or delete material.

Regardless if features are created as the default solid, or a thickened sketch, solids perform a Boolean operation, either adding or deleting material from the model.

Quilts

Most of the three-dimensional features you create in Pro/ENGINEER can be created as solids, as discussed earlier in this chapter, or they may be created as quilts. A quilt is basically a definition of shape, but has a null thickness. When creating the

extruded shape shown in Figure 8-2, we could have selected the **Surface** icon
from the feature dashboard, to create the shape as a surface (quilt) feature, as
shown in Figure 8-5.

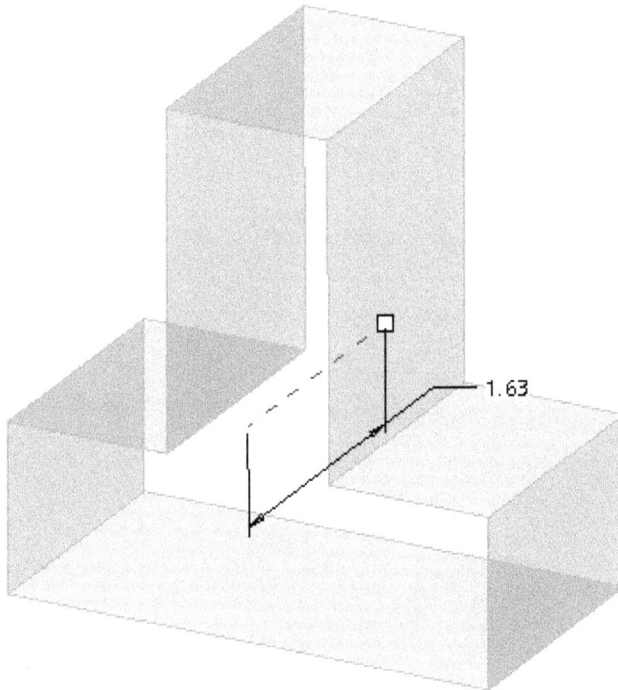

Fig. 8-5
Surface (quilt) feature

A quilt allows you to define three-dimensional geometry as a non-Boolean
operation, meaning you may create a three-dimensional shape in space without
adding or removing material. Quilts may be used to define regions, used as
references for solid features, or combined with other quilts to eventually be used to
define solid features (see Chapter 10).

Sketched Three-dimensional Features

Extrude

Revolve

Sweep

Variable Section Sweep

Blends

Swept Blend

Helical Sweep

Ribs

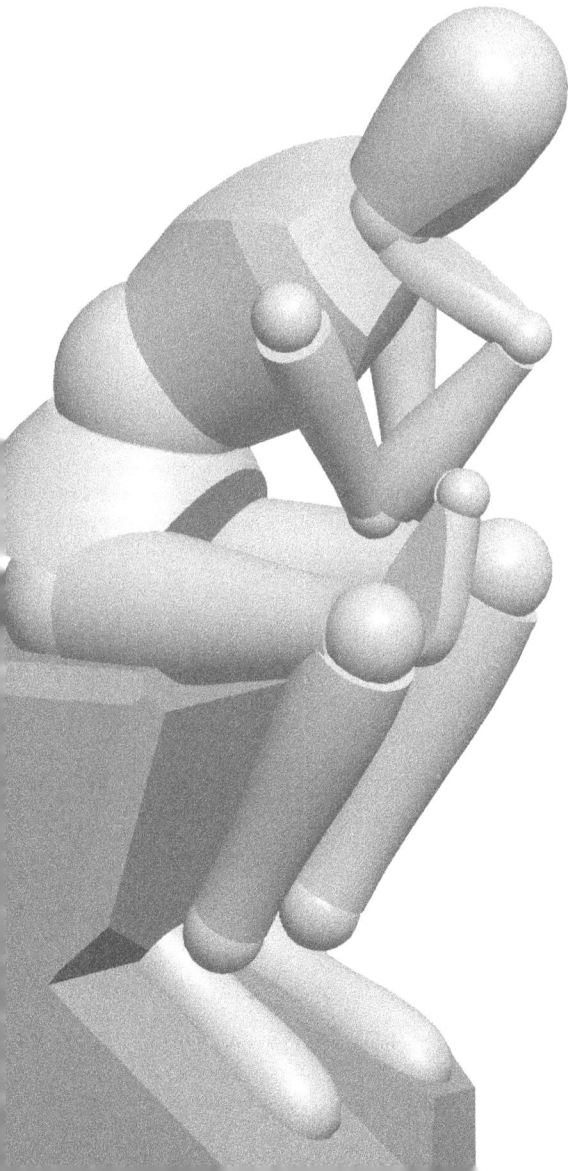

As discussed in Chapter 7, most of the three-dimensional shapes you will create in Pro/ENGINEER are first sketched as a two-dimensional shape, and then given the third dimension.

Extrude

Without realizing it, you have been creating extruded shapes every morning when you brush your teeth. When you squeeze your tube of toothpaste, the toothpaste is forced out the hole in the end of the tube, which takes on the shape of the hole.

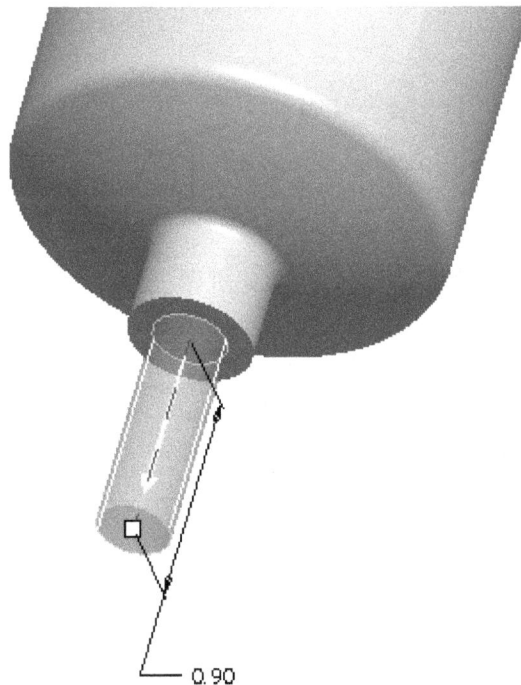

0.90

Fig. 9-1
Common extruded shape

The toothpaste doesn't start out shaped like a cylinder, but it becomes one by extruding the product through the two-dimensional shape, in this case a circle, to give it a three-dimensional shape (cylinder). What would the extruded toothpaste look like if the hole in your tube was in the shape of a star?

A Pro/ENGINEER extrude works exactly the same way as your tube of toothpaste. In fact, the example shown in Figure 9-1 is a Pro/ENGINEER extrude. To create an extrude, select the ⬚ **Extrude** icon from the Construction Toolbar. If you had already selected an existing Sketch feature (see Chapter 7), Pro/ENGINEER would assume that is the shape you wish to extrude, as well as using the location of the existing sketch as the starting point of the extrude, and provide you with the pre-construction highlight, as shown in Figure 9-1.

If however you do not have a Sketch selected, or you wish to define a unique shape, you may open the Placement tab on the feature dashboard, select an existing sketch, or Define an Internal Sketch (see Chapter 7).

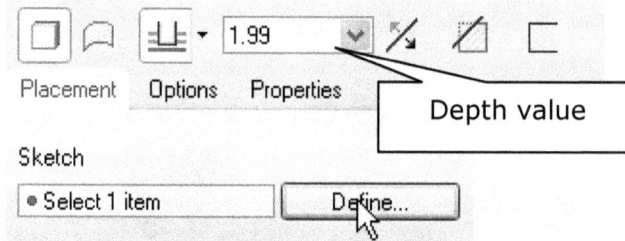

Fig. 9-2
Selecting or defining the sketch

Depth

After you have selected or defined the sketch, you need to control the depth (third-dimension). The three-dimensional shape will be extruded perfectly normal (perpendicular) to the sketching plane, without any bend, twist or taper. By default, Pro/ENGINEER will start to create the extruded shape with a single (blind) depth, as shown in Figure 9-2.

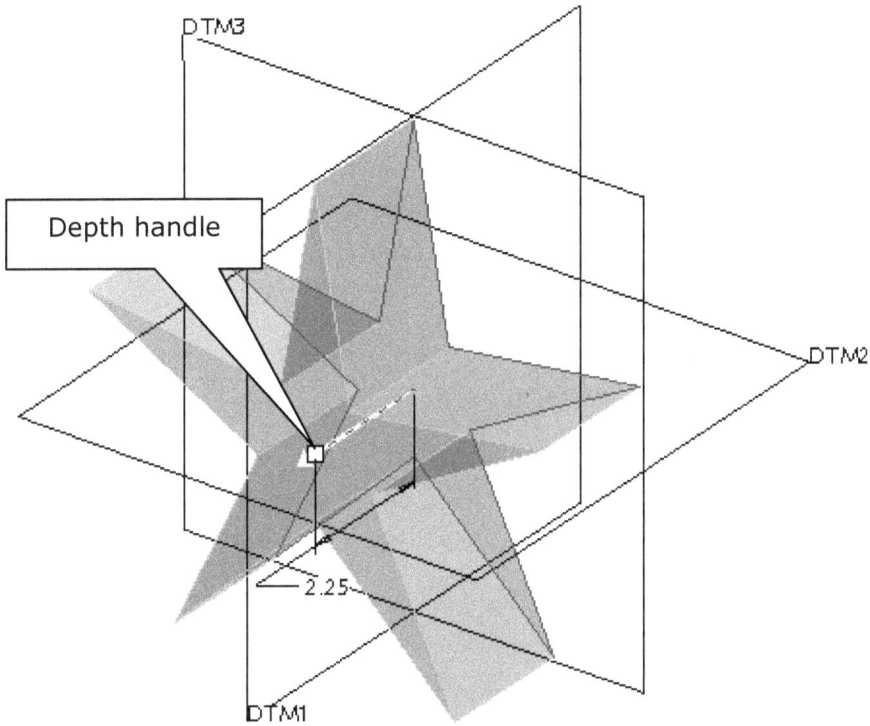

Fig. 9-3
Extruded blind depth

You may set the depth by dragging the depth handle, as shown in Figure 9-3, by double-clicking the value in the graphics area, or typing the value in the box in the dashboard. For additional depth options, open the Depth Option icon in the dashboard, as shown in Figure 9-4.

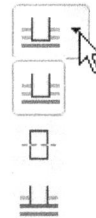

Fig. 9-4
Depth options

You may also change the direction of the extrusion by clicking on the arrow in the graphics area. The ⊟ **Both Sides** icon creates an extrusion a specified depth, symmetrically split in front and behind the sketching plane, as shown in Figure 9-5, and the ⊥⊥ **To Selected** icon allows you to lock the depth to an existing piece of geometry, as shown in Figure 9-6.

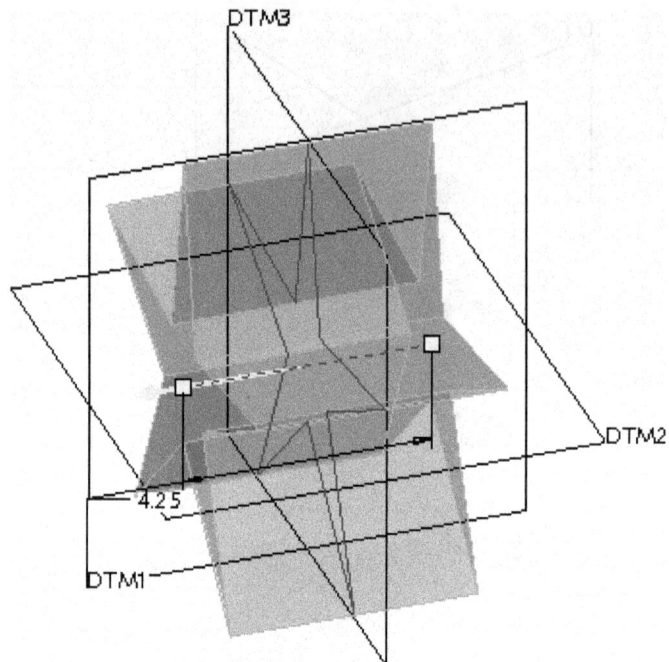

Fig. 9-5
Symmetrical depth

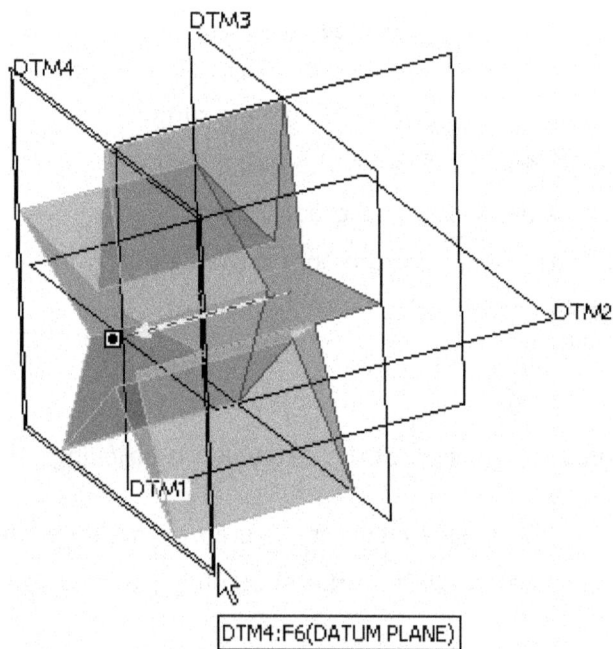

DTM4:F6(DATUM PLANE)

Fig. 9-6
Extrude to selected point, curve, plane or surface

Depth Two Directions

For even greater control of depth, you may open the Options tab in the dashboard, as shown in Figure 9-7.

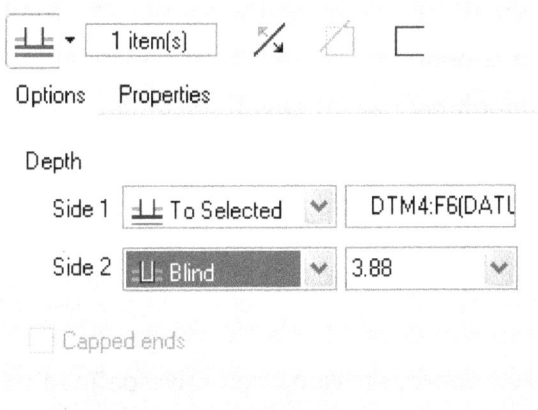

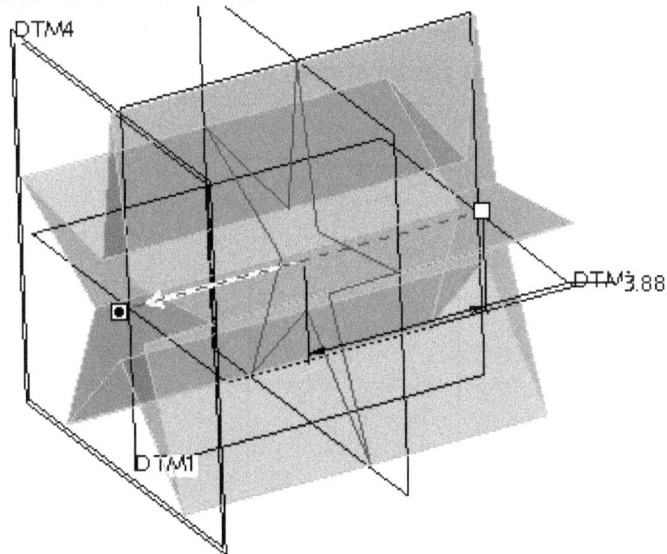

Fig. 9-7
Side 2 depth options

This will allow you to control the depth of the extrusion on either side of the sketching plane independently.

Remove Material

When opening parts that were created with a pre-Wildfire version of Pro/ENGINEER, you will see some features called PROTRUSION (adding material) and you will also see CUT (removing material). In Pro/ENGINEER Wildfire, the terminology has changed to indicate the way the shape is defined, i.e., extrusion, revolve, blend, etc.. When creating extrusions, the Default setting creates a three-dimensional boundary, and fills it with material (formerly called protrusion). (See Chapter 8 for discussions regarding solid and surface features.)

To use your extrusion shape to remove material (create a cut), simply select the

Remove Material icon from the dashboard. Provided you have defined the shape in the proper direction, and you have an existing solid to remove material from, you will define a cut as shown in Figure 9-8.

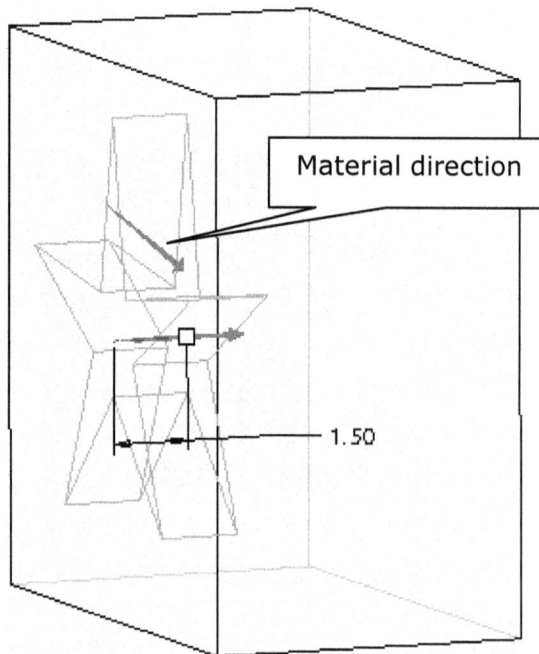

Fig. 9-8
Removing material (cut)

Notice the Material Direction arrows. These indicate not only which side of the

sketching plane the shape will be defined, but when you select the **Remove**

Material icon, the arrows indicate to which side (inside or outside) of the sketch

boundary the cut will be created. By flipping the arrow to the outside, all of the

material outside of the sketch will be removed to a specified depth, as shown in

Figure 9-9.

Fig. 9-9
Material removed to the outside

The part shown in Figure 9-9 was made by creating a solid block, then cutting away

some of the block to leave a star shape. The exact same geometry could have been

achieved by first creating a thinner block, then adding the star shape. Chapter 19

discusses capturing your design intent. You must decide which combinations of

adding and deleting material best define your design intent.

Revolve

A revolved feature can be defined to add or delete material, just as an extruded feature can, but rather than being created straight from the sketching plane at a depth, a revolve feature uses an axis of revolution to create a shape with an extent of rotation up to 360°.

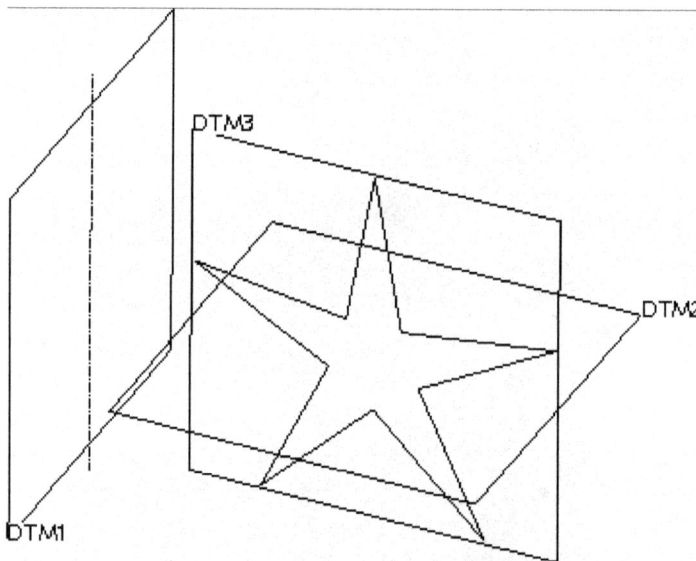

Fig. 9-10
Sketch to revolve

The axis of revolution must lie in the same plane as the shape to be revolved. This can be accomplished easily by including a centerline in your sketch, as shown in Figure 9-10. If you happen to create more than one centerline in your sketch, Pro/ENGINEER will automatically use the first centerline created, as the axis of revolution. If needed, you can select a different centerline and right-click to set it as the axis of revolution. To create a revolved feature, select the ⬡ **Revolve** icon from the Construction Toolbar. Once your sketch is selected, or created, you will see the pre-construction highlight, indicating the extent of revolution, as shown in Figure 9-11.

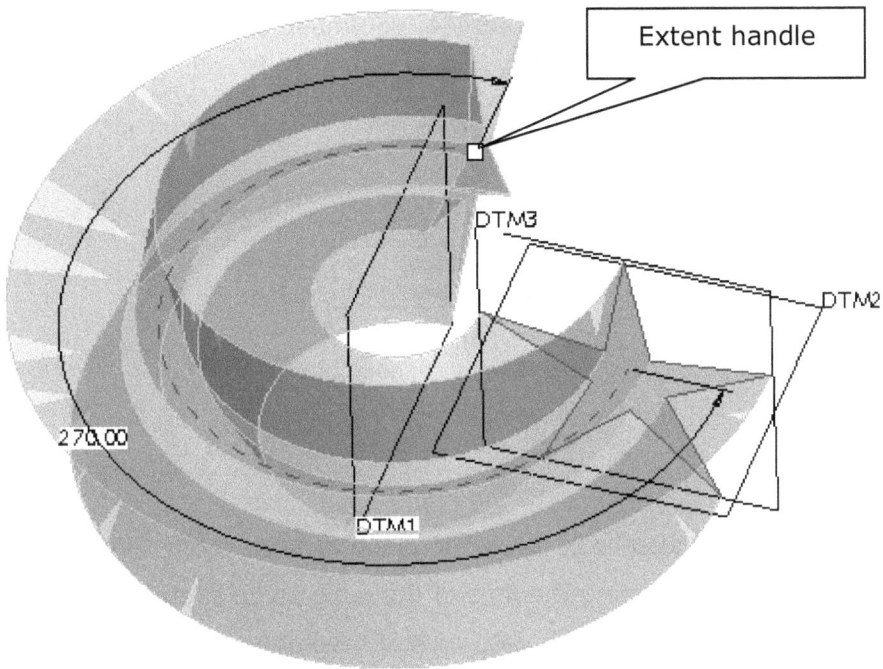

Fig. 9-11
Extent of revolution

If you define the extent of revolution to be 360°, the feature will form a completely closed loop, as shown in Figure 9-12.

Fig. 9-12
Complete loop

If your sketch does not contain a centerline, you must select an existing axis or edge as the axis of revolution, as shown in Figure 9-13.

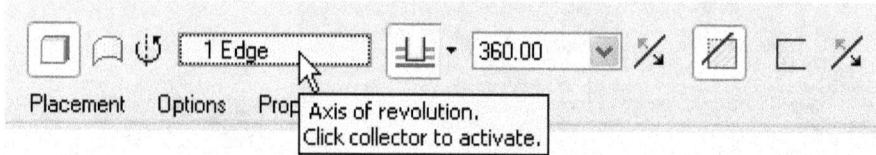

Fig. 9-13
Selecting axis of revolution

This selected axis must also lie in the same plane as the sketch. Figure 9-14 shows a sketch that was created using the face of the cube as its sketching plane, therefore the edge of the cube is a valid axis of revolution.

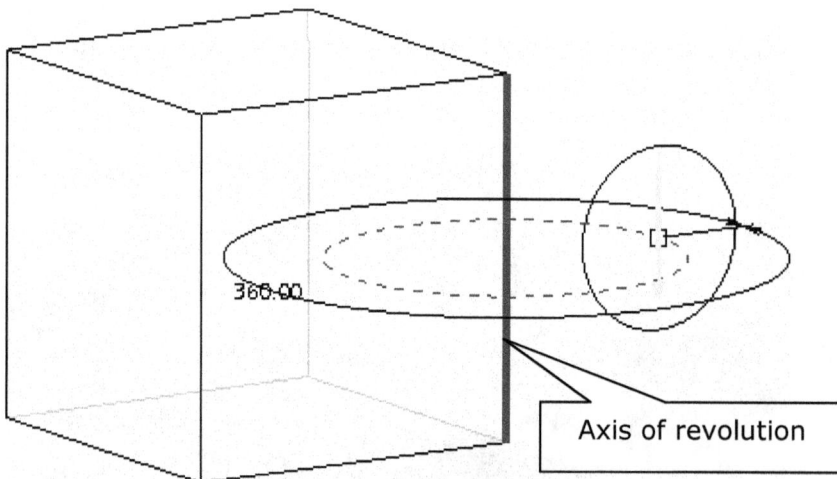

Fig. 9-14
Defining external axis of revolution

Figure 9-15 shows the result of using the sketch to remove material.

Fig. 9-15
Completed revolved cut

In addition to the requirement that the axis of revolution lies in the same plane as the sketch, all of the sketched entities must lie on or to one side of the axis. Figure 9-16 shows an example of an improperly defined sketch. Even though it is well defined, using an intended dimension scheme, it is impossible to revolve. A properly defined sketch is shown in Figure 9-17. Notice the sketch is closed off by creating a solid line directly on the axis of revolution, and all the other entities are to one side of the centerline.

To create the 0.375 and 0.13 diameter dimensions, start the dimension command, select the sketched entity, then the centerline (not the object line or reference), then select the sketched entity a second time before placing the dimension with the **MMB**. The same technique is used to create diameter dimensions on circles and arcs, by selecting the arc twice before placing the dimension with the **MMB**.

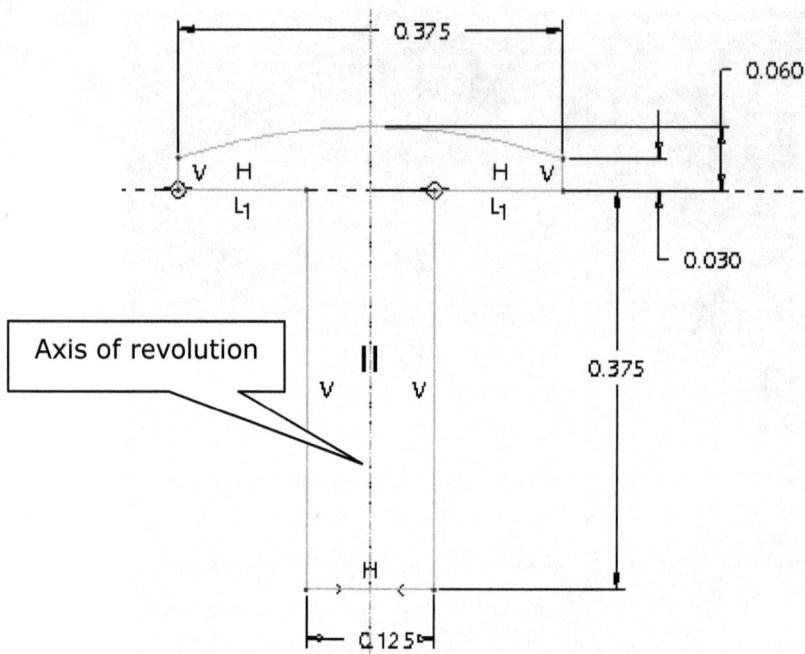

Fig. 9-16
Improper sketch

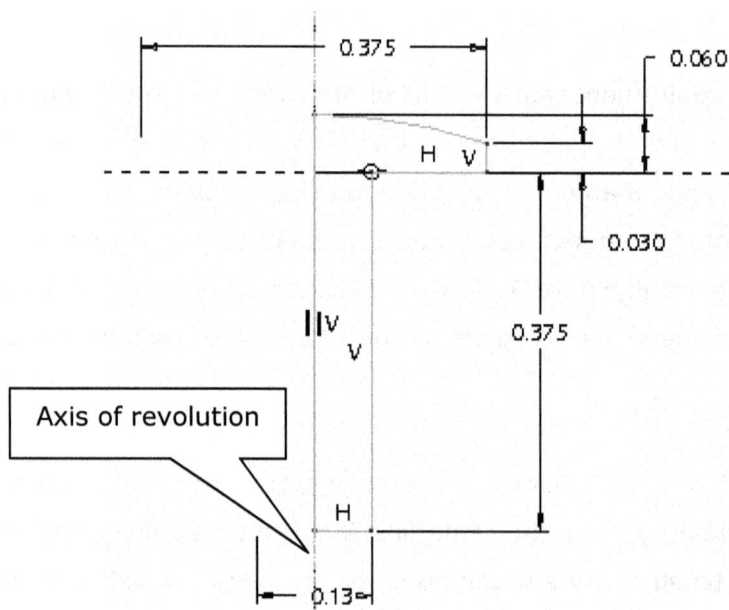

Fig. 9-17
Proper sketch

Sweep

Sweeps can be created to add or delete material, and also as surface features, but you must specify those operations at the start of the sweep definition by selecting **Insert** > **Sweep**, from the menu, then making the appropriate choice from the menu, as shown in Figure 9-18.

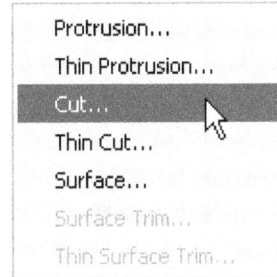

Protrusion...
Thin Protrusion...
Cut...
Thin Cut...
Surface...
Surface Trim...
Thin Surface Trim...

Fig. 9-18
Choosing sweep type

A dialog box will automatically open for you to fill in the required information:

Trajectory

The trajectory is what makes a sweep differ from an extrusion. Rather than extruding a sketch normal to its sketching plane, a sweep follows a sketched path. You may use a pre-existing sketch, or you may define the trajectory as an internal sketch, by making the appropriate choice from the pop-up menu, as shown in Figure 9-19.

Menu Manager
▼ SWEEP TRAJ
Sketch Traj
Select Traj

Fig. 9-19
Specifying Trajectory

Figure 9-20 shows a trajectory sketched on the top of a solid. It is considered 'open' because its starting and ending points do not meet. You can control which end you want to be used as the starting point (as indicated by an arrow) by selecting the endpoint, right-clicking, and selecting **Start Point**.

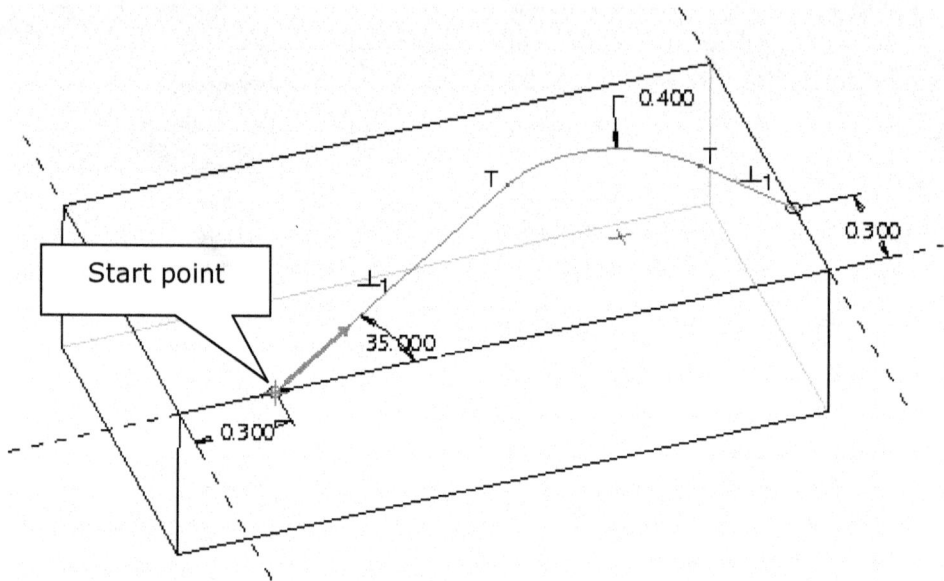

Fig. 9-20
Trajectory sketch

When a trajectory contains tangent continuous chains, the resulting sweep will be smooth, but when it contains non-tangent segments, the sweep will be created with a mitered corner.

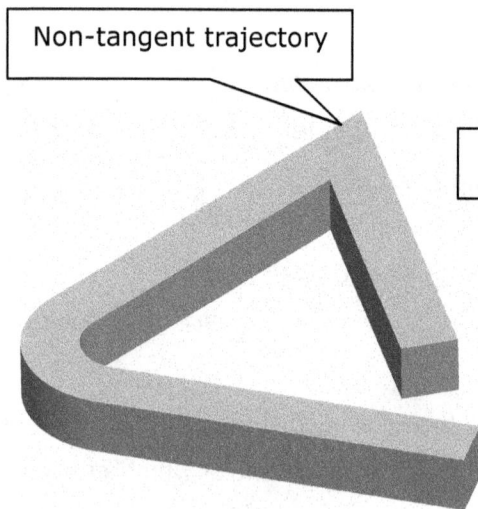

Fig. 9-21
Open trajectory

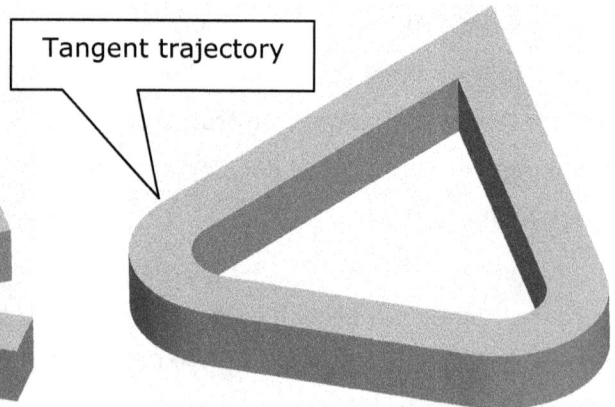

Fig. 9-22
Closed trajectory

Attributes

After the trajectory is defined, you will be prompted to specify either **Free Ends**, as shown in Figure 9-23, which terminate the extend of the sweep exactly at the ends of the trajectory, or **Merge Ends**, as shown in Figure 9-24, which continue the sweep to blend with the surfaces at the ends of the trajectory.

Fig. 9-23
Merge ends

Fig. 9-24
Merge ends

Section

After the attributes have been set, Pro/ENGINEER will prompt you to define the sketch for the section to sweep. It will automatically reorient the view so that the Start Point is facing you, as shown in Figure 9-25.

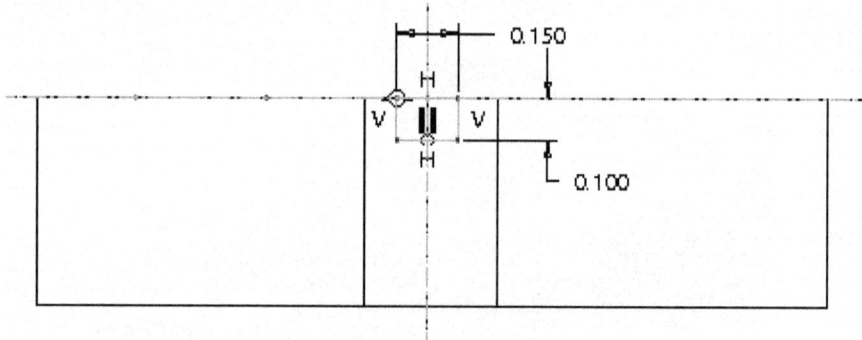

Fig. 9-25
Sweep section

A horizontal and vertical sketcher reference will be created at the starting point. You may define the sketch with the starting point in the center of the sketch, as shown in Figure 9-25, but it is not necessary. You may define the sketch anywhere you wish, as it will travel along the trajectory, relative to how you have it defined from the trajectory.

Fig. 9-26
Click OK to complete the feature

Variable Section Sweep

The Sweep tool keeps the section a constant shape as it travels along the trajectory.

If you would like to change the section as it is swept, you may select the
Variable Section Sweep icon from the Construction Toolbar. This will allow you to
select several trajectories, to not only control the path of the feature, but individual
entities (points. verticies, etc.) that can be dimensioned or constrained to the
additional trajectories, to alter the shape of the section as it travels along the path.

Figure 9-27 shows three individual sketches. When the **Variable Section Sweep** tools
is selected, you are prompted to select a curve to serve as the trajectory, with the
option of selecting additional curves to control the section.

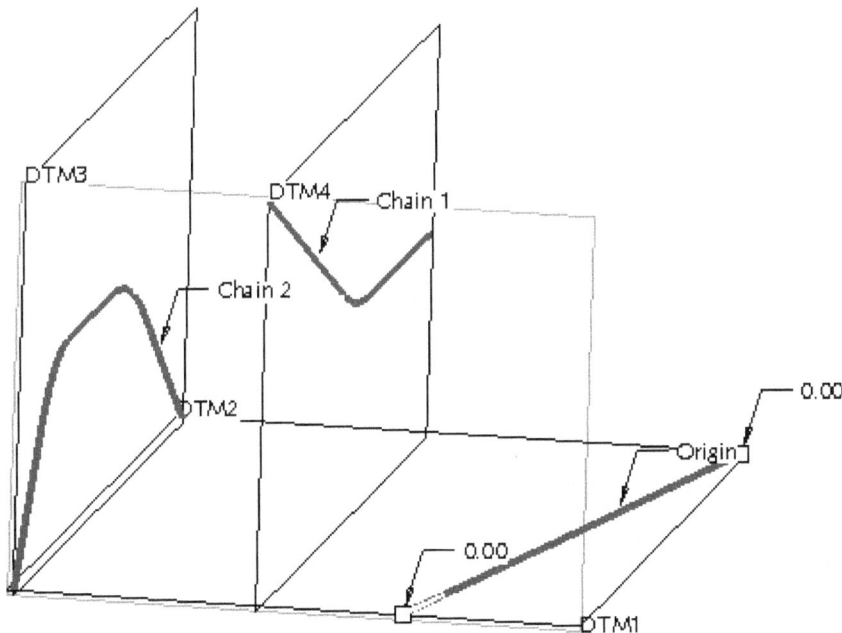

Fig. 9-27
Trajectory and control curves

By selecting the References tab in the feature dashboard, as shown in Figure 9-28, you can specify options for the orientation of the section.

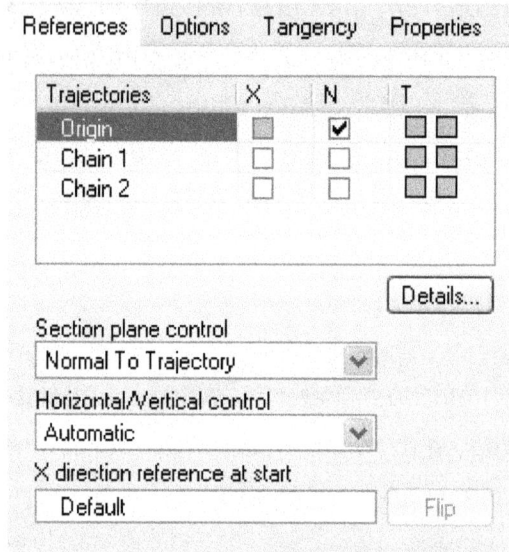

Fig. 9-28
Variable section sweep References

To create the section, select the ✎ **Section** icon from the feature dashboard. This will orient the view so that the starting point is facing you, but it will also provide you with indicators for the additional control points, as shown in Figure 9-29. By constraining or dimensioning the sketched entities relative to the origin and control points, the section will follow the trajectory and control curves, as shown in Figure 9-30.

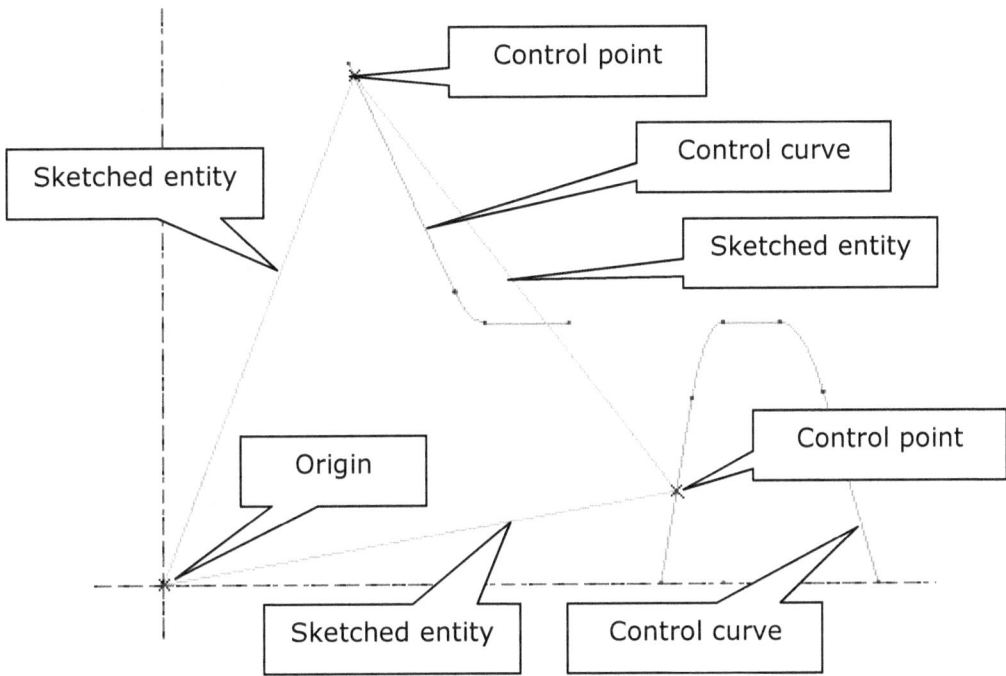

Fig. 9-29
Defining the section

Fig. 9-30
Completed Variable Section Sweep

You will notice that the default settings create a quilt (surface only) feature. You may change this to a solid in the dashboard, as well as specifying the feature to remove material (create a cut). It is interesting to note that if only the trajectory is selected, without any control curves, Pro/ENGINEER will create this feature exactly the same as a basic sweep, without any variation to the section.

Blends

A blend is a feature that is extruded a given distance, but it transitions between two or more distinct sections (shapes), as shown in Figure 9-31.

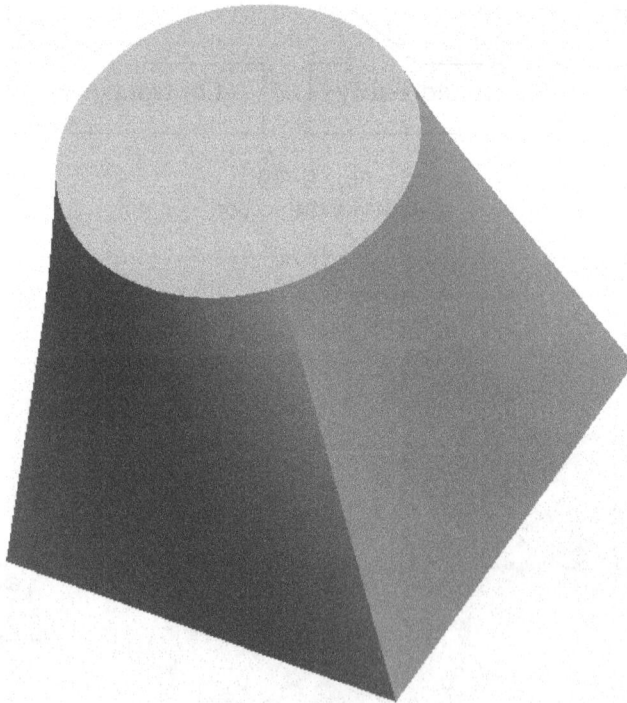

Fig 9-31
Square to circle blend

The two most important aspects to remember when creating blends is that the feature will be created by extruding normal to the sketching plane, and that each section (shape to blend) must contain the same number of entities. To create a blend, select **Insert** > **Blend** from the menu. Just like basic sweeps, you will choose up front if you want to create your blend feature as a solid, or surface, and whether you want to add or delete material. This will open a dialog box and the menu shown in Figure 9-32 where you may select several options (default settings shown). Select **Done**, and the menu shown in Figure 9-33 will open where you indicate if you want to make a straight or smooth blend (default setting shown).

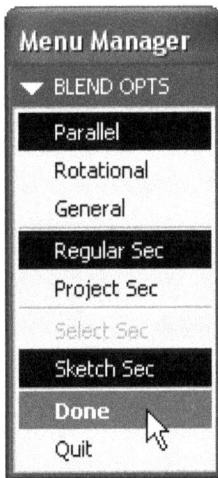

Fig. 9-32
Blend options

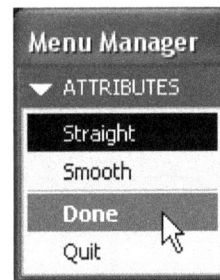

Fig. 9-33
Attributes

After selecting **Done** from the Attribute menu, you will be prompted to select a plane to sketch your first shape. Using the normal sketching tools, create the starting shape of your feature, as shown in Feature 9-34. You will see Pro/ENGINEER automatically places a start point at one of the verticies. The direction of the arrow is irrelevant, as it simply identifies which line's endpoint is being used. It is however, important to note the location. In this case, it is in the upper left-hand corner of our sketch. We must also take note of how many entities are in our sketch. In this case, we have four.

Start point

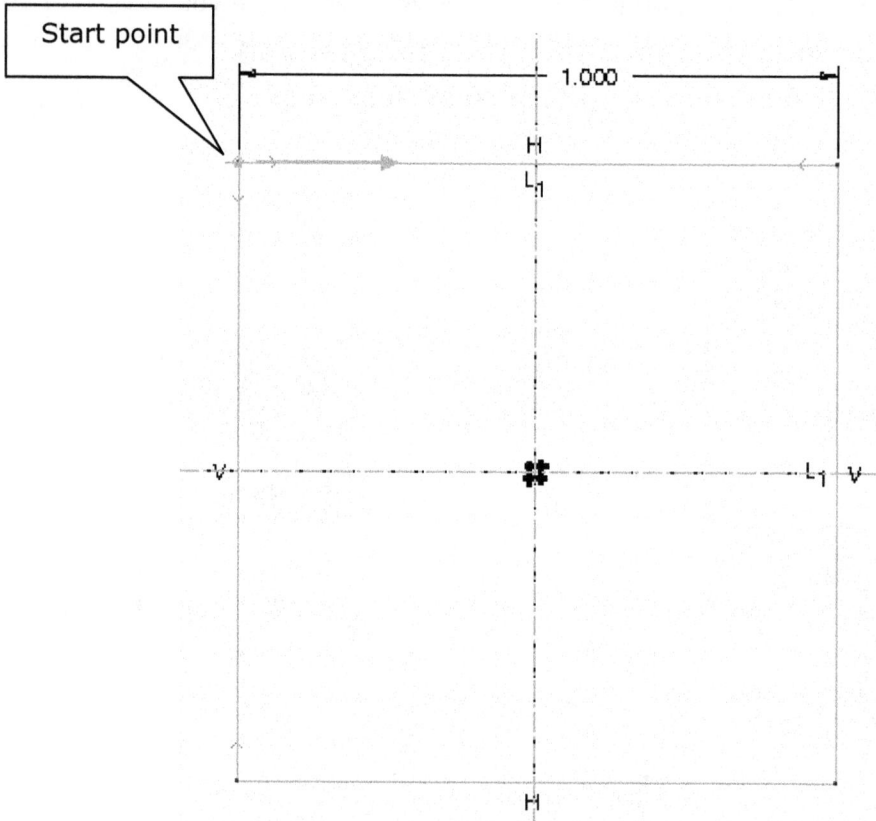

Fig. 9-34
First section

If we were to accept this sketch by selecting the ✓ **Done** icon, we would see the following in the message area:

"Must have more than one section. Select "Sketch", "Feature Tools", "Toggle Section" for next section".

This would be expected, as we are trying to create a blend from one section to at least one other. You may toggle to the next section by following the commands above, or you may simply hold down the **RMB** and toggle the section as shown in Figure 9-35.

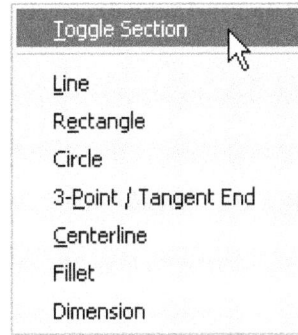

Toggle Section
Line
Rectangle
Circle
3-Point / Tangent End
Centerline
Fillet
Dimension

Fig. 9-35
Toggle to next section

You may then create the second section. Even though Pro/ENGINEER 'greys-out' the first section, it may be used as a reference if needed, as shown in Figure 9-36.

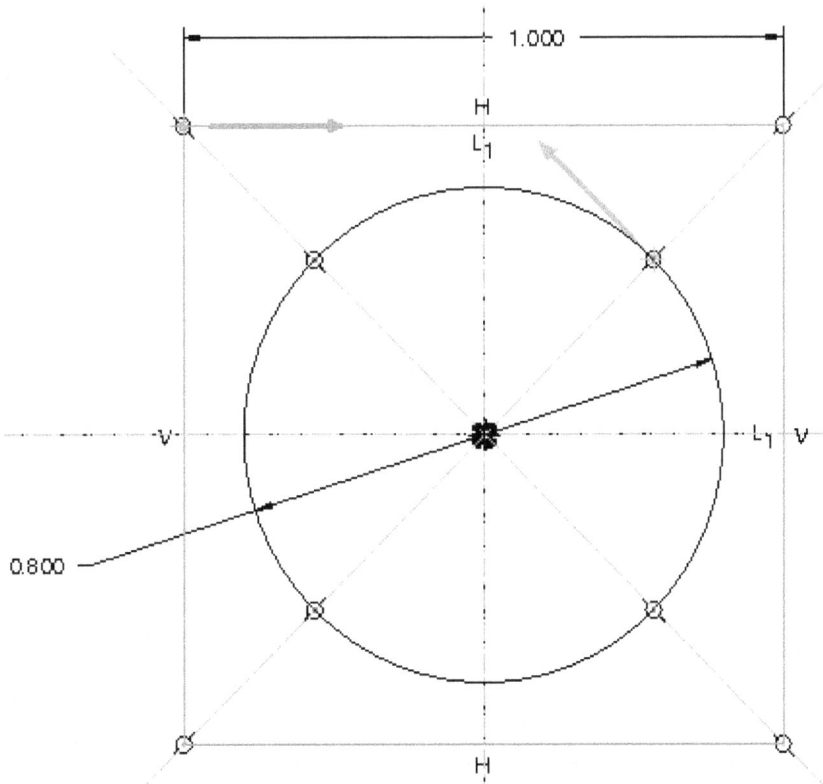

Fig. 9-36
Second section

In order to maintain the same number of entities in all your sketches, it may be necessary to create lines out of two or more segments and circles out of two or more arcs, etc.. In this example, a single circle was broken into four entities by using the 🖉 **Divide** tool.

You may toggle to add more sections, or select the ✔ **Done** icon to complete the section definition. You will then be prompted for the depth for Section 2. This is the distance from the sketching plane (where Section 1 is located) to the next section. In this case we will use 1.00 for the value.

To complete the feature, select OK in the dialog box, as shown in Figure 9-37.

The resulting blend feature is shown in Figure 9-38.

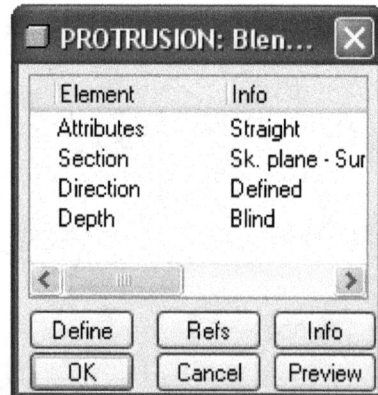

PROTRUSION: Blen... ✕	
Element	Info
Attributes	Straight
Section	Sk. plane - Sur
Direction	Defined
Depth	Blind

Define	Refs	Info
OK	Cancel	Preview

Fig. 9-37
Click OK to complete the feature

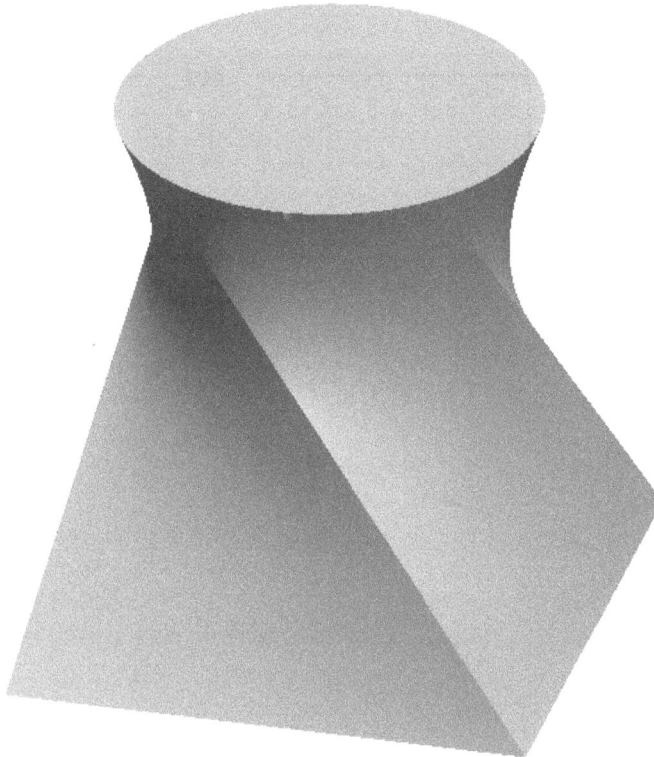

Fig. 9-38
Completed blend

Notice how the shape created is not only twisted, but also collapsed. Why is this? Examining the section shown in Figure 9-36, you will notice that even though we have the correct number of entities, we created a shape that blended from the upper left-hand corner of Section 1 to the upper right-hand corner of Section 2. To prevent this, the start points of each section should be specifically set by selecting them in the sketch, hold down the **RMB**, and selecting **Start Point**, as shown in Figure 9-39. The proper section is shown in Figure 9-40. Notice that it does not matter which direction the arrows are facing.

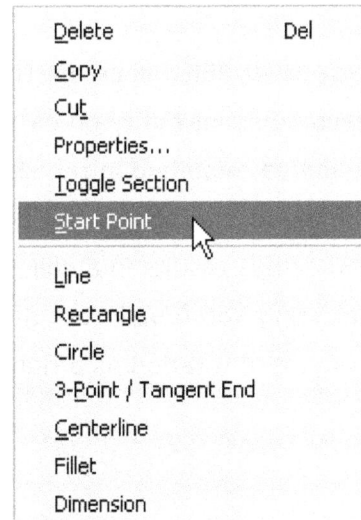

Delete	Del
Copy	
Cut	
Properties...	
Toggle Section	
Start Point	
Line	
Rectangle	
Circle	
3-Point / Tangent End	
Centerline	
Fillet	
Dimension	

Fig. 9-39
Start Point

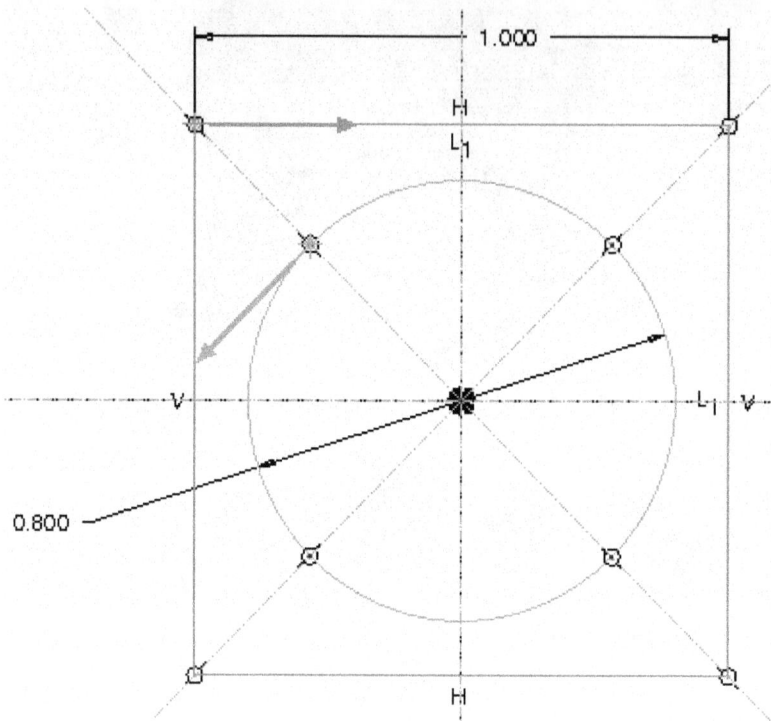

Fig. 9-40
Proper section definition

Pro/ENGINEER will create the blend by matching-up these two points first, then each adjacent entity on either side of the start point, until all the entities are matched, resulting in the shape shown in Figure 9-31. If it is your intention to 'twist' the blend, this should <u>not</u> be done by crossing the Start Points as shown in Figure 9-36, as this results in a collapsed volume (as shown in Figure 9-38), but rather selecting **Rotational** from the Blend Options menu, and specifying the desired amount of rotation as a numerical value.

The only exception to the equal number of entities rule is when you want to blend to a single point, as shown in Figure 9-41.

Fig. 9-41
Blending to a point

The shape blends directly (or straight) from one section to the next. By specifying **Smooth** from the Attributes menu, Pro/ENGINEER will create a shape that still passes through the section definitions at the distances specified, but it extrapolates the transition between sections to provide a smooth shape, as shown in Figure 9-42.

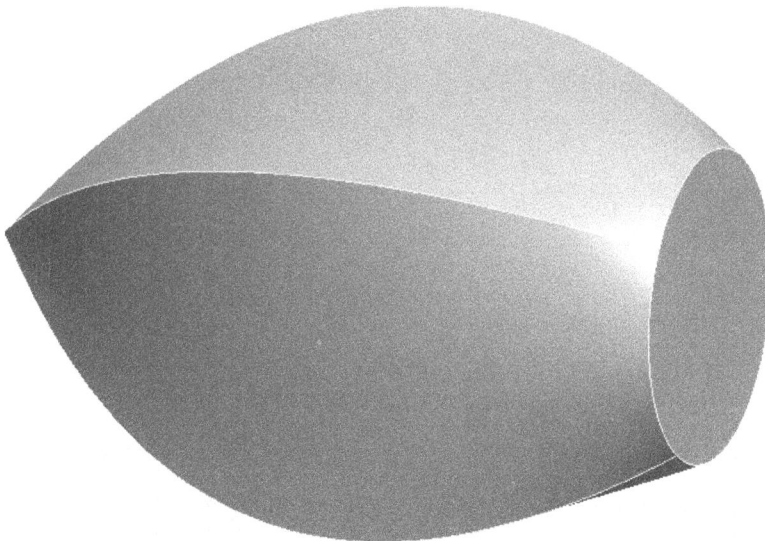

Fig. 9-42
Smooth blend

Swept Blend

A swept blend allows you to create a feature that is swept along a trajectory, but also blends from one section to another (or several). Because there are several entities and controls involved in creating a swept blend, it is recommended that you create these entities as individual features first, starting with a sketch to be used as a trajectory, as shown in Figure 9-43. Since the various sections used for blending will be located along the trajectory, it is also a good idea to divide the trajectory so that you have verticies that can easily be selected when locating the sections. Additional sketches can then be added a specific locations to control the shape of the sweep. These sections may be created during the sweep creation, but having them created first allows us to simply select them.

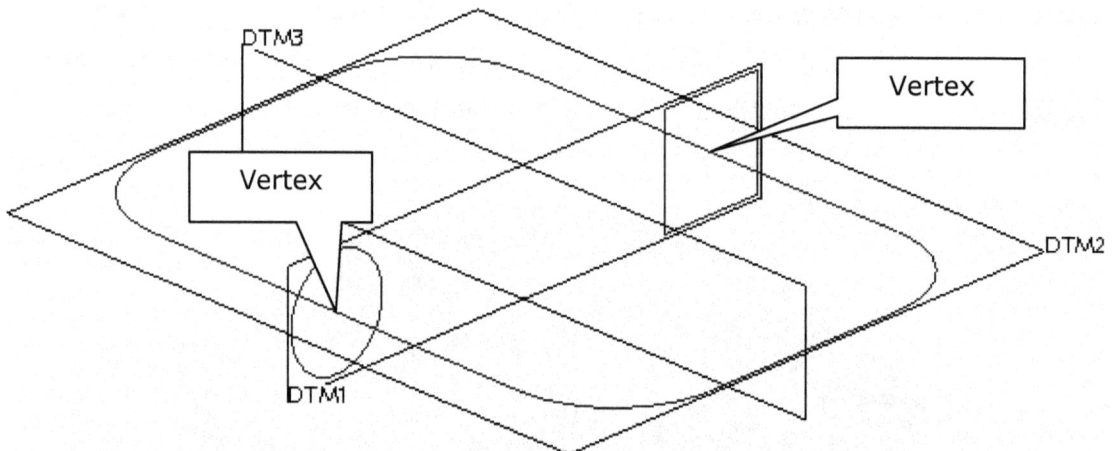

Fig. 9-43
Sketches to be used as trajectory and sections

To create the swept blend, select **Insert > Swept Blend** from the menu. Select the trajectory when prompted, and drag the starting point to one of the verticies specifically created for that purpose, as shown in Figure 9-44.

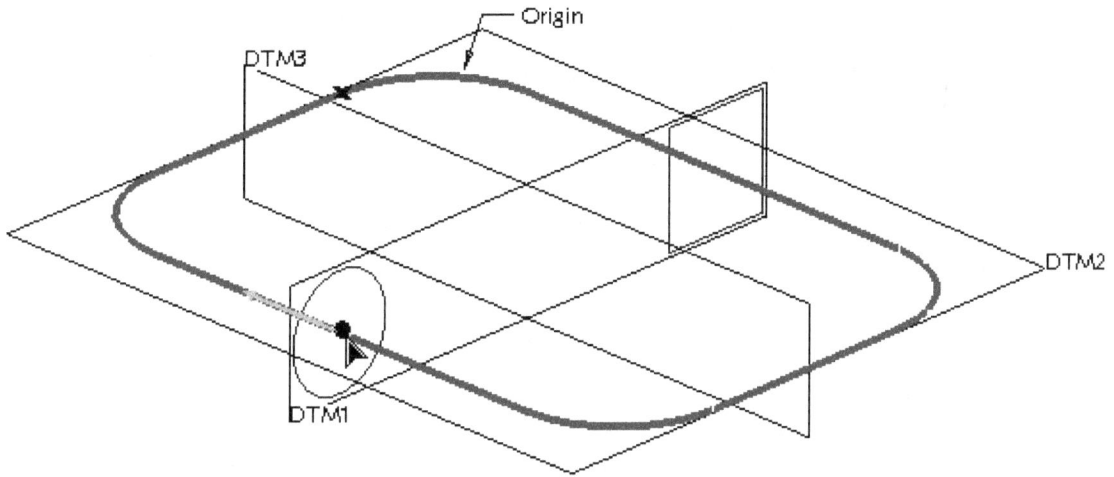

Fig. 9-44
Selecting the trajectory start point

To specify the sections to blend, open the Sections tab from the feature dashboard. You may create the sections now, or select existing sections, as shown in Figure 9-45.

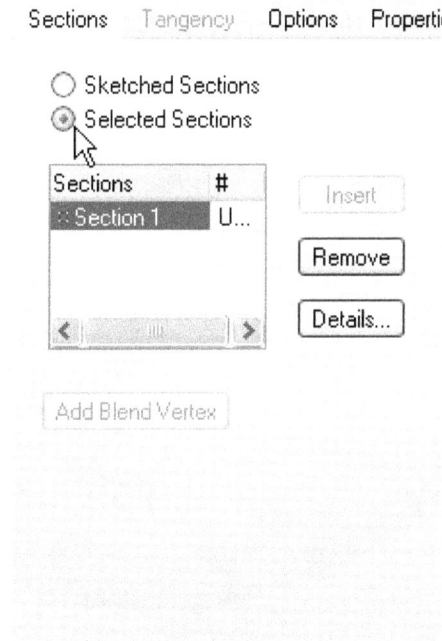

Fig. 9-45
Specifying sections

If the starting points of the sections need to be adjusted, you may drag them to the proper position with the **LMB**, as shown in Figure 9-46.

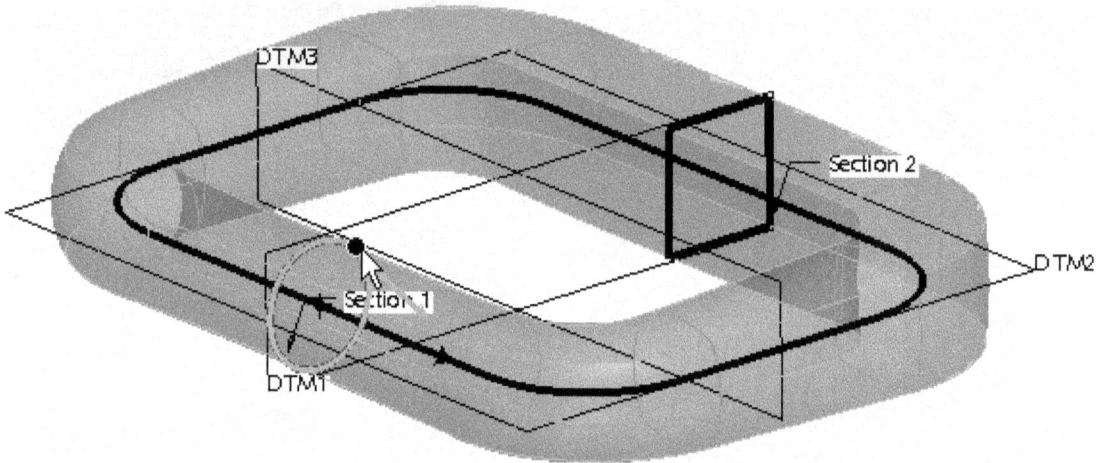

Fig. 9-46
Adjusting section start points

To complete the feature, select the ✅ **Accept** icon from the feature dashboard.

Fig. 9-47
Completed swept blend feature

Helical Sweep

Springs (coils) may be created by selecting **Insert** >
Helical Sweep from the menu. After choosing the feature
type you want (solid, surface, protrusion, cut), a dialog
box and the Attributes menu will appear, as shown in
Figure 9-48. After making the desired choices, select
Done, and you will be prompted to create a sketch for
the trajectory, such as the one shown in Figure 9-49.
Notice how it is similar to a sketch for a revolved feature,
with all the entities to one side of a center line, and that
the trajectory does not necessarily need to be parallel to
the center line.

Fig. 9-48
Attributes menu

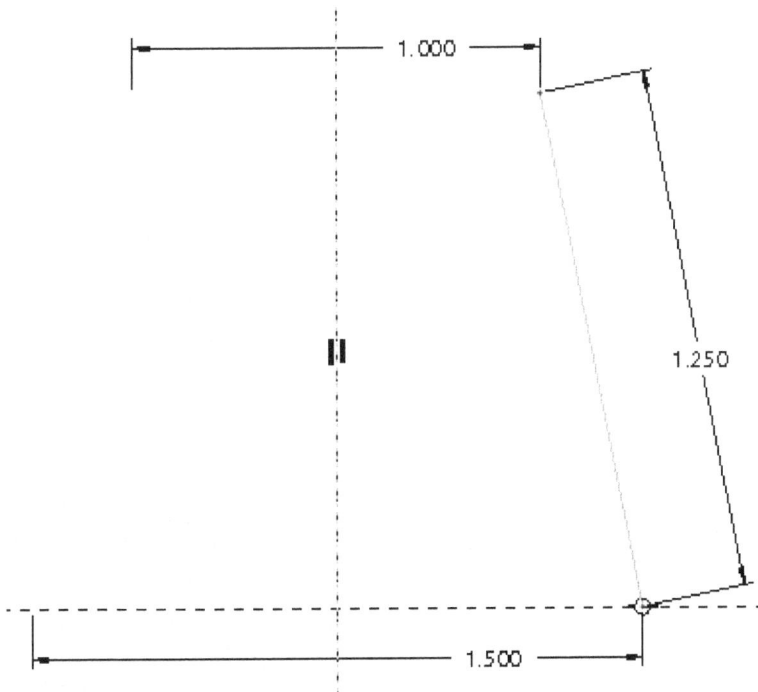

Fig. 9-49
Helical sweep trajectory

After the trajectory is created, you will be prompted to enter the pitch value
(distance between coils). Once the value is accepted, the view is reoriented to
sketch the shape of the section to revolve around the centerline, as shown in Figure
9-50.

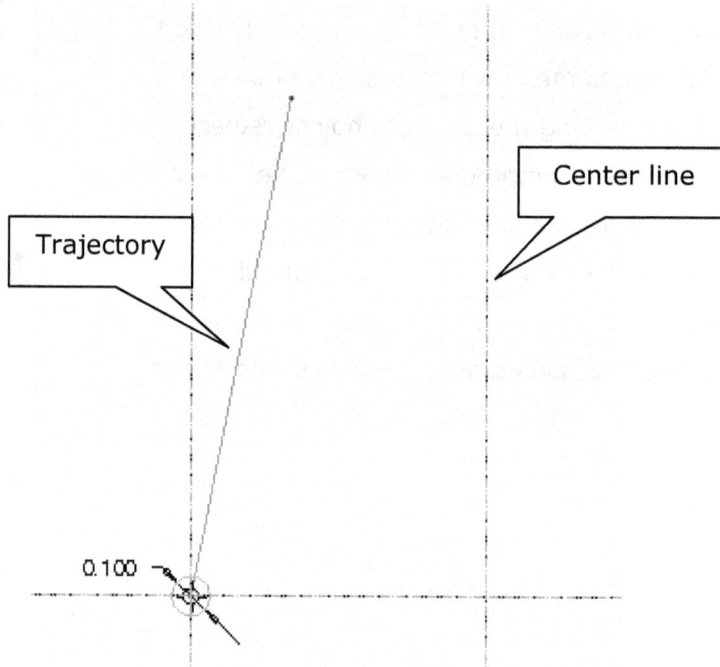

Fig. 9-50
Section definition

When all the Elements have been defined, the
dialog box may be closed by selecting **OK**, as
shown in Figure 9-51. The resulting geometry is
shown in Figure 9-52.

Fig. 9-51
Helical sweep dialog box

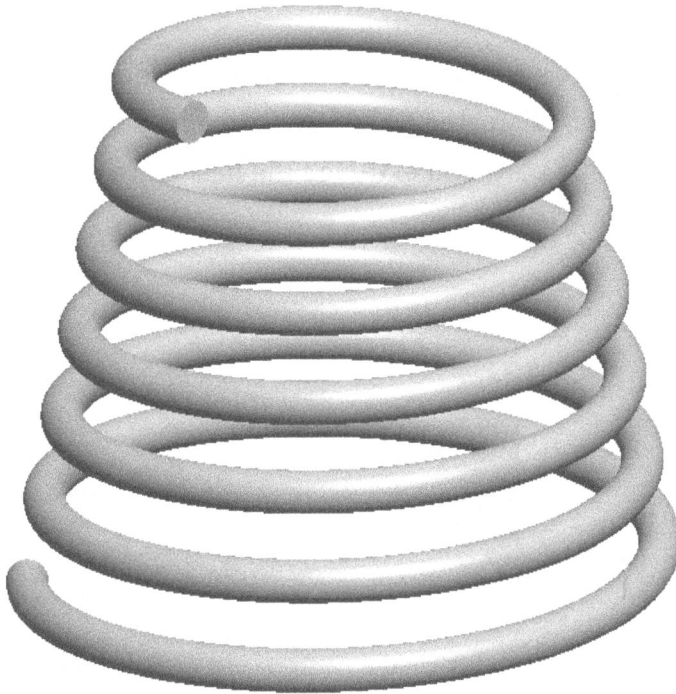

Fig. 9-52
Helical sweep

Caution should be used when defining the pitch value because if the value is not at least two times the section height, the resulting geometry will actually overlap itself, resulting in physically impossible geometry. However it is possible to use the variable pitch option as needed, and a pitch value that is larger than the length of the trajectory will allow you to create a feature such as the grooves in the cutter bit shown in Figure 9-53.

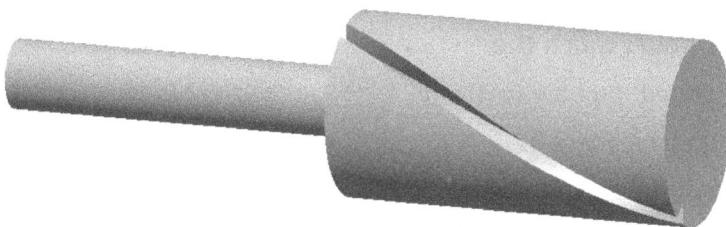

Fig. 9-53
Helical cut

Ribs

Figure 9-54 shows a rib, created on a revolved solid model. On first glance, it would appear that the rib could be created by simply sketching a triangle, with the legs of the triangle aligned to the part, and extruded the desired thickness.

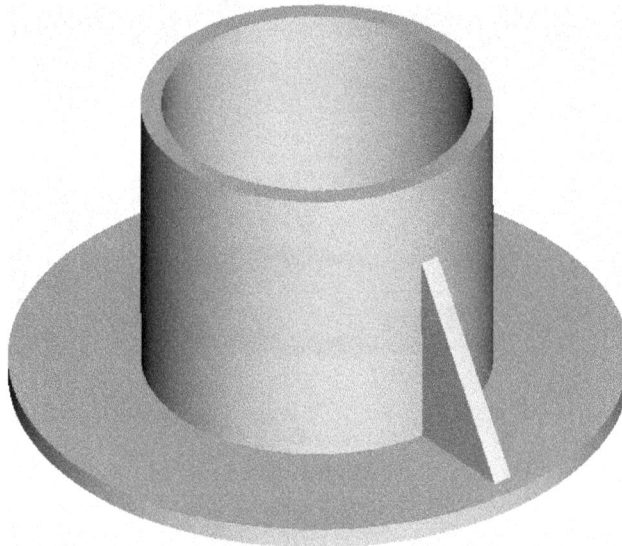

Fig. 9-54
Rib on revolved model

What happens as the thickness of the rib increases, as shown in Fig. 9-55? We certainly would not create a rib this thick, but it illustrates that only center of the rib would touch the cylinder, and it would 'pull away' from the cylinder as the thickness is added. What would happen if the bottom disc was wavy, instead of flat?

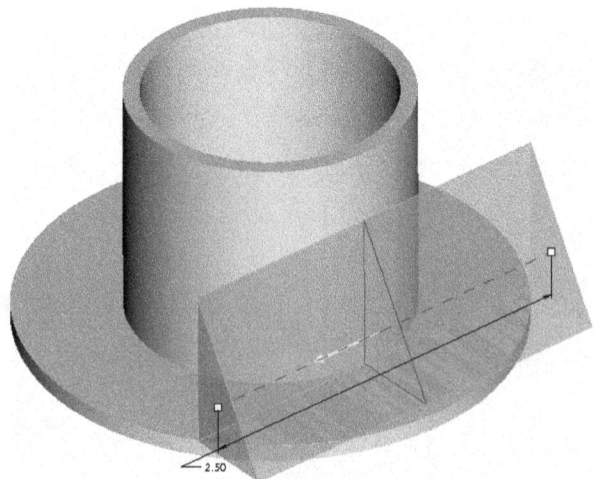

Fig. 9-55
Extruded triangle

Rather than creating an Extrude, select the ⬦ Rib icon from the Construction Toolbar. When creating the sketch for the rib, only the un-attached edge of the rib needs to be defined, and its ends should be aligned to the surfaces of the solid geometry, as shown in Figure 9-56.

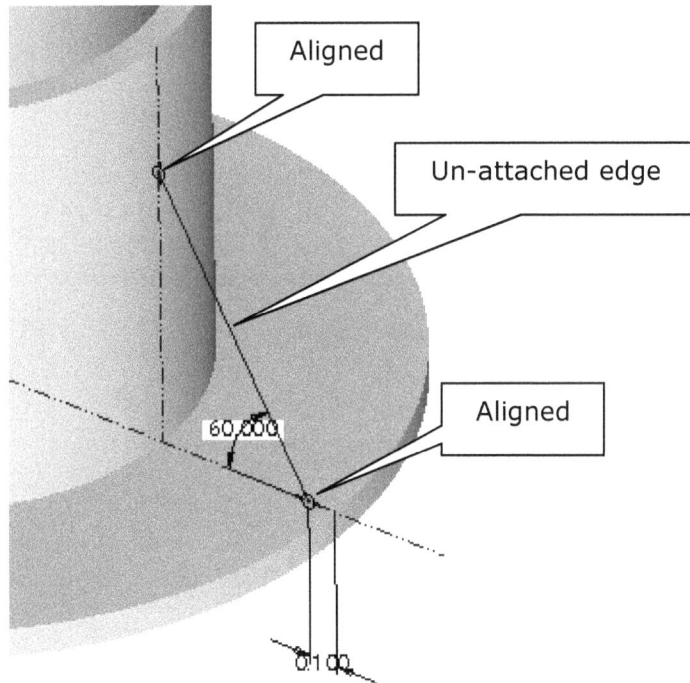

Fig. 9-56
Rib sketch

You will have an option in the dashboard to specify which side of the sketch the rib should be created, or symmetrically both sides, and as you adjust the thickness, the geometry will automatically follow the contours of its parent surfaces, as shown in Figure 9-57.

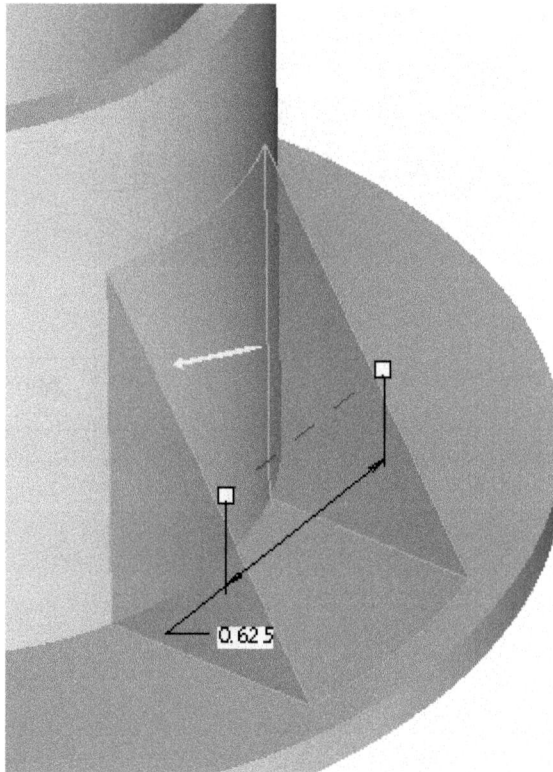

Fig. 9-57
Properly defined rib feature

Chapter 10

Quilts

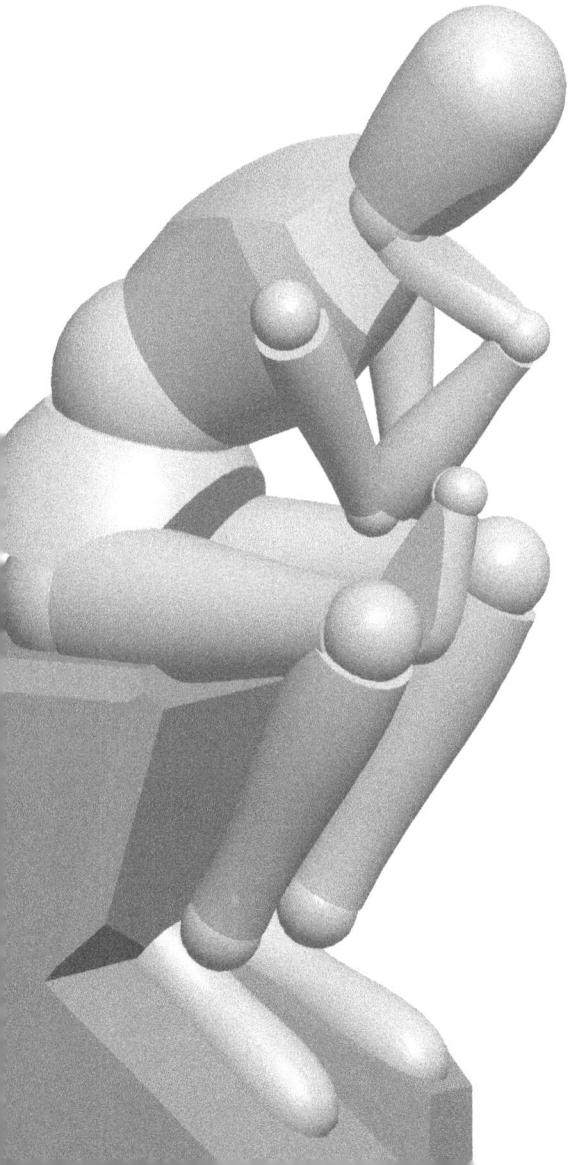

In Chapter 9, we discuss making three-dimensional solid shapes. When creating solid geometry, material is either added or removed from our model. It is however possible to create quilt (surface only) geometry to define shapes and boundaries without removing or adding material. This allows you to build extremely complex geometry by creating several simple portions of the geometry and manipulating those portions before combining them (if desired) to eventually add or delete material from your solid model.

There is a misconception among new and novice users of Pro/ENGINEER that quilts are only used for 'surfacing' operations, such as those required for Class A surfaces, when defining automotive body panels and aircraft design. In reality, surfaces can be used for any geometry or product design. Seasoned Pro/ENGINEER users will use the terms Quilt and Surface interchangeably.

Solid vs. Surface

As mentioned in Chapter 9, several shapes such as **Sweep** and **Blend** require you to indicate whether you wish to define a Solid or Surface (quilt) before creating the geometry. However, any three-dimensional shape tool that is controlled by a dashboard, i.e., extrude and revolve, can be defined as either a solid or a surface by selecting the **Surface** icon in the dashboard, as shown in Figure 10-1.

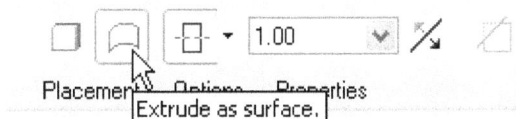

Fig. 10-1
Creating a surface feature

Rather than defining a solid, the entities used to define the shape are used to define the 'walls' of a quilt. These walls have no thickness, as shown in Figure 10-2.

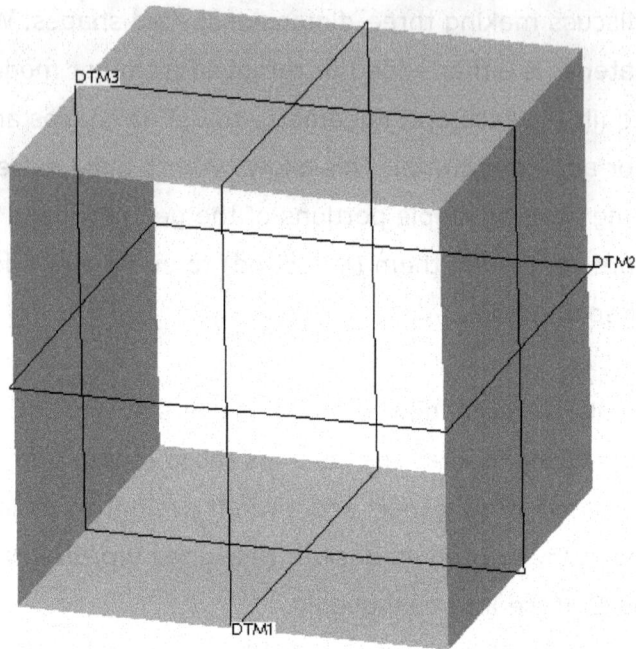

Fig. 10-2
Sketched square extruded as a surface

By default, Pro/ENGINEER will leave the ends of such features open. To close off the ends, check the **Capped ends** box under the Options tab, as shown in Figure 10-3.

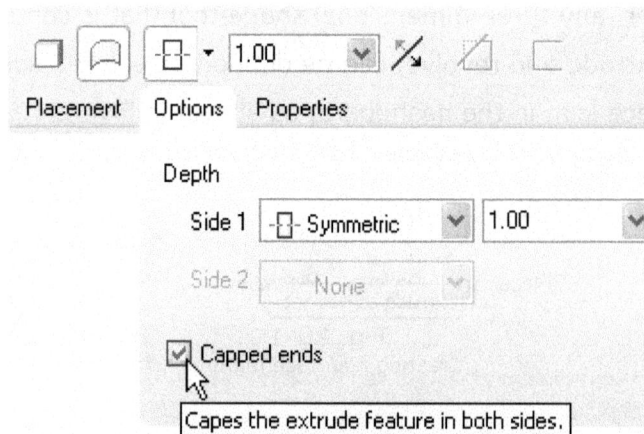

Fig. 10-3
Extruded surface with capped ends

This will create a completely defined, six-sided cube, but will not add or delete any material. It will simply be a definition of a shape. (Later in this chapter we will discuss how to use quilts to add or delete material.)

When using an open sketch, as shown in Figure 10-4, the **Capped ends** option is not applicable.

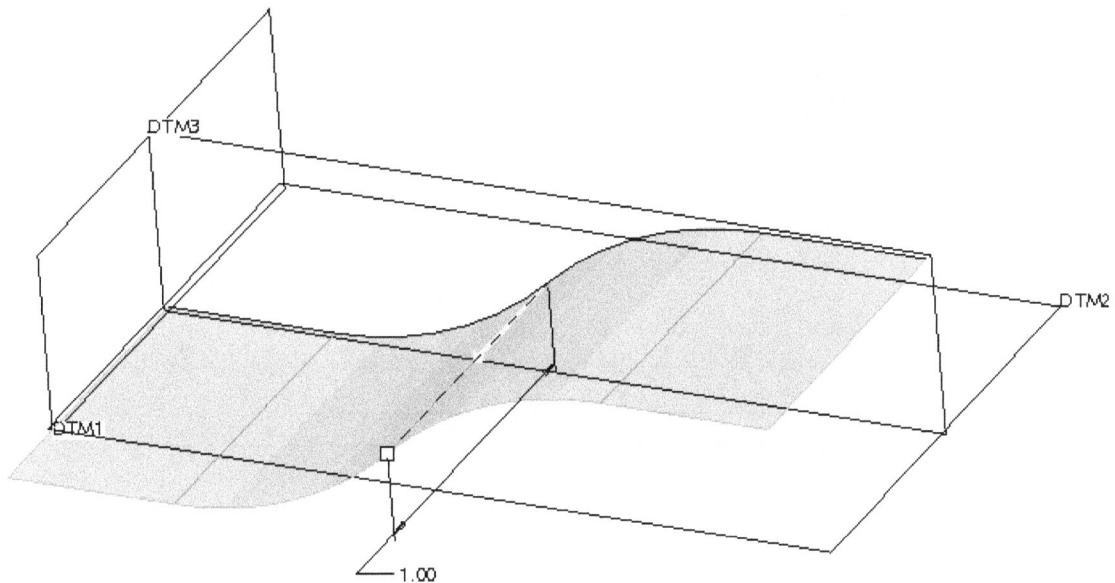

Fig. 10-4
Extruded open section

Fill

If the sketch used in Figure 10-4 was a single straight line, the resulting surface would be a flat, rectangular quilt. It is also possible to create a flat quilt by selecting **Edit > Fill** from the menu. You will be prompted to select any closed, planar sketch in your model, or you may define a new one. This will allow you to create a flat surface with any perimeter boundary, as shown in Figure 10-5. The idea is that the boundary is 'filled'.

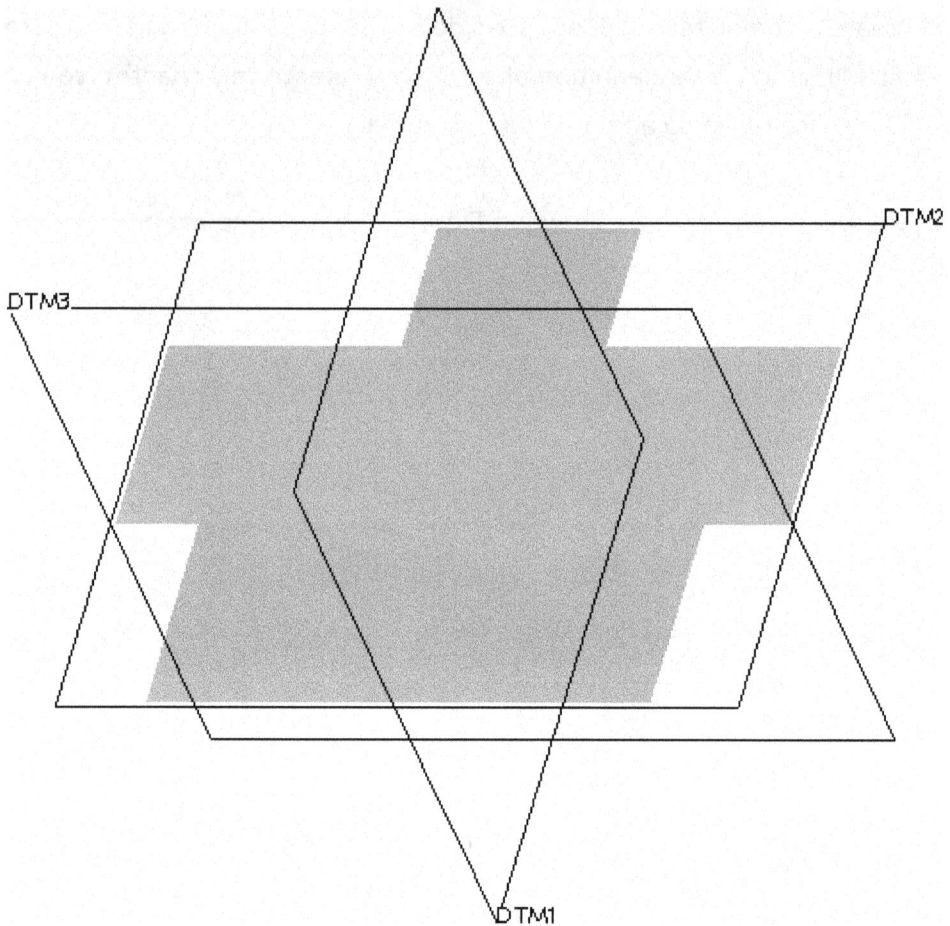

Fig. 10-5
'Filled' surface

Boundary Blend

The surface fill technique shown in Figure 10-5 requires all of the boundaries of the surface to lie in the same plane (two-dimensional). It is however, possible to create

a surface with three-dimensional boundaries by selecting the [icon] **Boundary Blend** icon from the toolbar. You will be prompted to select sets of boundary curves (sketches) like the ones shown in Figure 10-6.

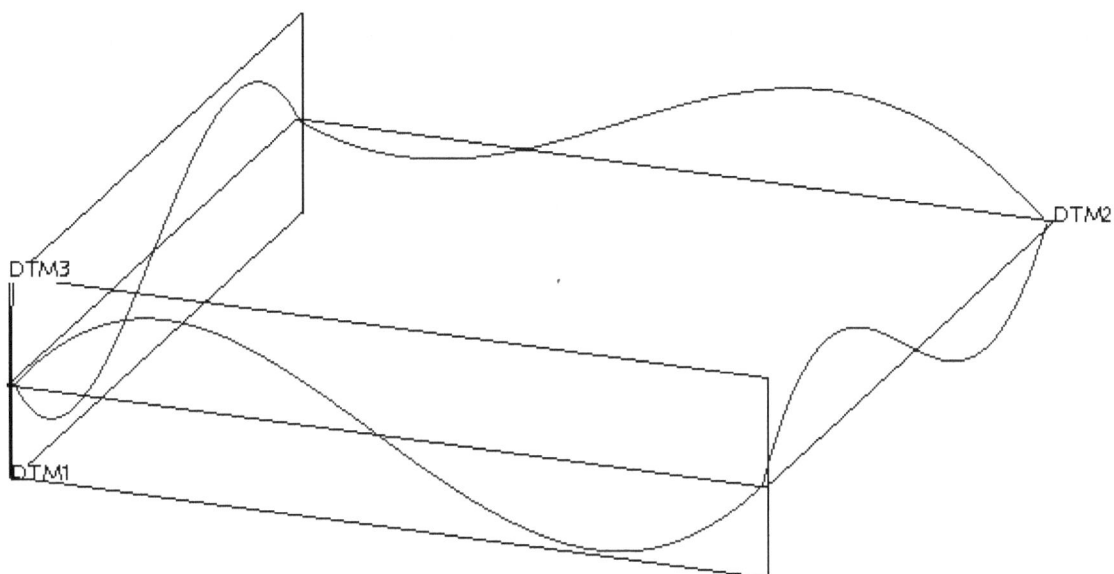

Fig 10-6
Four separate sketches

Using **Ctrl**, select boundary edges, as shown in Figure 10-7.

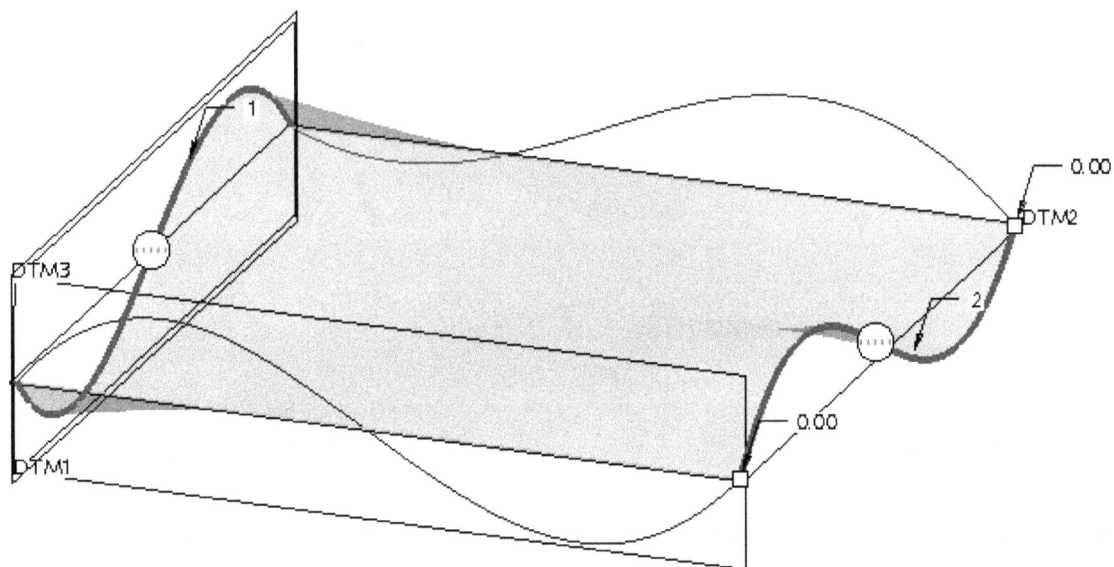

Fig. 10-7
Boundary blend in one direction

It is possible to create a surface using only one direction, as shown in Figure 10-7, but you may also define a second direction by clicking the **Second direction** chain collector box, as shown in Figure 10-8.

Fig. 10-8
Second direction chain collector

By selecting a second set of boundaries, as shown in Figure 10-9, complex shapes may be created from several simple shapes.

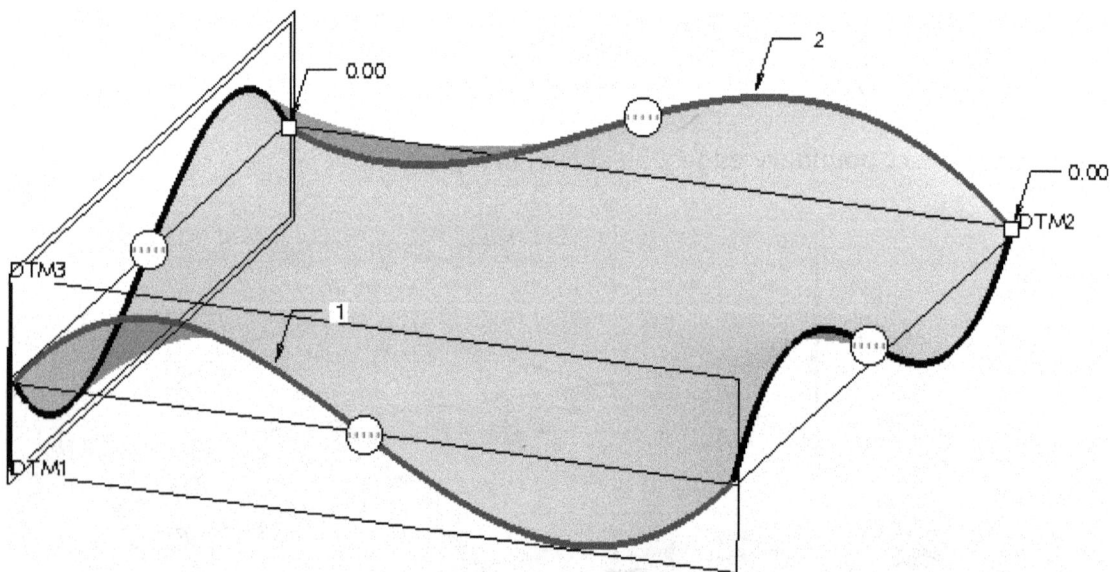

Fig. 10-9
Boundary blend using two directions

It is important to note that such shapes require the endpoints of the boundary chains to match, forming a closed loop. Also, the shape of the surface can be controlled by the shape of the curves (sketches) used to define its boundaries. For example, Class A surfaces are created by using continuous curvature splines in the sketches. Further controls may be placed on the surface (such as edge conditions) by making the appropriate choices in the dashboard, as shown in Figure 10-10.

Fig. 10-10
Complex controls for boundary blend surfaces

The subject of complex surfaces is much too large to further discuss in this book, and will be addressed in future volumes.

Copy

Individual surfaces or quilts may be created by copying the faces (surfaces) of solid geometry, or even other surfaces. To create a quilt from a solid, first select the surface of the solid, as shown in Figure 10-11.

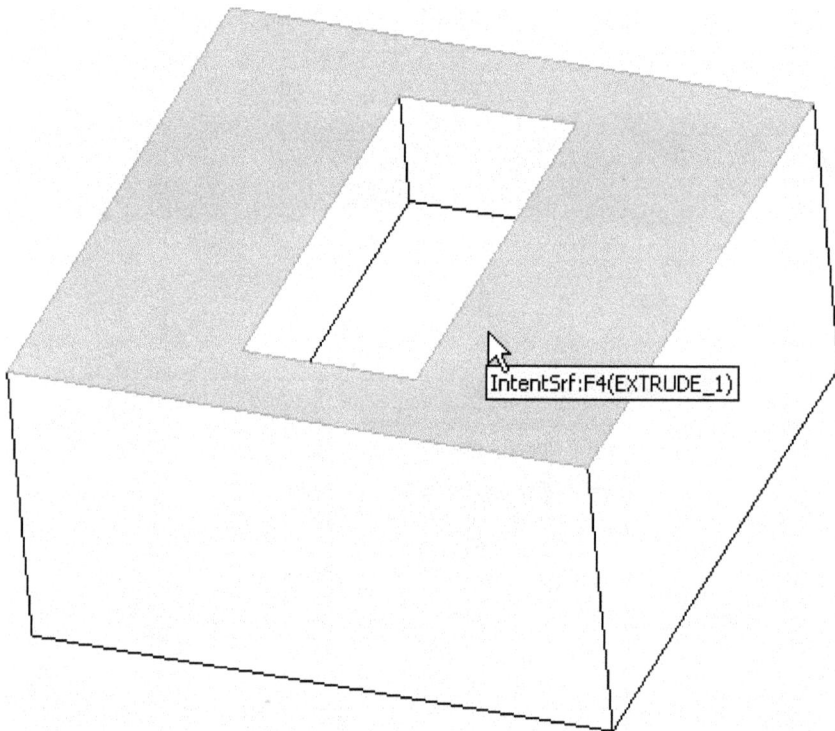

Fig. 10-11
Selecting the surface of a solid

Once the surface has been selected, select the ⊞ **Copy** icon from the Main Toolbar. This will copy the surface definition to the Windows clipboard. To create the surface feature, select the ⊞ **Paste** icon from the menu. Before closing the dashboard, it is possible to add additional surfaces to the quilt being created, by holding down **Ctrl** and selecting adjacent surfaces, as shown in Figure 10-12.

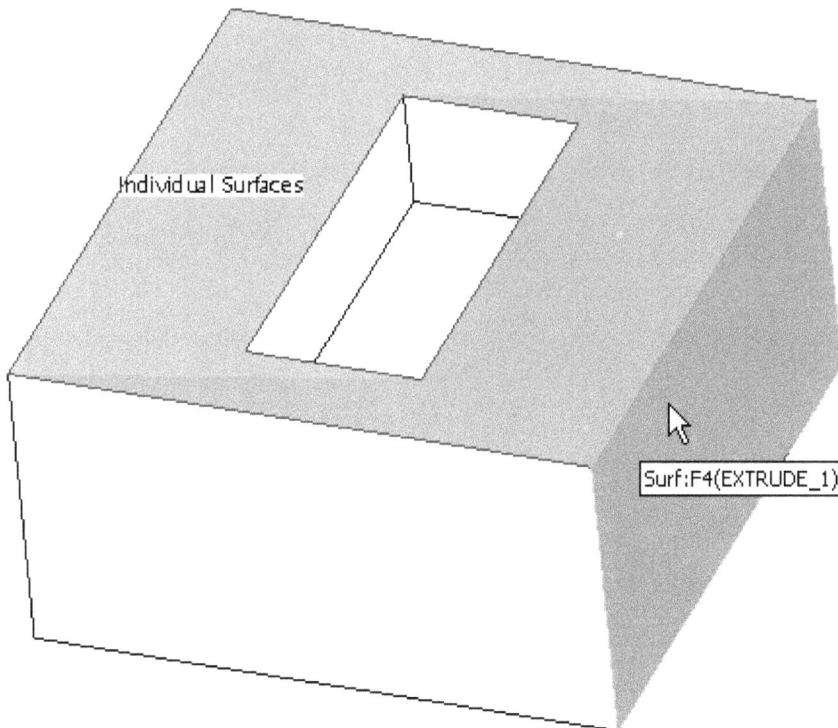

Fig. 10-12
Multiple-surface quilt

Offset

New surfaces may be created by offsetting existing surfaces and faces, as shown in Figure 10-13, by selecting the surface to offset, then **Edit > Offset** from the menu.

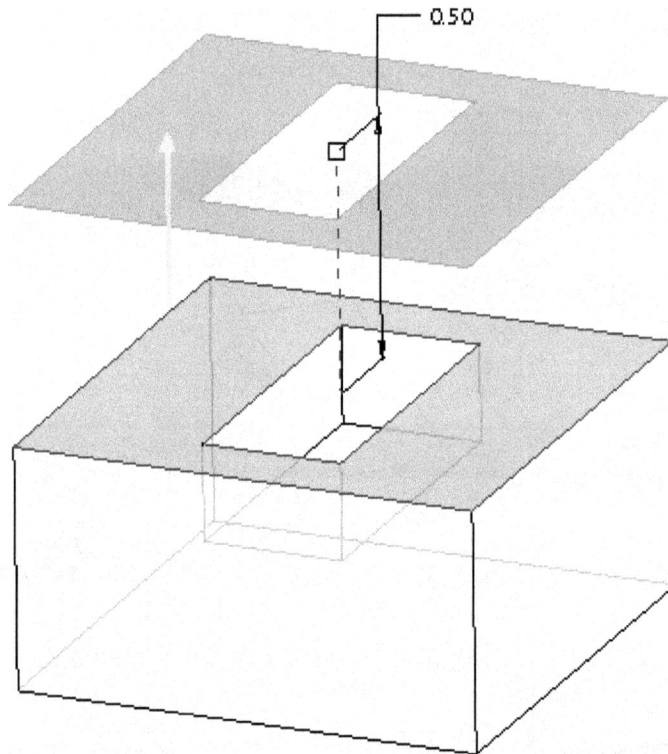

Fig. 10-13
Offsetting a surface

Extend

The edges of a quilt may be extended, as shown in Figure 10-14, by selecting the edge, then **Edit > Extend** from the menu.

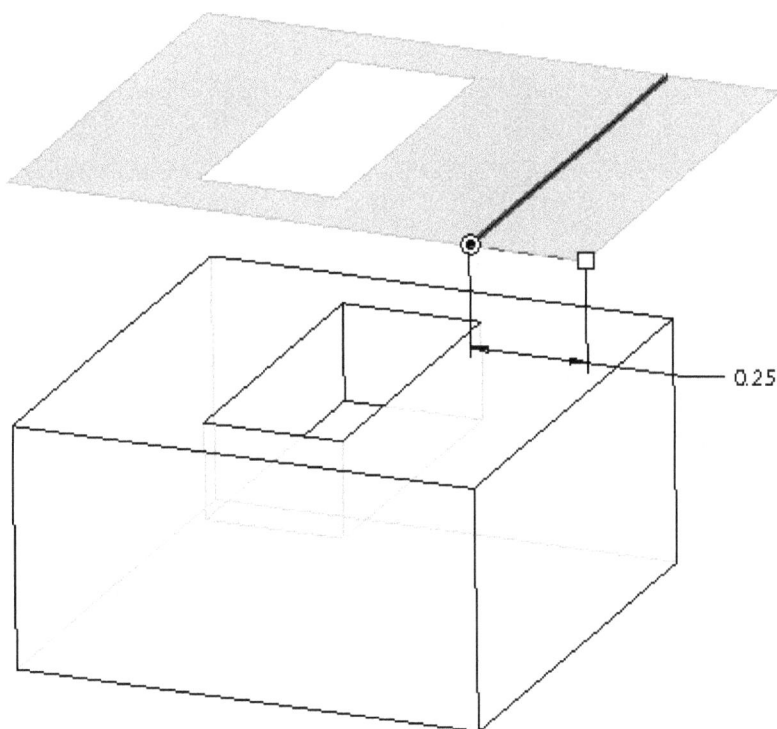

Fig. 10-14
Extending the edge of a quilt

Multiple edges may be extended at the same time, and the extent and direction of the extension may be controlled with the appropriate choices in the dashboard.

Trim

Since quilts do not have any material definition, solid cuts (remove material option) cannot be used when working with surfaces. To remove portions of a surface, select the surface, then select **Edit > Trim** from the menu. If an existing sketch already lies on the same plane as the surface, the sketch may be selected to define the trim boundary, otherwise a new sketch will need to be created, as shown in Figure 10-15.

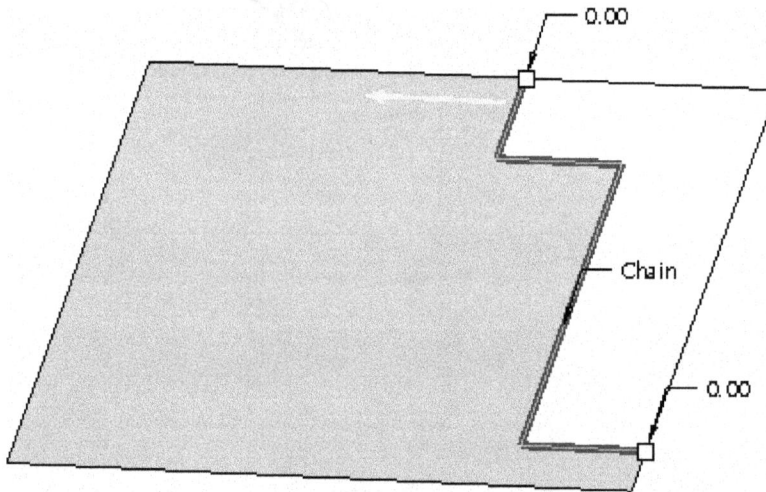

Fig 10-15
Sketch used to define trim

Many times, a three-dimensional quilt needs to be trimmed. Since it would be impossible to sketch a trimming boundary directly on the quilt, a second quilt can be created, which intersects the first, as shown in Figure 10-16.

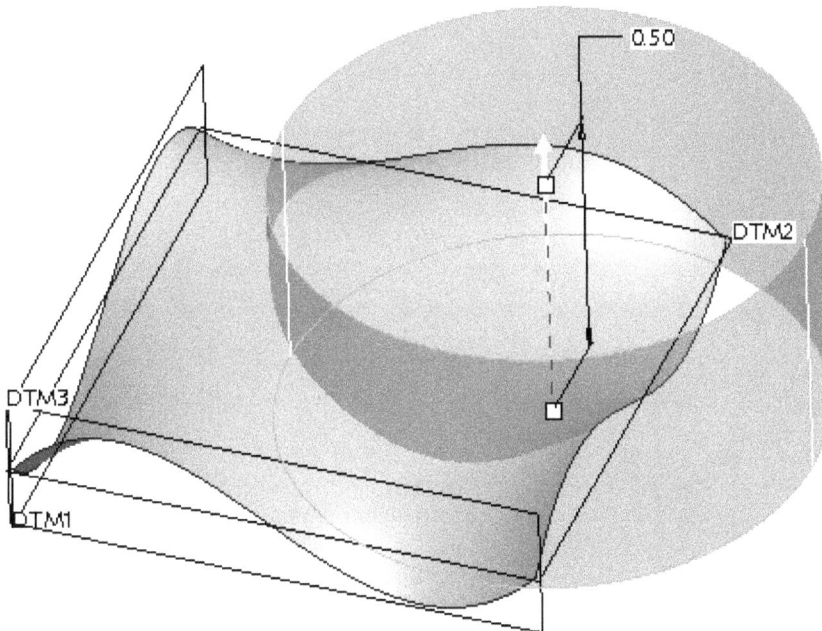

Fig 10-16
Quilt intersecting a quilt

The second quilt can then be used as a trimming reference, as shown in Figure 10-17.

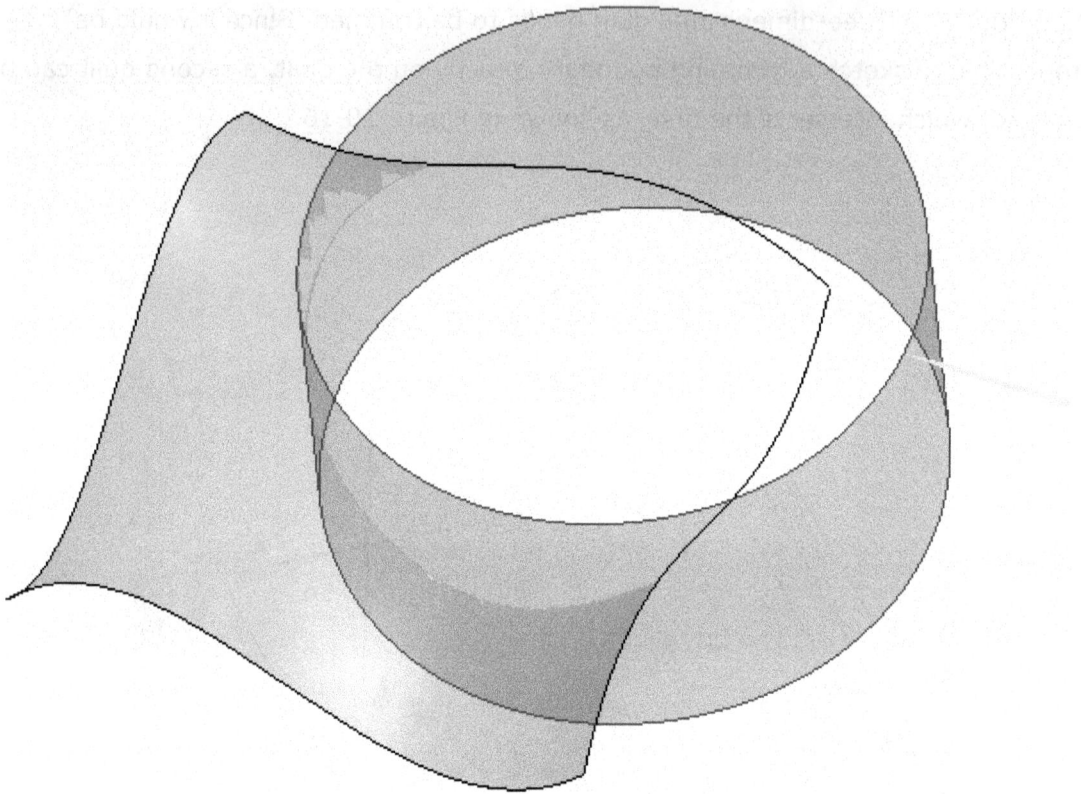

Fig. 10-17
Quilt used to define trim

The second (reference) quilt may be hidden (See Chapter 17), or you may also uncheck the **Keep trimming surface** box under the Option tab of the dashboard, as shown in Figure 10-18.

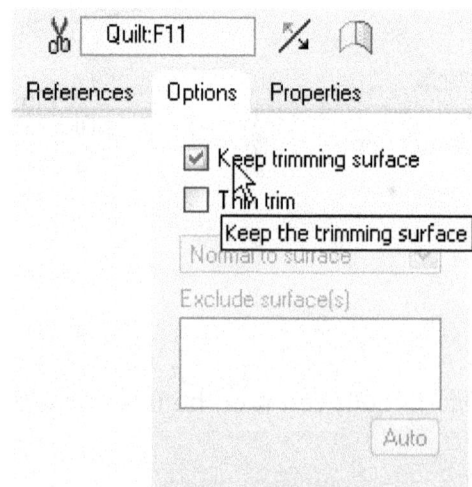

Fig. 10-18
Keep trimming surface option

Merge

Quilts that intersect each other, as shown in Figure 10-16, or those that share common boundaries may be joined together by selecting the two quilts, then selecting **Edit > Merge** from the menu. If the quilts intersect each other, you must decide which portion of each quilt will be trimmed away, and which will be joined to the other, by selecting the ⬚ **Side** indicator for each quilt in the dashboard, or by clicking on the direction arrow in the graphics area as shown in Figure 10-19.

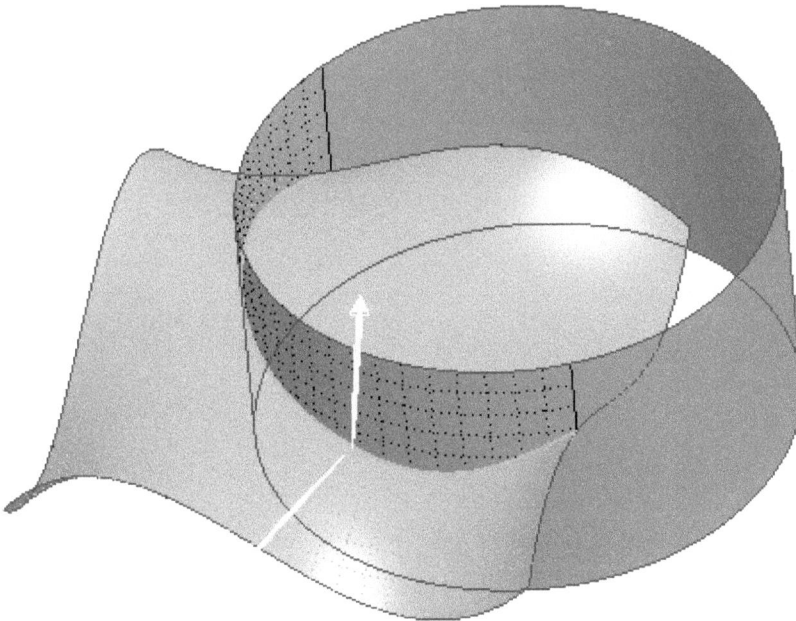

Fig. 10-19
Selecting sides of quilts to keep

By choosing different sides to keep, you may create the desired geometry, as shown in Figure 10-20.

Fig 10-20
Merged quilts

Thicken

A quilt, such as the ones shown in Figure 10-20 may be used to add or delete material, by selecting the quilt, then selecting **Edit > Thicken** from the menu. By selecting the **Material side** icon in the dashboard, you can control which side of the quilt the solid geometry will be created, or both sides, as shown in Figure 10-21.

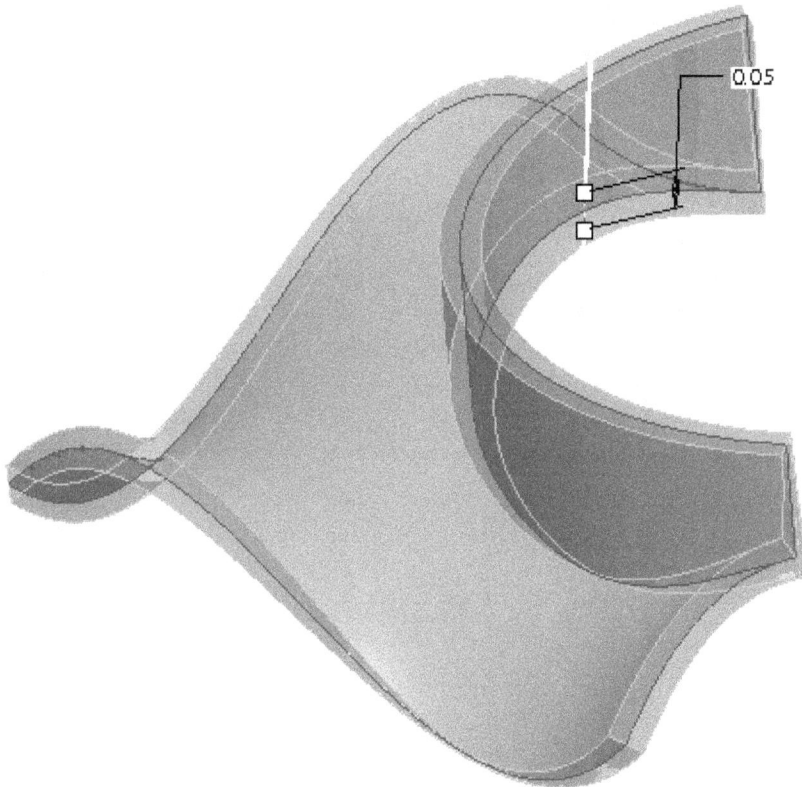

Fig. 10-21
Thickened quilt to add material

Figure 10-22 shows how the first quilt can be used to add material with the thicken option, while the second quilt is thickened to delete material.

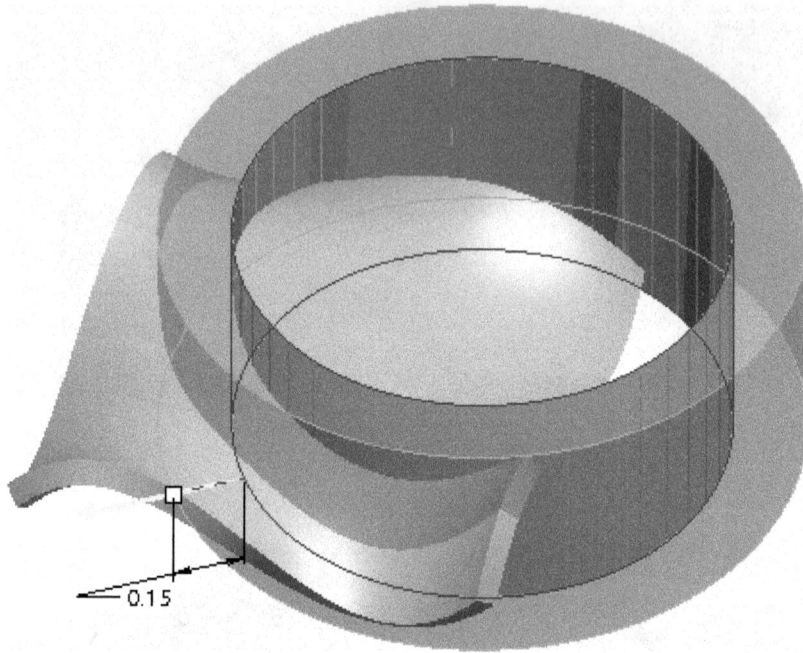

Fig. 10-22
Thickened quilt to remove material

The resulting geometry is shown in Figure 10-23.

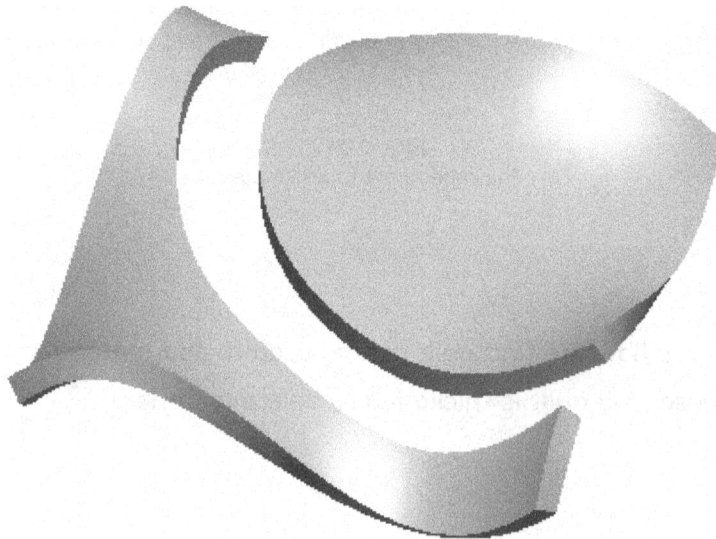

Fig. 10-23
Material removed by thickened quilt

Solidify

The name of the **Solidify** tool is somewhat of a misnomer, in that the tool can be used to both add material (as the name implies), but also to remove material, much the same way a solid extrusion can remove material. In order to solidify a quilt, it must be completely closed, i.e. forms a 'water tight' boundary. After creating, offsetting, extending and merging surfaces, you may be left with a surface such as the one shown in Figure 10-24. To create a solid feature, simply select the quilt, then select **Edit > Solidify** from the menu.

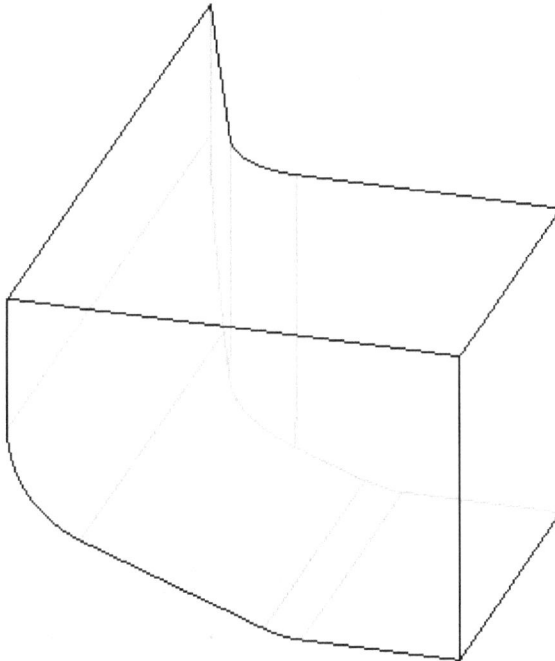

Fig 10-24
Closed boundary quilt

If however, the model contains solid features that occur before the quilt in the model tree, the same **Solidify** feature can be used to remove material as shown in Figure 10-25 by selecting the ▱ **Remove material** icon in the dashboard, with the resulting geometry shown in Figure 10-26.

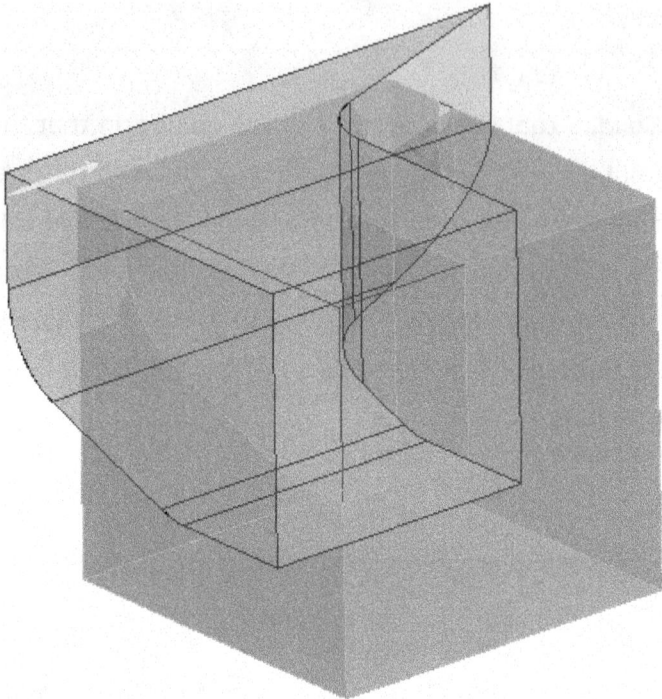

Fig. 10-25
Quilt to define material removal

Fig. 10-26
Solid with material removed using solidified quilt

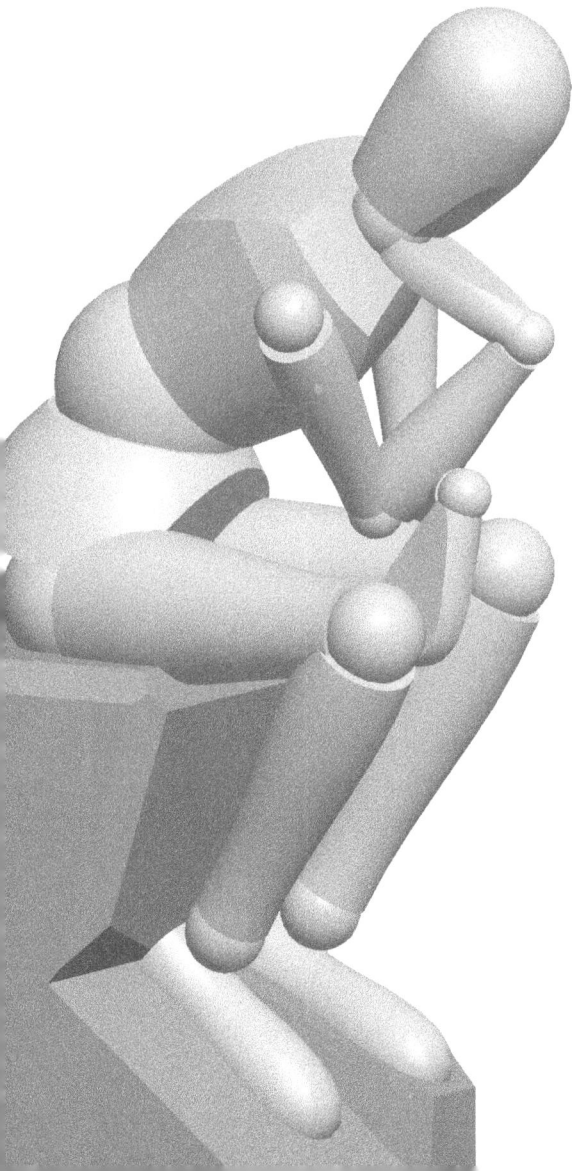

Chapter 11

Rounds

Round features can be created to remove material from outside edges, or add material to inside edges, as shown in Figure 11-1.

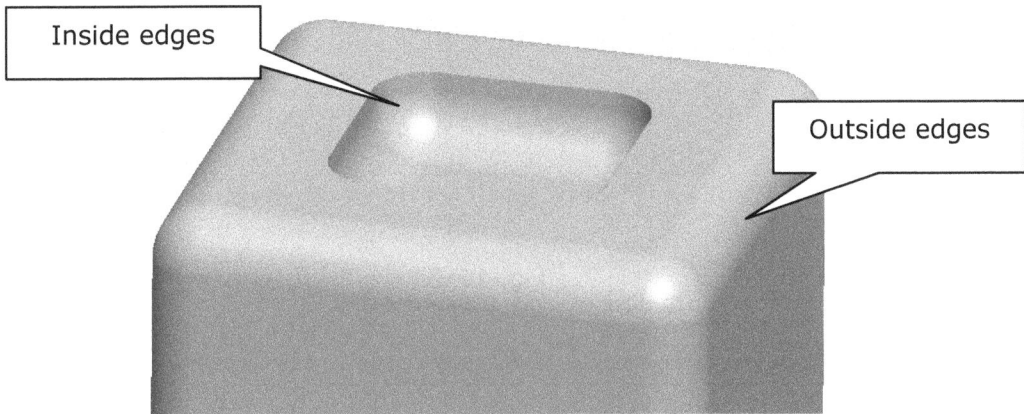

Fig. 11-1
Rounding inside and outside edges

Edge Rounds

Using Pro/ENGINEER's flexible work flow, you can create a round feature by

selecting the 🌙 **Round** icon from the Construction Toolbar, and then select an edge to round, or you may pick an edge first, and then select the icon. In either case Pro/ENGINEER will open the feature's dashboard control, and show a 'light weight' preview of the geometry to be created in yellow, as shown in Figure 11-2.

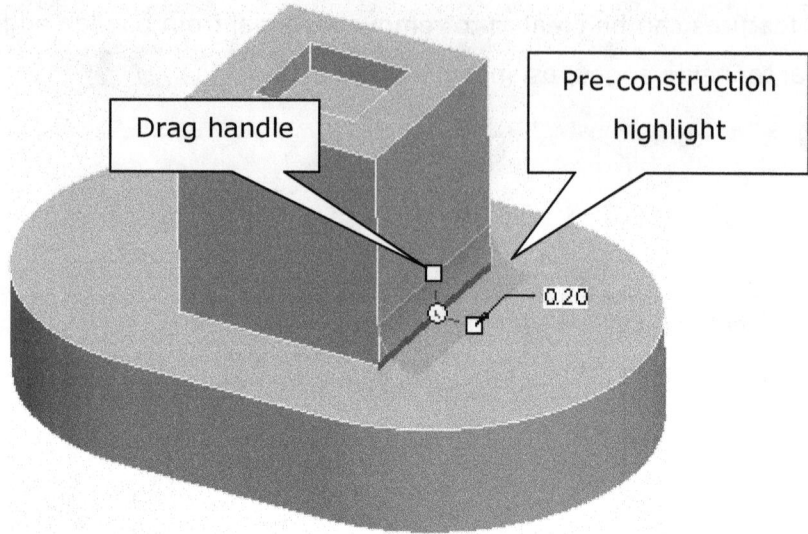

Fig. 11-2
Pre-construction preview of a round

The size of the round may be adjusted by selecting and dragging one of the drag handles, or double-clicking the value displayed in the graphics area, as shown in Figure 11-2, or in the dialog box, as shown in Figure 11-3.

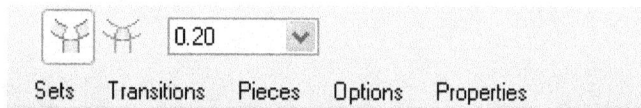

Fig. 11-3
Round dashboard control

The pre-construction highlight does not indicate the final feature, but rather serves as feedback to visualize what you are asking Pro/ENGINEER to create, and will update as you refine the definition of the feature. To accept the definition of the feature, select the ☑ **Apply** icon.

Fig. 11-4
Completed round

Surface to Surface Rounds

In addition to edges, you may select pairs of surfaces (using **Ctrl**), as shown in Figure 11-5, which will add or delete material accordingly.

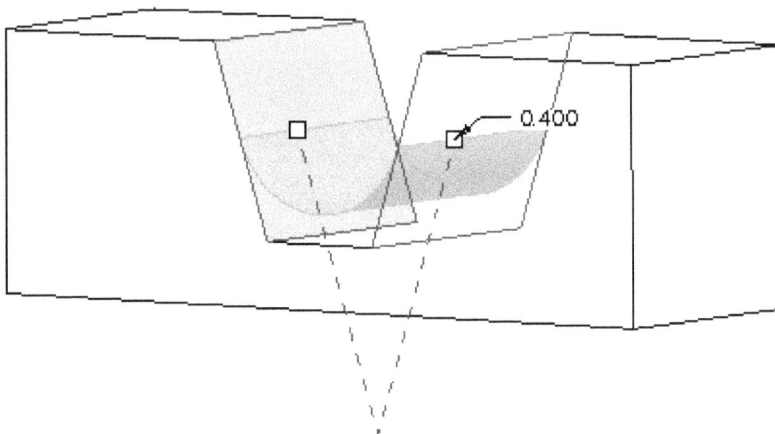

Fig. 11-5
Round tangent to two surfaces

Edge to Surface Rounds

Selecting a surface and edge together, will drive a round through the edge and tangent to the surface, as shown in Figure 11-6.

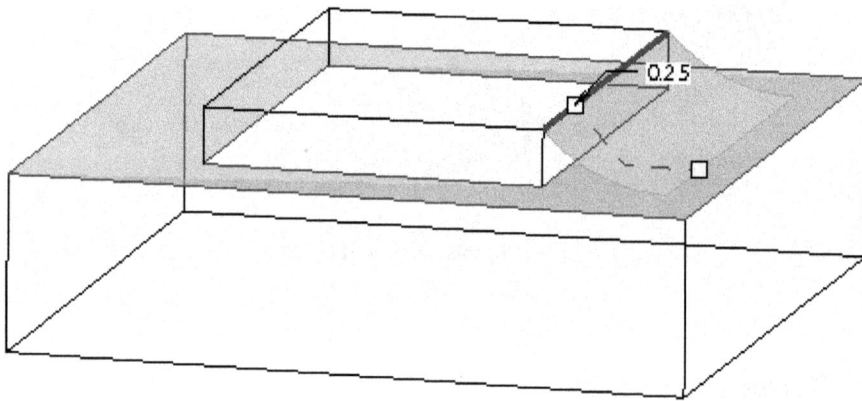

Fig 11-6
Round tangent to one surface and through an edge

Tangent Chain

If the edge you select is part of a chain of tangent edges, as shown in Figure 11-7, Pro/ENGINEER will automatically create a round feature, all along the chain, as shown in Figure 11-8.

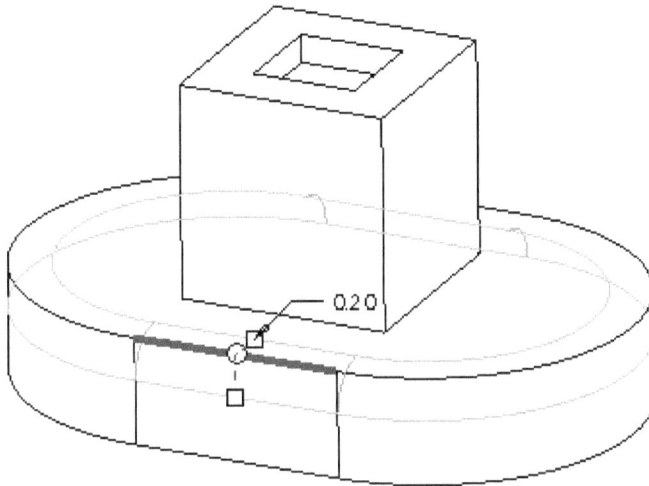

Fig. 11-7
Edge belonging to a tangent continuous chain

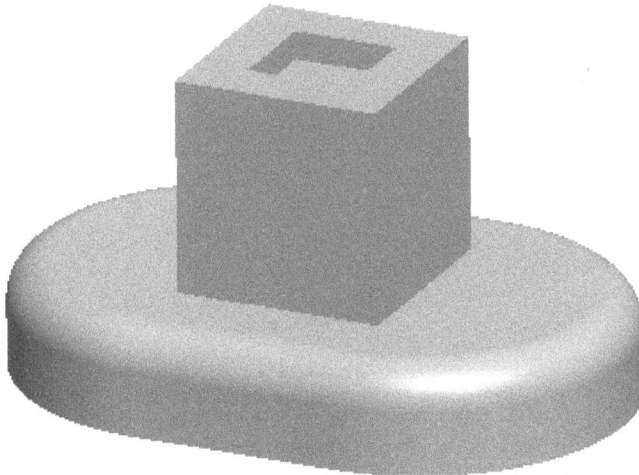

Fig. 11-8
Completed round feature

Depending on the overall part geometry and the edges selected, it may be possible to limit the extent of the round by clicking on the Pieces tab in the dashboard, as shown in Figure 11-9, and picking the appropriate edges.

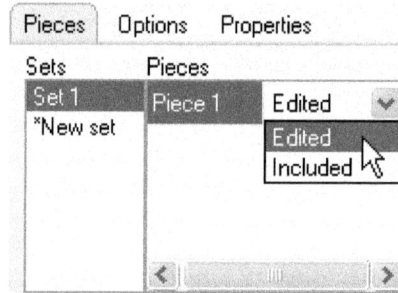

Fig. 11-9
Adjusting the extend of a round

Fig. 11-10
Rounding a single edge from a chain

Full Round

There are times when you may wish to completely round off the end or side of a feature or part. It would be possible to create two separate round features as shown in Figure 11-11, but if the part measures 1 unit tall, and you create two round features with radius values of exactly 0.50, then this would be fine.

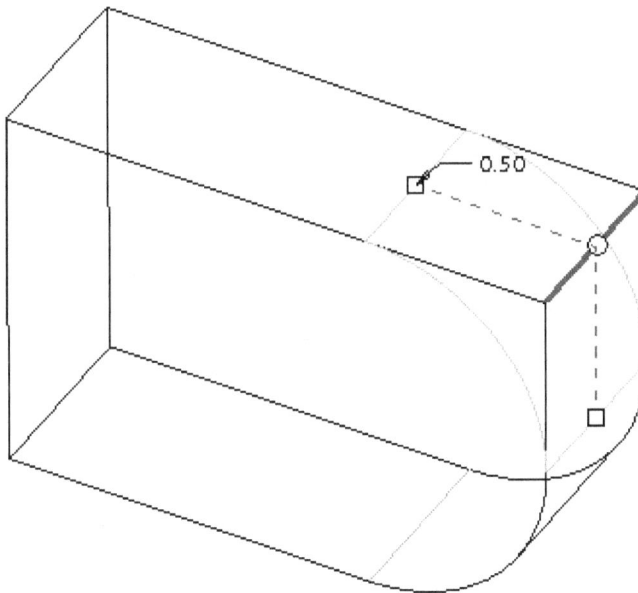

Fig. 11-11
Two round features

But what is your design intent? Is it that you have two 0.50 radius rounds, or that you round off the entire end of the part? What happens if the size of the part is modified to 1.347 units tall? You would end up with a flat spot, as shown on Figure 11-12, and you would have to remember to adjust each of the round features to 0.6735.

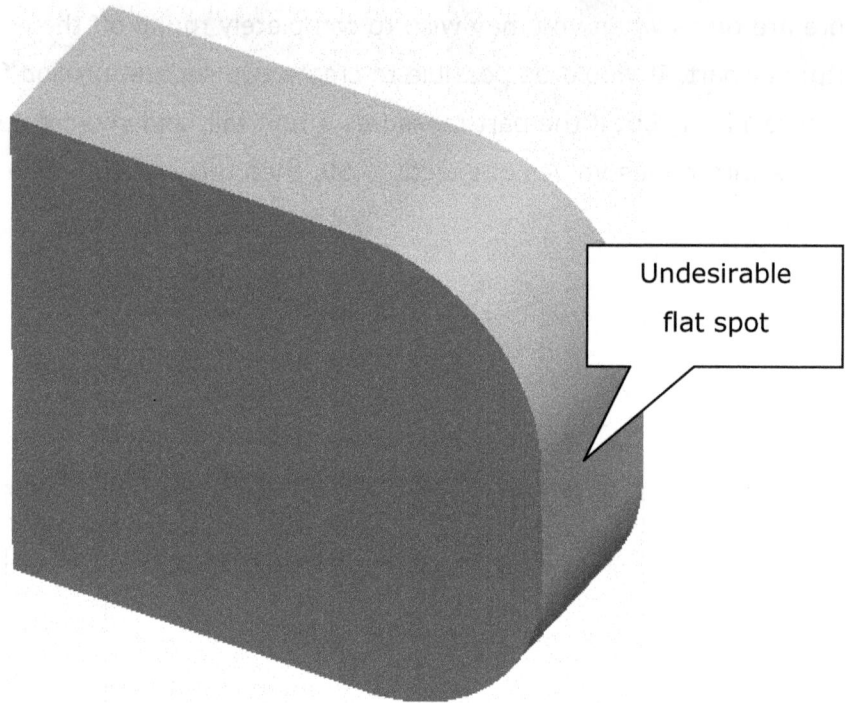

Fig. 11-12
Two separate round features

A more robust option would be to select both edges together (using **Ctrl** to place both items in the same selection set), then hold down the **RMB** and select **Full Round**, as shown in Figure 11-13. You may also select the top and bottom surfaces, then select the Driving Surface (surface to remove) when prompted. The resulting geometry is shown in Figure 11-14.

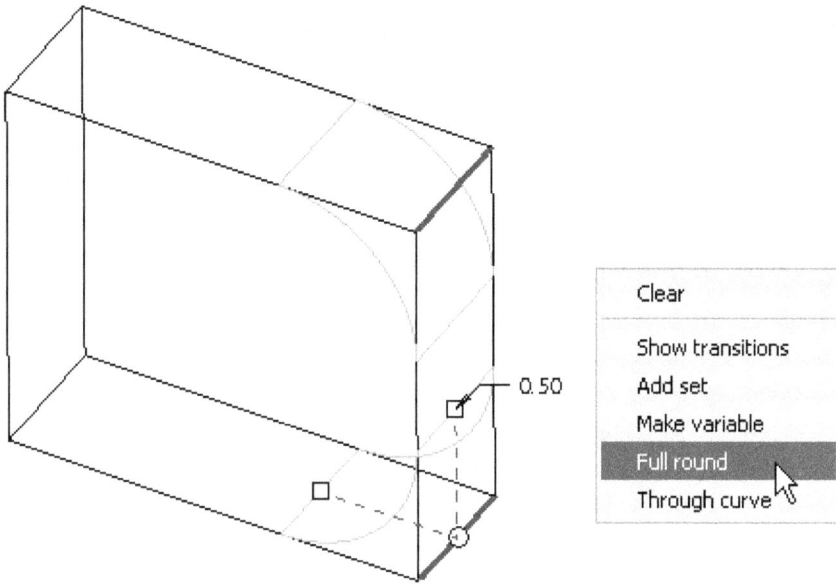

Fig. 11-13
Creating a full round

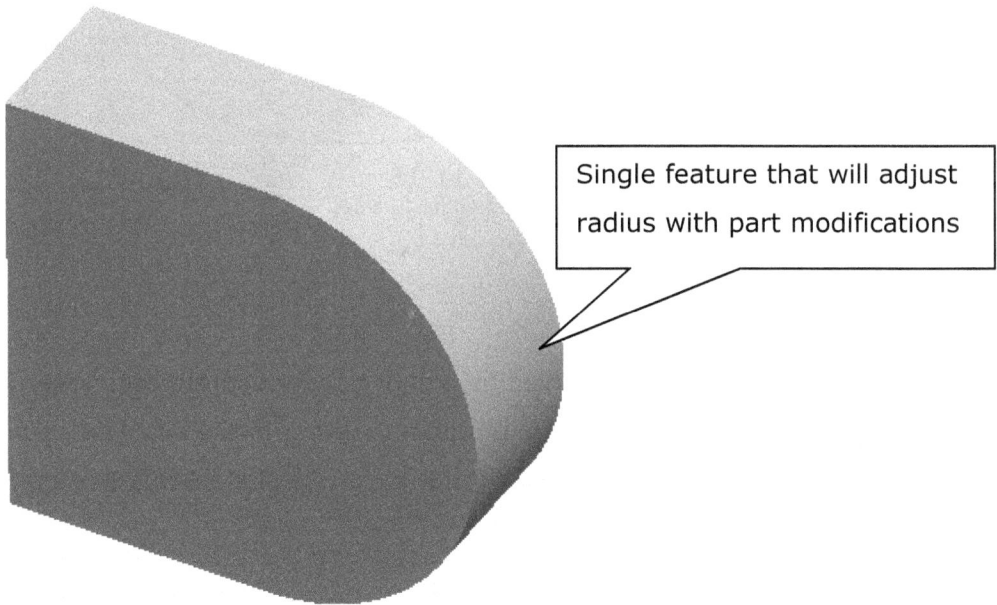

Single feature that will adjust
radius with part modifications

Fig. 11-14
Full round

Round Sets

When you first select an edge to round, you are establishing a set of edges. By holding down the **Ctrl**, you may add additional edges to the same set. By doing so, all of the rounded edges are part of the same feature, and each edge will have the same radius value, as shown in Figure 11-15.

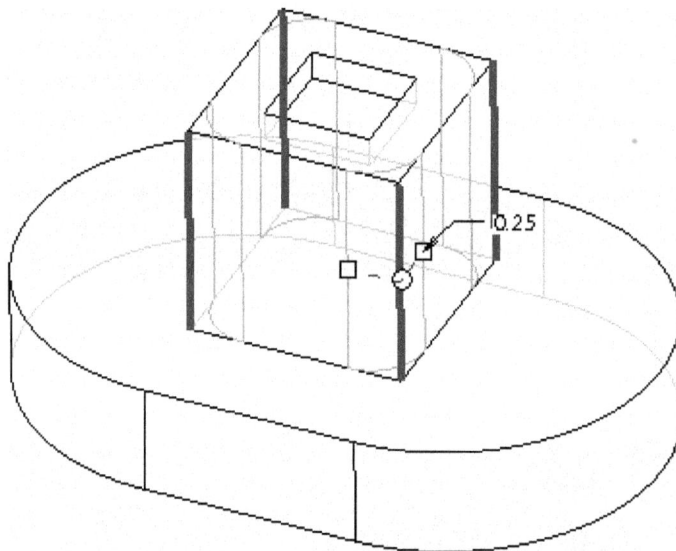

Fig. 11-15
Selecting edges in a set

The same geometry could be achieved by creating four separate round features, each with a single edge, but by grouping them together in the same set, you can easily maintain the same radius value (if that is your design intent) throughout the life of the part.

Each time you select a reference with the **Ctrl** held down, you will be adding that reference to your set. If you select a new reference without holding the **Ctrl**, then you will be starting a second set of references. By holding down the **Ctrl** now, you will be adding additional references to the second (current) set, and so on. Figure 11-16 shows the same part, but two separate sets of references in the same round feature.

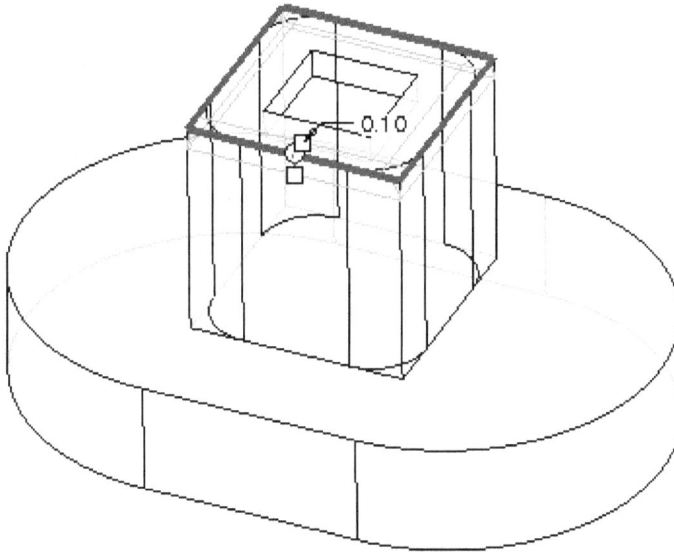

Fig. 11-16
Adding a second set of references

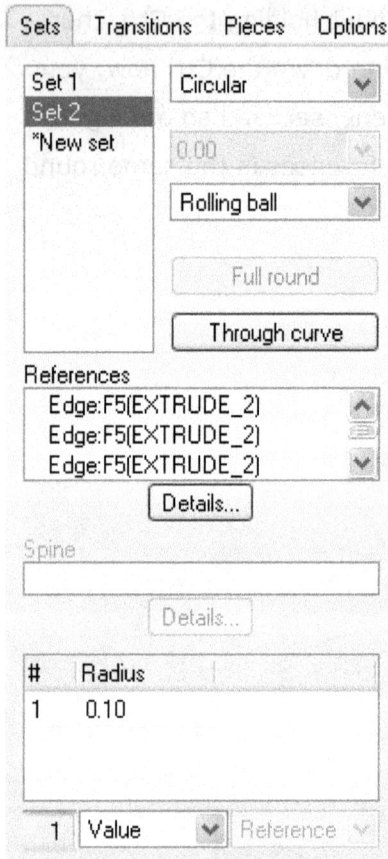

Fig. 11-17
Sets tab

Fig. 11-18
Single round feature with
Two sets of four edges

The advantage of creating multiple sets is that you may group all of the edges for a certain design feature together, but each group may have a unique radius value. To see exactly what sets are being created and their values, you may click on the Sets tab in the Dashboard, as shown in Figure 11-17.

Transitions

Another advantage to creating multiple sets is that you can control corner

transitions by selecting the [icon] **Transition Mode** icon in the dashboard and selecting

the corner you wish to control, as shown in Figure 11-19.

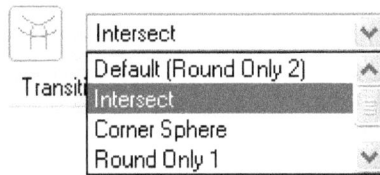

Fig. 11-19
Transition options

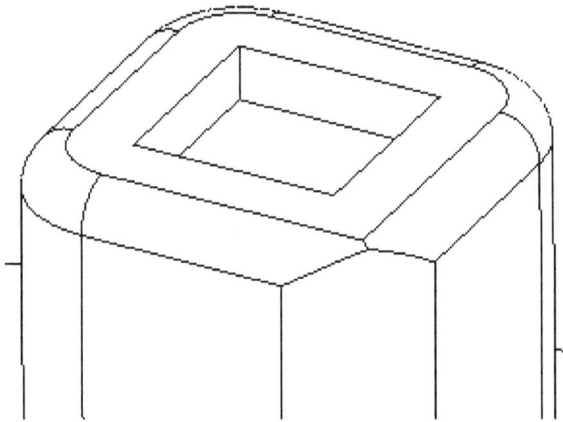

Fig. 11-20
Corner Intersect transition

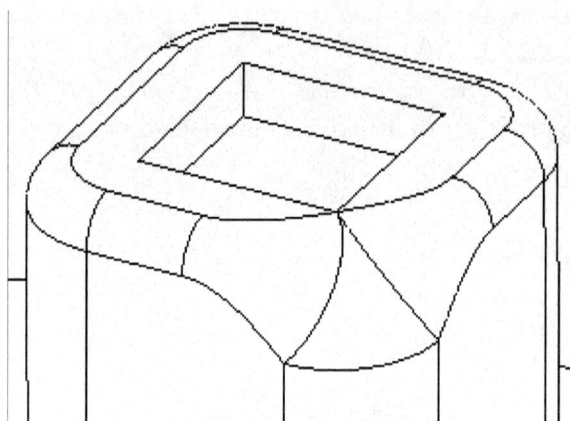

Fig. 11-21
Corner Sphere transition

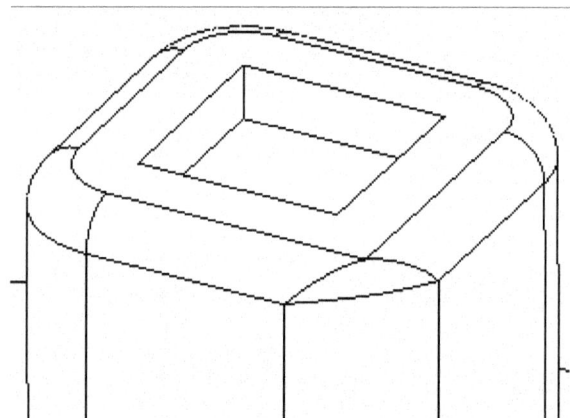

Fig. 11-22
Patch transition

Simply select the appropriate transition type, based on your design intent or manufacturing operation.

Variable Radius

There are times when you need a single chain of edges to vary its radius values, as shown in Figure 11-23.

Fig. 11-23
Continuous chain of edges with varying radius values

To create a variable radius round, first create the round, and while defining the edges (with the dashboard open), hold down the **RMB** and select **Make variable**, as shown in Figure 11-24.

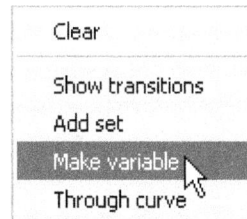

Fig. 11-24
Round options

An additional radius indicator (node) will be added, as shown in Figure 11-25. One drag handle controls the radius value (0.10 in the sample shown), and one controls its ratio (location) along the edge segment (0.65 in the sample shown).

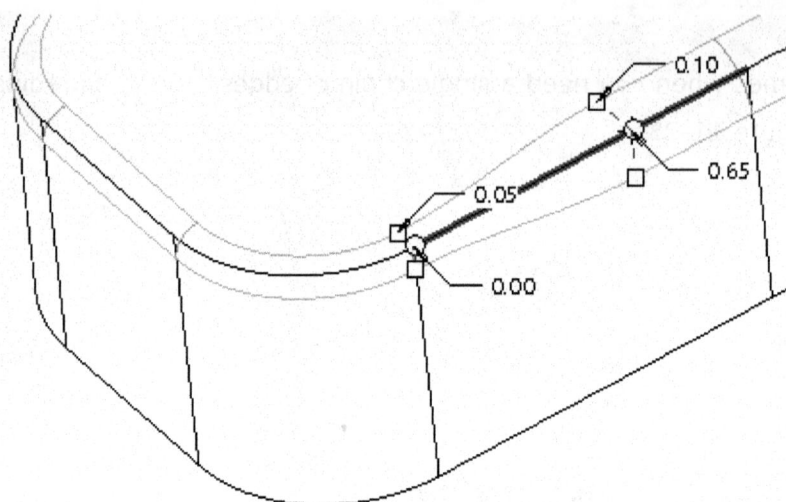

Fig. 11-25
Starting to add radii

If the ratio value in Figure 11-25 was set to 1.0 then it would move the node all the way to the end of the segment. To add additional radius nodes, select any one of the existing nodes and right-click to add a radius, as shown in Figure 11-26.

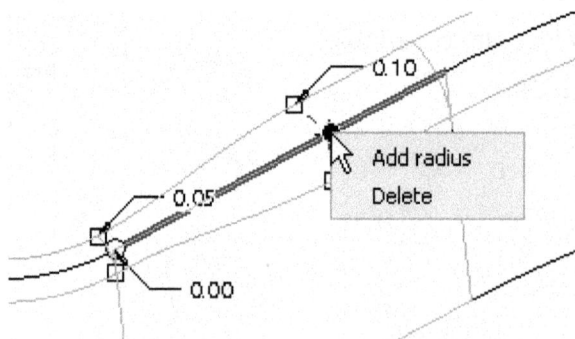

Fig. 11-26
Adding a radius node

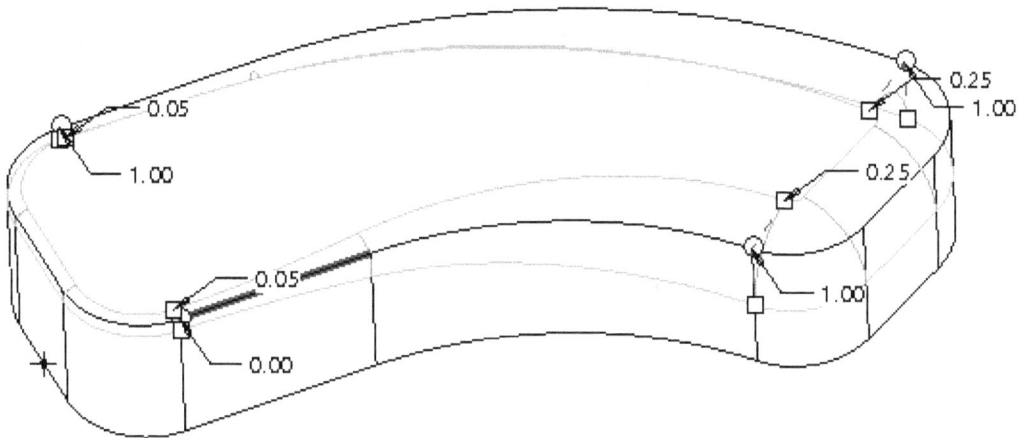

Fig. 11-27
Complete chain

Continue adding nodes, dragging them into position and adjusting the radii value until you have the desired result. If you have two adjacent nodes set to the same radius value, the edges in between will be a constant value. Any edges between two non-equal nodes will result in a taper.

Auto Round

There are times when you may wish to round all inside or outside edges of a part, as shown in Figure 28. Select **Insert** > **Auto Round** from the menu, and make the desired choices from the dashboard to round all concave (inside) and/or convex (outside) edges, and the radius values for each. You may also select any edges you wish to exclude from the feature.

Fig. 11-28
Single round feature

Chamfers

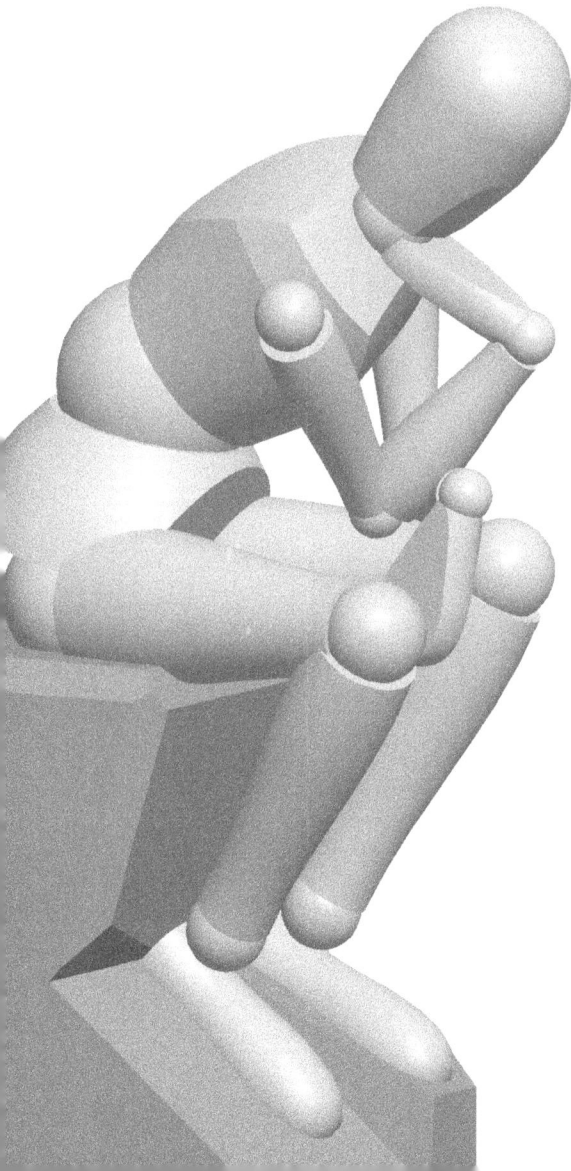

Chamfers work in much the same way as rounds (see Chapter 7), in that they can be created to add or remove material from edges. They are also created in much the same way regarding edge selection, tangent chains, etc.

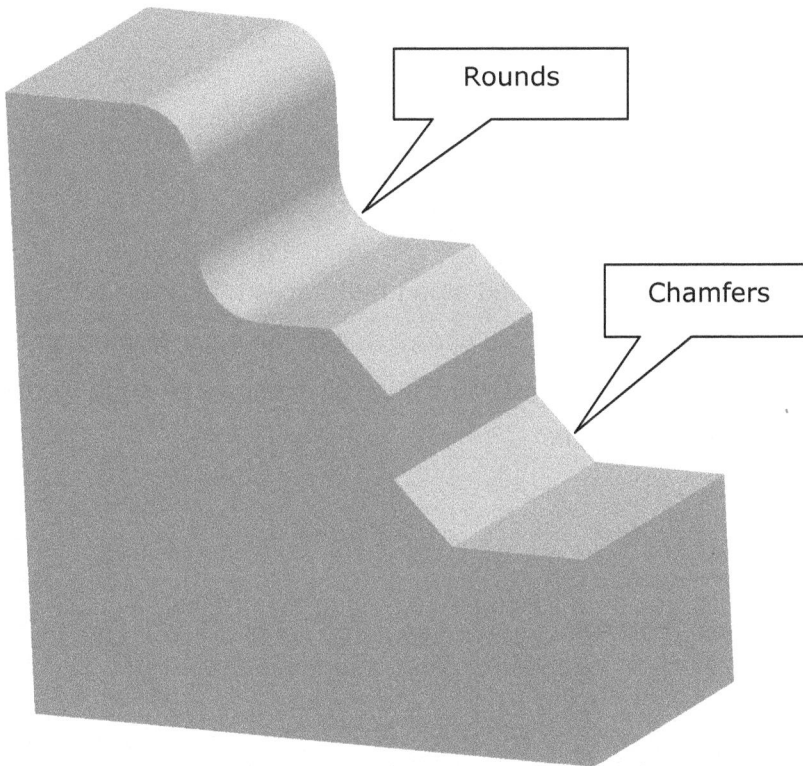

Fig. 12-1
Chamfers and rounds

The main difference between chamfers and rounds is that a chamfer feature creates a flat surface rather than a curved, 'rounded' surface. Therefore the dimensional controls are unique.

There are several dimensional options accessible from the dashboard, as shown in Figure 12-2.

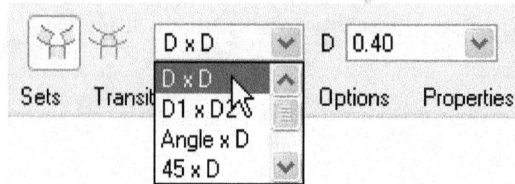

Fig. 12-2
Chamfer dimensional options

D x D

The same dimensional value will be used along both faces that intersect to form the edge that is being removed. Figure 12-3 shows this for an edge formed by two faces that are perpendicular to each other, while Figure 12-4 shows an edge formed by two faces that are not perpendicular.

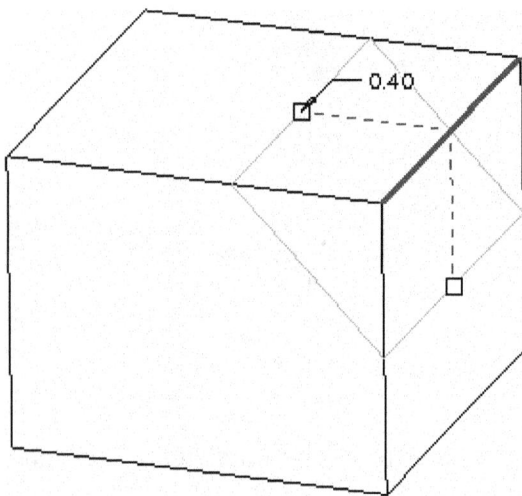

Fig. 12-3
Perpendicular faces

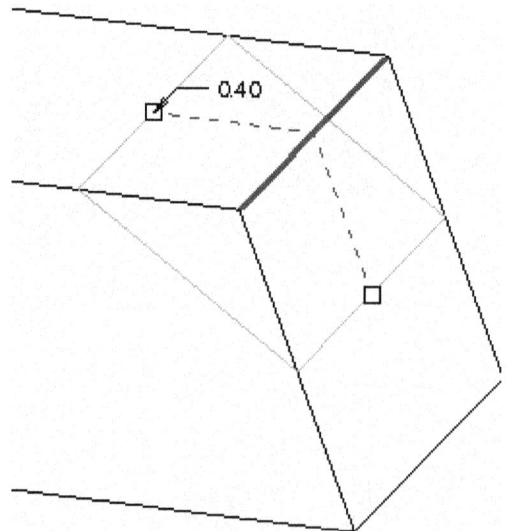

Fig. 12-4
Non-perpendicular faces

D1 x D2

This option allows you to use two separate dimensional values along each face, as shown in Figure 12-5.

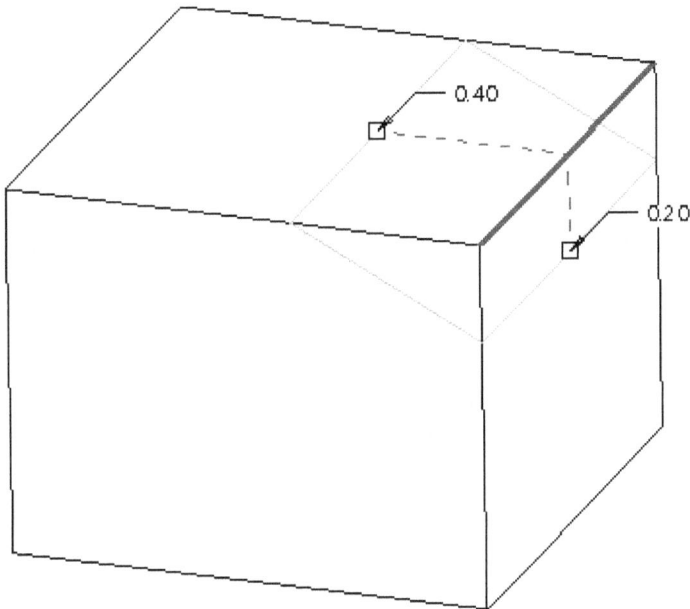

Fig. 12-5
Two separate dimensions

You can control the two dimensions individually and you may also switch the values from one to the other, by selecting the **Interchange** icon in the dashboard.

Angle x D

This option allows you to specify a distance along one face, and an angle relative to that face, as shown in Figure 12-6. You may also select the ![Interchange icon] **Interchange** icon in the dashboard to switch which face is the driving face.

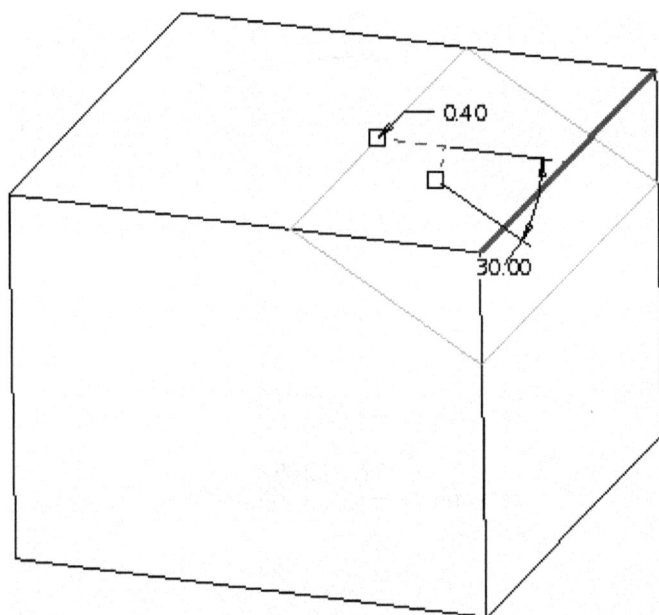

Fig. 12-6
Angle and a dimension

45 x D

This option is defined exactly they same way as Angle x D, except that the angle value is set to 45, and is not modifiable, as shown in Figure 12-7.

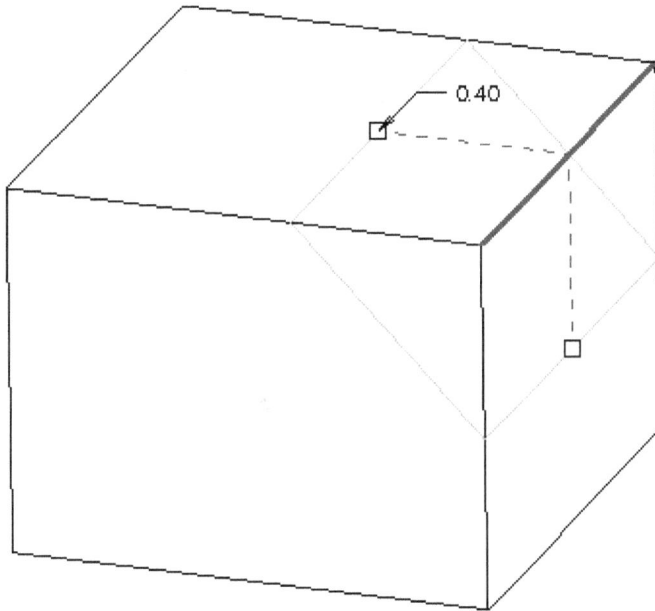

Fig. 12-7
45 degree angle pre-set

This option is most commonly used when chamfers are being placed on a model to remove sharp edges for harshness reasons. It is typically referred to as a 'break edge'.

O x O

O x O and O1 x O2 indicate offset values, and result in exactly the same geometry as D x D and D1 x D2 for perpendicular faces.

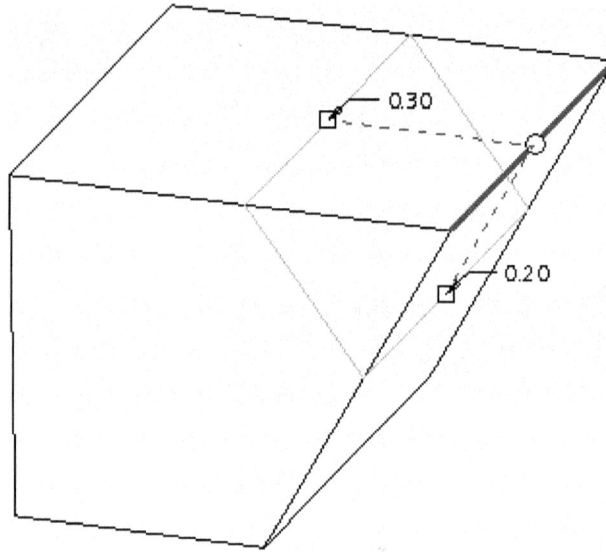

Fig. 12-8
O1 x O2 chamfer

However, when dealing with angled faces, as shown in Figure 12-8, Pro/ENGINEER does not use a linear distance, but rather uses the intersection of construction surfaces offset from the faces to determine the geometry, as shown in Figure 12-9.

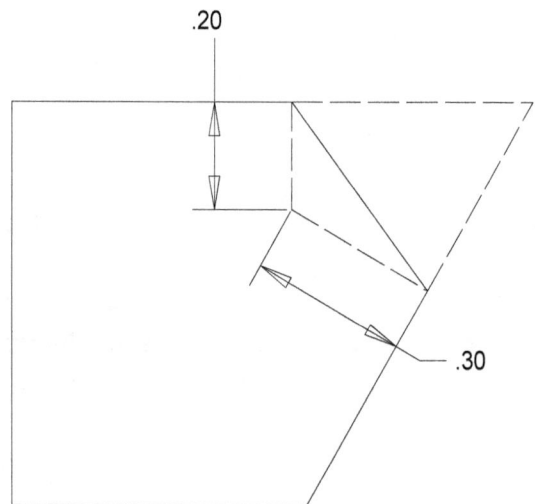

Fig. 12-9
Offset values

Chapter 13

Drafts

Draft Surfaces

Draft Hinges

Splits

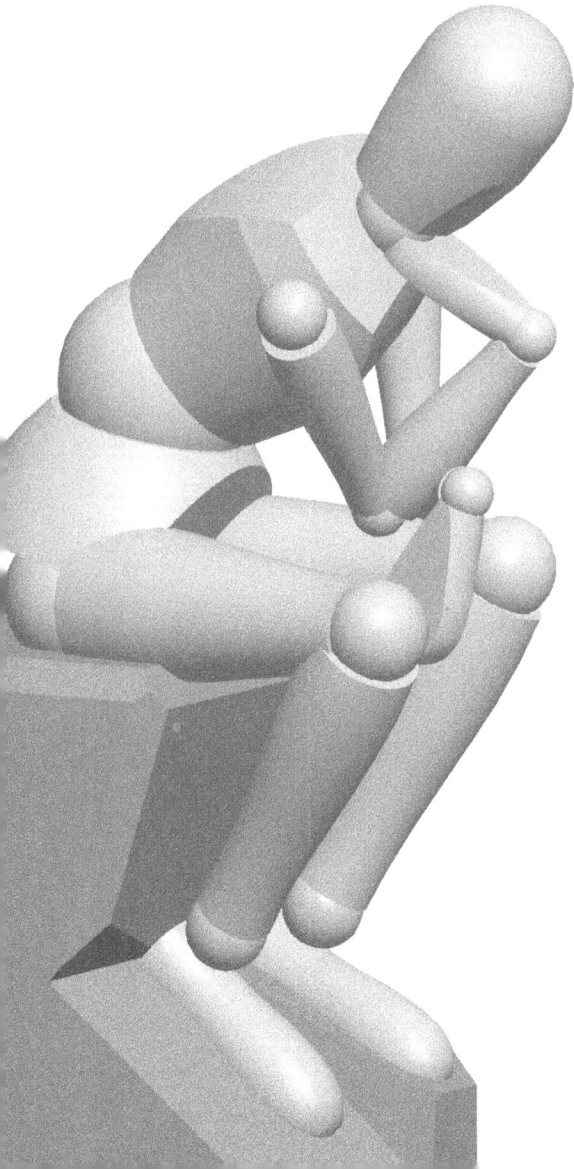

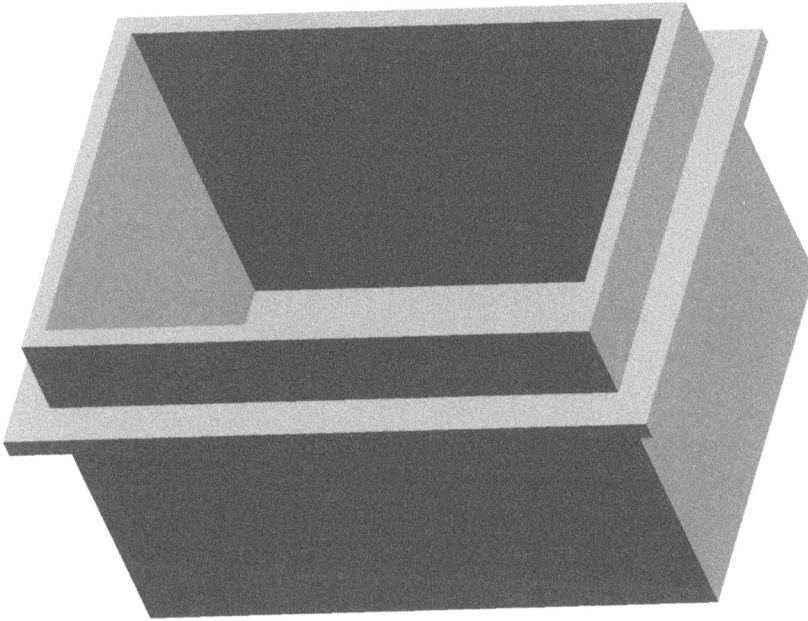

Fig. 13-1
Molded part

Figure 13-1 shows a part to be manufactured by a molding or casting process. Due to the geometry of the part, it will need to be formed from two halves of a mold that are placed together (closed) to form the geometry, as shown in Figure 13-2, then separated (opened) to release the part, as shown in Figure 13-3.

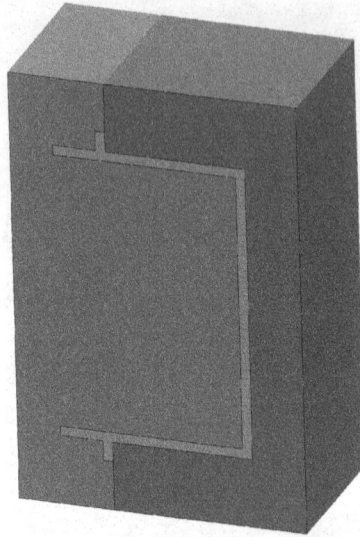

Fig. 13-2
Closed tool to form the part (cross section)

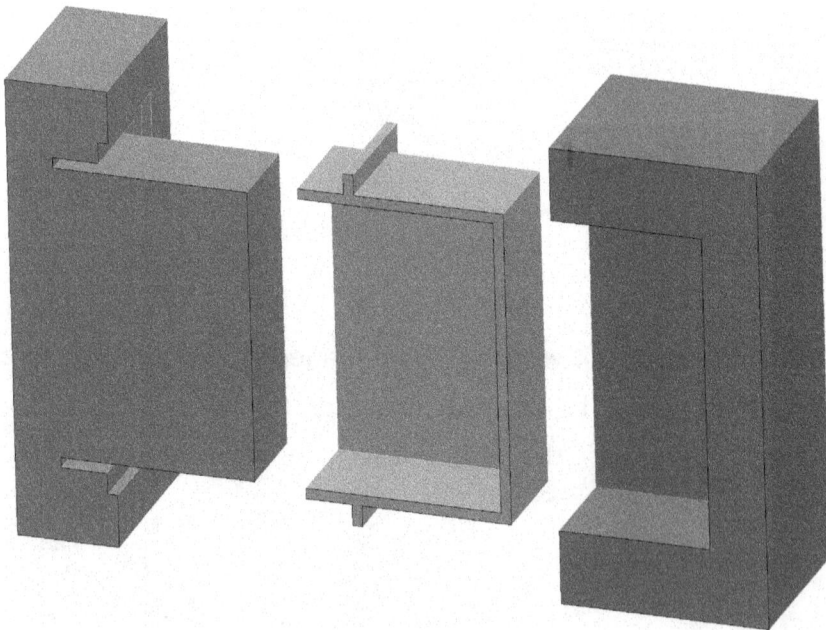

Fig. 13-3
Open tool to release the part (cross section)

Our design intent is that our part has straight, perpendicular walls, but this geometry may not be possible, due to the manufacturing method. When the two halves of the mold are opened, the friction and vacuum formed between the part and the tool will be too great, resulting in either a damaged part, or even worse, a locked tool. The solution is to draft (angle) the surfaces just enough to allow them to separate from the mold. This is not part of our design intent for the function of our part, but it is necessary for manufacturing, therefore we can add **Draft** features to our design model.

Draft Surfaces

Using Pro/ENGINEER's flexible workflow, you may select the surfaces you wish to add draft to, then select the ⬦ **Draft** icon from the Construction Toolbar, or select the icon first, then select the surfaces to add draft to, as shown in Figure 13-4.

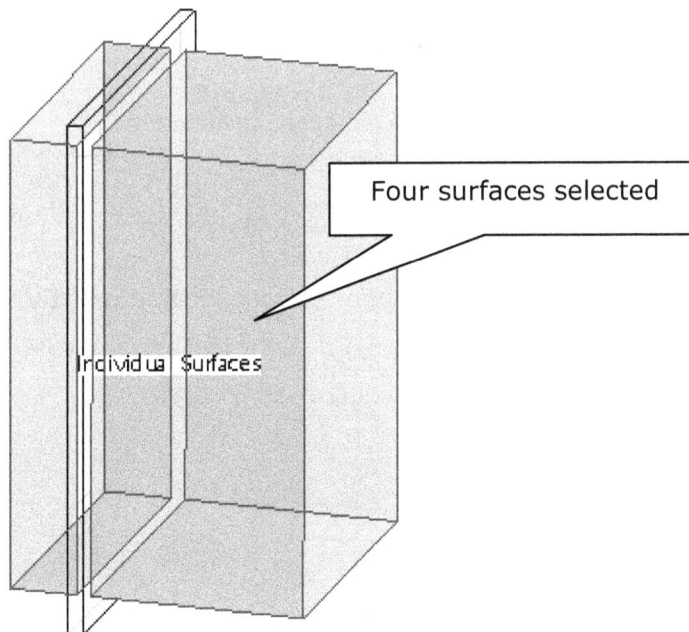

Four surfaces selected

Individual Surfaces

Fig. 13-4
Outside surfaces selected to draft

Draft Hinge

After you have selected the surfaces to draft, you need to select a draft hinge. The draft feature will either add or delete material from the selected surfaces, so the draft hinge is the point on the model where the original dimension is maintained. Figure 13-5 shows the draft dashboard. You may specify the draft hinge by clicking in the appropriate box, in the References tab.

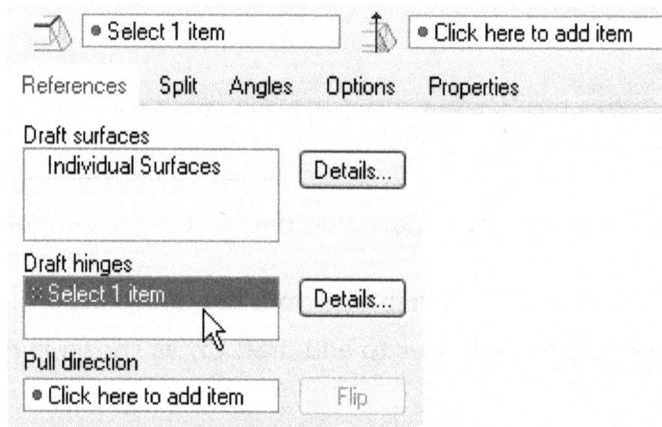

Fig. 13-5
Draft feature dashboard

Typically, the draft hinge is a planar surface located exactly where the two halves of the tool come together, commonly referred to as the parting line, as shown in Figure 13-6, but you may also select datum curves.

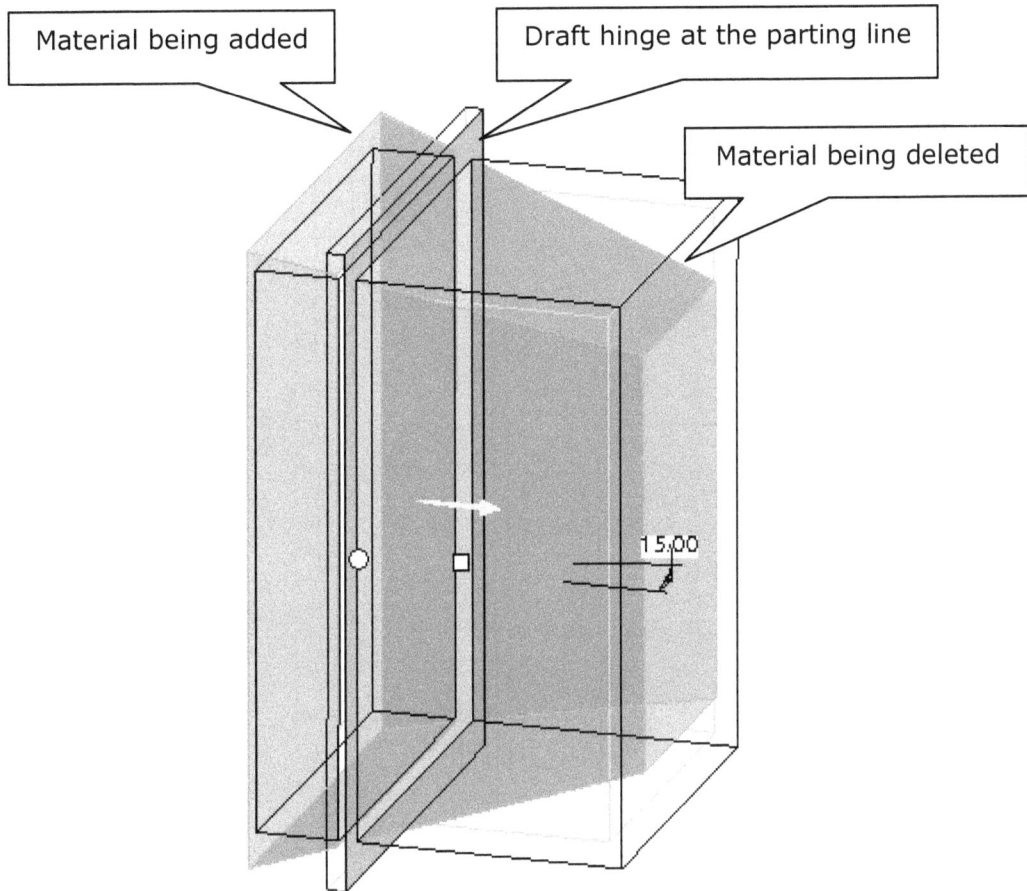

Fig. 13-6
Defining the draft hinge and amount of draft

The proposed geometry will highlight in yellow. Simply adjust the amount of draft to the desired value (typically only one or two degrees).

Split

The example shown in Figure 13-6 would be impossible to manufacture, because it would be adding material to the left side (as shown) of the parting line, causing a die-lock condition in the tool. We can solve this by clicking on the split tab on the dashboard, to break the draft feature into two controllable segments on either side of the draft hinge, as shown in Figure 13-7.

Split   Angles   Options   Properties

Split options
Split by draft hinge

Split object

Define...

Side options
Draft sides independently

Draft sides independently
Draft sides dependently
Draft first side only
Draft second side only

15:00

15:00

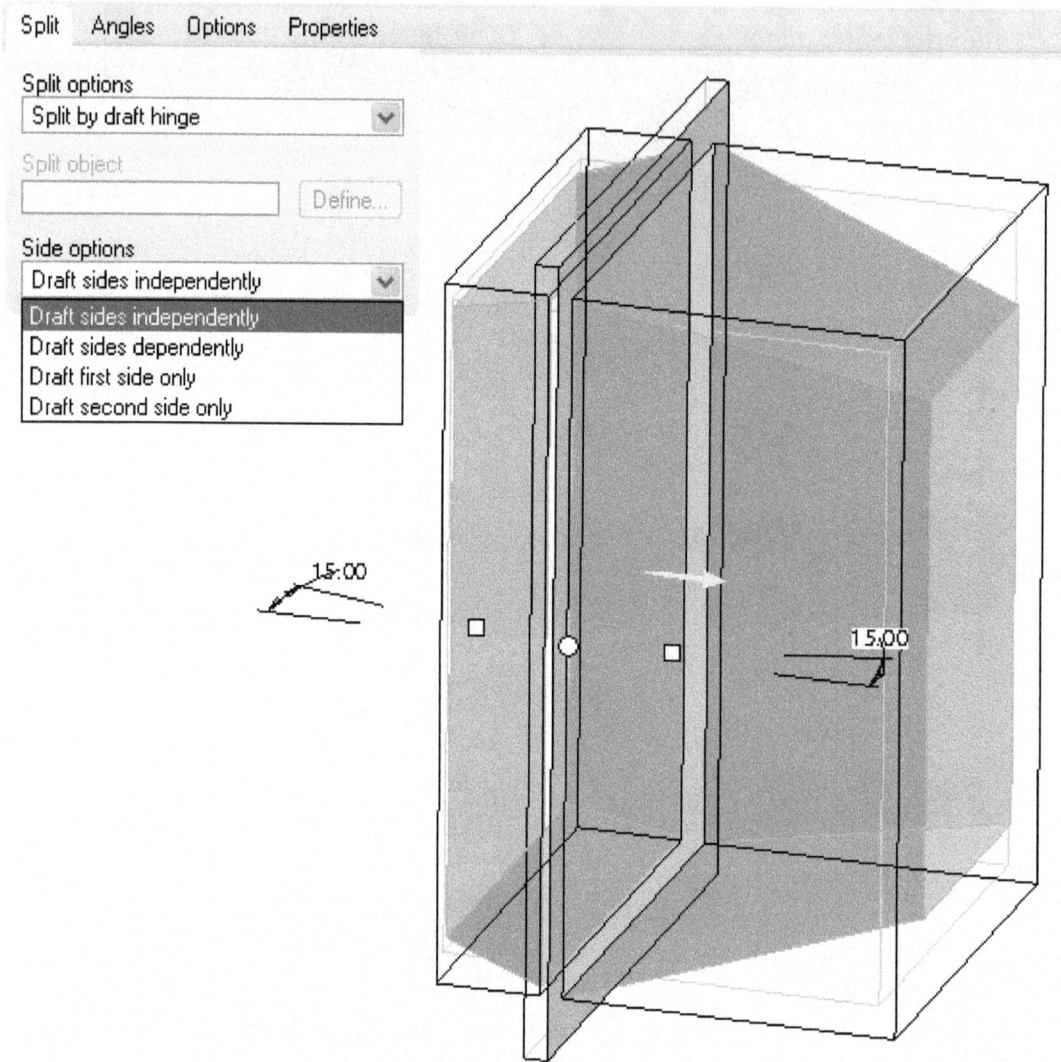

Fig. 13-7
Adding split at the draft hinge.

You may also select references to determine the pull direction (open/close of the tool) if different than the hinge. Continue adding draft to all of the surfaces as necessary to properly define a final shape suitable for manufacture, as shown in Figure 13-8.

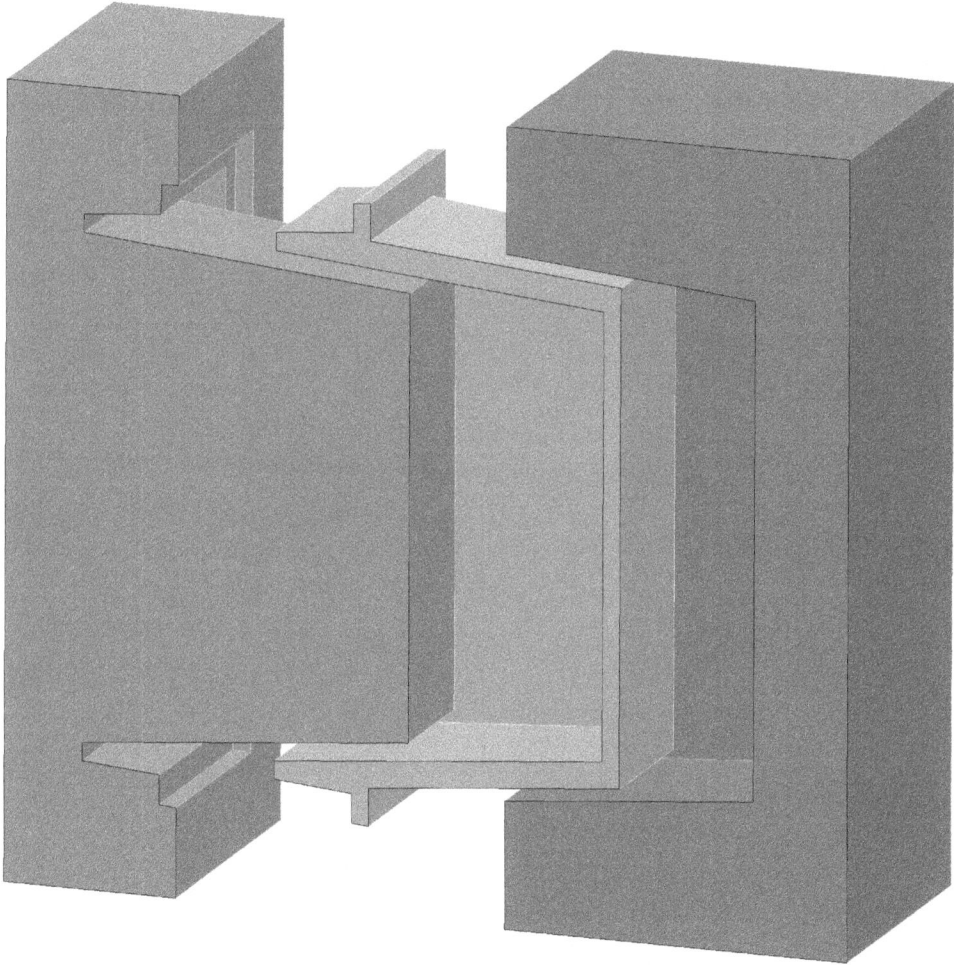

Fig. 13-8
Design with no surfaces perpendicular to the tool open/close direction

Chapter 14

Shells

Solid Definition

Removing Surfaces

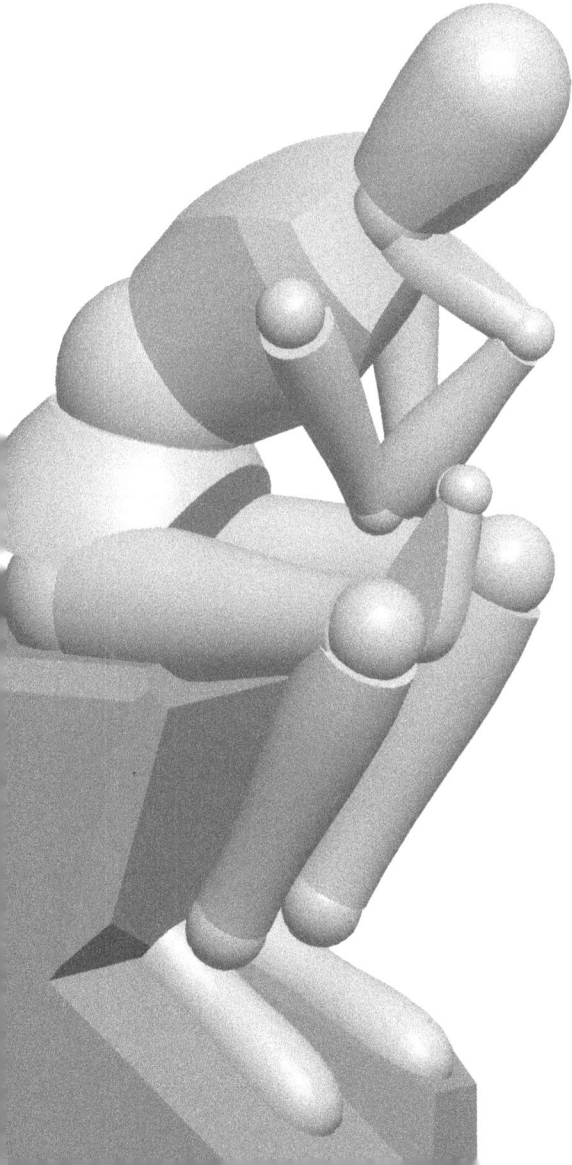

Figure 14-1 shows a bottle which will be manufactured utilizing a blow molding process. It has been cut in half to show the inside.

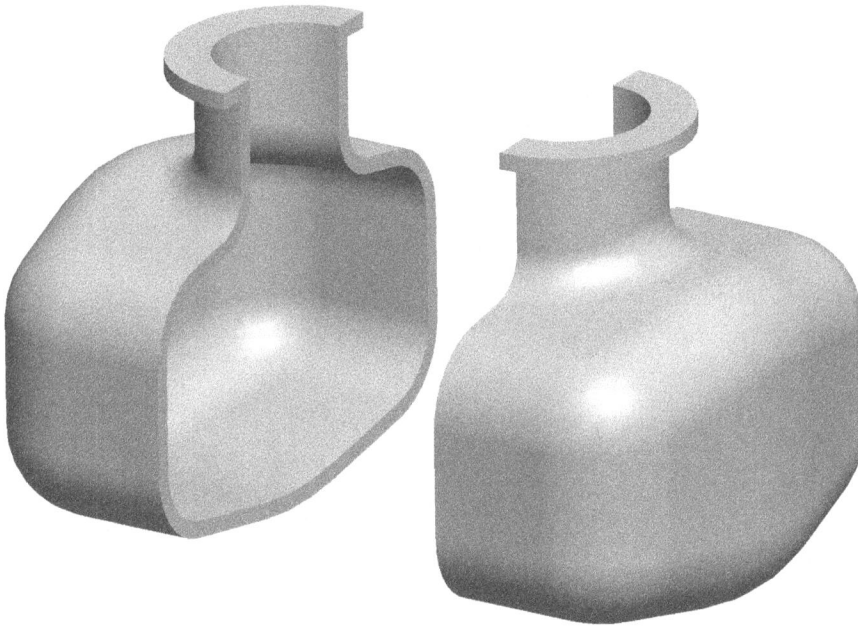

Fig. 14-1
Hollow part

It is important to create the model so that it maintains the same wall thickness at every point along the wall, but since it would be difficult or tedious to maintain a consistent wall thickness by using combinations of protrusions and cuts, we can start with a completely solid shape, as shown in Figure 14-2.

Solid Definition

Fig. 14-2
Solid model

In this case, we have created what will represent the exterior of our finished part, which is the geometry required to properly define and create the mold to manufacture it. Also notice that at this point, the model is completely solid, with no opening.

To create a Shell feature, select the ⬜ **Shell** icon from the Construction Toolbar. This is one of the few commands in Pro/ENGINEER that can be completed without selecting any references, because it applies the command to the entire part.

Figure 14-3 shows the initial result of using the Shell command. Pro/ENGINEER offsets every outside surface to the inside a nominal amount, and uses that new boundary to remove material.

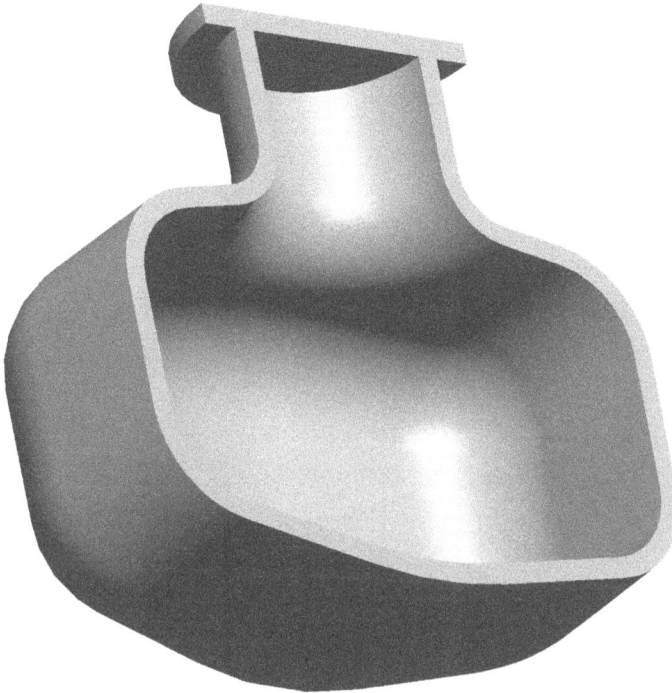

Fig. 14-3
Cross section of completely hollow part

Notice that since we did not select any references, it creates a complete void inside the part, with a single wall thickness. This is not a very useful design, as there is no way to fill it with liquid, so we must tell Pro/ENGINEER which face or faces should be removed in order to create an opening.

Removing Surfaces

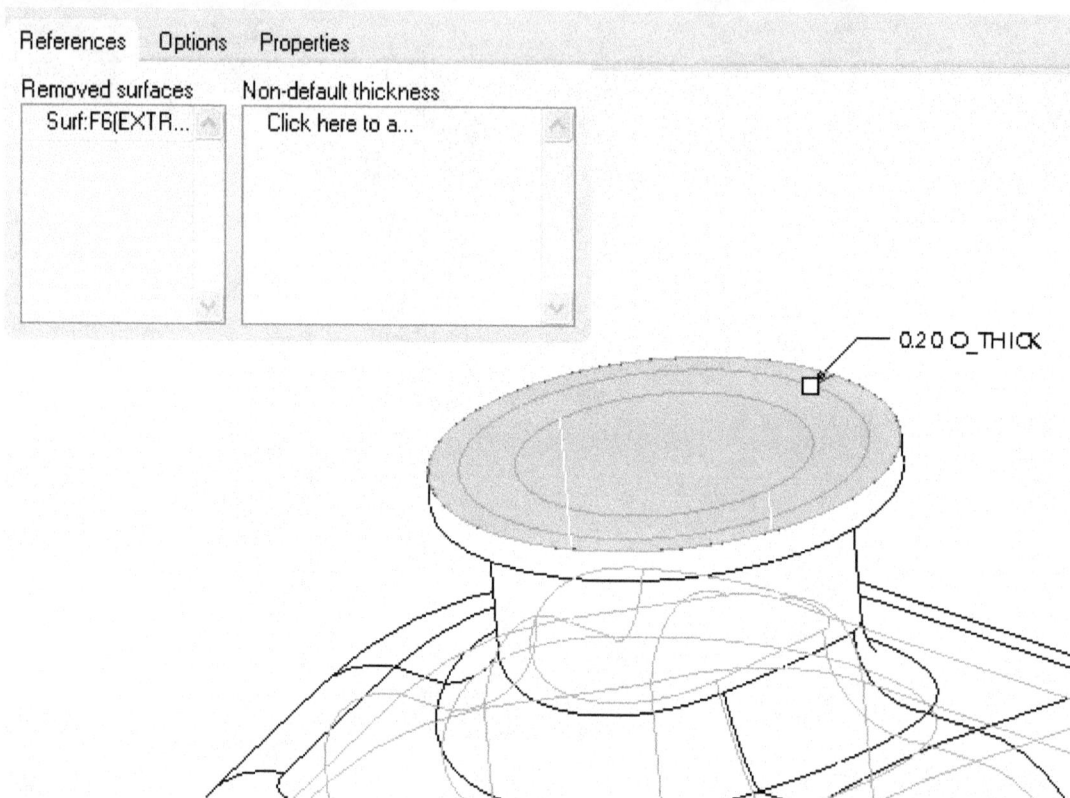

Fig. 14-4
Surface options

By making the appropriate choices from the dashboard, you may select which surfaces you wish to remove (create an opening), the nominal (default) wall thickness, and any walls you wish to create at non-default values.

By default, Pro/ENGINEER offsets the outside surfaces to the inside, and removes material from the inside, but a negative offset value will use the original model definition as the void, and add a thickness to the outside.

Holes

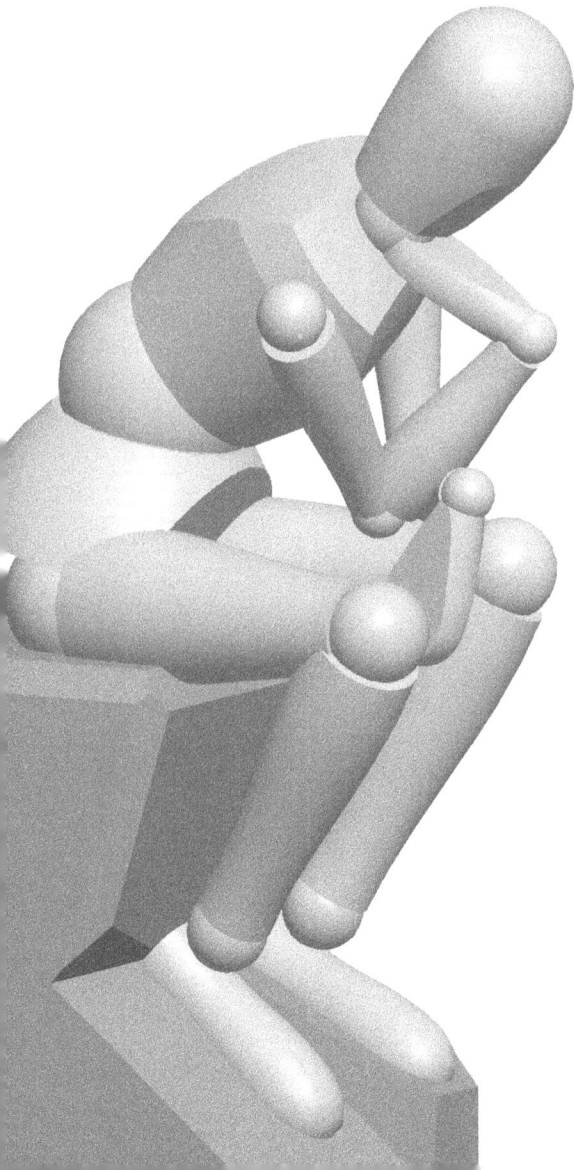

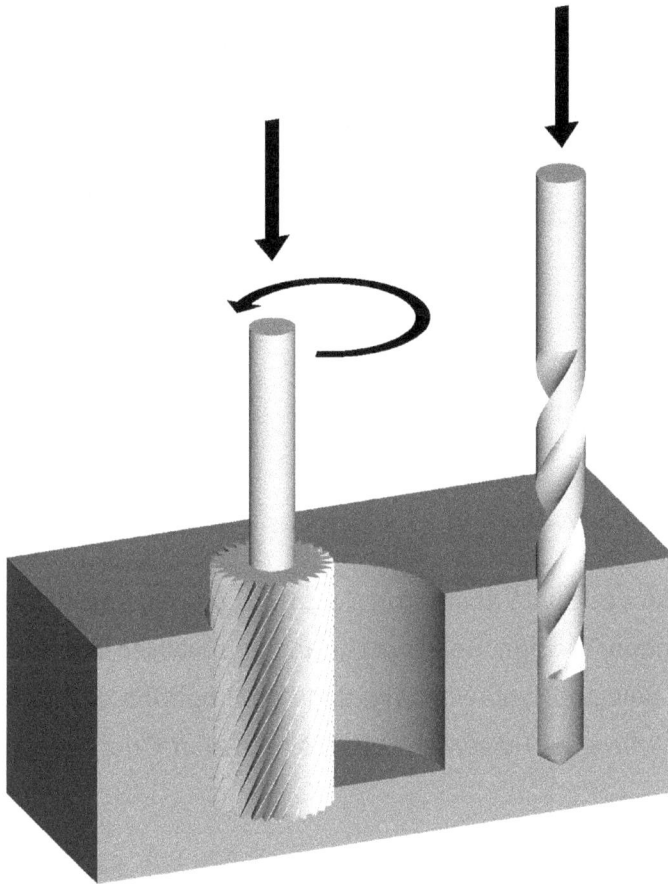

Fig. 15-1
Features created by cuts and holes

Even though we do not need to build our Pro/ENGINEER design models in the exact same steps as our manufacturing operations, we should keep manufacturing methods in mind. Figure 15-1 shows a section view of a block being cut. The feature on the left is being created with a milling bit, while the feature on the right is being created with a drill bit. Both of these features can be created in Pro/ENGINEER as either a cut or a hole, but since the feature on the right is going to be created with motion in only the Z direction, without any X or Y movement of the tool, then it should be created as a hole.

The advantage to using a hole is that they do not need to be sketched, therefore there is more flexibility in the placement of them on the model. You may also create ISO (metric) and standard UNC and UNF threaded holes, without needing to know the industry standard dimensions. When creating drawings, entire hole tables (charts) can be generated automatically, and standard hole notes indicating drill size and depth may be automatically displayed on the drawing.

Hole Placement

Holes may be placed anywhere on your parts as you wish, but the methods will vary, depending on your part geometry. To create a hole, select the ⊤ **Hole** icon from the Construction Toolbar. Select a surface you wish to drill into. Based on the type of geometry selected, you will have additional options to control the placement of the hole, by opening the Placement tab, as shown in Figure 15-2.

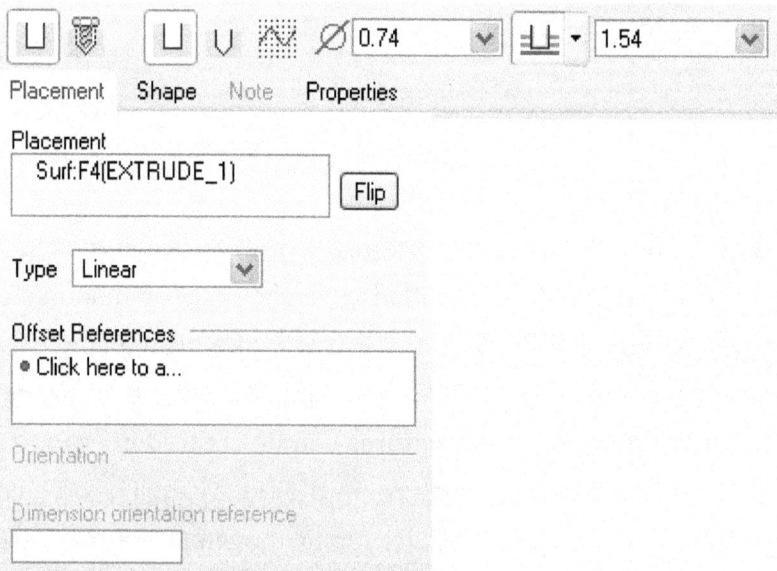

Fig. 15-2
Hole dashboard

Linear

When you select a planar surface as a placement reference, as shown in Figure 15-3, Pro/ENGINEER will automatically default to **Linear** as its placement type, but it may be changed by making the desired selection in the placement tab, as shown in Figure 15-2.

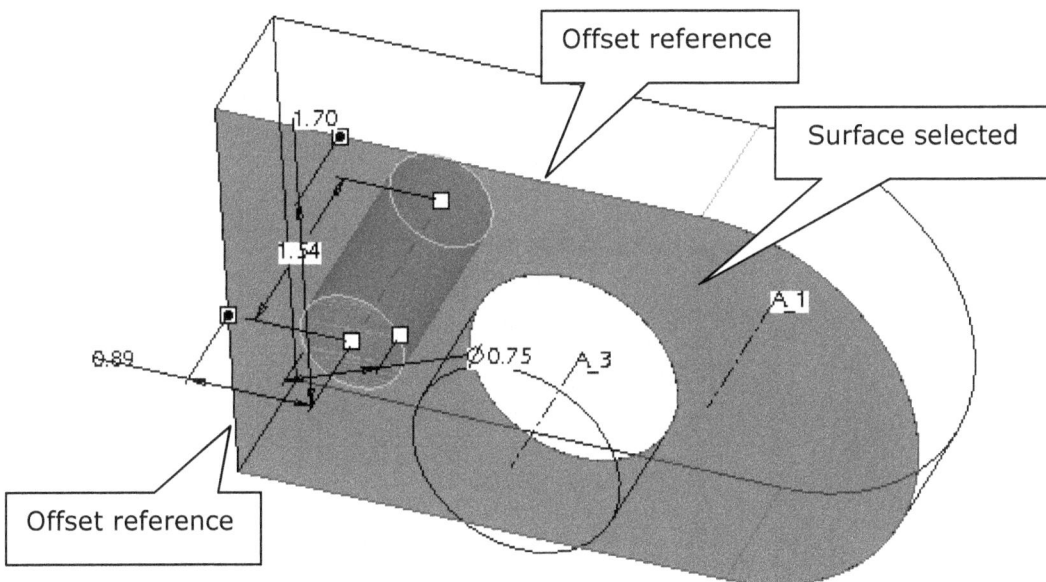

Fig. 15-3
Planar surface reference

Pro/ENGINEER will create the pre-construction highlight of the geometry in yellow. You will also notice several drag handles (white boxes) to control overall location on the surface, dimensional references, diameter, and depth. To locate the hole on the surface, click in the Offset Reference box in the placement tab, and select two pieces of geometry (surfaces, planes, edges, etc.), and specify the hole's distance from those references. You will also need to specify the holes diameter, and depth. (See later in this chapter for information on hole depth options.)

Coaxial

You may create a coaxial hole (a hole that shares the same axis as another feature) by selecting an existing axis, or cylindrical surface placement reference, in addition to a planar surface, as shown in Figure 15-4.

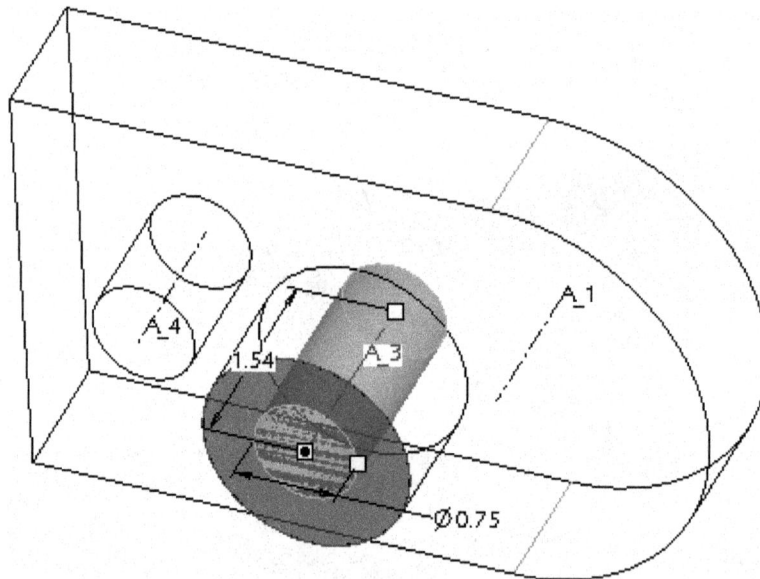

Fig. 15-4
Coaxial hole placement

If a cylindrical surface is the first placement reference selected, Pro/ENGINEER will use that reference as the surface to drill into, so the preferred method for a coaxial hole would be to select the face to drill into first, then the cylinder, or select a datum axis (not a surface) as the first placement reference.

Radial and Diameter

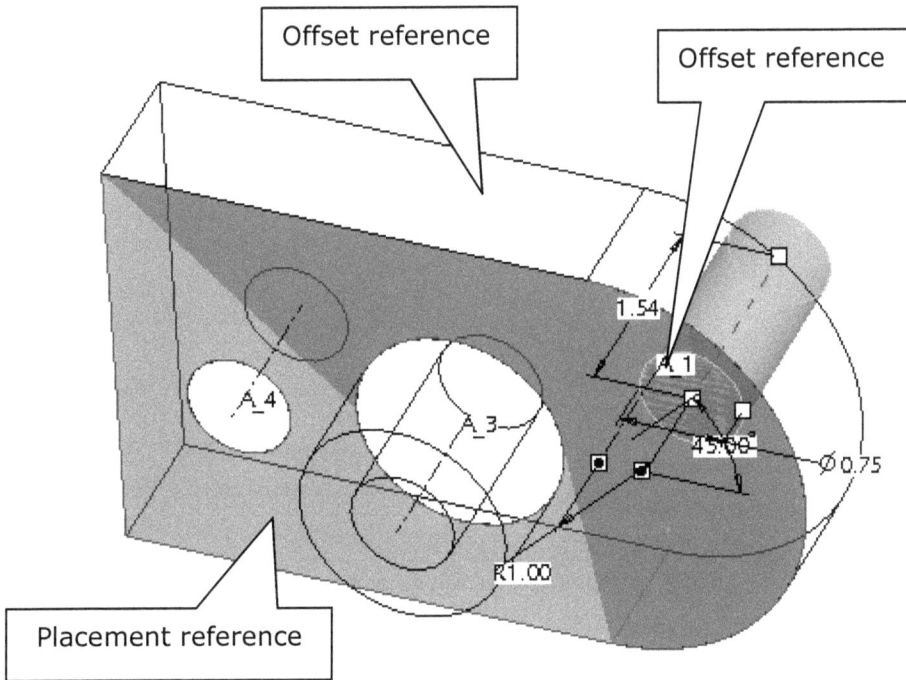

Fig. 15-5
Radial hole placement

By selecting a planar surface as the placement reference, and a combination of a datum axis and planar surface for offset references, you can create a hole as shown in Figure 15-5. In this example the hole is located 1.00 units from datum axis A_1 at a 45 degree angle from the horizontal offset reference.

Figure 15-6 shows the dimension scheme. The hole is located along a circle measuring a radius of 1.00 from the axis, and 45 degrees from horizontal. If the diameter placement type were selected, then the same hole would be located along a circle measuring a diameter of 2.00 from the axis.

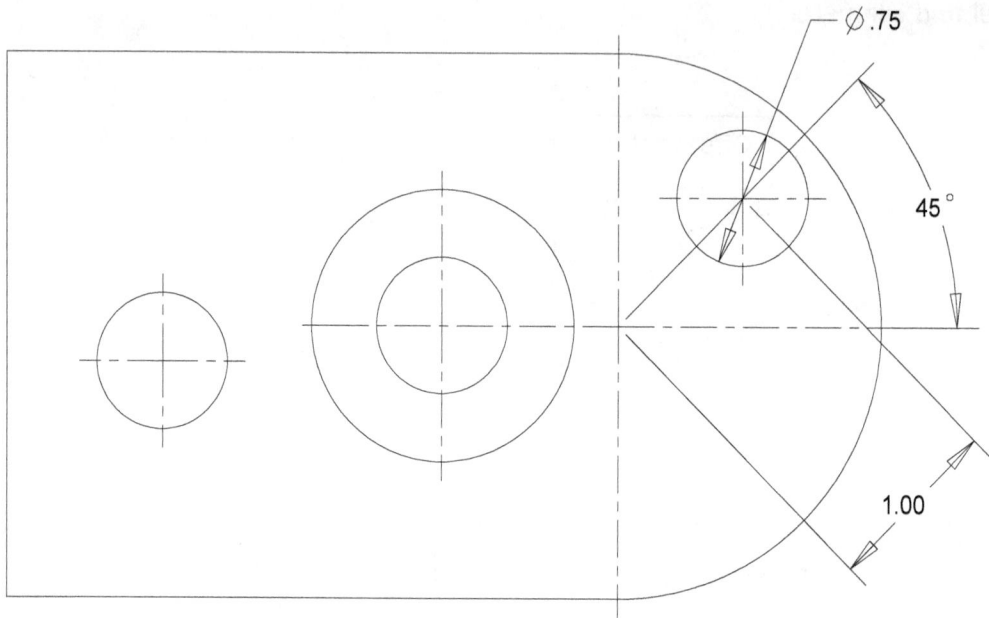

Fig. 15-6
Radial placement dimension scheme

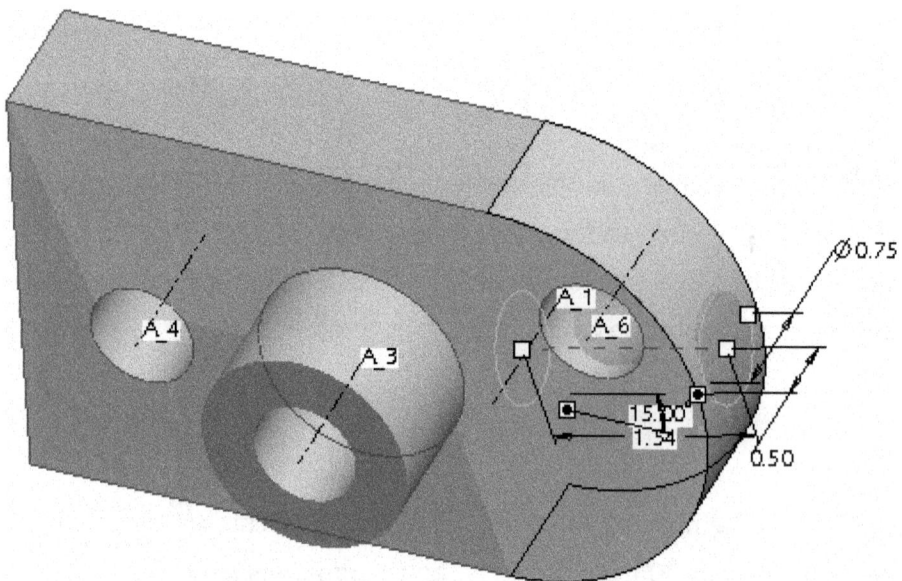

Fig. 15-7
Radial placement on a cylinder

If the placement reference selected was on a cylindrical or conical surface, then Pro/ENGINEER will use that surface as the face to drill into. You would then select a pair of offset references to control where along the face to locate the hole, as shown in Figure 15-7. In this case, the hole is located 15 degrees from horizontal, and 0.50 inches from the front of the part.

Depth Options

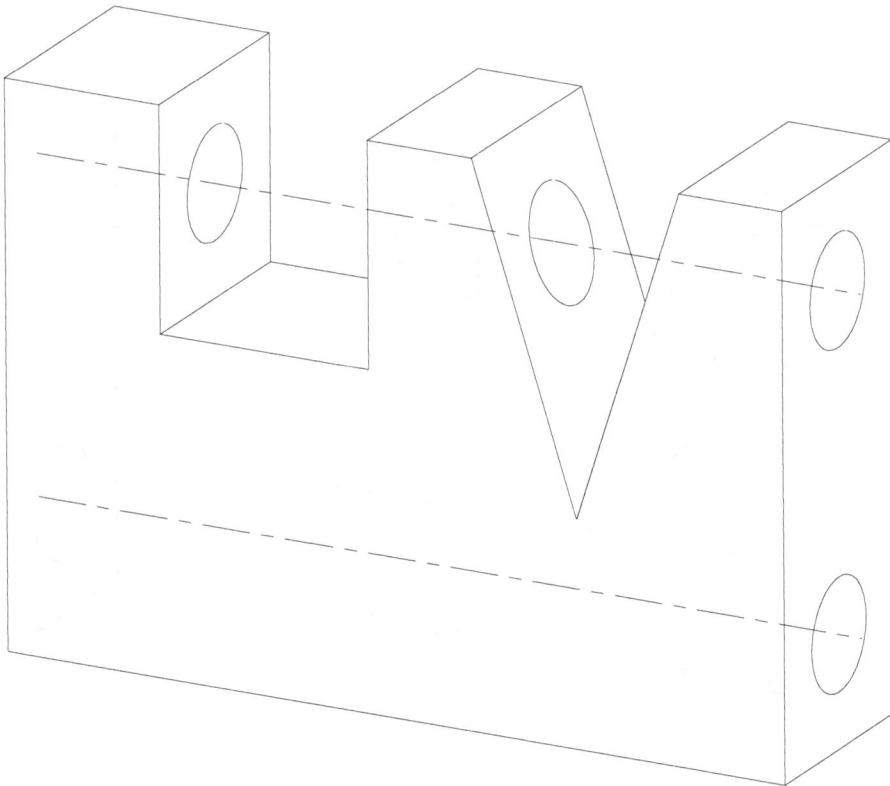

Fig. 15-8
Sample holes

For discussion purposes, both holes shown in Figure 15-8 are created in exactly the same way. Each is placed on the right side of the solid part, located the same distance from the front, and each is dimensioned from the top. The depth of each hole will be controlled exactly the same way in each of the following examples, to show how the depth of a hole can vary, not only by the controls we place on it, but the geometry of our part.

Blind

By default, when Pro/ENGINEER creates a hole, the depth option is set to blind, as designated by the ⊥ Depth icon on the dashboard. Basically this means that the hole starts at the placement reference, and continues to a depth as specified by a dimension, as shown in Figure 15-9.

Fig. 15-9
Blind depth

Different depth options may be selected from the dashboard, as shown in Figure 15-10, and the appropriate references may be selected as prompted.

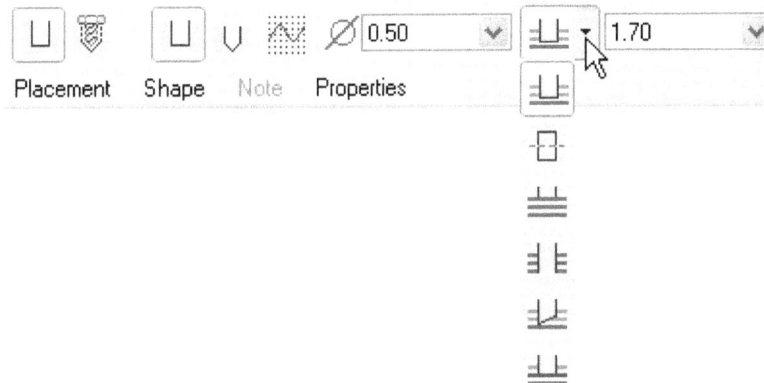

Fig. 15-10
Selecting depth options

Symmetrical

The symmetrical option may be specified by selecting the ⊟ **Each side** icon from the dashboard. This depth option works exactly the same as the blind depth, in that is uses a dimension from the placement reference, except it creates the hole in both directions along the axis, splitting the dimension value symmetrically, as shown in Figure 15-11. Caution should be used when selecting this option because it is possible to specify a drilling operation that cannot be duplicated by manufacturing. (You cannot drill in two separate directions from the center of a solid workpiece.)

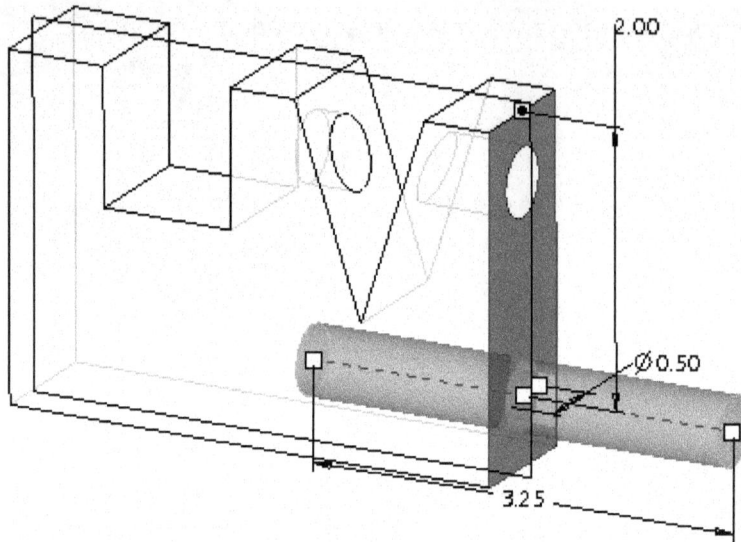

Fig. 15-11
Symmetrical depth hole definition

Next Surface

You may specify the depth of your holes to go up to the next surface by selecting

the ⬒ **Next surface** icon from the dashboard. This will start the hole on your

placement reference surface, and continue until it intersects another (next) surface.

When Pro/ENGINEER creates its pre-construction highlight, it does not perform any

math calculations yet, it is merely feedback for you, so that you can see what you

are asking Pro/ENGINEER to do (as discussed in Chapter 2). Since the calculation to

determine the 'next' surface has not been done yet, the pre-construction highlight

extends all the way through the part, to show you which surfaces may be

intersecting, as shown in Figure 15-12. When the feature definition is accepted, the

hole will be created, as shown in Figure 15-13.

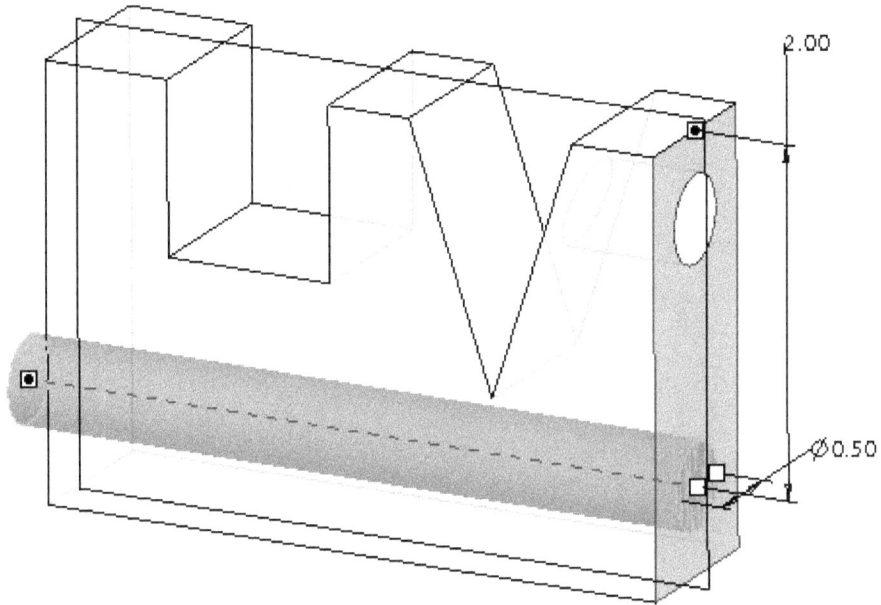

Fig. 15-12
Up to next surface depth definition

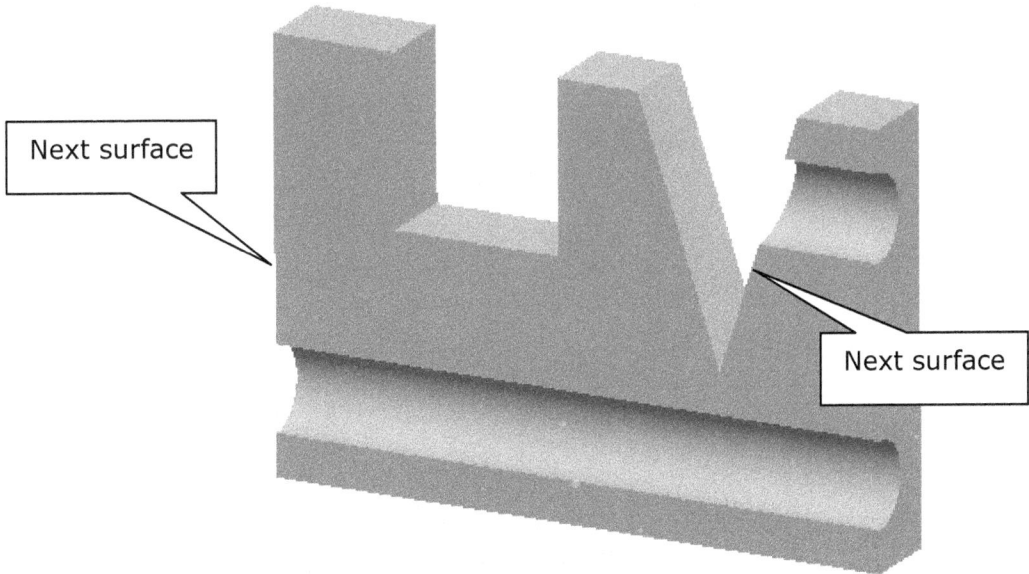

Fig. 15-13
Completed holes up to next surface

All surfaces

In industry, a hole that passes through the entire part is called a 'Thru' hole or

'Through' hole. This type of hole can be created by selecting the [icon] **All surfaces** icon from the dashboard. This sets the depth of the hole to intersect all surfaces of the part, therefore passing through the part, as shown in Figure 15-14.

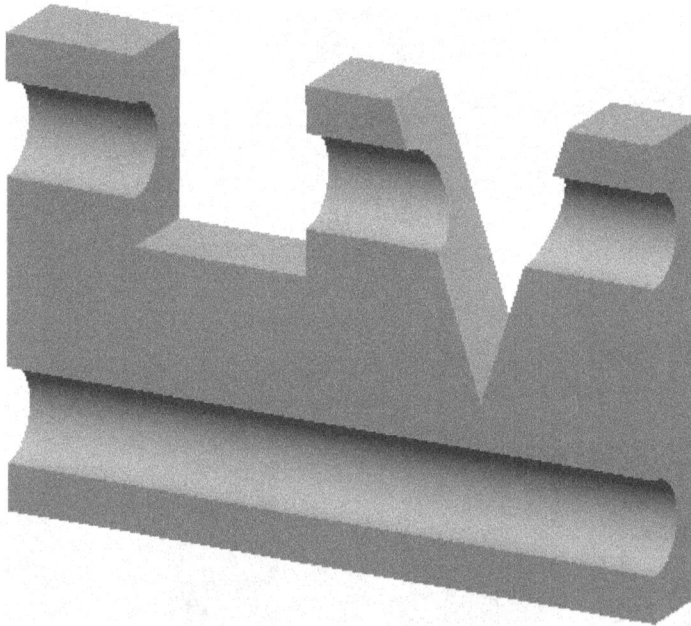

Fig. 15-14
Holes intersecting all surfaces (Through all)

Notice that there does not appear to be any difference between the bottom hole created using the **To Next** option (Fig. 15-13) and **All Surfaces**. This is because in this case, there was only one surface to intersect, but this was not the case for the upper hole.

Selected Surface

You may select a particular surface to set the depth of your hole by selecting the

⊥ **Selected surface** icon from the dashboard. This will allow the hole to pass through all surfaces until it intersects the selected surface, as shown in Figure 15-15.

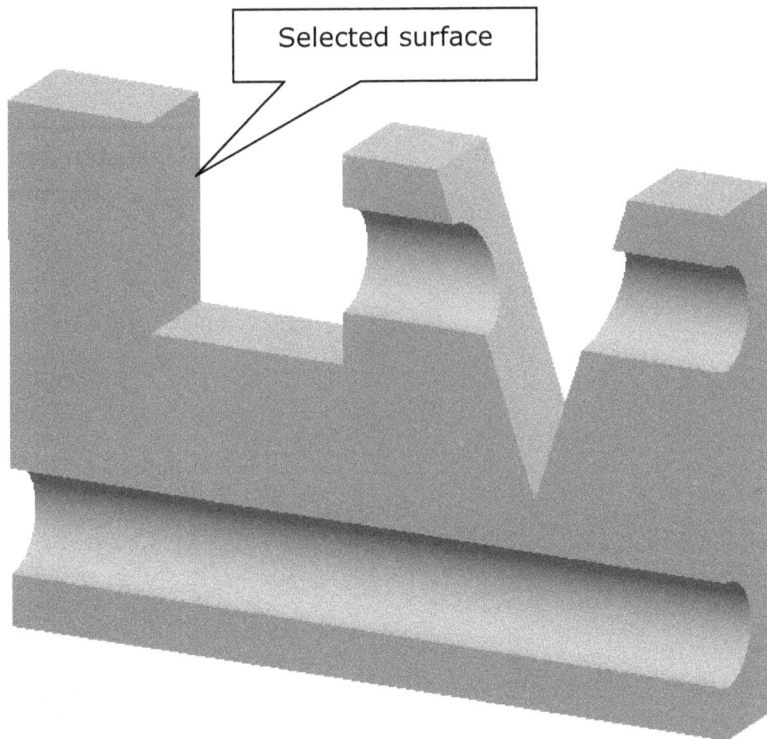

Selected surface

Fig. 15-15
Holes up to selected surface

Notice that the upper hole continued intersecting surfaces until it reached the selected surface. Since the lower hole does not intersect the surface, it continues all the way through the part.

Selected point, curve, surface or plane

To explicitly set the depth of your holes based on existing geometry, you may select

the ⊥ **Selected** icon from the dashboard. This will allow greater control of the

depth by treating surfaces as planes (which are infinite in size), as shown in Figure

15-16, and creates theoretical planes through selected edges and points, normal to

the hole axis, as shown in Figure 15-17.

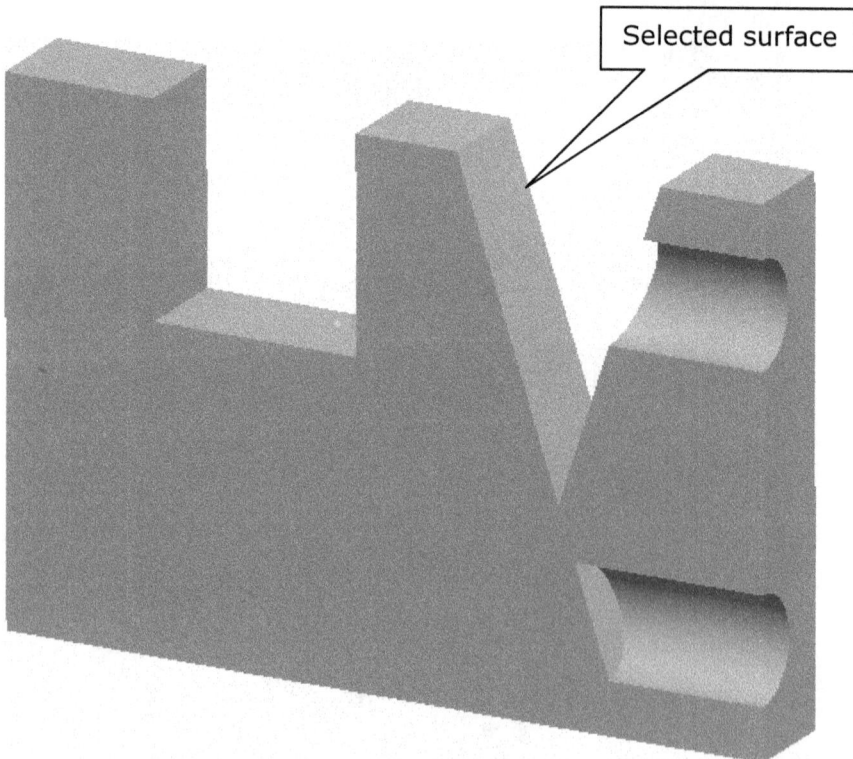

Selected surface

Fig. 15-16
Holes to selected surface

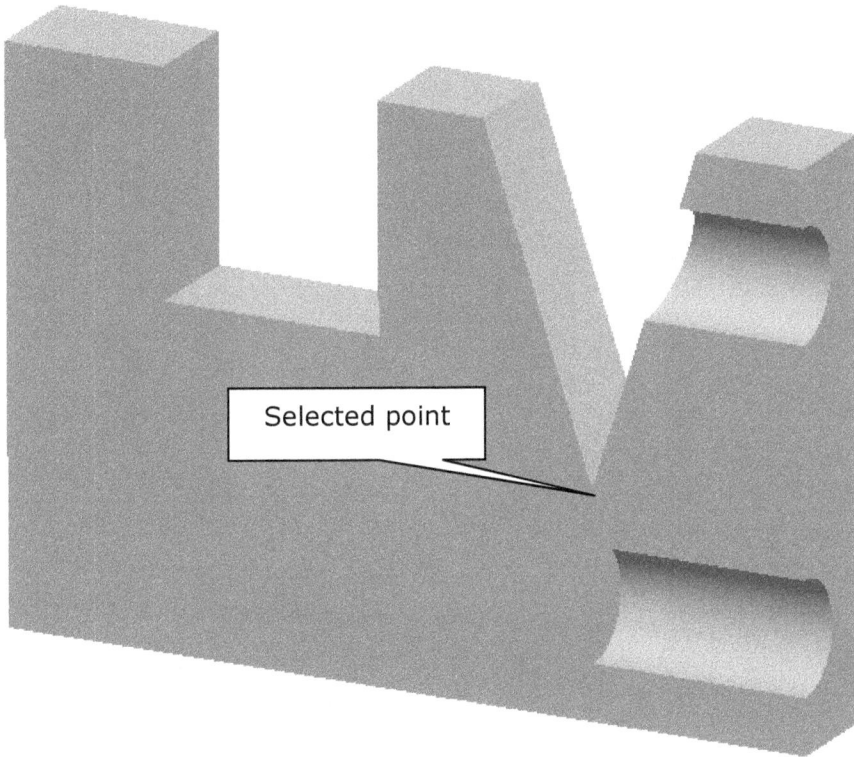

Fig. 15-17
Holes to selected point

Standard Holes

When creating holes that are intended to be used with standard fasteners in an

assembly, you may create a standard hole by selecting the ⬚ **Standard Hole** icon
from the dashboard. This will create a hole using industry standard pilot hole
diameters for ISO (metric), UNC and UNF (unified coarse and unified fine) threads.
By opening the Shape tab, you will be able to see exactly what the shape of the
hole will be, and also allow you to specify the depth of the thread, as shown in
Figure 15-18.

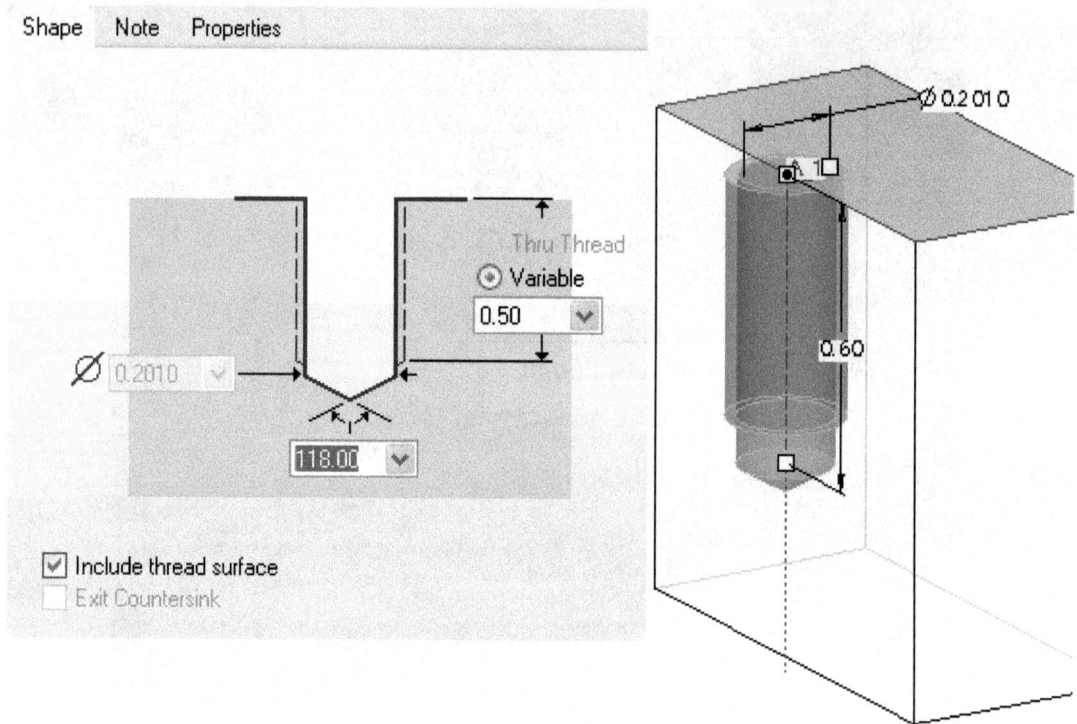

Fig. 15-18
Standard hole definition

By using a standard hole, Pro/ENGINEER automatically sets the hole diameter to the proper minor diameter of the standard machine thread selected. If you choose to include the thread surface, Pro/ENGINEER will create a cylindrical surface quilt at the depth specified, and the diameter set to the proper major diameter of the thread.

You may also choose to include a countersink by selecting the Υ **Countersink** icon from the dashboard, or a counterbore by selecting the **Counterbore** icon (or both). You may even create an exit countersink, all of which may be visualized in the Shape tab, as shown in Figure 15-19.

Shape   Note   Properties

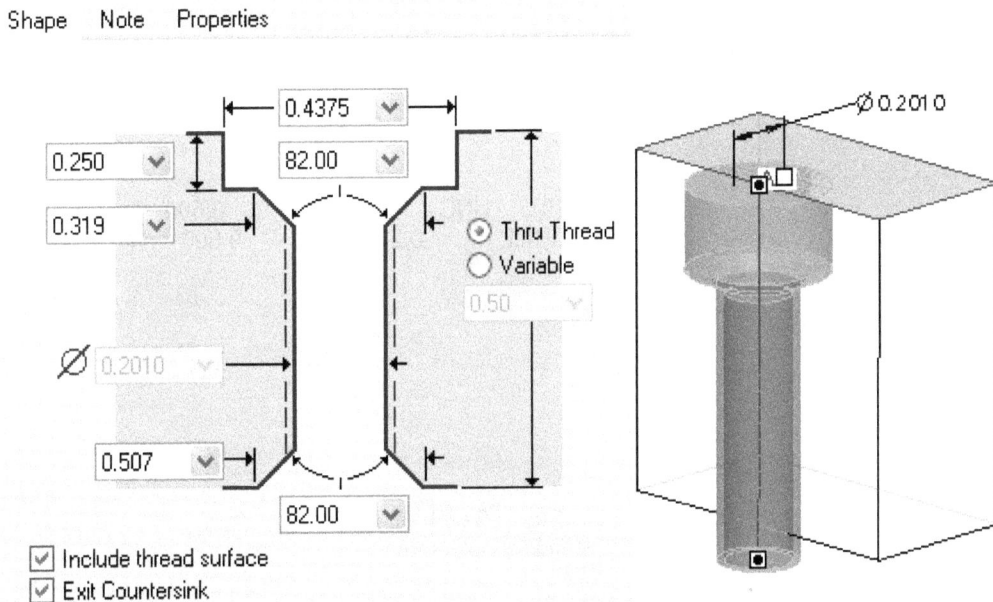

Fig. 15-19
Standard hole with thread, countersinks and counterbore

Using Pro/ENGINEER's automatic tool for creating standard holes has its advantages in that it will create a standard drill point, and proper diameters for the major and minor threads. All of the information necessary for machining is embedded into the feature. This information can be displayed on the manufacturing drawing automatically as a note (see Chapter 24) without needing to create dimensions for the same information, as shown in Figure 15-20.

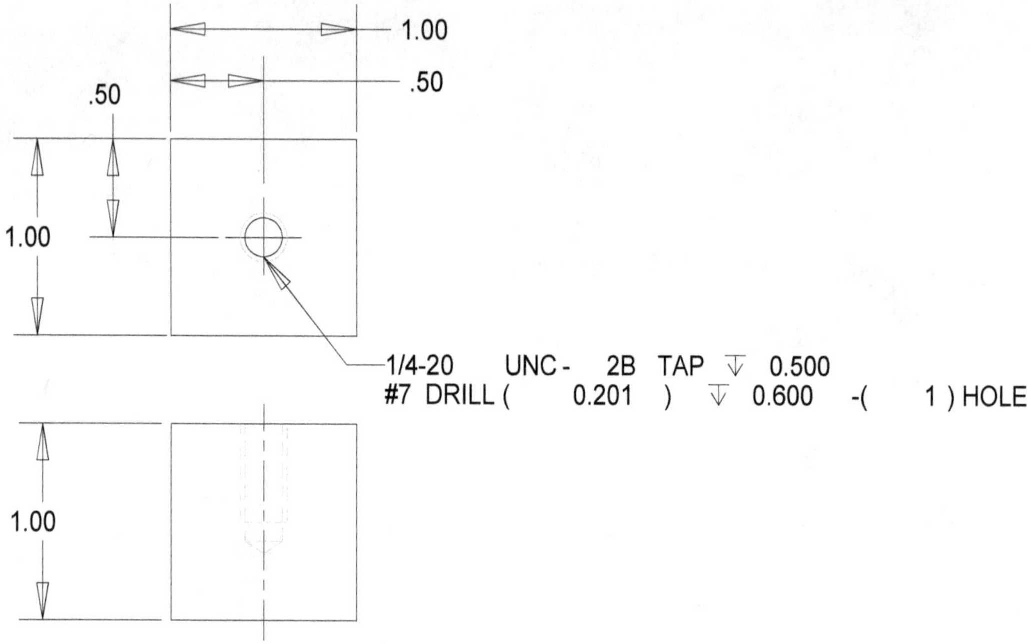
1.00
.50
.50
1.00
1/4-20 UNC - 2B TAP ⊽ 0.500
#7 DRILL (0.201) ⊽ 0.600 -(1) HOLE
1.00

Fig. 15-20
Standard hole note

Sketched Holes

Simple holes (Pro/ENGINEER's default) and standard holes are created with straight sides, with a variety of starting and ending shapes, but there may be times when you want to specify a special shape. This could be accomplished using a revolved cut (see Chapter 9), but if you want the feature type to be placed and classified as a hole, rather than a cut, you may sketch the shape of the hole by selecting the **Sketch** icon from the dashboard. You may then sketch and dimension the profile of the hole similar to a revolved cut, as shown in Figure 15-21.

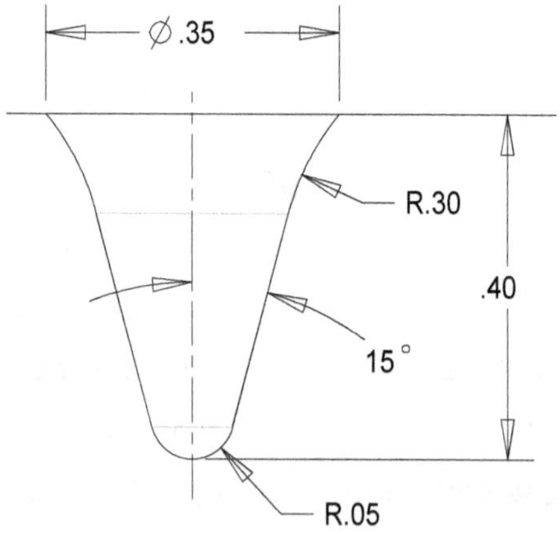
∅.35
R.30
.40
15°
R.05

Fig. 15-21
Sketched profile

Chapter 16

Duplicating Features

Copy
Paste
Paste Special
Mirror
Patterns

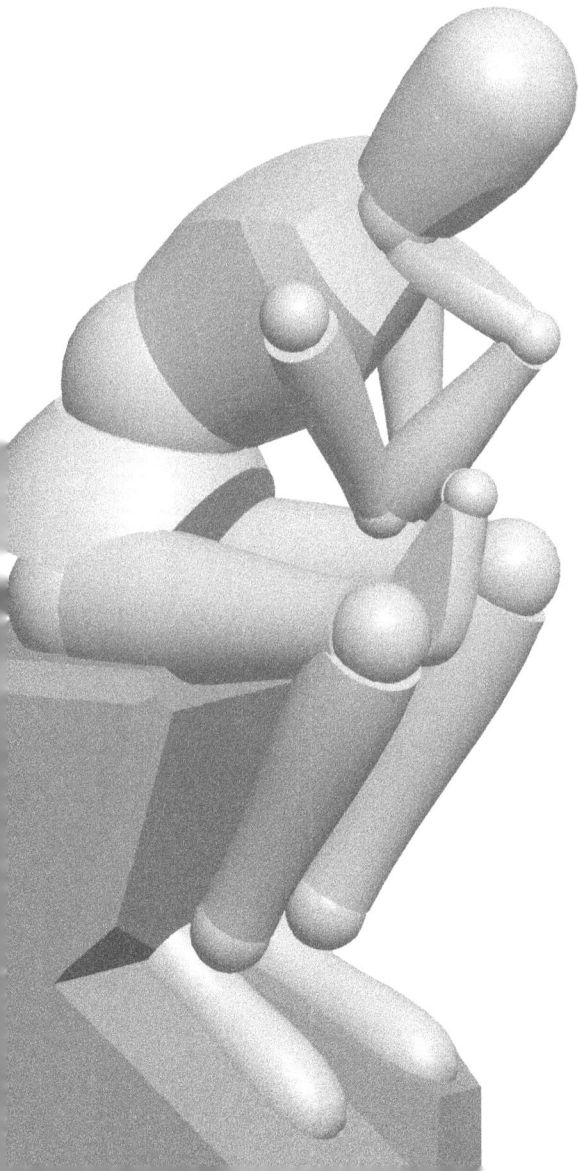

Pro/ENGINEER will allow you to create virtually any geometry imaginable. This may be accomplished with simple or complex features, but if you need to create more than one of a particular piece of geometry, there are several tools to help you save time and maintain accuracy and your design intent.

Figure 16-1 shows a D-shaped extrusion on top of a block. To create another D-shaped extrusion, we could certainly just create a new feature from scratch, or we could can make duplicates of the original.

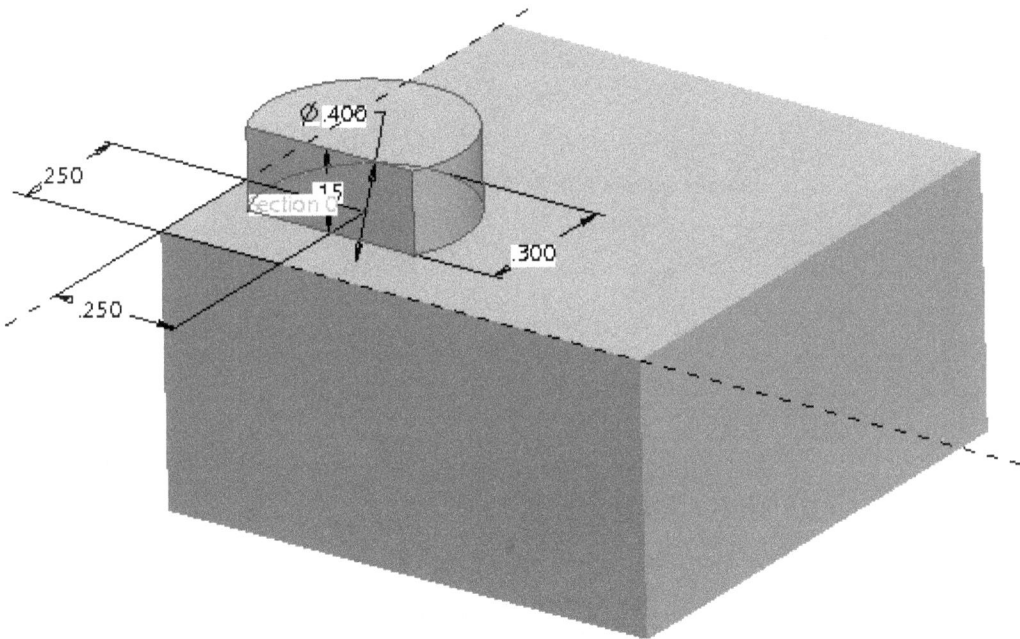

Fig. 16-1
Original feature to duplicate

Copy

You have the ability to copy existing geometry by simply selecting one or more individual features and selecting the ⬛ **Copy** icon from the main toolbar. This will copy the feature information to your computer's clipboard (temporary storage area).

Paste

Once you have placed information in your clipboard you may select the ▣ **Paste** icon from the Main Toolbar. The Paste operation will maintain the feature type and shape, but you will be prompted to select all of the necessary references for the new feature(s).

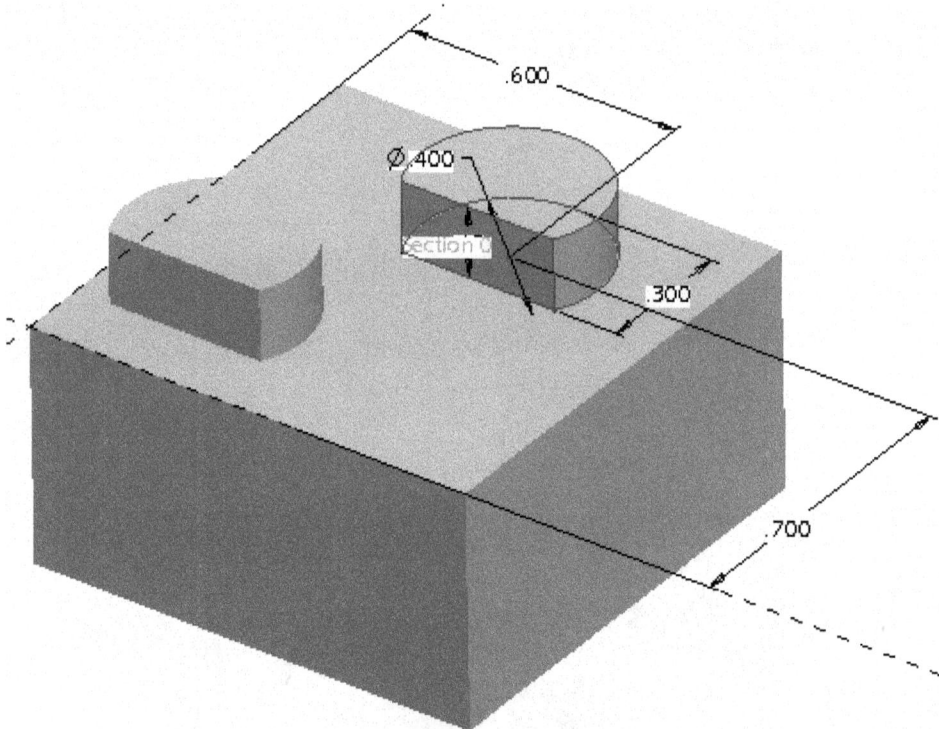

Fig. 16-2
Pasted feature

Figure 16-2 shows the D-shaped extrusion being pasted. The feature type, shape and original dimensions such as the height and Ø.400 are maintained, but you will need to select the sketching plane (even if you want to use the original again) and the references for the .600 and .700 location dimensions. For a part and feature as simple as the one shown in Figure 16-2, it may not save much time, but Figure 16-3 illustrates the same paste function, but by specifying unique sketching and reference planes, and by also modifying the feature dimensions and type (namely selecting the ⬜ **Remove Material** icon in the dashboard), we can create similar geometries in much less time than it would take from scratch, because we can eliminate all of the actual sketching operations. No parent/child relationship is created between the original feature(s) and the pasted feature(s). Each exist as separate entities, and either may be modified without affecting the other.

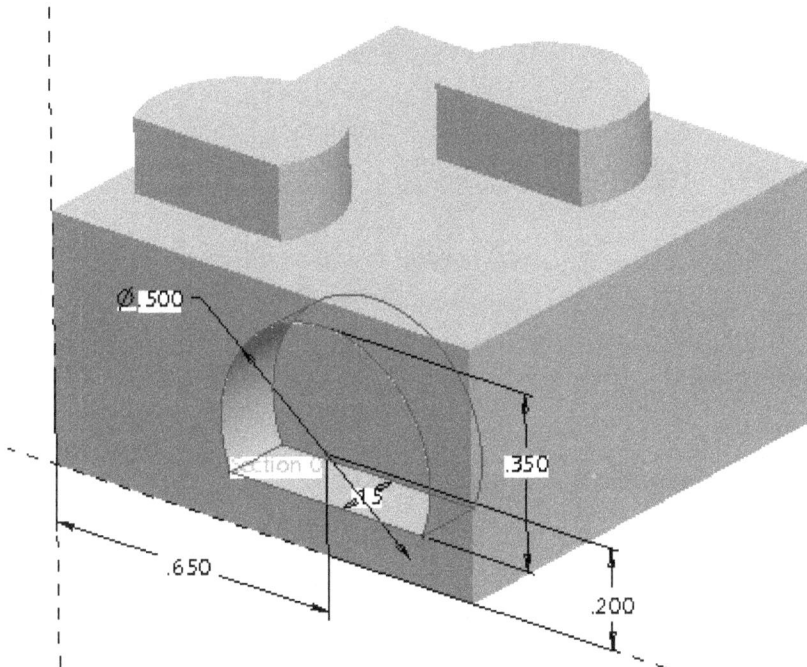

Fig. 16-3
Pasted feature with unique references and type

Paste Special

There are times when you may want to create an exact copy of a feature, and place it on the model relative to the original. In this case, after selecting the feature and

Copy, select the ⬜ **Paste Special** icon from the Main Toolbar. The dialog box shown in Figure 16-4 will open prompting you to make the desired choices.

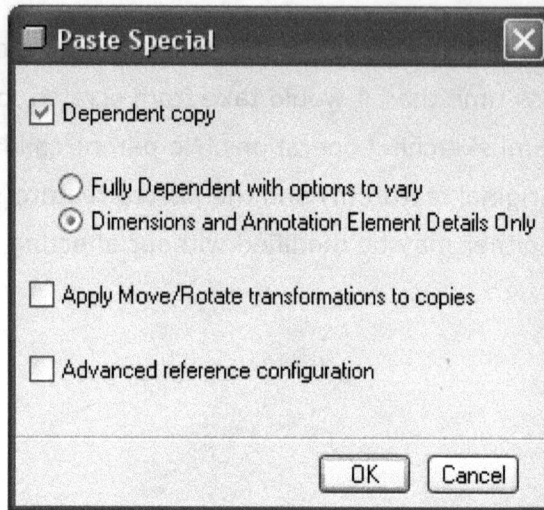

Fig. 16-4
Paste Special dialog box

Dependent copy (default)

Fully Dependent with options to vary

All elements of the copied feature definition will be dependent on the original. You can vary the dependence of certain elements after the Paste.

Dimensions and Annotation Element Details Only (default)

Only dimensions/sketch or annotation element details of the copied feature will be linked to that of the original.

Apply Move/Rotate transformations to copies

Placement of the new copies will be defined by translation and/or rotation from the position of the original features.

Advanced reference configuration

Review and specify the list of references of the new copies.

To paste a feature relative to its original, be sure to check the **Apply Move/Rotate** option. This will open a dialog box like the one shown in Figure 16-5 for you to specify if you want to translate along a reference (as shown) or rotate about an axis, as shown in Figure 16-6.

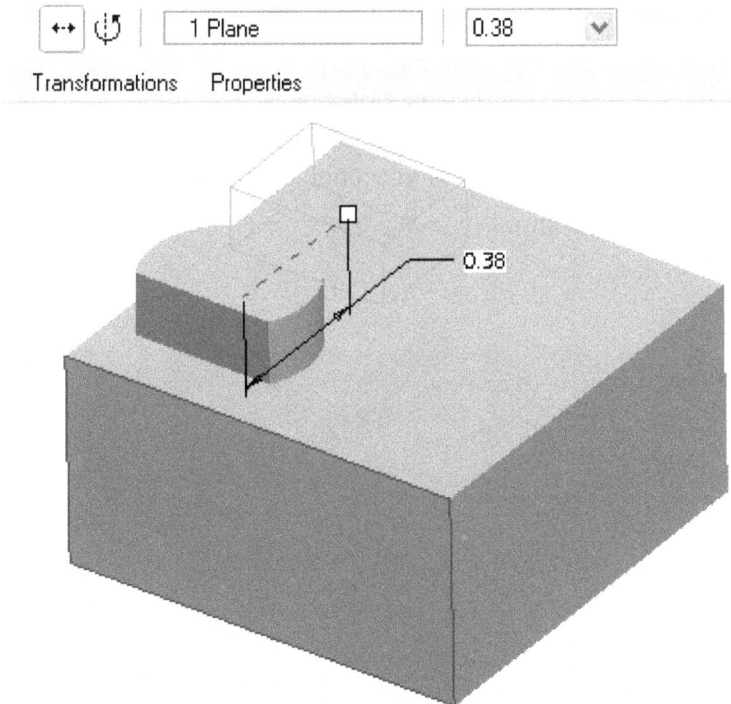

Fig. 16-5
Translated Paste Special

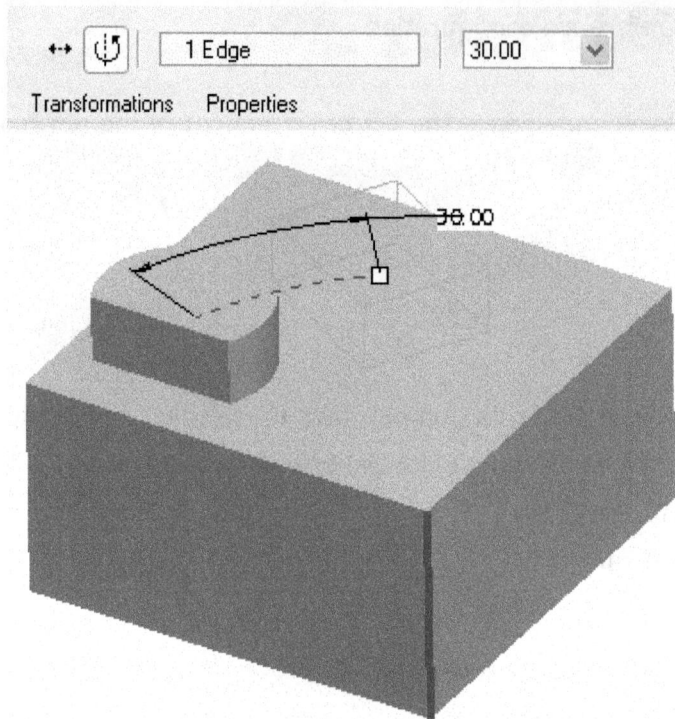

Fig. 16-6
Rotated Paste Special

Regardless of the dependency options you choose, the pasted feature(s) will start off as exact copies of the original.

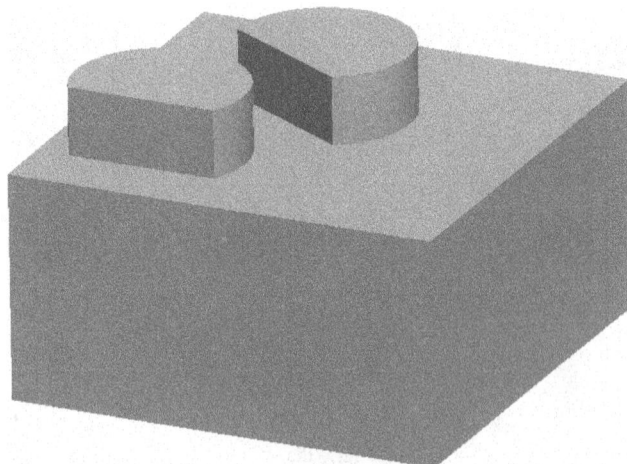

Fig. 16-7
Pasted feature

Mirror

Many products are designed with some sort of symmetry. While you are free to create each of your part's features individually, the **Mirror** tool allows you to create a feature or set of features, then create an identical set of features on the opposite side from a plane of symmetry.

Figure 16-8 shows a part with a tapered cylinder (created with an extrusion and a draft) with a hole and countersink.

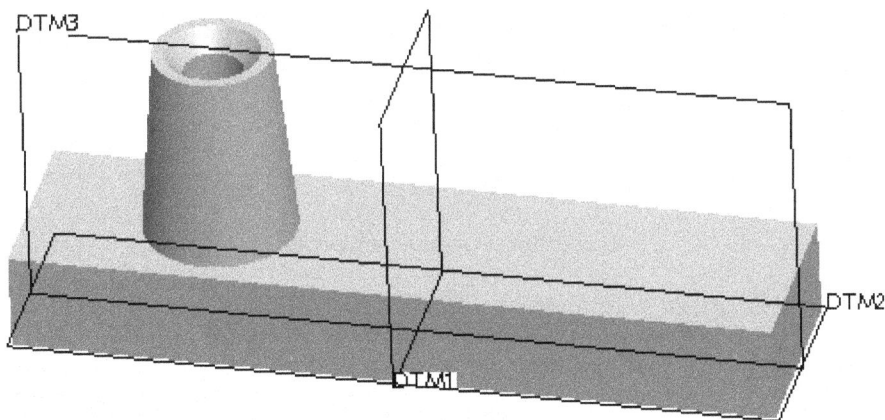

Fig. 16-8
Features to be duplicated

To duplicate the features symmetrically from the DTM1 datum plane, simply select the extrusion, draft, and hole, then select the ⊃|⊂ **Mirror** icon from the Construction Toolbar. When prompted, select a plane or surface you wish to mirror about (in this case, DTM1). The resulting geometry is shown in Figure 16-9.

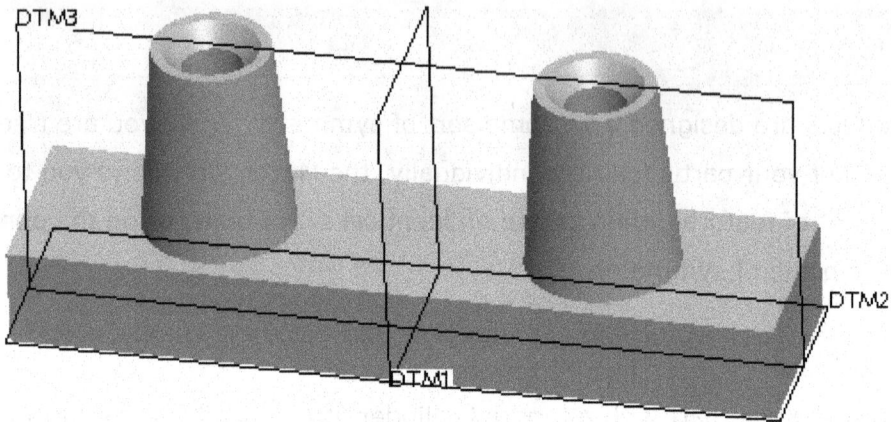

Fig. 16-9
Mirrored features

The mirrored features (children) are dependent on the originals (parents) by default, but the dependency may be broken by un-checking the appropriate box in the dashboard, as shown in Figure 16-10.

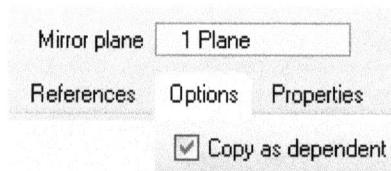

Fig. 16-10
Mirror without dependency

Each time the **Mirror** command is used, it creates a new feature or group of features in the model tree. Part geometry can be controlled by the order in which features and mirrors are created. It is also possible to create mirrors of mirrors.

Symmetrical parts

There are also times when you may wish to completely define half of a part, as shown in Figure 16-11, then mirror the entire model about a plane of symmetry.

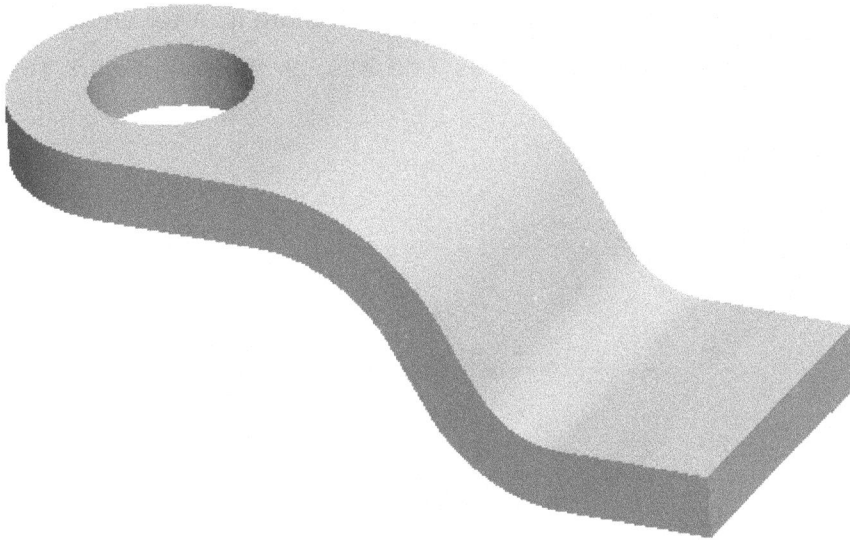

Fig. 16-11
Half of the intended design

It may be possible to select the first feature and create a mirror, then select the second feature and create a mirror, then the third, and so on but if you wish to create a completely symmetrical part, the more robust method is to select the entire mode at once by clicking on the name of the model at the top of the Model Tree. After selecting the ⊃|⊏ **Mirror** icon from the Construction Toolbar, select a planar surface on the model as the mirroring plane, as shown in Figure 16-12.

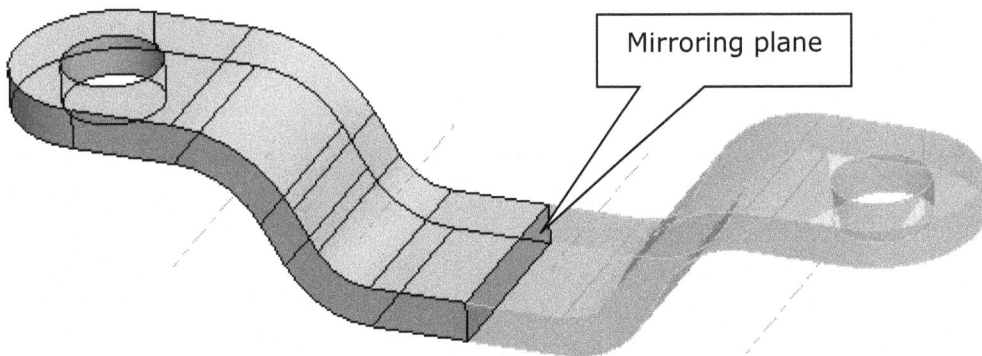

Mirroring plane

Fig. 16-12
Entire part mirrored

This again creates a single mirror feature in the model tree, however it is completely dependent on all of the features that are created before it. After creating the mirror, it is possible to continue adding features if desired, as shown in Figure 16-13.

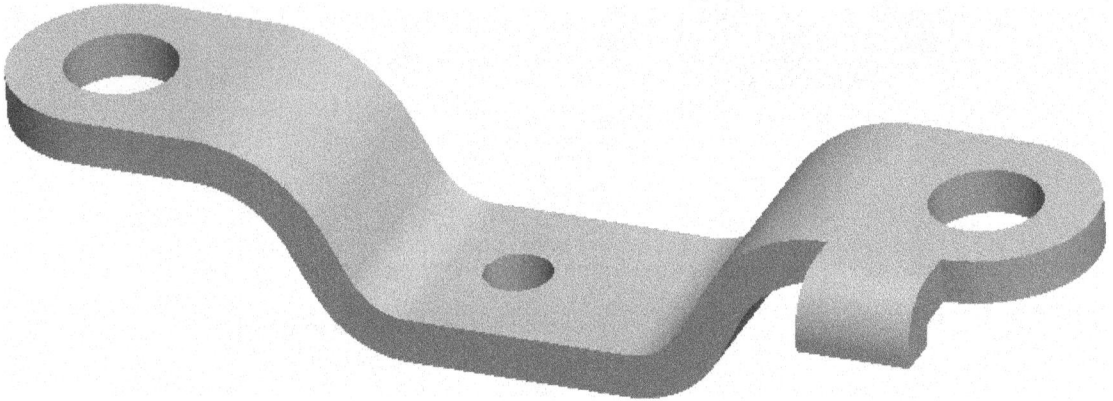

Fig. 16-13
Features added after mirror

Patterns

Patterns are used to create an array of features. To create a pattern, select a feature or group of features, and select the [icon] **Pattern** icon from the Construction Toolbar. This will open the pattern dashboard, as shown in Figure 16-14, from which you may choose one of several patterns types.

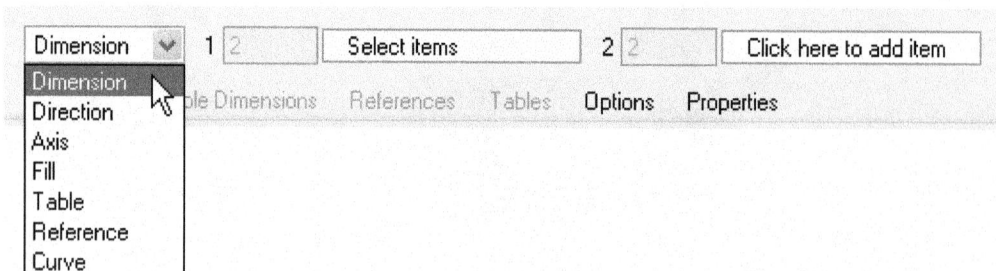

Fig. 16-14
Pattern dashboard

Dimension

When using this option the dimensions that are used to create the first (seed)
feature are used to control the layout of the pattern. This does not mean that the
spacing between the members needs to be set to the same value as the original
dimension, but rather that the dimensioning scheme or orientation of the members
will be driven by the original dimensioning scheme. You may also control patterns in
two directions, and use several dimensions in each direction. For example, Figure
16-15 shows an extrusion dimensioned with dimension d6 (See Chapter 20 for
discussions regarding dimension labels) from the left of the part, d5 from the front
of the part and a height of d3 from the top of the part.

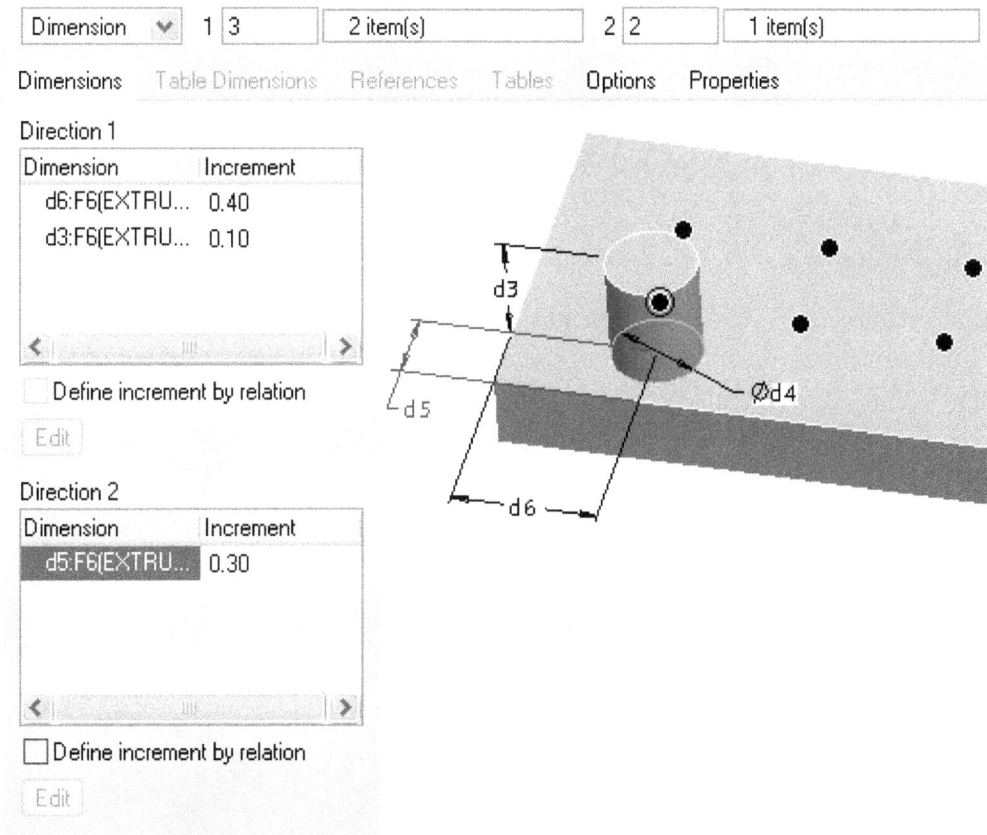

Fig. 16-15
Dimensional pattern control

By clicking on the Dimension tab in the dashboard, you will see that you may select existing dimensions of the feature to be added, and control boxes for either one or two directions. You may also specify an increment amount for each dimension. By default, Pro/ENGINEER will insert the dimension value as the increment value, but this value may be modified.

In Figure 16-15, you will see that we will be adding features from left to right in increments of 0.40 units and increase each member's height by 0.10 units. At the same time, we will be adding features from the front to the back in increments of 0.30 units. The number of members is controlled at the top of the dashboard where you will see that we are controlling 3 members (including the original) in the first direction (left to right) and two members (including the original) in the second direction (front to back). You will also see 'place holders' for the members to be created as a ● solid dot, with a ◉ dot and circle to indicate the original member. If you wish to omit any member (other than the original) from the pattern layout, you may simply click on the place holder, which will change the icon to an ○ open circle.

The pattern defined in Figure 16-15 is shown in Figure 16-16.

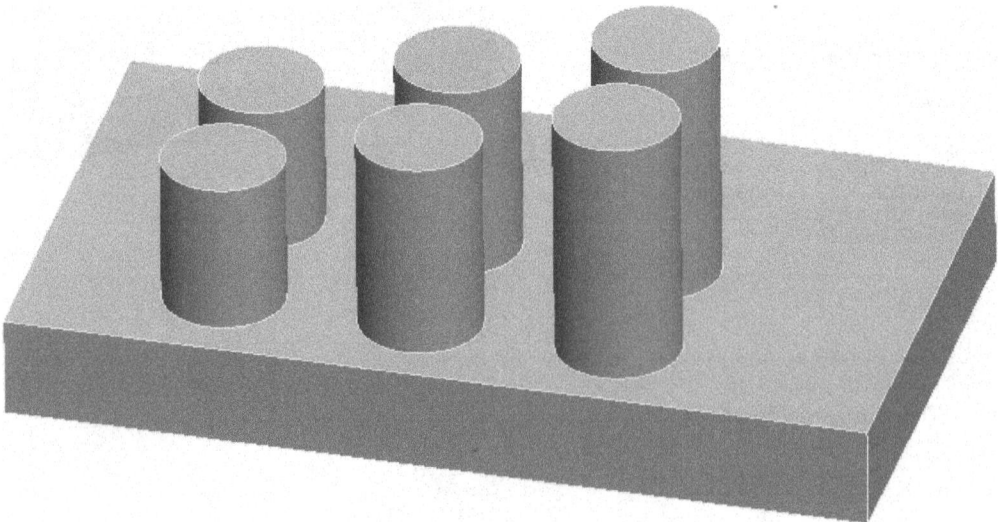

Fig. 16-16
Completed pattern

Direction

The Direction pattern type is very similar to the Dimension type, except that instead of selecting dimensions to control the orientation of the pattern, existing datum planes, surfaces, sketches, axes, and edges can be used as references. Figure 16-17 shows the same feature being patterned, but in this case, the selected edge is used to control the direction of the pattern members.

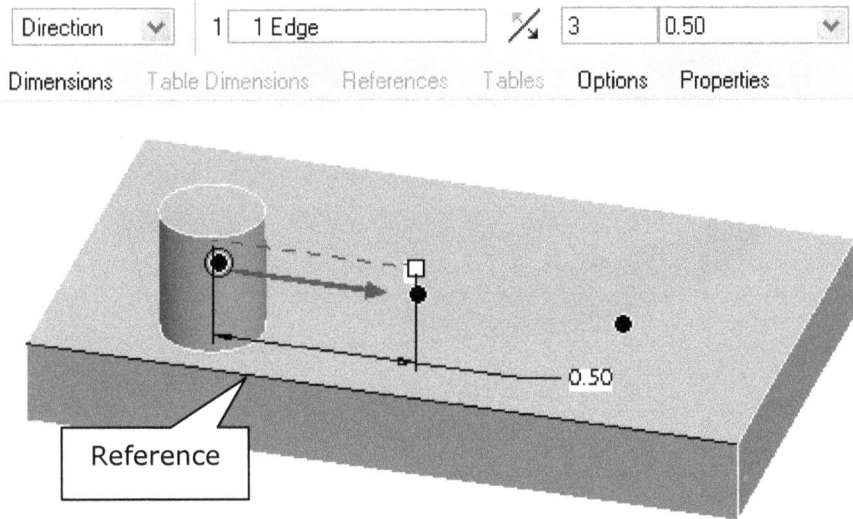

Fig. 16-17
Direction pattern definition

You may also add feature dimensions to the pattern definition to increment the geometry of the members in addition to the layout of the array.

Axis

The Axis pattern type allows you to create a circular array of pattern members about an axis or edge, as shown in Figure 16-18. By default, Pro/ENGINEER prompts for the number of members (including the original) and the desired angle between members. Figure 16-18 shows five members spaced 30° apart.

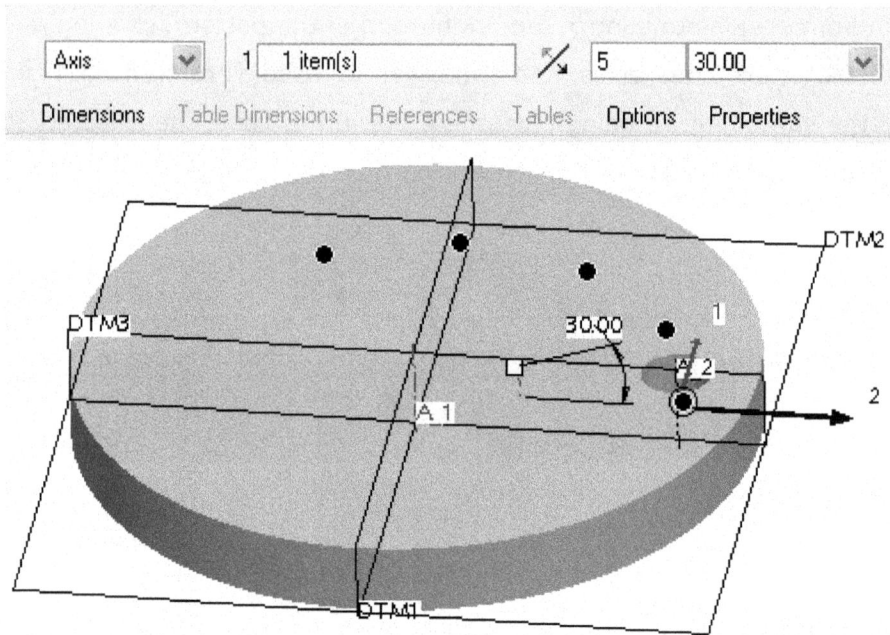

Fig. 16-18
Axis pattern definition

An alternate option for controlling the array is to activate the ◺ **Angular extent**
icon in the dashboard. This allows you to specify the number of members to be
equally spaced around a zone up to 360° from the start, as shown in Figure 16-19.

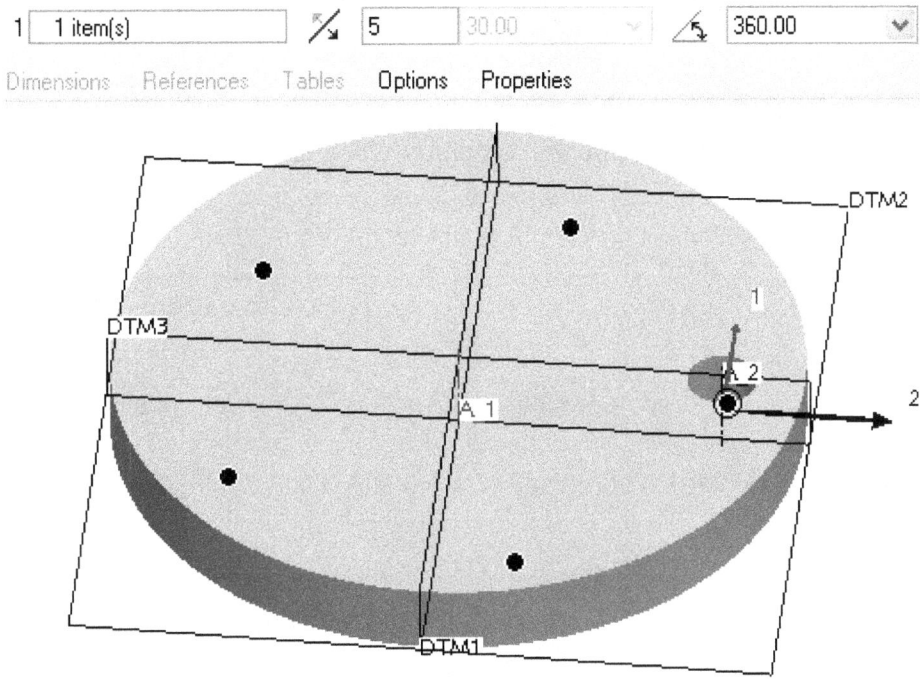

Fig. 16-19
Axis pattern with angular extent

As with the previous pattern types, a second direction may be specified, individual dimensions may be incremented, and individual members may be omitted, as shown in Figure 16-20, by making the appropriate selections in the dashboard and model.

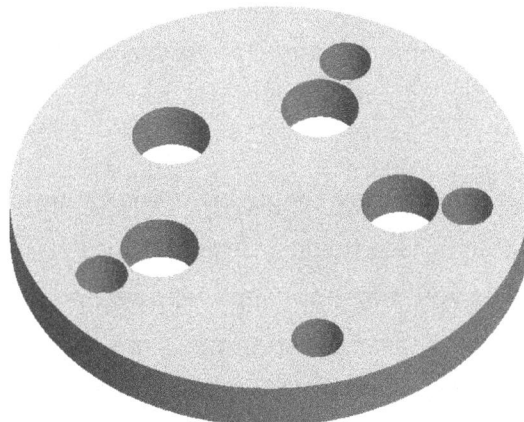

Fig. 16-20
Multi-directional, multi-dimensional Axis pattern with omitted members

Fill

Figure 16-21 shows a plate with a single hole in the center. A Fill pattern can be defined so that the pattern members completely fill a sketched boundary.

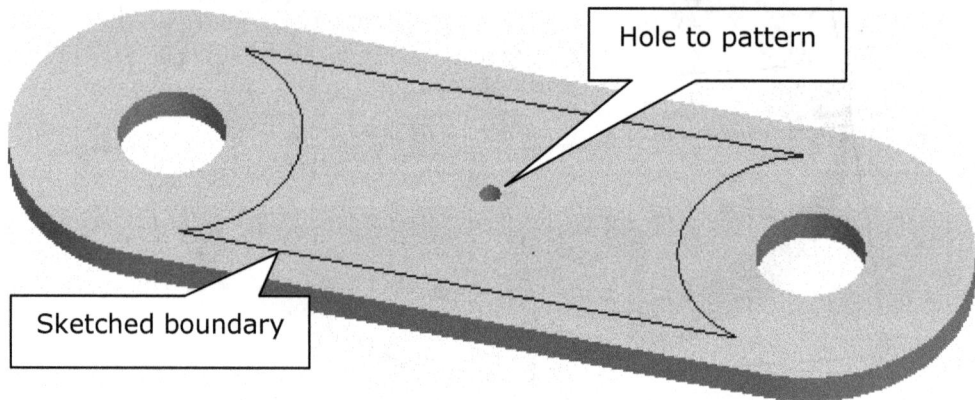

Fig. 16-21
Plate to fill will holes

After selecting the Fill pattern type and the reference sketch, Pro/ENGINEER will automatically fill the boundary with members with a specified pattern shape, as shown in Figure 16-22. You may also specify the spacing between members, the distance up to the sketched boundary a member may be placed (a negative value will place a member outside the boundary, if possible) and the angle of the entire pattern, relative to the part.

As with other pattern types, you may toggle off the creation of individual members by clicking on the ● solid dot place holder, turning it into an ○ open circle. But unlike other pattern types, you may not select feature dimensions to increment, as the members are created in all directions, and you may not specify the total number of pattern members. Pro/ENGINEER will automatically fill the boundary, based on the settings you choose.

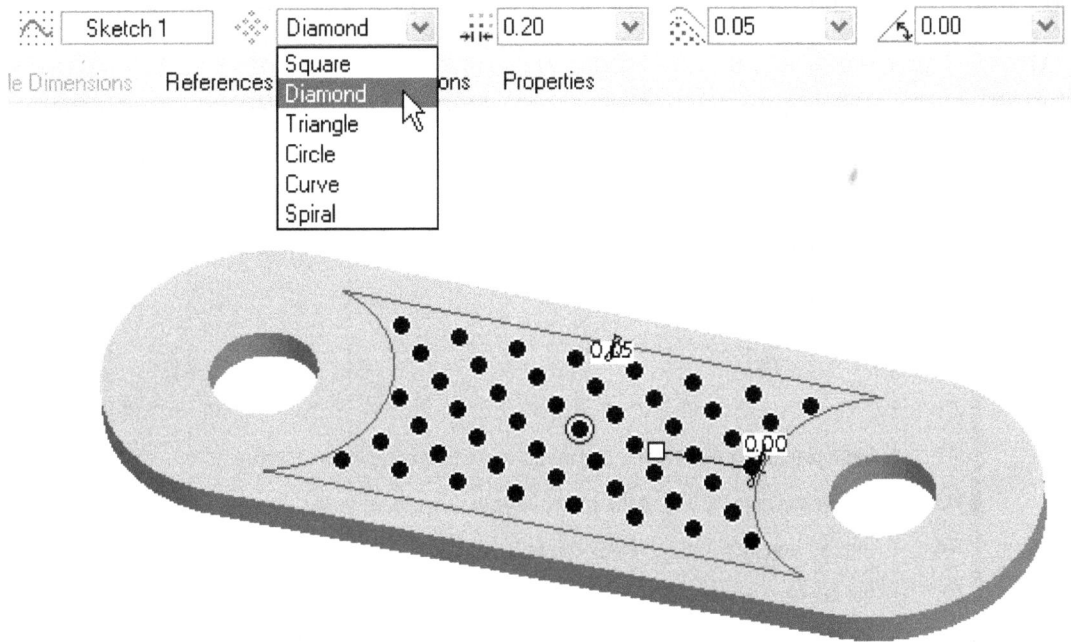

Fig. 16-22
Array of pattern members filling a sketched boundary

Table

Figure 16-23 shows a hole to be patterned.

Fig. 16-23
Feature to pattern

Table patterns are driven by dimensions only. After selecting the dimensions to control (in this case, the .18 and .16 dimensions), select the Edit **Edit** tab from the dashboard. This will open the Pro/TABLE text editor, as shown in Figure 16-24.

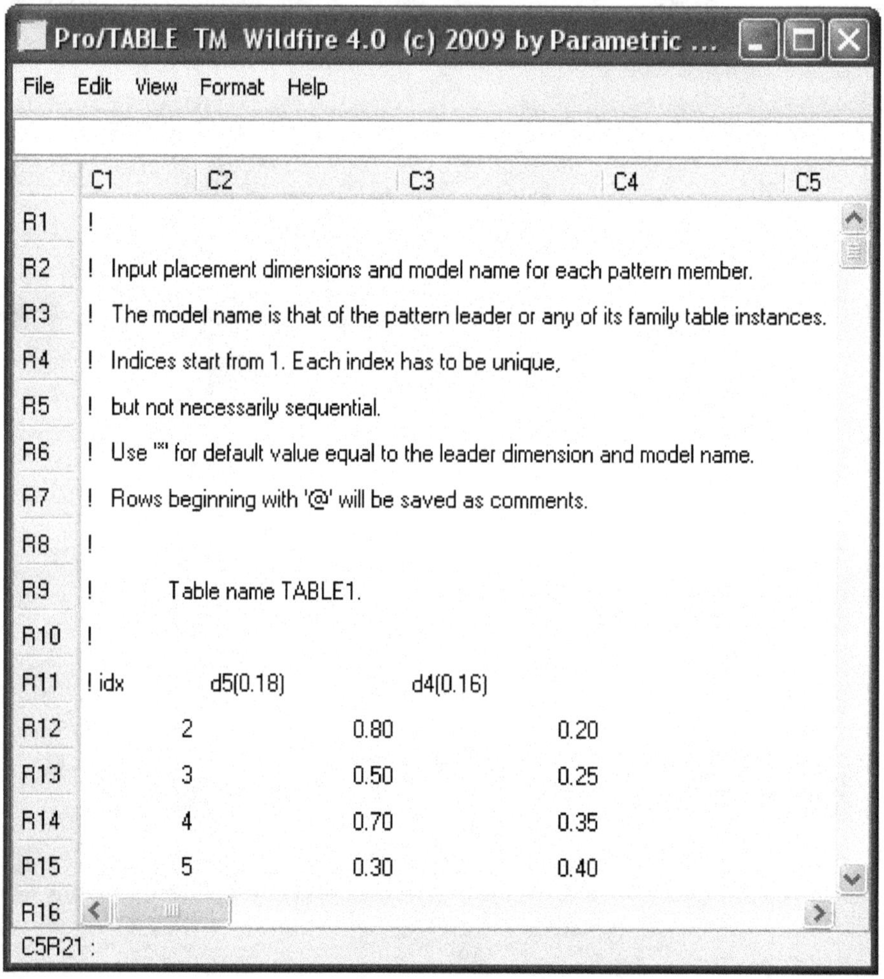
Pro/TABLE TM Wildfire 4.0 (c) 2009 by Parametric ...
File Edit View Format Help
C1 C2 C3 C4 C5
R1 !
R2 ! Input placement dimensions and model name for each pattern member.
R3 ! The model name is that of the pattern leader or any of its family table instances.
R4 ! Indices start from 1. Each index has to be unique,
R5 ! but not necessarily sequential.
R6 ! Use "*" for default value equal to the leader dimension and model name.
R7 ! Rows beginning with '@' will be saved as comments.
R8 !
R9 ! Table name TABLE1.
R10 !
R11 ! idx d5(0.18) d4(0.16)
R12 2 0.80 0.20
R13 3 0.50 0.25
R14 4 0.70 0.35
R15 5 0.30 0.40
R16
C5R21 :

Fig. 16-24
Table pattern definition

With all other pattern types, you specify the increment values of the dimensions or spacing between members, but with Table patterns you specify the actual dimension of each member from the reference used to create the original feature. This allows you to create an array of features that do not follow a sequential pattern, as shown in Figure 16-25.

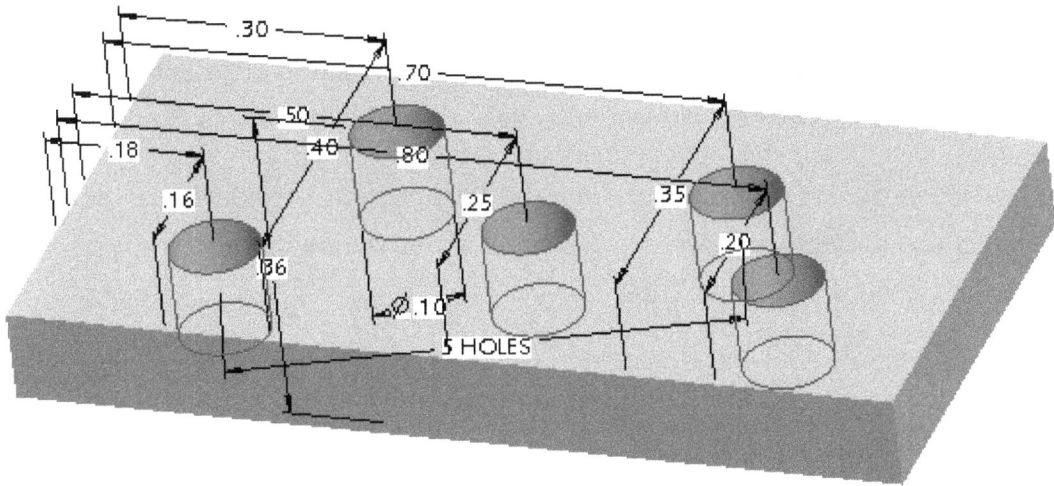

Fig. 16-25
Array of non-sequential features

Reference

Figure 16-26 shows a cylindrical feature on the left that has been patterned, creating a total of three members. A coaxial hole and two rounds have also been added to the model. If our intent was to have all three cylinders include the hole and rounds, it would have been best to select all four features together, when creating the pattern.

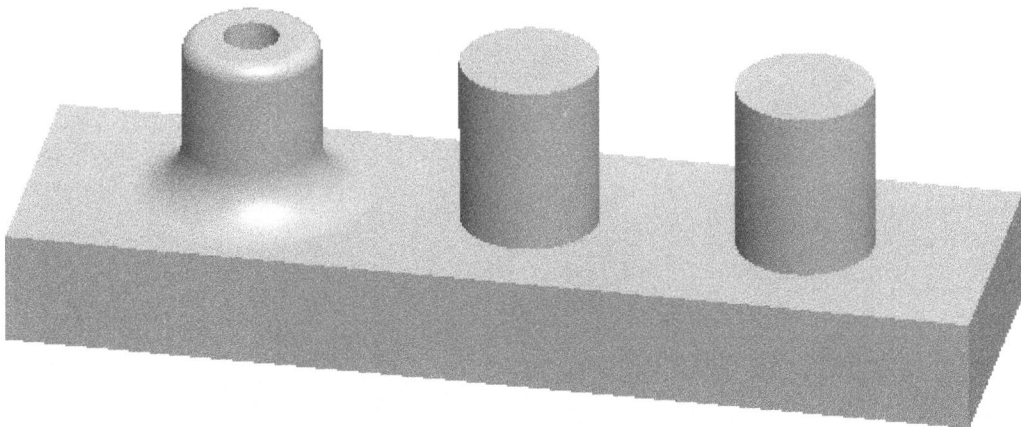

Fig. 16-26
Multiple features to pattern

Reference pattern allows us to pattern features using previous pattern definition information. This will only work however, if the parents of the additional features are included in the previous pattern. To create a pattern of the hole, simply select

the hole, then the ▦ **Pattern** icon from the Construction Toolbar. Since the parent (cylinder) was patterned, Reference pattern is set as the default pattern type in the dashboard, as shown in Figure 16-27.

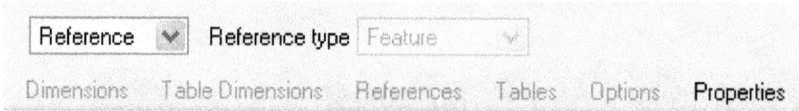

Fig. 16-27
Reference pattern dashboard

Notice that by using this pattern type, additional references or dimensions are not necessary. The resulting geometry is shown in Figure 16-28.

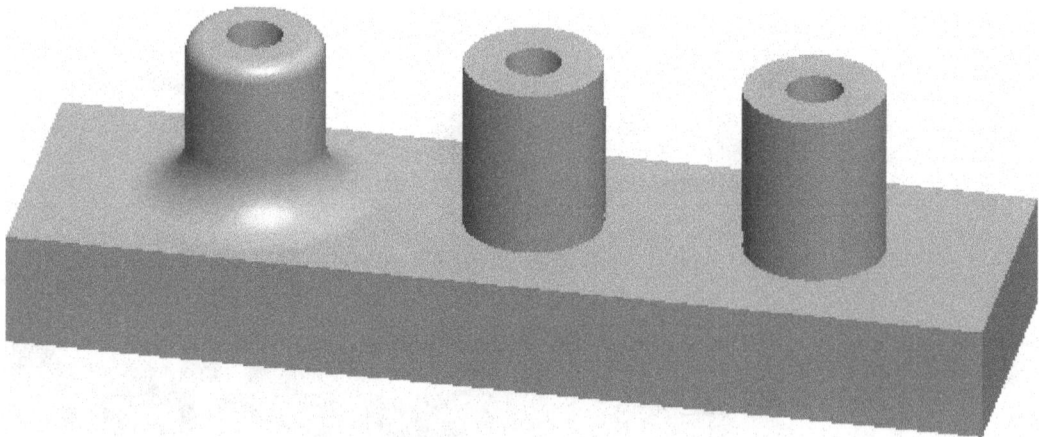

Fig. 16-28
Features created using Reference pattern

As with other pattern types, it is possible to turn off the creation of individual pattern types, as shown in Figure 16-29.

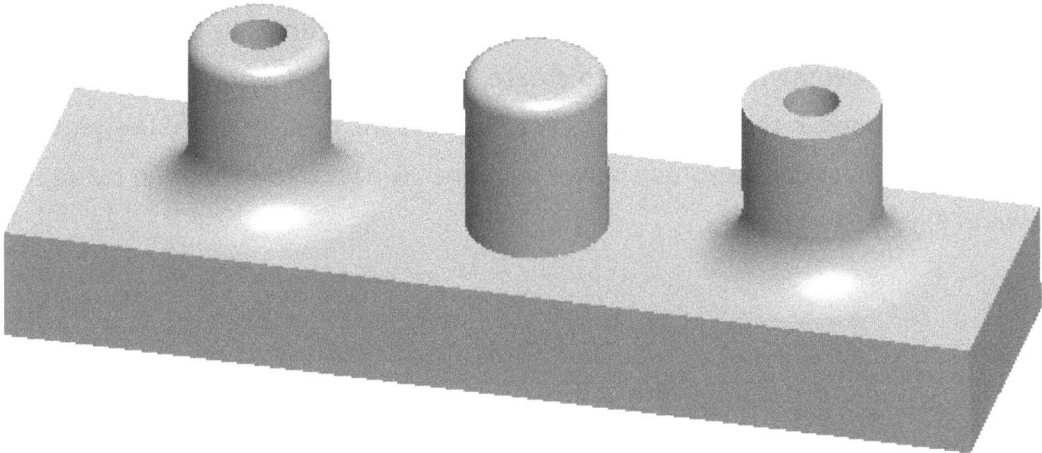

Fig. 16-29
Reference patterns with selective member creation

Curve

The Fill pattern option includes a Curve shape definition, which places pattern members along the perimeter of the boundary definition; however, this requires a closed boundary. When an array of features needs to be created along an open trajectory, as shown in Figure 16-30, a Curve pattern may be used.

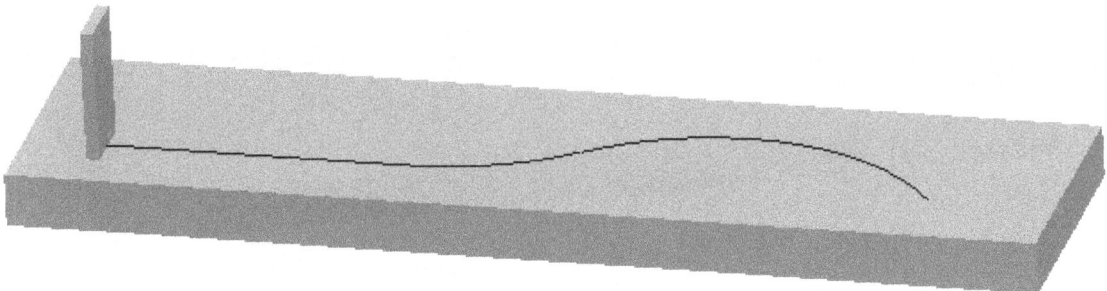

Fig. 16-30
Feature to be patterned along a trajectory

You may reference an existing sketch, or create a new sketch to define the trajectory, and similar to the Axis pattern type, you may select the ⬚ **Spacing** icon to specify the distance between members along the curve, or the ⬚ **Number** icon to specify how many members to create, evenly spaced along the curve. Among the settings in the Options tab, you may set the orientation of the pattern members to remain constant, as shown in Figure 16-31, or to follow the curve, as shown in Figure 16-32.

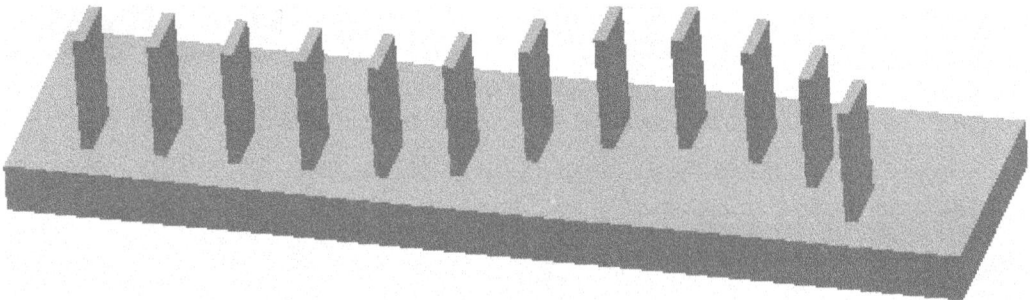

Fig. 16-31
Constant member orientation

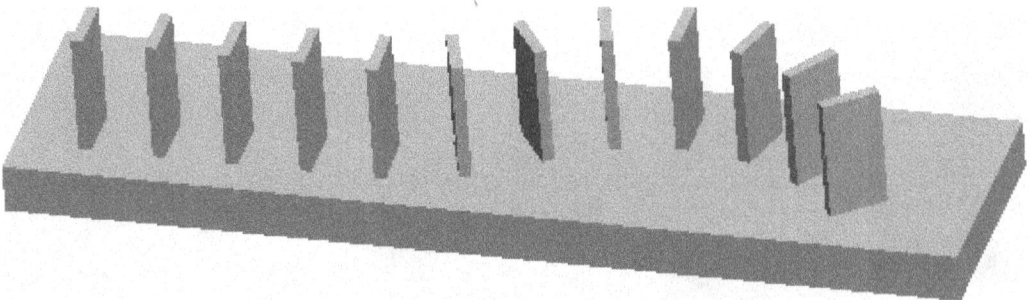

Fig. 16-32
Member orientation following the curve

Chapter 17

Removing Geometry

Hide

Suppress

Delete

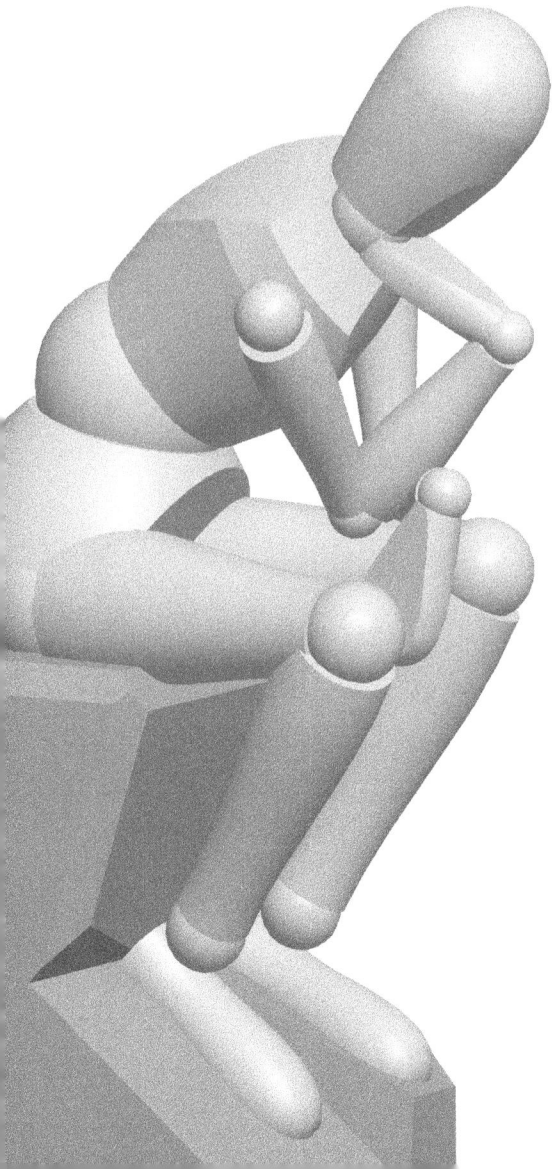

As you build your parts and assemblies, there will be times that you no longer wish to have certain aspects of the geometry. You may choose to remove these portions temporarily or permanently.

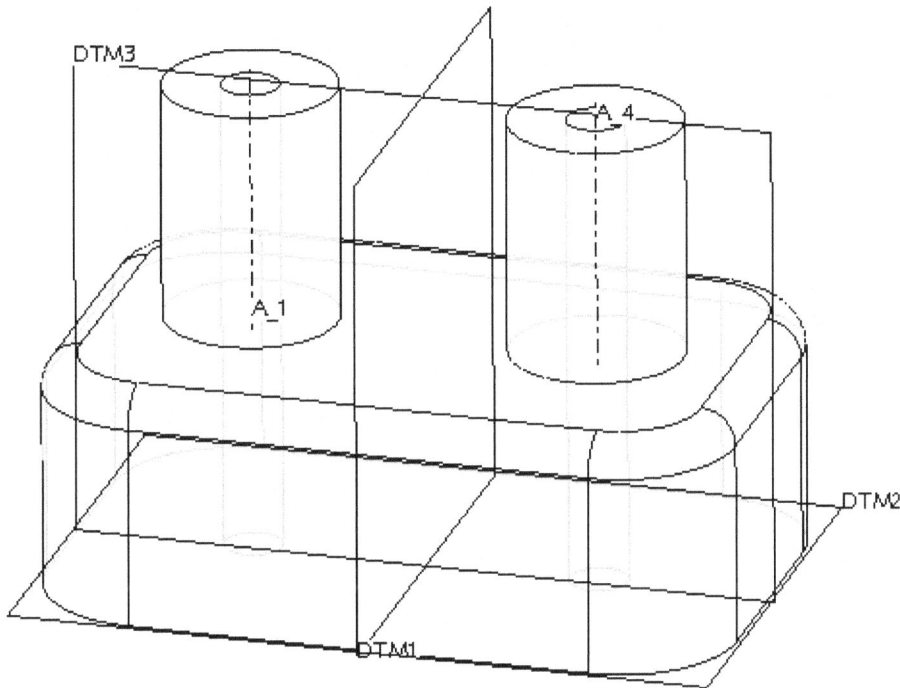

Fig. 17-1
Part with solid and non-solid geometry

Hide

If you have geometry that you need for your design, but you want to temporarily remove them from the display, you may choose to **Hide** them. When working on a part, you may hide non-solid geometry only. This means that any datum plane or axis shown in Figure 17-1 may be hidden, but not the extruded shapes or rounds, as they are solid features. Of course, if all you wanted to do was blank all axes or datum planes, you could select the ⌖ **Axis Display** or ▱ **Plane Display** icons from the Main Toolbar to toggle their display on and off, but this will control all of the axes at the same time. To individually blank features, select the feature, hold down the **RMB**, and select **Hide**.

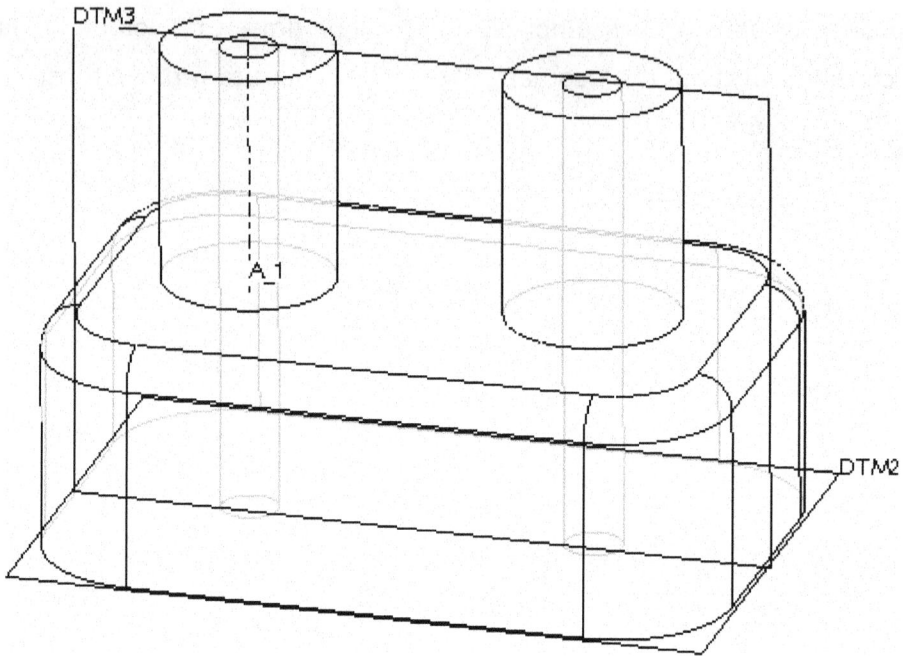

Fig. 17-2
Hidden geometry

In the example shown in Figure 17-2, the axes were created when the cylindrical shapes were extruded, they are not individual features. In order to **Hide** the axis, the protrusion can be selected, but since the **Hide** functionality only works on non-solid entities, only the axis will be hidden. Also, DTM1, as shown in Figure 17-1, was used as a mirroring plane to create one of the cylinders, but was still able to be blanked by using the **Hide** command. This works by leaving the geometry in place, but turning it invisible.

Hide is intended to be a temporary setting, to allow you to better visualize your designs, while you are creating and editing them. In fact, you may **Hide** several items, but the next time you open the file, you will find that all of those items have been returned to their original un-hidden state. To retain the hide status of your features, you may select **View** > **Visibility** > **Save Status** from the menu. As long as you remember to save the file before exiting, the model will retain your hidden status.

When working in an assembly, you may use the **Hide** function to control the display of non-solid geometry (planes, axes, points, coordinates, quilts), but you may also hide entire components, including entire subassemblies. Again, this works by turning the parts and subassemblies invisible. This will allow you to work on an area of the assembly which may be obscured from view. By using the **Hide** function, you may temporarily create a clear view of your work, without affecting the parent/child relationships of any of the components.

Unhide

Unhide simply returns items to be visible, but since hidden items are invisible, it is impossible to pick them from the graphics area again, but you may select them from the Model Tree, allowing you to then hold down the **RMB** and select **Unhide**. To display all previously hidden items, you may select **View** > **Visibility** > **Unhide All** from the menu.

Suppress

Like **Hide**, **Suppress** is intended to be a temporary setting, but unlike **Hide**, it may be used on both solid and non-solid features. It also differs from **Hide** in that, it removes the geometry from the model. Because **Suppress** removes the geometry from the model, it may be used to temporarily remove rounds, chamfers, and other features from a model to determine the mass properties (see Chapter 25) of a model prior to machine operations. You may also like to see what result completely removing a feature would have on your model, without permanently losing the feature definition.

Be aware however, that since **Suppress** removes geometry, it will have an effect on parent/child relationships. If you suppress a parent, the children will also be suppressed, and you will receive a warning like the one shown in Figure 17-3, with each of the affected children highlighted in the Model Tree.

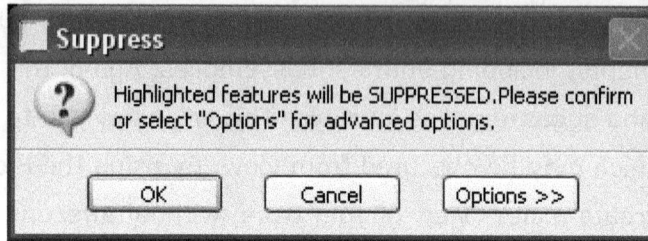

Fig. 17-3
Child suppression warning

There may be times however, that you do not wish the children to be suppressed. In that case, you may select the **Options** tab in the warning window. This will open the Children Handling dialog box as shown in Figure 17-4.

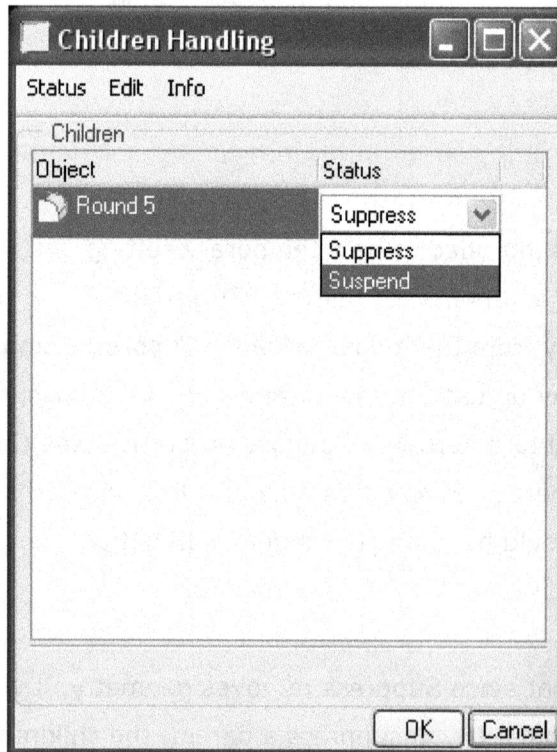

Fig. 17-4
Children Handling dialog box

Depending on the parent being suppressed, several objects may be listed. By choosing **Suspend** on any of the objects, you are telling Pro/ENGINEER to attempt to create that object without the parent. In some cases, this will work transparently, and in others it will not. For example, the Round 5 features shown in Figure 17-4 is the small round that goes around the perimeter of the part shown in Figure 17-1. It was created after the corner rounds, by selecting one of the straight edges, and allowing the round to be created as a tangent continuous chain. When one or more of the corner rounds is suppressed, as is the case in Figure 17-4, the original chain is interrupted. By choosing to **Suspend** the perimeter round, we are telling Pro/ENGINEER to construct the feature if possible. In this case, the feature can be constructed, as shown in Figure 17-5.

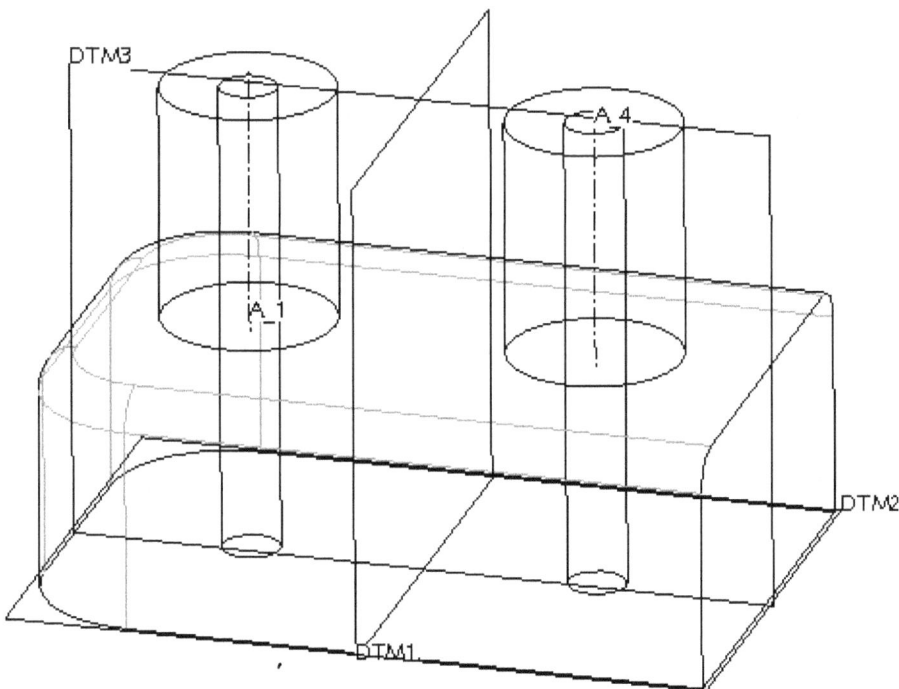

Fig. 17-5
Two corner rounds suppressed

Other times however, the suspended feature may not be constructed, due to the fact that too many of its references (parents) are no longer available. In which case, you must reroute or edit the definition of the feature (see Chapter 18).

Resume

Since **Suppress** only temporarily removes geometry, you may 'un-suppress' a feature by selecting it from the Model Tree, holding down the **RMB**, and selecting **Resume**.

By default, Pro/ENGINEER does not display suppressed items in the Model Tree, so in order to select them, you must change the settings of the tree by selecting from the top of the tree: **Settings > Tree Filters**. This will open the Model Tree Items dialog box, as shown in Figure 17-6.

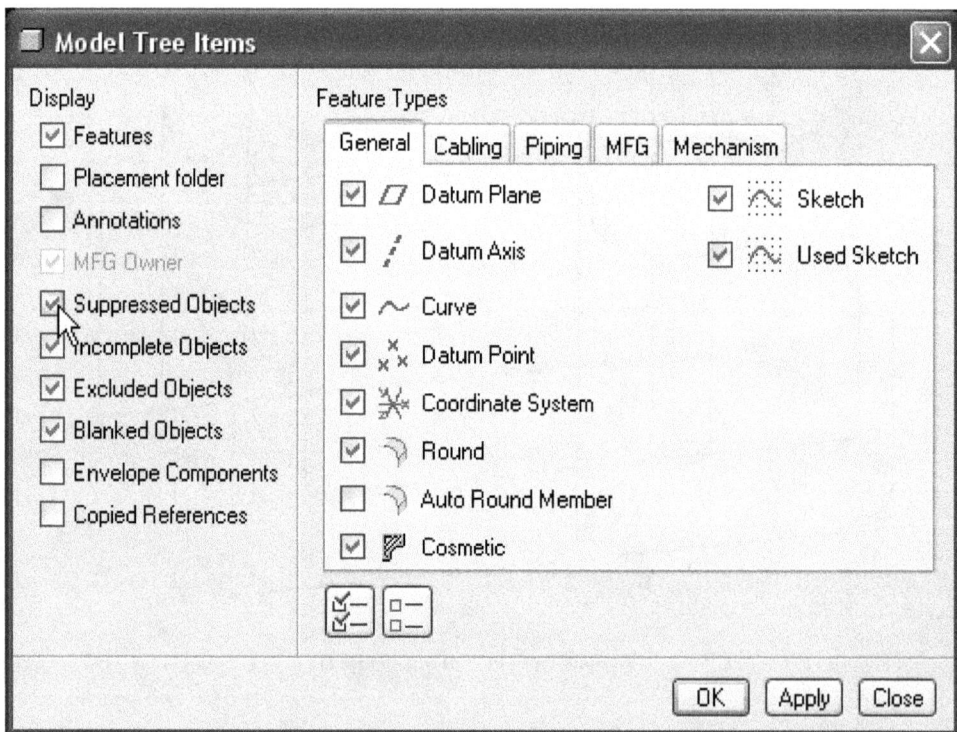

Fig. 17-6
Model Tree Items visibility

Delete

Features may be permanently removed by selecting a feature, then from the menu, selecting **Edit** > **Delete** > **Delete**. You may also select **Delete to End of Model** which will delete the selected feature(s) and all of the features that occur after them, or **Delete Unrelated Items** which will delete all the features in the model, except for the selected feature(s) and their parents.

Caution should be used with the **Delete** command, because there is no 'un-delete' command. If you delete a feature, but immediately realize that you would like the feature back, select the ↶ **Undo** icon.

Making Changes

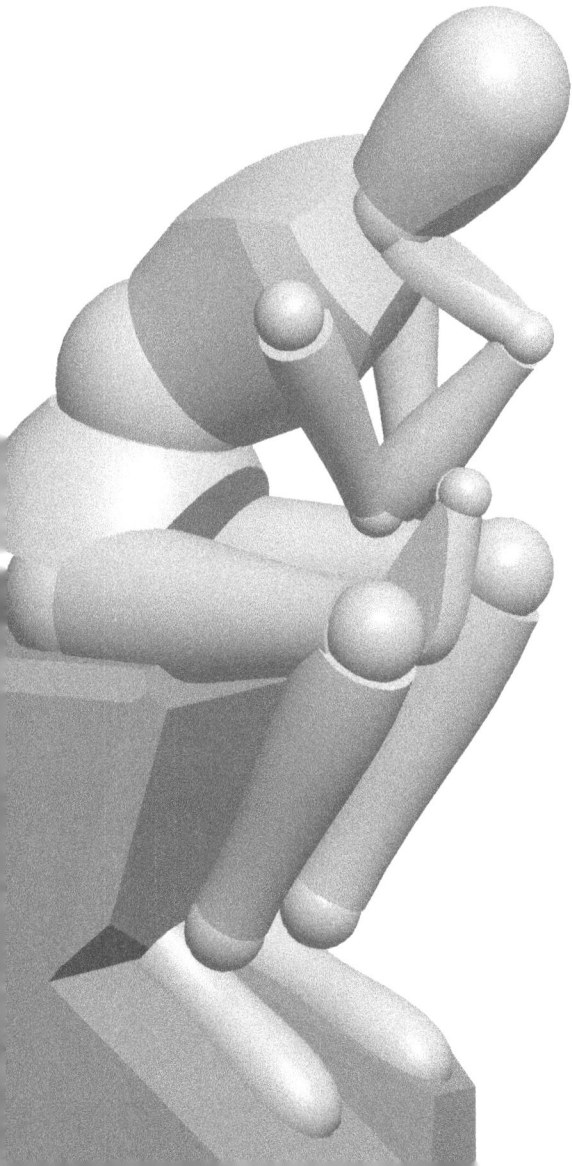

No matter how carefully you specify your features and dimensions, you will at some point want to change them. This is not a bad thing; in fact, one of the benefits to using Pro/ENGINEER over many other CAD applications is that you do not need to input the exact values for data at the time it is created. For example, if you know that you want to create a brick shape, as shown in Figure 18-1, but don't really know exactly how big to make it, go ahead and create your shape and give it any dimensions that simply 'look good'.

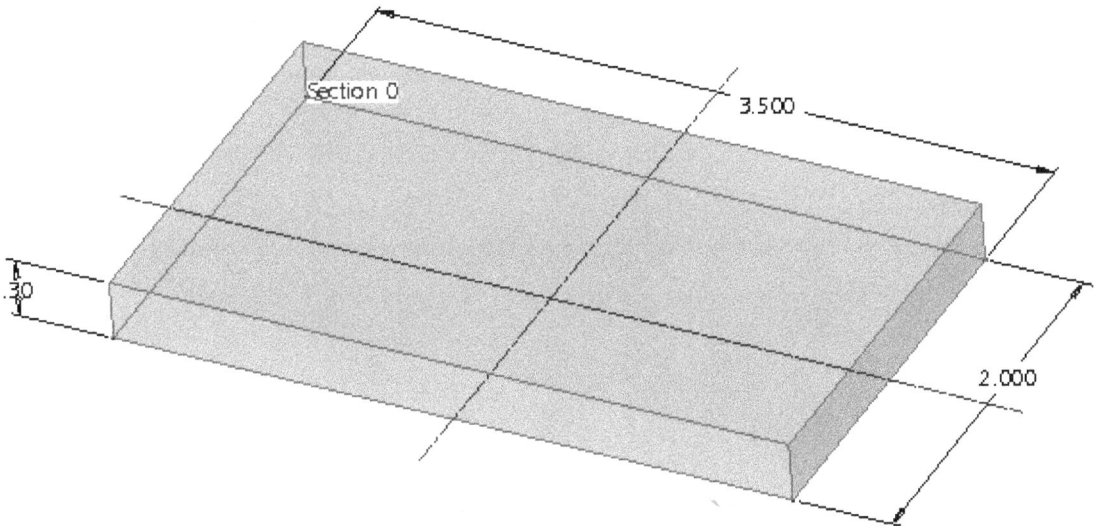

Fig. 18-1
Initial design

Edit (formerly known as Modify)

If at any point now, or even months or years from now, we decide that we need a different value for any of the dimensions, simply select the feature (in this case the brick shaped extrusion), hold down the **RMB**, and select **Edit**. This will display all of the dimensions used to create the feature, as shown in Figure 18-1. To change a value, select it, hold down the **RMB** and select **Value** as shown in Figure 18-2.

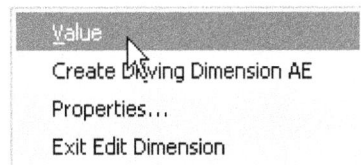

Fig. 18-2
Dimension edit menu

You may also simply double-click on the dimension. This will
open a value box, as shown in Figure 18-3. You may enter
any value you wish in the box, and if you have been editing
other dimensions, a pull down menu may be available for
you to select previously entered dimensions. Once you close
your Pro/ENGINEER session however, this clipboard of
values will be cleared.

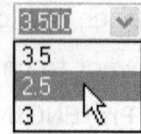

Fig. 18-3
Value box

After the dimension has been modified, it will turn from yellow to green and resize
itself, but the model will still be set at its original size, as shown in Figure 18-4.

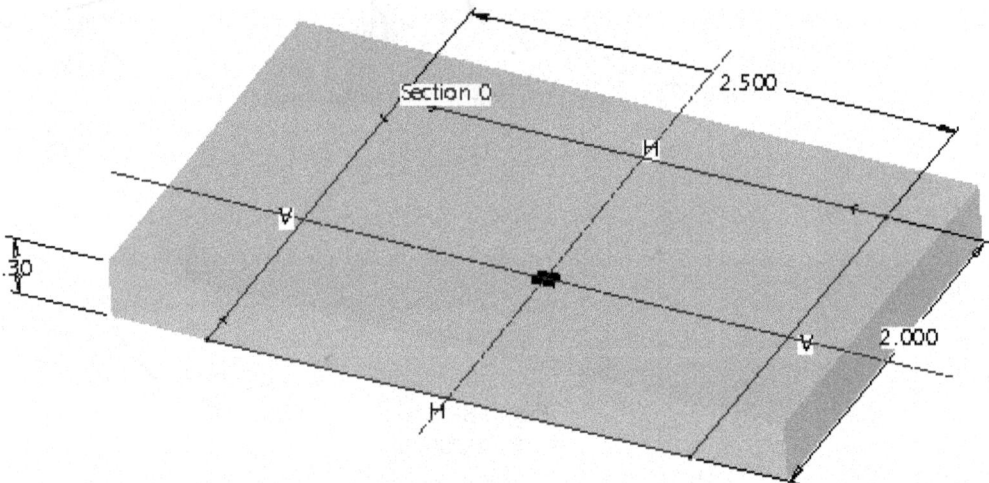

Fig. 18-4
Modified values

To update the three-dimensional model, select the ⬚ **Regenerate** icon. This will
force the three-dimensional model to be updated, or actually rebuilt if you will, from
all of its dimensions, parameters, and settings. Many Pro/ENGINEER beginners ask if
there is an 'auto regenerate' setting, and the answer is **No**, nor do you want one. In
a model as simple as the one shown in Figure 18-4, having the model rebuild itself
after every modification to the dimensions is not a big deal. If however, you are
modifying four dimensions of the first or second feature of a thousand feature

model, you do not want Pro/ENGINEER automatically regenerating a thousand features four times. Instead, you are able to make as many changes to the dimensions as you wish, then regenerate the entire model once, when you see fit. Just remember that you must regenerate the model in order to see the results of any dimension modification.

Edit Definition (formerly known as Redefine)

The **Edit** command will allow you to modify any dimension, but if you want to change more than a value, you may use **Edit Definition**. In simplest terms, **Edit Definition** allows you to go back in time, to the point at which a feature was created. All of the features that where created later in the Model Tree are suspended, and all of the feature's controls, such as its sketch and its type (extrusion or revolve, adding or removing material, etc.) are back to the state at which they were specified. For example, Figure 18-5 shows a cylindrical extrusion being created, along with its dashboard.

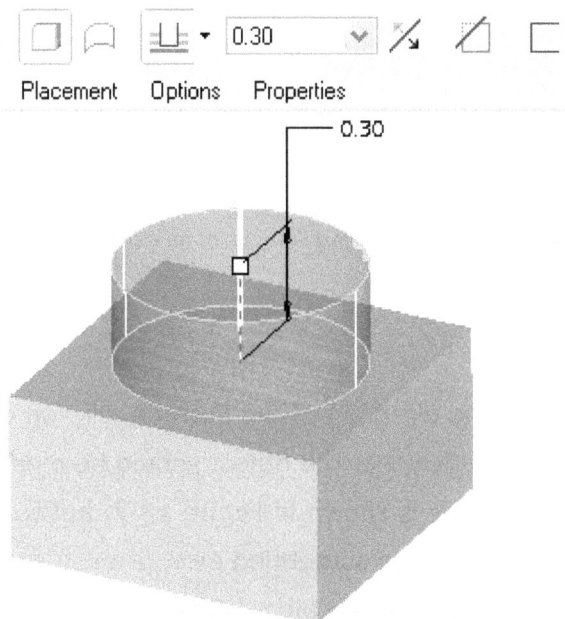

Fig. 18-5
Dashboard and preview of cylindrical feature creation

When a feature (or even a component in an assembly) is selected, then **Edit
Definition** is selected with the **RMB**, that feature's dashboard or dialog box is
opened, and the geometry preview is displayed, exactly as it did when the feature
was being created. By simply changing the controls in the dashboard, or even the
internal sketch, you may change anything you wish about the feature, as shown in
Figure 18-6.

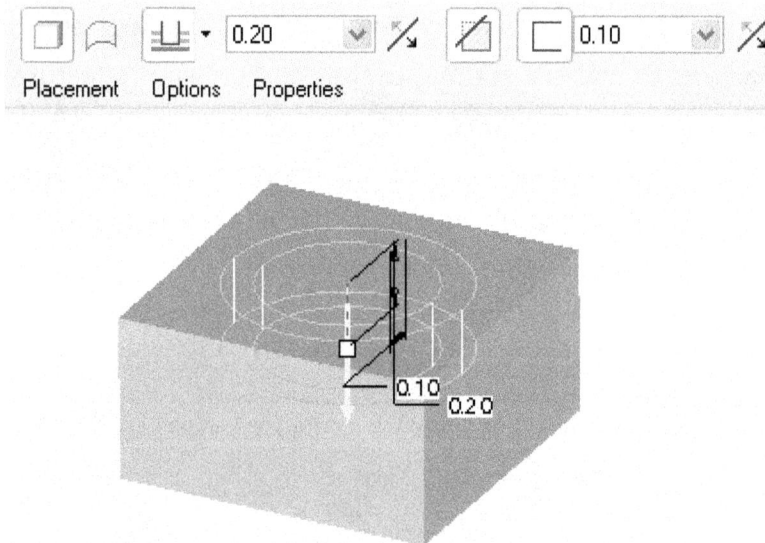

Fig. 18-6
Modifying the dashboard settings of an existing feature

In Figure 18-6, we flipped the direction of the **Extrude**, clicked on the **Remove
Material** icon, and even specified that the object should be made as a **Thickened
Sketch**. The resulting geometry is shown in Figure 18-7, but we could have also
changed the sketch from a circle to something else, or even redefined the sketch to
be created on a different surface of the block, if desired.

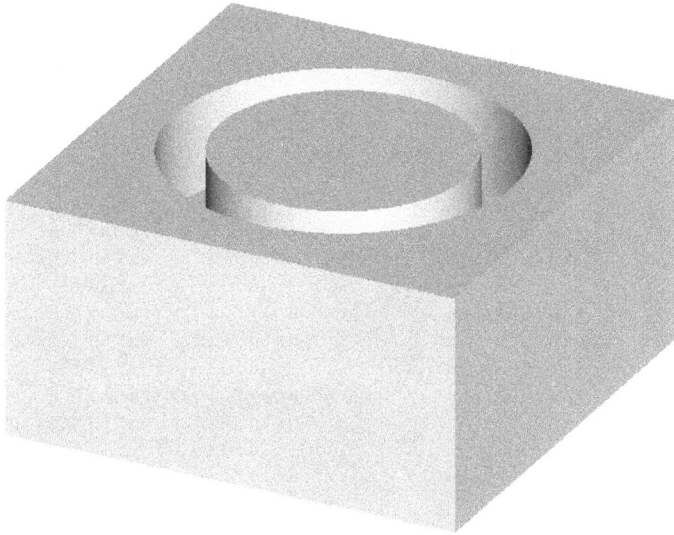

Fig. 18-7
Redefined feature

If you ever find yourself asking the question, *"How do I get back to the point where...?",* the answer is always **Edit Definition**. After the feature's definition has been modified, Pro/ENGINEER will then automatically resume all of the features that occur after it in the Model Tree. Keep in mind that if you change a feature that has children, the children may also be modified as a result. You may also find that the children may fail to regenerate if their parents have changed too much for them to be created the same way as before the change. When this happens, you must address this. (See **Resolving Failures**, later in this chapter.)

Edit References (formerly Reroute)

Simply put, **Edit References** is used to select different references (parents) for a feature. Figure 18-8 shows a cylindrical feature. It was created by selecting the upper surface of one of the rectangular protrusions as its sketching plane, and dimensioned from its edges. There are also several features (hole, chamfer, and round) that are children of the cylinder. If in the design process we decide that the cylinder should be built off of the other rectangular protrusion, we could simply delete it, and create new one, but what would happen to the hole, chamfer, and round? We would need to recreate them as well.

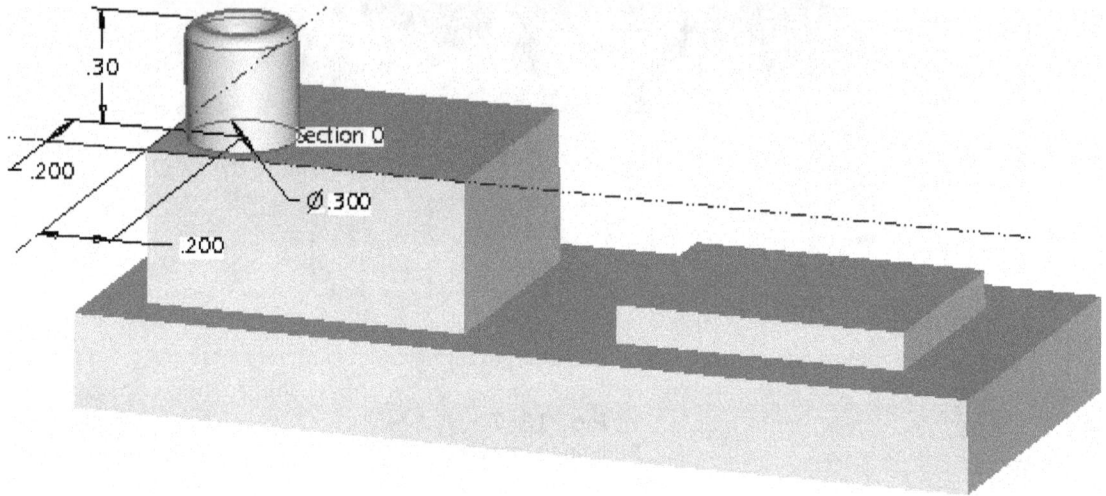

Fig. 18-8
Extrusion with parents and children

To change a feature's parents and keep its children, select the feature, hold down the **RMB**, and select **Edit References**. You will immediately be prompted, "Do you want to roll back the model?" If you answer **Yes**, Pro/ENGINEER will suspend all of the features that occur later in the Model Tree, similar to the way it does during **Edit Definition**. If you answer **No**, all of the model's features will remain intact. Depending on the feature you are attempting to reroute, a menu similar to the one shown in Figure 18-9 will open.

The first reference you selected to create the feature originally will highlight in the graphics window. If you would like to re-use this selection, select **Same Ref** in the menu. If you would like to choose a different reference,

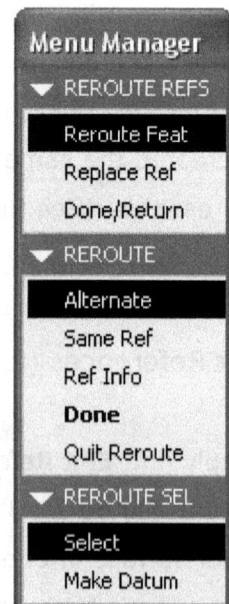

Fig. 18-9
Reroute menu

select **Alternate**, and choose the desired reference. This will be repeated until all of the references have been selected.

In Figure 18-8, the cylindrical extrusion was created using the top of the rectangular extrusion as the sketching plane, one of the default datum planes for orientation, and the left and forward edges of the rectangle for dimension references. Figure 18-10 shows the result of editing the references of the feature to use the other rectangle as a sketching plane, and the right and rear edges as dimensional references.

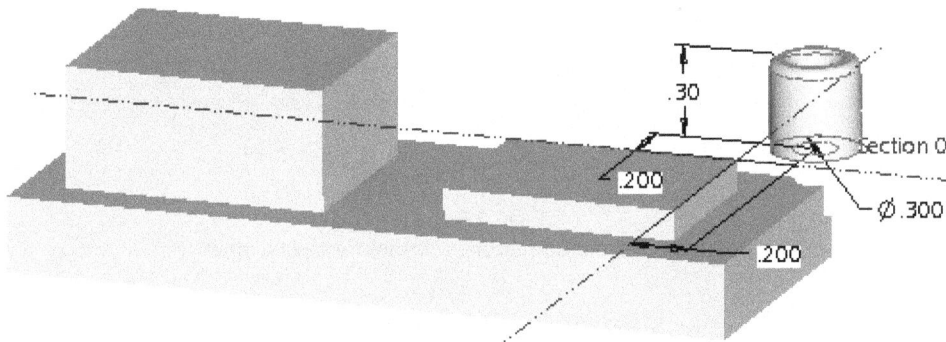

Fig. 18-10
Feature with new references (parents)

When first looking at Figure 18-10, it appears to be an error, (with the floating feature in space) but when you take another look, you will see that it was created exactly the same way it was originally, but with new parents. Originally it was located .200 units to the right and .200 units to the rear of its parents. In the rerouted version, it is still .200 units to the right and .200 units to the rear of its references. It just so happens that we selected an opposite corner from the original for its new references. This is not a problem, since we know that we can simply select the dimensions, and **Edit** them. In this case, we could simply set the values to be -.200 (negative). After the model regenerates, the dimension values will be returned to an absolute value, as shown in Figure 18-11.

Remember, the purpose of using the **Edit References** command is so that you can change any or all of the references (parents) of a feature, while avoiding deleting the feature and recreating it, which may have devastating effects on its children.

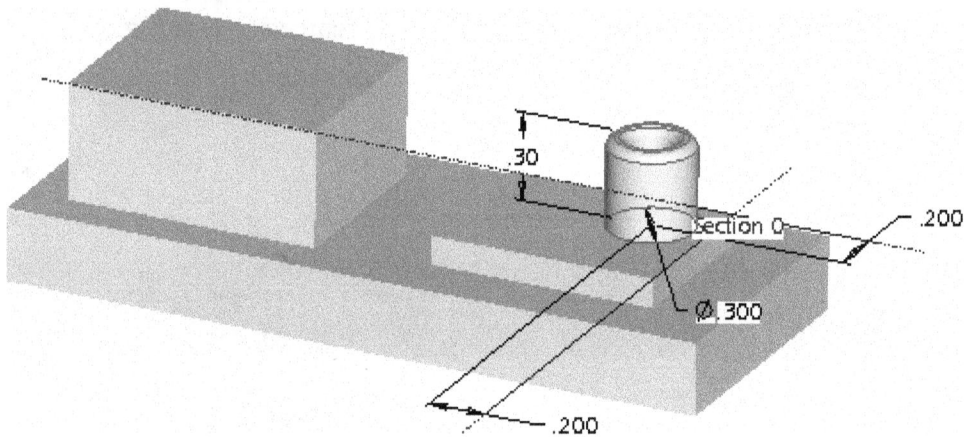

Fig. 18-11
Rerouted and edited feature with unaffected children

Reorder

Figure 18-12 shows a relatively simple part that can be described as a hollow brick, with rounded corners and bottom. It was created with exactly four features; one extrusion, one shell and two rounds.

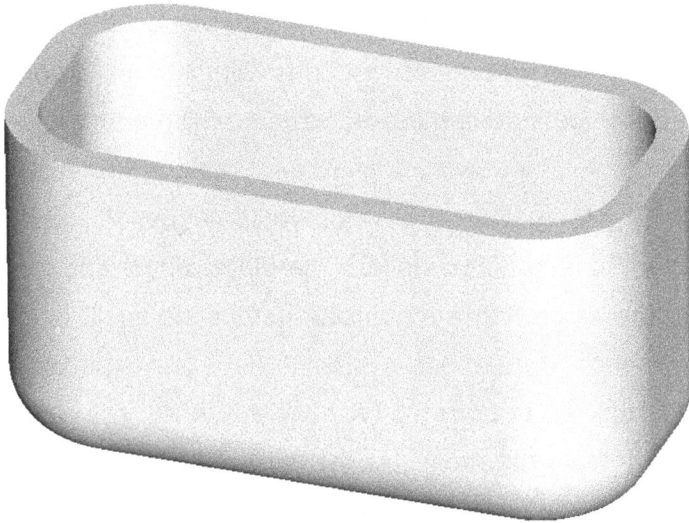

Fig. 18-12
Part with four features

Let's examine how the order in which we create features has an effect on the geometry. Figure 18-13 shows what happens when we create the extrusion, then the shell, then the bottom round (with four edges), then the corner round (with four edges), in that order.

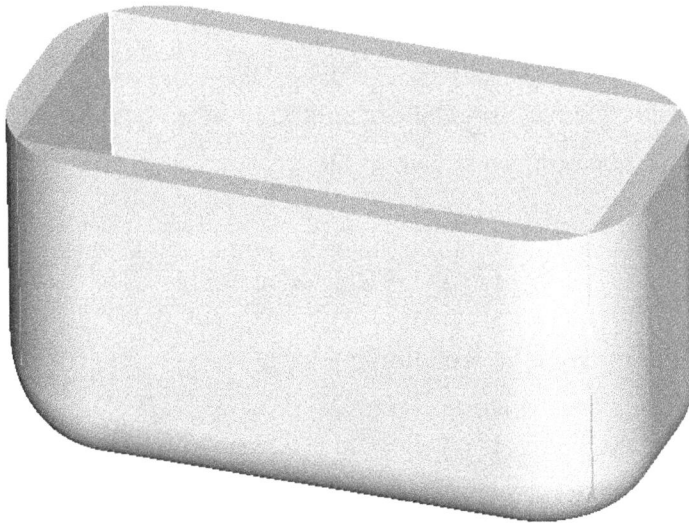

Fig. 18-13
Part with four features

After creating the part shown in Figure 18-13, it is obvious that the shell feature should be created <u>after</u> the round features. This will maintain a nominal wall thickness, and both the outside and inside corners of the part will be rounded at the same time. Of course, you can always delete features and recreate them so they occur at the end of the feature list, but what would happen if you did this to an early feature with children, in a complex model? The more robust and preferred method would be to move the round features to occur before the shell, or the shell feature to occur after the rounds. Remember, Pro/ENGINEER builds parts from its list of features, in order, from top to bottom. To move a feature, select **Edit > Feature Operations > Reorder** from the menu. At the prompt, select the feature or features that you want to move. You will then be prompted to select the existing feature that you want to insert the features before. A few rules to remember are that when moving more than one feature at a time, they must be consecutive features, and you will never be able to **Reorder** a feature to occur before any of its parents.

Rather than using the menu commands a more straight forward approach to reordering features is to simply select the feature(s) in the Model Tree, and while holding down the **LMB**, dragging them to the desired position, as shown in Figure 18-14.

This technique works equally well for moving features both up or down the Model Tree.

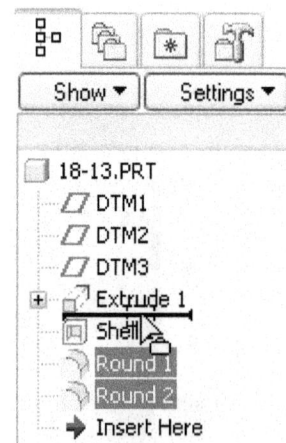

Fig. 18-14
Reordering features with the Model Tree

Insert

If at any time you are building geometry, and realize that it you would like to add a feature(s) in the middle of the Model Tree, you do not need to create the feature, then **Reorder** it as described above. Depending on the feature(s) that may not even be possible. Figure 18-15 shows the same hollow brick shape. It was created with an extrusion then a shell.

Fig. 18-15
Hollow brick

Upon examining it, we realize that perhaps we should have created some rounds before creating the shell. When this occurs, simply select **Edit** > **Feature Operations** > **Insert** from the menu, and select the feature to insert features after. The 'Insert Here' indicator in the Model Tree will move into the desired position, as shown in Figure 18-16, and all of the later features will be suppressed. Each and every feature created now will occur immediately before the indicator, as shown in Figure 18-17.

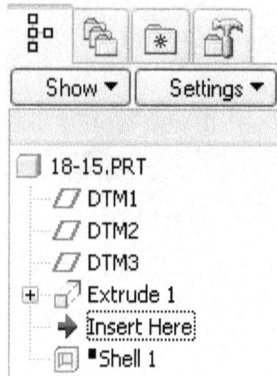

Fig. 18-16
Insert Here indicator

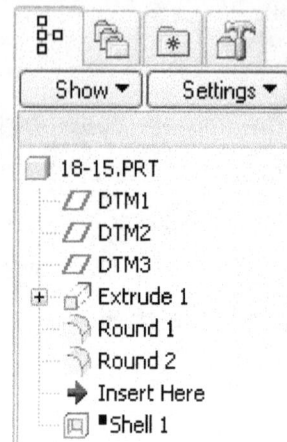

Fig. 18-17
Inserted features

To return to normal operation, select **Edit** > **Feature Operations** > **Insert** > **Cancel** from the menu, or select the indicator in the Model Tree, hold down the **RMB**, and select **Cancel**. You will be prompted to resume all of the features that were suppressed with the Insert command. If you answer **Yes**, they will of course resume. If you answer **No**, they will remain suppressed, but the next feature you create will occur after the suppressed features in the Model Tree. As with the reorder function, a more straight forward approach to the insert function is to simply select the 'Insert Here' indicator in the Model Tree, and drag it to the desired position. You may move the indicator up and down the Model Tree as you wish.

Resolving Failures

There is a misconception among beginners or casual users of Pro/ENGINEER that sometimes the software simply fails, or 'blows up'. **This is completely false.** If a model exists, and no changes are ever made to it, it will never 'fail'. What happens however is that we as Pro/ENGINEER users make changes to existing geometry. Perhaps we deleted a feature with children, making it impossible for the child to be created the same way it was before the change. Perhaps we changed a dimension of an existing feature to an impossible value. Perhaps we (or a co-worker) deleted a part file from our computer network, causing a drawing or assembly that referenced that part to fail to open.

Figure 18-18 shows a cube-shaped extruded feature. The surface of the recessed pocket was used as the sketching plane, and the sketch was dimensioned left to right, from the edge of the other protrusion.

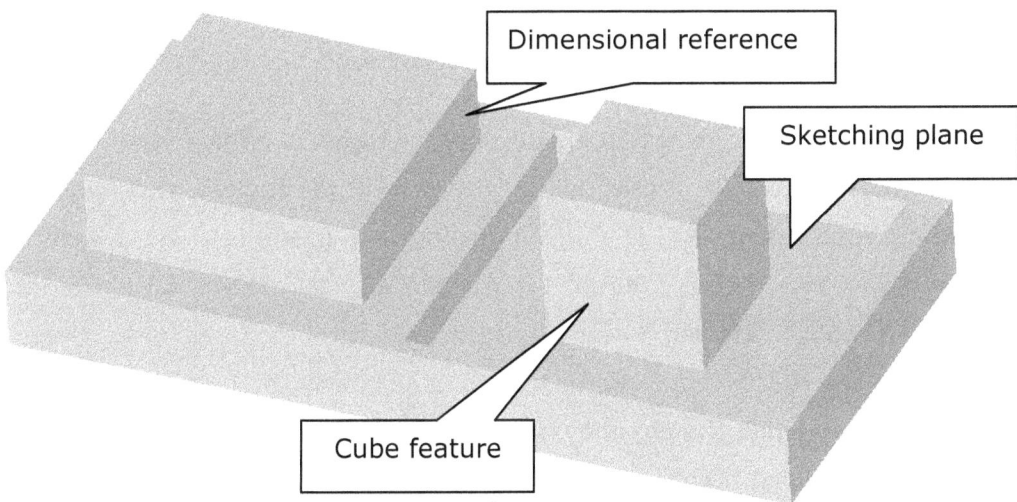

Fig. 18-18
Cube feature with references

There is nothing wrong with this, if this is our design intent. The feature will never fail, no matter how many times we open and close the model, and no matter how many times this model is used in a drawing or an assembly. But what if we were to delete the recessed pocket? By deleting the pocket, we are also deleting the surface that we specified as the sketching plane for the cube. We have destroyed the feature's parent; therefore it will fail to regenerate. When this occurs, a Failure Diagnostic window will appear, as shown in Figure 18-19.

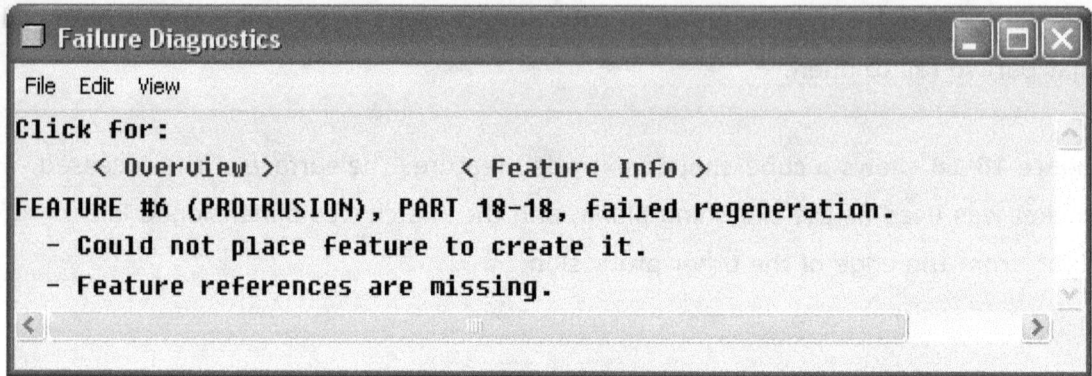

Fig. 18-19
Failure Diagnostics window

Take a few moments to read this, as it will tell you exactly which feature is failing, and why. In this example, it tells us that Feature #6 (a protrusion) cannot be created because it is missing one or more references (parents). That makes perfect sense, because we deleted it. You may also click on **Feature Info** for more detailed information about the failing feature. A Resolve Feature menu will also open, as shown in Figure 18-20. If you are unsure of exactly why the feature failed, or maybe you realize that the change you made was unintentional, you may simply select **Undo Changes**. If you want to explore the failure, you may select **Investigate**, at which point an un-modified version of the model can be opened and examined. Once you decide how you want to 'repair the damage' you can select **Fix Model**, which is exactly the same as if you where to invoke the **Insert** command immediately prior to the failing feature. You may then make changes to any of the earlier created features, if necessary.

Fig. 18-20
Resolve Feature menu

If you would rather change something about the failing feature, you would select **Quick Fix**, which gives you the option to **Redefine**, **Reroute**, **Suppress**, **Clip Suppress** or **Delete** the feature. (The **Clip Suppress** option will suppress the feature and every feature that occurs after it in the Model Tree.)

A beginner's first reaction is to simply delete the failing feature. If you know that you no longer want the feature, or any of its children, then there is nothing wrong with this, but what if it were Feature # 6, with several children, in a thousand feature model? How many children will fail, and how difficult will it be to rebuild your model if you simply deleted every failed feature? The model shown in Figure 18-18 is not too complex to deal with, but you should develop a more professional practice in dealing with geometry failures, such as rerouting the sketching plane of the cube to be the upper surface of the base protrusion, as shown in Figure 18-21.

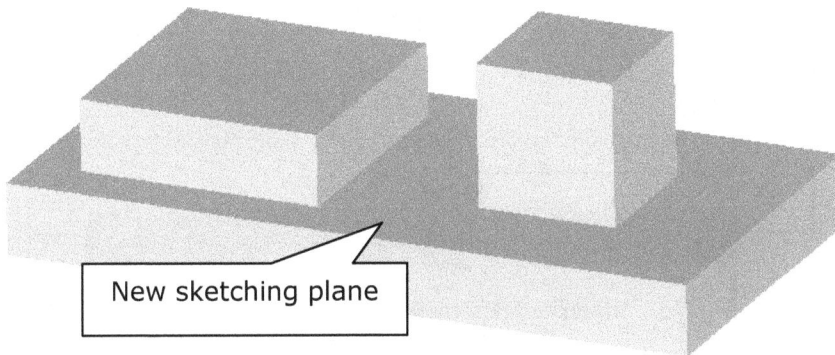

New sketching plane

Fig. 18-21
Failure resolved

In both Figures 18-18 and 18-21, the cube is dimensioned left to right, from the other extrusion. If we were to delete the extrusion, the cube would again lose one of its references, fail, and we would need to resolve it. So what if we decided we absolutely needed a different shape, such as a hexagon, for the first extrusion? Rather than just going ahead and deleting it (which would cause the cube to fail), we have a few options available.

First of all we already know that we can reroute a feature, so before deleting anything perhaps you want to reroute the cube to use different edges for its dimensions. That would break the parent/child relationship between the two, and you would be able to delete the first extrusion if you wish. If however you want to maintain a dimensional relationship between the two features, you could go ahead and edit the definition of the first feature. In our example we want to change the

shape of the first feature to a hexagon, so we will edit the definition of the sketch.
Figure 18-22 shows what happens when we delete the line that forms the edge that
the cube is dimensioned from.

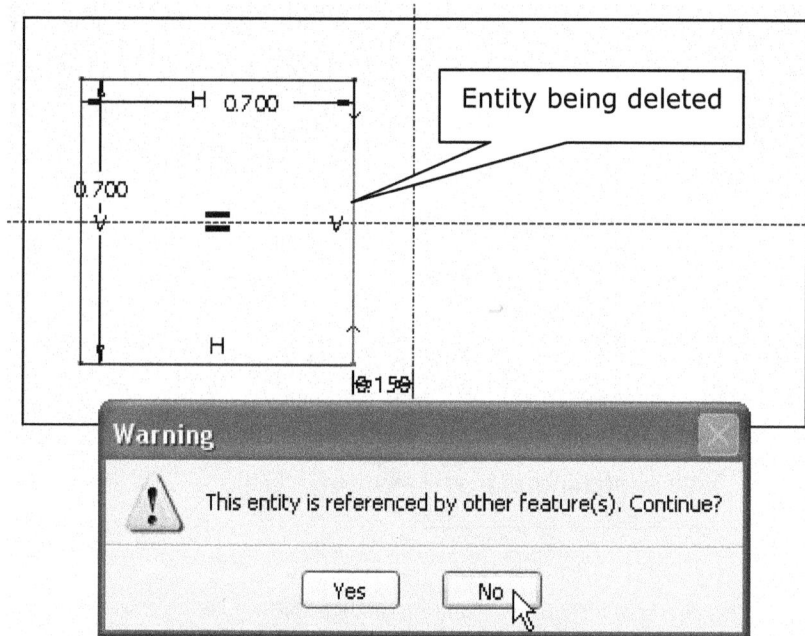

Fig. 18-22
Reference warning message

This is not a failure or error; it is simply warning you that if you delete this line, you
will need to deal with the consequences. If you are confident in your ability to
resolve regeneration failures, then perhaps you would like to select **Yes** and take
your chances. On the other hand you could select **No** to cancel the delete operation.
To accomplish our goal, without causing any failures, we could leave the square
sketch in place, and add additional entities, as shown in Figure 18-23.

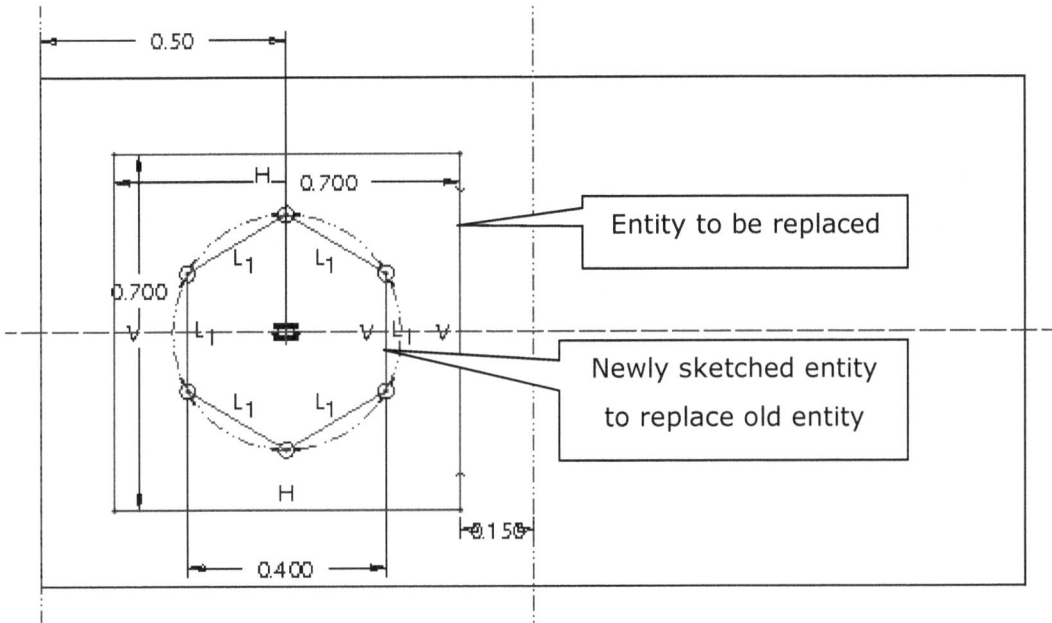

Fig. 18-23
Sketch with additional entities

Rather than deleting the vertical line from the square, we can select **Edit > Replace** from the menu. We are then prompted to select the entity to replace, at which point we would select the vertical line, then at the prompt, select the newly sketched entity to replace the old one. Generally an information window will pop up telling you that the dimensions of the old entity will be lost (in this case, the 0.150), but that also makes sense, since it will not be used any more. We can then continue deleting the other three lines from the square and complete the sketch.

The result is a cube that regenerates without any failures, referenced from the new hexagon shape, as shown in Figure 18-24.

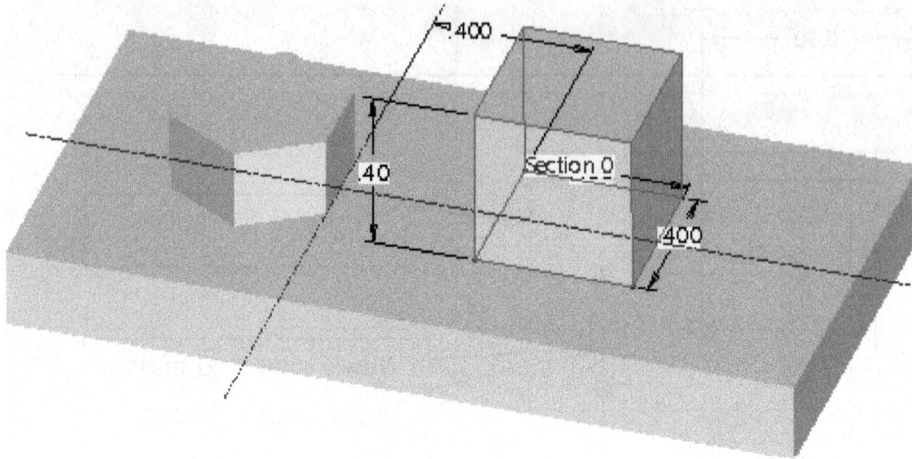

Fig. 18-24
Redefined parent

Assembly Failures

Features will fail for a variety of reasons as discussed earlier, but components in an
assembly will fail for one of only two reasons; failure to place the component and
failure to find the component.

Chapter 23 discusses how components in an assembly are placed and can have
references to each other. If we assemble the shaft of a bolt part to a hole in another
part, we create a necessary relationship between the shaft and the hole. If the hole
in the part were deleted or suppressed (again, by us or our co-workers) the bolt will
lose its assembly reference and will not be able to be assembled. When that
happens, you will see a Failure Diagnostic window similar to the one shown in Figure
18-19, except it will indicate that it failed to regenerate the component placement.
You will then have the same resolve options shown in Figure 18-20, where you can
undo the change, fix the assembly or fix the way the bolt is being assembled.

The other failure which may occur is when you or your co-worker deletes a component from your computer or network, renames the component outside of the assembly or PDM (Product Data Management) system, or moves the component to an unexpected location on your computer or network. In this case, Pro/ENGINEER will indicate that there is a failure to locate the component. When this happens, you may then browse to locate the component yourself. A Pro/ENGINEER assembly file only stores the names of its components, not their file paths. This is why it is important to be sure of the Working Directory, where you are opening files from, and where you are storing them. To avoid this problem, all of your components should be stored in the same location, or you may set up a search path in your *config.pro* file (See chapter 27).

When renaming components, it is best to do so in a PDM system, so that every assembly and drawing that uses that file will be updated to use the new model name. If you find yourself in the situation where someone (even yourself) improperly changed a component name, which causes a 'failure to find component' error, you can temporarily change the component's name back to the original, to be able to open the drawings and assemblies without failures. You may then use the PDM system to change the model name again. If you do not have a PDM system, you must open every single assembly and drawing that uses the model, change the model name in Pro/ENGINEER, then save all of the drawings and assemblies.

Chapter 19

Organizing Models

Feature Order

Feature Names

Groups

Layers

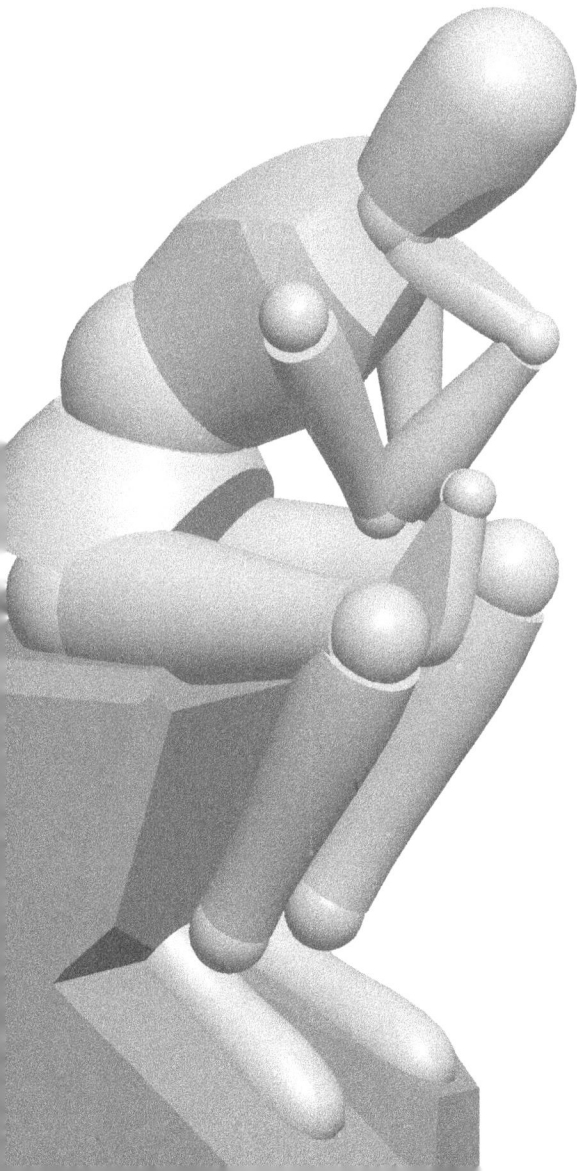

Pro/ENGINEER models may have an infinite number of individual features. To the uninitiated, working with such a model can be a bit overwhelming, but there are several techniques you can use to organize your models. It is important to maintain a well organized model because in most cases, you cannot be certain that you will be the only person to work with it. A well organized model can also be faster to develop and modify, and the original designer's intent is more obvious.

Feature Order

In Chapter 18 we discuss the effect feature order has on how geometry is formed, but feature order also has a direct effect on your speed and efficiency as a designer.

Gross vs. Fine Modeling

Figure 19-1 shows a model of a combined shaft and pulley. Many Pro/ENGINEER beginners fall back to the same techniques they needed to employ when using inferior CAD packages.

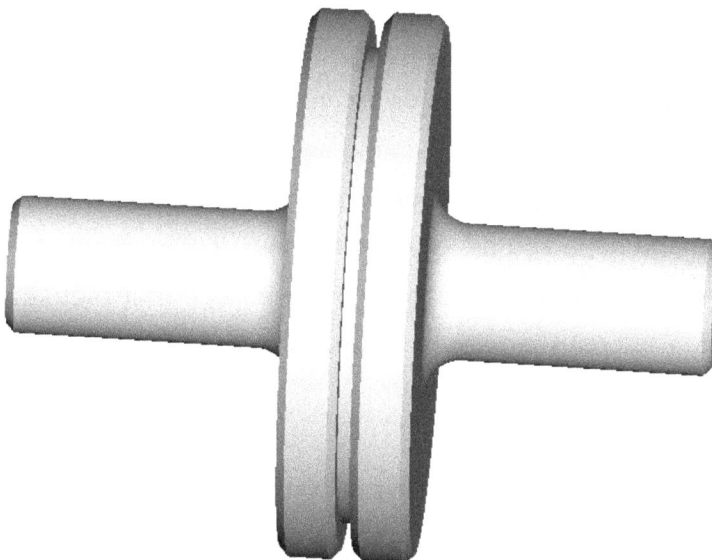

Fig. 19-1
Three dimensional design to be modeled

For example, former AutoCAD® users may try to make this part by revolving the sketch shown in Figure 19-2.

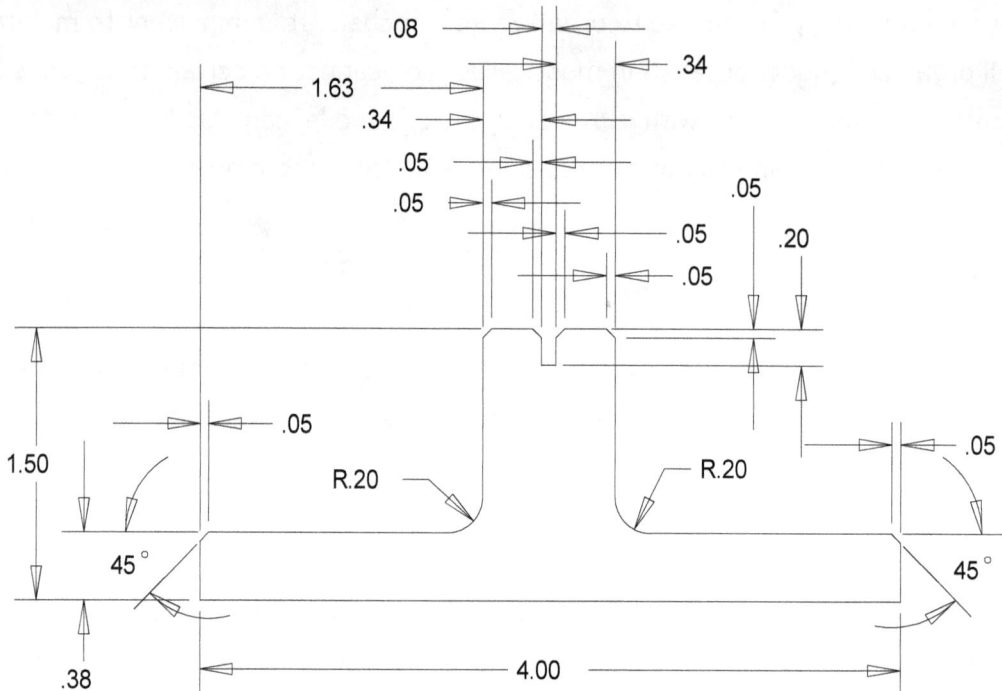

Fig. 19-2
Single, complex sketch

They do this for a few reasons, including the fact that in a program such as AutoCAD®, users need to place a line or arc in the exact location and size as the design requires. Making changes to existing lines requires a lot of time consuming moving, stretching, trimming, and re-dimensioning. The idea is that you place a line in a sketch once, and hope you never have to move it. The other reason beginners try to make a sketch like this is that they falsely believe that they are saving themselves time. They pat themselves on the back for being able to create the model in a single feature.

This approach has several flaws. The first is that the sketch shown in Figure 19-2 requires twenty individual lines and arcs to be created with precision, and dimensioned with at least nineteen individual dimensions. This takes a considerable amount of time to create. The second flaw is that there is no distinction of importance between any of the features. The lines that will become the shaft are just as important as the lines that will form the slot. If any of the dimensions are later modified, the entire sketch is affected simultaneously.

What if we no longer wanted the slot? We can't simply delete it. We would have to go back to the sketch, delete the lines that formed it, but also patch together the top of the sketch where we would be missing lines. What if we wanted to change the .20 radius rounds to .15 x 60° chamfers, or even worse, what if we decide that we do not even want the entire pulley shape at all? We would have wasted a lot of valuable time worrying about the size of each chamfer and round on a feature we end up deleting anyway. Don't believe it? Which do you think would be easier to deal with; 250 well organized sketches with four entities each built in a logical order, or a single sketch with 1000 entities?

A faster and more robust way of creating the same geometry is to follow the example shown in Figure 19-3, where we build up the part, starting with the most basic and important shapes first (this is Gross Modeling) then create more of the features necessary for the function of the part, such as bosses, holes, and slots, then finally the finishing features, such as drafts, chamfers, and shells (this is Fine Modeling).

Fig. 19-3
Geometry created from simple features

This example was created with just a few simple shapes, simple sketches, and minimal dimensions. If we no longer need the slot, it can be easily deleted, and the only downstream affect is that it would also delete the chamfers that were created on its edges (which we would need to delete anyway). The rest of the model remains intact.

Another advantage to placing finishing features (drafts, rounds, and chamfers) at the end of the feature list is that we will not create any unintentional parent/child relationships, such as dimensioning a very important piece of geometry from the edge of a round, or other insignificant features.

Big Rocks First

Another way to think about Gross vs. Fine Modeling is to apply Stephen Covey's (author of <u>The Seven Habits of Highly Effective People</u>) technique for time management. The idea is that with any project or design (represented by a jar), you will need to include some very important items or features (represented by big rocks). You will also have several detail items (represented by pebbles) and several somewhat trivial items that are not important to the function of the device, but a necessary evil of manufacturing, such as draft on molded parts, and inside radii on machined components (represented by sand). In a perfect world, we would like to not even have such items, but never the less, we need them.

If we put a big rock into the jar first, then a whole bunch of sand and pebbles, we may not have any room for more of the big rocks. The same is true for product design. If we spend vast amounts of time adding every single draft and round to a portion of our model, our delivery deadline will be fast approaching, without much to show for it. Even worse, if we spend time adding drafts and rounds (sand) to a feature we later delete (take out of the jar), we may not have enough time to put in the rest of the big rocks.

Simply put, don't waste time putting in sand, until all the big rocks are in the jar. Your Model Tree should also reflect this, so that the more important features are at the top of the list, and the lesser features are near the bottom.

Feature Names

The Model Tree for the model shown in Figure 19-1 is shown in Figure 19-4. By looking at it, you can see the different feature types, but it is not obvious which feature is which. On a model as simple as this one, it is not too hard to understand, but more complex models with many more features could be quite confusing. Also, you may wish to identify the purpose of any given feature for co-workers, vendors or customers. To change a name, simply select a feature in the Model Tree, hold down the **RMB**, and select **Rename**. You may then type in any alpha-numeric string you wish, as long as there are no spaces or special characters other than '-' (hypen) or '_' (underscore). Also, each name can only be used once per model.

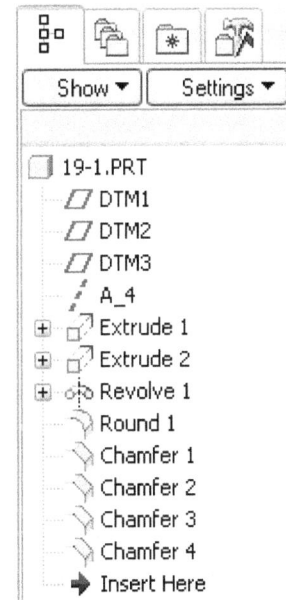

Fig. 19-4
Default names

Figure 19-5 shows the same Model Tree, but with
the important features labeled. Use your own
judgment in deciding which features need to be
labeled and which do not, so you don't become
consumed with the task of trying to label every
item. (Each name can only be used once.)

Rather than waiting until a feature is created then
renaming it, most features will allow you to specify
a name while you are defining it, by selecting on
the **Properties** tab in the feature's dashboard, as
shown in Figure 19-6.

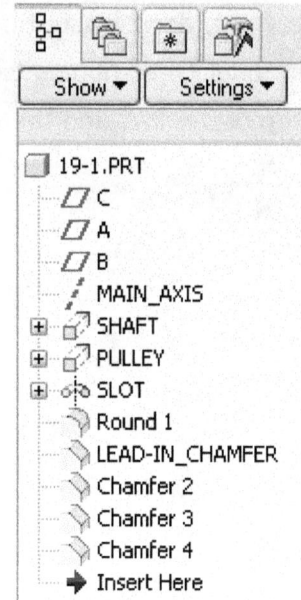

Fig. 19-5
Model tree with named features

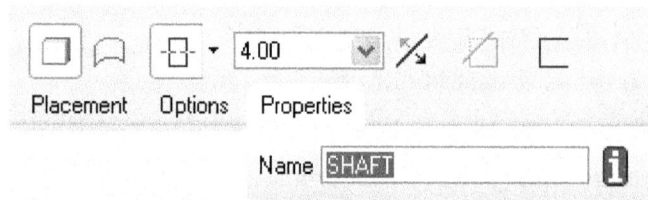

Fig. 19-6
Specifying a feature's name during its definition

Groups

Features that are consecutive in the Model Tree can be grouped together. In fact
Chapter 7 discusses how datum features created during the creation of other
features are automatically grouped together. To manually create a group, select the
features either from the graphics area or the Model Tree, hold down the **RMB**, and
select **Group**.

Figure 19-7 shows how all of the features associated
with the pulley can be grouped together. Unfortunately
not all of the features were originally consecutive in the
Model Tree, so before creating the group, the features
were reordered (see Chapter 18). Also the group has
been expanded to display its contents, but you may
also collapse the display of the group to make a shorter
or 'cleaner' Model Tree. You may also name the group,
using the technique described above.

So what does a group do for you? Basically,
Pro/ENGINEER will treat the group like a single feature.
This makes it easier to duplicate, without having to
duplicate each feature separately. You can also **Reorder**
the entire group in one operation, and if you decide to
Suppress or **Delete** the entire group of features, you
may do so without having to deal with any warnings or regeneration problems. If at
any time you no longer wish to have the features grouped together, simply select
the group, hold down the **RMB**, and select **Ungroup**. As long as you do not violate
any parent/child relationships, you may also use the Model Tree to drag features in
and out of groups.

Fig. 19-7
Grouped features

Layers

In Pro/ENGINEER, the term *Layer* is a misnomer. When two dimensional CAD
systems were introduced, they made use of layers to simulate sheets of clear
acetate with portions of the overall drawing on them. When all of the sheets of
acetate (layers) are stacked up, the complete drawing is visible, and portions of the
drawing could be isolated or blanked, by manipulating which sheets are in the stack.
This analogy does not carry over very well to the three-dimensional, solid modeling
world, so a better way to think about it is to use the term *Category*.

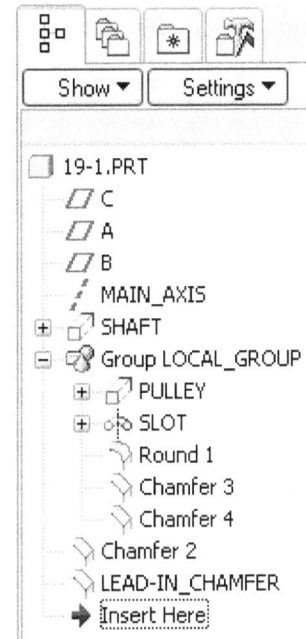

Layers differ from Groups in that features placed on a layer are done so because they share a similar type, rather than proximity to other features. Figure 19-8 shows a part with two bosses and four mounting holes, with an axis for each.

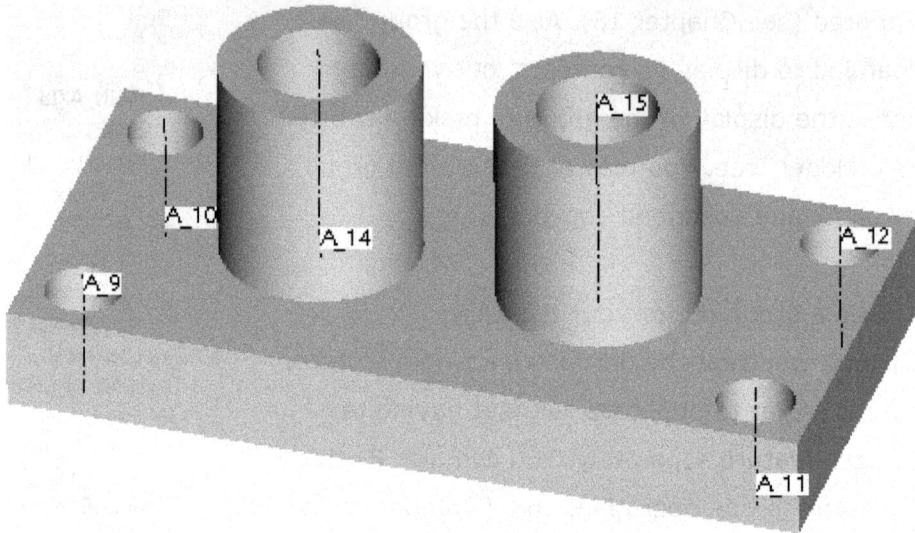

Fig. 19-8
Part with six axes

If we do not wish to see the axes, we could simply toggle them off by selecting the

 Axis Display icon from the Main Toolbar, but that would turn off all the axes. What if we only wanted to turn off the mounting hole axes? We could certainly select them, then use the **Hide** command, but on a more complex model, it would

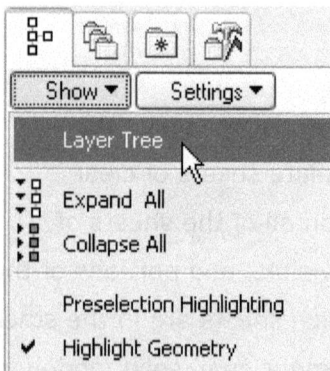

Fig. 19-9
Displaying the Layer Tree

be difficult to **Hide** and **Unhide** individual items over and over again, if needed. We can categorize these features by placing them in (on) a layer. Start by selecting the **Show** button from the top of the Model Tree, and selecting **Layer Tree**, as shown in Figure 19-9. This will change the Navigator Window to switch from the Model Tree to the Layer Tree. (You may switch it back to the Model Tree the same way.)

Manual Layers

To create a new layer, place your cursor anywhere within the Layer Tree, hold down the **RMB**, and select **New Layer**. This will open a Layer Properties dialog box, as shown in Figure 19-10.

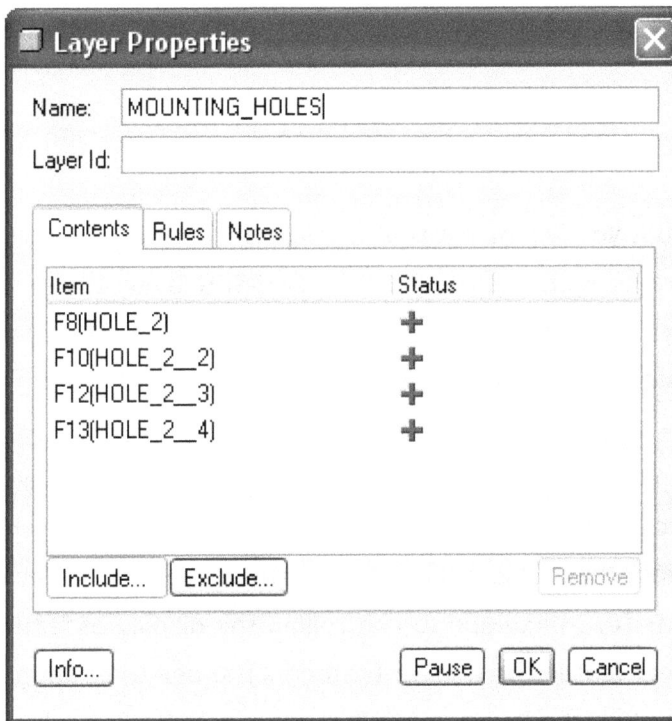

Layer Properties

| Name: | MOUNTING_HOLES| |
| Layer Id: | |

Contents | Rules | Notes

Item	Status
F8(HOLE_2)	+
F10(HOLE_2__2)	+
F12(HOLE_2__3)	+
F13(HOLE_2__4)	+

Include... | Exclude... | Remove

Info... | Pause | OK | Cancel

Fig. 19-10
Layer Properties

Enter a name for the new layer (category) and select any feature you wish to add to the category. Note that even though we were only concerned with adding axes, these features were internal to the holes, so we selected the holes. If we want to, we can repeat the process and create a layer for the bosses as well.

Now when we want to hide only the mounting hole axes, we can select the name of the layer from the Layer Tree, hold down the **RMB**, and select **Hide**. The result is shown in Figure 19-11.

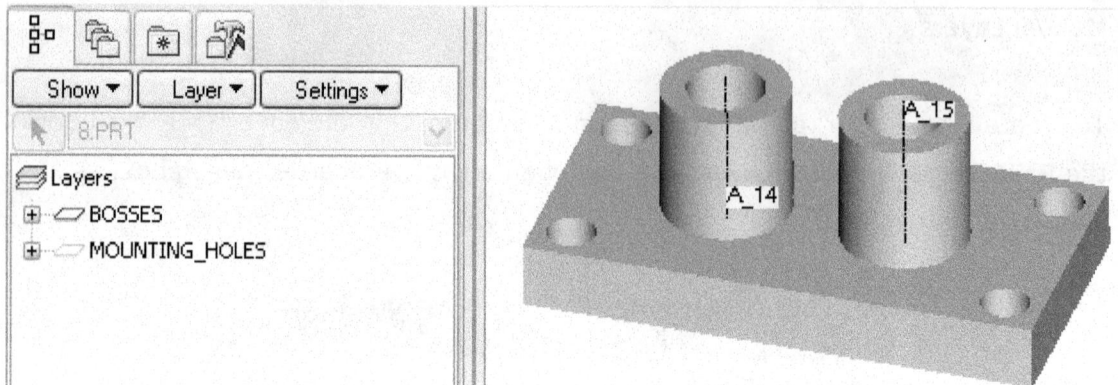

Fig. 19-11
Hidden layer

It is very subtle, but you will notice that the icon for the hidden MOUNTING_HOLES layer is slightly greyed-out, compared to the BOSSES layer. If you want to save the display status of your layers, you must place the cursor on the Layer Tree, hold down the **RMB**, and select **Save Status**.

At any time, you may expand the list to show the features that are on a layer, and also include or exclude features by selecting the layer, holding down the **RMB** and selecting **Layer Properties**. This will open the same Layer Properties dialog box, as shown in Figure 19-10. In addition to controlling the display of features, you might want to select every feature on a layer (category) to delete or suppress them. You can do this by selecting the layer, holding down the **RMB**, and selecting **Select Items**. This will go through the model and select every item on the layer, regardless of where the are on the Model Tree. By having these features categorized, you can save yourself a considerable amount of time searching throughout a complex model for features.

Rule-based (automatic) Layers

You may want to create a layer for a particular type of item, such as rounds, but it may be cumbersome to have to add each round to that layer, every time you create one. What if you forget one or two? To automate the process, you can create an automated layer by first searching for a particular type of feature (round). Start by selecting the 🔍 **Find** icon in the Main Toolbar. This will open the Search Tool as shown in Figure 19-12.

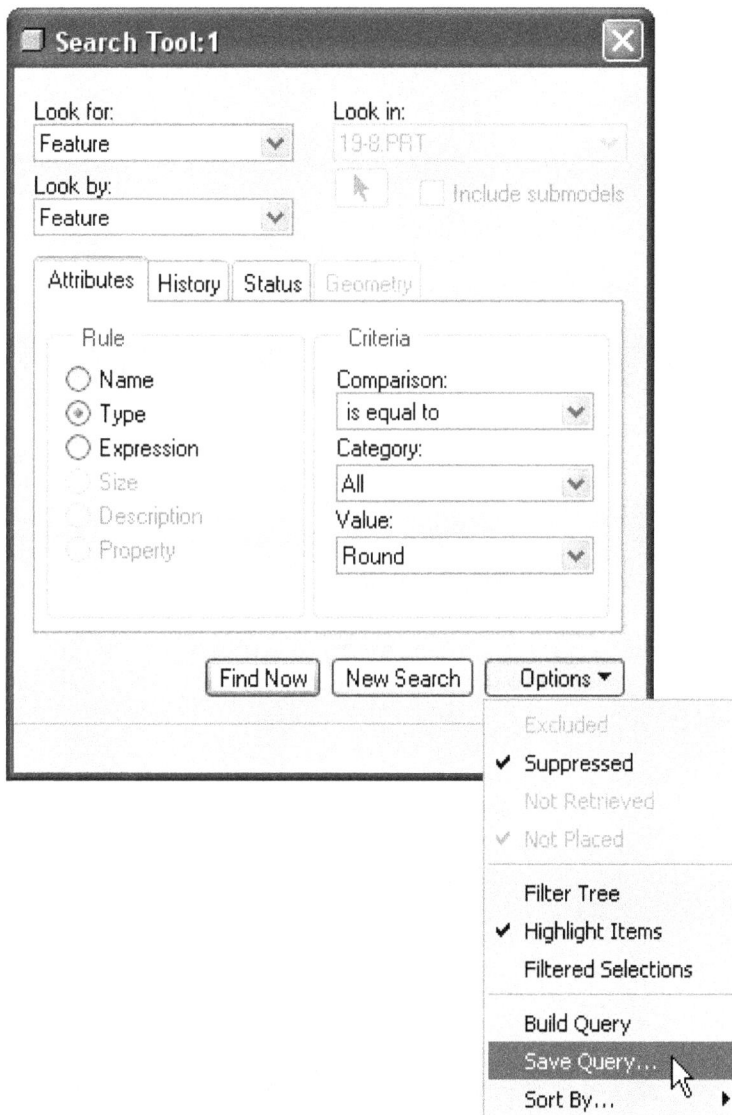

Fig. 19-12
Search Tool

After making the appropriate search selections, click
on the **Options** button, and select **Save Query**. This
will open a Save Rules dialog box, as shown in Figure
19-13. Notice that the box prompts you for a layer
name. After entering a layer name and selecting **OK**,
a new layer will be created. If there are any existing
features in your model that happen to match the
search criteria, those features will be automatically
placed on that layer.

Fig. 19-13
Save Rules dialog box

Now if any new feature matching the search criteria is created, it will also be
automatically placed on the layer. Any layer that is controlled by a rule is indicated
in the Layer Tree with special icon, as shown in Figure 19-14.

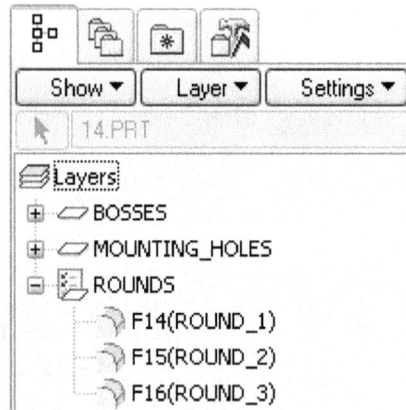

Fig. 19-14
Manual and rule-based layers

Assembly Layers

It is possible to create layers in an assembly, and place both features and components on those layers, however it is the recommendation of this author, that you <u>never</u> place components on a layer, for the purpose of hiding the components. Since you have the ability to create as many different layers with as many different names and include as many different components on these layers, there is not an administrative way to control what layers or components are hidden or displayed. Many times a user will place a component on an obscurely named layer, hide it, and save its status. The next person that opens the file sees that there is a component missing, doesn't know that is it just on a hidden layer, and mistakenly adds another one. Even if they knew there was a component on a hidden layer, what layer name should they select to unhide? What if there are dozens of layers? You may end up unhiding all of the layers, but then you'll have to figure out which layers to re-hide.

To control the display of individual components in an assembly, see **Simplified Representation** in Chapter 22.

Chapter 20

Smart Models

Parameters

Relations

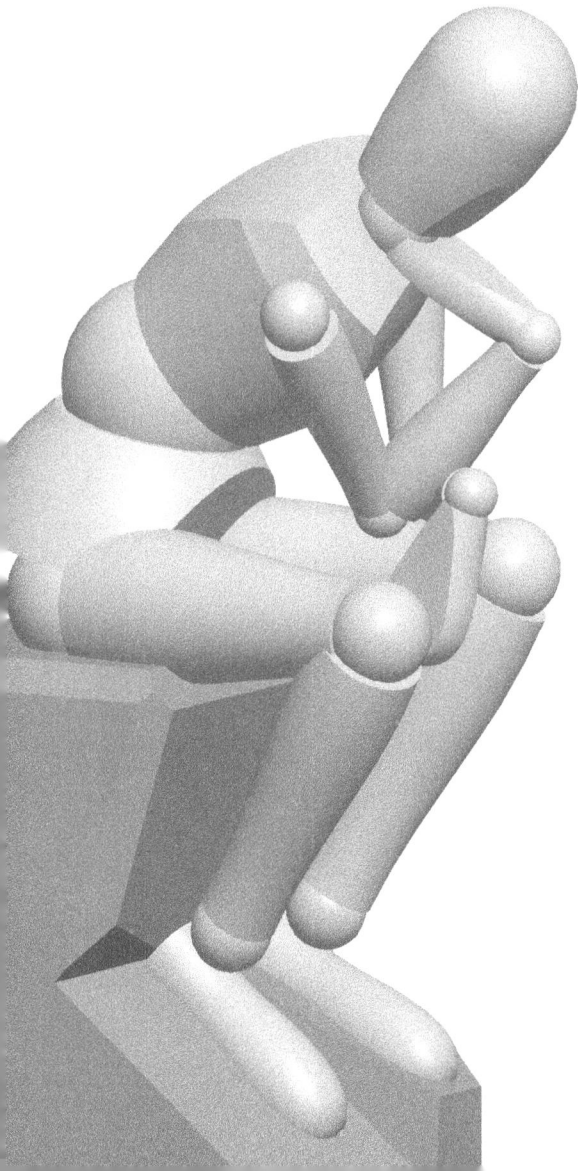

Parameters

Each Pro/ENGINEER part and assembly may contain any amount of geometric information you wish, but they can also contain non-geometric data. This data, called Parameters, is stored within the model, and can be accessed to control geometry and create reports. To create a parameter, select **Tools** > **Parameters** from the menu. This will open the Parameters dialog box, as shown in Figure 20-1.

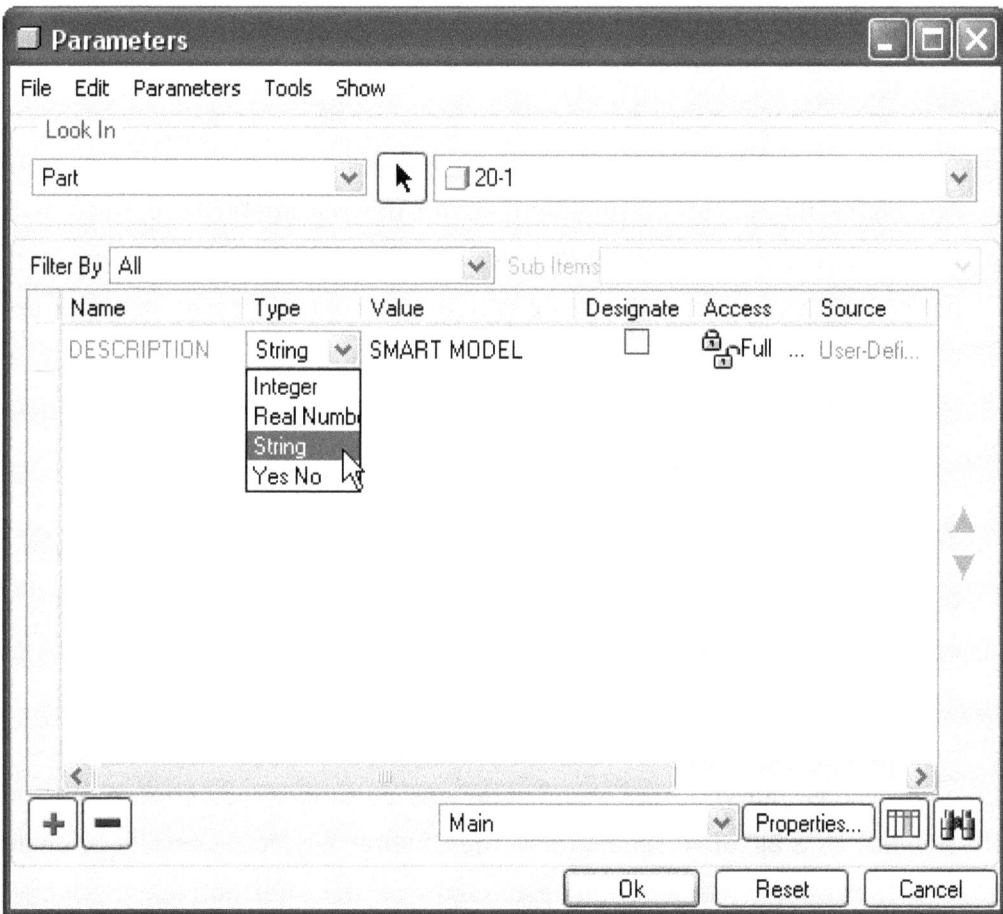

Fig. 20-1
Parameters dialog box

Select ➕ to add a new parameter. Specify the desired Name, Type, and Value.

Integer

Only integers are valid values for this parameter type, such as -1, 0, 1, 2, 3, etc., and can be used to control the number of instances in a pattern.

Real Number

Any numerical value expressed in decimal form may be used for this parameter type, such as -1.5, .0012, 6, etc.

String

Any alpha-numeric string may be used for this parameter type, such as HEX HEAD BOLT, JOHN SMITH, BLUE, etc. While the name of the parameter may not contain any spaces, the value can, and can be expressed in either upper or lower case.

Yes No

YES and NO are the only two values that may be used for this parameter type. This is useful for writing relations (see later in this chapter) that contain if/then statements.

Chapter 24 discusses displaying system parameters such as MODEL_NAME and SCALE on drawings, but you may also display any parameter you choose to include in your models. In a Bill of Materials (also see Chapter 24), it is possible to display parameters capturing a component's description, vendor information, revision level, color, cost, and whether it is a manufactured or purchased component. Since these are true values, and not just notes on a drawing, they will carry with the component whether there is a drawing or not, and always available no matter how many times it is used in multiple assemblies.

Relations

The part shown in Figure 20-2 was created using intelligent techniques which yield maximum results with minimum effort.

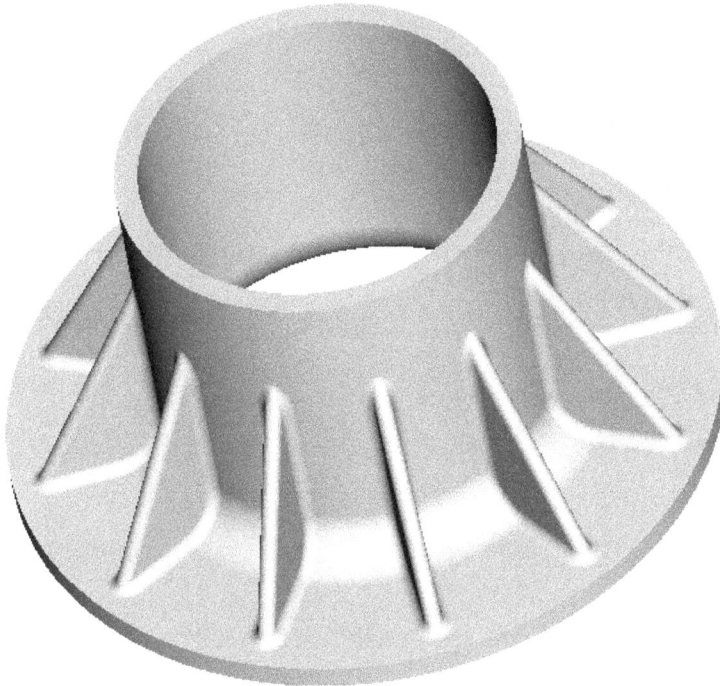

Fig. 20-2
Intelligently constructed model

The main portion was constructed as a **Revolve** (see Chapter 9) with a thickened sketch (see Chapter 8). This allows us to maintain a constant wall thickness (if that is our intent). A single **Rib** was constructed with only a single line (see Chapter 9) so that no matter what size the main portion may be modified to, the rib will always follow. The exposed edge of the rib was rounded off using a **Full Round** (see Chapter 11) so that no matter how thick or thin the rib becomes, it will always be completely rounded off. A single **Round** was created at the base of the rib, and since it was created after the full round, it created a tangent continuous chain of rounded edges.

The rib and both rounds were grouped together (see Chapter 19) and the entire **Group** was **Pattern**ed twelve times around the entire extent of the part (see Chapter 16), so that if the number of ribs were modified they will remain equally spaced. We've created this model with minimal effort, but what happens if we or our co-workers make a change to it? What is our 'design intent'?

- If the inner diameter of the part shrinks or grows, what should happen to the outside diameter?

- If either of the diameters change, should the height of the part change too?

- What about the wall thickness? Should it change or remain the same?

- If the wall thickness changes, should the thickness of the ribs change too? If so, by how much?

By using relations, we can create relationships (hence the name) between one or more dimensions within a sketch, or between dimensions of different features. We can use parameters to drive relations, and we can also drive parameters with our relations.

Functions

Any math equation may be used for your relations. The following functions can be used in relations, both in equations and in conditional statements:

```
    +   add
    -   subtract
    *   multiply
    /   divide
  cos ()  cosine
  tan ()  tangent
  sin ()  sine
 sqrt ()  square root
 asin ()  arc sine
 acos ()  arc cosine
 atan ()  arc tangent
 sinh ()  hyperbolic sine
 cosh ()  hyperbolic cosine
 tanh ()  hyperbolic tangent
   log()  base 10 logarithm
    ln()  natural logarithm
   exp()  e to an exponential degree
   abs()  absolute value
  ceil()  the smallest integer not less than the real value
 floor()  the largest integer not greater than the real value
```

Section Relations

While we are creating and modifying our sketches, we can create relations to tie together and control the dimensions algebraically. Later in this chapter, we discuss how dimensions have a default name placeholder, such as *d3* or *d59*. While we are sketching, these names are referred to as sketcher dimensions, such as *sd2* or *sd13*. Figure 20-3 shows the sketch used to define the main portion of the part shown in Figure 20-2. Notice that when **Tools > Relations** is selected from the menu, the relations dialog box is opened, as shown in Figure 20-4, and the dimensions switch from displaying their values to their names (sd7, sd*8*, sd9, etc.)

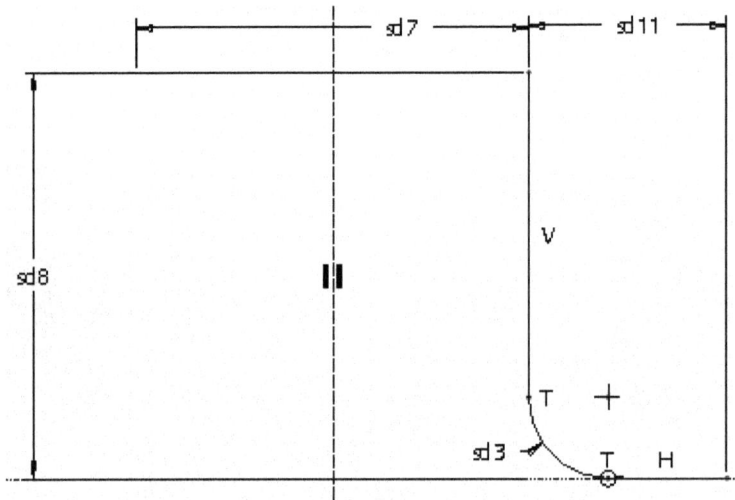

Fig. 20-3
Sketcher dimensions shown

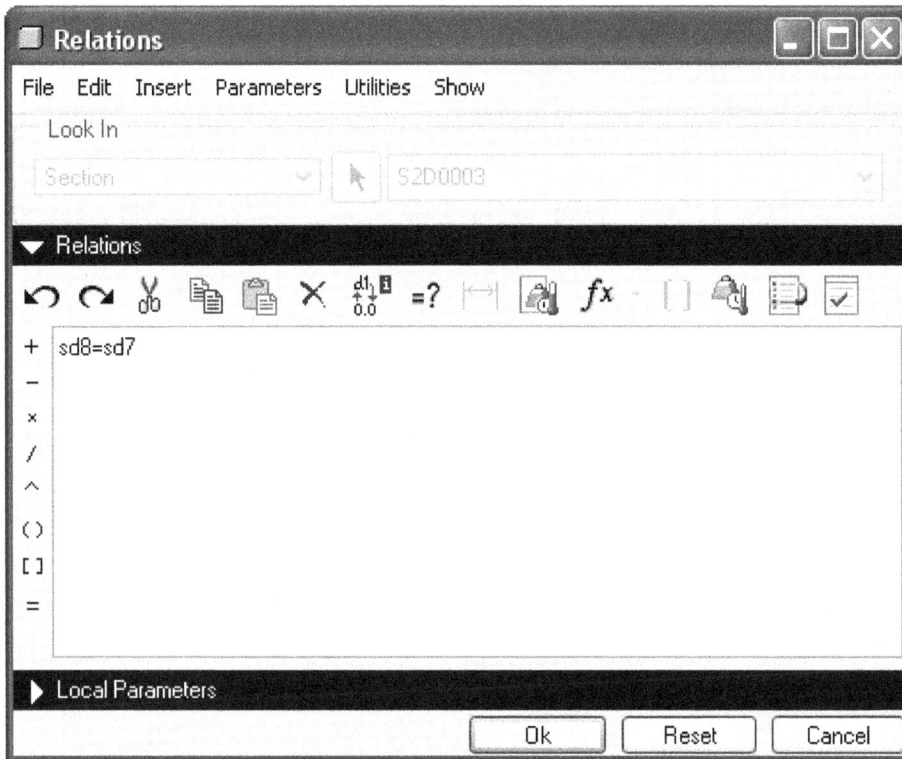

Fig. 20-4
Relation dialog box

If we want the height of our feature (controlled by sd8) to always be the same as the inner diameter (controlled by sd7) we could type a string in the relation dialog box such as:

sd8=sd7

This means that if the value for sd7 is ever modified, the value for sd8 will always be equal to it. The same relation could be written as:

sd8=sd7*1.5

This would set the height to be one and a half times the diameter.

Note that the dimension being controlled is always to the left of the equal sign. When this relation is in place, you will be able to modify the diameter (with the height to follow) but you will never be able to modify the height manually. This is how you capture and maintain your design intent. If you decide that you no longer wish for the height to be controlled by the diameter, simply delete the relation string.

Feature Relations

Relations may be used to control the dimensions of a feature that are not necessarily sketcher dimensions. For example, we may wish to set the thickness of our rib to be 75% or 50% of the thickness of the main revolved shape by selecting **Tools > Relations** from the menu. Change the setting in the **Look In** tab to **Feature**, and select the feature you want to control (in this case the first rib). The dimensions of the rib will be displayed, as shown in Figure 20-5.

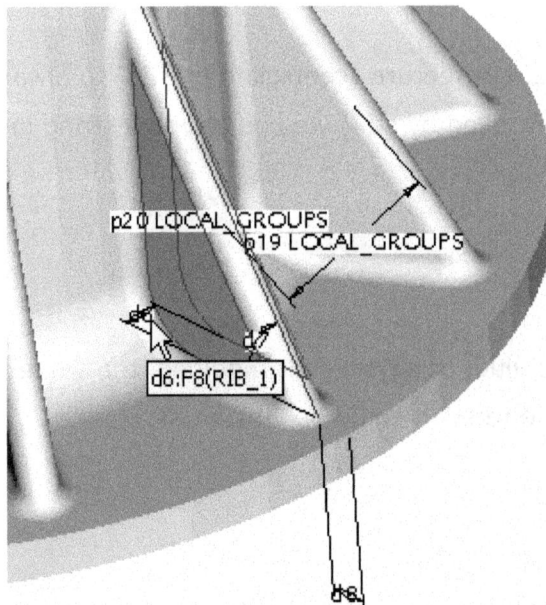

Fig. 20-5
Feature dimensions displayed

You may then pick the dimension from the graphics area (which automatically copies it to the relation dialog box) or you may type it manually along with the equal sign:

d6 =

If you know the name of the dimension that controls the wall thickness of the main feature, such as d1, you can simply type it in. If you do not already know the name, you can select the feature. Its dimensions will be displayed, which you can then select or simply type it in, and complete the equation:

d6 = d1 * .75

Part Relations

Sketcher and Feature relations not only control their respective dimensions, but the equations themselves are in a sense 'embedded' into the sketch or feature. If the sketch or feature is deleted, the equation is deleted as well. This helps to keep your lists of equations organized, and you won't have any obsolete equations.

Part relations on the other hand are stored at a higher level, but are created in exactly the same way as Feature relations. Some people choose to use this method, as all relations for a model are accessible from one place, but the list of equations could become quite long. Since your list of equations could control several dimensions for several features, it is a good idea to place comment lines preceded with ' **/*** ' (without the quotes) in your list of equations, such as:

/* THE FOLLOWING CONTROLS THE WIDTH OF THE RIB
d6 = d1 * .75

Parameters in Relations

In addition to dimensional values, you may use parameter names as variables in your relations. You may type the name of the parameter in the equation, or you may select the [ ] **Parameter Name** icon from the dialog box, and choose a parameter from the list, as shown in Figure 20-6. The resulting equation is:

d1= WALL

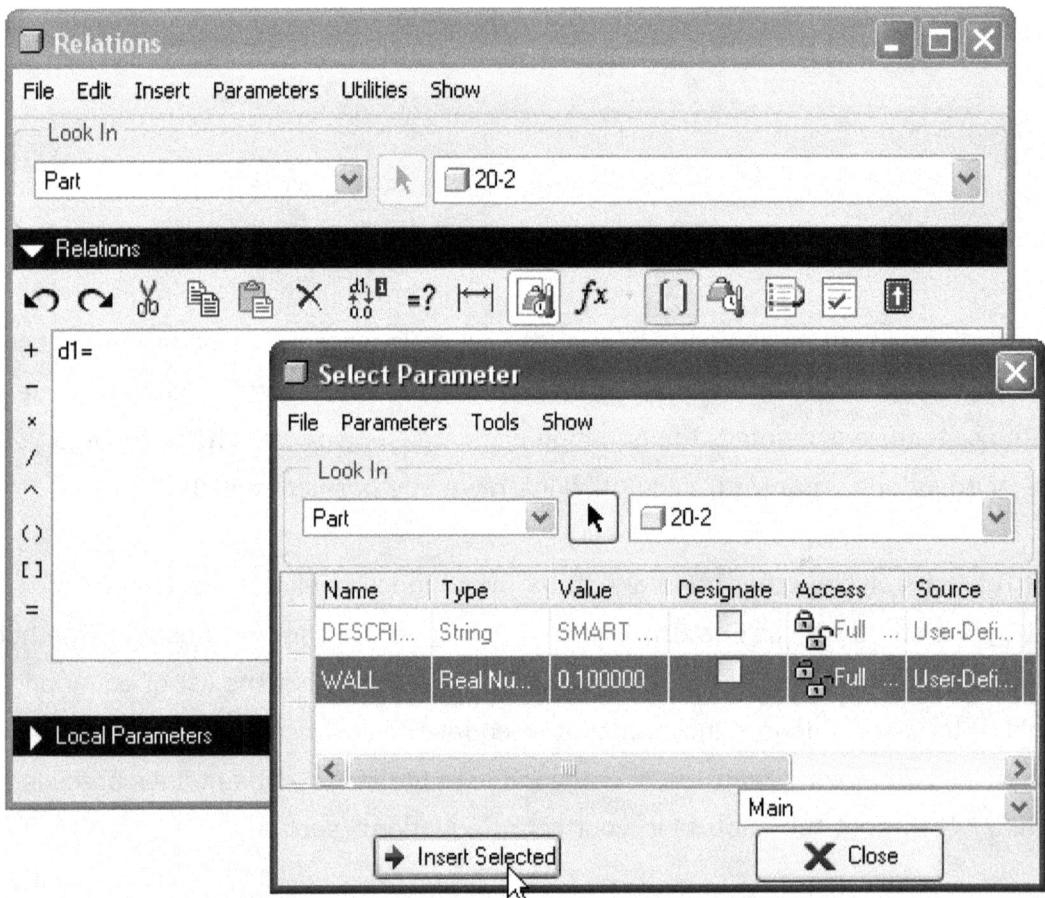

Fig. 20-6
Inserting parameter names into relation equation

In the earlier Part relation example, we set the width of the rib (d6) to be 75% of the thickness of the main feature (d1). We can leave this in place, because as the value of the parameter called WALL is modified, the d1 dimension will update, as will the d6 dimension, according to the equations in the relations. As an alternative, we could have just written the following relations:

d1 = WALL
d6 = WALL * .75

Dimension Names

When Pro/ENGINEER assigns dimension names (d#) to sketches and features, it does so in a sequential manner. If any features or dimensions are deleted, Pro/ENGINEER just ignores these numbers, and continues on with new numbers for new features. This results in a list of dimension names that are unique, but don't have much meaning to the user. To assist in both writing and maintaining your relations, you may want to change the default names of some of the dimensions to something meaningful.

To change a name, select a dimension as if you were going to change its value (see Chapter 18), but instead of selecting **Value** from the menu, select **Properties**. In the Dimension Text tab, as shown in Figure 20-7, replace the default name (d6) with any unique name, such as '**RIB**'.

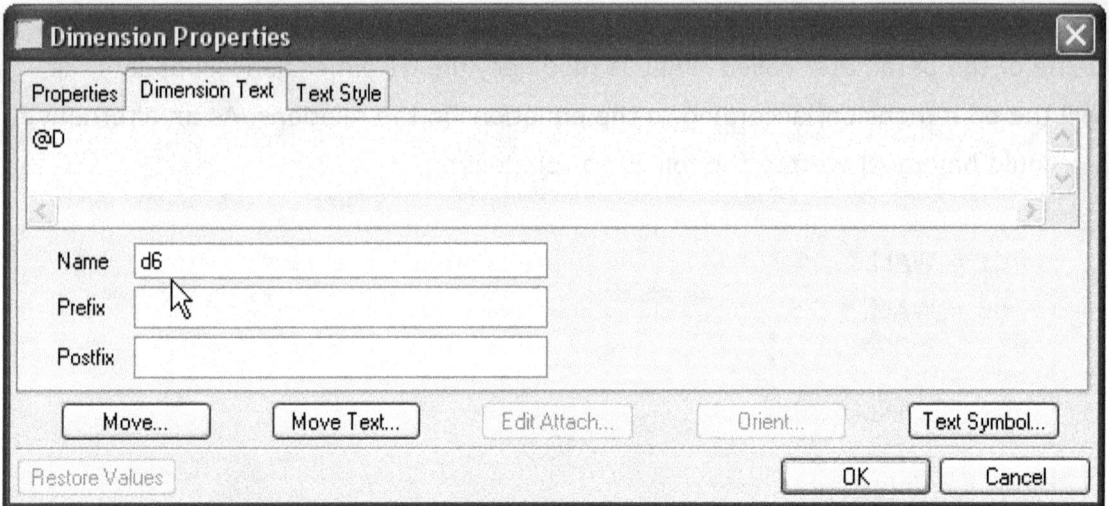

Fig. 20-7
Changing dimension name

This should make a more easily understood equation:

RIB = WALL * .75

Family Tables

Libraries

Nested Tables

Assembly Tables

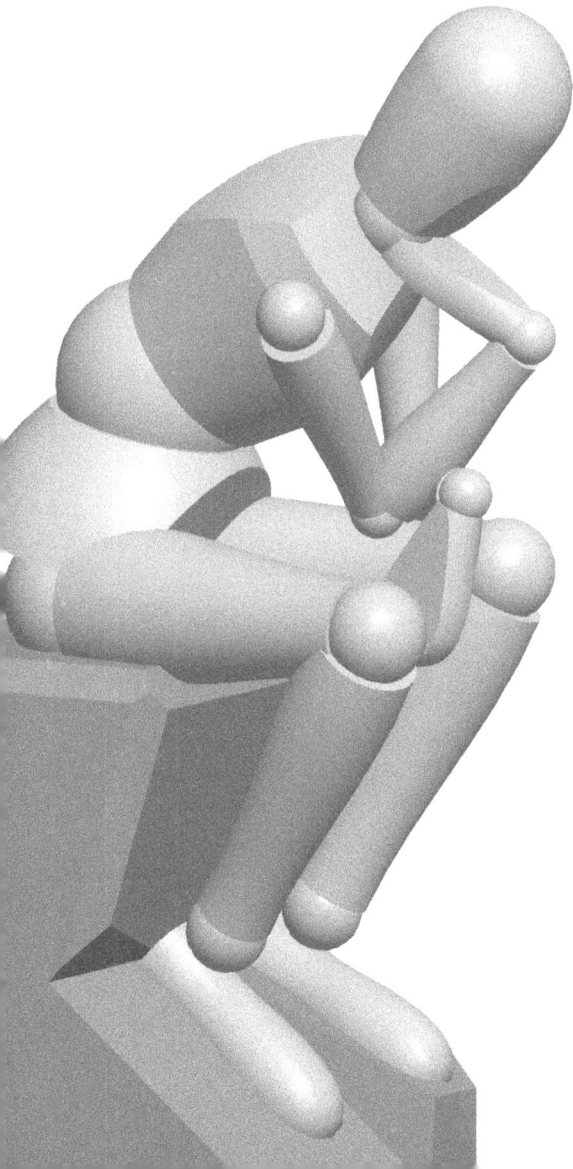

In nature, plants and animals inherit certain genes and traits from their parents. The offspring are very much like their parents, in that they of course are of the same species and class, but they are unique individuals. Siblings share the same parents, and may even share several of the same traits, such as eye color or gender, but unless they are identical twins, they are each unique. Both the parents, children and siblings are related to each other as a family but with variations.

When creating Pro/ENGINEER parts and assemblies, the same idea of family can be used to create two or more designs that are related to each other, that share certain aspects, but have variations in their design. Figure 21-1 illustrates a Hex Head Bolt. Using techniques discussed in Chapter 20, we have named the dimensions as shown, for clarity purposes.

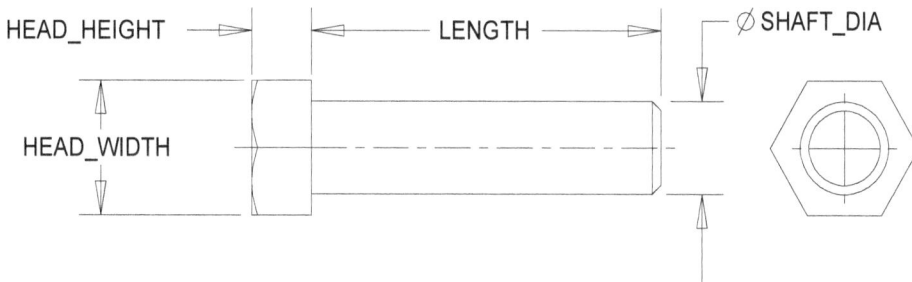

Fig. 21-1
Basic layout of a bolt

We could go ahead and create a Pro/ENGINEER model of this bolt, and use it in as many assemblies as we need to, but what happens when we need another one slightly shorter? We could create a second part file, either from scratch, or by copying and modifying this one, but what happens when we need another one slightly longer?

Each time we need another length, we would need to create another part file. Now what happens when we need another size (diameter), or if we need a set of bolts in stainless steel, and a set in nylon?

Libraries

Our bolt example is one of the most common uses of Family Tables. We can use a table to create and maintain a library of parts, driven from a single part file. To create a table, select **Tools** > **Family Table** from the menu. This will open the table for this part, as shown in Figure 21-2.

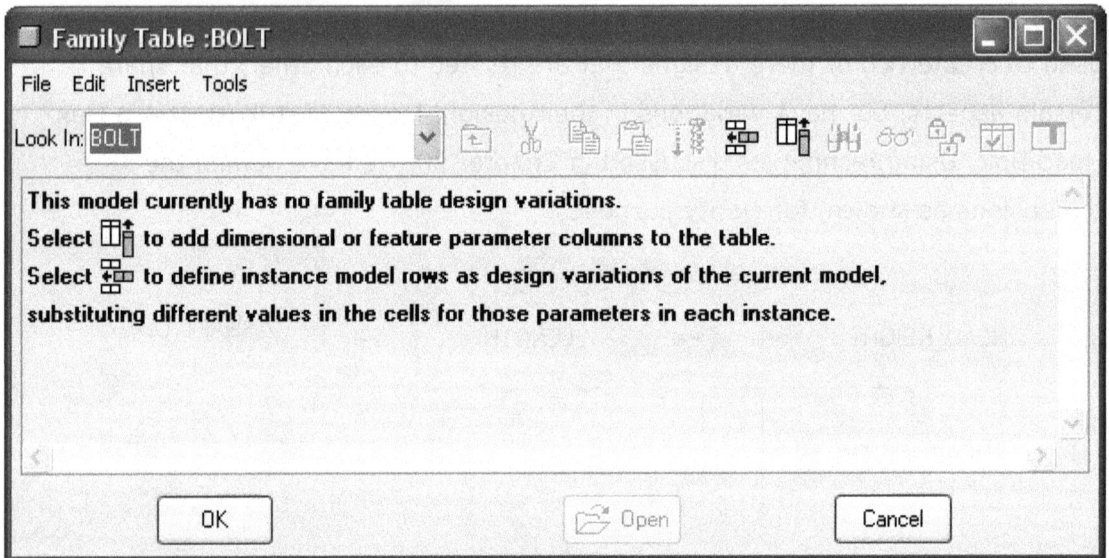

Fig. 21-2
Blank Family Table

Instances

The source model, in this case *BOLT.PRT* , is referred to as the generic model. Each version of the model we create is referred to as an instance, and is created in the Family Table as rows by selecting the ⊞ **Instance** (row) icon. This will add a row to the table, and automatically assign it a unique name. Each time the **Instance** button is selected, another row is added, as shown in Figure 21-3.

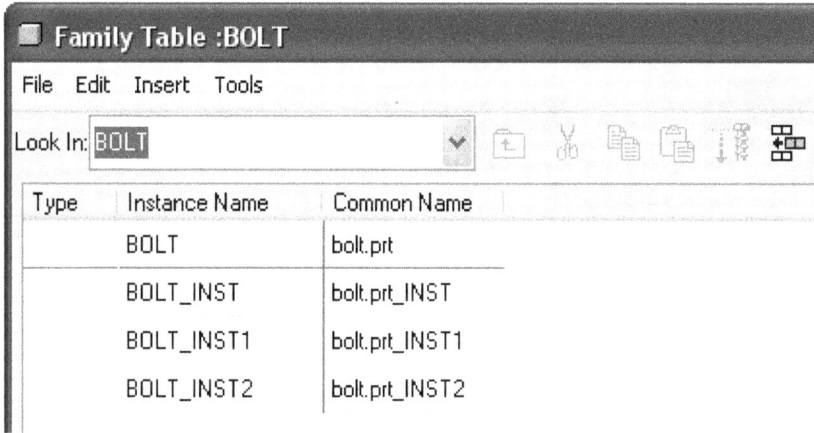

Fig. 21-3
Rows added to a table

The top row always indicates the generic (source) model. You may edit the names
of the instances as needed. In industry, you would most likely enter real part
numbers, but for our example we will keep it simple, and use *BOLT1, BOLT2,* and
BOLT3.

Family Items

Any feature or parameter that we want to vary between the generic and an
instance, or between instances are specified in the table by creating a column by

selecting the ⬚ **Column** icon. This will open the Family Items dialog box, as shown
in Figure 21-4. To add dimensions, simply click on a feature to display its
dimensions to the screen, then select the appropriate dimension. Each time, it will
be added to the Items list as shown.

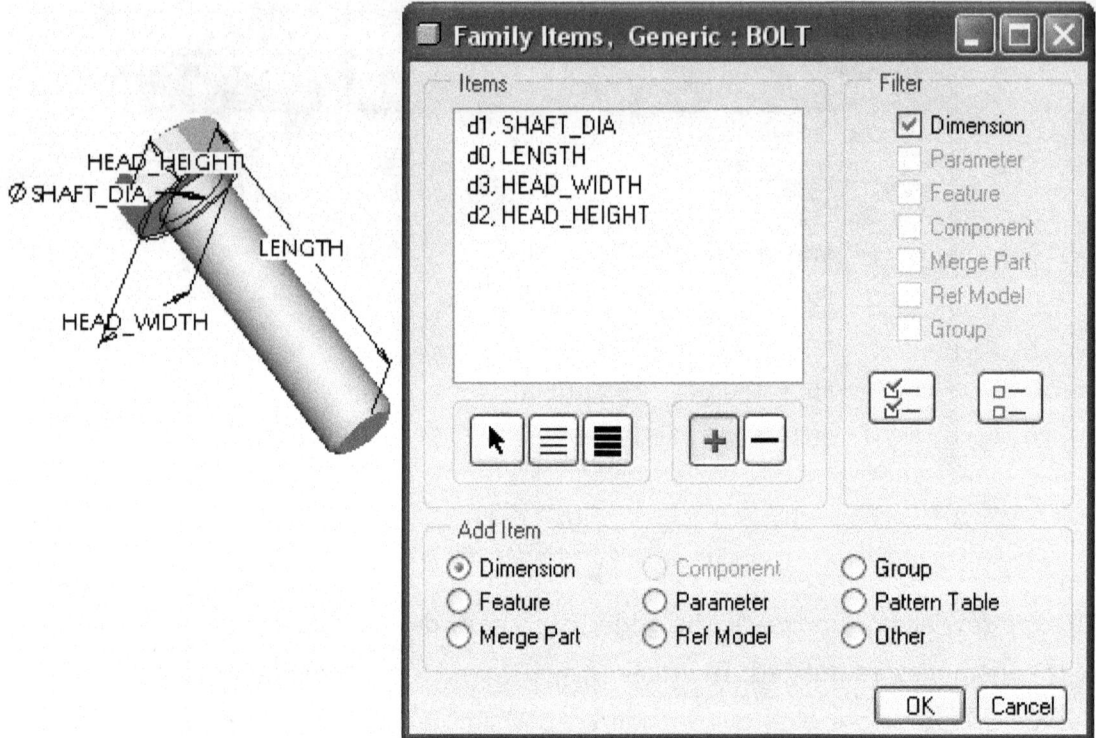

Fig. 21-4
Family Items dialog box

After selecting **OK**, the items are used as columns in the table, as shown in Figure 21-5.

Fig. 21-5
Family table columns

Notice that the generic row will indicate the actual value of the dimension of the source feature. Since Pro/ENGINEER must have a complete set of dimensions to create geometry, it goes ahead and fills in all of the cells of the table with an asterisk (*). This allows Pro/ENGINEER to apply whatever value is in the generic for that item to the instance.

It is the recommendation of this author that you never leave an asterisk in your table. You have placed your items in the table for a reason. You have decided that it was important to specify the diameter, length, etc. for a list of individual parts. If you leave an asterisk in place, and some time in the future, someone modifies the length of the generic part, your unique part will change. Doesn't that defeat the purpose? Even if one of your instances shares the value of the current instance, you should still enter the value specifically.

Figure 21-6 shows a completed table. We have added parameters and even a feature (the chamfer). By including features in your table, and setting their values to N (No), you can create instances of the model that do not contain the features at all. Technically the feature is suppressed in the instance, but it does not appear in the instance's Model Tree.

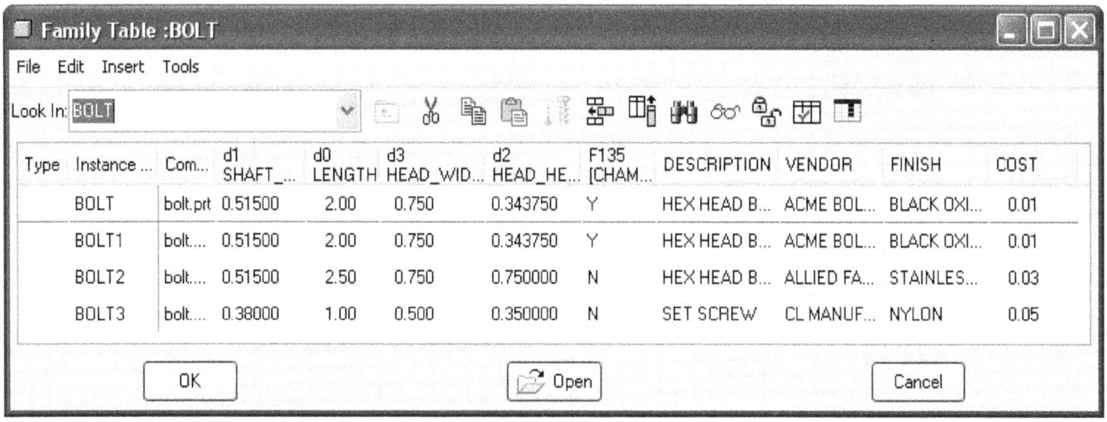
Family Table :BOLT
File Edit Insert Tools
Look In: BOLT
Type Instance ... Com... d1 SHAFT_... d0 LENGTH d3 HEAD_WID... d2 HEAD_HE... F135 [CHAM... DESCRIPTION VENDOR FINISH COST
BOLT bolt.prt 0.51500 2.00 0.750 0.343750 Y HEX HEAD B... ACME BOL... BLACK OXI... 0.01
BOLT1 bolt.... 0.51500 2.00 0.750 0.343750 Y HEX HEAD B... ACME BOL... BLACK OXI... 0.01
BOLT2 bolt.... 0.51500 2.50 0.750 0.750000 N HEX HEAD B... ALLIED FA... STAINLES... 0.03
BOLT3 bolt.... 0.38000 1.00 0.500 0.350000 N SET SCREW CL MANUF... NYLON 0.05
OK
Open
Cancel

Fig. 21-6
Completed Family Table

After filling in your values, or after every time you modify them, it is a good idea to

verify that you have specified valid combinations, by selecting the [⊞] Verify icon.

This will open the dialog box shown in Figure
21-7. When you select the **VERIFY** button,
Pro/ENGINEER will regenerate each instance
as a background operation. If the combination
of features and dimensions are possible
(meaning no regeneration failures) its status
will indicate **Success**. Any failed instance will
indicate **Failure**, letting you know that you
have an invalid combination, and that you
should modify the values for that instance.

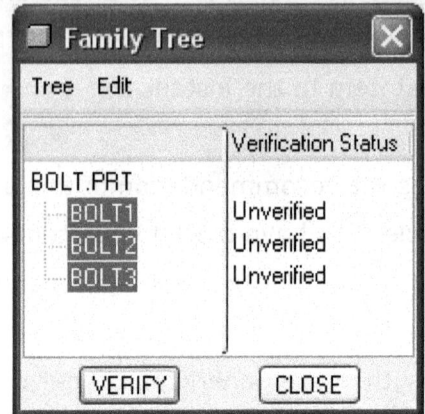

Fig. 21-7
Instance verification

After your table is complete, select **OK** to accept the values, and be sure to save
your model. You will now have a single Pro/ENGINEER part file, but three (four if
you include the generic) versions to use in your assemblies and drawings. The
advantage is that you will only need a single part file, and any modifications to the
generic will be propagated throughout the instances.

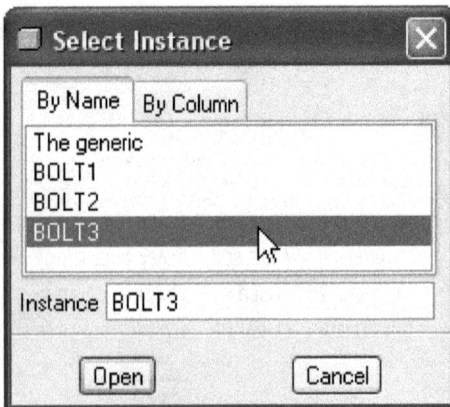

Fig. 21-8
Selecting an Instance

Each time you open or assemble a model
containing a Family Table, you will have a
choice as to which version you would like
to use, as shown in Figure 21-8. Once the
file has been opened or assembled, it
behaves exactly as if it were a separate
part. If you attempt to modify a
dimension that is controlled in a table,
Pro/ENGINEER will notify you of that fact,
and when you make the change, it
automatically updates the table.

Nested Tables

If we were to increase the size of our Family Table, shown in Figure 21-6, to include one hundred unique sizes of the bolt, we would need to create one hundred instances (rows). If we wanted to create a complete set of bolts in both UNC (Unified Coarse Thread) and UNF (Unified Fine Thread) we would need two hundred instances (rows). We would have to be sure that all of the dimensional values for BOLT3 with UNC matched all of the dimensional values for BOLT3 with UNF. If we make a change to one, we have to remember to make a change in the other.

Rather than maintaining large tables with hundreds of rows and columns, it is possible to create nested tables, essentially creating table driven versions of table driven versions of a single part.

Start by opening an instance of the model. (In this case BOLT3). Following the steps outlined earlier, create instances of this model, and add the additional items (in this case a thread callout parameter) to the table, as shown in Figure 21-9.

Type	Instance Name	Common Name	THREAD
	BOLT3	bolt.prt_INST2	THREAD
	BOLT3_UNF	bolt.prt_INST2_INST	UNF
	BOLT3_UNC	bolt.prt_INST2_INST	UNC

Fig. 21-9
Nested table

This technique is extremely useful for creating sheet metal parts, where the first table creates design version of the parts, and the nested tables create formed and flat pattern versions of the instances.

Assembly Tables

You may create Family Tables within assemblies, exactly the same way as within parts, but in addition to dimensions and parameters, you may also add components to the list of items. This allows you to have different instances of an assembly that may or may not contain certain components. By specifying **Y** (Yes), a component will be included, and by specifying **N** (No) a component will not. If you have a component that has its own Family Table (such as our Bolt), you can assemble the generic component in the generic assembly, and rather than using **Y** or **N**, you can specify which instance to use, by name, as shown in Figure 21-10.

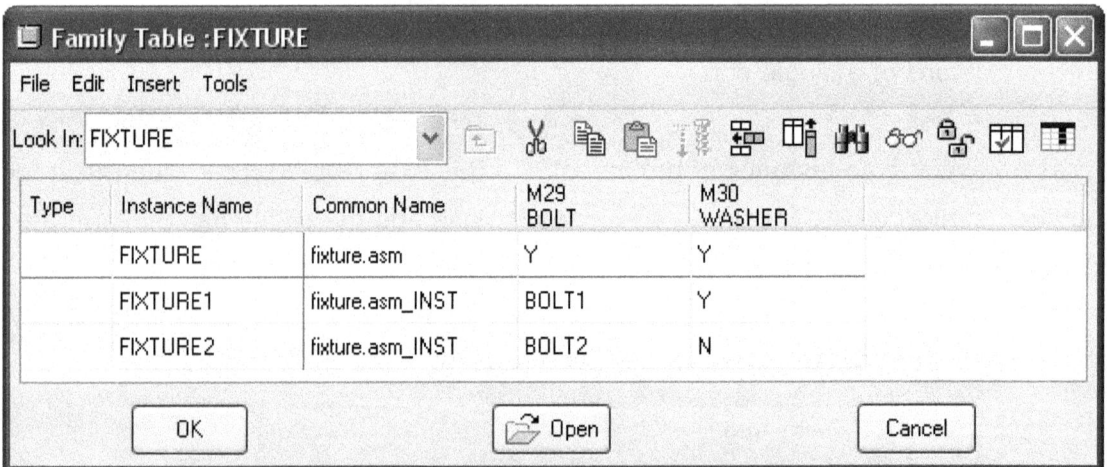

Type	Instance Name	Common Name	M29 BOLT	M30 WASHER	
	FIXTURE	fixture.asm	Y	Y	
	FIXTURE1	fixture.asm_INST	BOLT1	Y	
	FIXTURE2	fixture.asm_INST	BOLT2	N	

Fig. 21-10
Assembly table

The resulting assemblies are shown in Figures 25-11 and 25-12. Notice that by using Family Tables, we can create an unlimited number of design variations with a single part and a single assembly.

- Notice however, that since the Nut component was added to the assembly by mating it to the Washer, it cannot be generated without the Washer. When the Washer is omitted from the assembly, the Nut is omitted as well.

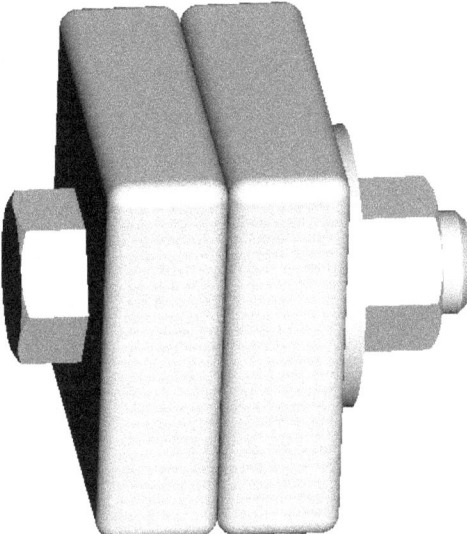

Fig. 21-11
Fixture1

Fig. 21-12
Fixture2

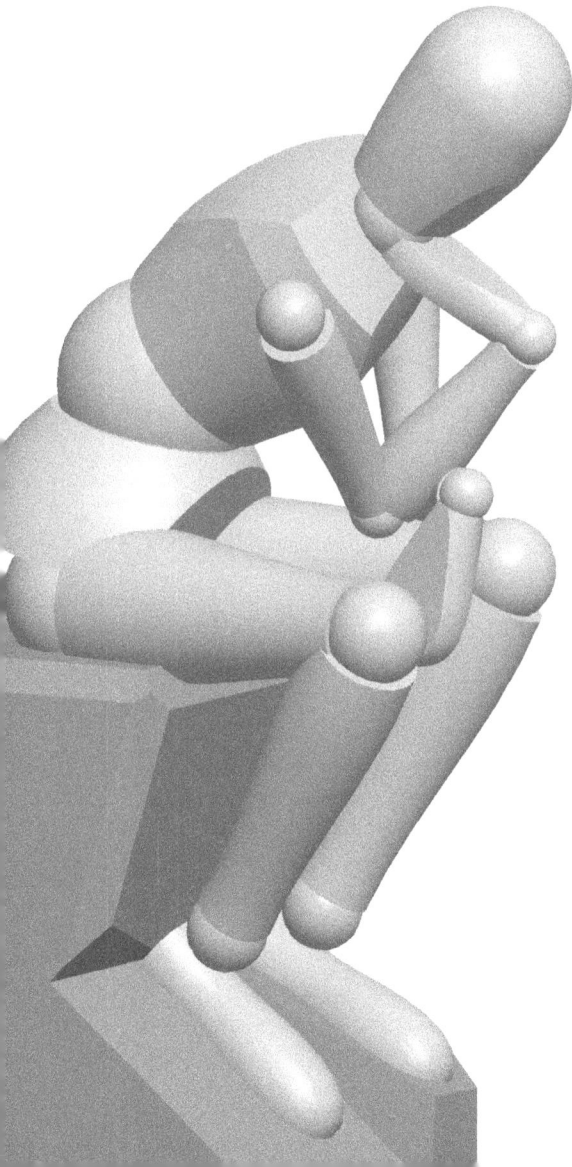

The **View Manager** gives you the ability to control how your Pro/ENGINEER model is displayed. Not only will it control how your design is displayed when others look at it, i.e. drawings, but you can use the **View Manager** as an invaluable tool to increase your productivity, while you are creating and modifying your designs.

It is important to note that the **View Manager**, and the tools contained within it, only control the way your designs are displayed (hence the name, View), and in no way affect your design's size or shape, nor can it add or delete any material.

The **View Manager** is available for both part and assembly files, but since the **View Manager** has a few additional tools (Explode and Style) available for assemblies only, we will use an assembly to discuss all of the tools. To access the **View**

Manager, and the tools described in this chapter, select the ⬚ **View Manager** icon from the Main Toolbar, which will open the **View Manager** dialog box, as shown in Figure 22-1.

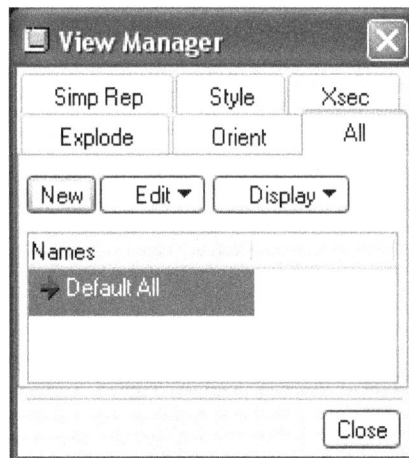

Fig. 22-1
View Manager dialog box

To access any of the tools discussed in this chapter, simply click on the appropriate tab in the dialog box.

Orientation (Orient)

In Chapter 4, we discuss methods for
zooming, panning, and spinning. If after you
manipulate the view of a model, you wish to
save it (so that you can return to it again),
select **New**, then accept either the default
name, or enter a new name, as shown in
Figure 22-2.

You will also notice a Standard Orientation and
a Default Orientation. The Standard
Orientation is Pro/ENGINEER's basic setting,
either isometric or trimetric (see Chapter 4),
while the Default Orientation is something that
you can adjust. This way, if you decide a
particular orientation is the way a model
should normally be viewed, you can edit the
Default to be that way.

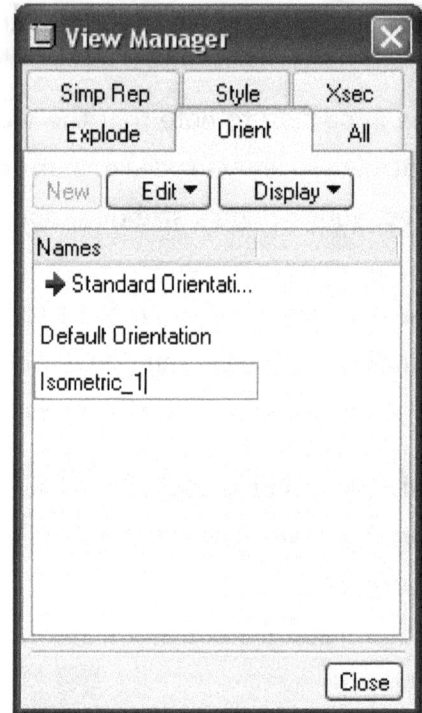

Saving an orientation
Fig. 22-2

Each saved orientation is available to you while you are working on your three-
dimensional model, by either double-clicking on the orientation name in the View

Manager dialog box, or by selecting the [AB] **Named View List** icon from the Main
Toolbar, and selecting the view name from the list. These views are also available
for your two-dimensional drawings (see Chapter 24).

If there is a specific orientation you would like to capture (rather than just from
spinning the model), select **View** > **Orientation** > **Reorient** from the menu. This will
allow you to specify a viewing plane and orientation, similar to the way you specify
a sketching plane (see Chapter 7).

Cross Sections (Xsec)

Cross sections, like the one shown in Figure 22-3, are used on two-dimensional drawings to illustrate how a part or assembly would look, if a portion of it were to be cut off, and viewed from the cut. This is used to show the detail or shape of a design that would otherwise be obscured from view.

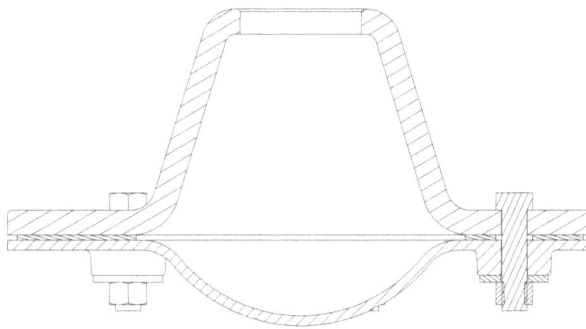

Fig. 22-3
Typical cross section

Not only can we generate these cross sections for use on our two-dimensional drawings (see Chapter 24), but since we generate these views from the three dimensional geometry, we can utilize them to assist us during the design of our models, as shown in Figure 22-4.

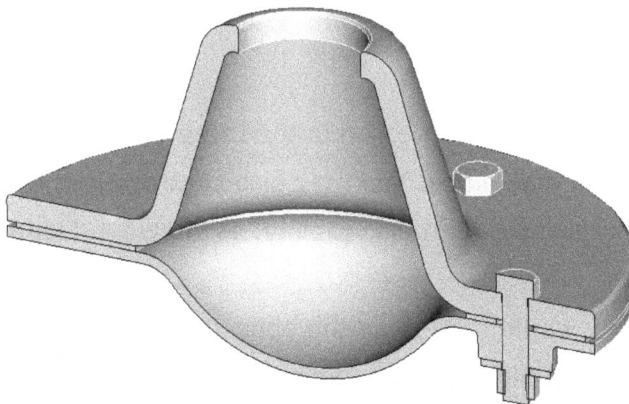

Fig. 22-4
Cross section in three-dimensional model

Planar section

To create a cross section, select **New** from the dialog box, and enter the desired name. Avoid using 'section' in the name, such as *SECTION-A*, as this is unnecessary and redundant. You should limit your names to A, B, C, etc.

After you have specified a name, choose the type of cross section from the Cross Section Options menu, as shown in Figure 22-5. In this example, we are selecting the **Planar** option, which then prompts use to either create or select an existing datum plane to use as a virtual cutting plane.

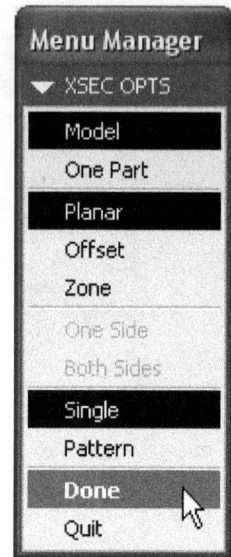

Fig. 22-5
Cross section option menu

Note that no matter what the section may look like, you are not actually removing any material. You are merely creating a 'view state' of the model. Also, if you choose to create a new datum, rather than selecting an existing one, it is good practice to name the new plane (see Chapter 19), such as *XSEC_A*, so that it will be obvious in the Model Tree.

If you would like to see the cross section in the three-dimensional model, double-click on its name in the dialog box. You may also control whether you want to see the cross hatching by turning on their **Visibility**, as shown in Figure 22-6.

If you decide that you would rather see the opposite side from the cutting plane removed, you may select **Flip** from the same menu. If you want to return to normal viewing with no section, simply double-click on **No Cross Section** in the dialog box.

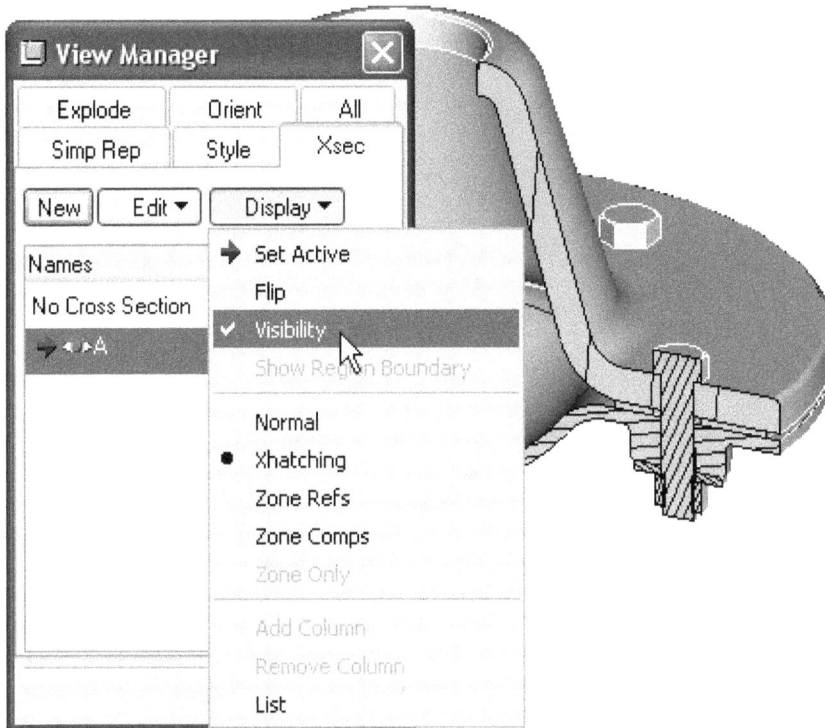

Fig. 22-6
Cross section display

Offset Section

You will notice that since our example assembly has five bolts equally spaced, any planar section that passes through the center of our design can only pass though one bolt at a time. If we wanted to show a section through more than one (or any other geometry that does not lie one same plane) we can create an **Offset** section by choosing that option from the menu shown in Figure 22-5.

This will prompt us to create a sketch to simulate a cut through our design. We can use any geometry as a reference, and your sketch should be created as an open sketch (see Chapter 9), as if we were specifying the path of a laser, as shown in Figure 22-7. Notice how the sketched lines pass through, and are aligned to the centers of the entire assembly, as well as the bolts.

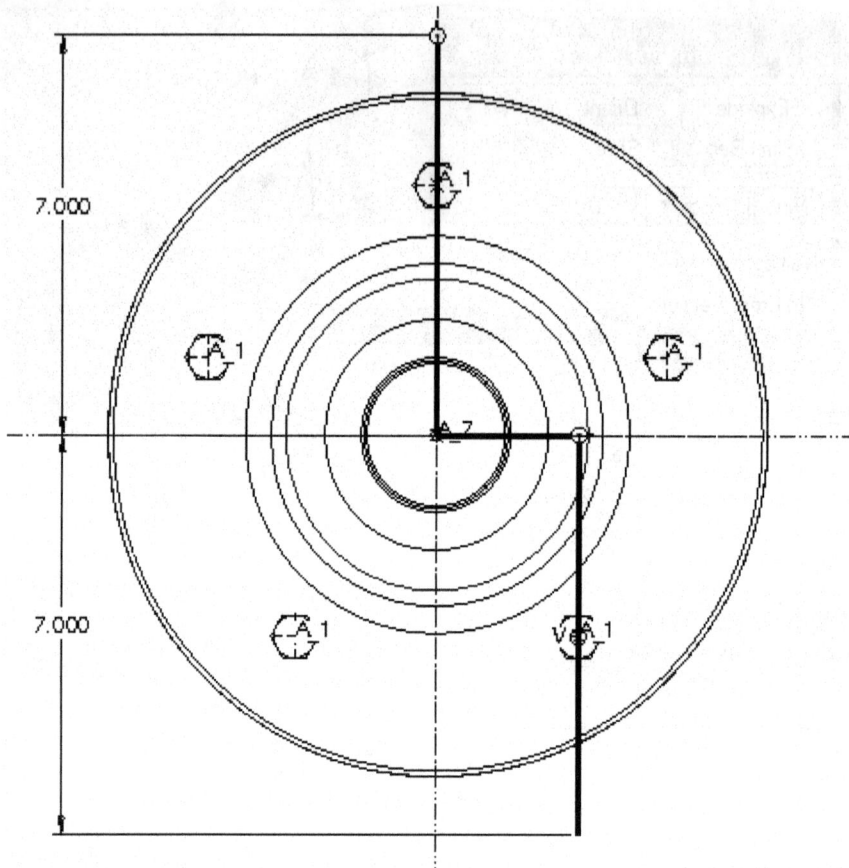

Fig. 22-7
Offset section definition

If you want to visualize the
resulting section in the three-
dimensional model, you certainly
may, as shown in Figure 22-8, but
it can also be used in a two-
dimensional drawing, as shown in
Figure 22-9.

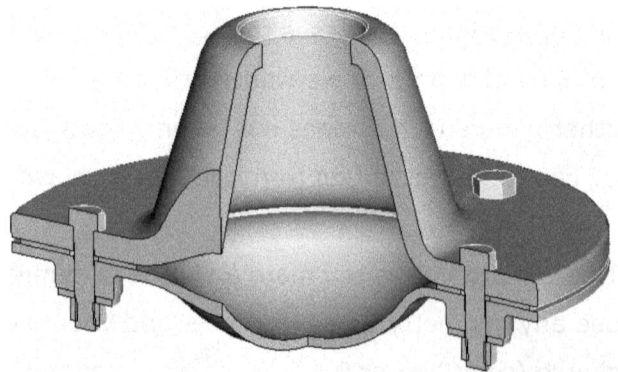

Fig. 22-8
Three dimensional offset section

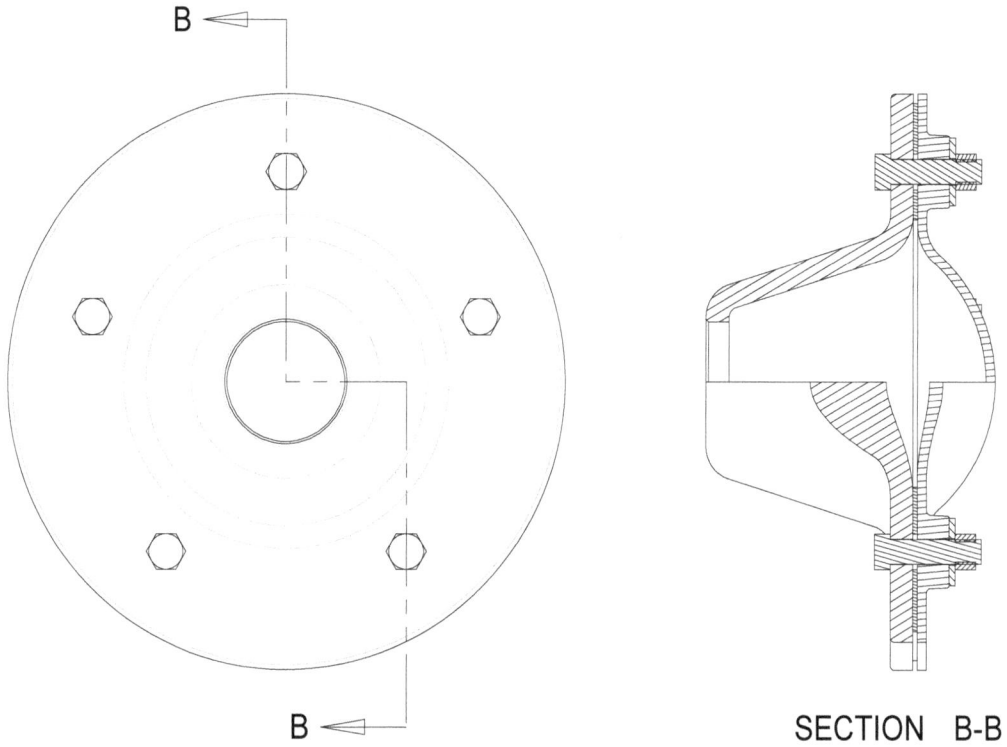

Fig. 22-9
Offset cross section in two-dimensional drawing

Notice that it was sufficient to simply name our cross section '*B*', as our two-dimensional drawing automatically places the name of the section at the cutting line arrows, and also labels the view with ' SECTION *name–name* '

You may create as many sections in a given part or assembly as you wish, and regardless of their display state, they will never alter the geometry in any way.

Explode

When we put several components together into an assembly, its structure and how the components fit together are obvious to us. We know exactly which parts we've used, and how many of them we've used, but it is not so obvious to any one else looking at it. You can create several views, including section views, such as the one shown in Figure 22-9, but an exploded view, as shown in Figure 22-10 can not only identify components, but also illustrate assembly sequences.

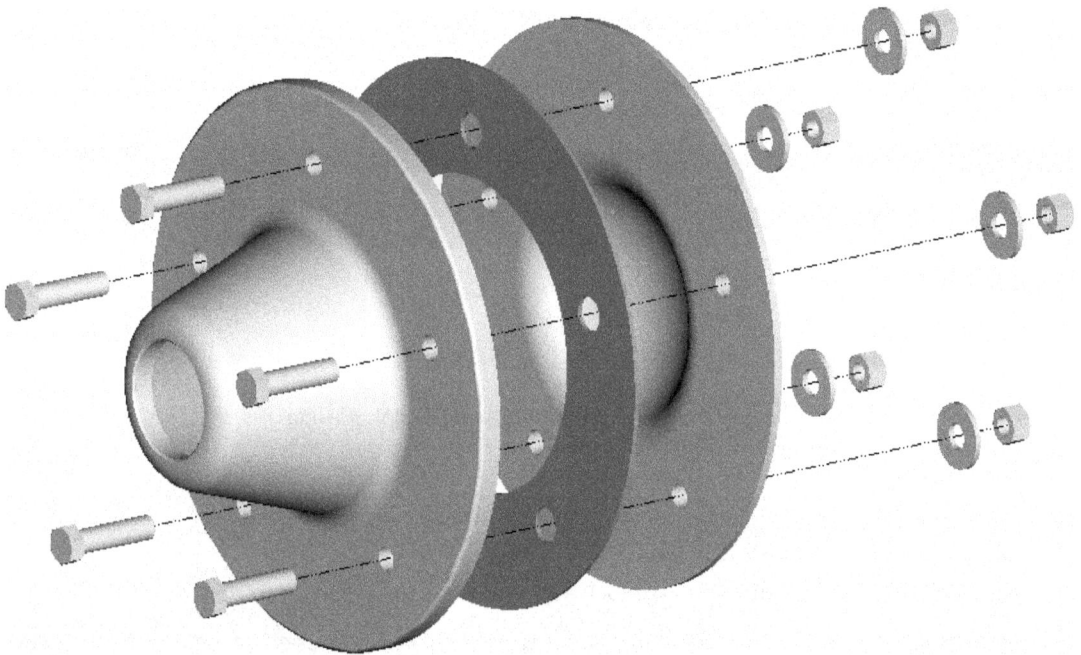

Fig. 22-10
Typical exploded view

As with all of the View Manager settings, a Pro/ENGINEER exploded view does not alter the actual three-dimensional design. The three disk shaped objects in our example have been assembled face to face (and still are) but an exploded view can simulate what the same assembly would look like if the components were pulled apart.

Pro/ENGINEER has a default exploded view built into every assembly, but since the program has no way of knowing what makes a 'good looking' view, you would most likely need to modify it considerably. It is recommended to just go ahead and create your own exploded view(s) by selecting **New** from the dialog box, and entering the desired name. This will create an exploded view, but since you haven't adjusted any positions yet, it will look normal.

To adjust the positions of the components, select **View** > **Explode** > **Edit Position** from the menu. This will open the Explode Position dialog box as shown in Figure 22-11. Choose the type of geometry you wish to use for the Motion Reference, such as normal to a plane (as shown), along an Edge, or coordinate system, and then choose the entity to use as a reference. With the **LMB**, select the component (part or subassembly) you would like to move. Release the button and drag the mouse. The component will move as you move the mouse. To place the component, click the **LMB** again. You may select additional components, and each will move along the same Motion Reference, until you select a new Motion Reference. The default Motion Type is Translate, but you may also copy the current position of a component, and apply it to another.

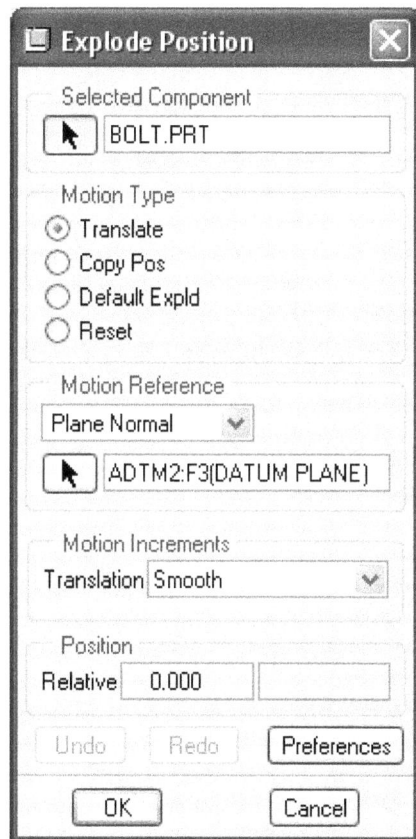

Fig. 22-11
Explode Position dialog box

You may also select options in the Preferences tab to move multiple components at the same time, or to move a component with all its children at the same time. After selecting **OK** to set the positions of the components, you must save the exploded view by going back to the View Manager, selecting the name of the exploded view, holding down the **RMB**, and selecting **Save**. You may create as many exploded views as you wish, and to modify any of them, just go back to the **View** > **Explode** > **Edit Position** menu to reopen the dialog box shown in Figure 22-11.

No matter how many exploded views you create, and no matter where you place components within the views, the actual assembled position of the components in the design will not be altered. (The components are not actually being relocated.)

If you no longer wish to view the model in an exploded state, place the cursor in the Names area of the dialog box, hold down the **RMB**, and un-check **Explode**, as shown in Figure 22-12.

Fig. 22-12
Un-exploding the assembly

Offset lines

To create the offset lines (also known as thrust lines) select **View** > **Explode** > **Offset Lines** > **Create** from the menu. You can choose to create the lines along an axis or edge, or normal to a surface.

The offset lines are created as assembly features, and are children of the components they are attached to. As the positions of the components are modified, the offset lines will follow.

Simplified Representation (Simp Rep)

Throughout this book, we have discussed the importance of parent/child relationships and the downstream effects of changes. When we delete or suppress a component in an assembly that has other parts referencing it (children), all of the children must be deleted, suppressed or rerouted to new parents.

Using Simplified Representations, you may create versions of your assembly that omit particular components, without affecting the parent/child relationships. A Simplified Representation can be created to represent all of the exterior components of an assembly, while another could represent all of the interior components. Perhaps you create one to represent all of the static components, while another represents all of the dynamic (moving) components, while yet another represents every component except the nuts and bolts. You can accomplish the same task by simply hiding the components (see Chapter 17), but Simplified Representations go beyond this in two significant ways.

First, you may create as many different representations in a single model as you wish. Each of these representations may be given a specific name, and you may toggle between them at any time. Detail drawings can be created from these versions of your model, and each of them can be used as sub assemblies in other models. None of the omitted components appear in a Bill of Materials (see Chapter 24). On the other hand, **Hide** merely turns the components invisible, therefore they will still appear in the Bill of Materials, and there is no way to save various combinations of hidden components.

Secondly, when a component is omitted from a representation, Pro/ENGINEER completely ignores its data. It is not considered during mass property or interference calculations (see Chapter 25). A hidden component still has mass and geometry, and Pro/ENGINEER retains its data. This data uses your computer resources, even if you cannot see it. Our examples are not very large or complicated, so even the least powerful computer can handle them, but once you omit a component, you can **Erase** it from your Pro/ENGINEER session. For extremely complex models, this can add up to a significant boost in your computer's performance, and at times, can make the difference between being able to work on an assembly, or not.

Master Rep

The Master Representation is the normal state for an assembly and all its components. Every feature and dimension of every part is present and modifiable. It is the Master Representation that retains all of the information necessary to build the model, so that when you create other representations with information omitted, that information is not lost forever.

Geometry Rep

A Geometry Representation retains a component's size, shape, and mass, but it ignores that fact that it has features with parents, children, and dimensions. It treats a component as a single, solid mass; essentially, as a 'dumb solid'. This gives you the ability to use it in an assembly while still maintaining its mass, and will also be included in any interference checking you may engage in. Since it does not maintain a list of features and dimensions, it will use less computer resources than the Master Representation.

Graphics Rep

A Graphics Representation contains absolutely no real geometry at all. It is simply a graphical placeholder for the component. It has no mass, merely a 'picture' of the component. This is useful for showing objects in your assembly that are for reference only, and use even less of your computer resources than a Geometry Representation.

Symbolic Rep

A Symbolic Representation allows you to replace a component with a single datum point. The amount of computer resources it requires is next to nothing and it allows you to maintain a valid Bill of Materials, without needing to display the actual component at all. This is extremely useful when your assembly contains a large number of the same item, such as the rivets in an aircraft. The rivets themselves may be simple, but multiplied hundreds or even thousands of times, then could become quite cumbersome.

Custom Representations

To create a representation, select **New** from the dialog box, and specify a name. In this example, we will omit the gasket from our assembly, so we can name it *No_Gasket*. After entering the name, the Edit dialog box will open, as shown in Figure 22-13. By default, you are prompted to select the components to exclude (remove) from the assembly. You may select parts and subassemblies, or even individual parts within the subassemblies. The selected components will not immediately disappear, so if you may select the [👓] **Preview** icon to see the results or your choices. When you are finished (you can always go back and edit it again later) select the check mark to accept the settings, and the components will be removed from the assembly.

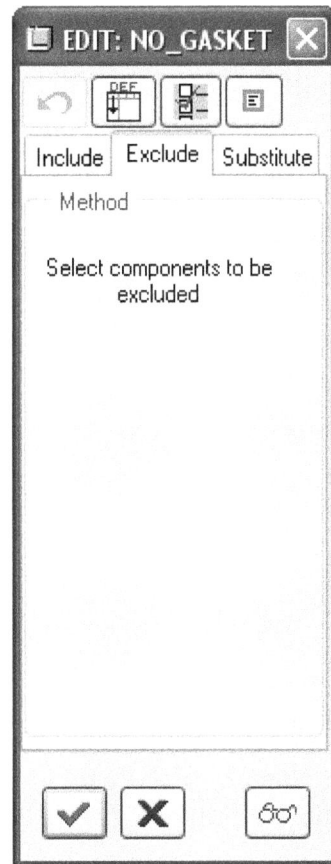

Fig. 22-13
Representation Edit dialog box

You may also select the Include tab. This is where you could choose a particular type of representation for an individual component. For example, in addition to excluding the gasket, you could decide to show the nuts and washers as datum points only, by selecting **Symbolic Rep** in the dialog box, then selecting the components from the graphics area or Model Tree. We could also choose to show one or more of the components as a **Graphics Rep** by following the same steps, as shown in Figure 22-15.

If you wish to isolate only a few components, you may Exclude every component and sub assembly first, then include individual components as a Master Rep, by selecting them individually in the Model Tree, as shown in Figure 22-16.

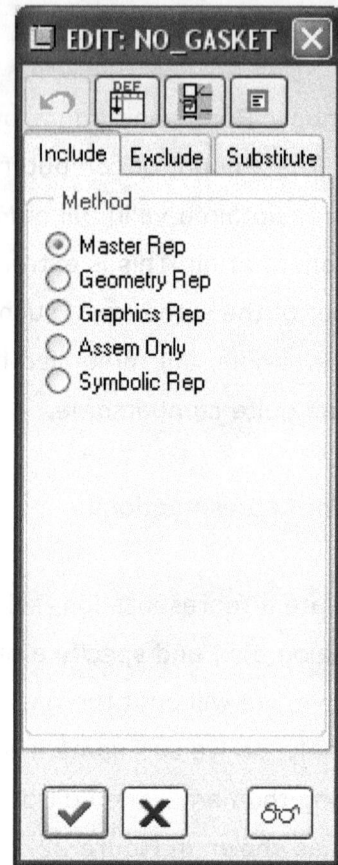

Fig. 22-14
Component Include states

As you are creating and editing your representations, a column will automatically open in the Model Tree to show you the status of each of the components, as shown in Figures 22-15 and 22-16.

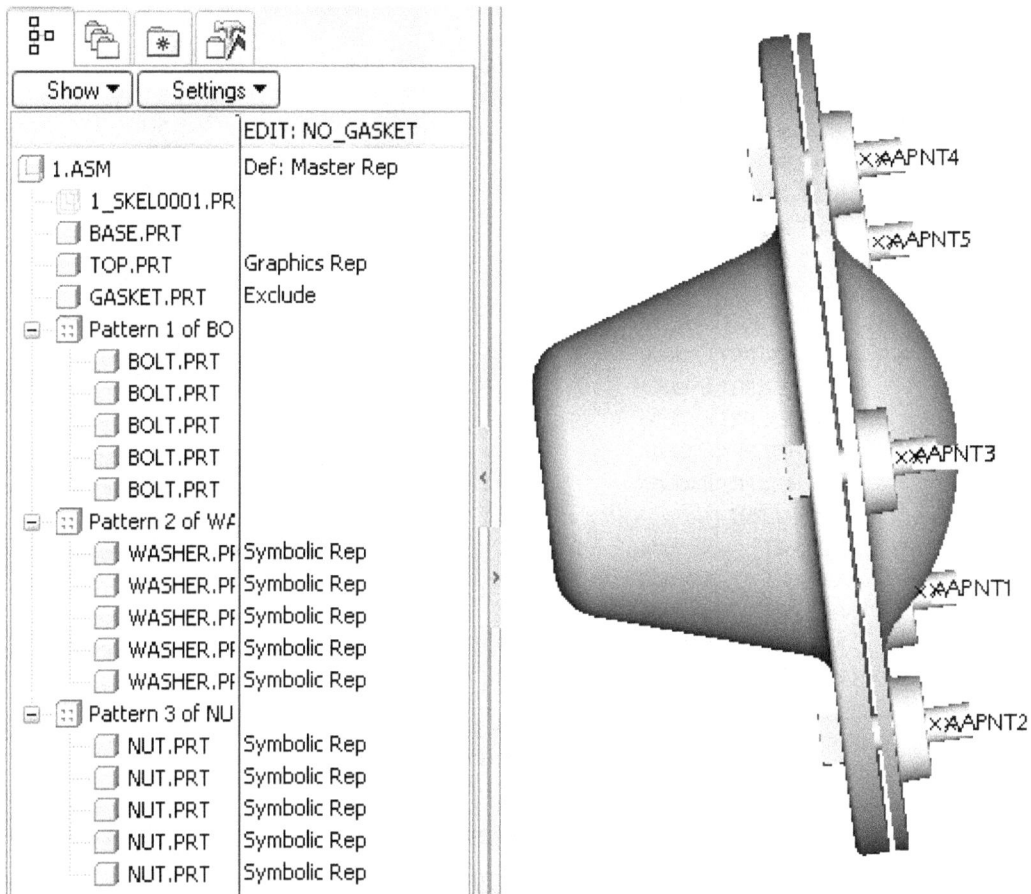

Fig. 22-15
No_Gasket Simplified representation

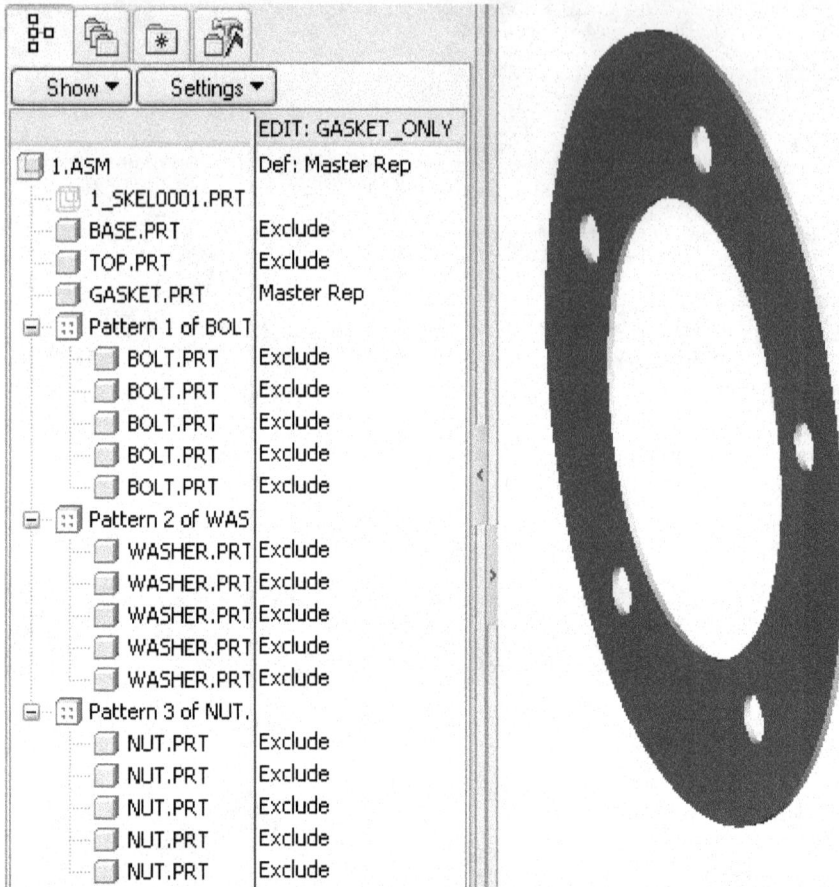

Fig. 22-16
Gasket_Only representation

To switch between representations, select them from the dialog box. Even if you have erased a model from memory, Pro/ENGINEER will retrieve it from the disk or network if necessary. To use a Simplified Representation as a sub assembly in another model, choose the Open Rep option when assembling it, as shown in Figure 22-17.

Fig. 22-17
Assembling a Simplified Rep

Style

As discussed in Chapter 4, you may toggle the display style between wireframe, hidden line, no hidden and shaded, by selecting the Display Style icons in the Main Toolbar. These settings are system settings, meaning that every component in every model will be displayed according to the current setting. By using the View Manager, you may create a unique display style that overrides this setting, may contain a variety of display styles for each component.

To create a style, select **New** from the dialog box. In this case we want to create a representation designating vendor supplied items as reference, so we will name it *Vendor_Supplied*. After saving the name, the Style Edit dialog box will open, as shown in Figure 22-18. By default, the system prompts you to select which items to blank, which is essentially a **Hide** command, but you may also select the Show tab, and choose individual style states for each component.

Again, these settings will override the system settings. Figure 22-19 shows the results of setting a single component to **No Hidden**, while the rest are set to **Shading**.

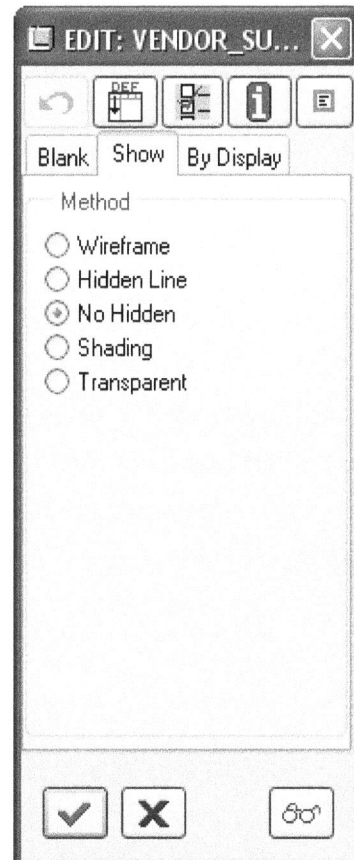

Fig. 22-18
Component style states

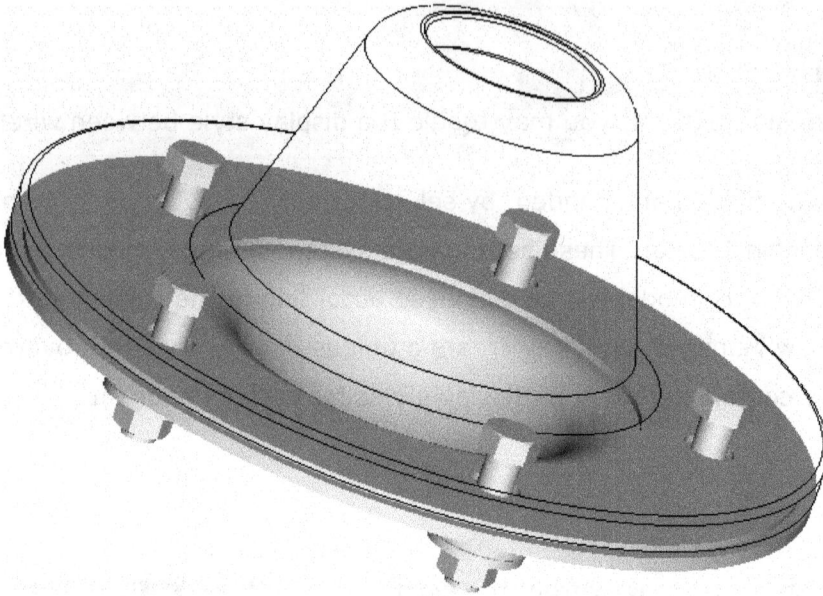

Fig. 22-19
Style representation showing a reference part

All

You may select the tabs across the top of the View Manager dialog box, as shown in Figure 22-1, and then choose the different saved states from the lists available at any time. If however you find that you want to go back to a particular combination of Simplified Representation, Cross Section, Orientation, Explode, and Style, go ahead and make all of those setting choices, then select the All tab, and create a state that combines <u>all</u> of the current settings. You will have a choice, as shown in Figure 22-20, to **Reference Originals**, which means it will update as the other settings are modified, or **Create Copies**, which will freeze the current settings.

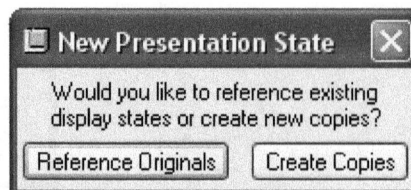

Fig. 22-20
Combination state reference control

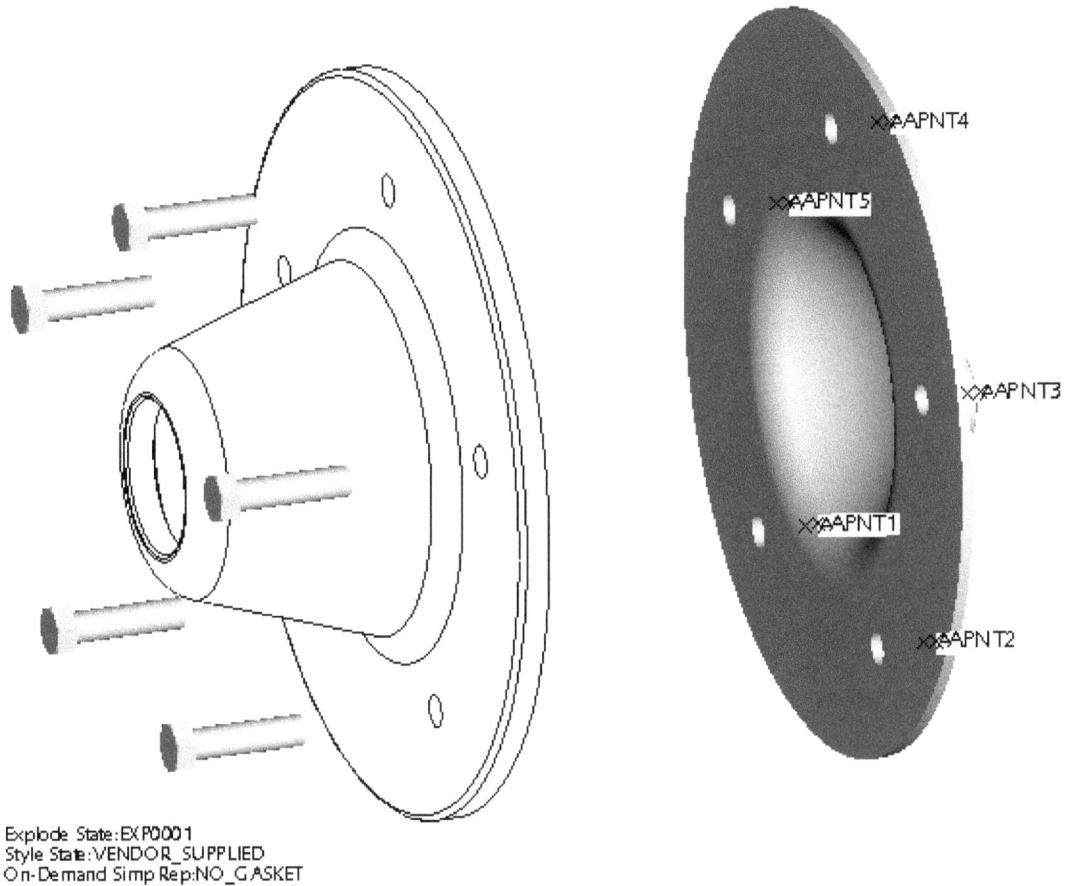

Explode State:EXP0001
Style State:VENDOR_SUPPLIED
On-Demand Simp Rep:NO_GASKET

Fig. 22-21
Combination of states

Figure 22-21 shows the result of combining various states. Notice that when a particular state is used, a tag will appear in the graphics window identifying the current state.

Assemblies

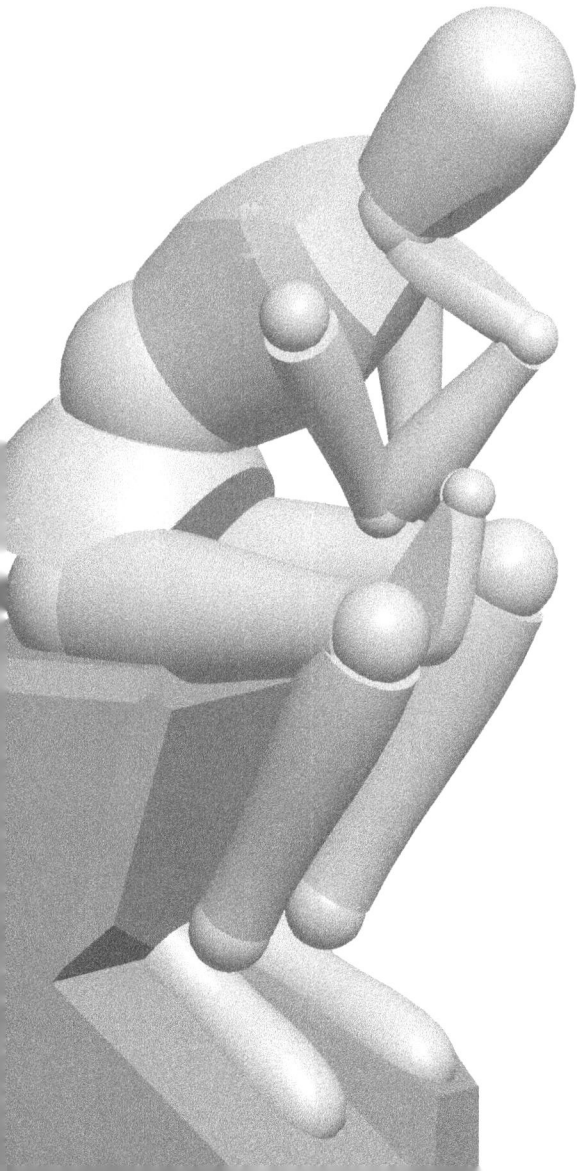

Any number of individual Pro/ENGINEER parts may be grouped together to form assemblies. The assembly file (*.asm) does not contain any part geometry, but instead is a collection of the various parts that contain the solid geometry; a virtual 'table of contents', if you will. Using Associativity, Pro/ENGINEER creates assemblies by pulling in the definition of the individual parts, from their respective files. It does not make copies, therefore any change to an individual part is automatically and immediately reflected in any assembly which may be referencing the part.

Any part may be added to a single assembly as many times as needed, and any part may be simultaneously added to as many different assemblies as desired. Subassemblies are simply assemblies that are added to higher level assemblies. For example, an automotive seat can be put together as an assembly, but as soon as it is placed in a vehicle, it is considered a subassembly.

Organization

It is best to create assemblies and subassemblies which represent the actual product to be manufactured. For example, Figure 23-1 shows a Pro/ENGINEER assembly consisting of a bolt, washer, and nut. Many novice Pro/ENGINEER users mistakenly believe that they can save time by creating a subassembly like this, then adding it multiple times to their higher level assemblies.

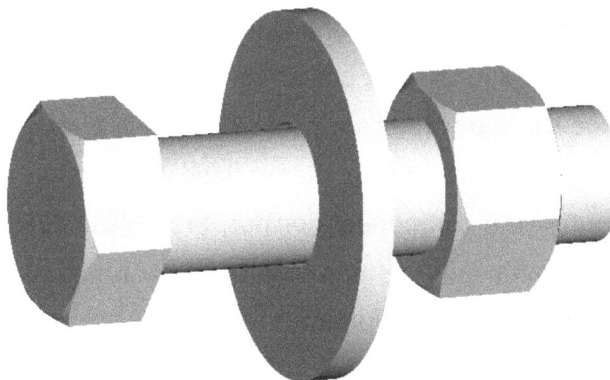

Fig. 23-1
Assembly containing three parts

The problem with this approach is that unless this is your final product being shipped to a customer (an assembly containing a bolt and a nut), this condition will never exist on the manufacturing floor. A technician will never pick up a bolt with a nut on it already, and install it into a product. They will however place a bolt in a product, then a nut, therefore your Pro/ENGINEER assemblies should reflect this. This will also allow for the automatic generation of an accurate Bill of Materials (see Chapter 24). Also, if two or more components are ever machined in the same operation, such as drilling through two parts at the same time, this operation may be defined in an assembly. (See later in this chapter.)

To create a new assembly, select the ▯ **New** icon from the **Main Toolbar**, specify **Assembly** as the file type and give the file the desired name. Just as when creating new part files, you have the option of starting with a completely blank (empty) assembly, or using any number of templates (see Chapter 27). Regardless of what you start with, your assembly should have at least default datum planes and perhaps a default coordinate system.

Adding Components

To add (assemble) a part (or subassembly), click on the ▱ **Assemble** icon from the **Construction Toolbar**. From the **Open** window, browse to and select the part or assembly you wish to add. There are many ways to locate components, but is very common and useful to use the **Default** placement. You may select **Default** from the pull-down menu in the dashboard, as shown in Figure 23-2, or you may hold down the **RMB** and select **Default** from the list. Regardless if you have a default coordinate system in your assembly and components or not, Pro/ENGINEER knows where the default coordinate systems would be, and how they are oriented. The **Default** position allows you to place the component in the assembly matching these positions and orientations. It is commonly only used for the first component in an assembly, but it may be used for additional components, if those components are designed appropriately.

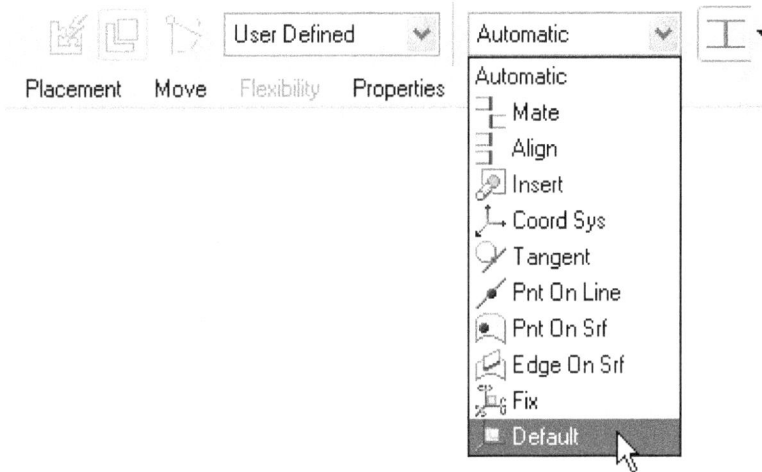

Fig. 23-2
Assembling a component in Default position

As additional components are added to the assembly, they will appear in the graphics area of the screen, along with the existing assembly (the collection of previously assembled components). To assist in placing the new component, hold down **Ctrl**, **Alt** and **MMB** to spin (orient) the model as desired, or **Ctrl**, **Alt** and **RMB** to drag the component into the approximate position, as shown in Figure 23-3.

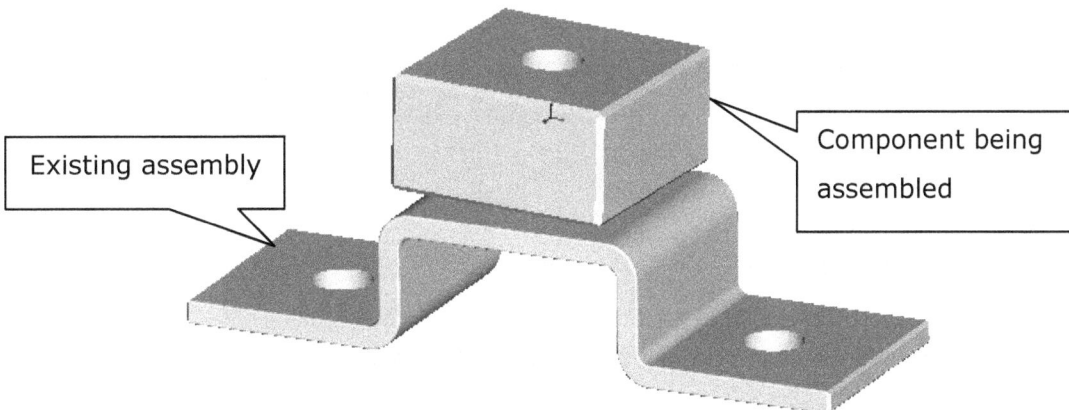

Fig. 23-3
Placing a component in an assembly

Depending on the component being added, and how you want to control its placement, you may define up to six degrees of freedom, although three is generally sufficient. Components may be controlled using joints, such as those used in assemblies with moving parts, or constraints which simulate parts that are held together.

User-defined Constraints

Mate   places two planar surfaces together. An example would be a postage stamp and an envelope. The adhesive side of the stamp is mated to the front of the envelope. The stamp surface and the envelope surface are Coincident (meaning there is no gap), which is one of the options available with the **Mate** constraint. You may also define an **Offset** value, if you want to create a gap between the surfaces. If the location of the stamp is controlled with a combination of other constraints, you may use **Orient** option of **Mate** to simply make the two planar surfaces face each other without controlling a gap distance.

Align   places two planar surfaces in the same direction. An example would be the steps of a ladder. The tread side of each step faces the same direction, and are evenly spaced (offset) from each other. You may also use **Coincident** or **Orient**. **Align** may also be used to attach two axes together, such as the center axis of a bolt and the center axis of a hole or nut.

Insert   places the centers of two cylindrical or conical surfaces together. An example would be a cap on an ink pen. This will locate the components as if the center axes where **Aligned**. This is useful if your component does not have an axis feature available.

Coord Sys places two coordinate systems at the same location and orientation. Any part or assembly may contain one or more coordinate systems, any of which may be used for assembly purposes.

Tangent places a non planar surface to another reference. An example would be a ball resting on a table.

Pnt On Line places a vertex or datum point along an edge or axis.

Pnt On Srf places a vertex or datum point on a surface.

Edge On Srf aligns a linear edge to a surface.

Fix locks the component in space, in its current position, without any geometry references. This is generally only used when first placing a component in the assembly, when its final position has not yet been determined, or when you are in the process or redefining the placement of a component, as a temporary placeholder.

First choose the constraint type you wish to use, and then select the appropriate geometry in both the existing assembly, and the component being added. It does not matter which order you choose, as you will need both assembly and component references. For clarity, you may wish to open the **Placement** tab in the dashboard, as shown in Figure 23-4. This will allow you to see the status of your constraint and reference selections. In this example, we chose the **Align** constraint, and then selected the axis in the hole of the bracket part (which is the assembly reference) and the axis in the hole of the block part (which is the component reference). Once this constraint is set, we can continue to drag and spin the component, but it will remain locked, axis to axis.

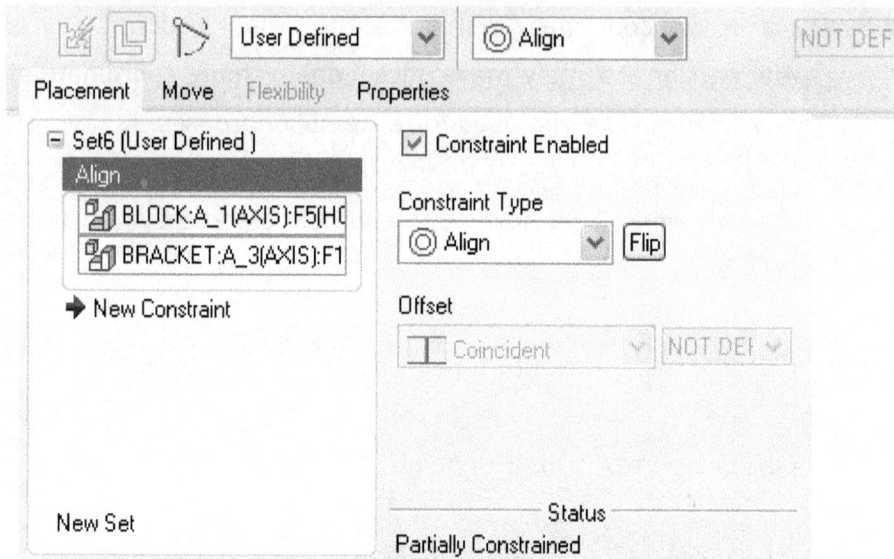

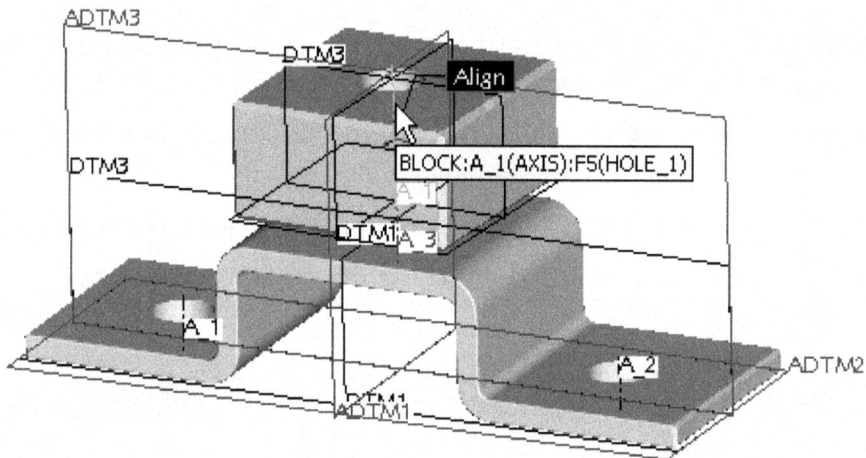

Fig. 23-4
Defining component and assembly references

Notice that the status of the component is 'Partially Constrained'. To continue, click on **New Constraint** and select an additional constraint type and references, such as using **Mate** to place the bottom surface of the block on the top surface of the bracket. After controlling a component in two degrees of freedom, Pro/ENGINEER will quite often give you the option to **Allow Assumptions** which uses the component's default orientation to define the third degree of freedom, as shown in Figure 23-5.

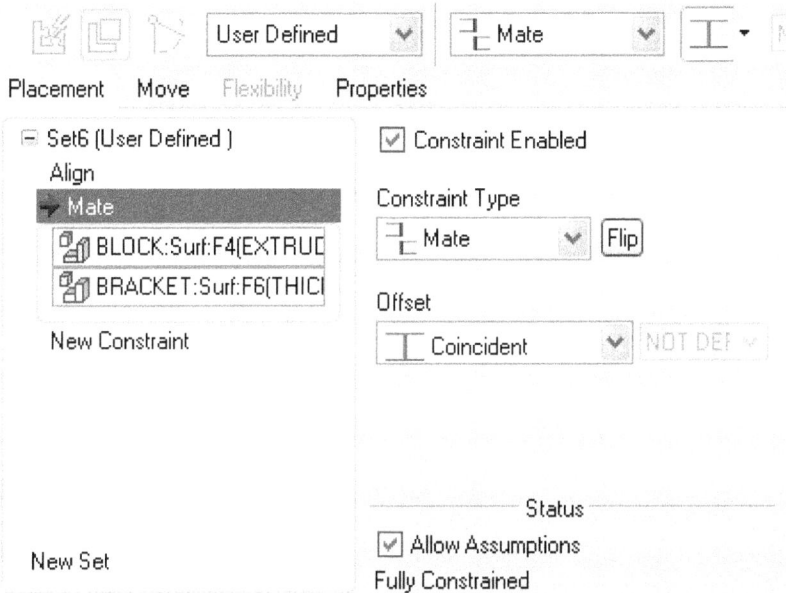

Fig. 23-5
Second constraint placed on component

This is typically used for items such as nuts and bolts, since their rotational orientation is not critical for the design of the assembly. If you uncheck the **Allow Assumptions** box, the component will again become partially constrained, at which time you would define a third constraint, as shown in Figure 23-6.

In this case we have selected the front surface of the bracket (assembly) and the front surface of the block (component) to be **Aligned**. If we wanted both surfaces to face exactly the same direction, then we would set the **Offset** to **Orient**, however we can specify any angle we wish, as shown in Figure 23-6. Similarly, if we wanted a gap between the top of the bracket, and the bottom of the block, we could specify an offset value for the **Mate**, rather than coincident.

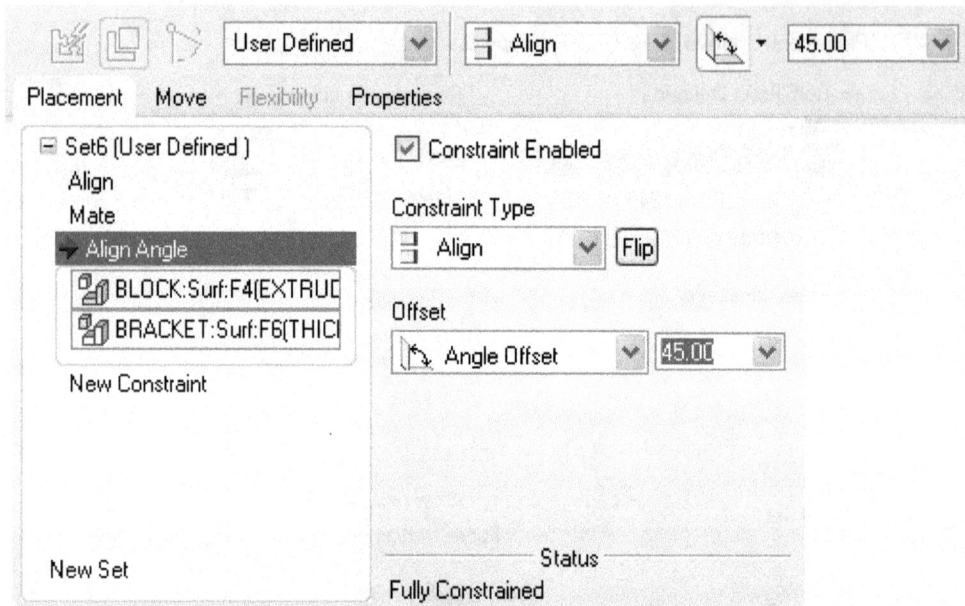

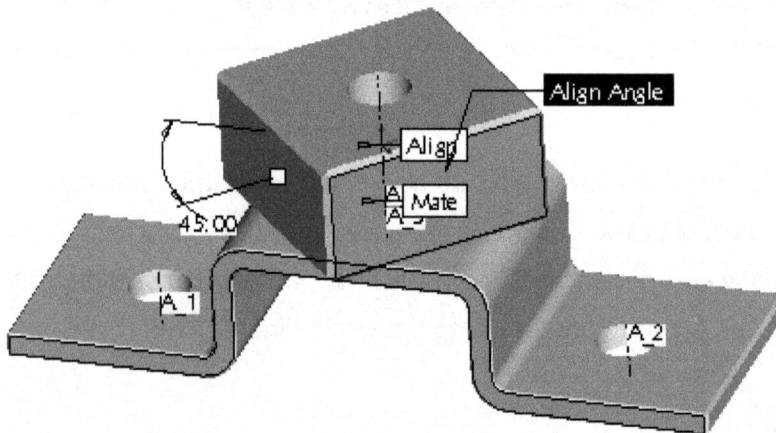

Fig. 23-6
Fully constrained component

You may use any number of constraint types and combinations of constraints and offset values, but Pro/ENGINEER will never allow you to define conflicting

constraints. When finished, click on the [✓] **Apply** icon. The component being added then becomes part of the assembly, as shown in Figure 23-7. Notice the Model Tree displays both assembly level features (datum planes) and components.

Fig. 23-7
Assembled components

Automatic Constraint Selection

You may specify the type of constraints to use, as discussed above; however you may let Pro/ENGINEER automatically select the appropriate type of constraint, based on the references you choose. For example, you may leave the constraint type set to the default, **Automatic**, and select two planar surfaces. If the two surfaces are generally facing each other, Pro/ENGINEER will assume that **Mate** is the best constraint to use. If the two faces are very close to each other, Pro/ENGINEER will most likely default to **Coincident** as the offset type. If the components are a considerable distance from each other, then Pro/ENGINEER will most likely use an offset value. If the two surfaces face in generally the same direction, Pro/ENGINEER will assume that **Align** is the best constraint to use, while two cylindrical surfaces will most likely default to **Insert**, and so on. If at any time, Pro/ENGINEER chooses a constraint type you do not agree with, you may simply change it to the desired type.

To reduce the number of incorrect assumptions, simply place the component being added in the approximate final position and orientation (you do not need to be exact) before selecting the reference geometry.

Repeat the process to assemble as many components as you wish. In this case we added a bolt, washer, and nut, as shown in Figure 23-8. Since the rotational orientation of these components is not critical, we allowed assumptions.

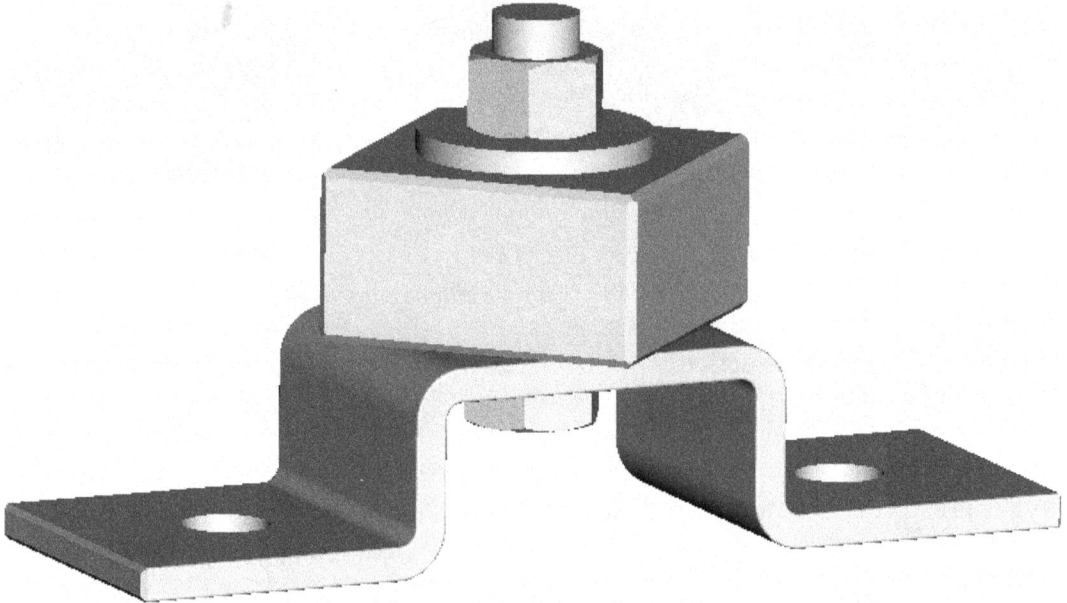

Fig. 23-8
Completed Assembly

Keep in mind that every assembly reference you choose becomes a parent to the placement definition of the component being assembled. For example, if you place a bolt in a hole, the placement of the bolt is dependant on not only the location of the hole, but the very existence of the hole. This means if the hole is ever deleted, then the placement of the bolt will fail. (See Chapter 18 for resolving failures). This also means that you should use good judgment in selecting references. You should avoid using references from unrelated components, so that unintentional parent/child relationships are not created.

Pre-defined Connections

Components that are intended to move, such as two halves of a door hinge, as shown in Figure 23-9, may be assembled using connections that simulate joints, rather than fixed constraints.

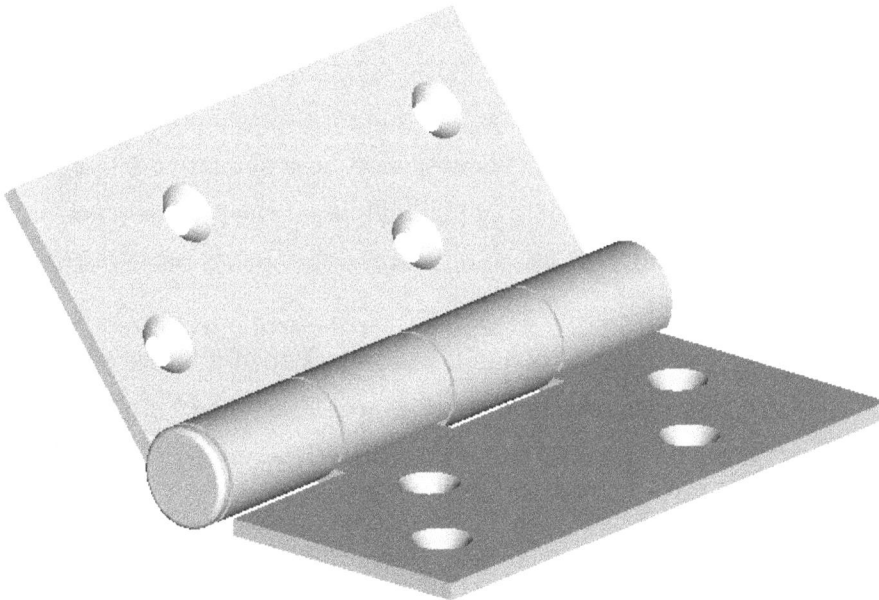

Fig. 23-9
A simple mechanism

Rigid   is similar to user-defined constraints to connect two components together, so that they do not move relative to each other.

Pin   allows a component to spin about an axis, with a specified translation (location) along the axis. An example would be the halves of the hinge shown in Figure 23-9.

Slider   allows a component to move along an axis, with a specified orientation. (The component always faces the same direction.)

Cylinder   is similar to both **Pin** and **Slider** in that a component is fixed to an axis, but it is free to both spin about, and slide along, the axis.

Planar uses mate and align two connect a planar surface of the component to a planar surface of the assembly, such that the component is free to move anywhere across the plane, but the surfaces will remain relative to each other.

Ball is a point-to-point connection that locates a datum point or vertex of the component to a datum point or vertex on the assembly, while allowing unlimited rotation about the point, in all directions.

Weld aligns a coordinate system on the component to a coordinate system of the assembly, such that the two do not move relative to each other.

Bearing connects one point to an edge or axis. It is similar to **Slider**, in that the component may slide in any location along the axis or edge, but it is not limited to a single orientation. It is free to spin in any direction, similar to a **Ball** connection.

General is used for when user-defined constraints such as **Mate** and **Align** are desired, in conjuction with other connection types.

6DOF aligns a coordinate system of the component to a coordinate system of the assembly, but allows for the component to have six degrees of freedom. The motion of the component is not affected by the motion of the assembly.

Slot creates a connection similar to **Bearing**, but requires a trajectory to follow a set distance from one end, to the other. The trajectory may be straight or non-straight and two or three-dimensional.

The hinge shown in Figure 23-9 could be assembled by aligning the pivot axes on both halves, aligning the bottom edges and allowing the rotation to be undefined, but the advantage to using a pin connection is that the hinge may be set at a nominal starting angle, and free to move within a minimum and maximum range. This means that when this hinge is assembled to a door and a frame, it can be mated to both sides, and the pin connection definition will limit the travel of the door, as desired.

The first half of the hinge is assembled at **Default** position, but Figure 23-10 shows the second half being assembled using a pin connection.

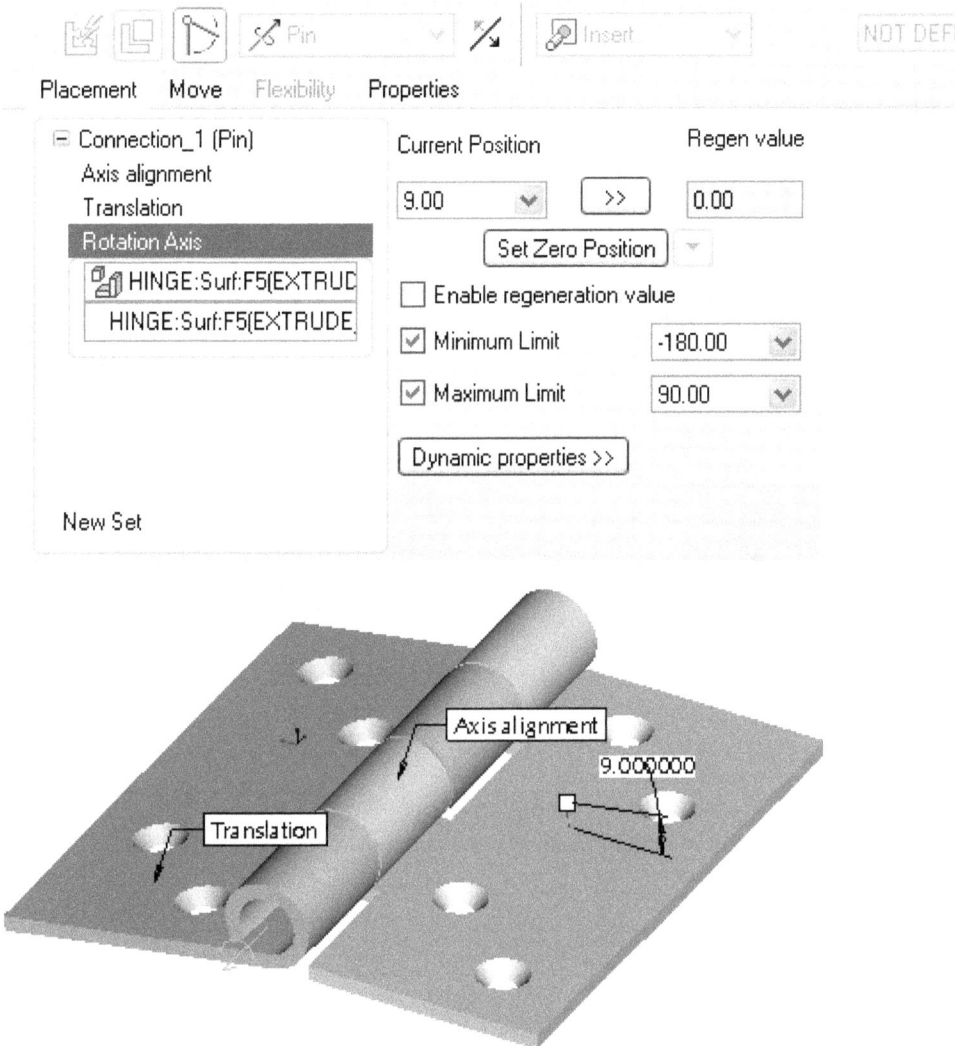

Fig. 23-10
Pin connection with rotational limit

The two top surfaces of each half are selected a rotational references. This allows you to enter a minimum and maximum amount of allowable rotation, if desired. You may also set the value you wish it to return to upon a regeneration. This allows you to 'reset' the assembly to a starting position.

To move the component through its range of motion, click on the ![Drag icon] **Drag Components** icon from the **Main Toolbar**, then select anywhere on the component and drag the component into position, as shown in Figure 23-11.

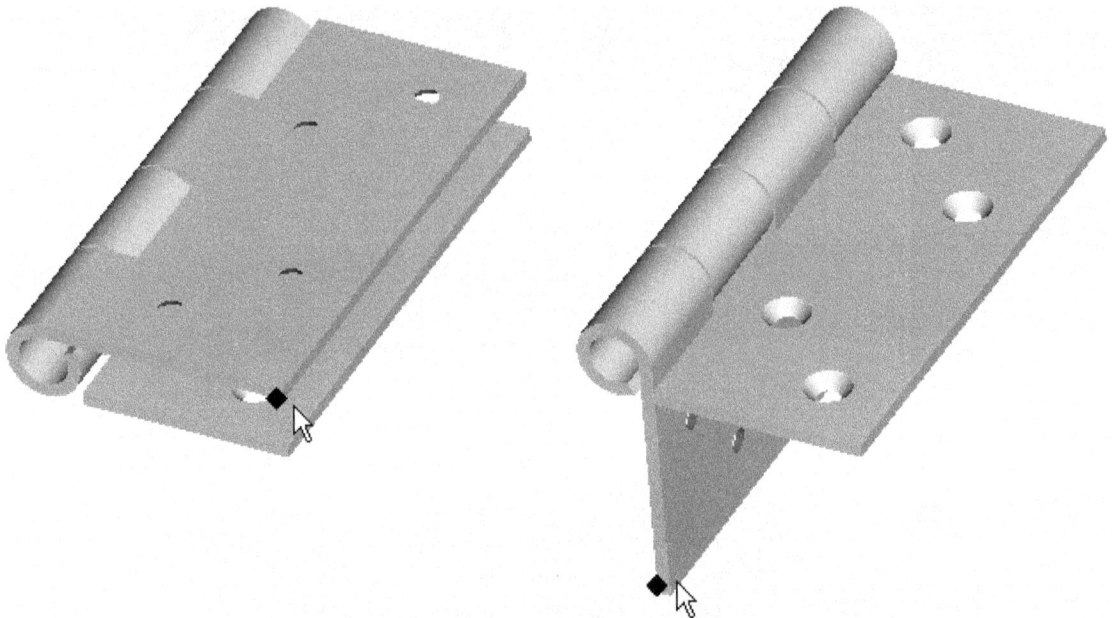

Fig. 23-11
Component minimum position (left) and maximum position (right)

Other connection types have similar range of motion controls that may be applied as appropriate. Once a component has been dragged to a position, a snapshot may be taken so that you can quickly return to the same position later, or it may be used when creating a particular view on a drawing.

Subassemblies

In addition to part models, you may also assemble existing assemblies into other assemblies, which then are automatically considered subassemblies. There is no distinction in the Pro/ENGINEER file between assemblies or subassemblies, as each can be defined separately from each other. All assemblies can be used as subassemblies for any other assembly.

Figure 23-12 shows a new assembly, with a part named *BASE* as the first component. The entire assembly created in Figure 23-8 is added as the second component. The same bolts, washers and nuts are then added as the third through eighth components.

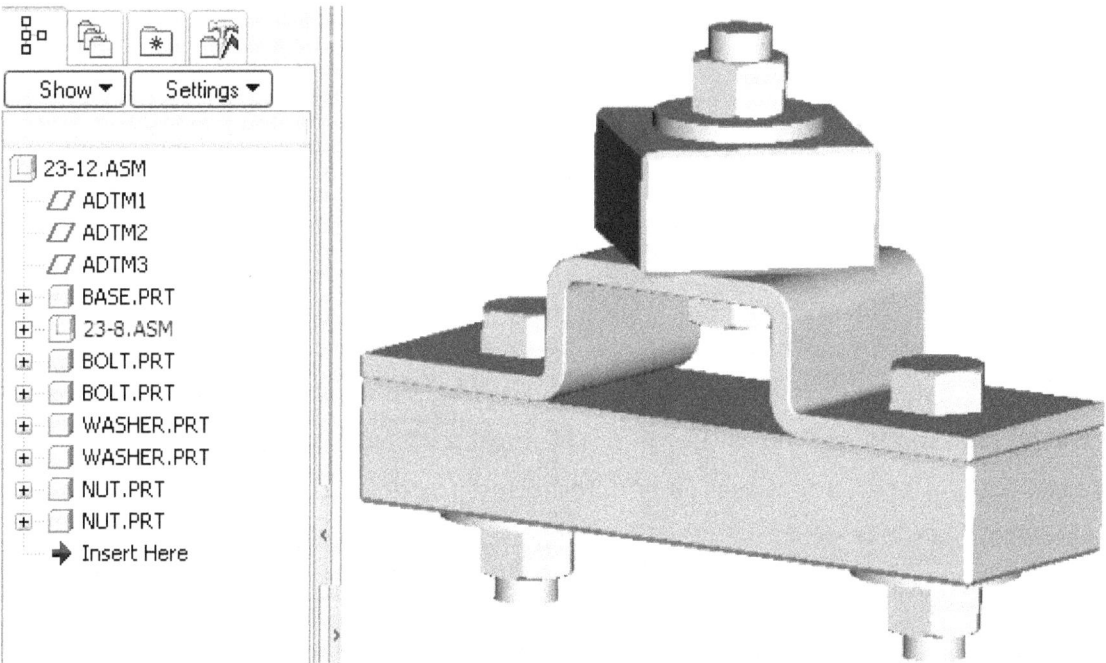

Fig. 23-12
Assembly with subassembly and parts

Interfaces

When the same component is added more than once, as in the case of the bolts, washers and nuts in Figure 23-12, Pro/ENGINEER will retain the component **Interface** information, so that you only need to specify the assembly references. For example, the first time the bolt was assembled, it was done so by inserting the cylindrical surface into the cylindrical surface of a hole, and the flat underside of the head was mated to the flat surface of the bracket. When it is added a second time, Pro/ENGINEER uses this interface information to pre-select the cylinder and flat of the additional bolt, and also assumes that they will be used in the same **Insert** and **Mate** constraints. If you wish to assemble the component manually, without reusing any temporary interface information, simply click on the ⬛ **Manual Placement** icon in the dashboard, as shown in Figure 23-13.

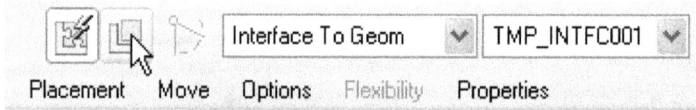

Fig. 23-13
Disabling Interface option

There may be certain components that you wish to pre-define their references for placing in assemblies. This is useful for standard parts which will be used over and over again, in possibly thousands of different assemblies. To create a permanent interface, open the component in Pro/ENGINEER. Select **Insert > Model Datum > Component Interface** from the menu.

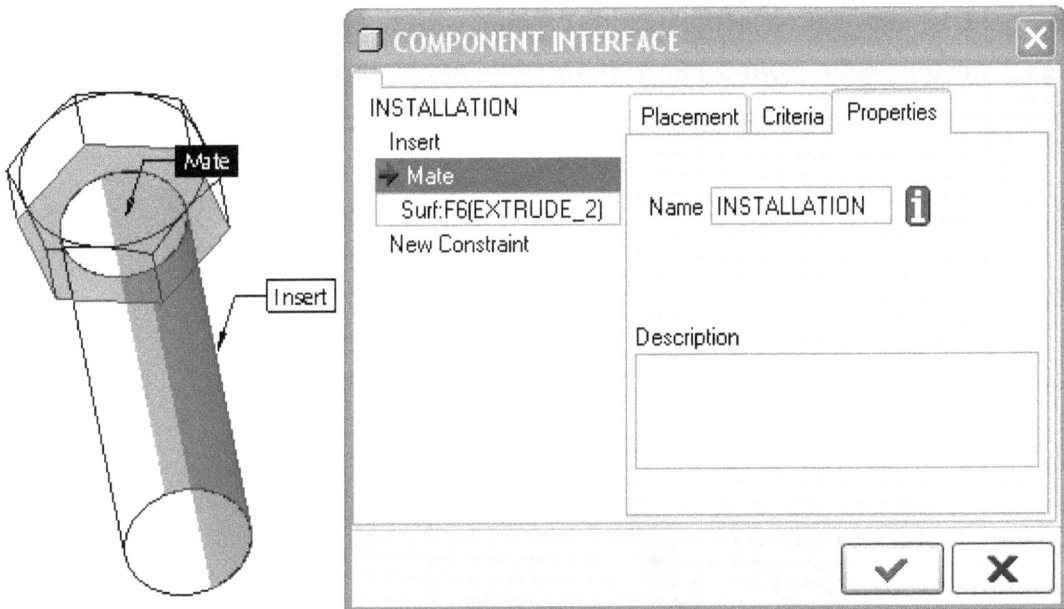

Fig. 23-14
Defining Component Interface

You may create more than one **Interface** in each component, with unique names and constraint types. It is important to note however that this information is stored within the component, not the upper level assembly, so you must save the component after the interface is defined. When adding this component to an assembly, you may choose the appropriate interface name from the available list.

Flexibility

There may be times when you wish to model a part such as a spring or gasket for manufacturing purposes, but when it is included in an assembly you want to show it in its expanded or compressed state. Since components in assemblies are not copies, but the actual part models, modifying the component's dimensions to match an assembly condition would alter the manufacturing design of the part. The solution is to use **Flexibility** to allow certain dimensions of the part to 'flex' when it is used in an assembly.

Figure 23-15 shows an assembly being created with two covers and a gasket. The gasket will be die cut from 0.25" thick material stock, but when the two covers are bolted together, the gasket is intended to be compressed to a thickness of 0.10".

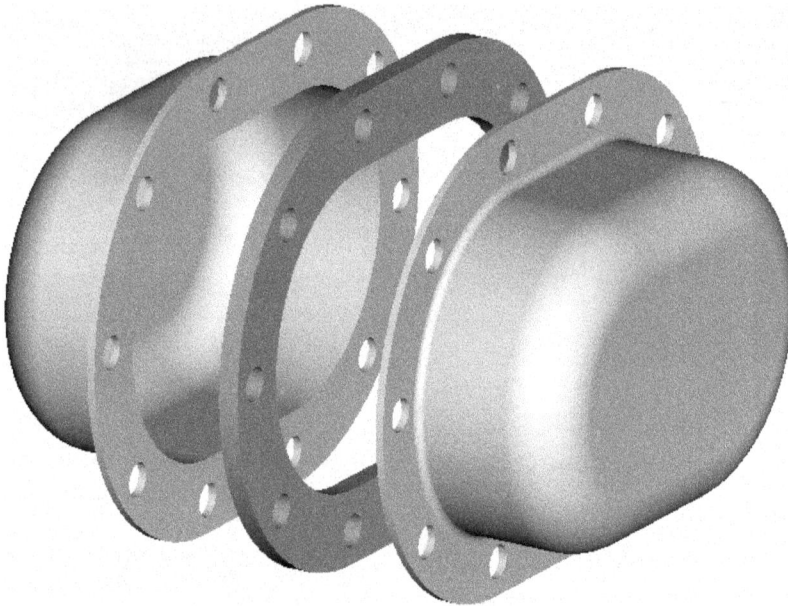

Fig. 23-15
Assembly with compressible component

If we mate the surface of the gasket to the surface of one cover, then the surface of the second cover to the other side of the gasket, all of the parts will be constrained, but they will not represent their final installed position. If we mated the two housings together with a 0.10" offset, they would be in their proper position, but if we placed the gasket in between the flanges, the gasket would appear to interfere with either one or both of the covers.

To allow the gasket to flex, open the part and select **Edit > Setup > Flexibility** from the menu. This will open a dialog box, as shown in Figure 23-16. Many aspects of the model may be controlled with flexibility, but in this example we will select the **Dimensions** tab, then the **+** icon to add a dimension, then select the appropriate feature and dimension from the model.

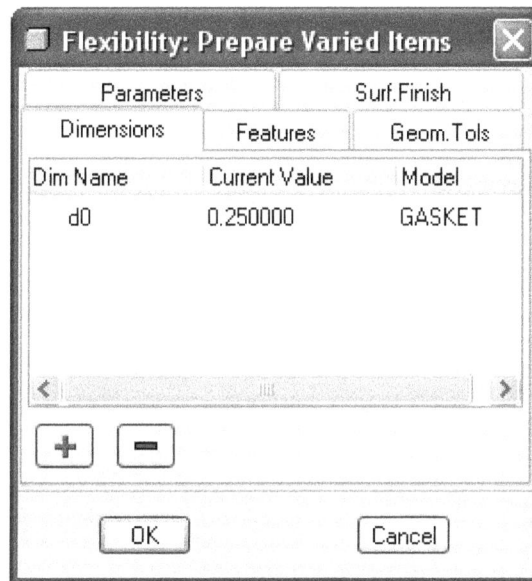

Fig. 23-16
Defining items to vary

Just as **Interfaces** are stored in the components, so are **Flexibility** controls, therefore the model must be saved, so that the controls may be used in the future.

In our example, we can first add the two covers, using a **Mate Offset** value of 0.10" between the two flanges. When adding the gasket to an assembly, Pro/ENGINEER automatically gives you the option to utilize the flexibility option, as shown in Figure 23-17.

This will open a dialog box, as shown in Figure 23-18, similar to the **Flexibility** definition box, but this time you are prompted for the values you wish to use in the assembly.

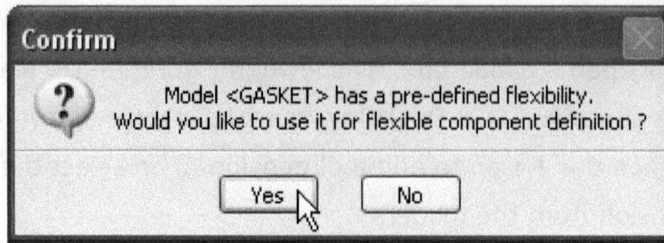

Fig. 23-17
Flexibility option

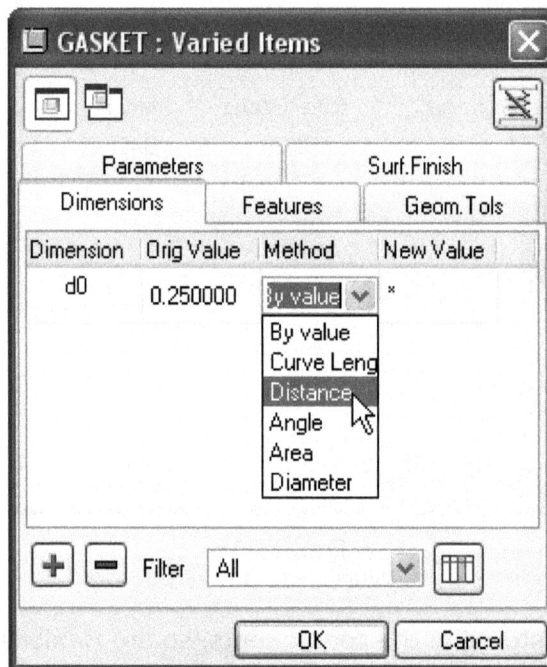

Fig. 23-18
Setting variables

You may manually enter 0.10 for the new value, but if the distance between the flanges is ever revised you will have either a gap or an interference. A more robust method would be to allow Pro/ENGINEER to dynamically measure the distance between the two flanges, as shown in Figure 23-18. You are then prompted to select the two pieces of geometry to measure (in this case the two faces of covers). Once the value has been set to the desired measurement, you will proceed to assemble the gasket using the appropriate constraints.

The gasket remains 0.25" thick in the part model, and any drawings of the gasket, but when it is represented in the assembly, it will measure 0.10", as shown in Figure 23-19, or whatever the current distance between the two flanges happens to be, as shown in Figure 23-20.

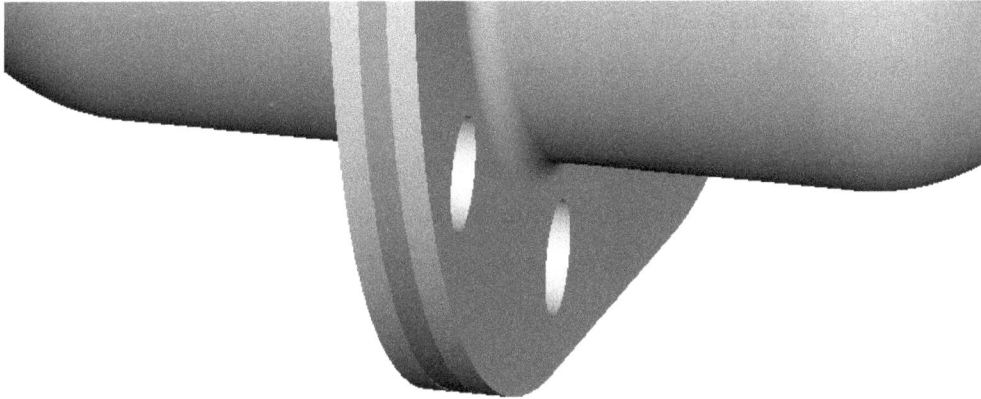

Fig. 23-19
Flexible component based on 0.10" gap

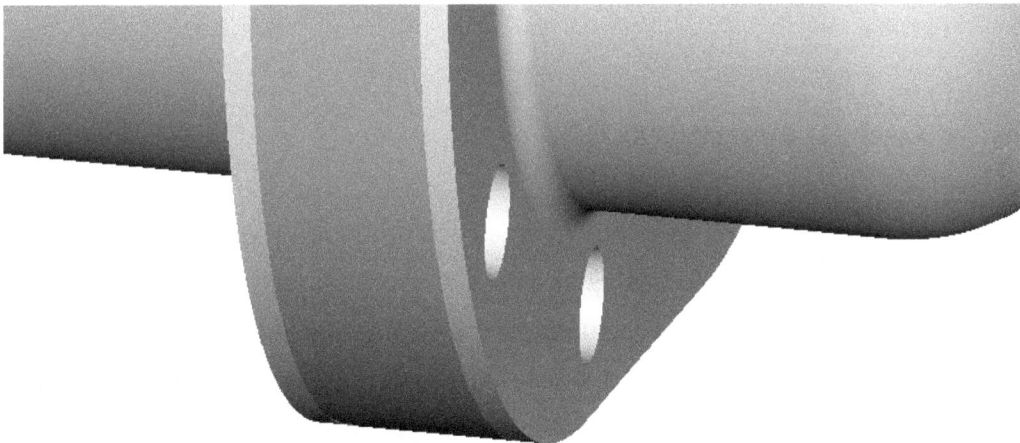

Fig. 23-20
Flexible component based on 0.60" gap

Regardless of the flexible value set in the assembly, the part model is not affected. This is particularly useful for including the same spring model in numerous different assemblies, in different states of compression or expansion.

Top Down Design

All of the assembly techniques discussed so far in this chapter are referred to as 'traditional' assembly techniques, in that we create a part, then another part, then we put them together in an assembly. We may do our best to be sure our parts will fit together, but each part and all their features are completely stand-alone, and have no real relationship with each other.

Top Down Design is an overall methodology, not any specific command or technique, where we create our parts and features with smart relationships, so that we know that they fit together, because we design them simultaneously.

Advanced Assembly Extension (AAX)

For truly robust models and assemblies, it is recommended that you utilize Pro/ENGINEER's 'Skeleton Models', along with 'Copy Geometry'. As of the printing of this book, those options are not included in the standard license of Pro/ENGINEER, and only available as part of the Advanced Assembly Extension. Since this is an 'add-on' to Pro/ENGINEER, Top Down Design will be explored fully in a future book. However, there are several tools that are part of the standard installation of Pro/ENGINEER that you can use as part of an overall Top Down approach.

Creating Models in Assembly Mode

Figure 23-21 shows a weldment assembly of three unique components. For proper fit, the base and side plate need to share the same length, and the end plates must not only have the proper height and width, but it must also share the same shape as the side plate.

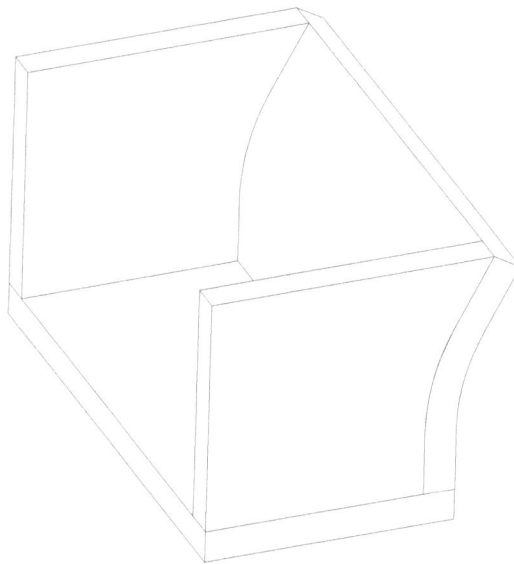

Fig. 23-21
Weldment

While it is certainly possible to create three separate parts, we would need to make sure we use the exact same dimensions during their creation. What happens if we change one dimension on one part? We would have to remember to make the same change on the others. What if we changed two or three dimensions?

We can start by creating the base plate and adding it to a new assembly, in the default position. While in assembly mode, we can select the **Create** icon from the Construction Tool bar. This will prompt us to enter a name and model type for a new component. When prompted for its placement, we can again use the default.

Since we are using the default position, we can have this completely blank part, fully constrained in the assembly, without any mate, align or inserts.

To add geometry to the new part that exactly matches the first, we can activate the new part by selecting it in the model tree, holding down the **RMB**, and selecting **Activate** from the menu. This allows for all the feature creation and modification commands to be executed to the active model, which is indicated by a green diamond attached to the part's icon in the Model Tree, as shown in Figure 12-22. (Activate the assembly to de-activate a component.)

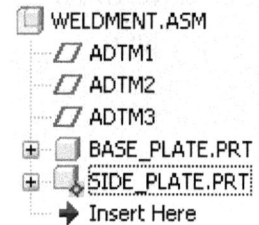

WELDMENT.ASM
    ADTM1
    ADTM2
    ADTM3
    BASE_PLATE.PRT
    SIDE_PLATE.PRT
    Insert Here

Fig. 23-22
Active model

When a model is activated, the rest of the assembly is displayed with stippled transparency, as shown in Figure 23-23. When selecting references, such as for the sketched extrusion shown, we can select any geometry from the assembly. In this example, we sketched our entities on a default datum plane, but the end of the sketched line is aligned to the top edge of the first component.

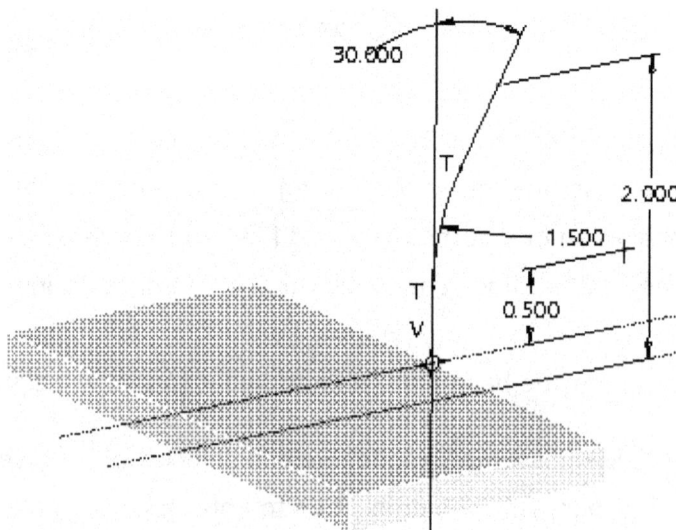

Fig. 23-23
Assembly features as sketch references

The extrusion's depth was set to the faces of the first component, as shown in Figure 23-24.

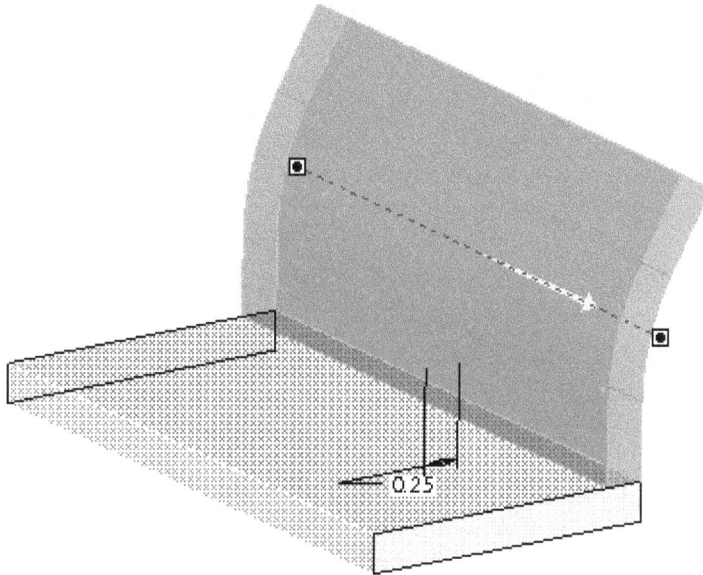

Fig. 23-24
Extrusion depth set to assembly references

By using another component's geometry as references, we are creating a parent/child relationship between the components and the assembly, but because these parts are necessary and unique to this assembly, there is nothing wrong with this.

When the third component is created, we are able to use assembly references to set the sketching plane, and also all the edges. By doing this, we can create a component with absolutely no dimensions (except for its thickness) that not only fits the other parts exactly, but it is also in the proper location, as shown in Figure 23-25.

To complete the assembly, another end plate can be added to the assembly using traditional mate and align constraints.

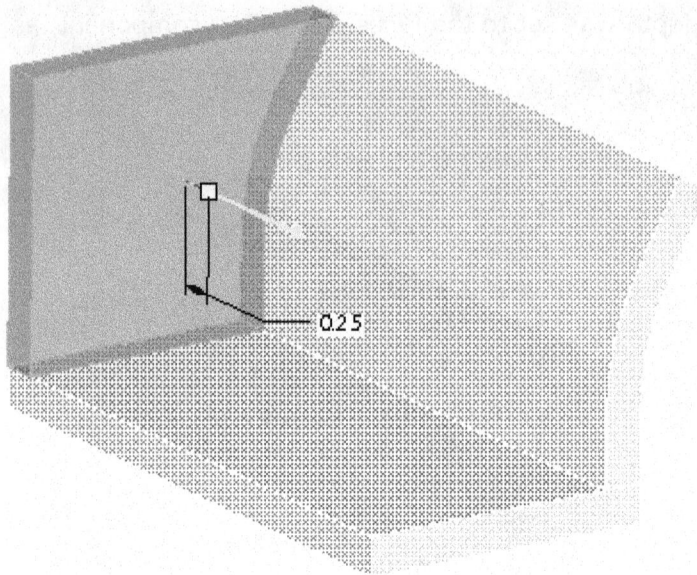

Fig. 23-25
Component with a single dimension

As the length of the base plate is modified, the length of the side plate will update, and the end plate's location will update. As the height and shape (bend) of the side plate changes, the height of the end place will change with it.

Assembly Features

In addition to adding components to an assembly, you may create features. You may use the features to remove solid geometry (cuts and holes), but not add. These assembly features can be used to specify actual manufacturing operations, such as machining two parts that have been welded together, or so that features occurring in multiple parts are in perfect position.

Figure 23-26 shows holes being added to an assembly. The default setting for assembly features is that they only exist in the assembly. If you would like an assembly feature to be included in the component, as a component feature, un-check the **Automatic Update** box in the **Intersect** tab, then right-click in the Display box to set the feature to occur in the **Part Level.**

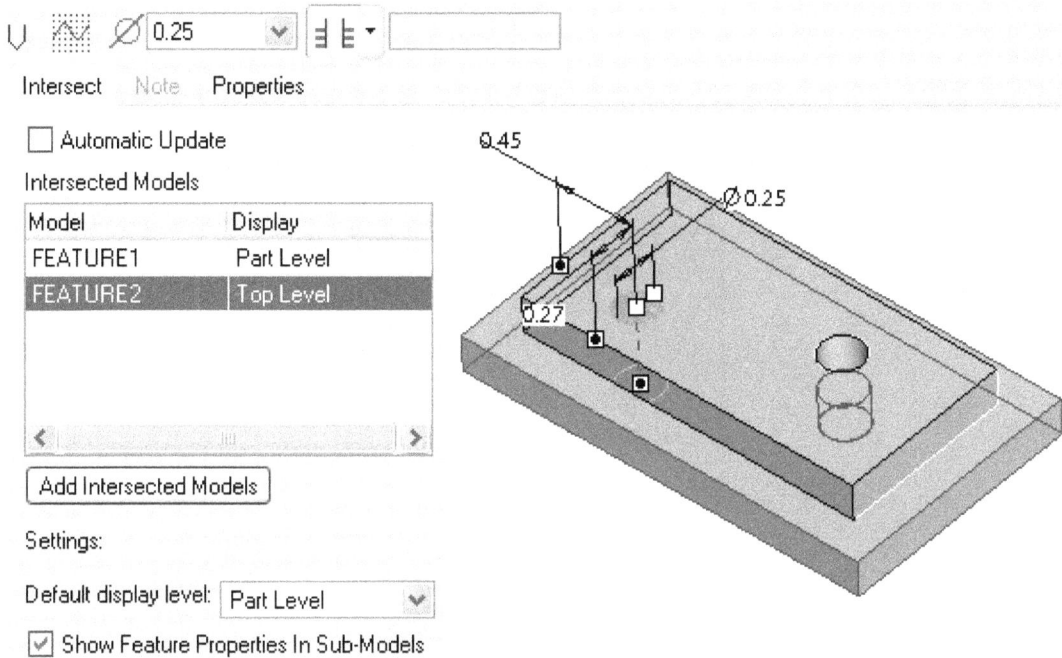

Fig. 23-26
Adding assembly features to the components

Mirror Parts

After creating a part and placing it in an assembly, as shown in Figure 23-27, we can create an exact mirror of the part, and also mirror its placement.

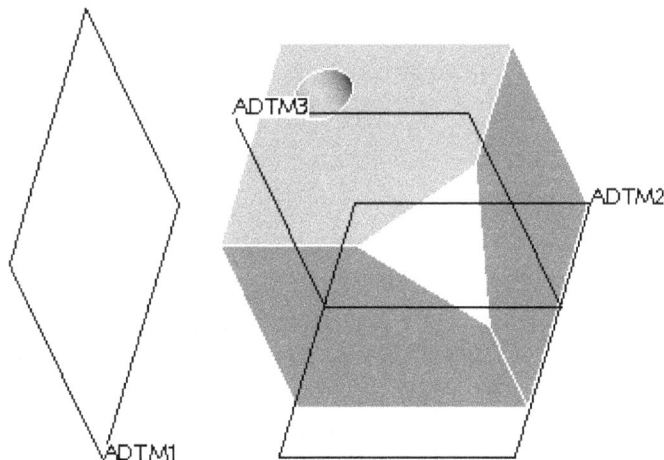

Fig. 23-27
Component to be mirrored

From the Construction Toolbar, select the ⬚ Create icon, and when specifying the name and type of component to create, check the Mirror sub-type, which will open the dialog box shown in Figure 23-28.

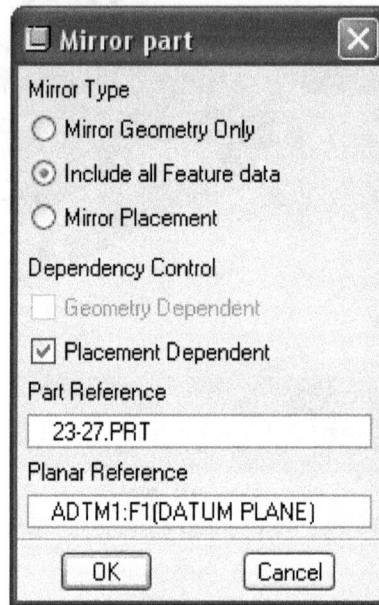

Fig.23-28
Mirror part controls

After making the desired choices for the part type, select the source part to copy, and a plane to mirror about (symmetry plane). The resulting part will then be an exact copy of the original, in the desired location, as shown in Figure 23-29.

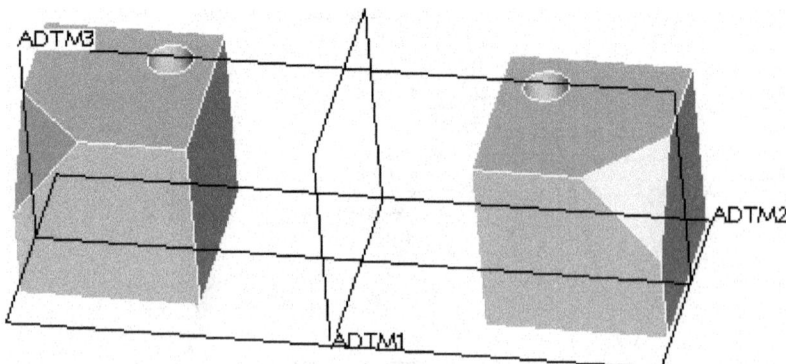

Fig. 23-29
Mirrored component

Chapter 24

Drawings

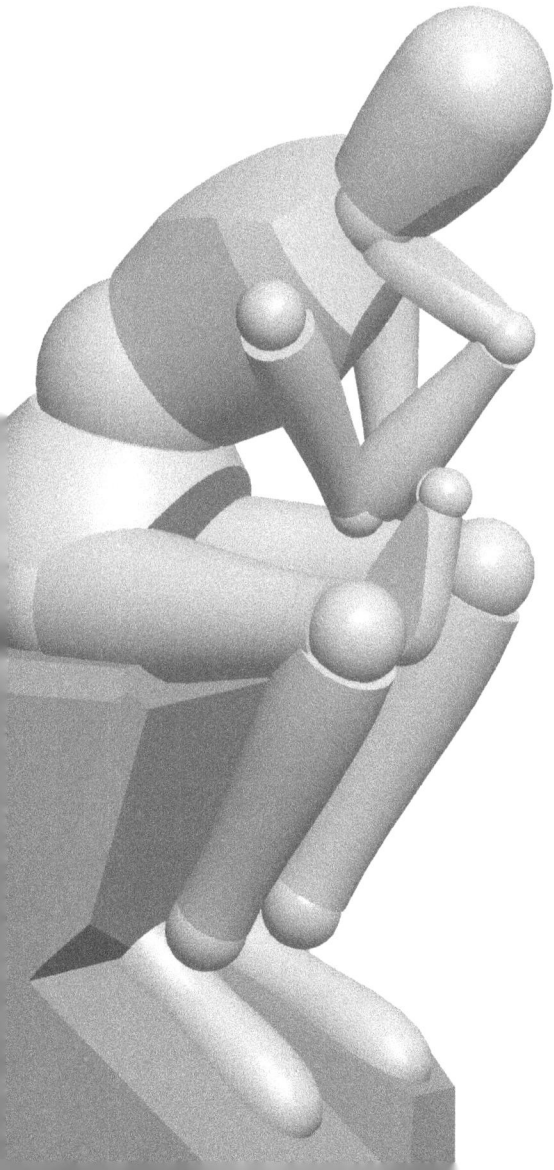

Associativity

Pro/ENGINEER drawing files (*.drw*) may be created as stand-alone files, with manually sketched entities, but typically a two-dimensional Pro/ENGINEER drawing is driven by one or more three-dimensional models. A single model may be represented in as many individual drawings, sheets or view as you wish, or not at all. Also, a single drawing can contain as many individual part and assembly models as you wish.

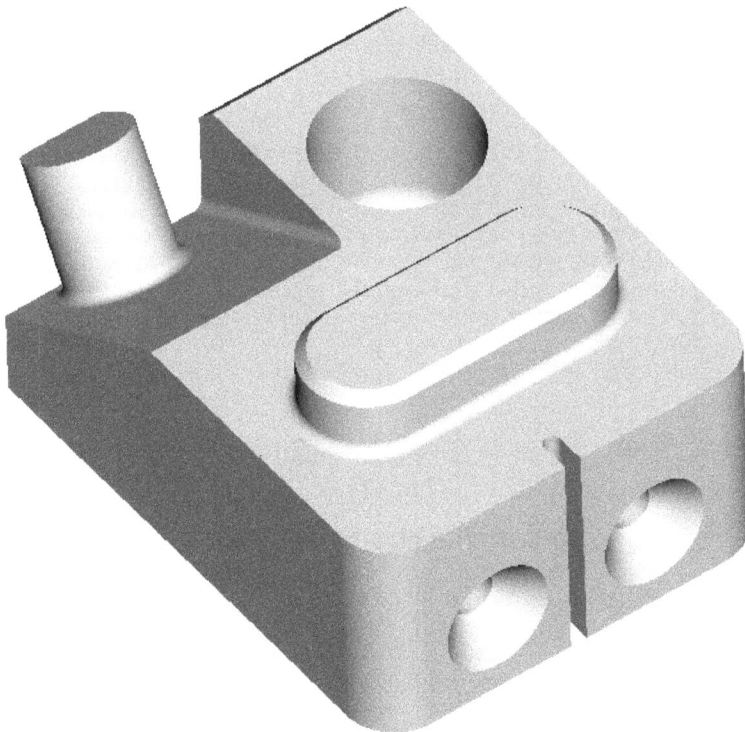

Fig. 24-1
Three-dimensional model to be represented two-dimensionally

The best practice is to associate a single three-dimensional model per drawing file. Typically, a part such as the one shown in Figure 24-1, will have a unique file name. In this case, it is filed as *widget.prt*. The drawing of this part may be named anything you wish, but common sense dictates that it be named *widget.drw*. The *.drw* extension is generated automatically when creating the file, designating it as a Pro/ENGINEER drawing.

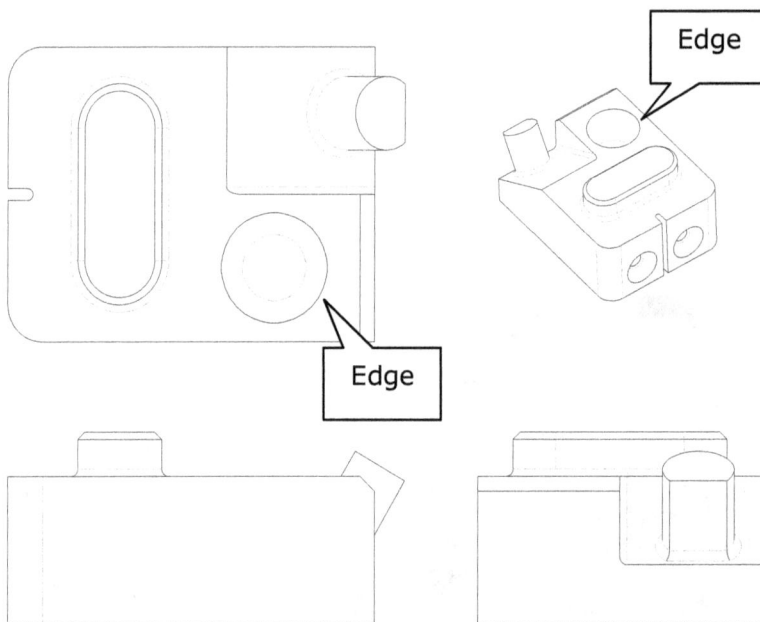

Fig. 24-2

widget.drw displaying the *widget.prt*

As discussed in Chapter 1, when viewing a Pro/ENGINEER drawing, such as the one shown in Figure 24-2, you are not looking at lines, arcs, and circles, but rather the edges of the three-dimensional model. As with the associativity related to parts in assemblies, the three-dimensional data displayed in a drawing is not a copy of the data, but the actual data. The views displayed on the drawing are driven by the three-dimensional model associated with the drawing. A change to the three-dimensional model is immediately reflected in every view of every drawing of the part.

Drawing Creation

To create a new drawing, select the ⬜ **New** icon from the Main Toolbar.

After selecting **Drawing** as the file type,
specify a file name. Until you are more
familiar with templates (see Chapter 27), it
is a good idea to uncheck the 'Use default
template' box, and click **OK**. This will open
the **New Drawing** dialog box, as shown in
Figure 24-3.

If you had a Pro/ENGINEER part or
assembly open, it will be used as the
default model (the model to be displayed),
or you may browse to find the appropriate
model. In addition to specifying the paper
size and orientation of the drawing, you
may choose to start with a completely
empty drawing, empty with a format
(border and title block) or use a copy of a
template.

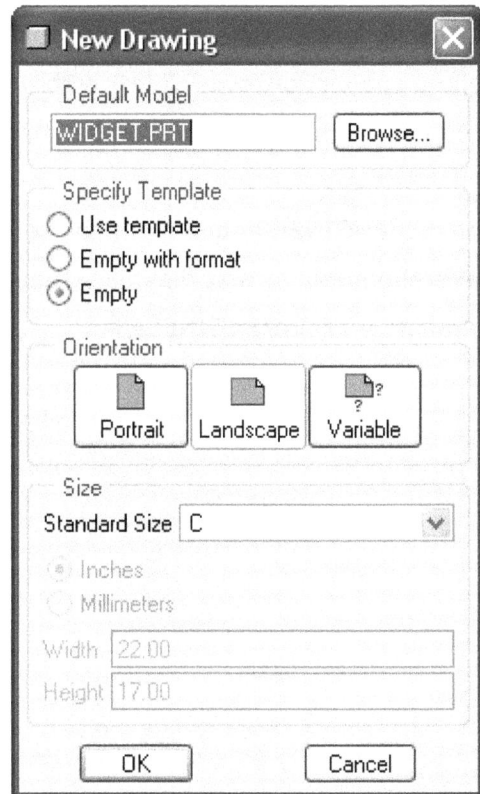

Fig. 24-3
New drawing dialog box

Drawing set up

Pro/ENGINEER utilizes ANSI (American National Standards Institute) guidelines for
drawing creation, but within those guidelines there are many optional settings you
may specify to suit the needs of your company. Also, you do not need to create
every drawing to the same standard, as you may have different drawing
requirements based on multiple product lines, vendors, and customers.

Formats

Technical drawings in some form have been used for centuries, but since the Industrial Revolution, drawings used for manufacturing purposes include a Title Bar or Title Block to convey general information about the design. Most drawings also include a border. Before the advent of CAD, most companies purchased drafting vellum (paper) or mylar (film) with a pre-printed title block and border. (These products are still available for purchase today.)

The Pro/ENGINEER equivalent to pre-printed drafting paper are format (*.frm) files. Several generic format files, like the one shown in Figure 24-4 are included with the installation of Pro/ENGINEER.

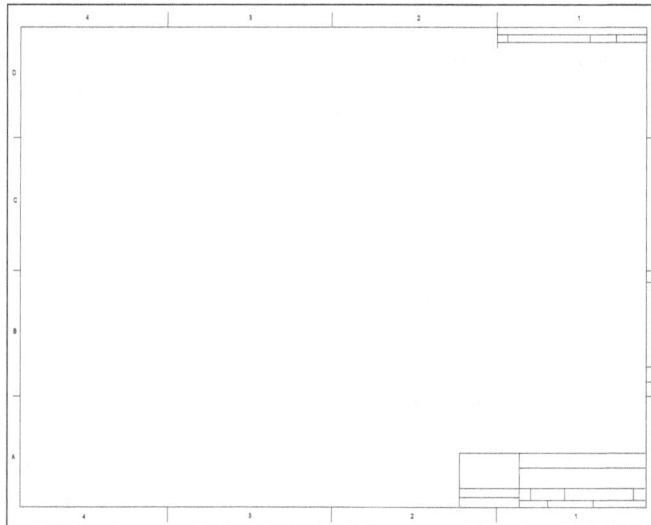

Fig. 24-4
Generic C size format

You may edit the generic format files to include your company information, or you may create a new format by selecting the ☐ **New** icon from the menu, select Format as the file type and specify the paper size. You may then add as many tables (blocks) and notes (see tables and notes later in this chapter) as you wish.

Pro/ENGINEER will retain associativity between your drawing and the format selected. This means that any changes to a format file will be reflected in <u>every</u> drawing that uses that file. Therefore, the best practice is to keep each format file as generic as possible.

Page Setup

To adjust the size of a drawing, or to add or replace a format, select **File** > **Page Setup** from the menu. From the dialog box shown in Figure 24-5, select the size you would like to use, or browse to select a format.

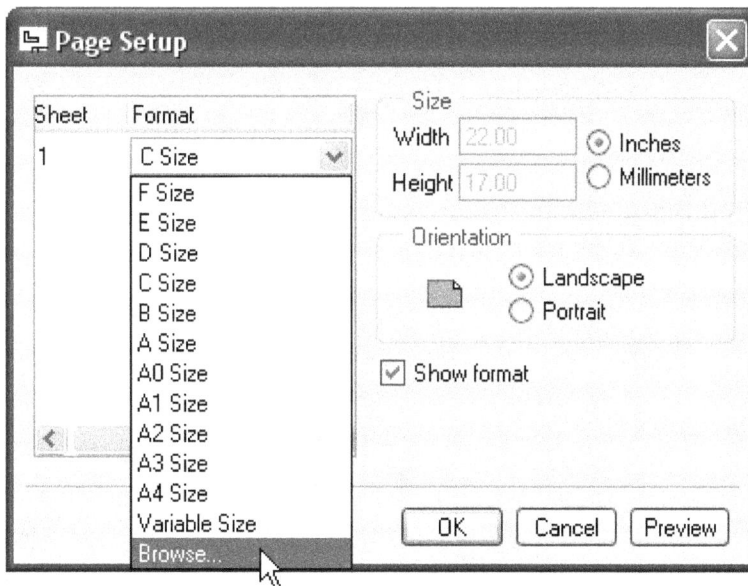

Fig. 24-5
Drawing Page Setup

Adding additional sheets is as simple as selecting **Insert** > **Sheet** from the menu. To choose which sheet to be active and display, click inside the 2 **Sheet** box in the Main Toolbar.

Properties

Pro/ENGINEER will create detail entities (dimension arrows, notes, etc.) based on default settings. For example, text will be displayed at a height of 0.15625 inches, and dimension arrows will be closed, 0.1875 inches long x 0.0625 wide. While the size and style of individual notes and dimensions may be modified, it is best practice to set all of the default values according your personal preference or company standards. Select **Properties** > **Drawing Options** from the menu. This will open a dialog box as shown in Figure 24-6.

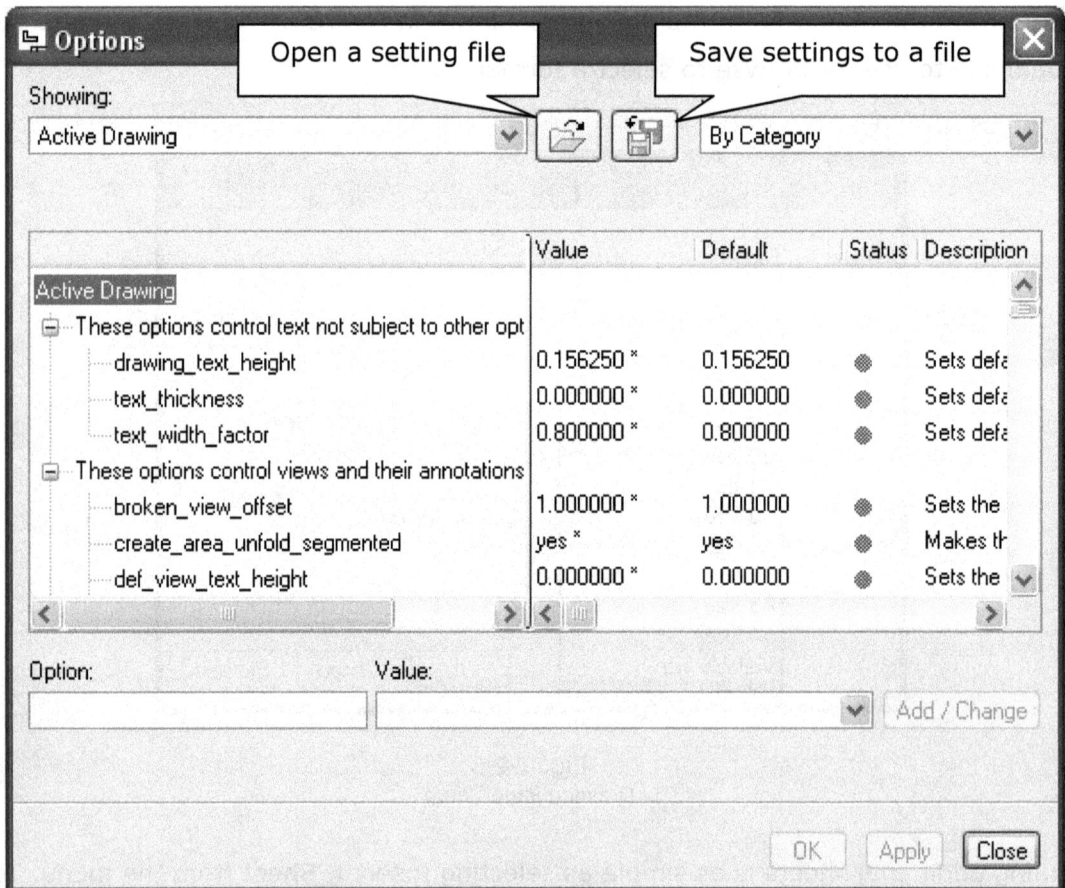

Fig. 24-6
Drawing options

You may change any individual value you wish. This information is stored within the drawing file. If you wish to use the same settings in another drawing, you may save the current settings to a file (*.dtl) as shown in Figure 24-6. To use previously saved settings, you may open and apply a .dtl file, also shown in Figure 24-6. Most companies will develop a standard set of .dtl files and place them in a central location for all users. (See Appendix C for a complete list of options and descriptions.)

Views

You may display as many views of your design, in any orientation, style or scale you wish. To add a view, select **Insert** > **Drawing View** > **General**. This will open the **Drawing View** dialog box as shown in Figure 24-7.

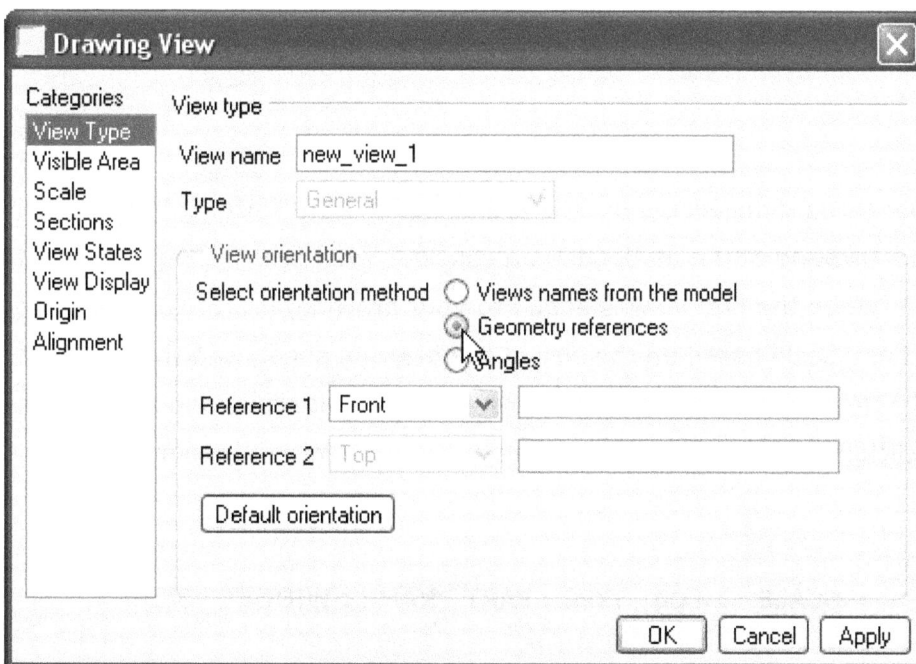

Fig. 24-7
Drawing View dialog box

You may select a predefined view name (See Chapter 22) from the list, or you may specify an orientation, as shown in Figure 24-7. This is exactly the same as specifying a sketching plane and orientation when sketching on the three-dimensional model.

View Properties

When a view is first placed on a drawing, it will be according to the drawing's default settings, therefore the view may or may not appear the way you wish. To change the way a view is displayed, select the view, hold down the **RMB**, and select **Properties**. This will open up the exact same dialog box shown in Figure 24-7. By clicking on the **Categories** list on the left side of the box, you can modify any aspect of the view, including the way hidden and tangent lines are displayed (View Display) and scale of the view.

Scale

All of your three-dimensional models are designed at full size. It is only when creating a drawing of the model do you consider what scale (size) you wish to display it. When the first view is added to your drawing, Pro/ENGINEER generally sets a 'sheet' scale based on the size of the drawing sheet, and the size of the three-dimensional model. This is the drawing's default scale, and can be adjusted by double-clicking the **SCALE** tag displayed in the bottom, left corner, as shown in Figure 24-8.

SCALE : 1.000   TYPE : PART   NAME : WIDGET   SIZE : C

Figure 24-8
Sheet control tags

The scale of individual views may be set to values other than the sheet scale, if desired, by adjusting the properties of the view, as discussed earlier. When changing the scale of a view, the three-dimensional model size remains the same. It is only the size of the view that changes. This allows you to have several views of the same three-dimensional model, at any scale you wish. Since drawing views are displaying edges of the model, not lines (as discussed earlier), Pro/ENGINEER retains the proper dimensional information at all times.

Moving Views

When Pro/ENGINEER is first started, the option for moving views is disabled. To allow the ability of moving views, simply hold down the **RMB** and uncheck **Lock View Movement**, as shown in Figure 24-9.

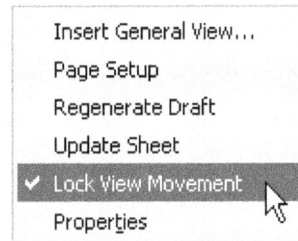

Insert General View...
Page Setup
Regenerate Draft
Update Sheet
✔ Lock View Movement
Properties

Fig. 24-9
Allowing view movement

To move a view, first select the view with the LMB. Notice that as your mouse passes over views, a view boundary box will be displayed in Cyan. This is the same as the pre-select highlight box used to select solid geometry (See Chapter 5). Once the view is selected, the boundary box will turn red, and a ✥ **Move** icon will appear, as shown in Figure 24-10. Hold the **LMB** down, drag the view to the desired location, and release.

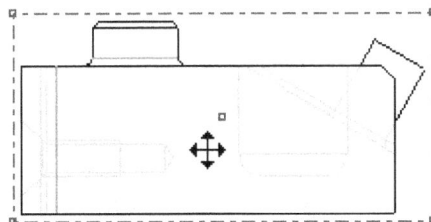

Fig. 24-10
Moving a view

Adding Views

You may add additional views by selecting **Insert** > **Drawing View** from the menu. Since a primary view already exists, you will have the option of creating views dependant on other views.

Projection View

To create a projection view, simply select **Insert** > **Drawing View** > **Projection** from the menu. After selecting a parent view, a view boundary box will apear, allowing you to place the new view anywhere on the drawing. Note that since this is a projection view, you will only be able to place the new view directly to the right, left, above or below the parent view. By default, Pro/ENGINEER utilizes third angle projection.

Auxiliary View

If you need a view projected normal to an angular piece of geometry, you may create an **Auxiliary** view. Based on the display settings you choose for this view, Pro/ENGINEER will automatically create the proper shapes and hidden lines.

Detail View

Depending on the scale of your sheet and views, you may find it necessary to create an enlarged area of a portion of your model. You can accomplish this by choosing **Detail** as the view type. At the prompt, select the center point for the detail on an existing view (pick a spot on the drawing that you wish to enlarge). Next, sketch a spline, without intersecting other splines, to define an outline, by clicking locations on the screen with the **LMB**. Click the **MMB** to close the loop. Finally, select the location for the new view being added. By definition, a detail view is a scaled view, which may be adjusted as necessary.

Section views

Section views are used to display and show detail of areas of your model that are physically hidden from view, such as the inside of a soda can. Pro/ENGINEER will allow you to display hidden lines in any view (hidden lines are shown in grey, but will print with dashes), but drafting standards do not allow you to dimension hidden lines. Yes, it is possible to create these dimensions in Pro/ENGINEER, but it is not best drafting practice. A section however, will allow you to display and properly dimension objects that are normally obscured from view, as shown in Figure 24-11.

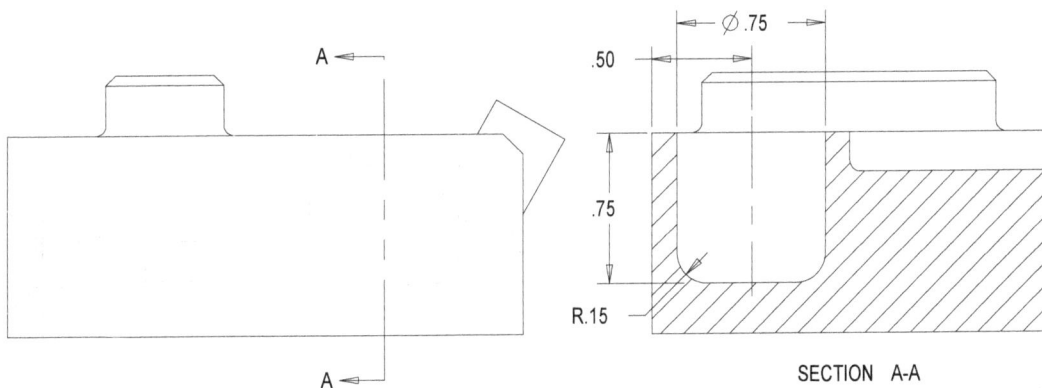

Fig. 24-11
Section view

Pro/ENGINEER allows you to create sections in views while working in drawing mode, or you may select a pre-existing section stored in the three-dimensional model. (See Chapter 22 for information regarding the creation of the sections.) The style, size, and orientation of the hatch pattern may be adjusted by selecting the hatching itself, holding down the **RMB**, and selecting **Properties**.

Detailing

You may add as much information to your drawings as needed to properly describe and document your design. This information may be manually added, or pulled

directly from the three-dimensional geometry by selecting the ![icon] **Show and Erase** dialog box from the Main Toolbar.

This will open the dialog box shown in Figure 24-12. Click on the **Show** button, then on any of the types of detail information, stored within the three-dimensional model, you wish to display. Note that the term 'show' is used, not 'create'. The associativity between Pro/ENGINEER drawings and the three-dimensional models allows us to display the actual dimensions used to create the three-dimensional geometry. This means that you may edit the dimensions of geometry from either the two-dimensional drawing, or the three-dimensional geometry, as they are one in the same.

You may choose to show all of the dimensions at the same time (**Show All**), or by individual features or views. Once detail items have been displayed on the drawing, you may choose items to remain, items to erase, keep them all, or erase them all. **Erase** only removes items from the display; it does not delete the item. Items that have been erased may be shown again.

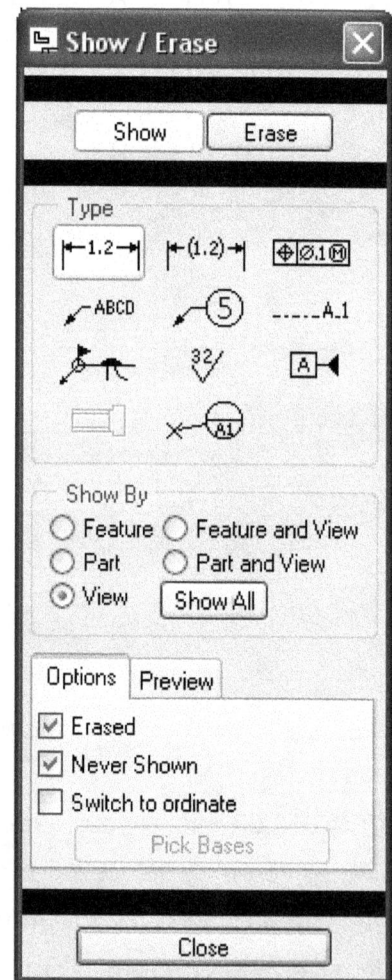

Fig. 24-12
Detail Show / Erase dialog box

Dimensions

Dimensions will be shown on the drawing based on the selections made in the **Show / Erase** dialog box, as shown in Figure 24-12. Figure 24-13 shows what our widget drawing looks like if we show all of the dimensions available for this view.

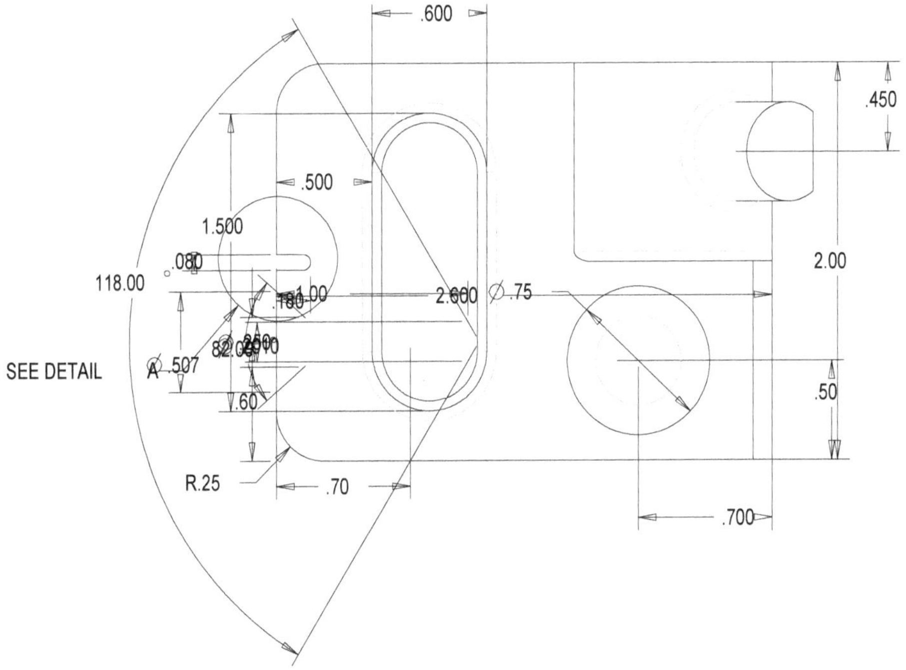

Fig. 24-13
Dimensions shown per view

Keep in mind that Pro/ENGINEER cannot possibly know how you, the designer, wants to display dimensions on your drawing. You can erase any dimension from the display by simply selecting the dimension, holding down the **RMB**, and selecting **Erase**. You may also show a dimension in one view, but decide that it would be better to show it in another. In this case you can simply select the dimension, and from the menu, select **Edit > Move Item to View** and pick the view to display the dimension. To move a dimension, simply click on the dimension, hold down the **LMB** and drag into position. Figure 24-14 shows the same drawing, but with the extra dimensions erased or moved.

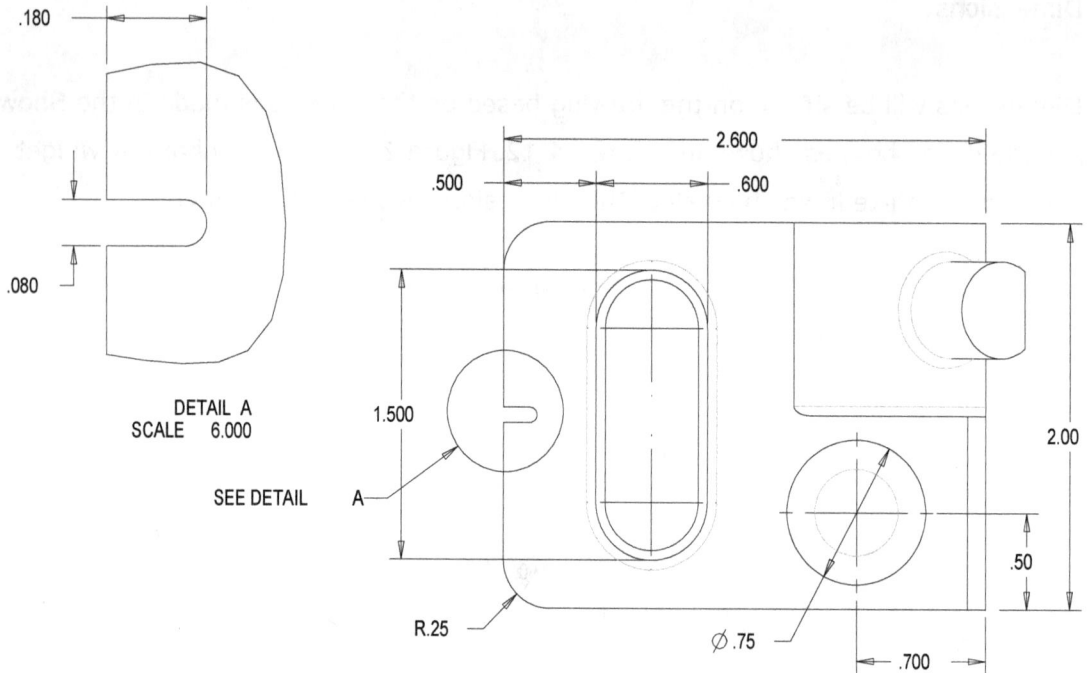

Fig. 24-14
Dimensions moved

In addition to moving the location of the dimensions, you can adjust the starting points of the extension lines by selecting the dimension, then selecting the end of the extension line and dragging it into position. While holding down the **RMB**, you may select **Flip Arrows** to flip the dimension arrows from one side of the extension lines to the other.

If additional dimensions are desired, you may select **Insert** > **Dimension** or **Reference Dimension** from the menu. These created dimensions can be added anywhere on the drawing, in the same manner dimensions are created in **Sketcher** (see Chapter 7).

Experienced Pro/ENGINEER users continue to debate the virtues of using only 'shown' dimensions versus only 'created' dimensions. This author will leave that decision up to the reader.

Tolerance

Once you have a dimension placed on the drawing, you may adjust its properties by clicking on the dimension, holding down the **RMB**, and selecting **Properties**. This will open the Dimension Properties dialog box, as shown in Figure 24-15.

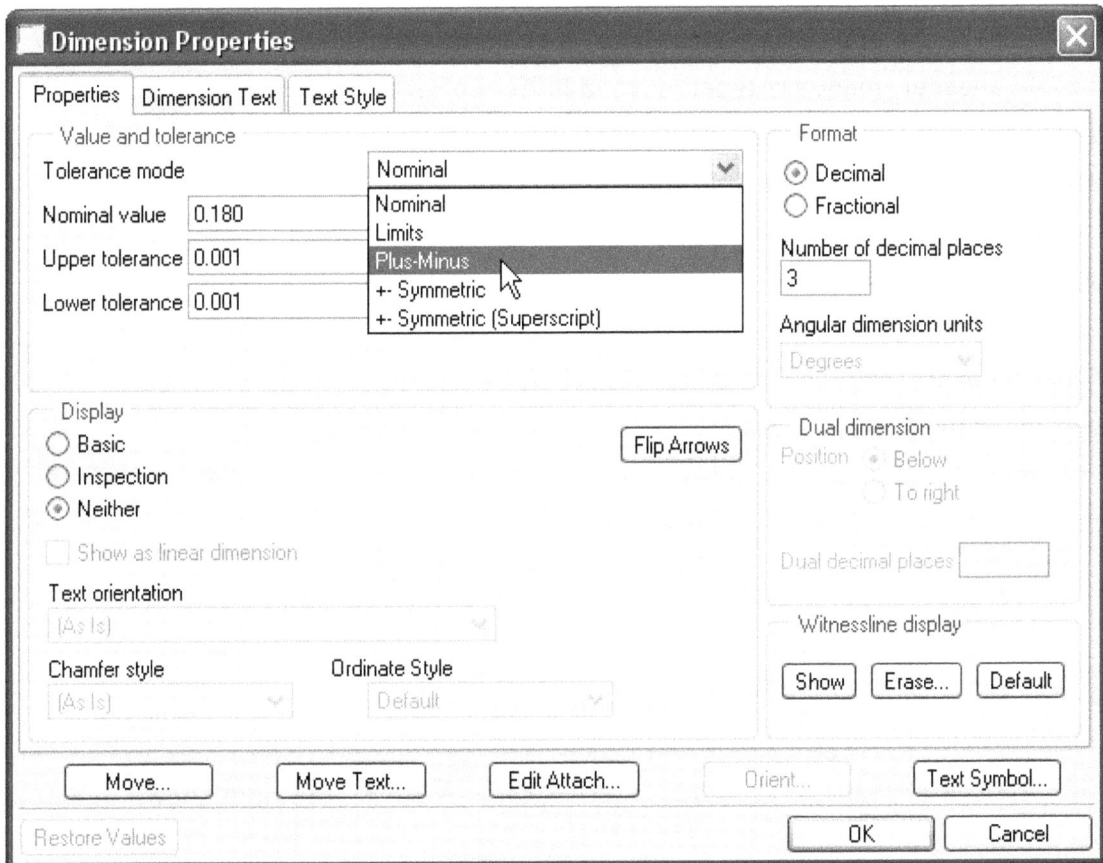

Fig. 24-15
Dimension Properties dialog box

The **Properties** tab within the dialog box allows you to adjust the number of decimal places and tolerance (tolerance mode must be enabled in the **Drawing Options**). The **Dimension Text** tab allows you to add notes to the dimension, while the **Text Style** tab controls the dimension's font, style, and size.

Notes

In addition to dimensions, you may create and place as many text notes on your drawing as you wish. A simple note may be created by selecting **Insert** > **Note** from the menu. This will open the Note Types dialog box as shown in Figure 24-16. Make the appropriate selections, such as whether to include a leader, manually typed or read in from a text file, and the style and orientation of the note (if other than default). Select **Make Note** from the box, and select the location on the drawing to start the note. A tab will open, as shown in Figure 24-17.

Type the exact text you would like. Selecting the **Check** button, or the **Enter** key will complete the line, and create a line return for multiple line notes. Selecting the **X** button or the **Enter** button twice will complete the note.

Menu Manager
▼ NOTE TYPES
No Leader
With Leader
ISO Leader
On Item
Offset
Enter
File
Horizontal
Vertical
Angular
Standard
Normal Leader
Tangent Leader
Left
Center
Right
Default
Style Lib
Cur Style
Make Note
Done/Return

➡ Enter NOTE: _____ ☑☒

Fig. 24-17
Text box

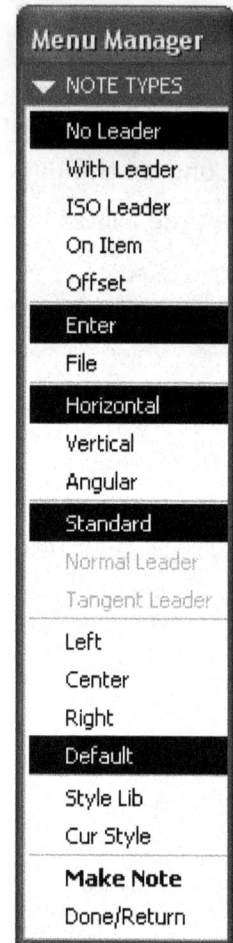

Fig. 24-16
Note types

The text will appear on the drawing as specified, such as the note shown in Figure 24-18.

UNLESS OTHERWISE NOTED:

1. REMOVE ALL BURRS AND SHARP EDGES

2. PAINT PER SPECIFICATION 5673-00987.

Fig. 24-18
Typical drawing note

If at any time you wish to modify the note, simply select the note, hold down the **RMB** and select **Properties**. This will open the dialog box as shown in Figure 24-19. You may manually type any text, add symbols from the Text Symbol pallet, cut and paste, and extra line returns.

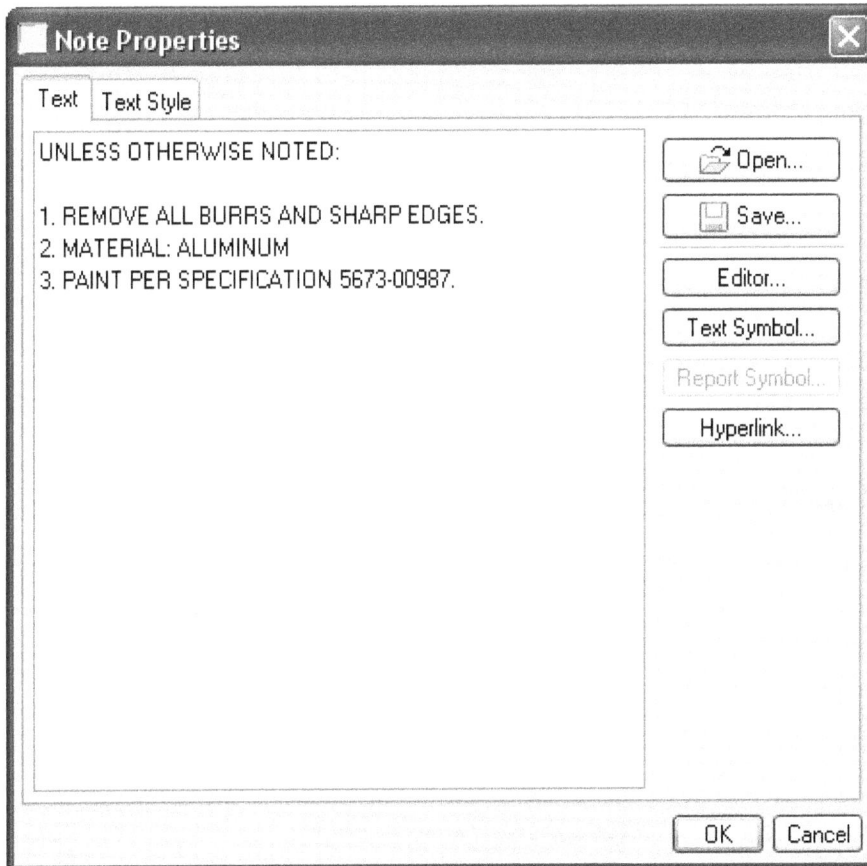

Fig. 24-19
Note Properties

You may also modify the style of the entire note, or if you would like to isolate and make changes to only a portion of the note, first select the entire note, then pass the cursor over the line or portion you wish to update. When you see the pre-select highlight (See Chapter 5), select that portion, and edit its properties.

Parametrics Notes

Parametric notes use dimensions or parameters stored in the models or drawings in place of manually entered text. (See Chapter 20 to add parameters to the model). A parametric note uses '**&**' (ampersand) followed by the name of the dimension or parameter. For example, we may have a parameter in our three-dimensional model named MATERIAL. The value for the parameter may be set to **AL6061**. To automatically use the proper value, the drawing note shown in Figure 24-19 could be modified to: **2. MATERIAL: &material**. On the drawing, the note would read: **2. MATERIAL: AL6061**.

The following system parameters may be added to formats and drawings to automatically read the values of the current model:

&todays_date — date as of the note's creation in the form dd-mm-yy.

&model_name — model file name associated with the drawing.

&dwg_name — file name of the drawing.

&scale — scale of the drawing.

&type — drawing model type (part, assembly).

&format — format size (A, B, C, etc.).

&linear_tol_0_0
through
&linear_tol_0_000000 — linear tolerance values for one to six decimal places.

&angular_tol_0_0
through
&angular_tol_0_0 — angular tolerance values for one to six decimal places.

&current_sheet — sheet number for the sheet on which the note is located.

&total_sheets — total number of sheets for the drawing.

All the dimensions in a three-dimensional model have a name. By default, the dimension begins with '*d*', followed by a number assigned by Pro/ENGINEER, such as '*d47*'. This is not the value of the dimension, only its name. You may determine a dimension's name by editing the dimension's properties (see Chapter 20), or when a dimension is displayed on the screen, select **Info** > **Switch Dimensions**. Pro/ENGINEER will also temporarily display the 'd' values of previously shown dimensions, when a note is being created. To use a dimension in a note, simply precede the name of a dimension with the ampersand, such as: *&d47*.

Figure 24-14 shows dimensions for a slot in the part. We could create the following note to capture the same information:

CUT A SLOT
&d47 WIDE X &d48 DEEP

Pro/ENGINEER only allows the display of an individual dimension once per drawing. When the parametric note is created, the dimension become embedded in the note, and is automatically erased from the view, as shown in Figure 24-20.

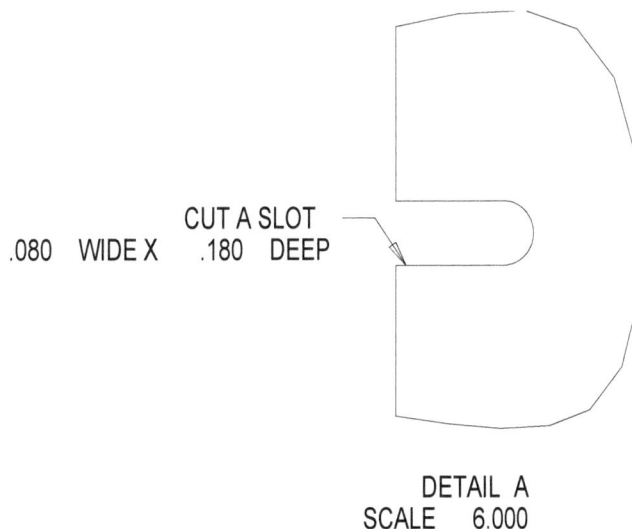

CUT A SLOT
.080   WIDE X   .180   DEEP

DETAIL A
SCALE   6.000

Fig. 24-20
Dimensions in a parametric note

Geometric Dimensioning and Tolerancing (GD&T)

Geometric dimensioning and tolerancing (GD&T) is used to define the nominal geometry of parts and assemblies, to define the allowable variation in form and possibly size of individual features, and to define the allowable variation between features. There are several standards available world-wide that describe the symbols and define the rules used in GD&T, such as American Society of Mechanical Engineers (ASME) Y14.5M-1994 and the International Organization for Standardization (ISO).

GD&T notes reference datums in the three-dimensional model. To use a model datum as a reference it must be set first. With the three-dimensional model open, select a datum plane or axis, hold down the **RMB**, and select **Properties**.

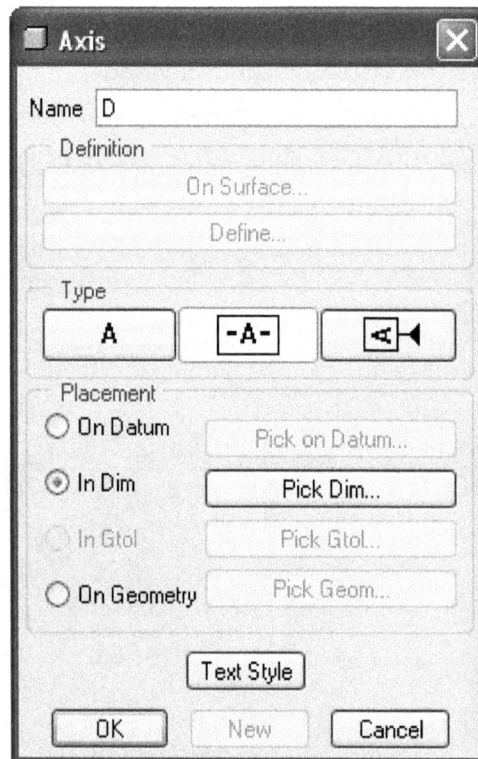

Fig. 24-21
Datum properties

This will open the Datum Properties box, as shown in Figure 24-21. Specify the name for the datum (generally a sequential letter, starting with A), the type, and how you would like to place the tag in the model. Select **In Dim** to attach the tag to a feature dimension.

Pro/ENGINEER will automatically display the datum tags on the drawing, as shown in Figure 24-22.

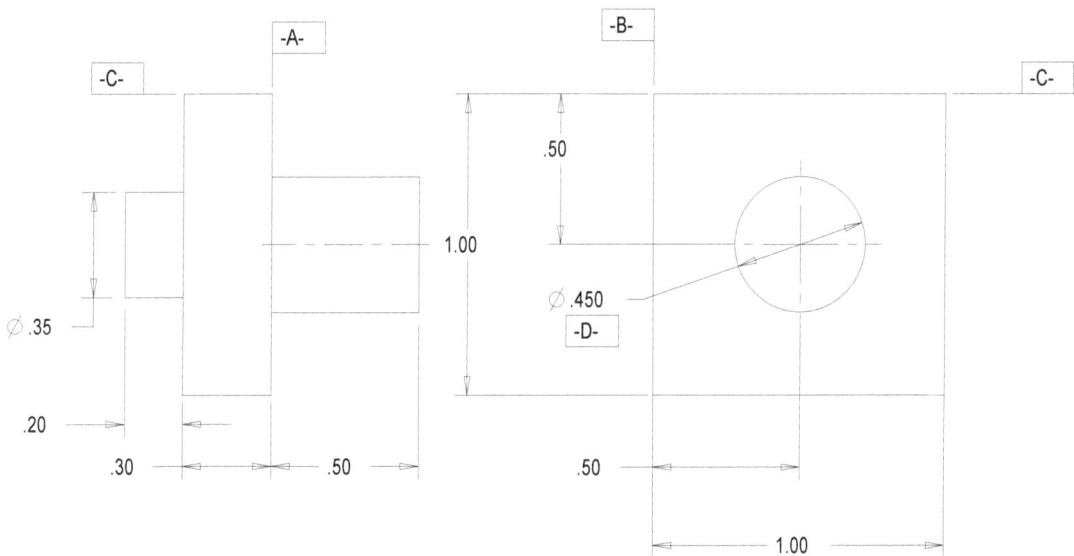

Fig. 24-22
Datums set and shown in a drawing

To specify a dimension to be a Basic Dimension, select the dimension, hold down the RMB, and select **Properties**. Select **Basic** from the Dimension Properties dialog box shown in Figure 24-15. This will place a box around the dimension. To create a tolerance, select **Insert** > **Geometric Tolerance** from the menu. This will open the Geometric Tolerance dialog box, as shown in Figure 24-23.

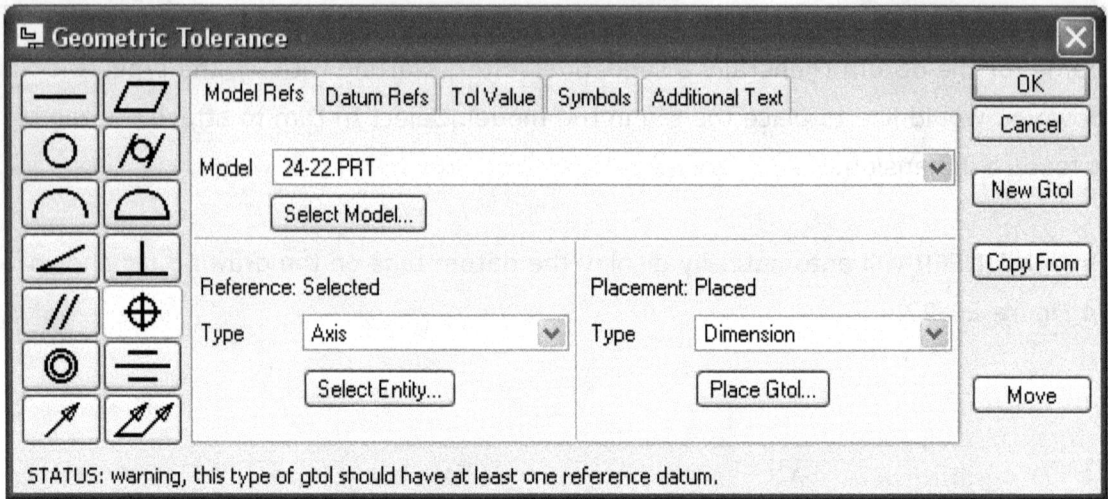

Fig. 24-23
Geometric Tolerance dialog box

Select the type of tolerance from the left pane of the box, then the appropriate geometry and dimension. To reference the appropriate datum, click on the Datum Refs tab to select the Primary, Secondary, and Tertiary datums, as shown in Figure 24-24.

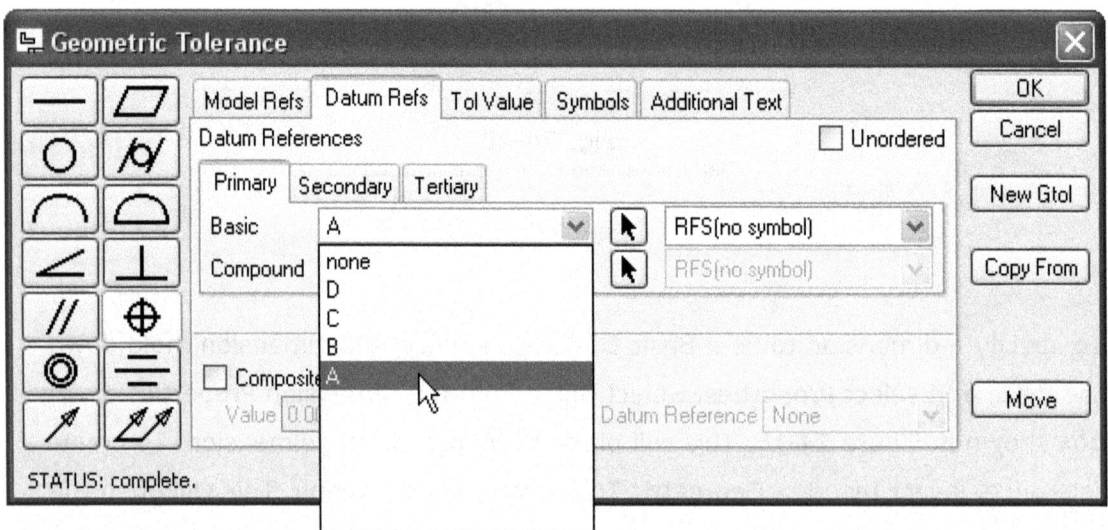

Fig. 24-24
Selecting datum references

Continue by specifying the amount of tolerance in the **Tol Value** tab, and any additional symbols or text in their respective tabs. The resulting drawing is shown in Figure 24-25.

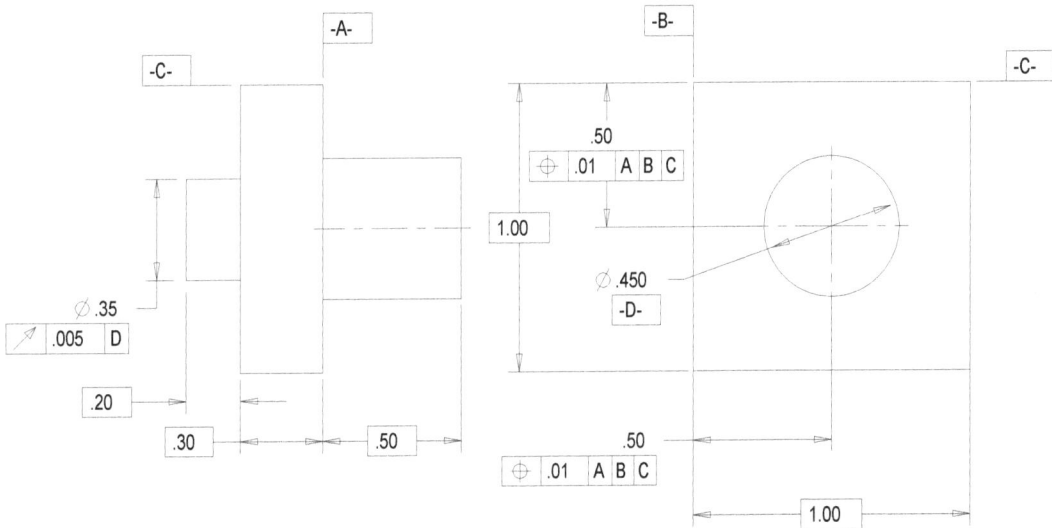

Fig. 24-25
Drawing with Geometric Dimensioning and Tolerancing (GD&T)

Symbols

A symbol is a collection of draft (sketched) geometry, text, or a combination of both. You may create and store custom symbols, or use several predefined System Symbols, such as standard welding symbols. To add a symbol, select **Insert > Drawing Symbol** from the menu.

From Palette

Pro/ENGINEER includes several pre-defined symbols. If the **From Palette** option is selected, the drawing shown in Figure 24-26 will automatically open in a pop-up window. Simply select the symbol you wish to use, and place it on your drawing.

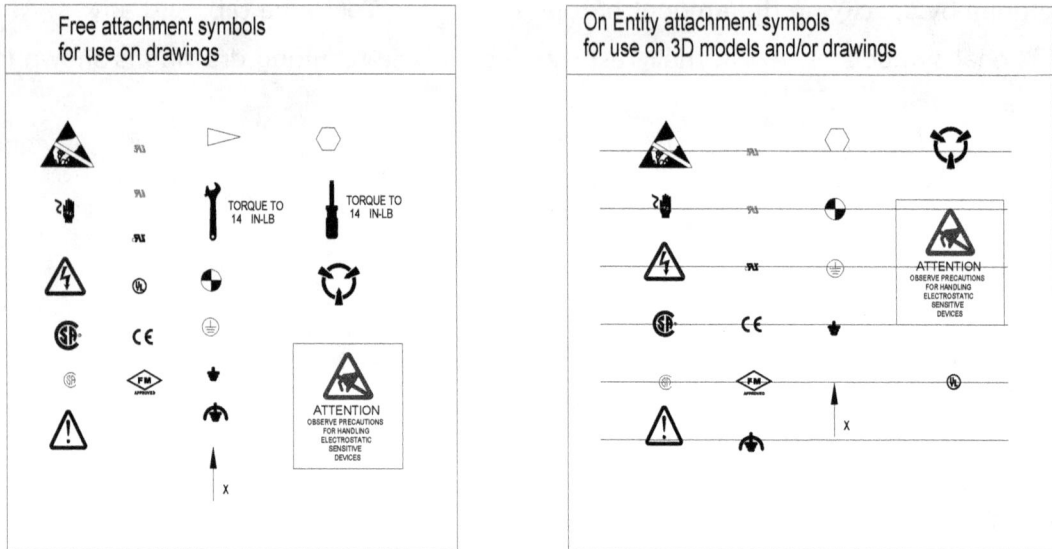

Fig. 24-26
Symbol palette

After defining your own custom symbols (see later in this chapter) you may add them to this symbol palette drawing for future use.

System Symbols

When creating a drawing of an assembly containing welds that were created using Pro/ENGINEER's **Welding** module, the appropriate weld symbols are displayed automatically. If the **Welding** module is not used, then the weld symbols may be added manually by selecting **Custom** from the **Drawing Symbol** menu. You may then browse to **System Syms > weldsymlib** and continue to select the desired weld symbol.

A **Custom Drawing Symbol** dialog box will open, as shown in Figure 24-27, displaying a preview of the symbol with placement controls.

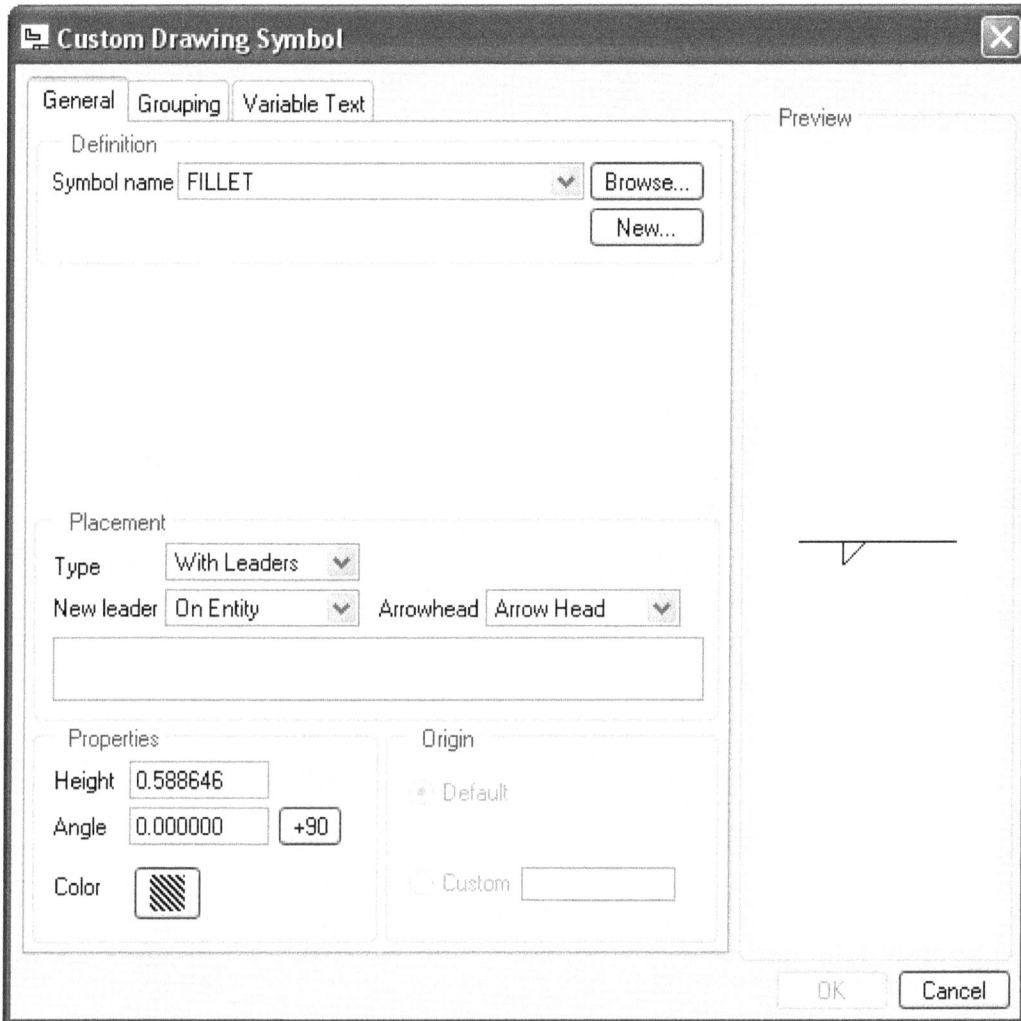

Fig. 24-27
Custom Drawing Symbol dialog box

To enter the proper information for the weld symbol, select the **Grouping** and **Variable Text** tabs and make the appropriate selections, as shown in Figure 24-28. The resulting symbol is shown in Figure 24-29.

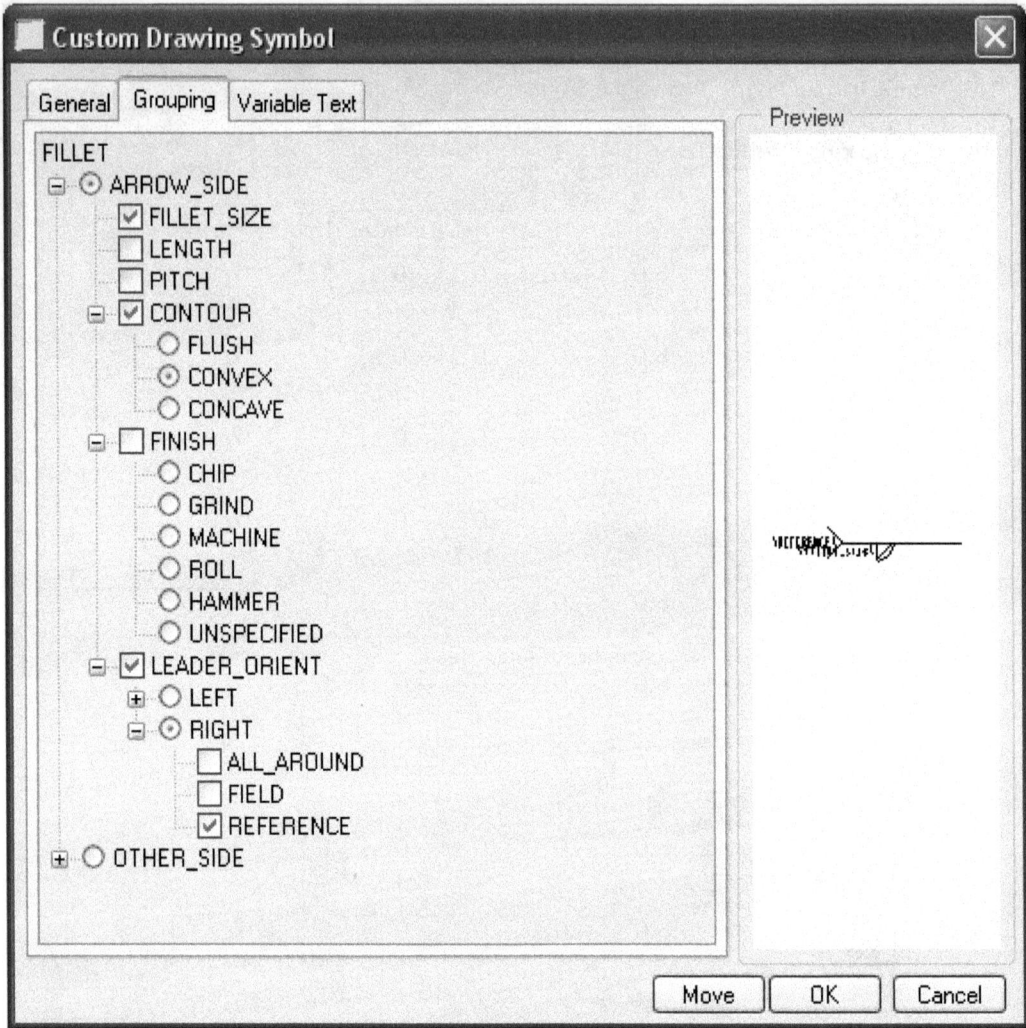

Fig. 24-28
Symbol details

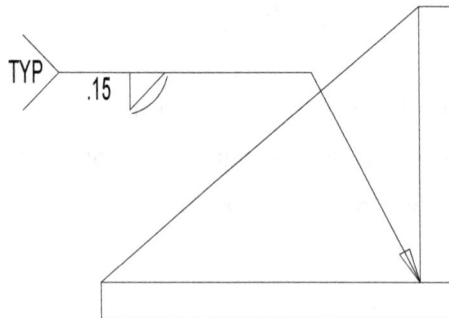

Fig. 24-29
Symbol placed on drawing

Custom Symbols

To create a new symbol, select **Format** > **Symbol Gallery** > **Define** from the menu.
After entering a name for the new symbol, Pro/ENGINEER will open a symbol edit
drawing window. Using common sketcher tools, you can create any two-dimensional
shapes you wish, including notes. If you would like to be able to vary the text of
notes when placed on a drawing, be sure to place a backslash before and after the
note, such as \X\. To control how the symbol is to be placed on the drawing, select
Attributes from the menu, to open the Symbol Definition Attributes dialog box, as
shown in Figure 24-30.

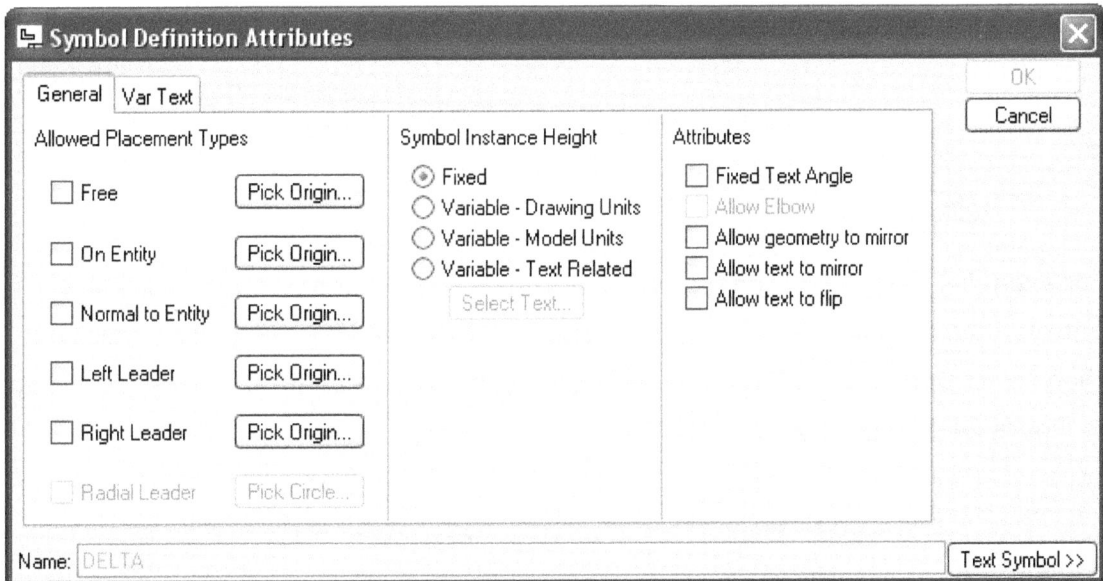

Fig. 24-30
Symbol Definition Attributes

When complete, select **Done** from the menu. This will create the symbol, and store
it in the current drawing for use. If you would like to use this symbol in other
drawings, or perhaps build a library of symbols, select **Write** from the menu, and
store the symbol in the desired folder. You may also add your symbol(s) to the
symbol palette drawing shown in Figure 24-26.

Tables

Tables in Pro/ENGINEER drawings are similar to tables in other Windows®
applications, in that they are made up of rows and columns, and contain text and/or
numeric values. They may be used to display design options and are also used to
construct title blocks in formats (see earlier in this chapter).

To create a table, select **Table** > **Insert** > **Table** from the menu. A Menu Manager
will open prompting you for how you want to define the table (ascending, left to
right, etc.). After selecting a point on the drawing to start the table, a string of
numbers will appear, as shown in Figure 24-31. To specify the size of the first
column, click the appropriate value.

₁12345678901234567890 1234567890

Fig. 24-31
Column width selection

For example, if you want the first column to be eleven characters wide, click in-
between the second 1 and 2. Continue until all of the columns have been specified,
then select **Done**. You will then be prompted to set the value for the rows, as shown
in Figure 24-32.

```
1 |         |          |          |
2
3
4
5
```

Fig. 24-32
Row height selection

When finished, simply select **Done** from the menu, and a table with the specified
number and sizes of rows and columns will be created. To change sizes or add and

delete rows and columns, select the table, then select the Table menu, and make the appropriate selections.

To add text to any table cell, simply double-click the cell with the **LMB**. This will open a note dialog box, where you may enter any text you wish. You may also modify the text style of any cell, as shown in Figure 24-33.

REV	DESCRIPTION	DATE	APPROVED
A	INITIAL RELEASE	05/10/2009	S.FREY

Fig. 24-33
Table with text

Repeat region

For assembly drawings, you may use a table to list all of the individual components, along with their individual attributes such as description, color, cost, etc. All of this information may be manually entered, but unfortunately the table will have no relationship to the assembly, therefore changes to the assembly will not be reflected in the table. An automatically updating table is created by utilizing a **Repeat Region**.

Begin by creating a table with at least two rows, using the techniques mentioned above. You may have one or more·rows that have static heading information, but one of the rows must remain blank, as shown in Figure 24-34.

BILL OF MATERIALS			
INDEX	QTY.	PART NUMBER	DESCRIPTION

Fig. 24-34
Sample Bill of Material table

After the table has been created, select **Table** > **Repeat Region** > **Add** > **Simple** from the menu. At the prompt, define the boundaries of the repeat region. In this case we would select the blank cell beneath the 'INDEX' cell and the blank cell beneath the 'DESCRIPTION' cell. Once the region has been created, double-click in any of the blank cells.

Instead of defaulting to manual text inputs, a Report Symbol dialog box will open, as shown in Figure 24-35. By following the selections, you may enter place holders in the cells. For example, entries such as quantity and index numbers are particular to the report itself, so you would select **rpt** > **index** or **rpt** > **qty**. This will create a text string in the cell such as *rpt.index*. To pull values from the components, you may select **asm** > **mbr** > **name** (for the file name of the component). If your components have embedded parameters (see Chapter 20) you may select **asm** > **mbr** > **USER DEFINED** and enter the name of the parameter, such as **DESCRIPTION**.

Because you are specifying a value place holder, and not manually creating text, the table will always create the proper amount of rows and pull its values from the assembly. As parts are added or deleted from the assembly, or if any of the parameter values are modified, the table will always update itself.

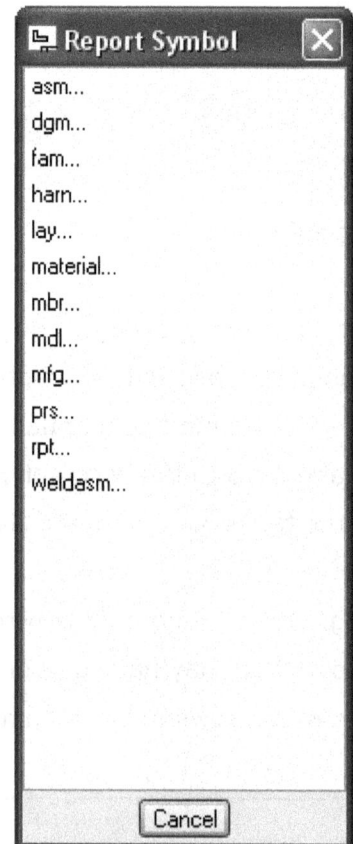

Fig. 24-35
Report Symbols

The display of multiple levels of parts and subassemblies and quantities may be adjusted by selecting **Table** > **Repeat Region** > **Attributes**.

Bill of Materials

To show BOM (Bill of Material) balloons in the drawing, select **Table** > **BOM Balloons** from the menu, and set the region (even if you only have one) that you want to use. From the menu, select **Create Balloon** and whether you want to show all the balloons, or by view or component. Once the balloon is created, you may move the balloon by selecting it and dragging it to a new location, and you may also change its attachment by selecting the balloon, hold down the **RMB**, and select **Edit Attachment**, and choose a new location for the arrow. The resulting table and balloons are shown in Figure 24-36.

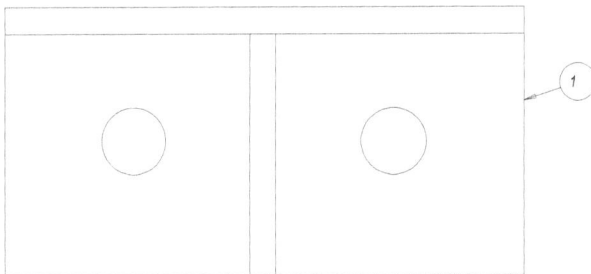

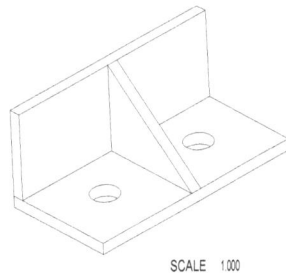

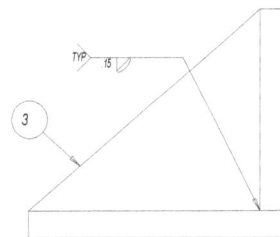

Fig. 24-38
Drawing with Bill of Materials

Printing and Plotting

In June, 1975, *Business Week* ran an article, "The Office of the Future", in which it predicted a paperless office. More than three decades later, we are able to create our three-dimensional designs electronically, but for some reason we still need to flatten them and put them on sheets of processed dead trees.

To send a drawing to your printer or plotter,

select the [icon] **Print** icon from the menu. You may choose to set up a particular engineering plotter at this time, by selecting **Add Printer Type**, as shown in Figure 24-39, but generally you would simply leave the type set at **MS** (Microsoft®) **Printer Manager**. You may select **OK** to accept all of the default settings, and move on to choosing which printer on your computer or network to use, or you may select **Configure** to set options.

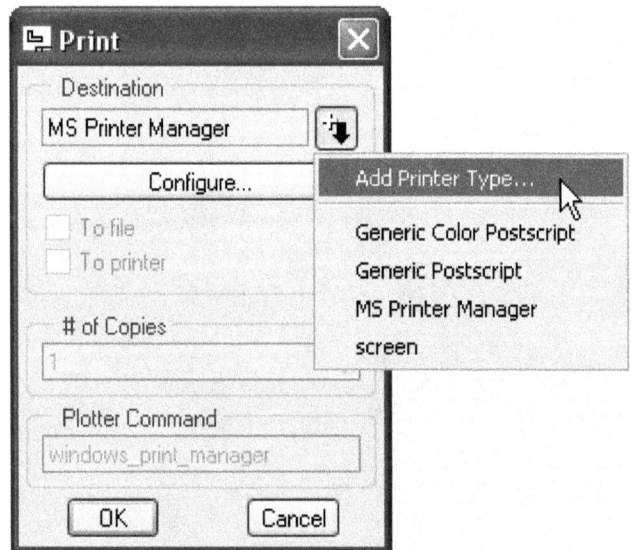

Fig. 24-39
Printer type

You may then choose several configuration options. The two most important settings are shown in Figures 24-40 and 24-41.

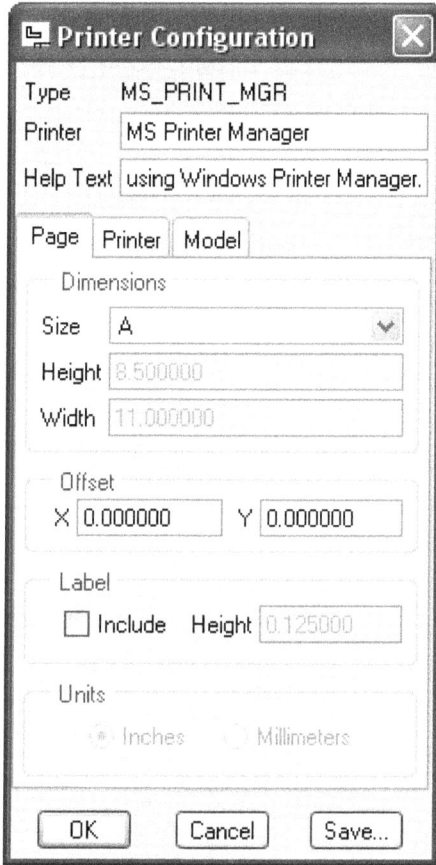

Fig. 24-40
Page setup

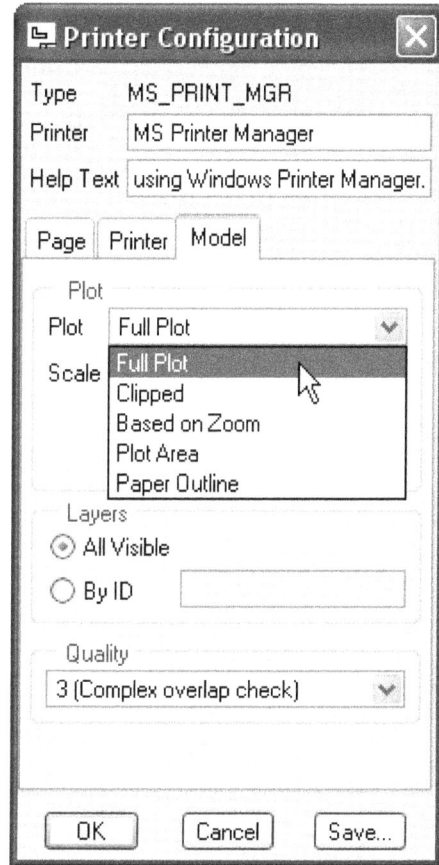

Fig. 24-41
Model setup

If your drawing set to a particular size, such as A, B, C, D, etc., the print will automatically be set to that size. If perhaps you have a D size drawing, but would like to print it on an 8 ½ x 11 printer, you may simply set the size accordingly, as shown in Figure 24-40.

The Plot and Scale settings shown in Figure 24-41 refer to how much of the original drawing will be sent to the printer, and at what scale. A scale factor of 1.0 means it will print the image at exactly the same size it is defined in the Pro/ENGINEER drawing file, provided you are printing on the same size sheet of paper as the drawing is set up for.

The default settings are to plot the original sheet size, **Based on Zoom** at a scale factor of **1.0**, so if you are looking to simply print your entire drawing, with the format, at the size it was defined, be sure to zoom out to the full extent of the drawing before selecting the ⬛ **Print** icon. Then simply accept all of the default settings, and choose which printer or plotter installed on your computer or network to send it to.

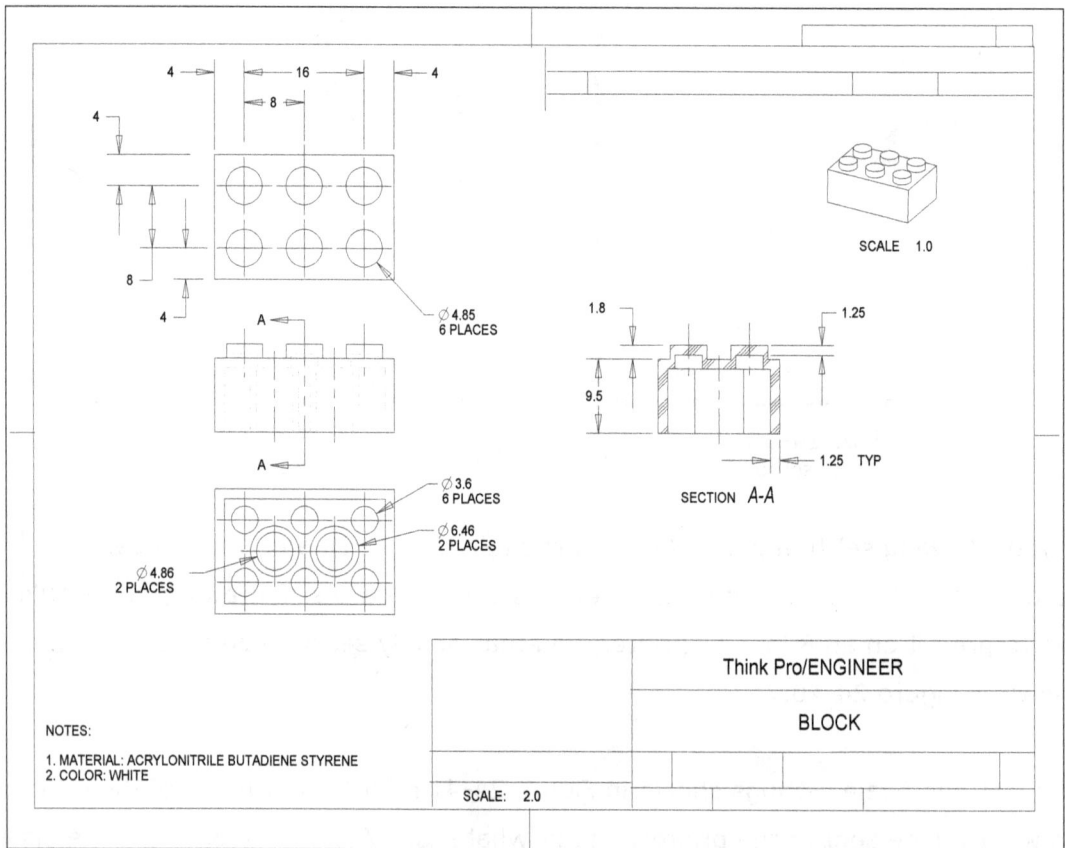

Fig. 24-42
Pro/ENGINEER printed drawing

Extracting Information

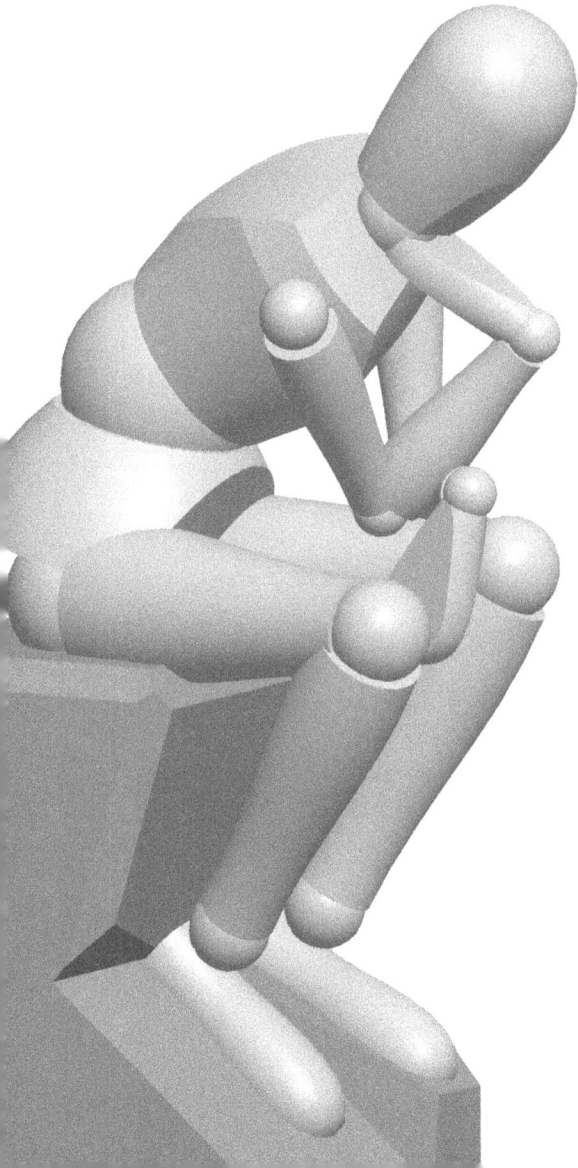

At some point during your design activities, you will want to be able to pull information from your models. This is especially true for models that someone else has created, and if you need to modify them. Knowing how the model is made is crucial.

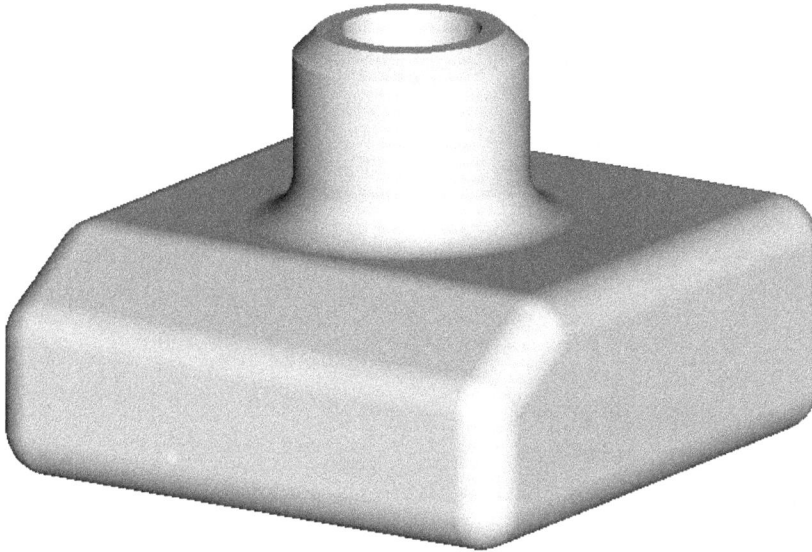

Fig. 25-1
Completed model

Figure 25-1 may be our own model, or it may have been created by a co-worker, vendor or customer. How big is it? How deep is the hole? Is it designed in inches or millimeters? If we need to make a design change, what feature(s) do we need to modify?

Information

Pro/ENGINEER builds the three-dimensional model from sets of features, controlled by dimensions and parameters. You may access that information to help understand how the model is constructed.

Model Info

To view general information about the model, select **Info** > **Model** from the menu. You will be prompted to choose whether you want the information displayed to the screen (as a browser window) or written to a text file in your working directory. Figure 25-2 shows the information for the model.

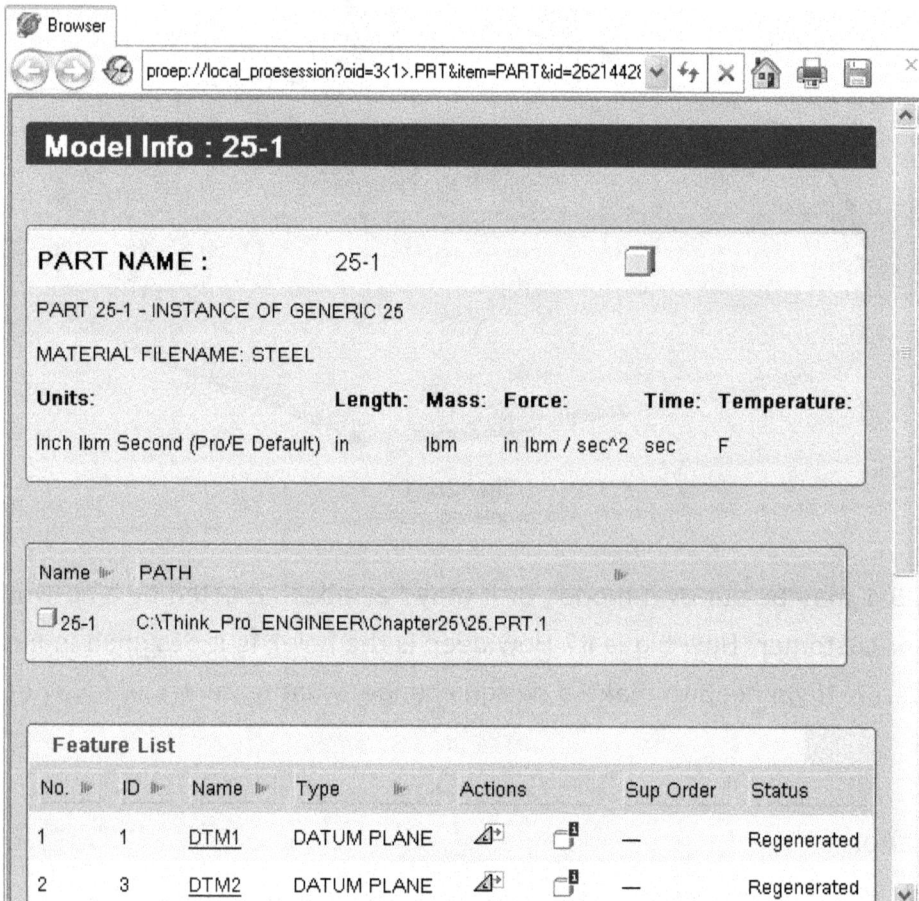

Fig. 25-2
Model Information

In addition to indicating the model name, material (if assigned), and the units used, the information window will also indicate if the model is an instance of a generic model (see Chapter 21) and the generic model's name.

The bottom of the window provides a complete list of the features contained within the model. When a feature name is selected in the window, the corresponding feature will highlight in the graphics area.

Feature Info

By selecting the ⬚ **Feature Info** icon in the Feature List, the browser window will switch to display information about the selected feature, as shown in Figure 25-3.

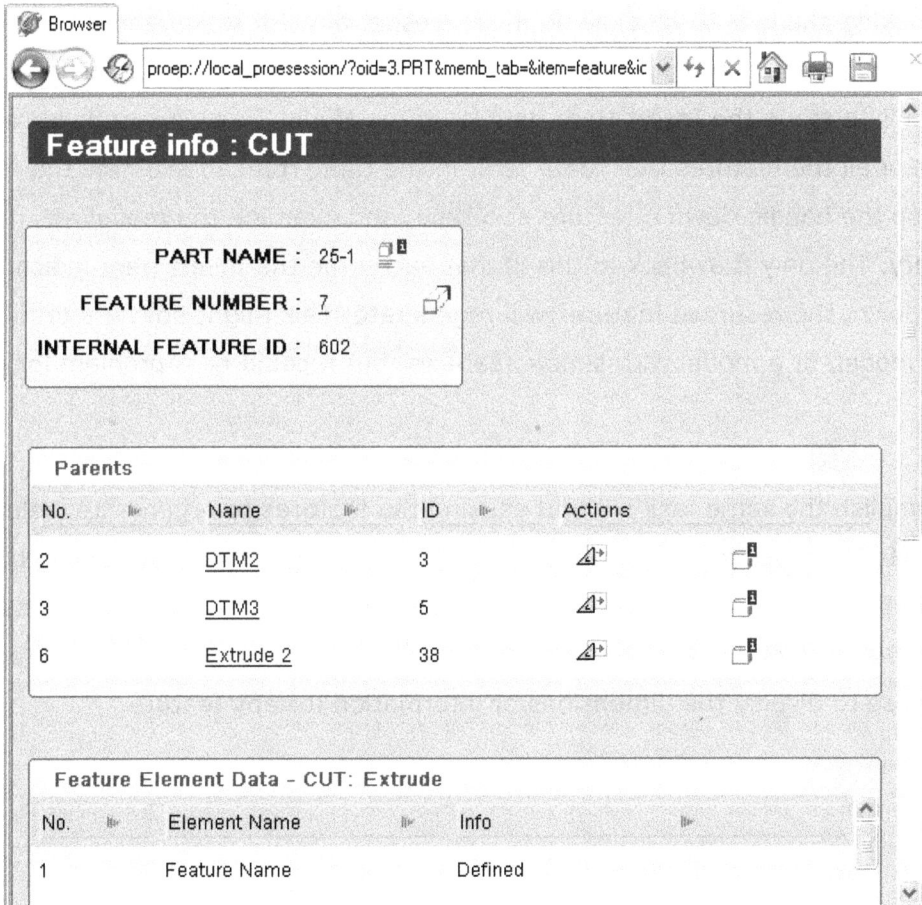

Fig. 25-3
Feature Info window

The Feature Info window will display details about what type of feature it is, what section was used (if any) and a list of dimensions. It will also provide a list of parents for the feature, and a list of children (if any). You may click on the Feature Info icon for any of these features, to display Information windows for each. You may also display feature information at any time by selecting a feature, holding down the **RMB**, and selecting **Info** > **Feature** from the menu.

Model Player

When making changes to an existing model (especially if it was created by someone else), it is extremely helpful to see the progression of the features. One way to do this is to is to move the **Insert Here** handle up the Model Tree. This suppresses the creation of all the features that occur later in the tree. You can examine the model, then drop the handle down a feature at a time, and examine the model as necessary. The only drawback to this is that each time the **Insert Here** indicator is moved down, the resumed features will regenerate. This might not be a problem for a small model, or a model with simple features, but it could be a problem for other models.

To accomplish the same task without causing the features to regenerate, select **Tools** > **Model Player** from the menu. This will open the Model Player dialog box, as shown in Figure 25-4. With the **Regenerate features** option unchecked, you can step through the creation of each feature one by one, or jump forward or back. You can also choose to display the dimensions or information for any feature.

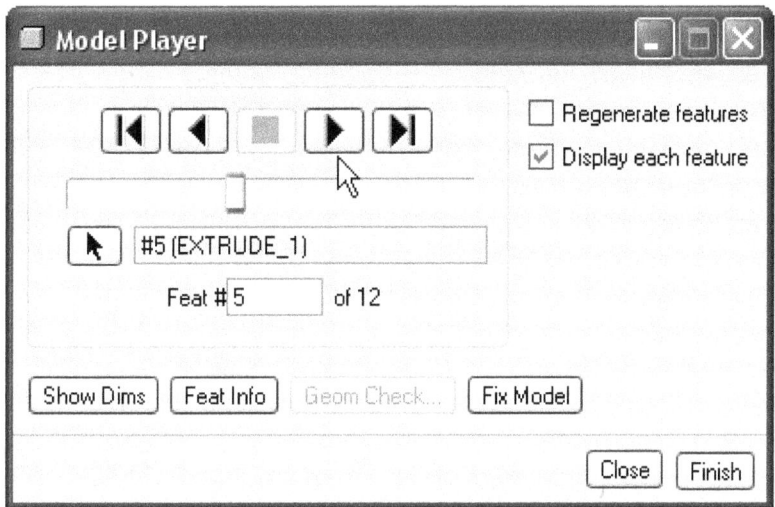

Fig. 25-4
Model Player

Measuring

If we want to know the outer diameter of the cylinder feature shown in Figure 25-1, we could simply select the feature, hold down the **RMB**, select **Edit**, and the dimensions would be displayed. We could also use the feature information techniques described earlier. Either way, we could easily see that its value is .500.

That works when we are trying to see the dimension of a feature, but the hole in the middle of the cylinder was not created with a diameter that we can simply display. It was created by sketching a circle offset from the outer diameter, and extruding to a depth. There is no diameter dimension to display, but we can still take a measurement manually by selecting **Analysis** > **Measure** from the menu, and selecting the desired measurement type from the list, as shown in Figure 25-5. Depending on the type of measurement you choose, a dialog box will open, prompting you to select the appropriate geometry.

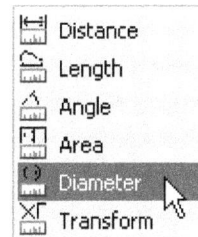

Fig. 25-5
Measurements

The inner diameter of the cylinder measures 0.300, as shown in Figure 25-6.

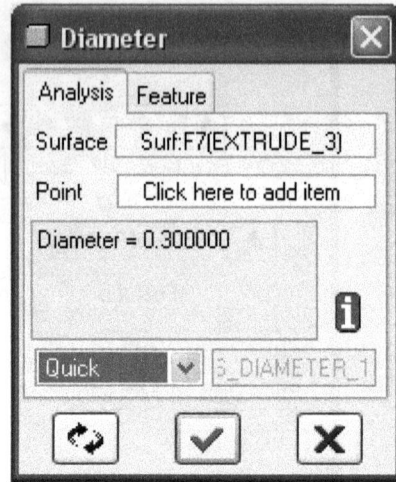

Fig. 25-6
Diameter measurement

Fig. 25-7
Distance measurement

Since that same inner shape was created by cutting down a blind depth from the top of the cylinder, there is no dimension that shows the distance from the bottom of the hole to the bottom of the part. If we need to know this information, we can select **Analysis > Measure > Distance** from the menu, and select the two surfaces, as shown in Figure 25-7.

If you are working in an assembly, you can take measurements between components, to check for proper fit.

Mass Properties

In addition to knowing the dimensions of your models, it is important to know how much your parts and assemblies weigh and/or how much material they require. To create a detailed report, simply select **Analysis** > **Model** > **Mass Properties** from the menu. Either select a coordinate system to use as a reference, or accept the default, then select the ⟨⟨⟨⟩⟩⟩ **Preview** icon. Pro/ENGINEER will perform the calculation, and indicate the location of the center of gravity, as shown in Figure 25-8. Selecting the 🛈 **Information** icon will display the full report, as shown in Figure 25-9.

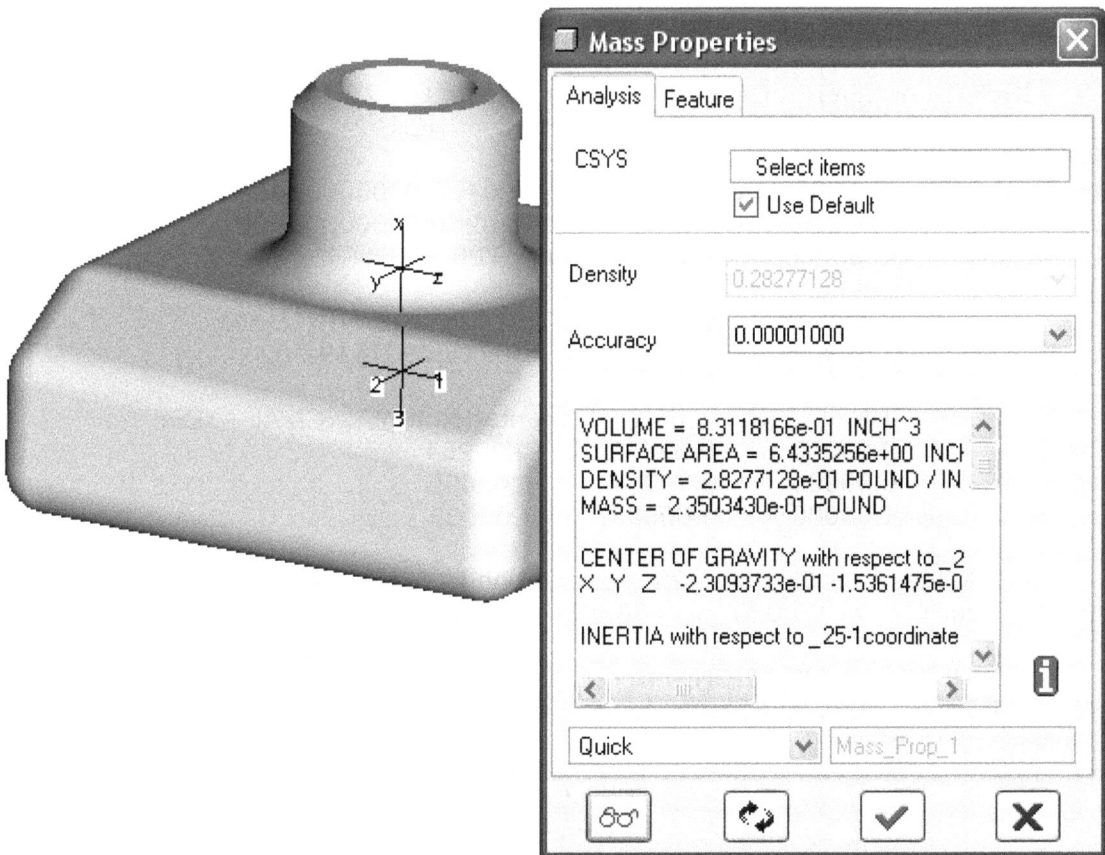

Fig. 25-8
Mass property calculation

MASS PROPERTIES OF THE PART 25-1

VOLUME = 8.3118166e-01 INCH^3
SURFACE AREA = 6.4335256e+00 INCH^2
DENSITY = 2.8277128e-01 POUND / INCH^3
MASS = 2.3503430e-01 POUND

CENTER OF GRAVITY with respect to _25-1 coordinate frame:
X Y Z   -2.3093733e-01 -1.5361475e-02 0.0000000e+00 INCH

INERTIA with respect to _25-1 coordinate frame: (POUND * INCH^2)

INERTIA TENSOR:
Ixx Ixy Ixz   6.0946361e-02 -2.2112849e-04 0.0000000e+00
Iyx Iyy Iyz   -2.2112849e-04 5.0720350e-02 0.0000000e+00
Izx Izy Izz   0.0000000e+00 0.0000000e+00 4.9580789e-02

INERTIA at CENTER OF GRAVITY with respect to _25-1 coordinate frame:
(POUND * INCH^2)
INERTIA TENSOR:
Ixx Ixy Ixz   6.0890899e-02 6.1266461e-04 0.0000000e+00
Iyx Iyy Iyz   6.1266461e-04 3.8185489e-02 0.0000000e+00
Izx Izy Izz   0.0000000e+00 0.0000000e+00 3.6990466e-02

PRINCIPAL MOMENTS OF INERTIA: (POUND * INCH^2)
I1 I2 I3   3.6990466e-02 3.8168969e-02 6.0907419e-02

ROTATION MATRIX from _25-1 orientation to PRINCIPAL AXES:
        0.00000   -0.02695   -0.99964
        0.00000   0.99964   -0.02695
        1.00000   0.00000   0.00000

ROTATION ANGLES from _25-1 orientation to PRINCIPAL AXES (degrees):
angles about x y z 90.000   -88.455   90.000

RADII OF GYRATION with respect to PRINCIPAL AXES:
R1 R2 R3   3.9671560e-01 4.0298566e-01 5.0906059e-01 INCH

Fig. 25-9
Mass property report

Interference Checking

Figure 25-10 is an exploded assembly view of our component from Figure 25-1, along with its mating component. We've added a chamfer to the hole in the mating component so that we do not have an interference with the base of the cylinder, and also measured the angles between the surfaces of the parts to be sure the beveled edge on our first component is large enough to not intersect the overhang on the other.

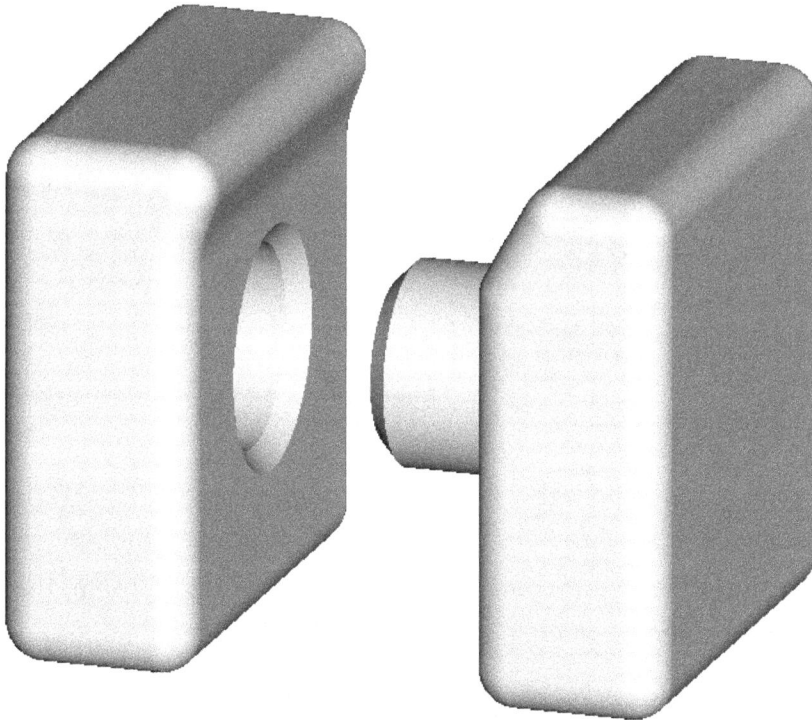

Fig. 25-10
Exploded assembly of mating components

To be absolutely certain that we do not have any interferences, select **Analysis** > **Model** > **Global Interference** from the menu. (It does not matter if the assembly is exploded, or not.) When the [⊙⊙] **Preview** button is selected, Pro/ENGINEER will compare every three-dimensional model in the assembly, create a report indicating which components are intersecting each other, and will highlight the intersecting geometry on the model, as shown in Figure 25-11.

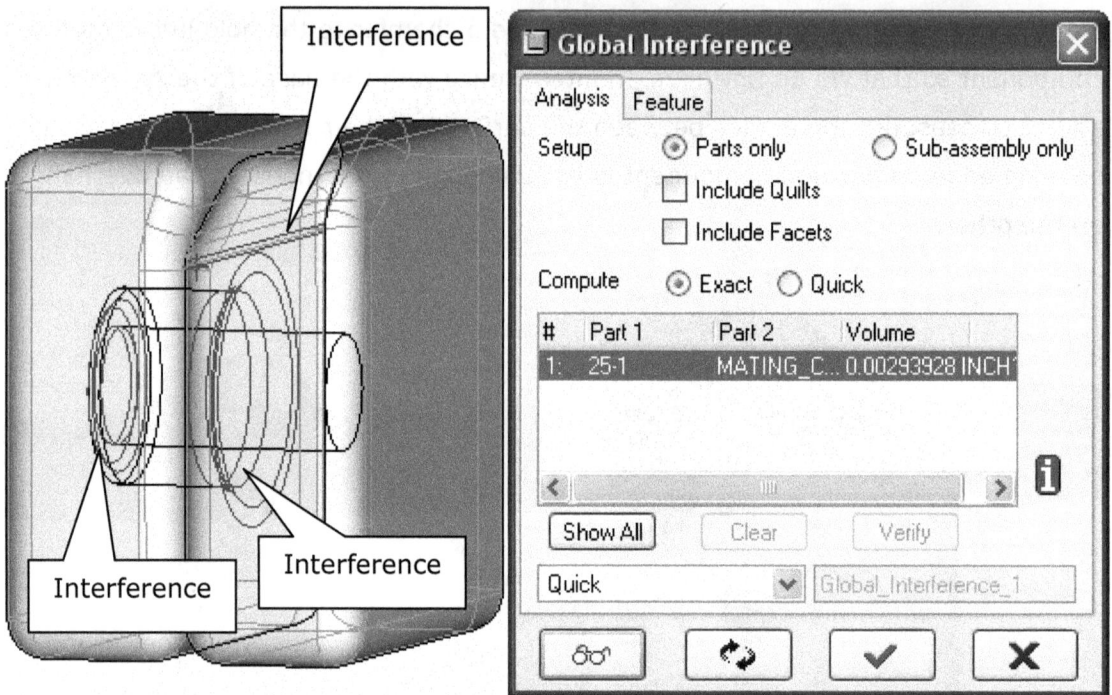

Fig. 25-11
Interference calculation

Upon examining the highlighted areas, we discover that even though we were mindful of the proper fit of our components when we designed them, the chamfer around the hole was not large enough, the round along the edge of the bevel was not large enough and the hole was not deep enough.

Many new Pro/ENGINEER users ask why the software can't just fix the problems it finds, and the answer is that even though the software is extremely powerful, you must still make your own design decisions. Is the hole not deep enough, or is the cylinder too long? Making a deeper hole or reducing the length of the cylinder can both result in a 'fix', but what is your design intent? After modifying the models, it is a good idea to go back and check for interferences again.

Chapter 26

Importing and Exporting Data

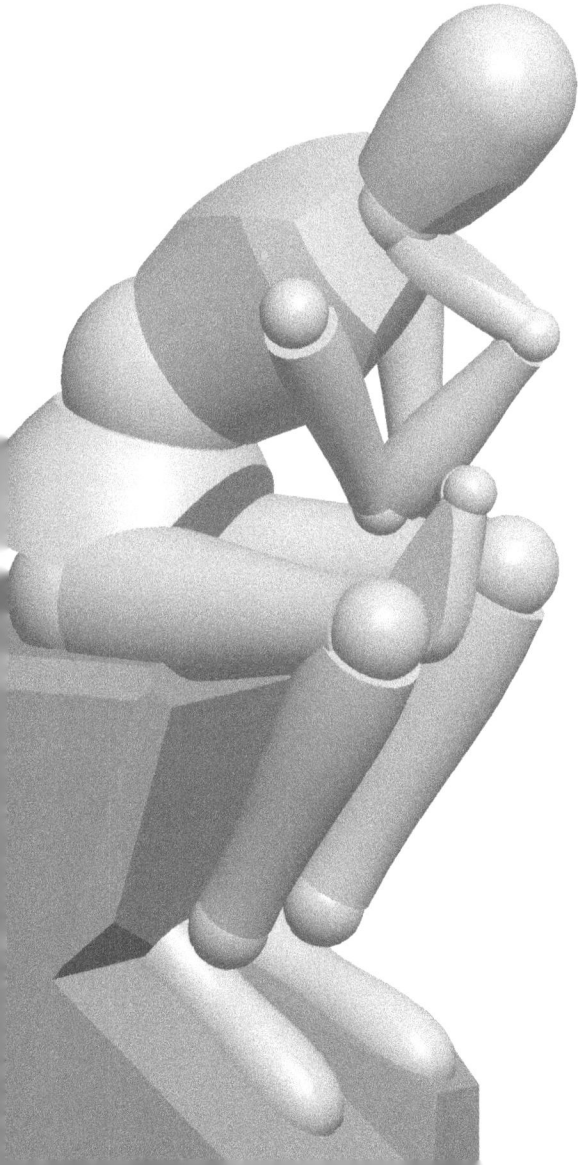

Pro/ENGINEER Releases

Importing Data

Exporting Data

In a professional environment, you will need to either receive data from customers, vendors, and co-workers, or you will need to send data to them, or both. Pro/ENGINEER offers several ways to accomplish this.

Pro/ENGINEER Releases

When Pro/ENGINEER files are created, they are specific to the release version being used. For example, if you are running Pro/ENGINEER Wildfire 2.0, all of the files you create are Pro/ENGINEER Wildfire 2.0 files. Each new release of Pro/ENGINEER will open the current and all previous release files, so you do not have to worry about bringing your legacy data up to date. If however you are running Pro/ENGINEER Wildfire 4.0 and you open, then **Save** an old file, the latest version of the file becomes a release 4.0 file.

Simply put, all Pro/ENGINEER files are upward compatible, not downward. When you attempt to open a Pro/ENGINEER file that is created with a higher release than you are using, you will receive the following in the message window:

File *path_file_name* was created in a newer release of Pro/ENGINEER.

The file *path_file_name* is not a valid PART file.

' path_*file_name*' cannot be retrieved.

'*file_name*' cannot be retrieved.

To determine the release level of a particular file, you may open the file in a text editor such as Microsoft® Notepad. Most of the file will be encrypted, but if you scroll down to the lines just before the encryption starts, you should find a line that indicates the release level and build code used to create the file:

#Pro/ENGINEER TM Wildfire 3.0 (c) 2006 by Parametric Technology Corporation All Rights Reserved. M110

If you are current with your PTC maintenance, you are entitled to the latest release version of the software at any time, so upgrading is not an issue. You may go to the PTC website and request a current copy of the software. If you are not currently on maintenance, you can contact your nearest PTC VAR (Value Added Reseller).

Importing Data

Pro/ENGINEER will read a variety of file types generated by other software products. There two basic ways of using imported data, and once the data has been accessed in Pro/ENGINEER, it can be saved as a Pro/ENGINEER file.

Open

Regardless of the type of file, if Pro/ENGINEER is able to read it, you may select **File > Open** from the menu. In the File Open dialog box, change the File Type to either **All Files (*)**, or the specific type, and select the desired file.

You will have the option to specify a name for the new Pro/ENGINEER file you are creating, and also the type, as shown in Figure 26-1. If you are opening a DXF (Drawing Exchange Format), it is most likely a two-dimensional drawing, so Pro/ENGINEER defaults to that file type. Likewise, if you are opening a STEP (Standard for the Exchange of Product model data) of multiple parts, then Pro/ENGINEER will default to Assembly as the file type.

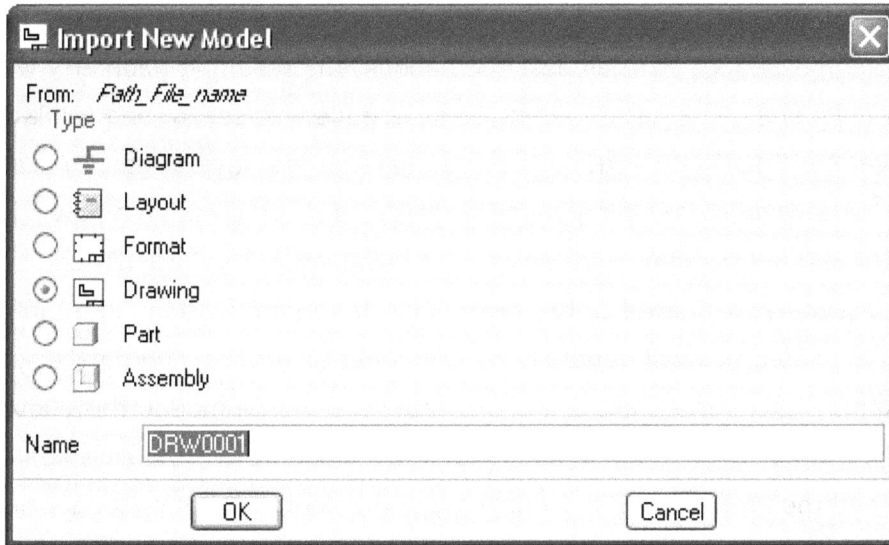

Fig. 26-1
Import New Model options

It is interesting to note however, that you are not limited to the default type. For example you may open a DXF of a two-dimensional drawing, as a part file. All of the entities contained within the drawing will be created as if they were a single sketch, on a default datum plane.

It is also important to note that when opening any three-dimensional file, such as STEP, IGES (Initial Graphics Exchange Specification) or Parasolid, the resulting model is comprised of a single feature. It will not contain separate features with dimensions that can be modified. It is referred to as a 'dumb solid'. You may of course add new features that add and remove material.

Once the new Pro/ENGINEER file is created and saved, the source file is no longer needed, and may be deleted from your file system.

Insert

When opening exchange data as described above, the resulting geometry will be in whatever units and coordinate system the source file was set to, and will lack any of your typical Pro/ENGINEER settings, such as parameters, layers, etc. To use the exchange data while maintaining your standards, start by creating a new Pro/ENGINEER file (drawing, part, assembly) using your standards. Then from the menu, select **Insert** > **Shared Data** > **From File**. If you are working in a three-dimensional model, you will generally be prompted to select a coordinate system. Since you may have more than one coordinate system in a model, this allows you to control the location of the import data within the model. Once the data has been inserted, and the Pro/ENGINEER model saved, the source file is no longer needed, and may be deleted from your file system.

Exporting Data

Pro/ENGINEER can create a variety of file types that may be used to transfer your design to companies that do not have Pro/ENGINEER capabilities. For example, you may need to send a manufacturing drawing to a machine shop that is still only running AutoCAD®, or some other archaic two-dimensional program. In which case you may send them a DXF file. You may need to send a customer your three-dimensional design for a packaging study, but they still haven't upgraded from Catia® or SolidWorks®, so you could send them a STEP file. You can even create an STL (stereolithography) file for rapid prototyping.

Save a Copy

To create an export file, first open the Pro/ENGINEER file. From the menu, select **File** > **Save a Copy**. After specifying a name and type, a dialog box similar to the one shown in Figure 26-2 will open for you to specify what type of geometry to include in the file, and which Coordinate System to reference. Note that once the file is created, it cannot be modified, but additional files can be created at any time.

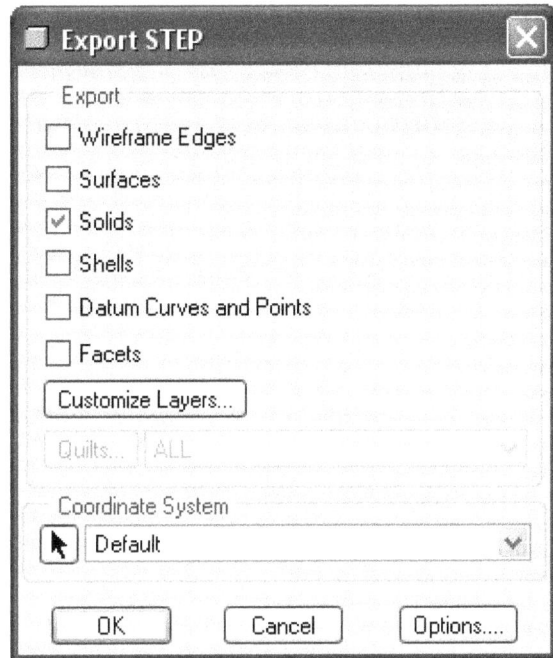

Fig. 26-2
File data options

Backup

In Pro/ENGINEER, the command name **Backup** is a misnomer. It is not intended to be a computer system backup utility to safeguard against catastrophic data loss. It is intended to provide you with a 'snap shot' of your current Pro/ENGINEER design. This is useful for creating a set of your 'latest and greatest' files to send to a customer or vendor.

To create a **Backup** (snap shot), open the source Pro/ENGINEER file. This could be an assembly, an individual part, or a drawing of an assembly or part. From the menu, select **File** > **Set Working Directory**, and select the folder where the new files should be created. (It is recommended that you either create a completely new folder, or choose an empty folder.)

Once the working directory has been set, select **File** > **Backup** from the menu, and select OK. Pro/ENGINEER will automatically create a new copy of every model that is in session and associated to the current file. For example, if you create a backup of an assembly drawing, Pro/ENGINEER will create a copy of the drawing file, the assembly file, all of the individual part files, and even the format file used for the drawing. This set of new files can then be transferred electronically to another user.

There are two caveats regarding **Backup** that you should be aware of. First, the new files will be created with a .1 version number. This means that even if your current part is *widget.prt.19*, your **Backup** file will be *widget.prt.1*. There is nothing wrong with this, but if this new file is placed in a directory with a file named *widget.prt.18*, Pro/ENGINEER will open the file with the highest version number (18), not necessarily the latest design.

The other common mistake made by beginners and experienced users alike, is that after the Working Directory is set, and the **Backup** models are created, users tend to forget that they are in the new Working Directory. The models that are currently in session are actually the new **Backup** models. This means that if you make a change to the Widget part and save it, you will create a *widget.prt.2* file in the new directory, instead of *widget.prt.20* in the original directory.

The best practice is to make sure all of your current files have been saved. Create the **Backup** as described above, then clear everything out of session and reset to the original Working Directory, or even better, exit Pro/ENGINEER entirely, and re-start the program.

Customization

Templates
Environment
Menu
config.pro File

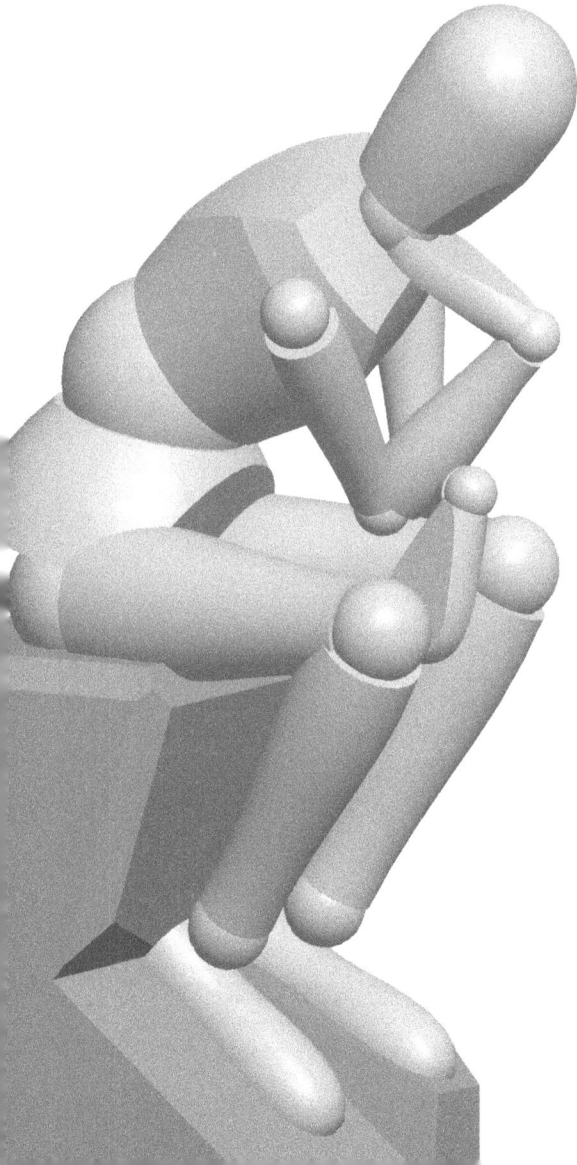

Pro/ENGINEER is fully functional right out of the box, but if you want or need something more than the 'plain vanilla' settings, there are several options you may set.

Templates

When you start to create Pro/ENGINEER files, and find that you are constantly setting the same information for the same types of files, it may be time to create one or more templates. A template is nothing more than a part, assembly or drawing that you would like to use as a starting point for new files. The Pro/ENGINEER term for these files are **Templates**, but they are commonly referred to as '**Start Parts**'.

Creating Templates

If your company produces part files in metric units, with a standard list of parameters and layers, go ahead and create a new part with all of those settings. In fact, if there are two or more standard ways you normally create parts, go ahead and make starting versions for each. While you are at it, go ahead and create a starting assembly and starting drawing if you would like. Be sure to store your templates in a common location on your computer or network, for easy access by yourself and your team.

Using Templates

Chapter 3 discusses creating new Pro/ENGINEER files. Figure 3-11 shows the creation of a new file, with the **Use default template** option checked. This means your new file will be an exact <u>copy</u> of whatever file is specified in your *config.pro* file (see later in the chapter) as the template for that file type. If you do not wish to use the default template, you can simply uncheck the box, and browse to select a different file, or none at all, in which case your new file will be completely blank.

Environment

All Pro/ENGINEER models and commands will operate the same, regardless of what your screen may look like, but many users choose to adjust their Pro/ENGINEER environment to suite their needs.

System Colors

The default Pro/ENGINEER graphics area for three-dimensional modeling utilizes a background that blends from grey at the top to lighter grey at the bottom. Dimensions to be edited are displayed in yellow. This lack of contrast, as shown in Figure 27-1, can be very difficult for some users to see.

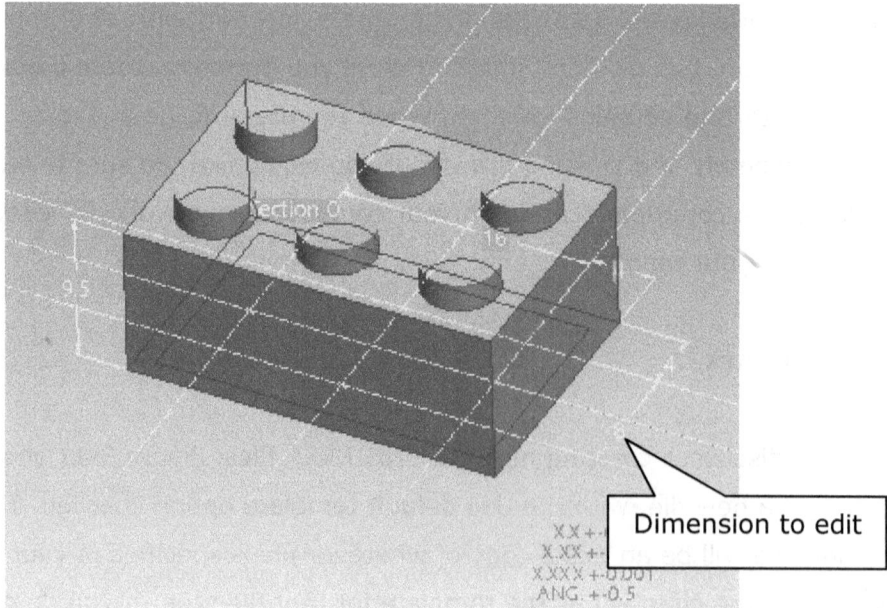

Fig. 27-1
Pro/ENGINEER default color scheme

To change the color settings, select **View**
> **Display Settings** > **System Colors** from
the menu. This will open the System
Colors dialog box, as shown in Figure
27-2.

You may set any color for any item, as
you wish. You may also change the two
colors used for the blended background,
or even decide to use a solid background
instead. Generally, setting the
background to a dark color is sufficient
to provide the necessary contrast to be
able to edit your Pro/ENGINEER models,
but you may also choose a pre-defined
color Scheme. (To produce most of the
figures in this book, the 'Black on White'
scheme was set prior to capturing the
images.)

This manipulation of settings is unique to
your current Pro/ENGINEER session. You
may choose to save your settings by
selecting **File** > **Save** and specifying a
location and name for a system color file
(*.scl*). To use it again, simply open the
same file, from the same menu.

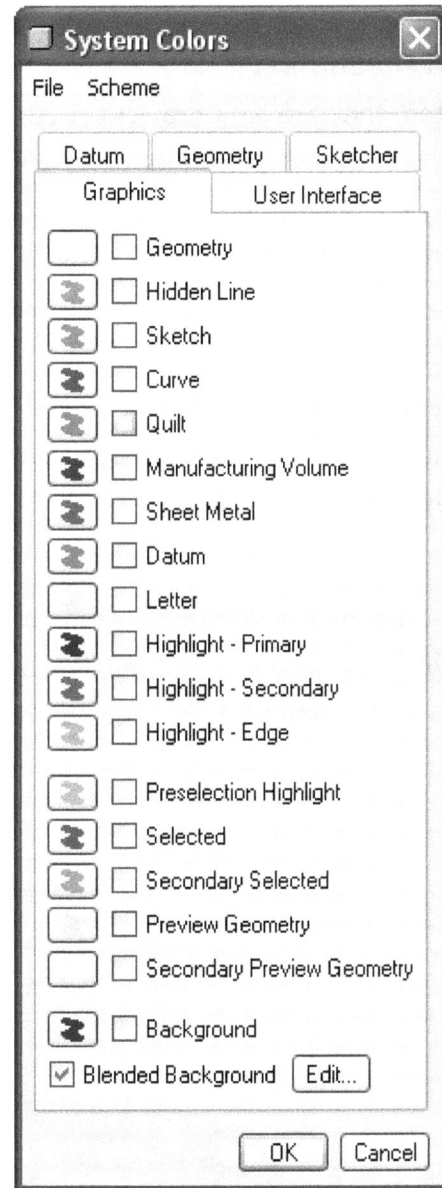

Fig. 27-2
System colors

If you would like to use this color setting every time you start Pro/ENGINEER, you
may include the path and name of the file in your *config.pro* file (see later in this
chapter).

Model Colors

When Pro/ENGINEER parts are first
created, they are light grey (RGB 224,
242, 255) but when a three-dimensional
object is displayed in shaded mode,
Pro/ENGINEER will provide a gradation
from light to dark, as shown in Figure
27-3. The default setting also has a
white highlight definition. This is why flat
surfaces displayed parallel to the screen
appear completely white.

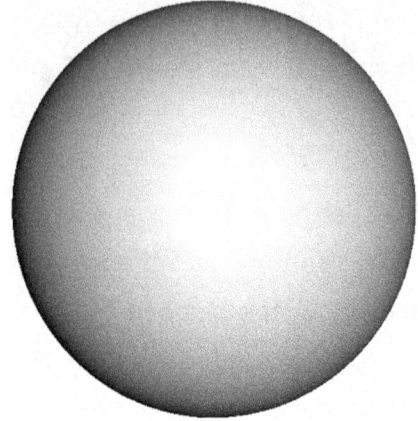

Fig. 27-3
White sphere

If you are only working on a single part, the color probably doesn't matter much,
but when working with assemblies, a single color may make it hard to distinguish
between individual components, as shown in Figure 27-4.

Fig. 27-4
Multiple components of the same color

To adjust geometry color, select **View >**
Color and Appearance from the menu.
This will open the Appearance Editor, as
shown in Figure 27-5.

You may choose a pre-defined color from
the list (palette), edit any of the existing
colors, or add your own. Under the
Properties section, you may specify the
RGB values of the color and its related
highlights. You may even use the
Advanced tab to control the amount of
transparency and the Map tab may be
used to create a texture from imported
bitmaps. Your palette (*.dmt) may be
saved by selecting **File > Save As.**

In the Assignment portion of the editor
you may choose to apply your new color
to the entire model, or select individual
surfaces only. Once the color has been
applied to a part, or a surface of a part,
that color will remain as long as you
save the part file. If you are working in
an assembly, you may choose to set
colors of individual components, which
would override any part colors that may
be set, without actually changing the
component file. (The assembly color
setting is unique to the assembly.)

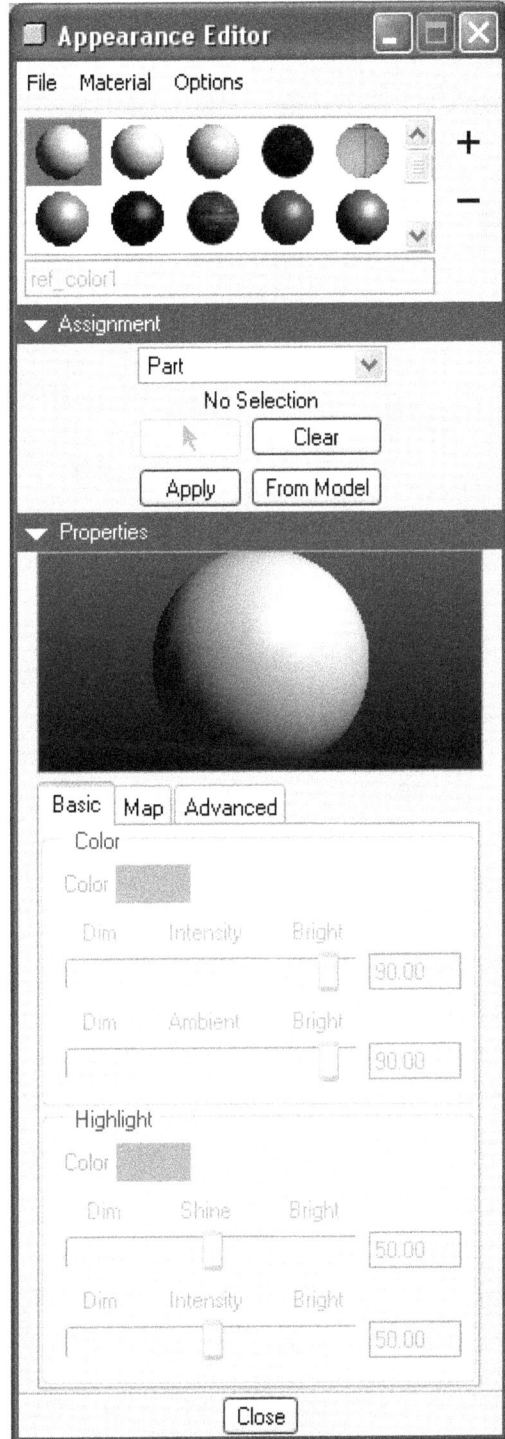

Fig. 27-5
Appearance Editor

Figure 27-6 shows the same assembly, but with a different color for each component. Even in the grayscale version of this book, you can easily see the difference between components.

Fig.27-6
Components of various colors

Note: Just because Pro/ENGINEER allows you to make photo-realistic colors, it doesn't mean you need to. Unless you are making images for your company website or catalog, your design images do not need to look realistic.

You may be able to create a perfect representation of polished aluminum, but it won't look much different than stainless steel, nickel, or zinc oxide. An assembly made up of red, orange, yellow, green, blue, and some weird purple part will convey your design intent, and will be easier to work with than one with five shades of silver.

Menu

Pro/ENGINEER is completely menu driven, but not every user will use all of the commands that are typically displayed with icons in the toolbars, and many users will repeatedly use commands that are not normally displayed. Because a Pro/ENGINEER file is a stand alone data file, it may be created and edited with any combination of commands, regardless of how you access them. To increase your productivity, it is possible to make the commands and combination of commands you use, more accessible.

config.win File

To alter the screen locations of your tools, select **Tools** > **Customize Screen** from the menu. This will open the Customize dialog box, as shown in Figure 27-7. With this utility, you can choose which icons to include on your toolbars. You may also decide which toolbars to display, and where they should be located on the screen. Once you have decided on your screen layout, you may save your settings as a configuration file (*.win*). The default name is *config.win*, but you could choose any name you wish. This allows you to have different settings that are unique to you the user, or possibly even per project.

You can load a saved window configuration file at any time, and if you would like to start with the same file each time you start Pro/ENGINEER, it can be added to your *config.pro* file (see later in this chapter).

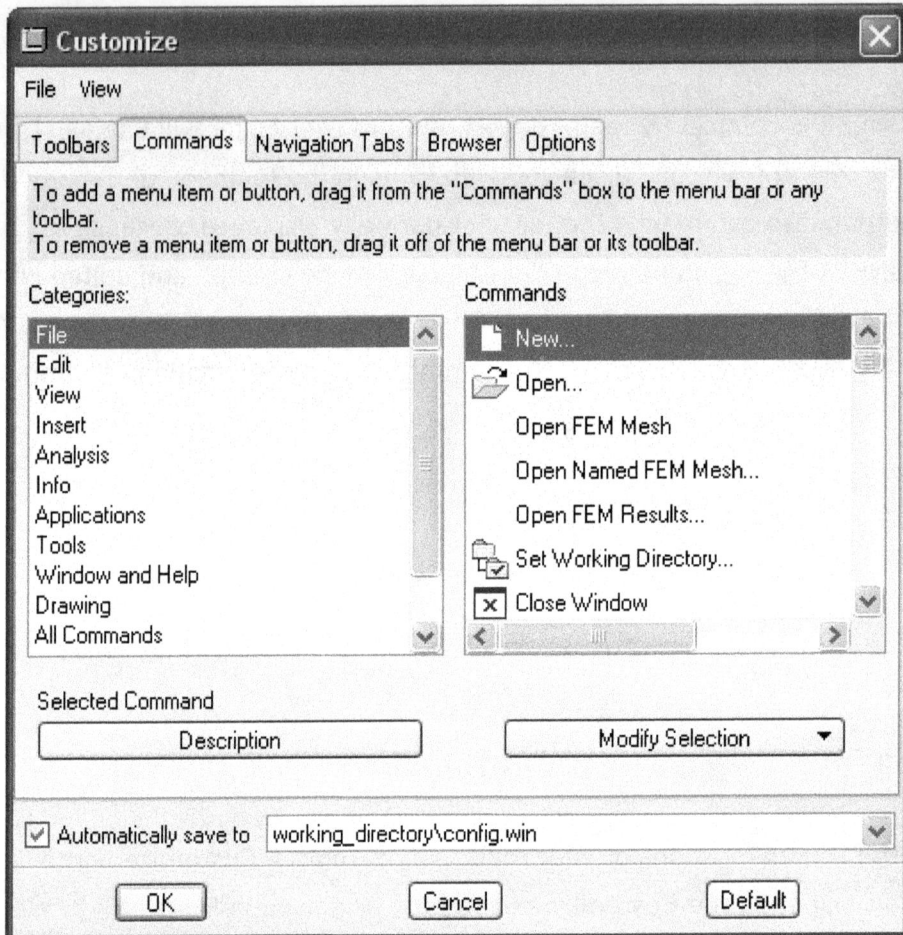

Fig. 27-7
Window customization utility

Mapkeys

Mapkeys, also referred to as 'macros', can be created for any string of commands (both menu selections and keyboard entries), by selecting **Tools** > **Mapkeys** from the menu, and select new from the list of Mapkeys. This will open the Record Mapkey utility shown in Figure 27-8.

First enter in a Key Sequence. This is a string of text that when entered will execute a set of commands. If you wish, you may also create a name and description for the Mapkey, but it is not necessary.

Select **Record**, then go ahead and make all of the menu picks, selections and data entries you wish to capture. When finished, select **Stop**, and go ahead and save the new Mapkey when prompted.

In this case, we want to create a macro so that any time we type '*aprint*', Pro/ENGINEER automatically zooms out to the extent of the display, starts the print command, and selects 'A' as the size of the output file.

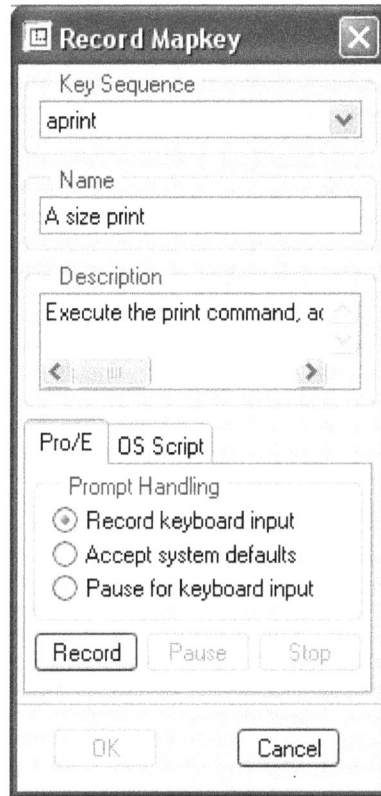

Fig. 27-8
Mapkey creation

Mapkeys are stored in your config.pro file (see later in this chapter), and the above example would appear as:

```
mapkey aprint @MAPKEY_NAMEExecute the print command, after zooming out the \
mapkey(continued) extents and selecting A size as the output;@MAPKEY_LABELA size print;\
mapkey(continued) ~ Command `ProCmdViewRefit` ;~ Command `ProCmdModelPrint` ;\
mapkey(continued) ~ Activate `print` `Configure`;~ Open `print_config` `o_size`;\
mapkey(continued) ~ Close `print_config` `o_size`;~ Select `print_config` `o_size`1 `A`;\
mapkey(continued) ~ Select `print_config` `r_opt_ctrl`1 `Model_sheet`;\
mapkey(continued) ~ Open `print_config` `o_plot`;~ Close `print_config` `o_plot`;\
mapkey(continued) ~ Select `print_config` `o_plot`1 `Full Plot`;\
mapkey(continued) ~ Activate `print_config` `OK`;~ Activate `print` `OK`;
mapkey $F1 @MAPKEY_NAMEsave;@MAPKEY_LABELsave;\
mapkey(continued) ~ Activate `main_dlg_cur` `ProCmdModelSave.file`;\
mapkey(continued) ~ Activate `file_saveas` `Current Dir`;~ Activate `file_saveas` `OK`;
```

config.pro File

Aside from the actual data you are creating, the config.pro file is arguably the most important, and often the least understood, file used in Pro/ENGINEER. It is quite simply, a basic text file that Pro/ENGINEER reads, which tells the software each and every setting to use. It is interesting to note however, that you do not necessarily need a config.pro file at all. If no such file exists, Pro/ENGINEER will operate using all of its default settings. A config.pro file is technically only needed if you want to change one or more default settings.

Loading

When Pro/ENGINEER starts, it will look for and find any file named *config.pro*, starting in the system default directory `<loadpoint>/text`, the home directory, and the current working directory, in that order. If more than one file is found along the way, the settings of the later files will override the settings of the earlier.

At any time, you may load a custom config.pro file by selecting **Tools** > **Options** from the menu, and browsing to the desired file, and applying its values. From that point forward, all of your Pro/ENGINEER program and data creation settings will be driven from the new config.pro settings. Note that changes to the configuration options only effect new files, and features, and have no affect on existing files. (When you save a model, it creates a new version number, therefore depending on the config.pro settings, the new file may be different than the previous.)

Contents

As mentioned above, Pro/ENGINEER will operate using default settings if no other setting is found, so config.pro files need only contain non-default settings. A config.pro file may be manually edited with a text editor, or it may be accessed by selecting **Tools** > **Options** from the menu. Figure 27-9 shows a sample config.pro.

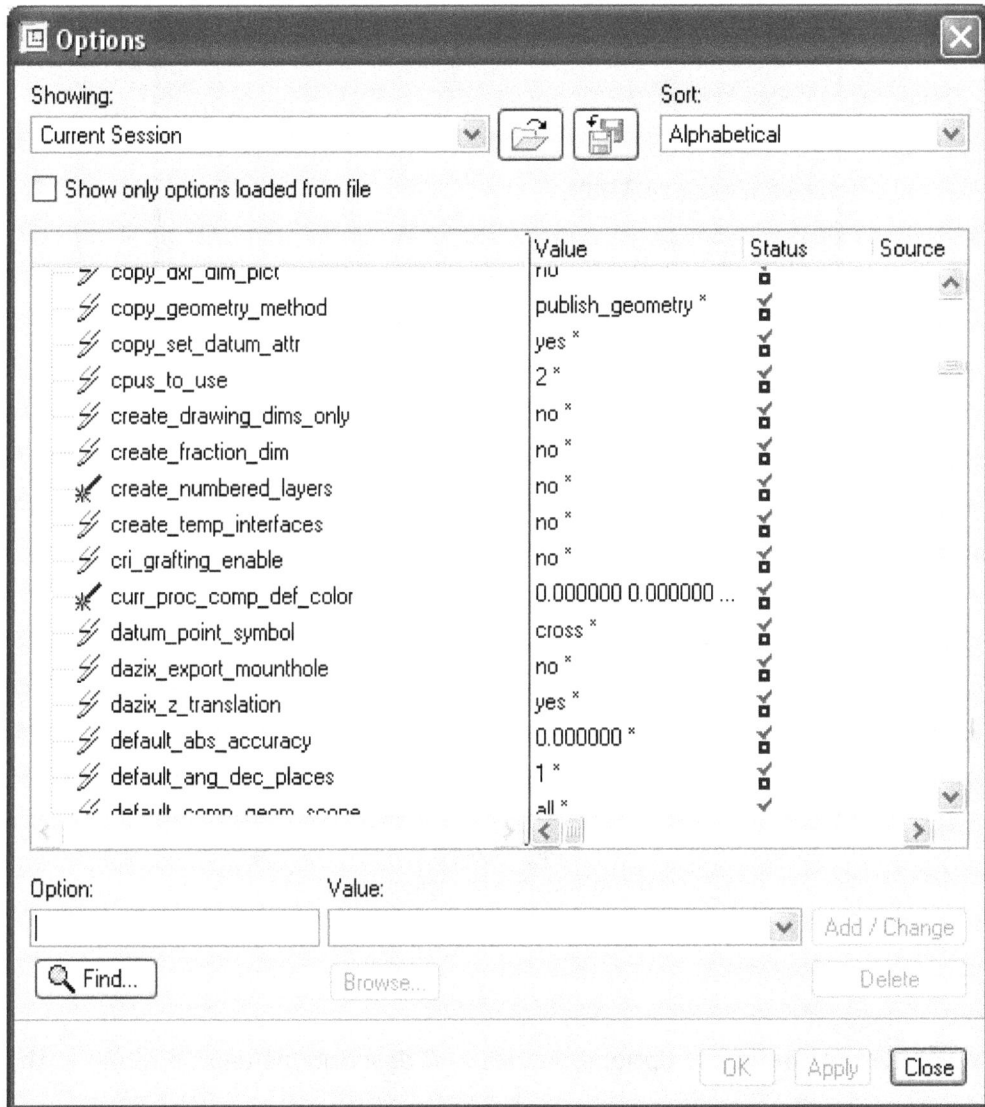

Fig. 27-9
Sample configuration options

Any value displayed with an asterisk (*) is set at Pro/ENGINEER's default value. To change a setting, select it (which will fill in the Option box) and enter or select an available Value from the list. To find a particular setting, you may select the

[Q Find...] **Find** button, which will open a search utility as shown in Figure 27-10.

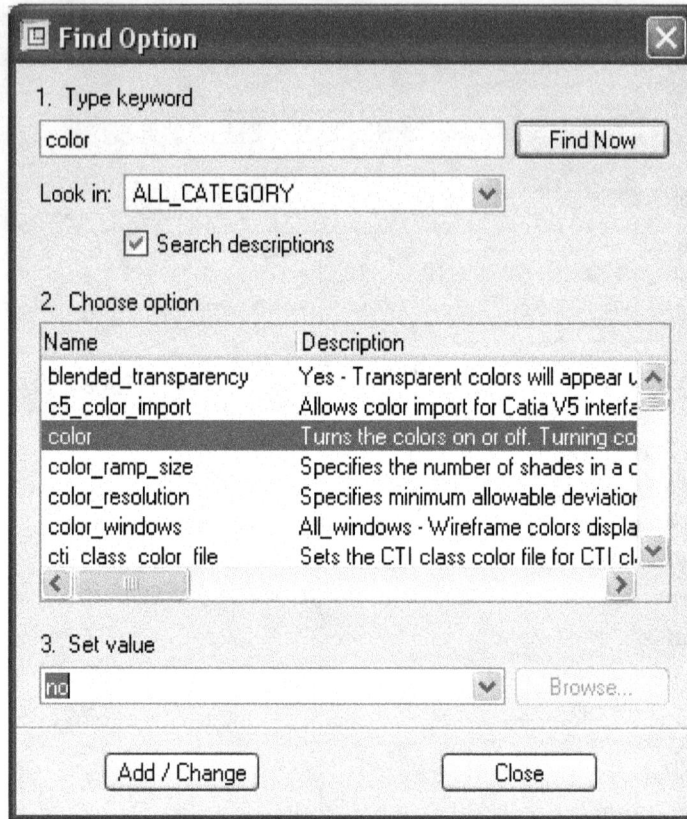

Fig. 27-10
Finding and setting a configuration option

A complete list of config.pro options, values and descriptions can be found in the Help Center (see Chapter 28) under Configuration Options, or you may open the document located on your computer directly:

<load point>\html\usascii\proe\helpSysTop\siteset\configoptions.pdf

Finding Help

Help Center

Parametric Technology Corporation

PTC/User

Pro/E Community

Frey Innovations, LLC

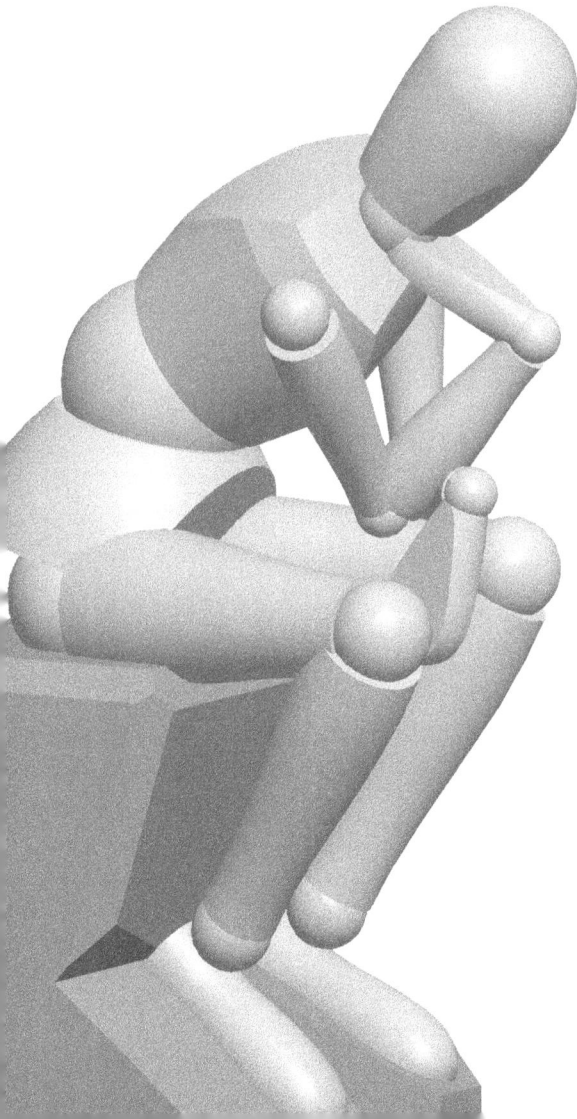

Whether you are a new user to Pro/ENGINEER or a seasoned professional, you will have questions (even after reading this book). Fortunately there are many resources available to you.

Help Center

Pro/ENGINEER release 20 (1998) was the last release of the software with a set of printed user manuals available. (Actually, it did not automatically ship with the software, but you could order a set.) Since that time, electronic versions of the manuals are included with the software. To access the information, select **Help** > **Help Center** from the menu. This will open a browser window, as shown in Figure 28-1.

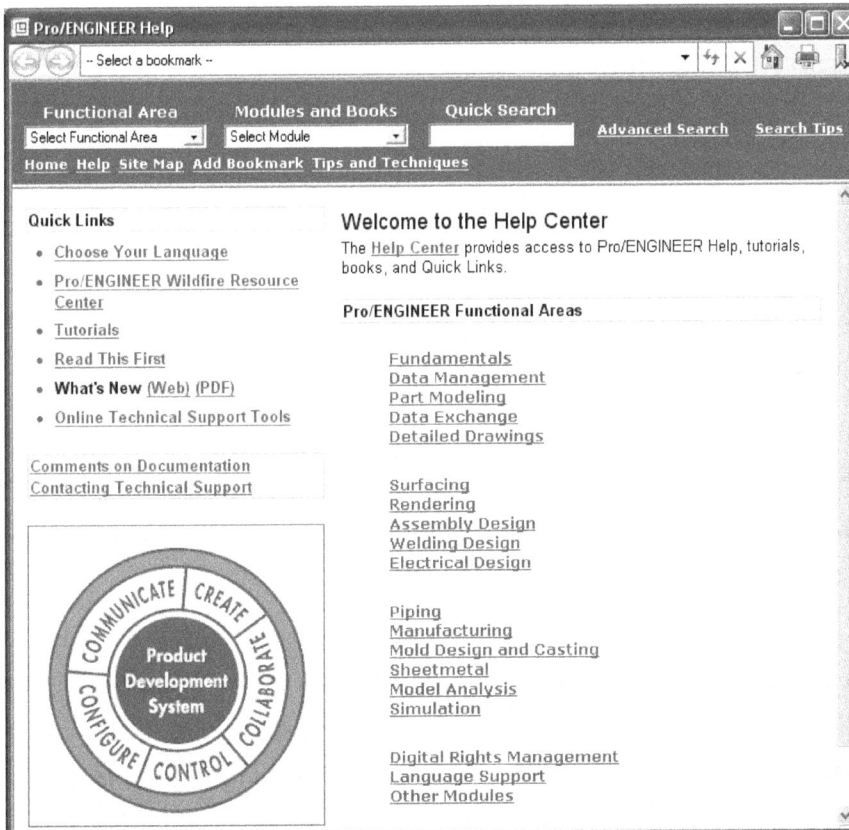

Fig. 28-1
Help Center

If you would like to, you may read through the volumes of information, by simply clicking on the links. You may also search for particular information by using the search utility at the top of the window. To narrow your search, you may want to specify a Functional area and Book to search.

When a search is initiated, the results are displayed in a new pop-up window, as shown in Figure 28-2.

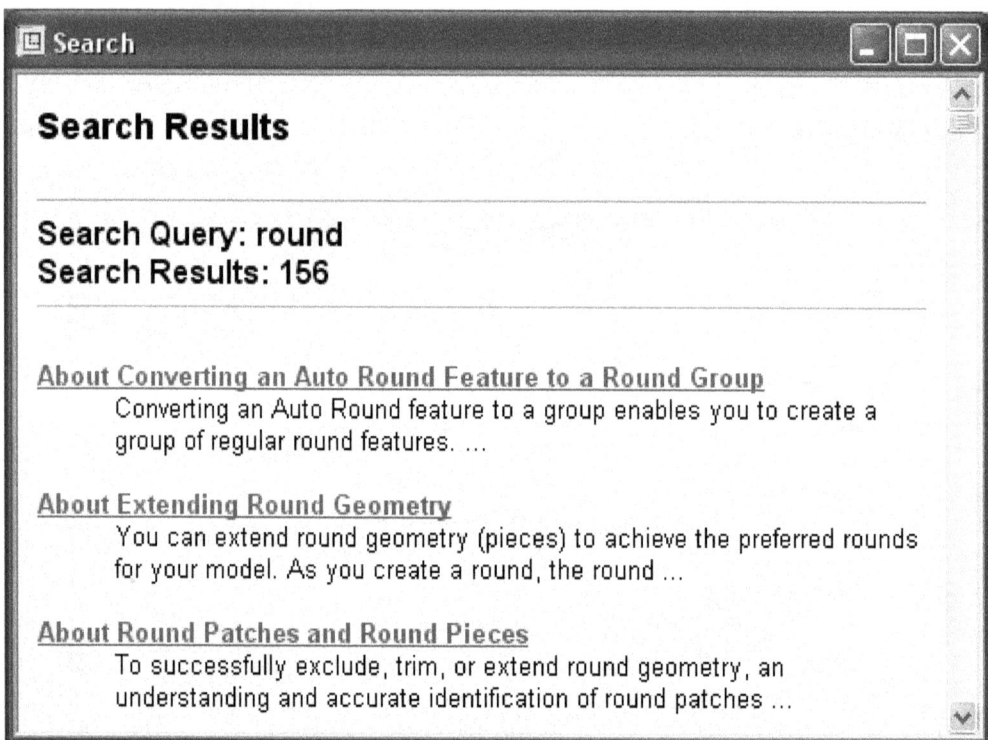

Search Results

Search Query: round
Search Results: 156

About Converting an Auto Round Feature to a Round Group
    Converting an Auto Round feature to a group enables you to create a
    group of regular round features. ...

About Extending Round Geometry
    You can extend round geometry (pieces) to achieve the preferred rounds
    for your model. As you create a round, the round ...

About Round Patches and Round Pieces
    To successfully exclude, trim, or extend round geometry, an
    understanding and accurate identification of round patches ...

Fig. 28-2
Search results for 'round'

Clicking on one of the results will display its contents in the original Help window, shown in Figure 28-1. The top of each page will indicate where in the electronic manual the document exists and allow you to advance page by page. The bottom of each page will also provide links to related topics.

Parametric Technology Corporation (PTC)

The PTC website located at **http://www.ptc.com** provides on-line tutorials and information for web based and instructor led training classes held at Authorized Training Centers around the world. It also hosts a forum for users to post and answer questions.

PTC/User

PTC/USER is an independent, not-for-profit corporation, and is the sole entity recognized by PTC as the official worldwide representative of its customers. It's main function is to organize an annual international technical conference, with seminars, tutorials and demonstrations. PTC/USER has approximately 70 regional user groups worldwide and operates several web and e-mail based discussion forums. For more information, go to: **http://www.ptcuser.org**.

Pro/E Community (formerly *Pro/E: The Magazine*)

Pro/E Community located at **http://www.proe.com** is a resource for users of Pro/ENGINEER, Windchill and other PTC affiliated products. The web site features articles, tips & tricks, industry spotlights, news and live, user-submitted questions and answers.

Frey Innovations, LLC

The author of this book is available for both Pro/ENGINEER mentoring, and product design services. For more information, go to: **http://www.freyinnovations.com.**

Appendices

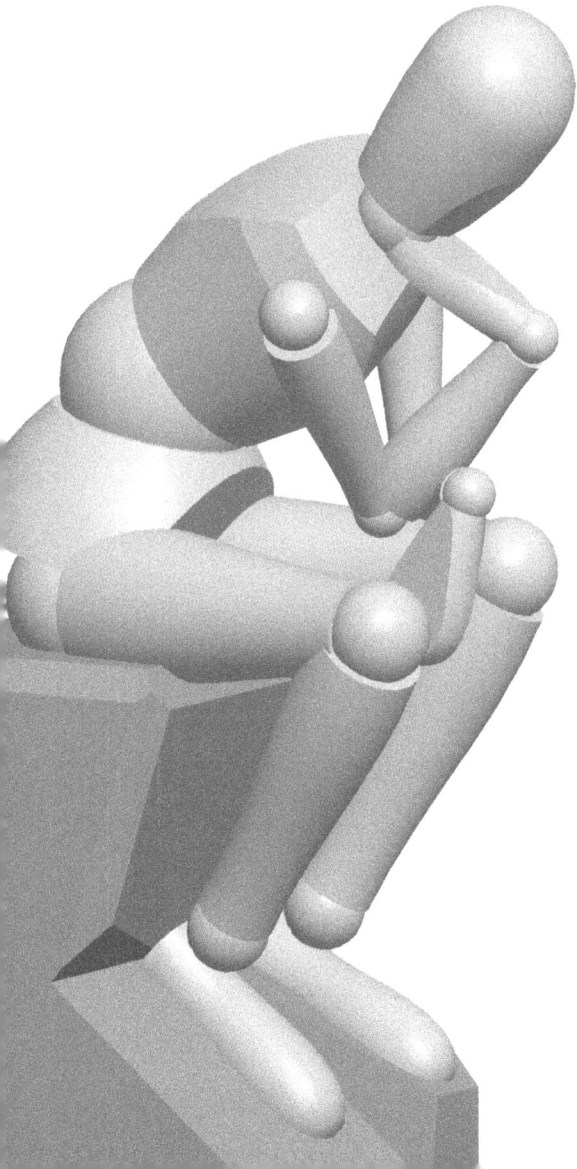

One-by-One (select items)

Line

Line Tangent

Centerline

Rectangle

Center and Point (circle)

Concentric

3 Point

3 Tangent

Ellipse

3-Point / Tangent End (arc)

Concentric

Center and Ends

3 Tangent

Conic

Circular (fillet)

Elliptical

Spline

Point

Coordinate System

Use (edge)

Offset

Normal (dimension)

Modify

Constrain

Text

Palette

Delete Segment (trim)

Corner

Divide

Mirror

Scale and Rotate

Done

Quit

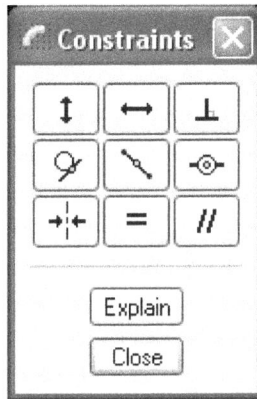

↕	**↔**	**⊥**
Make line or two verticies vertical	Make line or two verticies horizontal	Make two entities perpendicular
⟋	**⟍**	**-�⊙-**
Make two entities tangent	Place point on the middle of the line or arc	Create same points, points on entity, or collinear constraint
→¦←	**=**	**//**
Make two points or verticies symmetric about a centerline	Create Equal Lengths, Equal Radii or Same Curvature Constraint	Make two lines parallel

Option	Default Setting	Description
2d_region_columns_fit_text	NO	Determines whether each column in a two-dimensional repeat region is autosized to fit the longest piece of text.
all_holes_in_hole_table	YES	Include standard and sketched holes in hole tables. NO excludes standard and sketched holes from hole tables. YES includes standard and sketched holes in hole tables during creation and update.
allow_3d_dimensions	NO	Determines whether dimensions are shown in isometric views.
angdim_text_orientation	HORIZONTAL	Controls the placement of angular dimensions texts in drawings. Settings are relative to leader lines, dimension arc and the dimension.
asme_dtm_on_dia_dim_gtol	ON_GTOL	Controls the placement of a set datum attached to a diameter dimension. "on_dim" is ASME standard.
associative_dimensioning	YES	Associates draft dimensions to draft entities. Will only affect new dimensions.
axis_interior_clipping	NO	If set to "yes," you can clip an axis in the middle. If set to "no," you have to follow the ANSI Y14.2M standard which only allows clipping of end points.
axis_line_offset	0.1	Sets the default distance that a linear axis extends beyond its associated feature.
blank_zero_tolerance	NO	Determines whether to blank (not show) a plus or minus tolerance value if the tolerance value is set to zero.
broken_view_offset	1	Sets the offset distance between the two halves of a broken view.
chamfer_45deg_dim_text	JIS	Controls the display of 45 degree chamfer dimensions in a drawing.
chamfer_45deg_leader_style	STD_ASME_ANSI	Controls the leader type of a chamfer dimension without affecting the text.
circle_axis_offset	0.1	Sets the default distance that a circular cross-hair axis extends beyond the circular edge.

clip_diam_dimensions	YES	Controls the display of diameter dimensions in a detailed view. If set to "yes," dimensions which fall outside the view boundary will be clipped (not shown).
clip_dim_arrow_style	DOUBLE_ARROW	Controls the arrow style of clipped dimensions.
clip_dimensions	YES	Determines whether dimensions should be clipped or not displayed when one or more witness lines are outside the clipped view boundary.
create_area_unfold_segmented	YES	Makes the display of dimensions in area unfolded cross-sectional views similar to those in total unfolded cross-sectional views. If set to "yes," displays the View in segments when creating a new view. This option only affects new views.
crossec_arrow_length	0.1875	Sets the length of the arrow head on the cross-section cutting plane arrows.
crossec_arrow_style	TAIL_ONLINE	Determines which end of cross-section arrows - the head or the tail - touches the cross-section line.
crossec_arrow_width	0.0625	Sets the width of the arrow head on the cross-section cutting plane arrows.
crossec_text_place	AFTER_HEAD	Sets the location of cross-section text relative to the cross-section cutting plane arrows. If set to "no text," does not display any cross-section text.
crossec_type	OLD_STYLE	Controls whether appearance of planar cross-sections conforms to the style used prior to 2000i-2 ("old_style") or to the newer style that uses a z-clipping plane.
cutting_line	STD_ANSI	Controls display of cutting line. If set to "std_ansi," uses the ANSI standard. If set to "std_ansi_dashed," uses dashed lines. Otherwise, uses the DIN standard. If set to "std_jis_alternate" the display depends on setting of "cutting_line_segment".

cutting_line_adapt	NO	Controls display of line fonts used to show cross-sectional arrows. If set to "yes," all line fonts display adaptively, beginning in the middle of a complete line segment and ending in the middle of a complete line segment.
cutting_line_segment	0	Specifies the length in drawing units of the thickened portion of a non-ANSI cutting line. If set to "0," the length of the cutting line segment is 0.
dash_supp_dims_in_region	YES	Determines whether a display of dimension values in Pro/REPORT table repeat regions is suppressed (displays a dash instead).
datum_point_shape	CROSS	Controls display of datum points.
datum_point_size	0.3125	Controls size of model datum points and sketched two-dimensional points. This is always in inches.
decimal_marker	COMMA_FOR_METRIC_DUAL	Specifies character to be used as decimal point in secondary dimensions.
def_bom_balloons_attachment	EDGE	Sets the default attachment method for BOM balloons. When set to edge, balloons point to component edges. When set to surface, balloons point to component surfaces. For bulk and included component records, this option sets the default "Attach" selection.
def_bom_balloons_edge_att_sym	ARROWHEAD	Controls the default leader head when BOM balloons are attached to edges.
def_bom_balloons_snap_lines	NO	Determines whether snap lines are created around the view when showing BOM balloons.
def_bom_balloons_stagger	NO	Determines whether BOM balloons are shown staggered by default.
def_bom_balloons_stagger_value	0.6	Controls the distance between consecutive offset lines when BOM balloons are staggered.
def_bom_balloons_surf_att_sym	INTEGRAL	Controls the default leader head when BOM balloons are attached to surfaces.

def_bom_balloons_view_offset	0.8	Controls the default offset distance from the view boundaries on which to show BOM balloons.
def_view_text_height	0	Sets the height of text in view names used in view notes and in arrows in cross-sectional and projection detail views.
def_view_text_thickness	0	Sets default thickness for new text in view names used in view notes and in arrows in newly created cross-sectional and projection detail views.
def_xhatch_break_around_text	NO	Determines whether cross section/hatch lines break around text. Also affects the default setting in the dialog boxes.
def_xhatch_break_margin_size	0.15	Sets the default offset distance between the cross section lines and text; drawing unit is used.
default_dim_elbows	YES	Determines whether to display dimensions with elbows.
default_font	font	Specifies a font index that determines default text fonts. Do not include the ".ndx" extension.
default_pipe_bend_note	NO	Controls display of pipe bend notes in drawings. If set as text within quotation marks, uses that value when creating bend notes. Text may include parameters such as "&bend_name:att_pipe_bend", "&bend_num:att_pipe_bend" and "&bend_radius:att_pipe_bend"
default_show_2d_section_xhatch	ASSEMBLY_AND_PART	Controls the default crosshatch show state for 2D cross sections.
default_show_3d_section_xhatch	YES	Controls the default crosshatch show state for 3D cross sections.
default_view_label_placement	BOTTOM_LEFT	Sets the default position and justification for view label.
detail_circle_line_style	SOLIDFONT	Sets line font for circles indicating a detailed view in a drawing.
detail_circle_note_text	DEFAULT	Determines the text displayed in non-ASME-94 detail view reference notes.
detail_view_boundary_type	CIRCLE	Determines the default boundary type on the parent view of a detailed view.

detail_view_circle	ON	Sets display of a circle drawn about the portion of a model that is detailed by a detailed view.
detail_view_scale_factor	2	Determines the default scaling factor between a detailed view and its parent view. If set to 2, the detailed view scale is twice that of its parent view.
dim_dot_box_style	DEFAULT	Controls the arrow style display of dots and boxes only for leaders of linear dimensions. When set to "default," uses the draw_arrow_style" setting.
dim_fraction_format	DEFAULT	Controls the display of fractional dimensions in drawings. Unless set to "default," this option supersedes the configuration file option "dim_fraction_format". See documentation for details.
dim_leader_length	0.5	Sets length of dimension leader line when leader arrows are outside of witness lines.
dim_text_gap	0.5	Controls distance between dimension text and dimension leader line and represents the ratio between gap size and text height. For diameter dimensions, it controls the extension of an elbowbbeyond the text if "text_orientation" is "parallel_diam_horiz".
dim_trail_zero_max_places	same_as_dim	Sets the maximum number of decimal places trailing zeros will be extended to in the dimension primary value when dimension trailing zeros are used.
display_tol_by_1000	NO	For non-angular dimensions, tolerances will be displayed multiplied by 1000.
draft_scale	1	Determines value of draft dimensions relative to actual length of draft entity on drawing.
draw_ang_unit_trail_zeros	YES	Determines whether to remove trailing zeros (ANSI standard) when showing angular dimensions in deg/min/sec format.

draw_ang_units	ANG_DEG	Determines display of angular dimensions in a drawing. "ang_deg" indicates decimal degrees, "ang_min" indicates degrees and decimal minutes, "ang_sec" indicates degrees, minutes, and decimal seconds.
draw_arrow_length	0.1875	Sets length of leader line arrows.
draw_arrow_style	CLOSED	Controls style of arrow head for all detail items involving arrows.
draw_arrow_width	0.0625	Sets width of leader line arrows. Drives these: "draw_attach_sym_height," draw_attach_sym_width," "draw_dot_diameter."
draw_attach_sym_height	DEFAULT	Sets height of leader line slashes, integral signs, and boxes. If set to "default," uses value set for "draw_arrow_width."
draw_attach_sym_width	DEFAULT	Sets width of leader line slashes, integral signs, and boxes. If set to "default," uses value set for "draw_arrow_width."
draw_cosms_in_area_xsec	NO	Determines whether to display cosmetic sketches and datum curve features that lie in the cutting plane in planar area cross-sectional views.
draw_dot_diameter	DEFAULT	Sets diameter of leader line dots. If set to "default," uses value set for "draw_arrow_width."
draw_layer_overrides_model	NO	Directs drawing layer display setting to determine the setting of drawing model layers with the same name.
drawing_text_height	0.15625	Sets default text height for all text in the drawing using value set for "drawing_units."
drawing_units	INCH	Sets units for all drawing parameters.
dual_digits_diff	-1	Controls number of digits to the right of the decimal of the secondary dimension as compared to the primary dimension. For example, -1 indicate one less than the primary dimension.

dual_dimension_brackets	YES	Determines whether dimension units that occur second are shown in brackets. This option only applies when using "dual_dimensioning".
dual_dimensioning	NO	Determines whether values for dimensions should be shown in primary and/or secondary units. If set to "no," displays a single value for dimensions.
dual_metric_dim_show_fractions	NO	Determines whether the metric portion of a dual dimension will display fractions or not when the primary/model units are fractions.
dual_secondary_units	MM	Sets units for the display of secondary dimensions.
gtol_datum_placement_default	ON_BOTTOM	Determines whether the set datum will be attached above or below a geometric tolerance control frame.
gtol_datums	STD_ANSI	Sets drafting standard followed for displaying reference datums in drawings.
gtol_dim_placement	ON_BOTTOM	Determines location of a feature control frame of a geometric tolerance when attached to a dimension containing additional text.
gtol_display_style	STD	Sets the display style of profile gtols according to ASME Y14.41 standard.
gtol_lead_trail_zeros	SAME_AS_LEAD_TRAIL_ZEROS	Controls display of leading and trailing zeros in gtols.
half_view_line	SOLID	Determine the display of symmetry lines. If set to "solid," draws solid lines where material is present. "symmetry_iso," follows the ISO standard 128:1982 5.5. "symmetry_asme" follows the ASME Y14.2M-1992 standard.
harn_tang_line_display	NO	Specify whether or not to turn on the display of all the internal segment portions of cables when displaying "thick cables".
hidden_tangent_edges	DEFAULT	Controls display of hidden tangent edges in drawing views, when Hidden Line or No Hidden Line is selected from the Display Style list in the Pro/ENGINEER Environment dialog box.

hlr_for_datum_curves	YES	No - Datum curves will not be included when calculating display of hidden lines. Blanking and unblanking datum curves on a drawing will not cause hidden lines in views to be recalculated.
hlr_for_pipe_solid_cl	NO	Controls display of pipe centerlines. If set to "yes," hidden line removal affects pipe centerlines. Operates only on pipes created in Pro/PIPING, not on pipe Features in a part.
hlr_for_threads	YES	Controls display of threads. If set to "yes," thread edges meet ANSI or ISO standard for Hidden Line display. (ANSI or ISO set by the "thread_standard" option.)
ignore_model_layer_status	YES	If set to "yes," ignores changes to all layer status in the models of the drawing made in another mode.
iso_ordinate_delta	NO	Improves display of offset between an ISO-ordinate dimension line and witness line. If set to "yes," displays offset correctly as given in "witness_line_delta." (Otherwise "off" by about 2mm.)
lead_trail_zeros	STD_DEFAULT	Controls display of leading and trailing zeros in dimensions. It may also control other types of parameters, depending on the setting of "lead_trail_zeros_scope".
lead_trail_zeros_scope	DIMS	Controls whether only dimensions are affected by the setting of the drawing setup option "lead_trail_zeros."
leader_elbow_length	0.25	Determines length of leader elbow (the horizontal leg attached to text).
leader_extension_font	SOLIDFONT	Sets the font for leader extension lines.
line_style_standard	STD_ANSI	Controls text color in drawings. Unless set to "std_ansi," all drawing texts are displayed in blue, and boundary of detailed views in yellow.

location_radius	DEFAULT(2.)	Modifies radius of nodes indicating location, improving their visibility, particularly when printing drawings. Using "default" sets radius to 2.
max_balloon_radius	0	Sets the maximum allowable balloon radius. If set to "0," balloon radius depends only on text size.
mesh_surface_lines	ON	Controls display of blue surface mesh lines.
min_balloon_radius	0	Sets minimum allowable balloon radius. If set to "0," balloon radius depends only on text size.
min_dist_between_bom_balloons	0.8	Controls the default minimum distance between BOM balloons.
model_digits_in_region	YES	Controls display of number of digits in two-dimensional repeat regions. If set to "yes," two-dimensional repeat regions reflect the number of digits of part and assembly model dimensions.
model_display_for_new_views	FOLLOW_ENVIRONMENT	Determines line display style of model when creating views. If set to "Follow Environment", "Display Style" setting from environment is used.
model_grid_balloon_display	YES	Determines whether a circle will be drawn around the model grid text.
model_grid_balloon_size	0.2	Specifies default radius of balloons shown with the model grid in a drawing.
model_grid_neg_prefix	-	Controls prefix of negative values shown in model grid balloons.
model_grid_num_dig_display	0	Controls number of digits displayed in grid coordinates that appear in grid balloons.
model_grid_offset	DEFAULT	Controls offset of new model grid balloons from the drawing view. If set to "default," uses twice the current model grid spacing. Inches are always used for specified values.
model_grid_text_orientation	HORIZONTAL	Determines whether the model grid text orientation will be parallel to the grid lines or horizontal always.

model_grid_text_position	CENTERED	Determines whether the model grid text will be placed above, below or centered with the grid line. This option is ignored if model grid text orientation is horizontal.
new_iso_set_datums	YES	Controls display of set datums. If set to "yes," displays set draft datums in accordance with the ISO standard.
node_radius	DEFAULT	Sets the size of the nodes displayed in symbols.
ord_dim_standard	STD_ANSI	Controls the display of ordinate dimensions. If set to "std_ansi," shows dimensions without a connecting line. For other settings, the line is shown.
orddim_text_orientation	PARALLEL	Controls orientation of ordinate dimension texts. "parallel," indicates parallel to leader lines.
parallel_dim_placement	ABOVE	Determines whether dimension value displays above or below leader line when "text_orientation" is set to "parallel." Does not apply to dual dimensions.
pipe_insulation_solid_xsec	NO	Determines whether pipe insulation in cross-section displays as solid region.
pipe_pt_line_style	DEFAULT	Controls font of theoretical bend intersection points in a piping drawing.
pipe_pt_shape	CROSS	Controls shape of theoretical bend intersection points in a piping drawing.
pipe_pt_size	DEFAULT	Controls size of theoretical bend intersection points in a piping drawing.
pos_loc_format	%s%x%y, %r	This string controls the appearance of &pos_loc text in notes and report tables. The character pairs %%, %s, %x, %y and %r specify: a single `%', the sheet nu mber, the horizontal and vertical positions, and the end of the repeatable substring.
projection_type	THIRD_ANGLE	Determines method for creating projection views.

radial_dimension_display	STD_ASME	Allows display of radial dimensions in ASME, ISO or JIS standard formats, except when "text_orientation" is set to "horizontal", which forces display to be ASME format.
radial_pattern_axis_circle	NO	Sets display mode for axes of rotation that are perpendicular to the screen in radial pattern features. If set to "yes," a circular shared axis appears, and a xis lines pass through the center of a rotational pattern.
ref_des_display	NO	Controls display of reference designators in a drawing of a cabling assembly. If set to "DEFAULT," selects the Reference Designators checkbox in the Environment dialog box.
reference_bom_balloon_text	DEFAULT	Controls reference balloons text identifier. If set to DEFAULT, the word REF appears next to the balloon for simple balloons, and instead of the quantity value for quantity balloons.
remove_cosms_from_xsecs	TOTAL	Controls removal of datum curves, threads, cosmetic feature entities, and cosmetic cross-hatching from a full cross-sectional view. "total," removes features entirely in front of the cutting plane. They display fully only if intersecting it.
set_datum_leader_length	0.375	Controls the default leader length for set datums.
set_datum_triangle_display	FILLED	Determines whether the set datum triangle will be filled or open.
show_cbl_term_in_region	YES	Allows use of the report symbols "&asm.mbr.name" and "&asm.mbr.type" to show terminators in Pro/REPORT tables for cable assemblies having connectors with term inator parameters. If set to "yes" (and Cable Info for repeat region is set), shows terminators.
show_dim_sign_in_tables	YES	Controls display of the sign for negative tolerances in family table regions. "Yes" displays negative signs, "No" does not (default).

show_pipe_theor_cl_pts	BEND_CL	Controls display of centerlines and theoretical intersection points in piping drawings. "bend_cl," shows centerlines with bends only. "theor_cl," shows only c enterlines with theoretical bend intersection points.
show_quilts_in_total_xsecs	NO	Determines whether to include surface geometry such as surfaces and quilts in a x-section view. Including surface geometry means that it will be cut by the x-section.
show_sym_of_suppressed_weld	NO	Show symbols of suppressed welds.
show_total_unfold_seam	YES	Determines if seams (the edges of the cutting plane) in total unfolded cross-sectional views are shown.
shrinkage_value_display	PERCENT_SHRINK	Displays dimension shrinkage in percentages or as final values.
sort_method_in_region	DELIMITED	Determines repeat regions sort mechanism. String_only - sorts alphabetically. Trailing_numbers - logically evaluates trailing numbers (i.e. 1 < 02). Delimited XXX lcally evaluates sections between delimiters. Pre_2001 - reverts to pre-2001 sort method.
stacked_gtol_align	YES	Controls alignment in stacked gtols. If set to "yes," gtols comply to JIS standard, aligned on both ends of control frames.
sym_flip_rotated_text	NO	If set to "yes," then for new symbol definitions which allow rotation of text, by default any text which is rotated to be upside down will be flipped to make it right side up.
symmetric_tol_display_standard	STD_ASME	Controls how symmetric tolerances are displayed for the ASME, ISO and DIN standards.
tan_edge_display_for_new_views	DEFAULT	Determines tangent edge display of model when creating views. If set to tan_default, "Tangent Edges" setting from environment is used.
text_orientation	HORIZONTAL	Controls orientation of dimension texts. "parallel," indicates parallel to leader lines. "parallel_diam_horiz" is the same as "parallel," but with diameter dimensions showing horizontally.

text_thickness	0	Sets default text thickness for new text after regeneration and existing text whose thickness has not been modified. The value is in drawing units.
text_width_factor	0.8	Sets default ratio between the text width and text height. The system maintains this ratio until you change the width using the Text Width command.
thread_standard	STD_ANSI	Controls display of threaded hole with an axis (perpendicular to the screen as an arc (ISO) or as a circle (ANSI)).
tol_display	NO	Controls display of dimension tolerances. You cannot access the Pro/ENGINEER Environment dialog box if this option is set.
tol_text_height_factor	STANDARD	Sets default ratio between the tolerance text height and dimension text height, when showing tolerance in "plus-minus" format. "standard" is 1 for ANSI and .6 for ISO.
tol_text_width_factor	STANDARD	Sets default proportion between the tolerance text width and dimension text width, when showing tolerance in "plus-minus" format. "standard is .8 for ANSI and .6 for ISO.
use_major_units	NO	If using fractional dimensions and this option is set to "yes," dimensions will display as feet and inches (otherwise just inches). Does not apply to metric units.
view_note	STD_ANSI	If set to "std_din," creates a view-related note with the words "SECTION," "DETAIL," and "SEE DETAIL" omitted.
view_scale_denominator	0	When adding the first view of a model, if view_scale_format is decimal, the view scale chosen will be rounded to a value with the given denominator. If this would make the scale 0.0, "view_scale_denominator" will be multiplied by a power of 10.

view_scale_format	DECIMAL	Determines the display of a scale as either a decimal, a fraction or a ratio (e.g. 1:2). Make sure you set the "view_scale_denominator" option appropriately, even if you are using "ratio_colon".
weld_light_xsec	NO	Determines whether light weight weld x-section is showing.
weld_solid_xsec	NO	Determines whether weld in cross-section displays as solid region.
weld_spot_side_significant	YES	Set up placement of Weld Spot symbol for ANSI/AWS2.4 norm
weld_symbol_standard	STD_ANSI	Displays weld symbols in a drawing according to the ANSI or ISO standard.
witness_line_delta	0.125	Sets the extension of the witness line beyond the dimension leader arrows.
witness_line_offset	0.0625	Sets offset between a dimension line and object being dimensioned. This may be visible only when plotting (and on screen plot). Also controls the size of the line break at the intersection of witness lines.
yes_no_parameter_display	TRUE_FALSE	Controls display of "yes/no" parameters in drawing notes and tables. When set to "yes_no," parameters use "yes" or "no". "true_false," indicates using "true" or "false".
zero_quantity_cell_format	EMPTY	Specified the character to use in repeat regions cells that report a quantity of zero. If set to "empty", no character is displayed in the cell.

		Windows XP, Vista †	
Main Memory		Minimum	Recommended
		256 MB	1024 MB or higher
Available Disk Space	Pro/ENGINEER	2.0 GB	2.5 GB or higher
	Pro/ENGINEER with Pro/ENGINEER Mechanica Wildfire 4.0	2.0 GB	3.0 GB or higher
Swap Space		500 MB	2048 MB or higher
CPU speed		500 MHz	2.4 GHz or higher
Internal Browser Support		Microsoft Internet Explorer 6.0 or higher	
Monitor		1024 x 768 resolution or higher 24-bit or greater color	
Graphics Card		OpenGL	
Network		TCP/IP Ethernet Network Adapter	
Mouse		3-button mouse	
File systems		NTFS	
Misc.		CD-ROM or DVD drive	

* For a complete list, refer to the PTC web site

† For UNIX platform support and requirements, refer to the PTC web site